Elements of

Sociology

Elements of

Fourth Edition

Sociology

A Critical Canadian Introduction

John Steckley

OXFORD

UNIVERSITY PRESS

OXFORD
UNIVERSITY PRESS

Oxford University Press is a department of the University of Oxford.
It furthers the University's objective of excellence in research, scholarship,
and education by publishing worldwide. Oxford is a registered trade mark of
Oxford University Press in the UK and in certain other countries.

Published in Canada by
Oxford University Press
8 Sampson Mews, Suite 204,
Don Mills, Ontario M3C 0H5 Canada

www.oupcanada.com

Library and Archives Canada Cataloguing in Publication

Steckley, John, 1949–, author
Elements of sociology / John Steckley. — Fourth edition.

Previous edition had subtitle: A critical Canadian introduction.
Includes bibliographical references and index.
ISBN 978-0-19-901963-2 (paperback)

1. Canada—Social conditions—Textbooks. 2. Sociology—
Canada—Textbooks. I. Title.

HM586.S84 2016   301.0971   C2016-905061-0

Cover image: wundervisuals/Getty Images

Oxford University Press is committed to our environment.
Wherever possible, our books are printed on paper which comes
from responsible sources.

Printed and bound in the United States of America

1 2 3 4 — 20 19 18 17

Elements

Contents

PART TWO Social Structures　65

⓭ Health and Medicine   375

Tables and Figures

Tables

Figures

Introducing . . .
Elements of Sociology

In preparing this new edition of *Elements of Sociology*, we have, from the start, kept in mind one paramount goal: to produce the most dynamic and accessible introduction to sociology available to Canadian students.

This revision builds on the strengths of the highly acclaimed previous editions and incorporates new material designed to make the text even more engaging, more thought-provoking, and more relevant to students and instructors alike. I hope that as you browse through the pages that follow, you will see why we believe *Elements of Sociology* is the most exciting and innovative textbook available to Canadian sociology students today.

Six Things That Make This a One-of-a-Kind Textbook

A Canadian Textbook for Canadian Students

Written by a Canadian author for Canadians readers, *Elements of Sociology* highlights the stories of the figures and events at the heart of sociological inquiry in this country: John Porter, Elizabeth Bott, Dorothy Smith, Daniel G. Hill, the "Famous Five," Quebec's "Quiet Revolution," and much more.

82   PART TWO | Social Structures

Telling It Like It Is

The Hijab as Worn by Young Canadian Muslim Women in Montreal

MondiDT/Thinkstock

The Narrative of a 19-Year-Old Palestinian-Canadian Woman

The veil has freed me from arguments and headaches. I always wanted to do many things that women normally do not do in my culture. I had thought living in Canada would give me that opportunity. But when I turned 14, my life changed. My parents started to limit my activities and even telephone conversations. My brothers were free to go and come as they pleased, but my sister and I were to be good Muslim girls. . . . Life became intolerable for me. The weekends were hell.

Then as a way out, I asked to go to Qur'anic classes on Saturdays. There I met with several veiled women of my age. . . . None of them seemed to face my problems. Some told me that since they took the veil, their parents know that they are not going to do

anything that goes against Muslim morality. The more I hung around with them, the more convinced I was that the veil is the answer to all Muslim girls' problems here in North America. Because parents seem to be relieved and assured that you are not going to do stupid things, and your community knows that you are acting like a Muslim woman, you are much freer. (cited in Hoodfar, 2003: pp. 20–1)

The Narrative of a 17-Year-Old Pakistani-Canadian Woman

Although we did not intermingle much with non-Indian Canadians, I very much felt at home and part of the wider society. This, however, changed as I got older and clearly my life was different than many girls in my class. I did not talk about boyfriends and did

An Inclusive, Narrative Approach

Sociology is the study of people, and in *Elements of Sociology,* the people tell their stories. Students will read first-hand accounts of what it's like to fast during Ramadan, to come out to your family, to experience racism on campus, to meet the expectations of Italian parents, and to raise daughters in an era of Lingerie Barbie and La Senza Girl.

466   Glossary

McKay, Colin (1876–1939) prolific early Canadian socialist writer on issues of **class**.

McKinney, Louise (1868–1931) Canadian women's right activist and politician, the first woman to be elected in a legislature in Canada and the British Commonwealth, and a member of the **Famous Five**.

MacLean, Annie Marion (1869–1934) Canadian sociologist, the second woman to receive a PhD in sociology, and a pioneering researcher in using **participant observation**.

macrosociology an approach to sociological inquiry that involves looking at the large-scale structure and dynamics of society as a whole.

Malthus, Thomas (1766–1834) English minister whose contribution to the study of **political economy** and demography was his view that population growth would inevitably be checked by the opposing impact of famine and disease.

Mandell, Nancy Canadian sociologist who specializes in the study of family and gender.

manifest function (as described by **Merton**) the intended and widely recognized function of a social process or institution. *Compare* **latent function.**

manufacturing of need the creation of consumer demand for (1) items that were once produced in the home, or (2) products that were once considered inessential.

marginalization the experience of being treated as insignificant or of being moved beyond the margin of mainstream society.

marginalized masculinity (as described by R. Connell) those forms of masculinity that, owing to class, "race," sexual orientation, and ethnicity, are accorded less respect than other forms of masculinity.

marital roles *another term for* **conjugal roles.**

marked term a term with a qualifying or distinguishing label added to it (e.g. *field hockey* or *Aboriginal sociologist*), showing that it is not the usual or commonly accepted form. *Compare* **unmarked term.**

Market Basket Measure (MBM) an estimate of the cost of a specific basket of goods and services for a given year, assuming that all items in the basket were entirely provided for out of the spending of the household. Having an income lower than the MBM constitutes low income or poverty.

Marsh, Leonard (1906–1983) British-born sociologists who, while working at McGill University, produced groundbreaking work on **class** in Canada.

Martineau, Harriet (1802–1876) British sociologist who is generally considered to be the first woman in the discipline.

Marx, Karl (1818–1883) influential German economist and thinker, who viewed society primarily in terms of **class** and **social change** in terms of economic factors; he was the founder of modern communism.

mass culture the **culture** of the majority, when that culture is produced by big companies and powerful governments.

master status the **status** of an individual that dominates all of his or her other statuses in most social contexts, and plays the greatest role in defining the individual's social identity.

matrilineal denoting kinship determined along the mother's line.

matrilocal denoting a situation in which a man and a woman live together in or near the mother's family residence(s).

Mead, George Herbert (1863–1931) American founding figure of **symbolic interactionism** looked at how the self is constructed through personal exchanges with others.

mean a statistical figure usually calculated in the same way as the **average**, but for some purposes determined by taking the sum of the highest and lowest figures only and dividing by two. If I have six coffees one day, then two coffees another, and three another, the mean is (6 + 2) ÷ 2 = 4.

means of production (as described by **Marx**) the social means required for producing wealth (e.g. land in feudal times; capital—wealth, machinery—during the industrial period).

median the number that falls in the middle of a series of figures for a given population or group. I worked ten hours on Monday, ten hours again on Tuesday, five hours on Wednesday, two hours on Thursday, and one hour on Friday. The median of the set 10, 10, 5, 2, 1 is 5.

medical sociology the use of sociological research and data to analyze and improve public health, focusing primarily on how health care is administered and whether the medical system adequately supports both the providers and the recipients of health care and health services.

medicalization the process by which certain behaviours or conditions are defined as medical problems (rather than, say, social problems), and medical intervention becomes the focus of remedy and social control.

melting pot a metaphor for a country in which immigrants are believed or expected to lose their cultural distinctiveness and assimilate into the dominant society. *Compare* **cultural mosaic.**

Memmi, Albert (b. 1920) French social philosopher of Tunisian-Jewish origin, who is one of the foundational writers on the subject of anti-colonialism.

meritocratic describing the tendency to award power or rewards to people based on their demonstrated ability or achievements.

Merton, Robert K. (1910–2003) American sociologist whose many contributions to the discipline include his work in the sociology of science and his coining of important terms such as **reference group**, **role model**, and **status set**.

Métis a people of mixed First Nations and European ethnicity (usually Cree or Saulteaux and French) who took on a sense of nationality as well as a distinct legal status.

metrosexual a man (usually a heterosexual man) whose lifestyle, spending habits, and concern for personal appearance are likened to those considered typical of a fashionable, urban, homosexual man.

microsociology an approach to sociology that focuses not on the grand scale of society but on the plans, motivations, and actions of the individual or a specific group. *Compare* **macrosociology.**

middle class the social class made up primarily of small-scale businesspeople, educated professionals, and salaried employees possessing certifiable credentials.

Mills, C. Wright (1916–1962) influential American sociologist engaged in issues of class, whose work embraced **public sociology**, and who introduced the important concept of the **sociological imagination**.

Miner, Horace (1912–1993) Chicago School American sociologist and anthropologist whose work put the study of French Canada at the forefront of Canadian sociology.

minoritized denoting an identifiable social group that is discriminated against by mainstream society or the **dominants**.

Minturn, Ann Leigh (1928–1999) American social psychologist involved with cross-cultural studies of family and child-rearing.

NEW!   Names to Know Glossary

The new edition has incorporated biographical entries in the end-of-book glossary, providing an even richer and more useful resource for students as they review the material.

A Visual, Thought-Provoking Presentation

Students are challenged on every page to adopt a sociological imagination and see the sociology in everyday life. Carefully chosen photos and captions, provocative critical-thinking questions, and end-of-chapter review questions all invite readers to apply the theory and take a stance.

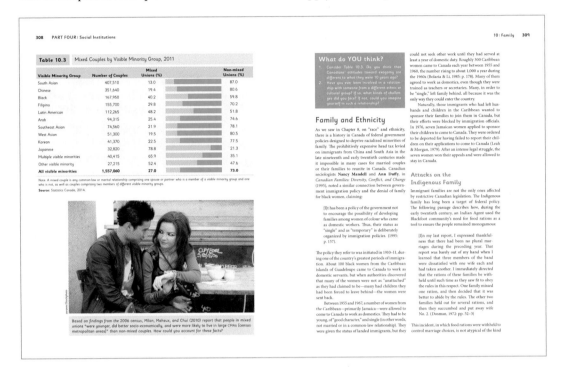

Coverage of Indigenous People in Canada

No sociology textbook can claim more extensive coverage of the issues that have affected and that continue to affect First Nations, Métis, and Inuit living in Canada.

Case Studies and Compelling Viewpoints

Elements of Sociology presents five different feature boxes, scattered throughout every chapter to highlight issues, events, and ideas at the centre of sociological debate and investigation.

POVs

Telling It Like It Is

Telling It Like It Is boxes feature first-person narratives that give voice to a variety of perspectives informed by different social factors—age, sex, gender, class, ethnicity, and so on.

Our Stories

Our Stories boxes examine research and events that are especially relevant to the practice and study of sociology in Canada.

The Point Is . . .

The Point Is . . . boxes present case studies and highlight important contributions to sociological research, past and present.

Quick Hits

Quick Hits sidebars supplement the author's narrative with relevant facts and data.

Going Global

Going Global boxes shed light on international issues of interest to sociologists in Canada and around the world.

For More Information: Online Resources

Elements of Sociology is part of a comprehensive package of learning and teaching tools that includes resources for both students and instructors.

For Instructors

- A comprehensive **instructor's manual** provides an extensive set of pedagogical tools and suggestions for every chapter, including overviews and summaries, concepts to emphasize in class, essay and research assignments, and links to relevant videos and online resources.

- Newly updated and enhanced for this edition, classroom-ready **PowerPoint slides** summarize key points from each chapter and incorporate graphics and tables drawn straight from the text.

- An extensive **test generator** enables instructors to sort, edit, import, and distribute hundreds of questions in multiple-choice, true-or-false, and short-answer formats.

- Carefully chosen **video clips**, matched to each chapter and available as streaming video, provide unique perspectives on themes and issues discussed in the textbook.

For Students

- The **Student Study Guide** includes chapter summaries, study questions, and self-grading quizzes, as well as explore-and-discuss exercises to help you review the textbook and classroom material.

 www.oupcanada.com/Steckley4e

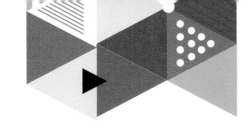

A Word or Two from the Author

Why Read a Sociology Text?

We live in times when it is more important than ever to be a critical consumer of social, political, medical, and environmental information. Your quality of life and the social health of your country depend on it. I know this sounds a bit extreme, but I believe it to be true. A sociology textbook (and, of course, your sociology instructor) can give you the intellectual tools that could make you such a critical consumer. Further, no matter what career you see yourself in three, ten, eighteen years down the line, you will have to be able to understand and communicate effectively with people. Again, your sociology textbook can help you here. Think of it as a literate, wise uncle/aunt, grandfather/grandmother whose opinion you value and whose advice you trust (even if you don't always take it).

Why Write a Sociology Text?

Why write a Canadian sociology textbook when there are so many out there already? I began with what I saw as an inability among introductory texts on the Canadian market to give proper voice to Indigenous and South Asian perspectives. I don't claim to have corrected the deficiency, but by incorporating the work of authors from each group, I hope I have made a significant departure from earlier Canadian sociology textbooks.

Making "Other" Voices Heard

I realized, too, that other voices needed to be heard. While I have included the work of authors representing different ethnic backgrounds, cultures, and sexualities, I have always felt that the best way to make different voices heard is through personal narratives, which I have incorporated in each chapter. These present a variety of perspectives informed by a variety of "social locations"—black, lesbian, Chinese, Italian, Muslim, Palestinian, and so on. I strongly believe that the narratives constitute one of the most important features of this textbook.

> "I have always felt that the best way to make different voices heard is through personal narratives, which I have incorporated in each chapter."

Celebrating My Heroes of the Discipline

The narrative approach is not the only way in which this textbook is a little different. Some of my views are provocative, but I was tired of the dry, conservative bent of other texts, and their general failure to include much or anything about my heroes of the discipline—Dorothy Smith, Michel Foucault, Franz Fanon, Antonio Gramsci, Albert Memmi, and (apart from a perfunctory nod to his sociological imagination) C. Wright Mills. I aimed for a more inclusive approach in covering theories and theorists, including the many women and sociologists of colour who have influenced and redirected the discipline.

> "I was tired of the dry, conservative bent of other texts."

Breaking Out of the Mould

The market imperative within the broader political economy of publishing means that there is little interest in doing something different from what has already been done. It wasn't until I began the publishing process that I realized how the conservative elements within the market influenced what materialized as the final product. A low tolerance for difference and little appetite for risk mean merely reproducing what is known to have worked before. I was fortunate that Oxford, constrained by its own market imperative and logic, has been so supportive of my unique views and approach.

Writing for Canadian Students

A textbook is typically considered Canadian when it uses Canadian figures, Canadian data, and Canadian research—this despite the fact the text may entirely overlook the history and emergence of sociology in this country. Canadian sociology is quite different from the sociology found in Europe and the US. For instance, the focus of early Canadian sociology was on rural life and the resource economy, which speaks to a society that is not highly urbanized or industrialized. Moreover, the influence of the social gospel movement and social work orients sociology in Canada, more than its counterparts elsewhere, around issues of social justice, even today.

> "Canadian sociology is quite different from the sociology found in Europe and the US. . . . I am confident that this is the most Canadian introductory sociology textbook on the market."

I am confident that this is the most Canadian introductory sociology textbook on the market. It is not an adapted American textbook with Canadian extensions, nor is it a North American textbook co-written by American and Canadian authors. I designed this book, from the ground up, as a text for Canadian students, to teach them about what I—a Canadian sociologist—have done, am doing, have failed to do, and hope to do in the future.

Introducing New Qualitative Research Methods

While contemporary sociology still engages in foundational methods, there has been an expansion of qualitative methodological approaches that have been influenced by feminism, queer theory, poststructuralism, postcolonialism, and cultural studies, many of which had been ghettoized into other disciplines, like anthropology and women's studies. These methods are not new, but they have not been part of the methodological lexicon in sociology. In order to represent contemporary sociology accurately, I went beyond a conventional discussion of quantitative and qualitative methods to include ethnographic research, case studies, and narratives, as well as content and discourse analysis, psychoanalysis, semiotics, and genealogy. I wanted to introduce students to concepts, ideas, and themes that will be recurring throughout their education, and in this way, to inspire their imagination.

Conveying the Discipline's Vitality

To give an accurate survey of sociology today means stressing what is current, what is being done, and whom is being studied. The discipline generally and the theory specifically are exciting, yet I feel this message is not conveyed to students, who often see sociology as boring or irrelevant. Sociological theory has shifted immensely, with influences from queer theory, feminist psychoanalysis, postcolonialism, and poststructuralism. Whether the exclusion of these influences is the result of the status quo or the belief that they are too complex for students to comprehend, it is a misrepresentation that in the end benefits no one, and one that I have tried to correct.

> "The discipline generally and the theory specifically are exciting, yet I feel this message is not conveyed to students, who often see sociology as boring or irrelevant."

Making Students Think

A casual flip through the pages of this text will reveal an abundance of photographs and other illustrations. The photos are not just pretty distractions to keep students looking at the book. They serve a purpose. I have chosen photos and have written captions that I hope will encourage students to adopt a sociological perspective. The same objective is served by the numerous critical-thinking questions scattered throughout the chapters.

My Thanks

It takes a number of people to put together a book of this size and scope. First, I would like to thank the people at Oxford University Press who made major contributions to this project. David Stover I thank for suggesting (twice) that I write this book. Darcey Pepper, who signed me on for the new edition, deserves to be acknowledged for setting things in place, as does in-house editor Eric Sinkins, who, with amazing effort and diplomatic skill, always gets the manuscript across the goal line. For this new edition, I would thank Amy Gordon for her gentle nipping at my heels (she was obviously a border collie in a past life). I would like to acknowledge the following reviewers, as well as several anonymous reviewers, whose thoughtful comments and suggestions have helped to shape this edition of *Elements of Sociology*:

- Jim Cosgrave, Trent University
- Stephen Decator, St Clair College
- Seema Ahluwalia, Kwantlen Polytechnic University
- Annette Tézli, University of Calgary

For helping me write the initial draft of this book, I would also like to thank several of my colleagues at Humber. Les Takahashi, Jim Jackson, John Metcalfe, and Joey Noble all contributed to this work with their support and helpful ideas. Librarians Jennifer Rayment and Marlene Beck worked major feats of magic to make obscure articles and books appear. And I would like to thank Guy Letts for his invaluable help in earlier versions of this text.

Closer to home, there is the Steckley household menagerie: Wiikwaas and Trudy—the dogs that are—and Egwene and Cosmo, the beloved and terribly missed dogs that were; the parrots: Quigley, Tikkifinn, Stanee, Louis, Lime, Sam, Juno, and Gus, as well as Benji, Misha, Finn, and Tika, who provided support on earlier editions. No joke—I couldn't write without their wonderful distraction.

Finally, there is my wife, Angie. She supported me through the lows and highs of this project, when I was not the easiest person to live with (either low or high). When the sands of my life shift, there is always a rock I can depend on.

John Steckley
September 2016

PART ONE

Foundations of Sociology

Introduction to Sociology

The Gist

Reading this chapter will help you to . . .

- Understand how sociology differs from other disciplines.
- Describe what the sociological imagination is.
- Cite some key ideas of sociology's trailblazers: Durkheim, Marx, and Weber.
- Trace the development of sociology in Canada.
- Distinguish the three "functions" identified by Robert Merton.
- Explain why sociology by approach is different from sociology by audience.
- Identify the main aspects of the feminist and postmodernist perspectives.
- Know the basic ideas of Michel Foucault and Dorothy Smith.

Terms of the Trade

- archaeology of knowledge
- back stage
- bourgeoisie
- capital
- class
- conflict theory (or approach)
- critical sociology
- cultural mosaic
- discourse
- disproportionate representation
- dramaturgical approach
- egalitarian
- ethnography
- folk society

- front stage
- ideological
- impression management
- intersectionality
- latent dysfunction
- latent function
- macrosociology
- manifest function
- melting pot
- microsociology
- narratives
- objective
- policy sociology
- political economy
- professional sociology

- proletariat
- Protestant (work) ethic
- public sociology
- social fact
- social gospel
- social location
- sociological imagination
- sociology
- standpoint theory
- structural functionalism
- subjective
- symbolic interactionism
- total institution
- totalitarian discourse
- vertical mosaic

Names to Know

- Helen C. Abell
- Herbert Blumer
- Samuel Delbert Clark
- Auguste Comte
- Carl Addington Dawson
- W.E.B. Du Bois
- Émile Durkheim
- Michel Foucault
- Erving Goffman
- Everett C. Hughes

- Ibn Khaldûn
- Harold Innis
- Annie Marion MacLean
- Thomas Malthus
- Leonard Marsh
- Harriet Martineau
- Karl Marx
- George Herbert Mead
- Robert K. Merton
- C. Wright Mills

- Horace Miner
- Friedrich Nietzsche
- Robert Park
- John Porter
- Aileen Ross
- Georg Simmel
- Dorothy Smith
- Herbert Spencer
- Thorstein Veblen
- Max Weber

For Starters

Doughnut Shops, Drive-Throughs, and the Value of Sociology

I am a big fan of coffee-and-doughnut shops. When I go to a doughnut shop, I tend to savour the experience: I park my car, walk in, chat with the server, and generally enjoy the social aspect of the transaction. I have never used a drive-through (or a "drive-thru"). I feel that pulling up to the drive-through window limits the overall experience—the socializing with fellow patrons, the customer service, the ritual of surveying the assortment of doughnuts and then choosing the perfect one. For that matter, it doesn't really save any time—I've done an informal study.

I wondered why some people use the drive-through instead of parking and coming into the shop. Just who are these people who would rather interact over an intercom and receive their orders through a pickup window? I long thought it was either young men whose most significant relationships were with their cars, or else lazy, unfit, older men who drive everywhere rather than walk.

My opinion changed, however, because of a student in one of my sociology classes. The student carried out his own study, in Newmarket, north of Toronto. He spent an hour one morning at a doughnut shop taking notes on who was using the drive-through and who was walking in through the front door. Over that period he observed 91 people walk into the doughnut shop and 95 people drive through. He did notice a gender difference in the two groups, but not the one I had predicted: in terms of the counter sales, 42 of the customers were women and 49 were men, but of the drive-through patrons, 70 were women and just 25 were men. The student also observed that compared with middle-aged and older women, *young* women were much more likely—by a ratio of nearly 7 to 1—to use the drive-through. This was in stark contrast to the male drive-through customers, among whom there was a roughly 1 to 1 ratio of the two age-determined groups.

Another statistic enabled the student to come up with a hypothesis to account for the results of his research. He observed that compared with the parked cars of the walk-in clientele, the cars entering the drive-through were more likely to have child seats in them. Further, he often identified young children among the passengers of the drive-through vehicles.

The student's hypothesis was that at that hour and at that location, young mothers with infants and toddlers were significantly more likely to use the drive-through because it was easier than going through the complicated process of unbuckling their children and bringing them into the restaurant. To be really convincing, his hypothesis would have to be tested for other times and locations, but it presented a compelling example of how sociology can be used to understand everyday life.

Introduction: Why This Textbook Is a Little Different

This textbook is not like the others. It will offer candid observations, occasional humour, and lots of stories told from the perspective of the author, his students, and his colleagues in sociology. In keeping with contemporary sociological terminology, we are calling these stories narratives. Narratives make up an important branch of sociological literature, one recognizing that to understand someone's situation, you need to listen to the words, the "voice," of that person. For this reason, every chapter of this textbook will make use of narratives to illustrate key points and concepts.

There are two basic strategies that textbook writers can take. One is to create a kind of reference book that touches on pretty much every conceivable topic within the discipline. That sort of book can be good for students who need support outside of the classroom or away from the instructor. The other approach is to write a book that arouses the curiosity of the reader as a student of the discipline, even if only for one semester. That is what I'm trying to do here. My aim is to hook you on the subject of sociology, to get you interested in reading and learning about it. I feel that—to use a baseball analogy—if you try to round the bases too quickly, you might get picked off. I'd rather get you safely on base. You may not touch all the bases this inning, but there's a better chance you will in your next at-bat. In other words, I've tried to avoid writing a textbook you will lose interest in because it tries to introduce you to too much, too quickly.

Introduction to Sociology

Sociologists notice social patterns. Things tend to happen differently to you depending on your sex, age, class, ethnicity, "race," religion, and sexual orientation. If you are a woman, for instance, you typically pay more in Canada for a haircut and to have your shirt dry-cleaned than you would if you were a man (Vermond, 2016). You are not paying more because the service you receive is any different: it's just that your hair and your shirt, because they are designated as "female," are subject to what we call the "pink tax," making them more expensive to cut and to clean (respectively). If you are a young black man driving in Canada, you are more likely than a young white male driver to be pulled over at night by the police: you are guilty of the offence known facetiously as "driving while black"; that's another social pattern.

What if you are a young, white, heterosexual male? If you are, you might think that all the "other groups" are ganging up on you. Insurance companies make it very expensive for you (and your parents) to pay for your driving. You read that white males have privilege in terms of getting jobs, but it is often difficult for you to find the jobs that white male privilege is supposed to help you with.

Sociologists also investigate and challenge the social patterns that other people perceive. For example, why do so many people, even those in the medical profession, assume that male nurses are gay? This stereotype has never been demonstrated statistically, in part because it would be highly unethical to ask a male nurse about his sexual preferences ("On a scale of 1 to 10, how gay would you say you are?"). Sociologists studying the subject might investigate the effects of movies like *Meet the Parents* (2000), where characters declare that all male nurses are either gay or, at the very least, "sissies." Does this stereotype discourage men from entering the nursing profession for fear of being seen as *deviant* (by which we mean simply deviating from what is seen as normal or usual)? As a sociologist, I have noted that male nursing students taking my classes are typically mature students who were born outside of Canada and who are not white; those few who are young, white, and English-Canadian often defy a number of societal norms in ways that might lead others to call them eccentric or unconventional.

Why are young men afraid of nursing? Could it also reflect the fact that the nursing profession is thought of as "naturally feminine" because it involves care-giving and is a chronically underpaid profession involving responsibilities that we in the West consider less important than the work of (typically male) doctors? Sociologists look carefully at social patterns such as these to learn more about what causes them and what effect they could have on society.

Sociology and Issues

Sociology can help students understand issues facing society today. One divisive social issue of recent years is same-sex marriage. Since July 2005, same-sex marriage has been legally recognized across Canada, although many Canadians remain strongly opposed to the idea. What can sociologists tell us about this issue?

Sociology can't say what is moral, or "right." There isn't a scientific way of measuring that. But sociology *can* tell us about who tends to be in favour of same-sex marriage: younger people, those with more education, women more than men, French Canadians more than English Canadians. As well, sociology can speak about who tends to be against same-sex marriage: those with fundamentalist religious views versus the more liberal members of Canada's many faiths, and people from rural rather than urban communities. Beyond this, sociology might also help students understand the impact that socializing influences such as parents and the media have on their own opinions concerning same-sex marriage. You can have more choice in forming your own opinion when you understand what has helped to shape it in the past.

This relates to a question that sociology students often ask: How come I got a low mark when it's just an opinion and there are no right or wrong answers? Everyone has a right to an opinion; however, people should become knowledgeable about issues before forming opinions on them. Sociology gives us the means to form considered opinions on social issues. In this way, sociology helps students distinguish between a well-argued, informed opinion and an uninformed viewpoint spouted off without careful thought (say, by peers who aren't taking sociology).

Ann Worthy/iStockphoto

Would you take a $20 haircut from this barber? Or would you pay considerably more to receive the same haircut from a stylist at a salon? Women typically pay more than men do to have their hair cut: how do you account for this social pattern?

Sociology as a Discipline

Academic disciplines are artificial constructions. There is nothing "natural" about the borderlines that separate sociology from other established disciplines such as anthropology, economics, history, psychology, philosophy, or political science. These various fields have much in common, as Table 1.1 shows. There is a lot of cross-referencing in the books and articles written by specialists in each discipline. Students who have taken courses in psychology, anthropology, or philosophy will notice that sociology regularly encroaches on their territory, just as those disciplines often "poach" on sociology's hunting ground.

Still, artificial or not, the discipline of sociology does exist and is unique. It has its own history, a distinct vocabulary and set of tools, and a

Table 1.1   Sociology and Related Disciplines

Discipline	Emphasis
anthropology	The comparative study of human societies and cultures and the way they developed.
economics	The production and consumption of wealth, including the distribution of goods and services among individuals and groups.
philosophy	Major thinkers and turns of thought in particular societies, and how they have addressed the major questions of life.
political science	Systems of government and how they serve citizens.
psychology	The human mind, the social and biological influences on it, and its functions, especially those affecting behaviour.
social work	The way our understanding of society and individuals can be applied to improving peoples' well-being.
sociology	The development, structure, and functioning of human society, especially as seen in group interaction, social relations, social institutions, and social structures.

separate department in most colleges and universities in Canada. You'll find that people teaching such varied subjects as Canadian studies, communication, criminology, cultural studies, education, Native studies, international relations, and women's studies often have degrees in sociology. In order to understand sociology—its weaknesses and strengths, and the ways in which its perspective has broadened over recent decades—we need to understand it as a discipline.

What Is Sociology?

You may have noticed that so far I have cleverly avoided defining what sociology is. That's because it's not a straightforward thing to do, and in some ways not particularly useful. Defining something is very different from understanding it. I could give you a simple (but not terribly useful) definition by saying that *sociology is the systematic or scientific study of society*. Can you imagine the multiple-choice questions that could come from that?

Sociology is

a)   the systematic study of society;
b)   the unsystematic study of society;
c)   "statistical stuff and heavy duty theoretical bullshit" (see Mills, p.10);
d)   all of the above.

The answer could easily be the final one, "all of the above." I could just as easily refer you to the glossary at the back of this book, where sociology is defined

as "the social science that studies the development, structure, and functioning of human society." Does that help?

The truth is, giving a precise, all-encompassing explanation of what sociology *is* would be much more difficult (and probably less useful) than explaining what sociology *does*. This is why I've begun our introduction to sociology by highlighting some of its uses. At this point it is enough to know that sociology involves looking for and looking at social patterns

•   in social variables, such as age, gender, "race," ethnicity, religion, ability, and sexual orientation;
•   in social institutions, such as education, religion, and the family; and
•   in social interactions.

By the time you've reached the end of this textbook, I hope that you will have formed your own idea of what sociology really *is*.

Why Study Sociology?

Studying sociology helps you obtain a greater understanding of the *social world*, which is essentially the social practices, attitudes, and institutions that surround us. Studying sociology will also help you to better understand yourself in terms of whether you follow or do not follow patterns of social behaviour predicted by sociological variables. Think, for

The Point Is...

Can Sociology Help Someone Studying to Be a Police Officer?

I have taught sociology to many students in the Police Foundations Program (PFP), where it is a required course. They typically enter the classroom with the same question: *How can sociology help me as a police officer?* This is my typical response.

Police officers deal with people all the time in their jobs. Sociology gives PFP students a set of tools that can help them understand people representing different social categories (based on ethnicity, gender, age, and so on); these tools enable police officers to relate to people more effectively and with greater justice.

An example will illustrate. One summer, my wife and I had to drive to downtown Toronto to tend to a family emergency. My father-in-law had disappeared while looking for his car. He had been missing for over an hour. He did not have a cell phone. My wife and I spent the hour-long journey exchanging grimmer and grimmer explanations to account for her father's disappearance. He could have been injured and taken to hospital. He could have been beaten up by thieves. He could have become disoriented and fallen into the lake. One of us mentioned zombies. (Downtown Toronto, if you haven't been there, can be a scary place.)

By the time we arrived on the scene, we were distraught, and so was my mother-in-law. My immediate suggestion was to call the police. My perspective, as a white, middle-class, older man, was that the police were there to help—that they would be working *with* us in a situation such as this. My mother-in-law's position, that of someone who had grown up in Nazi Germany, was that police were agents of oppression: you did not ask for their help; you did not want them knowing about you. This is the position of many people who have come to Canada, sometimes as refugees, from countries run by oppressive, authoritarian regimes.

My mother-in-law strongly opposed calling the police. We called them anyway, and I explained why my mother-in-law was nervous around them, and reluctant to give them information. I like to think that my knowledge of sociology helped me present her position in a manner the officers could relate to, having themselves taken sociology courses as part of their training. Together, we shared an understanding of the situation rooted in sociology.

And, yes, we found my father-in-law. He had found his car and driven home, where he was waiting for us, safe and sound.

Michael Matthews—Police Images/Alamy Stock Photo

Would you find the sight of police officers patrolling your neighbourhood comforting or intimidating? How do you think your perspective is shaped by your age, your "race," your appearance, and other social characteristics?

instance, of a young Latin woman who likes salsa dancing—quite predictable—and a black youth from the city who enjoys line dancing—not so predictable. Sociology helps you develop an understanding about others around you in the multicultural and generally diverse social world that is Canada, as well as in the smaller social worlds of neighbourhoods, chat groups, classrooms, pubs, and workplaces. Thinking more globally, sociology helps you better understand the larger world of nations and their social institutions. You can look, for example, at how the price of oil can affect the relative presence or absence of democratic social practices in oil-producing countries such as Saudi Arabia and Iran. Political jurisdictions whose lands are rich in oil tend to have the same group or political party in power for a long time. Alberta did before the election of the NDP in 2015.

The Heart of Sociology: The Sociological Imagination

One of sociology's most useful instruments is the sociological imagination. The term was coined by **C. Wright Mills** (1916–1962), who sums it up nicely as:

> the capacity to shift from one perspective to another—from the political to the psychological; from examination of a single family to comparative assessment of the national budgets of the world. . . . It is the capacity to range from the most impersonal and remote transformations to the most intimate features of the human self—and to see the relationship between the two. (Mills, 1959: p. 4)

Mills argues that when we create and communicate sociological knowledge, our ideas must show "how society works" in terms of our own personal lives. If you go to buy a good pair of rubber boots (as my wife did), and the only ones you can get are yellow and relatively flimsy, then you are a woman, and your own frustrating shopping experience reflects the way society thinks of and treats women in general.

What happens when we fail to exercise our sociological imagination is discussed by Henry

Giroux in *Beyond the Spectacle of Terrorism: Global Uncertainty and the Challenge of the New Media* (2006). Commenting on the lack of sociological imagination in the post-9/11 political posturing of George W. Bush, Giroux warns that "[d]emocracy begins to fall and political life becomes impoverished when society can no longer translate private problems into social issues" (Giroux, 2006: p. 1). He spells this out in detail in the chapter "Acts of Translation":

> As the very idea of the social collapses into the private realm of the self and its fears, it becomes more difficult for people to develop a vocabulary for understanding how individual insecurity, dread, and misery could be translated into concerns of an engaged and critical citizenry. Instead, they are told that their privately held misery is a fall from grace, a flaw in character that must be suffered in isolation. Poverty, for example, is now imagined to be a problem of individual failing. Racism is rationalized and represented as simply an act of individual discrimination or prejudice. Homelessness is reduced to a freely chosen decision made by lazy people. (Giroux, 2006: p. 4)

In other words, without the sociological imagination, the individual, not society, becomes the primary focus of blame. The sociological imagination enables us to see an individual's circumstances in the context of broader social forces that affect us all and warrant our attention.

The Origins of Sociology

People since ancient times have contemplated social systems and looked for patterns in human social relationships. The first person to carry out a systematic study of sociological subjects and set his thoughts down in writing is most likely Arab scholar **Ibn Khaldûn** (1332–1406). In *Al Muqaddimah* (*An Introduction to History*), he examined various types of societies—tribes, cities, nations, and dynasties—and their histories, cultures, and economies. Many of his ideas and much of his research are still relevant. For instance, in *Al Muqaddimah*, he provided insight into the cyclical rise and fall of power and status among desert tribes in the Middle East:

The Point Is...

The Sociologist as Hero: C. Wright Mills

In my first year of university, the sociologist who captured my imagination was C. Wright Mills. He took on the rich and powerful and challenged his conservative colleagues and his country's government in the staid and stuffy 1950s. His public critique of American society caught the attention of the FBI, who started a file on him. He rode a motorcycle to work, and dressed in plaid shirts, old jeans, and work boots. Mills became my first sociologist hero.

Mills published seven books. These include two trilogies and an important stand-alone volume that gave its name to a key characteristic of the very best sociologists and sociology students: *The Sociological Imagination* (1959). His first trilogy, a study of the three main socioeconomic classes in the United States, comprises *The New Men of Power: America's Labor Leaders* (1948), *White Collar: The American Middle Classes* (1951), and *The Power Elite* (1956). The last of these found a wide and varied audience that included the then young Cuban revolutionary Fidel Castro, who, after he had overthrown the American-backed dictator Fulgencio Batista, invited Mills to visit so they could discuss his ideas. After the book was translated into Russian, Mills was asked to visit Moscow.

In the early 1950s, Mills issued a challenge to those writing sociology. Responding in a letter to a question about whether sociology writing could be improved, Mills wrote:

> It doesn't look good. I think for two reasons: First, there is no real writing tradition in sociology, as there is, for example, in history. It just doesn't exist. Second, the field is now split into statistical stuff and heavy duty theoretical bullshit. In both cases, there's no writing but only turgid polysyllabic slabs of stuff. So, because that is now the field, no men get trained, have models to look up to; there is no aspiration to write well. (Mills, 2000: pp. 154–5)

While Mills himself has disproved the first point, the second critique stands. So much of sociological writing is mired in theory and fails to resonate with a broad audience. So sociologists and sociology students, your duty is clear. Prove him wrong and aspire to write well, avoiding the "theoretical bullshit" and "polysyllabic slabs"!

Photo by Yaroslava Mills

Consider this photo of C. Wright Mills: does he look like an educator to you? Why or why not?

[W]hen a tribe has achieved a certain measure of superiority with the help of its group feeling, it gains control over a corresponding amount of wealth and comes to share prosperity and abundance with those who have been in possession of these things. It shares in them to the degree of its power and usefulness to the ruling dynasty. If the ruling dynasty is so strong that no one would think of depriving it of its power or of sharing [its power] with it, the tribe in question submits to its rule and is satisfied with whatever share in the dynasty's wealth and tax revenue it is permitted to enjoy. . . . Members of the tribe are merely concerned with prosperity, gain, and a life of abundance. [They are satisfied] to lead an easy, restful life in the shadow of the ruling dynasty, and to adopt royal habits in building and dress, a matter they stress and in which they take more and more pride, the more luxuries and plenty they acquire, as well as all the other things that go with luxury and plenty.

As a result, the toughness of desert life is lost. Group feeling and courage weaken. . . . Their group feeling and courage decrease in the next generations. Eventually group feeling is altogether destroyed. Eventually . . . [i]t will be swallowed up by other nations. (Ibn Khaldûn, 1981: p. 109)

Essentially, Ibn Khaldûn was arguing that as societies acquire more affluence, they also become more soft and senile and fall into demise. Replace "tribe" with "country" and "dynasty" with "empire," and Ibn Khaldûn's observations could have been written any time in the past century.

What do YOU think?

Even if you're new to sociology, you might have heard of people like Marx, Durkheim, and Weber before picking up this textbook, yet you probably hadn't heard of Ibn Khaldûn. Why do you think that Ibn Khaldûn has only recently been recognized for his contributions to the development of sociology?

The Development of Sociology in Europe

Sociology became an area of academic interest in nineteenth-century Europe, specifically in France, Germany, and Britain. It developed in response to the dramatic social changes taking place at that time: industrialization, urbanization, and significant population increases. Cities were growing rapidly, both because of the dramatic influx of people from the countryside looking for jobs in newly minted factories and because of natural population increases. Concerned scholars like the economist **Thomas Malthus** (1766–1834), a forerunner of modern sociologists, began to wonder whether Europe's cities could cope with such tremendous population growth. The politics of the time were also favourable to the growth of sociology, with the French Revolution in particular providing evidence that citizens could bring about social change swiftly and on a massive scale.

What do YOU think?

1. Why do you think it was that sociology developed in Europe rather than Africa, the Middle East, China, or South Asia?
2. How might sociology have developed differently as a discipline if the early thinkers had been African, Middle Eastern, Chinese, or South Asian?

Max Weber: A Founder of Modern Sociology

One example of the intellectual impact of early sociology is seen in the work of German sociologist **Max Weber** (pronounced VAY-ber; 1864–1920). One of his most important and well-known contributions was his identification of a set of values embodied in early Protestantism, which he called the Protestant (work) ethic. He believed that these values contributed significantly to the development of modern capitalism.

Weber's theory was based on a number of related ideas. One is the notion, popular among early Protestants, that there is a predestined "elect," a group of people who have been chosen to be "saved" during the Second Coming of Christ.

Telling It Like It Is

Not a Sociological Phenomenon, Eh?

In August 2014, after 15-year-old Tina Fontaine's lifeless body was found wrapped in a bag in the Red River in Winnipeg, Indigenous rights groups, along with women's rights activists and federal opposition parties, called on the government to hold an inquiry into why Indigenous women are disproportionately targeted for murder and other forms of violence. In response, Prime Minister Stephen Harper said that violent crime involving Indigenous women was not a "sociological phenomenon" but a series of more or less isolated incidents best left to the police. Sociology instructors across the nation said, "Thank you, Stephen, for helping me write my first lecture of the semester."

Sociology, as we've just seen, involves looking for patterns of social behaviour predicted by sociological variables—variables like age, "race," sex and gender (*not* the same thing, as we'll see in Chapter 9), and class (upper, middle, lower). These variables, or traits, combine to make up your **social location**, which gives you a unique set of experiences and outlook on the world around you. When one of these traits sets you apart from the mainstream—say, you identify as transgender, or you use a wheelchair—we can predict a pattern of social behaviour that involves discrimination against you because these traits tend to be negatively valued by society generally. We can also predict that the discrimination you face will be different if your social location involves two or more variables that set you apart from the mainstream—say, you identify as transgender *and* you use a wheelchair. The idea that the way two or more negatively valued traits

combine or "intersect" can make your experience of discrimination worse is known as **intersectionality**.

When we consider Indigenous women living in Canada, we can see that they have three strikes of social location against them: "race," class, and gender. They are Indigenous, they are usually poor, and they are women, embodying three traits that mainstream society judges negatively. This makes it easier for people to treat them violently and to exploit them sexually; it makes it easier for politicians and the media to neglect their problems and for police to treat them like non-humans. It makes it easy for someone like Stephen Harper, who is white, wealthy, male, and powerful, to say that the killing of Tina Fontaine was just an isolated crime; after all, the variables that make up his social location rule. Imagine if powerful white men started to disappear and turn up dead in disproportionate numbers. Do you think these would be treated as isolated crimes?

Indigenous women are far more likely than other women, and other Canadians, to be victims of homicide, domestic violence, and violence generally; they are more likely to go missing or enter the sex trade; they are more likely to have grown up in foster care; and they are more likely to be teenage parents and lone (i.e. single) parents. That Indigenous women are represented in unusually large numbers in these statistical findings is an example of what sociologists call **disproportionate representation**. This is a sociological phenomenon. It does not take a lot of sociological imagination to realize that.

Naturally, it was important to early Protestants to be seen as part of this exclusive group. Success through hard work was considered one proof of membership; another was the accumulation of capital (money and other assets used to generate money, like factories) through thriftiness. Working hard, making profitable use of one's time, and living a materially *ascetic* (self-denying) life by acquiring property and saving rather than spending lavishly

are all principles of Weber's Protestant work ethic. As Weber explained:

> The span of human life is infinitely short and precious to make sure of one's own election. Loss of time through sociability, idle talk, luxury, even more sleep than is necessary for health . . . is worthy of absolute moral condemnation. . . . [Time] is

infinitely valuable because every hour lost is lost to labour for the glory of God. Thus inactive contemplation is also valueless, or even directly reprehensible if it is at the expense of one's daily work. For it is less pleasing to God than the active performance of His will in a calling. ([1904]/1930: pp. 157–8)

Weber later elaborated on how demonstrating these values represents proof of being one of God's chosen few, and how these values supposedly fuelled the rise of capitalism:

The religious valuation of restless, continuous, systematic work in a worldly calling, as the . . . surest and most evident proof of rebirth and genuine faith, must have been the most powerful conceivable lever for the expansion of . . . the spirit of capitalism. ([1956]/1958: p. 172)

Although the idea of the Protestant (work) ethic took hold firmly enough that it entered popular thought and speech, it was never demonstrated sociologically that capitalism developed primarily in Protestant rather than in Catholic countries, or that the work ethic Weber associated with Protestantism was somehow missing from other religions. Latin American scholars argue that the rise of capitalism began with colonialism, a movement in which Catholic Spain and Portugal were major early players. Weber paid little attention to the role that colonialism played in the rise of capitalism as an instrument for exploiting colonized countries. Spain looted Aztec and Inca gold to become, for a time, the richest country in Europe. Weber, by attributing the development of capitalism to the strength of the Protestant will, might have been trying too hard to account for the relatively recent economic and political superiority of European Protestants.

What do YOU think?

1. Do you think that Weber would have advanced this theory if he had been a devout Catholic, Muslim, or Buddhist, rather than a liberal Protestant?
2. Does being religious enhance one's ability to become rich?

The Spread of Sociology to North America

During the late nineteenth and early twentieth centuries in North America, the emergence of conditions similar to those that existed already in Europe—the arrival of millions of immigrants, the development of cities and urban life, and the growing impact of technology on the daily lives of individuals—spurred the growth of sociology. In the United States, one of the country's oldest sociology departments, at the University of Chicago, arose primarily as a way of understanding the problems associated with the rapid immigration of thousands of Europeans to the city. During the 1920s and 1930s, the "Chicago School" became synonymous with both the specialized sub-discipline of urban sociology and a number of prominent sociologists including Everett C. Hughes, George Herbert Mead, Robert Park, Ruth Cavan, Edwin Sutherland, W.I. Thomas, Florian Znaniecki, and Jane Addams.

What do YOU think?

Look at the list of early sociologists in Table 1.2. Why are most of them men?

The Development of Canadian Sociology

While there is no distinctly Canadian way to carry out sociological research and practice, the way the discipline developed in this country and its primary focal points are unique. The relationship between French and English, the development of the Canadian West, the connection between class and ethnicity, and a close working relationship with anthropology have all been fundamental to the development of a Canadian perspective on sociology.

As we will see in later chapters, sociology began in this country long before the establishment of departments of sociology in Canadian universities and colleges. However, we will focus here on Canadian sociology as it developed in postsecondary institutions across the country.

Table 1.2   Some Early Sociologists and Their Contributions

Sociologist (years, nationality)	Key Works	Contribution
Auguste Comte (1798–1857, French)	• *The Course in Positivist Philosophy* (1830–42) • *A General View of Positivism* (1848)	A proponent of positivist philosophy, he aimed to develop a social science that could be used for social reconstruction.
Harriet Martineau (1802–1876, British)	• *Illustrations of Political Economy* (1834) • *Society in America* (1837)	Widely viewed as the first woman sociologist, she wrote extensively on social, economic, and historical topics and translated several of Comte's works.
Karl Marx (1818–1883, German)	• *The German Ideology* (1846) • *The Communist Manifesto* (1848, with Friedrich Engels) • *Capital* (1867)	The founder of modern communism, he viewed social change in terms of economic factors.
Herbert Spencer (1820–1903, British)	• *Social Statics* (1851) • *First Principles* (1862) • *The Study of Sociology* (1873)	Social evolutionist sought to apply Darwin's theory of natural selection to human societies and coined the term "survival of the fittest."
Friedrich Nietzsche (1844–1900, German)	• *Human, All Too Human* (1878) • *Beyond Good and Evil* (1886) • *On the Genealogy of Morals* (1887) • *The Will to Power* (1901)	Philosopher rejected Christianity's compassion for the weak and championed the "will to power" and the *Übermensch* ("superman"), who could rise above the restrictions of ordinary morality.
Thorstein Veblen (1857–1929, American)	• *The Theory of the Leisure Class* (1899) • *The Theory of Business Enterprise* (1904)	Economist and social critic attacked American "conspicuous consumption."
Émile Durkheim (1858–1917, French)	• *The Division of Labour in Society* (1893) • *The Rules of Sociological Method* (1895) • *Suicide* (1897) • *The Elementary Forms of the Religious Life* (1912)	Among the first to consider society as a legitimate subject of scientific observation, he studied society in terms of "social facts" such as ethics, occupations, and suicide.
Georg Simmel (1858–1918, German)	• *On Social Differentiation* (1890) • *The Philosophy of Money* (1900) • *Sociology: Investigations on the Forms of Sociation* (1908)	Father of microsociology studied the way people experience the minutiae of daily life.
Max Weber (1864–1920, German)	• *The Protestant Ethic and the Spirit of Capitalism* (1904–5) • *Economy and Society* (1922)	Identified a set of values, the "Protestant (work) ethic," to which he attributed the rise of capitalism.
George Herbert Mead (1863–1931, American)	• *Mind, Self, and Society* (1934)	Father of "symbolic interactionism" looked at how the self is constructed through personal exchanges with others.
Robert Park (1864–1944, American)	• *Introduction to the Science of Sociology* (1921) • *The City: Suggestions for the Investigation of Human Behavior in the Urban Environment* (1925)	Urban sociologist was a founding member of the "Chicago School" of sociology.
W.E.B. Du Bois (1868–1963, American)	• *The Souls of Black Folk* (1903) • *Black Reconstruction in America* (1935)	Documented the experience of American blacks from a sociological perspective.

Note: All works have been identified by their English titles, although several of these works first appeared, in the years indicated, in languages other than English.

McGill University: Dawson, Hughes, and Miner

The first professional, institutionalized sociologist in Canada was **Carl Addington Dawson** (1887–1964). Born in Prince Edward Island, Dawson completed his MA and PhD at the University of Chicago. In 1922, shortly after joining the faculty at McGill, he founded the university's sociology department, an accomplishment not without opposition. Senior administrators worried about the left-wing political leanings of sociologists (they still do), and academics in other departments did not want their scholarly territory infringed upon. Dawson succeeded in spite of these objections. McGill's remained the only independent department of sociology until 1961.

Dawson's work reflected two elements of early Canadian sociology: (1) the social gospel movement and (2) hands-on social work. The social gospel movement developed as an attempt by people trained for the ministry to apply Christian principles of human welfare to the treatment of social, medical, and psychological ills brought on by industrialization and unregulated capitalism, not just in Canada but in the United States, Britain, Germany, and other European countries during the late nineteenth century. Out of the social gospel movement came the Social Service Council of Canada (1912), which through various churches carried out the first sociological surveys of Canadian cities.

Dawson's affinity with the social gospel movement was natural—his first degree was in divinity—but his inspiration to become involved early on in social work came as well from the methods and philosophy of the Chicago School of sociology. The Chicago School put an emphasis on going out into communities—what sociologist Robert Park called "living laboratories"—to observe them first-hand. Dawson took this approach and, with his students, applied it to the living laboratory of Montreal. Their research was given a jump-start in 1929, when they were awarded a $110,000 Rockefeller Foundation grant to study unemployment in the city.

That same year, Dawson and Warren E. Gettys became the first Canadians to write a sociology textbook (three cheers for sociology textbooks!). The text was an instant success, adopted by over 150 colleges and universities across North America within a year. While there was not a great deal of Canadian content, it helped legitimize the study and practice of sociology in Canada.

Another figure vital to the development of sociology at McGill was **Everett C. Hughes** (1897–1983). Like Dawson a graduate of the University of Chicago, the Ohio-born Hughes joined the sociology department at McGill in 1927. Hughes was a firm believer in community research. While at McGill, Hughes focused on the "ethnic division of labour," a situation that enabled English Canadians to rise above French Canadians in large companies, creating a disparity that he wished to correct. Out of this research came *French Canada in Transition* (1943). By the time the landmark study was published, Hughes had already returned to the States to take a position in the faculty of his alma mater.

Horace Miner (1912–1993) was another American sociologist who put the study of French Canada at the forefront of Canadian sociology. As a graduate student at the University of Chicago, he came to Quebec to study the parish of St Denis. His book *St Denis: A French-Canadian Parish* (1939) shows the blurred distinction between sociology and anthropology in Canada. His work is best described as an ethnography, a study of a community based on extensive fieldwork, whose primary research activities include direct observation of and interaction with the people observed. Ethnography is the main research method used in social anthropology. Miner described the rural peasants and farmers of his study as a folk society, following the model of University of Chicago anthropologist Robert Redfield, who coined the term. The close connection between sociology and anthropology can still be seen in some Canadian universities where the two disciplines are joined in the same department.

The University of Toronto: Harold Innis and S.D. Clark

Around the same time, a different sociological tradition, that of political economy, was beginning at the University of Toronto. Political economy is an interdisciplinary approach involving sociology, political science, economics, law, anthropology, and history. It looks primarily at the relationship between politics and the economics of the production, distribution, and consumption of goods. It is often Marxist in nature, pointing to the

What kind of work do you think is being performed at this Montreal office c. 1920? Are the people you see here more likely to be anglophones or francophones?

tensions that arise in the extraction and distribution of goods.

A Canadian pioneer in this field was **Harold Innis** (1894–1952), who joined the University of Toronto in 1920. Innis was more economic historian than sociologist, but his work has exerted a strong influence on Canadian sociology. He argued that the availability of staples—resources such as fish, fur, minerals, and wheat—shaped the economic and social development of Canada. I wonder what he would think of the oil projects in northern Alberta today.

Innis was also a mentor to the first person hired at the university specifically as a sociologist, **Samuel Delbert Clark** (1910–2003). Born in Alberta, S.D. Clark received his first two degrees from the University of Saskatchewan before joining the Department of Political Economy at the University of Toronto in 1938. Sociology remained a branch of that department until 1963, when it became a stand-alone department, with Clark as its chair. Summarizing Clark's influence, sociologist Deborah Harrison wrote:

The importance of S.D. Clark within the development of Canadian sociology is universally recognized. Clark's publications span more than forty prolific years, with at least the first fifteen occurring when almost no other sociologists were writing in Canada; he is generally acknowledged as the father of the Canadian approach to the discipline. . . . For reasons of both his scholarly engagement and his articulation of a "Canadian" sociology, Clark is the most important sociologist Canada has yet produced. (Harrison, 1999)

Clark can be considered a "sociological historian": consider a selection of his chapter headings in *The Developing Canadian Community* (1962):

- The Farming–Fur-Trade Society of New France
- The Rural Village Society of the Maritimes
- The Backwoods Society of Upper Canada

- The Gold-Rush Society of British Columbia and the Yukon
- The Prairie Wheat-Farming Frontier and the New Industrial City
- The Religious Influence in Canadian Society
- The Canadian Community and the American Continental System
- History and the Sociological Method.

Social Class and Ethnicity: John Porter

Fundamentally missing from the work of both Innis and Clark are the themes of class and ethnicity. These themes received their definitive treatment in what is generally recognized as the best-known work of Canadian sociology, *The Vertical Mosaic: An Analysis of Social Class and Power in Canada* (1965), by **John Porter** (1921–1979). Porter joined the faculty of Carleton University in 1949, becoming the university's first full-time appointment in sociology. The title of his book plays on the term cultural mosaic, a metaphor frequently used to characterize Canada's multicultural society. A mosaic is a type of artwork composed of many small tiles that lend different colours to the picture. A society that is a cultural mosaic is one "in which racial, ethnic, and religious groups maintain a distinct identity, rather than being absorbed into a 'melting pot'" (Lundy & Warme, [1986]/1990: p. 583). A melting pot encourages the "rapid assimilation of recent immigrants into their new society" (Lundy & Warme, 1990: p. 586).

Porter coined the term vertical mosaic to describe the situation he observed in Canada, in which systemic discrimination produced a hierarchy of racial, ethnic, and religious groups. To stay within the metaphor of the mosaic, we can say that Porter's study found that the different tiles were stacked and not arranged evenly. Tiles representing white Anglo-Saxon Protestants were at the top of the hierarchy, followed by French-Canadian tiles, the tiles of the more successful ethnic groups (notably Jewish, Chinese, and Italian), and finally those of everyone else, with the racially marginalized groups at the bottom. Porter concluded that ethnicity was the main factor determining how the tiles were ranked.

Melting pot or cultural mosaic?

AP Photo/Matt Rourke

Three Early Women Sociologists and the Writing of Gender in Canada

Annie Marion MacLean

Annie Marion MacLean (*c.* 1870–1934) was the first Canadian woman to obtain a PhD in sociology. Born in Prince Edward Island, she received her first two degrees from Acadia University before earning her PhD at the University of Chicago. She also taught there, although, despite her excellent qualifications, in a very subordinate position.

MacLean pioneered the sociological study of working women, especially in *Wage-Earning Women* (1910), which was based on a survey of some 13,500 women. She conducted her research in department stores, in "sweat shop" factories, and among hop-pickers in rural Oregon. Though born in Canada, she was never hired by a Canadian university.

Aileen Ross

The first woman hired as a sociologist at a Canadian university was **Aileen Ross** (1902–1995), a Montrealer, who taught sociology at the University of Toronto for three years before joining the faculty at McGill. She earned her first degree at the London School of Economics, and her MA (in 1941) and PhD (in 1950) from the University of Chicago.

Ross devoted her books to two of her foremost concerns: women and India. She published *The*

Hindu Family in an Urban Setting (1962) after carrying out several years of research in India. *The Lost and the Lonely: Homeless Women in Montreal* (1982) was the first study of homeless women in Canada. Her research strategy for that study is discussed in the next chapter, on pages 46–7.

Helen C. Abell

Alberta-born **Helen C. Abell** (1917–2005) has been called the founder of rural sociology in Canada. After receiving a degree in human nutrition at the University of Toronto (1941), she worked as a nutritionist for the Ontario Department of Agriculture, and then as an officer in the Canadian Women's Army Corps during World War II. She received her PhD in rural sociology (the first Canadian to do so) in 1951. She then established a rural sociology research unit in the federal Department of Agriculture. Her research, notes Jenny Kendrick:

> played an important role in identifying systematically the roles women played on the farm. This was an invaluable contribution to the policy arena, virtually forcing society and policymakers to lay aside their stereotypes of the marginal contributions of farm women to agriculture. (Quoted in Eichler, 2001: p. 382)

The Growth of Sociology in Canada

In 1958, there were fewer than twenty sociology professors in Canada, teaching in just nine universities (Clark, 1976: p. 120). Sociology did not become a significant area of study and teaching in Canada until the 1960s and 1970s, as baby boomers entered universities and colleges. The growth of sociology during that time is astounding. Hiller and Di Luzio, for example, report that the University of Alberta "had no sociology majors in 1956–7, but a year later had nine, followed by 24 (1957–8), 44 (1959–60), and 62 (1960–1). The number of majors there reached a peak for the twentieth century at 776 in 1987" (Hiller & Di Luzio, 2001: p. 490).

During this era of growth in sociology, most of the sociologists hired to teach in Canadian postsecondary institutions were from the United States and Britain. Of those with doctorates teaching sociology and anthropology in Canada in 1967, 72 per cent

had PhDs from the US, 10 per cent from Britain, and only 6 per cent from Canada (Gallagher & Lambert, 1971: p. vii). In 1973–4, 45 per cent of the full-time sociology faculty in Canada was made up of non-Canadians (Hofley, 1992: p. 106). This should not be surprising given that only 22 doctorates in sociology were conferred at Canadian universities between 1924 and 1967 (Gallagher & Lambert, 1971: p. vi).

The lack of Canadian sociologists meant that sociology textbooks lacked a Canadian perspective. When John Hofley was hired to teach sociology at Carleton University in 1966, he saw "very little about Canada in the sociology texts that were available" (Hofley, 1992: p. 104). The 1970s saw a big movement to "Canadianize" sociology textbooks. Today most introductory sociology textbooks used in Canadian schools are either Canadian in origin or "Canadianized" versions of American textbooks.

What do YOU think?

How might an introductory sociology textbook written in Canada be different from a "Canadianized" one originally written in the US?

Different Kinds of Sociology

Sociology did not take on a uniform appearance as it grew as a discipline during the nineteenth century: instead, it diversified. European and North American social thinkers had differing views of what sociology was, what it could do, and how it should be applied. Consequently, sociology developed into several different schools that varied according to their particular applications and the perspectives (historical, political-economical, feminist, and so on) of those who were using it.

In this section we will explore two ways of distinguishing the various kinds of sociology. The first is based on the approach used; the second is based on the intended audience for the work and how socially critical the sociologist is.

1. Sociology by Approach

The traditional way of representing different kinds of sociology in introductory textbooks is to break it down into the different approaches sociologists use to pursue their inquiries:

- structural functionalism
- conflict theory
- symbolic interactionism
- feminist theory
- postmodern theory.

These terms are typically presented in the introductory chapter of a textbook and then repeated throughout most, if not all, of the subsequent chapters. The linguist Edward Sapir said, "all grammars [i.e. explanations of language] leak." We feel that this particular "grammar of sociology" leaks too much (like a flooded basement) to sustain using it throughout the text. Nevertheless, these distinctions do reveal some key differences in philosophy, so they are worth explaining and illustrating here.

Structural Functionalism

The structural-functionalist approach has deep roots in sociology. As the name suggests, the approach contains two dimensions. *Functionalism* focuses on how social systems, in their entirety, operate and produce consequences. The work of Émile Durkheim, Robert Merton, and Talcott Parsons (discussed in Chapter 13, on health and medicine) represents the functionalist approach.

The functionalist approach was fused with *structuralism* (grounded in the work of anthropologists Bronisław Malinowski and A.R. Radcliffe-Brown) as a way of explaining social forms and their contributions to social cohesion. It uses an *organic*, or biological, analogy for society. How? Nursing students, when they take the dreaded Anatomy and Physiology course, have to learn all the different *structures* of the human body as well as the *functions* each one performs. The structural-functionalist approach treats society in a similar way: *This is the part of society we call "organized religion." This is what it does for society . . .*

While the structural-functionalist approach was popular for most of sociology's history, it has lost favour during the last few decades. It is too much of a stretch, for example, to talk about the *functions*

ZUMA Press, Inc./Alamy Stock Photo

Vancouver's Downtown Eastside is one of the poorest urban neighbourhoods in North America. A functionalist would argue that homelessness is a natural social consequence of our economic system, and that it benefits society by providing citizens with an incentive to work hard. Would you agree?

of poverty or inequality and how they contribute favourably to social stability. Poverty and inequality don't really serve the interests of society at large, just the narrow class interests of those who profit from others' misfortunes. In addition, functionalism is not good at promoting an understanding of conflict or social change. While sociologists still draw on the classic works and essential concepts of structural functionalism, few contemporary sociologists are committed to the theoretical practice itself in their research and writing.

Durkheim and Social Facts

To get a better sense of the functionalist approach, look at the work of **Émile Durkheim** (1858–1917), one of the founders of sociology. An important early sociological concept is Durkheim's social fact. Social facts are patterned ways of acting, thinking, and feeling that exist outside of any one individual but exert social control over all people. Think about how different social characteristics—aspects of your social location such as gender, age, religion, ethnicity, "race," sexual orientation, your role as sister or brother or as student or teacher—exert a compelling social force over you and lead you to act in sociologically predictable ways. These ways of acting based on social characteristics are social facts.

Every social fact has three essential characteristics:

1) It was developed prior to and separate from any individual (i.e. *you* didn't invent it).
2) It can be seen as being characteristic of a particular group (young Canadian men, for instance, like to watch sports while drinking beer—a social fact that explains why so many beer commercials feature young men watching sports).
3) It involves a constraining or coercing force that pushes individuals into acting in a particular way (like when young men watching sports succumb to "beer pressure" and begin yelling, high-fiving, and displaying other behaviour associated with this social fact).

You can see how looking for social facts would be a useful way for a sociologist to get beyond focusing on individuals to examine larger social forms and how different parts of society function.

In *Suicide* (1897), Durkheim examined suicide as a social fact. He found that in late nineteenth-century France, certain groups were more likely to commit suicide than others: military officers more than enlisted men, Protestants more than Catholics, and unmarried people more than married people. He drew a correlation between suicide and the degree to which individuals were connected or committed to society, finding that those with a very strong dedication to society were more likely to commit suicide than those with a weaker commitment. Officers are responsible for the soldiers in their charge. It makes sense that a heightened sense of honour might make them suicidal when they make a mistake that results in the death of one of "their men." On the other hand, Durkheim also concluded that having too weak a connection to society could produce suicide. Protestants were in the minority in France and thus had weaker bonds to both the country in which they lived and its culture.

In Canada today, men commit suicide more often than women do. This is a social fact. Why men commit suicide more often than women do is a complicated matter. It has to do in part with the fact that women are more likely to share their problems with other people than to "suck it up" and remain silent. Women are more likely to have a network of friends with whom they can communicate about serious matters, and they are more likely to go to a therapist with an emotional problem, which lowers their likelihood of committing suicide. Women attempting suicide are also more likely to use less efficient means: pills and slashed wrists over the more deadly male choice of guns.

> ## What do YOU think?
>
> The author of this textbook considers himself fairly enlightened, with feminist sympathies. Yet a woman reader commented that it was obvious this commentary was written by a man: women, she pointed out, are less likely to commit suicide because of their child care responsibilities, not because they're incapable or are more likely to "share their feelings." Do you agree?

Since the start of this century, and particularly since the start of the War in Afghanistan in 2001, a number of high-profile suicides among Canadian soldiers have made the subject of suicide in the Canadian Forces a topic of concern among public health officials, veterans' groups, and the public

A woman holds a message as Canadian soldiers who served in Afghanistan are recognized during the National Day of Honour on Parliament Hill in Ottawa (9 May 2014). How do you think a show of public support like this might affect a returned soldier's connection to society?

generally. In response, the Surgeon General commissioned a study of suicide among Canadian Forces personnel from 1995 to 2012, comparing the suicide rate among male soldiers with the suicide rate among male civilians in the general population (Bogaert et al., 2013). What the study showed was that in each age group, the rate of suicide among male soldiers was actually lower than the rate among non-soldiers (see Table 1.3). How can we account for the unexpected result? The authors of the report suggested that the screening process used by the Canadian Forces plays a significant role: in assessing candidates, the military chooses only those who exhibit a high degree of emotional and mental stability. Do you think we could also argue, following Durkheim, that men in the Canadian Forces feel a greater degree of attachment to a larger group than their male civilian peers do?

When examining Table 1.3, you should note that the difference between the projected number of suicides and the actual number of suicides was shrinking as Canada's participation in the Afghanistan mission continued. We also know that public support for Canada's mission was falling during that time. Do you think that the lack of support here at home might have played a role in narrowing the gap?

Merton's Manifest and Latent Functions

Robert K. Merton (1910–2003), one of the leading American sociologists of the mid-twentieth century and a major contributor to functionalist thinking, identified three types of functions:

1) **Manifest functions** are both intended and readily recognized, or "manifest" (i.e. easily seen).

Table 1.3	Suicides among Male Canadian Forces Personnel: Actual versus Expected, 1995–2009

	Suicides		Difference between Actual and Expected	
Years	Actual	Expected*	Number	Percentage
1995–9	56	78	−22	72
2000–4	50	63	−13	79
2005–9	50	59	−9	85

* Based on the rate of suicides among Canadian civilians within the same age groups studied.

Source: Adapted from Bogaert et al., 2013, Table 1 (p. 3) and Table 2 (p. 4).

2) Latent functions are largely unintended and unrecognized.

3) Latent dysfunctions are unintended and produce socially negative consequences.

This last group is often studied using the conflict approach, making Merton's brand of functionalism something of a bridge to conflict theory (which we will examine in the next section). The three examples in Table 1.4 illustrate the differences among Merton's three functions.

Conflict Theory

Conflict theory (sometimes called the conflict approach) is based on the "four Cs":

- conflict
- class
- contestation
- change.

The approach is based, first, on the idea that *conflict* exists in all large societies. The stress lines are factors such as sex and gender, "race" and ethnicity, religion, age, and class—the sociological ingredients of a person's or group's social location. Second, it asserts that *class* divisions exist and are a source of conflict in all large societies. Third, it contends that

the functions of society, as laid out in traditional structural-functionalist theory, can be *contested*, or challenged, based on the question, *What group does this function best serve?* Finally, the approach involves the assumption that society either will or should be *changed*.

A major figure in the early history of sociology was German economist and political philosopher **Karl Marx** (1818–1883). For Marx, conflict was all about class: the division of society into a hierarchy of groups, with each group's position determined by its role in the production of wealth. Marx saw class conflict as the driving force behind all major socio-historical change. He believed that conflict between the class of capitalists (the bourgeoisie) and the class of workers (the proletariat) would initiate a socialist revolution that would produce a classless,

---

What do YOU think?

1. Could you challenge, amend, or add to any of the functions presented in Table 1.4? How?
2. What would be the three different functions for the following?
   a) children's organized sports in Canada
   b) large organized walks, runs, or bike rides for social causes.

Table 1.4   Examples of Robert Merton's Three Functions

Example 1	**Postsecondary Education**
manifest function	Postsecondary education provides students with the skills and knowledge to find a profitable career in order to become productive, self-sufficient citizens.
latent function	It provides a social network that will make the search for employment and a marriage partner easier.
latent dysfunction	From a left-wing perspective, postsecondary education reinforces class distinctions, since people in the lower socioeconomic classes cannot afford to attend; from a right-wing perspective, it exposes students to (dangerous!) socialist ideas.
Example 2	**Religion**
manifest function	Religion fulfills spiritual and emotional needs, and answers important existential questions that many people have.
latent function	Religion creates a social support network and marriage market.
latent dysfunction	Religion provides justification for judging outsiders ("non-believers") negatively.
Example 3	**Canadian Doughnut Shops**
manifest function	Doughnut shops provide customers with coffee, snacks, and light meals, served quickly and conveniently.
latent function	Doughnut shops serve as places to meet and socialize with others.
latent dysfunction	Doughnut shops provide late-night venues for drug dealing.

bonnie jacobs/iStockphoto

The relationship between a teacher and her students is a social fact. What patterned ways of acting influence this teacher's behaviour toward her students? How might the teacher, should she not conform to the behaviour expected of her, be punished, either in some formal way (i.e. by the school board) or in some informal way (i.e. by her peers or her students or their parents) depending on the nature of the transgression? What are some of the patterned ways of acting that influence students' behaviour?

or egalitarian, society. A classless society has never existed in more complex societies, but many of Marx's insights about class conflict and capitalist production are still valid. This is true on a global scale, if you think of transnational corporations headquartered in Western societies as the capitalist "owning class" and underpaid workers in poorer countries (say garment workers in Bangladesh producing cheap clothes for Canadian shoppers) as the ultimate "working class."

The territory of conflict theory now stretches well beyond Marxism and incorporates applications in feminist sociology, critical disability thinking, "queer" theory, anti-colonialism, and other approaches that fall under the umbrella of "critical sociology," which we'll encounter shortly.

Symbolic Interactionism

Symbolic interactionism is an approach that looks at the meaning (i.e. the symbolism) of our daily social interactions. For example, two male students approach each other and, with a slight incline of the head, say, "'Sup, yo?" lightly bringing their fists together in greeting. What are they communicating to each other about their relationship, their shared interests, and their role models?

The symbolic-interactionist method was pioneered by American social psychologist **George Herbert Mead** (1863–1931), who examined the way the self is constructed as we interact with others and how the self allows us to take on social roles, reflect on ourselves, and internalize social expectations. **Herbert Blumer** (1900–1987), a pupil of Mead's, coined the term "symbolic interaction." He (1969) argued that social systems are simply abstractions that do not exist independently of individual relations and interactions. In other words, social systems (friendship patterns, education, the economy, etc.) are simply byproducts of our personal dealings with one another.

The symbolic-interactionist approach, with its focus on individuals rather than larger social structures, differs from the approaches described

vitchanan/iStockphoto

In this conversation, how is meaning being generated? Words are simply one aspect of constructing meaning in our day-to-day interactions.

earlier—functionalism and conflict theory. It represents one part of another distinction used to differentiate various kinds of sociology: the distinction between macrosociology and microsociology. When sociologists engage in research and writing that focus primarily on the "big picture" of society and its institutions, they are engaging in macrosociology. Weber, Durkheim, Merton, and Marx were all primarily macrosociologists. When the focus is, instead, more on the plans, motivations, and actions of the individual or a small group, then a microsociological approach is involved.

A good example of how microsociology and a symbolic-interactionist approach are used to understand people's actions comes from the work of **Erving Goffman** (1922–1982). Born in Alberta, Goffman received his BA from the University of Toronto and his MA and PhD from the University of Chicago. His work was highly original, as evidenced by the many terms he introduced to sociology. One example is total institution, an expression he coined in *Asylums* (1961). He defined it as any one of "a range

of institutions in which whole blocks of people are bureaucratically processed, whilst being physically isolated from the normal round of activities, by being required to sleep, work, and play within the confines of the same institution" (quoted in Marshall, 1998: pp. 669–70). Examples include psychiatric hospitals, prisons, army barracks, boarding schools, concentration camps, monasteries, and convents—institutions whose residents are powerfully regulated, controlled, or manipulated by those in charge.

Goffman carried out his research for *Asylums* in 1955–6, when he engaged in fieldwork at a mental hospital in Washington, DC. He wanted to learn about the day-to-day social world of the inmates. He did this by pretending to be an assistant to the athletic director, a position that allowed him to pass his days with the patients. Goffman stressed the importance of learning the *subjectivity* of people, meaning the views and feelings they have. He denied both objectivity and neutrality in his research methodology, and sided with the patients rather than the professionals who managed them in the hospital.

Our Stories

Applying Goffman to Research

I'm a Goffman fan. His books are readable, and his concepts are readily adaptable to research, as I discovered in 1972, when I spent a year studying a religious group in downtown Toronto for my honours thesis. I needed a theoretical base for my research, and so I turned to Goffman's *The Presentation of Self in Everyday Life* (1959). In this book he introduced the **dramaturgical approach**, a way of conducting research as if everyday life were taking place on the stage of a theatre. According to an often-told anecdote, Goffman was on the Hebrides Islands, off the coast of Scotland, looking for a topic for his doctoral dissertation. While sitting in a restaurant, he noticed that the waitstaff acted differently when they were on the "**front stage**"—that is, in the public eye—than when they were "**backstage**" in the kitchen, away from the dining customers. They presented themselves differently depending on which stage they were on, an example of what Goffman called **impression management**. Impression management refers to the ways in which people conduct themselves in specific roles and social situations. His doctoral thesis and best-selling book were born that day—or so the story goes.

The religious group I was studying was managing their impressions for two different audiences. One included street kids and other youthful lost souls who might be in need of spiritual guidance. For this audience, representatives of the religious group put on a hip, anti-establishment face. However, in order to obtain food donations from supermarket chains to feed their flock, and to achieve respectability in the eyes of both corporate sponsors and the neighbouring businesses in their rather exclusive downtown area, they had to present a more conservative face.

I predicted that the group would split according to the two "stages," the two audiences to which they were presenting themselves. This happened just a year later, when the organization developed two distinct branches, one dealing with youth outreach and the other handling charitable donations. Thanks, Erving.

Brian Losito/Air Canada

Can you apply Goffman's dramaturgical approach to the work of a flight attendant? Who makes up the "front stage" audience? Where is the "back stage"? Which audience(s) are the pilots part of?

Feminist Theory

Two branches of conflict theory now comprise such an extensive collection of research and literature that they demand to be considered in their own right. These two branches are feminist theory and postmodern theory.

Feminism, it could be argued, began with Mary Wollstonecraft's *A Vindication of the Rights of Women* (1792). Like anything that has existed and evolved for well over two hundred years, it is difficult to pin down with a tidy, hard-and-fast definition. We can say that feminism involves correcting centuries of discrimination and male-dominated conceptions of gender roles in order to gain and present an accurate view of the social condition of women. Contrary to what some male students believe, you don't have to be a woman to be a feminist. You do have to accept that recognizing a female perspective (or "standpoint") is absolutely critical to forming an accurate appraisal of the roles women play in society (or so says the bearded feminist John Steckley).

One of the earliest sociologists to carry out a careful examination of women's roles in society was British writer and social theorist **Harriet Martineau** (1802–1876). She wrote over 6,000 articles, many of them on the social condition of women. In 1834 she began a two-year study of the United States, which she documented in the three-volume *Society in America* (1837) and in *Retrospect of Western Travel* (1838). Her feminist thinking can be seen in her comparison of women to slaves in a chapter of the former work revealingly called "The Political Non-Existence of Women." After travelling to the Middle East, she published *Eastern Life: Present and Past* (1848), in which she briefly departed from her intended sociological spirit of impartiality to condemn the practice of polygyny (one husband with more than one wife).

Martineau's goal of remaining impartial was in keeping with the sociology of her time. In contrast, most feminist theorists today believe that the best way to understand the social condition of women involves trying to view life through the eyes of the women they're studying. It sounds obvious, but it was a revolutionary idea, and a foundational figure in the movement was a Canadian sociologist, **Dorothy Smith** (b. 1926). While doing graduate work at the University of California, Berkeley, Smith experienced first-hand the kind of systemic sexist discrimination that would become the subject of her first work. She moved to Canada in the late 1960s, when she was given a rare (for a woman) teaching opportunity at the University of British Columbia. Fortunately, as she jokes, departments of sociology in this country were "scraping the bottom of the barrel." It was the start of a distinguished academic career that also includes slightly less than 20 years at the University of Toronto's Ontario Institute for Studies in Education. She is currently (2016) an adjunct professor of sociology at the University of Victoria.

Smith developed standpoint theory directly out of her own experience as a woman discriminated against by male colleagues in the academic community. Her standpoint theory challenged traditional sociology on two fronts, both relating to sociology's preference for objective (depersonalized and distanced from everyday life) as opposed to subjective (personalized and connected to everyday life) research and analysis. Her first criticism attacked the traditional position that the objective approach to research is more scientific and therefore truthful, while the subjective position is ideological, based on biases and prejudices, and therefore distorted. According to Smith, knowledge is developed from a particular lived position, or "standpoint." Sociology, having developed from a male standpoint, had long denied the validity of the female standpoint and overlooked the everyday lives of women—an oversight that feminist researchers today are still working to correct.

What do YOU think?

1. How does Smith's standpoint theory fit with Mills's notion of the sociological imagination?
2. Do you agree with Smith's view that sociology developed from a male standpoint? Why or why not?
3. Consider the list of early sociologists and their contributions provided in Table 1.2. How might early developments in the growth of sociology have differed if the female standpoint had been given greater consideration?

Feminism's "Waves"

Some historians have attempted to trace the development of feminism through successive generations, or "waves," each characterized by a different agenda. According to this conception, first-wave feminism is associated chiefly with the campaign for civil and political rights, specifically the rights to vote and hold political office, which began in the nineteenth century. Canada's "Famous Five," a group of social leaders and activists who petitioned to have women recognized as "persons" under British and Canadian law in the early twentieth century, are examples of first-wave feminists in this country (see Our Stories on page 274 of Chapter 9 for more on the Famous Five).

After securing political rights in most North American jurisdictions, the women's movement began to wane in the first half of the twentieth century. It gained new life during the civil rights movement that began in the 1960s, fuelled by the fight for equality in the home and in the workplace, including equal opportunities for employment and pay. The activists of this generation saw themselves as successors to the "first wave" of activists, who had won voting and other rights. Second-wave feminism differed, though, by tackling not just public rights—like the right to take a job in traditionally male-dominated professions—but also private rights, including reproductive rights and freedom from domestic violence (Hunter College & Simalchik, 2017).

Beginning during the 1980s, third-wave feminism is associated with the campaign for social justice for women left out of the more mainstream agenda of second-wave feminism, traditionally set by white women from middle- and upper-middle-class backgrounds. Some critics view it as a backlash against second-wave feminism. Third-wave feminism represents the interests of LGBTQ women, as well as women from racial and ethnic minorities and women living in poverty. It is closely tied to the notion of intersectionality defined earlier in this chapter.

So where are we now? Many feminist activists today are using social media as a way to draw attention to issues including sexual harassment and violence, online bullying and shaming, media representations of women, and unethical versus ethical pornography. Some see this millennial-driven activism as a fourth wave. Others say it's merely third-wave feminism carried out using the tools of technology. Others still argue that the idea of waves is an outdated concept that was problematic to begin with: after all, where do you situate black feminists of the 1960s and 1970s, who were arguing that race was being left off the feminist agenda (Hunter College & Simalchik, 2017)? What is clear is that there are many feminisms, defined by different (sometimes competing) interpretations of the movement and its objectives. We will revisit different kinds of feminism in Chapter 9, on gender and sexuality.

Postmodern Theory

A good way to think of postmodern theory is to consider the concept of *voices*. In all societies, there are different voices that speak, and together they represent a diversity of life experiences and social locations. Postmodern theory is concerned with recognizing that there are many such voices, and that they should not be drowned out by the powerful voice of those who are dominant in society (traditionally, white heterosexual men from middle- and upper-class backgrounds).

A leading figure in postmodern theory was the French philosopher and historian **Michel Foucault** (1926–1984). In his groundbreaking article "Two Lectures" (1980), Foucault talked about the misleading nature of what he termed totalitarian discourse. A totalitarian discourse is any universal claim about how knowledge or understanding is achieved. Western science, for example, is at the centre of a totalitarian discourse used by those who claim that it is the only legitimate path to discovering the "truth" about the causes and cures for different diseases, while dismissing alternative forms of medicine that are popular and trusted in many non-Western cultures.

"Totalitarian" in this context should be easy enough to understand: it describes a set of beliefs or ideas that dominates ("totally") all others. The other part of this term, "discourse," is not as easily understood. A discourse can be defined as follows:

> A conceptual framework with its own internal logic and underlying assumptions that may be readily recognizable to the audience. A discourse involves a distinct way of speaking about some aspect of reality. [Use of the term] also suggests that the item under discussion is not a natural attribute of reality but socially constructed and defined. (Fleras & Elliott, 1999: p. 433)

A discourse is not necessarily wrong or false. The term really just refers to a particular treatment of a topic that has been created through a given set of assumptions, a vocabulary, rules, logic, and so on. However, to call something a *totalizing* (or *totalitarian*) discourse is to condemn it as overly ambitious and narrow-minded. Consider the common observation that the brain is like a computer. We can create a discourse comparing the functions and capabilities of the brain to those of a computer. Both store memories—sounds, images, video—and both acquire and process "data." We can all relate to a time when we felt that our brains had "crashed."

But the discourse fails when we consider how poorly computers handle translation. Computers cannot translate well—not as well as humans—since they cannot deal with the complicated input of cultural context. Very few words or phrases from any given language can be translated directly and perfectly into another. Our discourse, then, is problematic: the brain may be *similar* to a computer *in certain ways*, but it would be wrong to say that the human brain is *just like* a computer. A discourse becomes totalitarian when it is promoted by those with power and influence until it becomes widely accepted as the only "right" interpretation.

In *The Archaeology of Knowledge* ([1972]/1994), Foucault wrote about the importance of discovering how individual discourses developed as a way of examining their strengths, weaknesses, and limitations. He called this process of discovery an archaeology of knowledge. The sociologist must dig through the layers of presented information considered to be factual (a discourse) in order to discover how the supposed fact was established or constructed.

Through this process of excavation the sociologist may find that some parts of the discourse have been distorted along the way, which affects how people interpret and act upon the discourse. The Our Stories segment on page 29 presents an example of how an archaeology of knowledge can lead us to reassess our understanding of a supposed historical fact.

Foucault's challenge to students of sociology is to understand that knowledge is constructed, and that it is important to investigate the question, *How do we know that?* Because there are conceptual constraints that both determine and limit our thinking in ways that we are not aware of, there may be alternative constructions of knowledge on a particular subject that are just as valid as—or even more valid than—our own.

2. Sociology by Audience

Another way of categorizing sociology is based on the *audience* for whom the work is intended and how critical the sociologist is. We borrow here from

Stephanie Sinclair/VII

Tahani (*left*), married at the age of six, and Ghada, also a child bride, stand with their husbands in Hajjah, Yemen. Every year, millions of girls under 18 enter arranged marriages. The tradition spans continents, religion, and class. Girls who marry early often abandon their education, and the incidence of maternal and infant death is high for women under 18 who give birth. How important are the factors of "race" and gender in telling the story of these girls? What might a Western, white, male sociologist, or female journalist miss? What insights might a sociologist raised with child marriage as part of her culture add that could otherwise be missing?

Our Stories

Abandoning Inuit Elders: An Archaeology of Knowledge

Several introductory sociology textbooks assert that among Inuit populations, it was once customary to abandon the elders when times got tough, such as during food shortages. The discourse of abandoning elders, presented as fact, has been reinforced and perpetuated through the disciplines of sociology and anthropology, and internalized within popular culture. By conducting an archeological excavation of this discourse, we are able to see how this "fact" was constructed.

The first step is to check the relevant footnotes and the bibliographies contained in the textbooks. Most of the sociology textbooks studied obtained their information from three earlier studies: one on Inuit (Weyer [1932]/1962), one on suicide (Cavan [1928]/1965), and one on primitive law (Hoebel [1954]/1965). When you look at these studies, you discover that none of the writers actually did their own research on Inuit. They were merely citing earlier works.

The next step is to track down the works written by those earlier scholars to find out what they actually said. Some researchers studying the Inuit merely assumed that the practice occurred, even though they hadn't observed it. A few mentioned times when elders were temporarily left behind while others who were more fit went ahead to look for food before returning to feed and resume travel with the elders. In fact, there is no direct observation or ethnographic account of the practice of elder abandonment. The reported custom never really existed.

We could take a further step by questioning who benefited from this particular discourse of elder abandonment. This line of inquiry might lead us to large and celebrated Canadian institutions, such as mining companies, the Hudson's Bay Company, and the RCMP—all of which moved into Inuit territory without respecting their Indigenous rights—and to sociologists and anthropologists in need of sensational examples to illustrate cultural differences between the Inuit and mainstream North American society.

Michael Burawoy (2004), who divided sociology into four types:

- professional
- critical
- policy
- public.

Professional Sociology

Professional sociology has as its audience the academic world of sociology departments, scholarly journals, professional associations, and conferences. The research carried out by professional sociologists is typically designed to generate very specific information, often with the aim of applying it to a particular problem or intellectual question. Consider some of the articles that appeared recently in the *Canadian Review of Sociology* (2015):

- "The Rise and Stall of Canada's Gender-Equity Revolution"
- "Social Class, Economic Inequality and the Convergence of Policy Preferences: Evidence from 24 Modern Democracies"

- "Home Care Workers' Skills in the Context of Task Shifting: Complexities in Care Work"
- "Critical Nexus or Pluralist? Institutional Ambivalence and the Future of Canadian Sociology."

These articles address specific sociological questions, centring around the key issues of gender, specifically in the work world, class, and the state of sociology in Canada. Written in technical or specialized language, they target an academic or professional readership, but can usually be read by interested students.

Critical Sociology

The main role of critical sociology, according to Burawoy (2004), is to be "the conscience of professional sociology." It performs this role in two ways:

Critical sociology reminds professional sociology . . . of its value premises and its guiding questions. It also proposes alternative foundations upon which to erect sociological research. In other words, critical sociology is critical in two senses, first in bringing professional sociology into alignment with its historical mission and second in shifting the direction of that mission. (Burawoy, 2004)

Critical sociology, then, addresses the same audience that professional sociology does, but with a different purpose. Its aim is to make sure that professional sociologists do not lose sight of the goals of sociological inquiry, specifically to bring about meaningful social change.

Much of what we call conflict theory would fit into this category. Two giants of critical sociology, Michel Foucault and Dorothy Smith, are known for having examined the production of knowledge in relation to power—in other words, which groups in society get their views heard and accepted as true. Foucault discussed the conflict between "scientific experts" and other producers of knowledge, whose voices tended to be drowned out by the former group, while Smith discussed conflict in terms of gender relations.

Policy Sociology

Policy sociology is about generating sociological data for governments and large corporations, to be used in developing laws, rules, and long- and short-term plans. A government might commission a study on crime prevention to see if tougher sentences or better rehabilitation programs are more likely to reduce the rate of criminals reoffending: this would be an example of policy sociology. Think-tanks are policy organizations that try to bring about social change by persuading governments to adopt or amend certain laws (the right-wing Fraser Institute and the left-leaning Broadbent Institute are two examples). When they commission studies to generate findings that support their lobbying efforts, this is another example of policy sociology. Education, health, and social welfare are three main areas that policy sociology serves.

A classic work of Canadian policy sociology is the *Report on Social Security for Canada*, prepared by **Leonard Marsh** (1906–1982). Based on research Marsh had done in the 1930s while acting as research director for the McGill Social Science

Research Project, it set the stage for a number of major social policy initiatives that we now take for granted. The report offered:

a dense and detailed plan for comprehensive social programs, constructed around the idea of a social minimum and the eradication of poverty. The realization of this ideal, according to Marsh, meant the recognition that individual risks were part of modern industrial society, and that they could be met by collective benefits throughout the lifecycle. . . . "Employment risks" were to be met through income-maintenance programs, such as unemployment insurance and assistance, accident and disability benefits, plus paid maternity leave. . . . "Universal risks" were addressed through national health insurance, children's allowances, and pensions for old age, permanent disability, and widows and orphans. (Maioni, 2004: p. 21)

None of these social policies existed in Canada at the time. A particularly notable aspect of Marsh's report, as Antonia Maioni points out, was his "holistic view of social security that considered health as a central part of the welfare state, rather than a separate item and expense" (2004: p. 21). Our system of health insurance can be traced to this important piece of policy sociology.

Public Sociology

Public sociology addresses an audience outside of the academy (i.e. universities and colleges) and the political establishment. Herbert Gans (1989) has identified three key traits of public sociologists:

One is their ability to discuss even sociological concepts and theories in the English of the college-educated reader. . . . Their second trait is the breadth of their sociological interests, which covers much of society even if their research is restricted to a few fields. That breadth also extends to their conception of sociology, which extends beyond research reporting to commentary and in many cases social criticism. . . . [T] heir work is intellectual as well as scientific. A third, not unrelated, trait is the ability to avoid the pitfalls of undue professionalism. (Gans, 1989: p. 7)

By "undue professionalism" Gans is referring to professional sociology's overly cautious style, its tendency to footnote everything, and its inclination to bury analysis in statistics. My nominee, as the consummate public sociologist, is C. Wright Mills, introduced earlier in this chapter. The recently published *The Public Sociology Debate: Ethics and Engagement* (2014), by Canadian sociologists Ariane Hanemaayer and Christopher J. Schneider, presents a powerful discussion of public sociology as it relates to the Canadian context.

Professional, Critical, Policy, and Public Sociology: A Review

Distinctions among the four types of sociology are not watertight. It is common for individual sociologists to engage in more than one area, even on a single piece of work. Criticisms can flow easily from people who see themselves as practitioners of one form only. Professional sociologists criticize critical sociologists for low professional standards and for being "troublemaking radicals." Critical sociologists accuse professional sociologists of being far too conservative, and of taking small bits of data and over-analyzing them, dazzling their reading audience with statistical science while actually saying little. Public sociologists could accuse professional sociologists of speaking only to a very small audience made up exclusively of peers; at the same time they accuse the policy sociologists of selling out to corporate and government "mouthpieces." But policy and professional sociologists can counter-accuse the public sociologists of being in it just for the fame, of being no more than "pop sociologists" or simply "popularizers"—a dirty term among many in the academy.

What do YOU think?

1. Consider the four types of sociology we've just discussed. Where do you imagine your sociology instructor would fall in this scheme? Where would you place the author of this book?

2. Have you ever seen or heard a broadcast interview with a sociologist? If you haven't, why do you think this is so? Is "popular" sociology—sociology for the masses—any more or less important than the other kinds (professional, critical, policy)?

WRAP IT UP

Summary

In this chapter, I tried to give you a sense of what sociology *looks like*. You likely won't have formed a really good opinion of what sociology *is* until you've reached the end of the book. You've learned a bit about what my approach to writing sociology is like, and my aim of making this a textbook not like the others. You have been introduced to some of the main players that will strut the stage in the chapters that follow: Marx, Durkheim, Weber—three of the modern discipline's founders; Goffman, Foucault, and Smith, pioneers of critical sociology; the structural-functionalist Merton and the symbolic-interactionist Mead. Others you have met only in passing, but you can expect to read a lot more about them in later chapters.

In addition to becoming familiar with some of the discipline's key figures, you have discovered two different ways of categorizing sociology: by approach (structural functionalism, conflict theory, and symbolic interactionism, along with the growing perspectives of feminism and postmodernism) and by audience (professional, critical, policy, and public). References to these categories turn up frequently throughout the book. Finally, you have tasted some of sociology's Canadian flavours. Expect plenty more Timbits and maple syrup in the chapters to come.

THINK BACK

Questions for Critical Review

1. Outline some of the differences and similarities between sociology and other social science disciplines, such as anthropology, political science, women's studies, and Indigenous studies. What are some of the places where these disciplines intersect?
2. Identify the key ideas of Durkheim, Marx, and Weber, as outlined in this chapter.
3. Distinguish between the structural-functional, conflict, and symbolic-interactionist approaches to sociology.
4. What do the "newer" perspectives of feminism and postmodernism add to sociology?
5. Distinguish between professional, critical, policy, and public sociology.
6. Articulate the basic ideas of Erving Goffman, Michel Foucault, and Dorothy Smith, as outlined in this chapter.

READ ON

Suggested Print and Online Resources

Online

C. Wright Mills [1916–1962]

www.genordell.com/stores/maison/CWMills.htm
- This very useful website features a short profile of the eminent sociologist, as well as lists of works by and about Mills and links to online copies of some of his books and articles.

The Durkheim Pages

http://durkheim.uchicago.edu/
- Created by University of Illinois historian and sociologists Robert Alun Jones, this site contains abundant information on the French sociologist, including a biography, summaries of some of his works, and a glossary of terms important to understanding Durkheim's work.

Marx & Engels Internet Archive

www.marxists.org/archive/marx/
- This is a comprehensive guide to the works of the two fathers of socialism, complete with an image gallery and a sophisticated search feature that allows readers to find specific words and phrases.

Max Weber [1864–1920]

www.sociosite.net/topics/weber.php
- Created by Dutch sociologist Albert Benschop, this site contains links to books and articles by and about Max Weber.

From Cradle to Cane: The Cost of Being a Female Consumer

www1.nyc.gov/assets/dca/downloads/pdf/partners/Study-of-Gender-Pricing-in-NYC.pdf
- New York City's Department of Consumer Affairs commissioned a study of gender pricing in 800 products sold at over two dozen retailers in the Big Apple. Released in December 2015, the report documented evidence of the "pink tax" on everything from toys and children's clothing to adult apparel and personal care products.

In Print

CJS (2009), *Canadian Journal of Sociology* 34 (3); also online at https://ejournals.library .ualberta.ca/index.php/CJS.
- This special issue of CJS devoted to professional, critical, policy, and public sociology features articles by and about Michael Burawoy, as well as features on sociological practice in French Quebec and what public sociologists do.

Gary Gutting (2005), *Foucault: A Very Short Introduction* (Oxford: Oxford).
- This is a reasonable and concise introduction to Foucault's life and ideas. It's not for every reader, though, as it is a fairly heavy read and dense in terminology.

Michael Hviid Jacobsen, ed. (2009), *The Contemporary Goffman* (New York: Routledge).
- This collection of readings by various authors imagines what kind of research Goffman might be involved in if he were living in the twenty-first century.

Allan G. Johnson (1997), *The Blackwell Dictionary of Sociology: A User's Guide to Sociological Language* (Oxford: Blackwell).
- This is a very useful reference work that outlines some of the basic terms in sociology.

Kathryn Mills, ed. (2000), *C. Wright Mills: Letters and Autobiographical Writings* (Los Angeles: University of California).
- Gathered and edited by a daughter of C. Wright Mills, this collection makes clear connections between the famous sociologist's life and work.

Dorothy Smith (1987), *The Everyday World as Problematic: A Feminist Sociology* (Boston: Northeastern University).
- This is probably the most often read work by the Canadian pioneer of standpoint theory.

John Steckley (2013), *Learning from the Past: Five Cases of Aboriginal Justice* (Whitby, ON: de Sitter).
- Chapter 2, The Helen Betty Osborne Case (pp. 55–86), offers a good discussion of *disproportionate representation*, a term introduced in relation to Indigenous women earlier in this chapter.

Social Research Methods

The Gist

Reading this chapter will help you to . . .

- Understand the difference between fact, theory, and hypothesis.
- Distinguish between qualitative and quantitative social research.
- Recognize the defining features of the various qualitative research methods.
- Explain why it is important to identify the individual informant in ethnographic research.
- Outline the value of narratives to sociological research.
- State the significance of operational definitions in quantitative research.
- Recognize and give examples of spurious reasoning.

Terms of the Trade

- absolute poverty
- anomie
- average
- best practices
- case study approach
- causation
- content analysis
- correlation
- cultural artifact (or event)
- dependent variable
- direct correlation
- discourse analysis
- disjuncture
- ethics
- ethnography
- experiential
- fact
- genealogy

- hypothesis
- independent variable
- informant
- informed consent
- insider perspective
- institutional ethnography
- inverse correlation
- low income cut-off
- Market Basket Measure
- mean
- median
- narrative
- negative correlation
- operational definition
- Orientalism
- outsider perspective
- participant observation
- positive correlation

- positivism
- poverty
- poverty line
- qualitative research
- quantitative research
- relative poverty
- research methodology
- ruling interests
- ruling relations
- semi-structured interview
- spurious reasoning
- statistics
- theory
- third variable
- triangulation
- variable
- voice

Names to Know

- Auguste Comte
- Michel Foucault
- Aileen Ross
- Edward Said
- Dorothy Smith

For Starters

epicurean/iStockphoto

Fact, Theory, Hypothesis, and Wondering Why People Speed Up When I Pass Them

It's easier to *observe* than it is to *explain*. I can observe people speeding up on the highway when I pass them, but I can't really explain why they do it. Is it because the bee-like buzz of my car's engine wakes them up from a semi-sleeping state? Or is it their competitive spirit that awakens when I—an aging hippie in a Toyota Corolla—pass them in their shiny, high-priced, high-powered vehicles?

That people speed up when I pass them is a **fact**: an observation that, as far as can be known, is true. It does not happen all the time. I have observed it often enough to call it at least a *tentative* fact. But if I want to use important qualifiers such as *almost all of the time*, or *most of the time*, or the easier to prove *often*, then I have to find a way to *quantify* this fact—for example, by saying: "I passed 100 vehicles, and 37 were observed to speed up." I should also be more specific about the situation involved by adding "on Highway 50, northwest of Toronto"; "while driving in the slow lane, passing someone who is in the passing lane"; "while driving home from work, travelling north around four o'clock." This is how I quantify and qualify my fact: by giving details about how often it occurs and under what conditions.

Now I need a theory. A **theory** is an attempt to explain a fact or observed phenomenon. My theory of

why people speed up when I pass them is that I make them aware that they are travelling more slowly than they thought they were. My theory becomes a **hypothesis** when I set out to verify it by providing some kind of concrete test of its validity. What kind of test can I provide? Obviously I can't pull people over on the highway and ask them why they just sped up when I passed them. However, I could develop a questionnaire for people who use that highway. First, I might ask a question such as, "Do you frequently speed up when people pass you on a highway?" I might follow up with a multiple-choice question such as the following:

What is your best explanation for speeding up when people pass you on a highway?

a) Being passed makes me realize that I am driving slower than I thought.
b) I do not like people passing me.
c) I am very competitive.
d) Other: explain _____. (e.g. I use the highway to re-create my favourite movie scenes from *The Fast and the Furious*.)

Then I would proceed to test the hypothesis.

Introduction: Research Methodology Is No Joking Matter

Nothing is more contentious in sociology than research methodology, the system of methods a researcher uses to gather data on a particular question, hence the following joke:

> **Question:** How many sociologists does it take to change a light bulb?

> **Answer:** Twenty: one to change the light bulb and nineteen to question that person's methodology.

There is no single best way to do sociological research. Researchers often combine several research methods in their work. In this chapter we'll take a look at some of the different methods used in sociological research, pointing out the pluses and pitfalls of each one. We begin, though, with a few comments about the history of sociology research and some challenges to be aware of.

Insider versus Outsider Perspective: Challenging Sociology's Positivist Tradition

French philosopher **Auguste Comte** (1798–1857) coined the word *sociology*. The basis of Comte's sociology was positivism, a belief that the social sciences could be studied using the methods used to study the natural sciences, namely experiment, measurement, and systematic observation. Positivism also assumes that the supposed objectivity of these methods can be applied just as well to the social sciences with no accommodation made for the biases, or any other aspects of the social location (gender, age, ethnicity, etc.), of the social scientist.

Although the positivist mode of thinking had a long run, many sociologists today do not believe it is possible for an "outsider" to study a group with complete objectivity. Indeed, one way to contrast the different methods of sociology research is to look at how researchers treat insider and outsider perspectives. In Comte's view, the outsider was the "expert" and occupied a privileged position over the subjects of study. Most of sociology's history reflects this privileging of the outsider perspective. Of the four audience-based types of sociology discussed in the previous chapter—professional, critical, policy, and public—policy sociology is the one most likely to reflect the outside expert ideal.

By contrast, critical sociology, particularly feminist sociology, rates the insider view highly while questioning the outsider's presumed objectivity. Dorothy Smith's standpoint theory, introduced last chapter, states that social characteristics such as gender, "race," ethnicity, age, and sexual orientation strongly condition both the questions sociologists ask and the answers they receive. **Michel Foucault**, in *The History of Sexuality, Volume I* (1978), criticized the outsider approach in his discussion of the "sexual confession." Foucault described the sexual confession as an approach to treating sexual deviance in which the "deviant" patient admits to "impure" thoughts, fantasies, and taboo sexual practices in the presence of an "expert"—typically a doctor or psychotherapist. The subjects being treated provide information based on personal experience. But according to Foucault, this information is not recognized as "authentic" until it has been interpreted by an "objective" outsider expert. This individual is placed in the privileged position of deciding which parts of the insider's account are true and which are fabricated or imagined. The subject is not allowed to have a voice that is heard without translation from the outsider/expert. This is how sociologically important messages get lost.

To see how an outsider perspective can be flawed, imagine yourself as a non-Aboriginal sociologist studying a First Nation reserve. Taking an outsider approach, you conduct your study by looking only at statistics, covering such subjects as unemployment, housing, crime rates, and suicide. Not including the voice of the people who live on that reserve means that you will miss key elements of interpretation. First, some definitions could be problematic. Take "unemployed." Is a man providing for his family by hunting, trapping, fishing, gathering plants for food and medicine, and cutting wood for home heating and cooking "unemployed"? Technically he is, as he does not have a "job" that pays money. Second, typical statistical surveys of Aboriginal reserves leave unanswered the question of why so many people choose to live on reserves when there is so much more unemployment, crime, and overcrowding than in non-Native communities of comparable size. You need to hear the people's voices to answer this question.

Brian Maracle is a Mohawk who left his home reserve when he was five years old but returned as an adult. *Back on the Rez: Finding the Way Back Home* (1996) is his account of the first year of his return to the Six Nations reserve near Brantford, Ontario. This reserve is very different from the more troubled Aboriginal communities—Davis Inlet and Attawapiskat, for example—commonly described in sociology textbooks. The people of the Six Nations reserve have lived there for over 220 years, since the land was granted to them for siding with the British during the American Revolution. In the introduction to *Back on the Rez*, Maracle points out that reserves can be considered homelands because they function as refuges from non-Aboriginal society:

> The reserves mean many things. . . . On one level, these postage-stamp remnants of our original territories are nagging reminders of the echoing vastness of what we have lost. On another, they are the legacy and bastion of our being. They are a refuge, a prison, a madhouse, a fortress, a birthplace, a Mecca, a resting-place, Home-Sweet-Home, Fatherland and Motherland rolled into one. (Maracle, 1996: p. 3)

Maracle writes of the importance of the reserve as the home of the Mohawk elders, who interpret past traditions and adapt them to the present. In this way, he emphasizes that the reserve is the home of Aboriginal culture. However, reserves are not always homeland to everyone. They can be places where men with physical strength and social connections can oppress women and sexually abuse children. They can be places where young people feel despair and alienation, caught between the ancient traditions that make up their heritage and the rapidly modernizing practices of a globalizing world. While recognizing the importance of the insider's view in sociological research, remember that a range of voices have to be heard.

My position is that complete objectivity is impossible whenever one human being studies others. However, complete subjectivity can be blind. A judicious balance of insider and outsider vision is the ideal.

What do YOU think?

Think of a community that you are particularly involved in—a club or team, a religious group, your college or university residence, or some other. How easily could it be studied by an outsider? Which insider voices would an outsider need to listen to in order to get an accurate picture of it? What biases would be reflected if they asked only you?

Qualitative versus Quantitative Research

An ongoing debate in sociology concerns the relative merits of qualitative research and quantitative research. Quantitative research focuses on social elements that can be counted or measured, which can therefore be used to generate statistics. It often involves working with surveys, questionnaires, and polls. Qualitative research involves

Quick Hits

The Weaknesses of the Insider View

Have you ever been told you were too close to a situation to judge it fairly? Many of Maracle's insights come from his position as both an insider *and* an outsider. Imagine the weaknesses of a study of the Harper government written by Stephen Harper himself or one of his cabinet ministers. Think of how a marriage counsellor can see the flaws in a marriage that are invisible to the couple. The point is, while insider views are vital to a proper sociological understanding of a situation, a critical view often requires a certain measure of distance.

the close examination of characteristics that cannot be counted or measured. Unlike quantitative research, which is typically used to find the patterns governing whole structures or systems, communities, and so on, qualitative research may be used to study those smaller cases that don't fit into the larger model.

Proponents of quantitative research accuse qualitative researchers of relying on data that is "soft," "anecdotal," "too subjective," or "merely literary." In turn, champions of the qualitative approach dismiss quantitative researchers as soulless "number crunchers" operating under the delusion that it is possible for humans to study other humans with complete objectivity. It's wrong to think that the two methods are mutually exclusive. Good quantitative researchers know that their research always has a subjective component to it and always involves choice and some personal bias. They usually make statements to that effect in introductory comments. Qualitative researchers, similarly, often benefit from using quantitative data. We'll now take a closer look at different methods of qualitative and quantitative research to see how they measure up.

Qualitative Research

Qualitative research permits—often encourages—subjectivity on the part of both researcher and research subject in a way that quantitative research oriented around "hard data" does not. Among the various qualitative methods are ethnography and the case study approach, which differ mainly in their breadth of focus. The former typically takes a broader view by attempting to describe the entirety of a culture, while the latter adopts a narrower focus to study individual cases.

Ethnography

Robert P. Gephart, who teaches research methods at the Alberta School of Business, describes ethnography as relying on

> direct observation and extended field research to produce a thick, naturalistic description of a people and their culture. Ethnography seeks to uncover the symbols

and categories members of the given culture use to interpret their world. . . . (Gephart, 1988: p. 16)

A classic example of the ethnographic approach in sociology is William Whyte's *Street Corner Society: The Social Structure of an Italian Slum* (1955). Beginning early in 1937, Whyte spent three-and-a-half years living in the neighbourhood of Boston that he called "Cornerville," following a standard research practice of assigning a fictitious name to the community studied in order to preserve the anonymity of the subjects. Whyte spent 18 months living with an Italian-American family. His research methodology involved semi-structured interviews—informal, face-to-face interviews designed to cover specific topics without the rigid structure of a questionnaire but with more structure than an open interview—and participant observation, which entails both observing people as an outsider would and actively participating in the various activities of the studied people's lives. Participant observation enables the researcher to achieve something resembling an insider's perspective.

Researchers engaged in ethnography typically depend as well on informants, insiders who act as interpreters or intermediaries while helping the researcher become accepted by the community studied. Whyte's informant was a gang leader in his late twenties who went by the name "Doc." Whyte met Doc through the latter's social worker in a meeting Whyte describes in the book:

> I said that I had been interested in congested city districts in my college study but had felt very remote from them. I hoped to study the problems in such a district. I felt I could do very little as an outsider. Only if I could get to know the people and learn their problems first-hand would I be able to gain the understanding I needed. (Whyte, 1955: p. 291)

Doc replied:

> "Well, any nights you want to see anything, I'll take you around. I can take you to the joints—gambling joints—I can take you around to the street corners. Just remember

that you're my friend. That's all they need to know. I know these places, and, if I tell them that you're my friend, nobody will bother you. You just tell me what you want to see, and we'll arrange it." (Whyte, 1955: p. 291)

Doc and Whyte would discuss Whyte's research interests and findings to the point where Doc became "in a very real sense, a collaborator in the research" (Whyte, 1955: p. 301). Whyte learned to speak Italian so that he could talk directly to the older generation from Italy. He participated in the second generation's activities of going to "gambling joints," bowling, and playing baseball and cards. He called his work "participatory action research" because he wanted his research to lead to actions that would improve the lives of the people studied.

In Canada, Whyte's study influenced Carl Dawson's work with Prairie communities, as well as the Quebec community studies of Everett C. Hughes (*French Canada in Transition*, 1943) and Horace Miner (*St Denis: A French-Canadian Parish*, 1939).

Institutional Ethnography

Institutional ethnography is a relatively new method of research, based on the theories of **Dorothy Smith**. This method of research differs from traditional sociological research in that it does not reflect the view that a neutral stance is necessarily more scientific than an approach that explicitly involves "taking sides" (Campbell & Gregor, 2002: p. 48).

Institutional ethnography recognizes that any organization can be seen as having two sides, each associated with a different kind of data. One side represents ruling interests: the interests of the organization, particularly its administration, and/or the interests of those who hold power in society. The data associated with this side are text-based, comprising the institution's written rules and practices. When the workers in the institution follow these rules and practices, they are activating ruling relations: that is, they are helping to serve the needs of the organization, often at the cost of their clients and themselves.

A soup kitchen in the basement of a Montreal church in the 1930s, around the time of William Whyte's study of Italian slums in Boston. How would you engage in ethnographic research in this kind of setting?

The other side of an organization is that of the informant, someone who works in the institution outside of management. The data associated with the informant's side are experiential, based on the informant's experience. Institutional ethnography recognizes that there is a disjuncture, or separation, between the knowledge produced from the perspectives of these two sides. In pointing out this disjuncture, institutional ethnographers generate information that they hope will lead to institutional change.

Schools offer a good example of the kind of organization that institutional ethnographers study. York University professor Alison Griffith asserts that teachers rely on parents (typically mothers) to get children to do the work and acquire the skills necessary to succeed at school. Campbell and Gregor refer to this reliance on parents as "downloading educational work" (2002: p. 43). This practice serves the ruling interests of boards of education and provincial governments, who can then spend less on schools and teachers. Teachers and parents, by complying with the demands of school administrators, are activating ruling relations. At the same time, they are also biasing the system in favour of students from upper- and middle-class households, whose parents are in a better position to provide the resources (including their own time and knowledge, as well as computers and high-speed Internet access and a quiet study space) to best serve this end. Lower-class students are poorly served by the system, as they are more dependent on the school and its resources. The problem is made worse in provinces like Ontario, where it is illegal for school boards to pass deficit budgets. Local boards, meeting the ruling interests of the provincial government, have been forced to consider closing pools and cutting music and athletic programs, putting more pressure for children's health and enrichment onto the parents. So there's a second disjuncture—between the provincial government and its boards—in addition to the one between boards and administrators and parents/children. This kind of information, generated

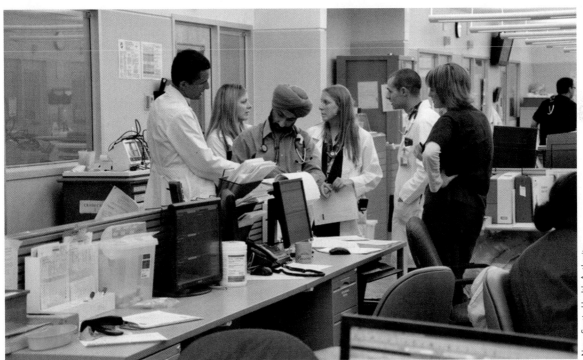

Nova Scotia Health Authority

Managers and charge nurses at the QEII Health Sciences Centre in Halifax meet to identify how many beds will be available for patients coming from scheduled surgeries and the emergency room. The hospital is a common subject for institutional ethnography. Who represents the ruling interests? Who is responsible for ensuring that those ruling interests are met? Who gets caught in the middle?

through institutional ethnography, can be used to recommend improvements to the school system.

The Case Study Approach

British sociologist Gordon Marshall describes the case study approach as

> [a] research design that takes as its subject a single case or a few selected examples of a social entity—such as communities, social groups, employers, events, life-histories, families, work teams, roles, or relationships—and employs a variety of methods to study them. . . . Case studies include descriptive reports on typical, illustrative, or deviant examples; descriptions of good practice in policy research; evaluations of policies after implementation in an organization; studies that focus on extreme or strategic cases; the rigorous test of a well-defined hypothesis through the use of carefully selected contrasting cases; and studies of natural experiments. (Marshall, 1998: p. 56)

The case study approach is often used to identify and describe best practices—strategies with a proven history of achieving desired results more effectively or consistently than similar methods used in the past by a particular organization or

Our Stories

Case Study of a Best Practice: First Nation Policing in Kitigan Zibi Anishinabeg

Located about 130 kilometres north of Ottawa, Kitigan Zibi Anishinabeg, with a registered population of 1,401 (as of the 2011 census), is the largest of nine communities that make up the Algonquin Nation in Quebec. The community first had its own policing services in 1981, when, like other Quebec First Nations, it began operating a community police force under the auspices of the Amerindian Police Service (the APS). The APS is usually seen as a failure by First Nations in Quebec, owing mainly to the fact that Aboriginal officers were given limited, second-class roles as "special constables." In 1985, the Kitigan Zibi community moved ahead of other Aboriginal communities by transferring police services to its own independent force.

Following the introduction of the federal First Nation Policing Policy in April 1992, the community entered into a three-year tripartite agreement that allowed the Kitigan Zibi Police Department (KZPD) to become a fully functional force, with powers equivalent to those of any non-Aboriginal force in Canada. By 2002, the KZPD had a chief of police, five full-time officers, and one part-time officer. Community satisfaction with the department's work was high: in a 2002 survey, 91 per cent of community members surveyed felt that the KZPD was the best police organization to meet the needs of the community. This compares favourably to the 55 per cent of community stakeholders who, in a First Nation Chiefs of Police Association survey, felt the self-administered police services in their communities were effective.

There are four keys to the success of the KZPD. Unfortunately, two of them cannot be replicated in most other First Nations. First, Kitigan Zibi has a very stable political environment. At the time of the study, the chief councillor of the band had been in the position for over 20 years. During that time there had been few changes in the makeup of the band council. Further, there were no apparent political factions within the community, making it unlike many First Nations. Second, the KZPD has a reasonably harmonious relationship with the Quebec provincial police, a rarity for a First Nation force in Quebec.

currently by similar organizations. The case study typically begins by introducing an organization or department that exemplifies the best practices under review, before describing the practices in terms of the organization's success. The case study is often geared to finding out whether certain best practices can be applied with comparable success elsewhere.

Narratives

The narrative is perhaps the purest form of the insider view. Narratives are the stories people tell about themselves, their situations, and the others around them. They have long been part of sociology. An early Canadian example of narrative research is **Aileen Ross**'s *Becoming a Nurse* (1961), based on her analysis—for an introductory sociology course—of 259 term papers written by nursing students between 1948 and 1959.

In spite of their history and the value of narratives to sociological inquiry, the positivism of early sociology and the discipline's emphasis on statistical evidence kept narrative study in a minor role until the late 1980s. In 1993, D.R. Maines proclaimed the growing interest in narratives among sociologists as "narrative's moment." He saw in this trend a dual focus for sociological study, aimed at both examining the narratives of the subjects of study and at the same time "viewing sociologists as narrators" (Maines, 1993: p. 17). He put forward 10 propositions on which to base narrative sociology:

1) Since all socialized humans are storytellers, they are always in a potential storytelling situation when interacting with or encountering others.
2) The vast majority of all speech acts and self-representations contain at least some elements of narratives.
3) Variation in situation, audience, individual perspective, and power/authority relations will

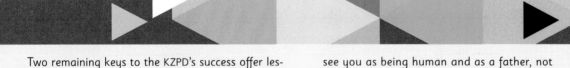

Two remaining keys to the KZPD's success offer lessons for police forces operating in other First Nations. One is the strong relationship between the KZPD and the youth of the community. In 1995, the KZPD took part in a pilot project with Aboriginal youths aged between 12 and 24, who were paired with police officers to ride in cruisers, observe police duties first-hand, and visit the homes of their police mentors. Commenting on the mentoring experience, one officer said, "I took great pride in seeing the barriers fall and the sense of openness that developed in our communication" (First Nations Policing Update, July 1995, #3). In 1996, Chief of Police Gordon MacGregor (still in office in June 2016) stressed:

> [t]he importance of being among the people, being visible and approachable especially to the youth and young children. . . . [P]eople see you as being human and as a father, not just as a police figure. (Stewart, 1996)

The final key is the KZPD's dedication to training. One condition of the 1992 tripartite agreement signed with federal and provincial governments was that constables already in the force would earn the basic training equivalency diploma. This would enable the officers to assume powers equal to those of any other officer in Quebec. All of the KZPD's officers successfully completed the training. The chief of police went beyond the qualifications required in the agreement, taking managerial courses for senior officers and additional courses offered at the Canadian Police College in Ottawa. When the Quebec Police Act was amended to include more training for provincial officers, the chief of police prepared a five-year forecast of the training needs of his force.

What do YOU think?

1. What indicates that the KZPD is a good choice for a best practice case study?
2. What factors in the KZPD's success cannot be readily replicated in other First Nation communities in Quebec? Which ones can?
3. The case study approach combines quantitative and qualitative research. How is that evident in this case?

produce the universal condition of multiple versions of narrated events.

4) Narratives and narrative occasions are always potential sites of conflict and competition as well as of co-operation and consensus.

5) All narratives are potentially rational accounts, but because of inherent human ambiguity and variation in linguistic competence, all narratives are ultimately incomplete.

6) Narratives exist at various levels of scale, ranging from the personal to the institutional to the cultural; they exist for varying lengths of time; and they inevitably change.

7) All social science data are already interpreted data; the uninterpreted datum does not exist.

8) All sociological facts are narrated facts insofar as they have been processed through some form of story structure that renders events as factual.

9) The act of data collection is an act of entering respondents' lives that are partly formed by still unfolding stories. Therefore, in the name of honesty, research subjects will likely tell different stories about the same thing at different times and to different people.

10) A major implication of the above nine propositions is that sociology can only be a science of interpretations and to some extent must constitute itself as an interpretive science. (Maines, 1993)

The use of narratives in research is important because it can give voice to people who do not usually get to speak directly in research. Voice is the expression of *a* (not *the*) viewpoint that comes from occupying a particular social location—a unique vantage point influenced by a person's gender, "race," ethnicity, sexual orientation, class, professional status, and so on, which give a person a unique perspective).

Consider the two narratives presented below. Both give voice to viewpoints not often heard. In the first, a young, male Muslim college student talks about fasting. His voice is different from the voices of other Muslims—those of young women, or of local religious leaders, but it speaks a truth because it reflects the speaker's life experience. We value it because it gives the non-Muslim reader a sense of what it is like to be a young, male Muslim living in Canada. In the second narrative, we hear the voice of a young Palestinian-Canadian woman. We know of

A Student's POV

Telling It Like It Is

Fasting

"Hey Moe, come join us for lunch."

"I can't, guys. I'm fasting."

"Fasting, what's that?"

This passage may be heard every year, asked by anyone and almost everyone. It bothers me to consider that the average person doesn't know what fasting for Muslims is. Fasting is an Islamic tradition practised for centuries, where a Muslim is subjected to no food or drink from sunrise to sunset. This is done to remind Muslims where we came from, to remind us that we started with nothing. It teaches us to value what we have and to value our gracious religion. There is fasting in almost every religion, yet the people who know the basic term of fasting don't

know what type of fasting Muslims commit to. Many people [I have spoken to] were shocked to hear that during Ramadan [fasting month] you cannot only eat, but also [not] drink. Many people thought that water was allowed in any fasting, but it isn't for the Muslim type of fasting.

When someone asks me what fasting is for Muslims, I reply with such fatigue from saying it over and over that I simply reply, "Well, we (Muslims) basically can't eat or drink anything when the sun is up." I simply gave a quick answer because I get that question asked every year, by anyone and almost everyone."

—Mohamed Abseh

the long-standing struggles involving Palestinians in the Middle East, but we hear little about Palestinians living in Canada. Consider the factors shaping her *social location*, the vantage point from which she speaks: age, gender, ethnic background, nationality, the site of her upbringing, her status as a student, even the political climate at the time of writing. All contribute to her unique perspective.

If you wanted a more detailed picture of what it's like to be a young Muslim or Palestinian living in Canada, you could gather additional narratives and link them through triangulation, a process involving the use of at least three narratives, theoretical perspectives, or investigators to examine the same phenomenon.

What do YOU think?

Consider an issue raised in one of the two narratives you've just read. How do you think triangulation—the use of at least three narratives—would help you gain a different understanding of the issue?

Telling It Like It Is   A Student's POV

Canadian by Birth, Palestinian by Culture

My name is Nadine and I am Canadian-born, but Palestinian by culture. My father was born in Palestine and my mother was born in Egypt to Palestinian refugees. Nowadays, being of Palestinian origin is quite difficult, even when you're living in a so-called multicultural nation. I guess it's not as hard for me as it has been for my parents because I am Canadian-born and my parents came to Canada knowing little about the country. However, the difficult aspect in my life was that I grew up in a one-cultured town [the predominantly Italian-Canadian town of Woodbridge, in southern Ontario] which made it extremely difficult for my brothers and I to fit in. I have never been able to have any close relationship with anyone. Why? I guess that children needed a common ground in order to establish a relationship, and not possessing the same culture as those around me made my assimilation even more difficult. Within homogeneous groups one can be easily singled out and that happened to me. Furthermore, as I grew up it became harder for me to engage in any real relationship with boys or girls because my culture became stronger for me and as well for them, which made us even grow farther apart. Maybe it was because I didn't speak or dress like them, or because I was darker than them, it didn't matter—basically I was just different.

Entering college, it was a bit easier for me to make acquaintances, though I realized how uneducated and ignorant people could be. It was particularly difficult for me after the events of 9/11 because, automatically, the Arab world would get blamed for it and most people, ignorant as they are, believed everything that the media's propaganda had been telling them. I was in college at that time, and explaining to people my point of view was tremendously challenging. Media brainwash had its toll on the majority of those around me. Furthermore getting into debates with individuals about what's occurring in Palestine and my views as a Palestinian was almost impossible. Right now my oppressed and displaced people who have been legitimately resisting occupation since 1948 are the bad guys. Maybe in a couple of years it will be another group, but for me now it's hard because I'm still singled out by my friends and the media. Maybe it would be a little bit easier if individuals would become open-minded about what goes on in the world. Then people could understand who we are and who I am. Knowledge is responsibility and to most, responsibility is a heavy burden to take. It is pretty sad what's going on in the twenty-first century is that people like me, Canadian-born, have difficulties growing up because of who they are and where they're from!

—Nadine Dahdah

Our Stories

Aileen Ross's Research on Homeless Women in Montreal

In 1977–8, Canadian sociologist Aileen Ross engaged in pioneering sociological research in two women's shelters in Montreal, one run during the day, the other at night. Both shelters had just opened when she began her research in the summer of 1977. The methodology she chose, and her reasons for choosing it, are instructive in understanding the limits of sociological research as she saw them:

> This study began without case histories that could be analyzed in terms of the usual neat hypotheses gleaned from previous studies. One reason for this omission was that very little sociological research has been done which throws light on Skid Row men, still less on homeless women. Another reason was that the staff of the day shelter held tenaciously to their basic philosophy that

the women would not be questioned about themselves. . . . "Don't sit eyeball to eyeball with them. If they think the shelter is being researched, they won't come back. No questions, please, and _no_ questionnaires" (Staff member).

The data were collected through careful observation of and informal interviews with the women and through accounts of their behaviour by the staffs of the two shelters and several other shelters. Interviews also were obtained from the directors of the Women's Shelter Foundation and from many professionals, including psychiatric, medical, and other social workers. . . . The records kept at the night shelter and the log written up each night at the day shelter were other sources of information. (Ross, 1982: p. 107)

Why might a homeless person fear being questioned by someone in a position of authority?

Alternative Qualitative Research Methods

Content Analysis

Content analysis involves studying a set of cultural artifacts or events by systematically counting them (to show which ones dominate) and then

interpreting the themes they reflect. Cultural artifacts include children's books, billboards, novels, newspaper articles, advertisements, artwork, articles of clothing, clinical records—even textbooks. These items all have two distinct properties not normally found in the subjects studied using other types of qualitative methodology. First, they have a "found" quality because they are not created specifically to

What do YOU think?

1. What were the restrictions on her research?
2. What would be the value of subsequent research on those two shelters?
3. What additional research strategies might be tried to get more information (keeping in mind the ethical restrictions put on sociological research)?
4. Why do you think that no one studied homeless women in Montreal before the 1970s?
5. Would you call this institutional ethnography?

In the description of her methodology Ross notes that she gathered information not just from observations and interviews but from logs kept by the staff of the shelter. These kinds of records can be valuable to social research as they provide clues to what goes on in a person's life. Consider "Lily," one of the homeless women Aileen Ross wrote about. Lily was about 30, and an Anglophone resident of Montreal. She had held a steady job until she injured her leg skiing. During a painful recovery, she became addicted to painkillers, which led her to homelessness. The following is just part of an account of her interactions with local institutions during the period of Ross's study:

Date	Institution	Problem	Result
1977			
19 June	hospital	drugs—couldn't speak	discharged
2 July	hospital	stomach pains	discharged
6 August	night shelter	crying at door in early morning frightened, scratches and bruises	—
7 August	hospital	stoned, shaky, grave condition	discharged
19 August	night shelter	strongly medicated, couldn't stand	—
23 August	hospital	drug overdose	discharged next day
26 August	hospital	could not stand, poor respiration	discharged next day
28 August	detention centre	upset as she had to go to court	did not show in court
29 August	hospital	stomach ulcers	discharged
1 September	jail	one day for shoplifting	sent to hospital
9 September	hospital	drugs and sore legs	discharged next day
23 September	hospital	suicide attempt (set fire to room)	sent to another hospital
28 September	hospital	drug overdose	left

What do YOU think?

What can you learn from examining the record of Lily's interactions with institutions? What questions does it leave unanswered? Does it only show the negative side of her life?

be studied. Second, they are *non-interactive* in that there are no interviews used or behaviours observed to gather the data (Reinharz, 1992: pp. 146–8).

Feminist approaches to content analysis attempt to expose pervasive patriarchal ("male-dominated") and misogynist ("woman-hating") culture. American sociologist Elaine Hall, in "One Week for Women? The Structure of Inclusion of Gender Issues in Introductory Textbooks" (1988), demonstrated how women's issues are treated as an afterthought in introductory-level texts. Judith Dilorio, in a paper presented in 1980, used content analysis to examine scholarly articles on gender role research and found that their methods *naturalized*, or normalized, social facts that diminished women and promoted male-oriented conservatism (in Reinharz, 1992: pp. 147, 361).

In *Gender Advertisements* (1976), Erving Goffman undertook a content analysis of commercial pictures depicting gender in print media. The women in the magazine ads he examined were overwhelmingly shown as subordinate and submissive. The magazines Goffman used represented both mass media and popular culture, having been selected on the basis of their availability and their circulation size. Taken together, these magazines (available in supermarkets, convenience stores, and drug stores) act as cultural objects, reflecting the social world. This relationship, however, is bidirectional: cultural objects such as magazines reflect the social world, and the social world, in turn, is influenced by cultural objects (Griswold, 1994: pp. 22–3). Popular magazines give us both a snapshot of the social world and also, if we look carefully, an indication of how the social world is being constructed through mass media.

Sut Jhally (1990) argues that magazine ads are neither completely true nor completely false reflections of social reality. They are partial truths and falsehoods. Ads depicting gender do not truly or falsely represent "real" gender relations or ritualized gender displays. Rather, for Jhally, they are "hyper-ritualizations," exaggerations that emphasize certain aspects of gender display and de-emphasize others (1990: p. 135).

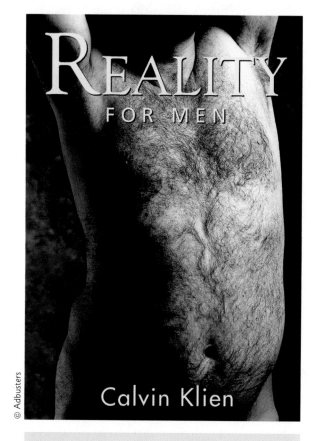

© Adbusters

Ritualized displays of gender in advertising often assert stereotypes, exaggerating certain aspects of our social reality while de-emphasizing others. What gender stereotypes, promoted in advertising, are critiqued in this spoof ad from Adbusters? What aspects of social reality does it suggest advertising exaggerates or de-emphasizes?

Discourse Analysis

Foucault defined *discourse* as "a conceptual framework with its own internal logic and underlying assumptions that are generally recognizable." There are two types of discourse analysis used by sociologists. One analyzes discourse as the term is commonly understood: that is, as a conversation, a speech, or a written text. Sociologists may examine the "discourse" found in a given ethnography, in an open-ended interview, or in a narrative. They might also focus on other kinds of "text," such as court transcripts, newspaper stories, movie trailers, and advertisements.

Another type of discourse analysis considers a broader definition of "text," going beyond individual works and authors to include large "fields" of presentation of information over a period of time, such as movies in general or in the early twenty-first century, reality shows, introductory sociology textbooks, Canadian historical writing, and so on. A "field" comprises all known discourse on a particular cultural concept or idea—"masculinity," for instance. The role of the researcher is to trace the discourse through time, looking at the representation, naturalization, change, and influence of the discursive field. An example would be a discourse analysis of changing popular cultural representations of masculinity in Hollywood films over the past fifty years.

Genealogy

In discourse analysis, genealogy is a method of examining the history of the second type of discourse defined above. Foucault, in his later works, used a genealogical method to trace the origins and histories of modern discourses as they collide, fragment, and adhere to other cultural practices and discourses over time. Foucault's genealogical work captures the dynamic nature of such discourses as mental illness (1961), the penal system (1975), and sexuality (1978).

Edward Said's study of Western attitudes toward Eastern culture, *Orientalism* (1979), offers another example of genealogical research. The Palestinian-born Said (1935–2003) developed the genealogy of Orientalism, broadly defined as a Western fascination with or romanticization of the "exotic" culture of Middle and Far Eastern societies. For Said, Orientalism could not be studied or understood without the concept of discourse:

> My contention is that without examining Orientalism as a discourse one cannot possibly understand the enormously systematic discipline by which European culture was able to manage—and even produce—the Orient politically, sociologically, militarily, ideologically, scientifically, and imaginatively during the post-Enlightenment period. (1979: p. 3)

Orientalism refers to "a corporate institution for dealing with the Orient—dealing with it by making statements about it, authorising views of it, describing it, by teaching it, settling it, ruling over it: in short, . . . a Western style for dominating, restructuring, and having authority over the Orient" (Said, 1979: p. 3). Orientalism, then, refers to the ways in which the "Orient" was, and continues to be, constructed in the western European imagination.

Mary Evans/Grenville Collins Postcard Collection

What does this postcard from Turkey, dated 1904, tell you about how Westerners thought of "the Orient" at this time? In what sense would you call this a form of "romanticism"? Has the Western image of this region of the world changed?

What do YOU think?

Now decidedly old-fashioned, "Oriental" was once the common term to describe what many people today consider "Asian." But what does "Asian" mean to you? If you're North American, it likely refers mostly to China and Japan. If you're British, you probably associate it with India and Pakistan (countries we in Canada might refer to as "South Asian"). What countries do the terms "Southeast Asian" and "East Asian" suggest to you? What term might you use for someone from Siberia or Mongolia?

Quantitative Research

Understanding Statistics

Sociologists have mixed feelings about statistics, a science that, in sociology, involves the use of numbers to map social behaviour and beliefs. Social scientists relish the opportunity to show off by quoting numbers. And yet, sociologists are also critical of other people's statistics. There are more jokes about the science of statistics than about any other kind of sociological research method—and we can prove that statistically. But here is some anecdotal evidence:

- "It shames me some to hear the statistics about us in class. The shame burns holes in whatever sympathy I may have for Indians, not my mom though."—the

Native protagonist of Aboriginal writer Lee Maracle's novel *Sun Dogs* (Maracle, 1992: p. 3)

- "There are three kinds of lies: lies, damned lies, and statistics."—Benjamin Disraeli
- "There are two kinds of statistics: the kind you look up, and the kind you make up."—Rex Stout
- "An unsophisticated forecaster uses statistics as a drunk man uses lampposts—for support rather than illumination."—Andrew Lang
- "Smoking is one of the leading causes of statistics."—Fletcher Knebel
- "Statistician: A man who believes figures don't lie, but admits that under analysis some of them won't stand up either."—Evan Esar, *Esar's Comic Dictionary*
- "Statistics: The only science that enables different experts using the same figures to draw different conclusions."—Esar

Measuring the Centre: The Median, the Average, and the Mean

Let's take a moment to consider that last statement and the idea that experts can draw different conclusions from the same statistics. How is that possible? One way is by using different measures of centre to analyze the statistics. A measure of centre is a way of taking all of the data you have gathered on a particular subject and finding the most representative result. Two of the most common measures of centre are the median and the average. The median represents the number, score, or result that separates the higher half from the lower half of a given set of data. If you have a set of five scores, the median will be the one in the third position. In the series 6, 8, 10, 11, 14, 16, 18, the median is 11: it is the number in the fourth position, separating the bottom three scores from the top three scores.

How is the median different from the average? You find the average by adding up all the scores and dividing the total by the number of scores you have. In the series above, the average would be 6 + 8 + 10 + 11 + 14 + 16 + 18 = 83 ÷ 7 = 11.9. The average is not always higher than the median. For the sequence 4, 7, 9, 11, 12, 14, 16, the median would be 11, and the average would be 10.4. Another measure of centre is the mean, which is usually calculated in the same way as the average. However, for weather (and other

purposes), it can be determined by taking the two extremes and dividing by two. If the daily low is 0 degrees Celsius and the daily high is 10, then the daily mean is 5.

To see why this matters, let's consider an example. A small hardware store employs seven sales associates to help customers with their purchases. Two of the sales associates believe they are significantly underpaid: they both make $14.75 an hour. They pluck up the courage to talk to the store's owner, who explains that the median salary of the seven employees is $15.00—not much more than what the two employees make. The two employees decide to ask their co-workers what their hourly wages are, and this is what they discover:

Employee	Hourly Wage
1	$22.50
2	$21.00
3	$19.75
4	$15.00
5	$14.75
6	$14.75
7	$14.00

The median hourly wage really is $15.00, but the average salary is $17.39—quite a bit more than what the two employees make. The employees would make good sociologists: they did their own analysis of the data and came up with a different interpretation to the one they were given. The average is not necessarily more reliable than the median: the two scores can be very different, though, so it's good to look at both if you can.

The Value of Using the Median: All Those Indian Chiefs Making So Much Money

Amid Indigenous claims for a greater degree of self-government, the conservative media (the *National Post*, the various *Suns*, and many radio and television stations) have made an issue of "all those Indian chiefs making so much money." An analysis of band leaders' salaries that appeared in the Toronto *Star* gave me material for a good reply, and a teaching moment for readers. The numbers shown in Table 2.1 come from the federal Department of Aboriginal Affairs and Northern Development.

What you can expect from elements of the conservative media critical of Indigenous people would be a focus on "all those chiefs" getting paid $240,000, or else the $180,000+ earned by the list's top ten. However, when analysts at the *Star* looked for the median salary earned by First Nation chiefs they arrived at a figure of $64,697. Other figures could have been used to get across the same idea that most band leaders make far less than $180,000: for instance, 79 per cent are paid less than $80,000, and about 67 per cent (or roughly two-thirds) received between $20,000 and $79,999. This approximates the pay of a low-level bureaucrat or a lower middle manager in a large company.

Using Operational Definitions

Knowing that different measures of centre can produce different interpretations of the data is one area of quantifiable research in which a sociology student can learn to challenge the research of professionals. Another involves the use of operational definitions. These definitions take abstract or theoretical concepts—"poverty," "abuse," or "middle class," for example—and transform them into concrete, observable, measurable, and countable entities. This can be difficult to do.

The *Handbook for Sociology Teachers* (1982), by British sociologists Roger Gomm and Patrick McNeill, contains a brilliant exercise illustrating the importance of operational definitions. Students are presented with a table showing the number of thefts that have occurred at a number of schools. Included in the table are the following factors that may have a bearing on the number of thefts at each school:

- size of the school
- social class of the school's students
- whether the school is single-sex or co-educational.

Students are asked to determine if there may be a cause-and-effect relationship between any of these factors and the number of thefts. Once they have reached tentative conclusions, the teacher gives them a handout showing that each school in the study defined "theft" differently. With no consistency in the operational definition, the students' efforts to compare schools were sociologically worthless (although pedagogically rewarding).

Table 2.1	Median Pay for First Nation Band Leaders	
Salary Range ($)	Number of First Nation Chiefs	Total
0	8	8
1–9,999	34	42
10,000–19,000	41	83
20,000–39,999	100	183
40,000–59,999	140	323
60,000–79,999	190	513
80,000–99,999	70	583
100,000–119,999	28	611
120,000–139,999	14	625
140,000–159,999	8	633
160,000–179,999	4	637
180,000–199,999	5	642
200,000–209,999	2	644
210,000–219,999	0	644
220,000–239,999	0	644
240,000+	3	647

Source: Smith, 2015: pp. A1, A8.

To get a sense of how operational definitions are used, consider poverty. There is no standard definition for "poverty" or "poor." There are, however, various conventional methods for defining poverty. One is to establish a poverty line, an income level below which a household is defined (for statistical or governmental purposes) as being "poor."

How is a poverty line established? There is no universally accepted procedure, though a few methods are prevalent. One is to link it to the availability of basic material needs: food, clothing, and shelter. Anything below the minimum income level needed to secure these necessities is considered absolute poverty. But this varies across countries and provinces. Consider, for example, how housing costs vary across Canada. It costs more for a resident of Vancouver to pay rent on an apartment than it costs a citizen of Halifax living in a comparable dwelling.

Since 1997 Statistics Canada has used the Market Basket Measure (MBM) to establish a poverty line for different regions across the country. As Giles explains:

The MBM estimates the cost of a specific basket of goods and services for the reference year, assuming that all items in the basket were entirely provided for out of the spending of the household [i.e. that none of the items were purchased for the householders by family or friends]. Any household with a level of income lower than the cost of the basket is considered to be living in low income. (Giles, 2004)

The "basket" includes five types of expenditures for a reference family of two adults and two children:

- food
- clothing and footwear
- shelter
- transportation
- "other" (school supplies, furniture, recreation and family entertainment, personal care products, and phone and Internet access).

Different levels are calculated for 19 specific communities in Canada and 30 theoretical communities based on province and population size (Statistics Canada, 2013c). To give you an idea of what the Market Basket Measure looks like, Table 2.2 shows the MBM thresholds for Saskatchewan.

Another way to define "poor" is to use a relative poverty scale, which defines poverty relative to average, median, or mean household incomes. An example is the low income cut-off, which is calculated based on the percentage of a family's income spent on food, clothing, and shelter. Since 1992, Statistics Canada has judged any household that spends more than 63 per cent of its total after-tax income on food, clothing, and shelter to be in low income (Statistics Canada, 2011a). Conservative-minded analysts such as Christopher Sarlo, who developed the basic needs poverty line, a measure of absolute poverty similar to the MBM, argue that measures of relative poverty are really just measures of inequality, a condition that exists even in

Quick Hits

So You Think You Know What a Single Parent Is?

Arriving at an operational definition for a concept that appears to be obvious can sometimes be difficult. Take a category as seemingly self-evident as "single parent" (now often referred to as "lone parent"). Identify which of the following you would count as a single parent, and then address the questions below.

		Yes	No
a)	a mother whose husband is dead	❏	❏
b)	a 41-year-old separated mother who lives with her 22-year-old son	❏	❏
c)	a father whose 4-year-old daughter sees her mother every weekend	❏	❏
d)	a mother whose 10-year-old son lives with his father every summer	❏	❏
e)	a father whose two daughters live with their mother every other week	❏	❏
f)	a mother whose husband lives in the same house but contributes nothing financially or in services to the raising of her children from a previous marriage	❏	❏
g)	a gay man who, along with his live-in partner, is raising his two sons without any assistance from the children's mother	❏	❏
h)	a mother who, along with her son, is completely supported by her ex-husband	❏	❏
i)	a mother whose husband is away at work most of the year	❏	❏

What do YOU think?

1. How would you define "single parent"?
2. Do you think that "single-parent family" is a category that would be easy to do research with? Why or why not?

Table 2.2 MBM Thresholds for Saskatchewan, 2010

MBM Region	Persons Not in Economic Families	2 Persons	3 Persons	4 Persons	5 Persons
Rural areas	16,269	23,008	28,179	32,538	36,379
Small population centres with less than 30,000 persons	16,755	23,695	29,021	33,510	37,465
Medium population centres with a population between 30,000 and 99,999 persons	15,499	21,918	26,844	30,997	34,656
Saskatoon	16,531	23,378	28,632	33,061	36,963
Regina	15,939	22,540	27,606	31,877	35,640

Source: Statistics Canada, Income Statistics Division, www12.statcan.gc.ca/nhs-enm/2011/ref/dict/table-tableau/t-3-5-eng.cfm

prosperous societies. The focus, he argues, should be not a person's standard of living compared to that of a neighbour but rather a person's "absolute level of well-being and ability to acquire basic necessities" (Sarlo, 2013: p. 3). Sarlo, in turn, has been criticized for devising a measure of poverty that sets the bar very, very low (see The Point Is... on page 54). The debate over how to define a concept like poverty shows that operationalizing abstract concepts is an exercise that is as political as it is statistical.

Research Surveys and a Lesson in Interpreting Poll Results

Polls, surveys, and questionnaires are frequently used in both quantitative and qualitative research. Quantitative research uses *closed-ended questionnaires*, in which respondents are asked to reply to set questions by selecting the best answer from a list of possibilities. "What college or university do you presently attend?" would be an example of a closed-ended question, and you can see how the results would be easy to summarize in numbers. Closed-ended questionnaires can be administered online, over the phone, or in person. They are generally administered to a sample, a selection of the population under investigation, such as a sample of college and university students or a sample of Canadians. The sample must be representative of the broader population so that the results of the survey can be extrapolated and applied to the whole. You could not do a study of student debt by interviewing only students from families with a total household income of over $175,000: that would not be a representative sample.

Qualitative research relies on open-ended questionnaires, in which respondents are encouraged to answer freely to each question without having to select a predetermined response from a list. Open-ended questions are most effective when they cannot be answered with a simple *yes* or *no*. "How would you describe your first year of college or university?" is an example of an open-ended question. You can see how this question might give you a more informative response than one that asks you to rate your first year of college or university on a scale from 1 to 5, although it can be more difficult to summarize the results of open-ended questionnaires.

The term *poll* usually refers to a quantitative survey designed to measure respondents' views on a particular topic or set of topics. The wording of poll questions is important, since polls are often subtly manipulated for political ends, and not for scientific accuracy. Our example of how polls can be manipulative comes from *The Appeal* (2008), a novel by popular American crime writer John Grisham, who was a lawyer and a Democratic representative in the Mississippi legislature before he became a writer. The novel takes place in conservative Mississippi, where a powerful chemical company goes to great lengths to appeal a conviction for cancer-causing pollution. Part of their plan involves getting an unknown but sympathetic candidate elected to the state's supreme court to help swing the court's vote in favour of their appeal. (Judges in the United States are elected rather than appointed; it doesn't make them less susceptible to bias or corruption.) To get their candidate elected, the chemical company launches a campaign to discredit a moderate rival named Sheila McCarthy. Here is how their poll contributes to that end. They ask the following questions, all of which produce the expected conservative responses.

Would you vote for a supreme court candidate who is opposed to the death penalty? Seventy-three per cent said they would not.

Would you vote for a candidate who supports the legal marriage of two homosexuals? Eighty-eight per cent said no.

Would you vote for a candidate who is in favor of tougher gun-control laws?

Eighty-five percent said no. . . . (Grisham, 2008: p. 255)

The death penalty, gay marriage, and gun control are hot-button issues among conservative voters, and so the questions are a surefire way to engage Mississippi's conservative electorate—even though they are irrelevant to the election of state supreme

The Point Is...

Two Very Different Measures of Absolute Poverty

Statistics Canada's Market Basket Measure (MBM) is a way to measure poverty based on whether a family's total household income is sufficient to buy a specified set of essential goods and services. The MBM thresholds are adjusted higher for families living in larger cities and lower for those living in rural areas.

While this may sound straightforward and objective, it's important to note that other agencies have their own versions of the Market Basket Measure, which may give a very different impression

of what it means to be living in poverty. Consider the Basic Needs Poverty Line (BNL), developed by Christopher Sarlo and favoured by the Fraser Institute. Like the MBM, the BNL is based on a household's ability to purchase a certain set of necessities. Regional variations are not considered; in Table 2.3, the BNL thresholds for households of 1 to 5 people are compared with the MBM thresholds for the most and least expensive regions, according to Statistics Canada.

| Table 2.3 | MBM and BNL Thresholds for Households Ranging in Size from 1 to 5 Members |

Household Members	Statistics Canada's Market Basket Measure (2010) ($)		Fraser Institute's Basic Needs Poverty Line (2014) ($)
	High[a]	Low[b]	
1	18,431	14,641	13,310
2	26,065	20,706	18,824
3	31,923	25,359	23,054
4	36,861	29,282	26,619
5	41,212	32,738	29,762

[a] Province of Ontario, Toronto census metropolitan area
[b] Province of Quebec, medium population centre with a population between 30,000 and 99,999

Source: Statistics Canada, Income Statistics Division, www12.statcan.gc.ca/nhs-enm/2011/ref/dict/table-tableau/t-3-5-eng.cfm; Lammam & MacIntyre, 2016: p. 3, Table 1.

The table shows that Statistics Canada considers a family of four in Toronto to be living in poverty if its total household income after taxes is less than $36,861. The Fraser Institute considers the same family to be in poverty only if its total household income is less than $26,619. There's a difference of over $10,000 in these two measures of poverty. Why? Statistics Canada is a public organization that gathers

and supplies statistics based on the federal census and other means. The Fraser Institute is a private "think-tank" appealing to conservative policy-makers with policy recommendations that promote free enterprise and limit social programs. The lower the poverty line, the lower the number of people considered poor in the analysis of statistics, and the lower the need for social programs such as welfare and legal aid.

Going Global

Defining the World: Labels for Rich and Poor Countries

There are rich countries and poor countries. Both have been given various names. For a long time they were known, respectively, as "First World countries" and "Third World countries." The latter term was coined in 1952. The First World included the wealthy capitalist countries, while the Third World comprised those countries without social or economic power. The USSR and the eastern European countries under its power (sometimes called the Soviet bloc) were identified as the Second World.

More recent terminology distinguishes between "developed nations" and "developing nations." This is problematic. Not all of the so-called developing nations are developing. They could be called "underdeveloped nations," or perhaps more accurately "underdeveloping nations," since they are being exploited and running up huge debts incurred as a result of one-sided globalization.

More recently, theorists have divided the world conceptually into "the North" and "the South," as almost all of the powerful and rich nations are in the northern hemisphere, while the less powerful and poor nations are typically found in the southern hemisphere. Of course, this has flaws, too: Australia and New Zealand are not among the world's poorest nations, and a number of the northern hemisphere's central Asian countries are considerably poorer than their immediate neighbours.

Despite its flaws, I have, for the most part, used "the North" and "the South" to refer to the world's wealthiest and poorest countries. When devising your operational definitions, it's sometimes necessary to rely on conventional categories even if they aren't ideal. The important thing is that you spell out as clearly as possible how you intend each of your key terms to be understood in your discussion.

---

court judges, who have no jurisdiction over such matters. Then the direct attack begins:

> Would you support a liberal candidate for the supreme court? Seventy per cent would not.
>
> Are you aware that Justice Sheila McCarthy is considered the most liberal member of the Mississippi Supreme Court? Eighty-four per cent said no. (Grisham, 2008: p. 256)

Grisham summed up the purpose of the poll in the following way:

> The trick, of course, was to convert Sheila McCarthy from the sensible moderate she was into the raging liberal they needed her to be. (Grisham, 2008: p. 257)

The moral is that polls can be used to guide, rather than gauge, public opinion. As a sociologically aware consumer of polls, you should always ask yourself, *who funded this poll?* In 2015 Conservative member of Parliament Lawrence Toet sent a pamphlet out in his Winnipeg riding to promote the federal Conservatives' anti-terrorism legislation, Bill

C-51. The mailer included the following poll question designed to be answered by the recipient and returned to the riding office:

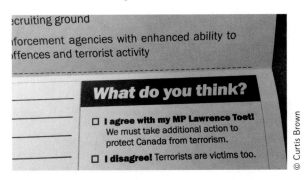
© Curtis Brown

Can you see the problem with this question? In logic terms it represents the fallacy known as a false dichotomy, where two positions are presented as though they were opposites and mutually exclusive, so that if you disagree with one premise, you must naturally agree with the other. In fact, this is not a choice between two opposites.

What do YOU think?

How would you turn the question in Lawrence Toet's pamphlet into an unbiased poll question?

Variables and Correlations

Here are a few concepts necessary for understanding and carrying out quantifiable research (and even certain forms of qualitative research). The first one is variable: a concept with measurable traits or characteristics that can vary or change from one person, group, culture, or time to another. One variable can cause another variable to change, or it can be affected by another. The average temperature of Nunavut's capital, Iqaluit, can be a variable, as can the average amount of clothing a resident of Iqaluit wears. Clearly the first variable can affect the second one.

Sociologists commonly refer to two different types of variables: independent variables and dependent variables. Independent variables are presumed to have some effect on another variable. In the example given above, the average temperature of Iqaluit is the independent variable. Dependent variables are those that are assumed to be affected by an independent variable. In our example, the average amount of clothing worn by the Iqalungiut ("people of Iqaluit") would be the dependent variable. Table 2.4 presents a list of possible independent and dependent variables from examples presented in this chapter.

Another key term is correlation. A correlation exists when two variables are associated more frequently than could be expected by chance. Both variables might increase together, or one might increase while the other decreases. A direct or positive correlation exists when the independent variable and the dependent variable increase or decrease together. Table 2.5 shows some examples. An inverse or negative correlation exists when the two variables change in opposing directions—in other words, when the independent variable increases, the dependent decreases, and vice versa. Table 2.6 gives examples of inverse correlation.

Table 2.4 — Independent and Dependent Variables: Three Examples

Study	Independent Variable		Dependent Variable
opening narrative	Car passes another car	➡	The passed car speeds up.
schoolwork	Middle-class parents take an active role in children's education	➡	Middle-class children achieve better results.
level of support for same-sex unions	Postsecondary education	➡	Higher level of support

Table 2.5 — Direct Correlation of Independent and Dependent Variables: Three Examples

Independent Variable		Dependent Variable
smoking	➡	rates of lung cancer
education level	➡	(1) income level (2) tolerance for difference (e.g. regarding "race" and ethnicity, sexual orientation, etc.)
parents' income level	➡	likelihood of child becoming a dentist, doctor, or lawyer

Table 2.6 — Inverse Correlation of Independent and Dependent Variables: Three Examples

Independent Variable		Dependent Variable
average temperature	➡	average amount of clothes worn
woman's education	➡	number of children she will have
age (of an adult)	➡	support for same-sex marriage

Spurious Reasoning: Correlation Is *Not* Causation

In the discussion of correlations above I've said nothing about causation, the linking of effects to causes. We may *observe* that women with postsecondary education have fewer children than those who don't, but we can't assume, based on that correlation, that being involved with postsecondary education *causes* them to have fewer children. We have to prove it, by testing hypotheses about why this is so (for example, women who attend college and university delay childbirth while they complete their studies and begin a career).

While correlation is relatively easy to prove, causation is not. Claiming that a cause-and-effect relationship exists based on correlation alone, without sufficient evidence, is known as *spurious reasoning*. Spurious reasoning is a concept that's hard to grasp with just the definition. Sociology instructors are challenged to explain and identify it. It usually takes lots of examples. So I'll begin here with the definition and then present examples.

Spurious reasoning exists when someone sees *correlation* and falsely assumes *causation*. Remember that a correlation is easy to determine; causation is not. The journey from one to the other is long and difficult. It involves proving—or else disproving—the existence of the critical third variable, the outside factor that influences both correlating variables.

Here are the examples, some silly, some serious.

Example #1: Birds and Leaves

There is a correlation in Canada between birds flying south and leaves falling. We can see both phenomena occurring roughly at the same time. It would be spurious reasoning to say that the birds see the leaves falling and therefore decide to migrate. If we look for a third factor, we'll find that the angle of the sun's rays affects both dependent variables.

Example #2: Fire Trucks and Fire Damage

There is a direct correlation between the number of fire trucks that go to a fire and the amount of damage that takes place at the fire. The greater the number of fire trucks, the greater the damage the fire *causes*. It would be spurious reasoning to say that the large number of fire trucks *causes* the extensive damage done at the site of the fire. Seek out the third variable: the seriousness of the fire affects both the number of fire trucks that appear and the amount of damage caused.

Example #3: Older Men and Younger Wives

Older men who marry significantly younger women tend to live longer than the cohort of men their own age. Spurious reasoning would lead us to conclude that marrying young women keeps old men active and healthy. But before declaring that we've found the fountain of youth for old men, we must look for a third variable. If the older man is relatively strong and healthy for his age, then he is both more likely to attract and keep a younger bride and also more likely to live longer.

Example #4: Cohabitation and Divorce

There is a direct (but not strong) correlation between a couple's living together prior to marriage and the likelihood of divorce. People who live together first

tyler olson/iStockphoto

Spurious reasoning might lead us to conclude that this man will live long because he is married to this young woman. What do you think?

are more likely to divorce than those who go from living apart to living together in marriage. It would be spurious reasoning to say that a couple's greater likelihood of divorce comes from the fact that they lived together first. Seek out the third variable and you will find it in social liberalism and social conservatism (the latter possibly a cause or effect of that difficult-to-pin-down social factor "religiosity"). Socially liberal people are more likely *both* to live together *and* to leave a marriage if they feel it is bad. More socially conservative people are *both* more likely to begin living together with marriage *and* more likely to stay in a marriage, even if it is horrible.

Example #5 Divorce and Suicide

Durkheim detected a direct correlation between divorce rates and suicide rates during a 10-year period from 1870 to 1880; some of his findings are recorded in Table 2.7.

There was a positive correlation between divorce rates and suicide rates over this period. However, it would be spurious reasoning to say that greater rates of divorce produced higher suicide rates. For Durkheim, the third variable was anomie, a societal state of breakdown or confusion, or a more personal one based on an individual's lack of connection to society. Anomie, concluded Durkheim, was the real cause of increases in both divorce and suicide rates.

Critical Thinking and Statistics

Sociologist Joel Best, author of *Damned Lies and Statistics: Untangling Numbers from the Media, Politicians, and Activists* (2001), presented the following example illustrating why we should approach statistics critically. He was on the PhD dissertation committee of a graduate student who began his dissertation with a questionable statistic. The student cited the following stat from an article published in 1995:

> Every year since 1950, the number of American children gunned down has doubled.

This certainly gains the reader's attention. But wait a minute, said Best: do the math. Say the 1950 figure was one. Here is how it would add up from 1950 to 1983:

Year	Value
1950	**1**
1951	**2**
1952	**4**
1955	**32**
1957	**128**
1959	**512**
1960	**1,024**
1961	**2,048**
1965	**32,768** (there were 9,960 homicides in total that year)
1970	**1 million +**
1980	**1 billion** (approximately more than four times the total population of the United States at the time)
1983	**8.6 billion** (nearly one-and-a-half times the world's population)

Source: Adapted from Best (2001)

What the author of the original article—the one cited by the PhD student—had done was misquote a 1994 document stating (accurately) that the number of American children killed each year by guns

Table 2.7	Correlation between Divorce and Suicide Rates in Four Countries, 1870–89	
Country	**Divorce Rate (per 1,000 marriages)**	**Suicide Rate (per 1 million people)**
Italy	3.1	31.0
Sweden	6.4	81.0
France	7.5	150.0
Switzerland	47.0	216.0

Source: Reprinted with the permission of The Free Press, a Division of Simon & Schuster, Inc., from *Suicide: A Study in Sociology* by Emile Durkheim, translated by John A. Spaulding and George Simpson. Copyright © 1951 by The Free Press; copyright renewed (c) 1979 by The Free Press. All rights reserved.

had doubled since 1950; the number itself had not doubled *each year*.

Best then warns the reader that bad statistics come to support all political stripes, from the political right wing (our Conservative Party) to the left wing (the NDP), from wealthy corporations to advocates for the poor, the sick, and the powerless. To cite an extreme Canadian example, in the late 1990s, the Mike Harris Conservative government of Ontario officially stated that the number of people on social assistance in the province had gone down, implying that the situation for poor people had improved under their administration. It hadn't. The numbers were down because the government had changed the criteria for programs like employment insurance, lowering the number of successful applicants. As a result, government-run agencies had closed the "welfare door" on a number of people. The statistic was presented as though all the people no longer collecting social assistance had obtained jobs and were, as a result, better off. Lost behind the statistic were the people who didn't apply for social assistance because they had become homeless, had moved out of the province (to find work, family support, or better provincial assistance programs), had moved in with family members or friends, or had resorted to criminal activity for a living because they were no longer eligible for Ontario's welfare programs.

Best advises us to approach statistics critically. That involves recognizing that all statistics have flaws, and that some flaws are more significant than others. Best presents the following useful series of questions for sociology students to consider when encountering a statistic in a news report, magazine, newspaper, or conversation:

> What might be the sources for this number? How could one go about producing the figure? Who produced the number, and what interests might they have? What are the different ways key terms might have been defined, and which definitions have been chosen? How might the phenomena be measured, and which measurement choices have been made? What sort of sample was gathered, and how might that sample affect the result? Is the statistic properly interpreted? Are comparisons being made, and if so, are the comparisons appropriate? Are there competing statistics? If so,

what stakes do the opponents have in the issue, and how are those stakes likely to affect their use of statistics? And is it possible to figure out why the statistics seem to disagree, what the differences are in the ways the competing sides are using figures. (Best, 2001)

Ethics and Research

An important consideration in sociological research today, and one that is more important now than it was historically, is the ethics of research. Practising good research ethics largely involves demonstrating respect for the research subjects, specifically concerning their privacy, their understanding of what the research will require of them, and their capacity to choose to be researched or not. When participants indicate their understanding and acceptance of the research conditions, they are providing what is known as informed consent. Colleges and universities now have research committees or entire departments responsible for vetting the research that sociologists and other faculty members engage in. Two examples will illustrate how standards of ethics in research have changed over the past 50 years.

"Unethical" Fieldwork in Religion, 1972–3

In Chapter 1 I described how I applied the theories of Erving Goffman to a newly formed religious group as part of my honours thesis. What I didn't mention was how I conducted my research. The group was known as the Process Church, or the Church of the Final Judgement. The *Toronto Sun* had labelled them a Satanist cult. They weren't, as it turned out, but the rumour alone was enough to make them particularly interesting to me.

My research method was *undisclosed* participant observation. This means that I did not tell them that I was doing research. I was working "undercover." I presented myself as an unemployed drummer (which I was); I did not tell them I was also an undergraduate sociology student. My research subjects were not willing participants who knew that they were being studied. I felt that my research had to be undisclosed because the Process Church had received negative publicity from the local media, and were nervous about outsiders, especially if they felt they might be reporters posing as faithful congregants to observe their meetings.

The Process Church was located in downtown Toronto, where they operated a soup kitchen and held different services every night. Once a week from September to February, I would participate in the evening activities, which could include their own music (think guitars and bongos, not traditional church choir or organ) and a sermon. The speaker did his best to "keep it real," in the words of the day. He would be hip and funny, but he also dispensed good advice. On some nights there would be workshop sessions in which people in groups would talk to each other, sometimes at a very personal level. I grew close to a number of people there, including those who worked in the soup kitchen, where I often hung out. Once the evening's session was over, I would head to the subway, take a pad of paper out of my pocket, and write notes like crazy.

What do YOU think?

1. Why might this kind of research be considered unethical today?
2. How would the research have changed if informed consent had been sought? Do you think that the information gathered would have been as useful?

Ethical Work in Disability Studies, 2014–15

I am currently engaged in assembling an anthology of stories told by students who have different disabilities. It took me over a year to get permission to proceed from the college's research ethics board (REB). The students are given an information letter to read, and then a consent form advising them that they are not waiving their legal rights or releasing me or the

Speed Bump

When the need for informed consent gets in the way of research progress, it can be tempting to forgo or lessen ethical standards in order to get things done. Why is it important to retain your ethical integrity, even at the cost of potential sociological insight? Who do ethics policies benefit?

college from our legal and professional responsibilities. The form, which they are asked to sign, explains that they have the right to ask the chair of the REB what "ethics approval" implies. They also have the right to ask any questions about the research and to modify or withdraw their contribution to the anthology, even after the form is signed. In signing the form they are agreeing that they have been well informed about the intent and general nature of the work.

Quick Hits

Alice Goffman's Ethical Dilemma

Alice Goffman (b. 1962), Erving's daughter, is an American sociologist whose recent book *On the Run: Fugitive Life in an American City* (2014) involved fieldwork she carried out to study the impact of policing on the lives of young black men in Philadelphia. During the course of that fieldwork, she heard about and may have witnessed various plans to break the

law. She even drove around a young armed man who was out for revenge on an individual he suspected of killing one of his gang members. However, she felt that her duty as a sociologist was to protect the confidentiality of her research subjects, not to uphold the law. What was her ethical dilemma as you see it?

Social Research Methods: A Final Word

In this chapter we've considered a number of ways to carry out sociological research. In all the talk about quantitative and qualitative methods, independent and dependent variables, correlation and statistics, it's easy to lose sight of an important point: the subjects under investigation are people, and the moment you begin to study them, you start a relationship that will not always be equal. Students, soldiers, and inmates of prisons and asylums are often studied because they have little power to say no. If I can ask questions about your life but you can't ask questions about mine, then I have a kind of power over you that you do not have over me. People who are poor, who belong to racialized (e.g. black), or colonized (e.g. Indigenous) groups when studied by white middle-class researchers have often been studied for purposes that serve more to control or exploit the subjects of the research than to give them power over their lives. The Maori of New Zealand have been through that experience. Maori researcher Linda Tuhiwai Smith, in *Decolonizing Methodologies: Research and Indigenous Peoples* (1999), wrote:

> From the vantage point of the colonized . . . the term "research" is inextricably linked to European imperialism and colonialism.

The word itself, "research," is probably one of the dirtiest words in the indigenous world's vocabulary. When mentioned in many indigenous contexts, it stirs up silence, it conjures up bad memories, it raises a smile that is knowing and distrustful. . . . The ways in which scientific research is implicated in the worst excesses of colonialism remains a powerful remembered history for many of the world's colonized peoples. . . . It galls us that Western researchers and intellectuals can assume to know all that it is possible to know of us, on the basis of their brief encounters with some of us. It appalls us that the West can desire, extract and claim ownership of ways of knowing, our imagery, the things we create and produce, and then simultaneously reject the people who created and developed those ideas and seek to deny them further opportunities to be creators of their own culture and own nations. (Tuhiwai Smith, 1999: p. 1)

If your interest in sociology comes from a desire to effect positive social change, the bitter tone of this statement might shock you. Let it serve as a reminder. Treat research subjects with respect and represent the data fairly. You will go a long way toward sociology's goal of bringing clarity to social issues.

WRAP IT UP

Summary

Ideally, the study of sociological research can lead students to develop reliable "fact checkers" or "bullshit detectors" that will automatically kick in when it comes to assessing the many forms of social information they receive through a variety of media. Asking such questions as *How did they define . . . ?*, *What social voices or locations were being heard or excluded?*, *How do they know that?*, and *Who paid for the research?* should enable you to be critical of even professional researchers. Keep these questions in mind as you read the chapters that follow.

As you encountered the diverse and, at times, opposing research strategies presented here, it has hopefully become clear to you that the facts do *not* speak for themselves. Knowledge is created: social "facts" and hypotheses are tested by human researchers with human biases who occasionally (and perhaps unintentionally) allow these biases to manufacture distortions rather than the ever-elusive "facts" or "proof." In short, be critical.

THINK BACK

Questions for Critical Review

1. Distinguish between qualitative and quantitative research. Give examples of each.
2. Explain the importance of narratives to sociological research.
3. Explain spurious reasoning. Furnish some examples of your own.
4. Outline the different methods of sociological research.
5. Identify the importance of operational definitions in quantitative research.
6. You have received scores of 30/40, 22/30, and 20/30 in three sociology tests. Which would you rather have as your mark: your average percentage or your median? And shouldn't you have studied harder for the third test?

READ ON

Suggested Print and Online Resources

Online

Canadian Sociological Association

www.csa-scs.ca

- The CSA's website has a separate page for student members (see Students@CSA), with news on events and workshops, student work, and employment opportunities.

Sociology and Legal Studies

http://subjectguides.uwaterloo.ca/sociology

- Maintained by the University of Waterloo, this site features a useful guide to conducting effective research, outlining the key steps from defining your topic to citing your sources.

Statistics Canada

www.statcan.gc.ca

- We're fortunate to have a wealth of data, derived from censuses and other polls, on all kinds of information relevant to Canadians, from where we live and where we're from to how we spend our money.

In Print

Joel Best (2012), *Damned Lies and Statistics: Untangling Numbers from the Media, Politicians, and Activists*, updated edition (Berkeley and Los Angeles: University of California).

- Now in an updated edition, this relatively light-hearted but helpful sociological guide to understanding the manipulation of statistics was so popular that it spawned a sequel, *More Damned Lies and Statistics: How Numbers Confuse Public Issues* (2004).

Michael Blastland & Andrew Dilnot (2007), *The Tiger That Isn't: Seeing through a World of Numbers* (London: Profile Books).

- A Scottish journalist and an English economist teamed up to produce this useful guide to interpreting statistics.

James Paul Gee (2014), *How to Do Discourse Analysis: A Toolkit*, 2nd edition (London: Routledge).

- A relatively accessible introduction to discourse analysis by a professor of literature.

Marie Campbell & Frances Gregor (2002), *Mapping Social Relations: A Primer in Doing Institutional Ethnography* **(Aurora, ON: Garamond).**

- The insights of Dorothy Smith inform this insightful work on institutional ethnography.

John L. Steckley (2008), *White Lies About the Inuit* **(Toronto: University of Toronto).**

- This genealogical work puts to rest three discourse myths about the historic Inuit: that Inuit elders are sometimes abandoned on ice floes; that there are blond, blue-eyed Inuit descended from Norse ancestors; and that the Inuit have 52 (or more) words for snow.

Helen Thornham (2011), *Ethnographies of the Videogame: Gender, Narrative and Praxis* **(Farmham, UK: Ashgate).**

- This work presents a British sociologist's use of several methods of research to investigate standard sociological issues such as gender, power, identity, and relationships to media.

PART TWO

Social Structures

Culture

3

The Gist

Reading this chapter will help you to . . .

- Recognize the differences between
  a) dominant cultures and subcultures/countercultures;
  b) high culture, popular culture, and mass culture;
  c) reading and decipherment; and
  d) folkways, mores, and taboos.
- Identify the intellectual traps of Eurocentrism, exoticism, and the biases of Western medicine.
- Explain what it means for culture to be "contested."
- Discuss how ethnocentrism has affected mainstream sociology's interpretation of the potlatch.
- Cite some of the reasons that Muslim women in Canada choose to wear the hijab.
- Contrast the linguistic expectations of speakers of Algonquian and Indo-European languages.

Terms of the Trade

- actual culture
- agency
- Algonquian
- authenticity
- contested
- counterculture
- cultural capital
- cultural relativism
- cultural studies
- culture
- decipherment
- dialect
- dominant culture
- dominants
- ethnocentrism
- Eurocentrism
- folkways
- high culture
- ideal culture
- Indo-European
- linguistic determinism (or causation)
- mass culture
- mores
- negative sanction
- *niqab*
- norms
- patriarchy
- popular culture
- positive sanction
- potlatch
- reading
- reverse ethnocentrism
- Sapir–Whorf hypothesis
- simulacra
- sociolinguistics
- subculture
- symbol
- taboo
- values

Names to Know

- Jean Baudrillard
- Pierre Bourdieu
- William Graham Sumner

Martin New/www.montrealinpictures.com

For Starters

Culture and Claiming Space

I saw the conflict coming, but I could do nothing to stop it. It was all about culture.

It was 1981, and I was in Edinburgh, Scotland, in one of the few decent hamburger joints in the city. It was a popular spot, both for locals and for tourists, commanding a beautiful full view of the castle on the top of the hill across the street. I was waiting in line with my Scottish friends when I saw the incident that would precipitate the conflict.

A pair of American tourists set their jackets on two of four chairs attached to a table, and then slowly walked to the lineup. I sensed trouble coming. As I stood in line I saw a Scottish couple looking for a place to sit with their meals. Their eyes fixed on the chairs opposite the ones the tourists had laid claim to with their jackets. The couple went over, sat down at the unoccupied chairs, and began to eat.

The tourists had been distracted by the view of the castle. When then turned around and saw the couple at the table, they reacted instantly.

"What are you doing?! That's our table! Didn't you see the jackets?" The Scots looked up at them, dumbfounded, and unprepared to move. This was their country, and they weren't about to be booted from their seats by tourists.

Witnessing the conflict, my Scottish friends asked me (as a Canadian, an obvious expert in things North American): "What's wrong with them? Do they think they bought the table? Bloody tourists!"

The tourists continued to argue with the Scots before storming out of the place.

A few months earlier, I might have sided with the tourists, sympathizing with their typically North American sense of space. But having spent time in Scotland, I understood why the Scots were surprised. In Canada, when two people in a bar are sitting at a table with four chairs, and someone asks them, "Are these seats taken?", the unseated patrons will take the two extra chairs and sit at a vacant table. In Scotland, they will sit down right at "your" table, perhaps joining you in conversation or ignoring you altogether.

It was all about culture.

Introduction: What We Mean by Culture and Why It's Contested

The word *culture* has a lot of different meanings. Some people equate it with a sophistication of manners and tastes, something you either have (if you enjoy, say, the opera, ballet, and fine dining) or are sadly lacking in (if your idea of a good breakfast is cheap domestic beer and leftover pizza). But that's just one kind of culture, *high culture*, which we'll get to a bit later on.

More broadly, culture is a system of behaviour, beliefs, knowledge, practices, values, and concrete materials including buildings, tools, and sacred items. In this sense, everyone has a culture. Many people can claim more than one. But although I've described culture as a system, I'm not suggesting there is total agreement concerning any one culture and its constituent parts. Those who belong to a particular culture may disagree about what it does or should include.

Let's talk hockey. Just about everybody would agree that hockey is part of Canadian culture—but that's where agreement ends. Does success by Canada's national teams in international hockey mean we've succeeded as a culture? Not everyone would say so. Is fighting an integral part of the Canadian game? You don't have to be Don Cherry to get into an argument on that point. Does the sport's long history in this country make it more culturally important than soccer, even though the latter has higher youth participation rates and tends to be played by boys and girls in more equal numbers, representing a far broader range of ethnic and socioeconomic backgrounds? Hockey as part of our national culture is contested.

In more serious cases, aspects of a culture may be contested when they become instruments of oppression. Anne McGillivray and Brenda Comaskey, in *Black Eyes All of the Time: Intimate Violence, Aboriginal Women, and the Justice System*, argue that we should not assume that Aboriginal women who have suffered spousal abuse "will view 'cultural' solutions in the same way as Aboriginal men" (McGillivray & Comaskey, 1999: p. 18). Aboriginal justice typically calls for forgiving offenders and reintegrating them into the community. This is part of Indigenous culture. However, many of the women McGillivray and Comaskey interviewed said that they would prefer that their male abusers spend time in jail to give the abused time to feel safe again. Under these circumstances, these aspects of Aboriginal justice—forgiveness and keeping offenders in the community—become contested.

Culture often becomes contested over the question of authenticity. Culture involves traditions but is not confined by them. It is dynamic, changing over time. Authenticity carries the idea of being true to a particular culture, yet think of how broadly the word "authentic" can be applied and understood. For some, an "authentic Italian meal" may be something you'd have to fly to Tuscany to experience; for others, it comes from the pizzeria down the street. Authenticity becomes a problem when a colonial society studies a colonized culture and claims to know the secret of its authenticity. Edward Said, in *Orientalism*, criticized Western intellectuals for forming their impressions of the Middle East and central Asia from historical accounts written by nineteenth- and twentieth-century Western scholars. Once they had formed an idea of what "the Orient" was, these intellectuals negatively compared their rather romanticized (think *Aladdin*) notions of the Eastern world's traditions to their negative perceptions of its present. In effect, they said: "You are a corruption of what you used to be." That's like someone saying to you: "I understand you better than you do, and you were better before."

It is a common mistake to view one's own culture as being contested, in a way that makes it dynamic and complex, while holding a narrow view of other cultures as somehow simple and fixed. This leads to unhealthy cultural stereotypes—"All Americans are ethnocentric, warmongering bullies; we Canadians are far more tolerant and diverse." It is important to appreciate that all cultures are contested and subject to change.

What do YOU think?

In 2016, NFL quarterback Colin Kaepernick knelt during "The Star-Spangled Banner" to protest the oppression of blacks and other racial minorities. Critics, sidestepping the substance of his protest, charged that football was no place for politics and called his action disrespectful to all Americans, the country's military, and the game of football itself. How does the criticism reveal the contested nature of aspects of American culture, notably the anthem, the flag, and football?

foodpix/Alamy Stock Photo

How authentic do you imagine this Mexican restaurant in Bucks County, Pennsylvania, is? Would you expect the proprietors to be Mexican? To have lived in Mexico? To have studied Mexican cooking at a US-based culinary arts school? How should authenticity be judged?

What Kinds of Cultures Are There?

As noted at the outset, there are different kinds of culture, apart from culture in the general sense just outlined. These can be seen in terms of two oppositions:

1) dominant culture *versus* subculture and counterculture
2) high culture *versus* popular culture and mass culture.

As we examine each of these oppositions, you will gain a better idea of why we say that culture is contested.

Dominant Culture versus Subculture and Counterculture

Defining Canada's Dominant Culture

Look around, and it isn't hard to see the signs of the dominant culture in Canada. The dominant culture is the one that, through its political and economic power, is able to impose its values, language, and ways of behaving and interpreting behaviour on a given society. The people most closely linked with the cultural mainstream are sometimes referred to as dominants. Although statistically their share of the overall population has dropped significantly in the last 20 years, it is fairly safe to say that white, English-speaking people of Christian and European stock make up the dominant culture in Canada. It is also fair to say that the dominant culture is middle-class. How do we know what the dominant culture looks like? Think of what culture is typically represented in Canadian morning shows like *Breakfast Television*, in commercials played on Canadian airwaves, and in television programs generally. Think of the expectations they express about what people own, what their concerns are, and how they live.

We can narrow our picture of Canada's dominant culture by taking a regionalist perspective. People living in the Atlantic provinces have good reason to suspect that the dominant culture lies in central or western Canada, where most big companies have their head offices, and where the greatest share of the national population is situated. But western Canada has several times produced political parties (the Social Credit, Reform, and, most recently, Wildrose parties, for instance) to protest the West's exclusion from the dominant political culture and its unfair treatment at the hands of institutions dominated by and situated in central Canada (like the big banks and the agencies of the federal government). Power and wealth tend to be concentrated in large cities, and central Canada is home to the country's two largest metropolitan areas, Toronto and Montreal.

Feminists argue that Canada's dominant culture is male. Let's look at our House of Commons for an example. Of the 306 people who were members of Parliament in Canada in October 2014, 230 were male and just 76 were female; in other words, the ratio of men to women in the House of Commons was 3 to 1, and women held just 25 per cent of the seats. How did things change one year later, following the most recent federal election, in October 2015? On the plus side, a record 88 women were elected to Parliament. However, the number of seats in the House of Commons was increased from 306 to 338, so women make up just 26 per cent of all MPs—a very small year-over-year increase. However, there was a change in the prime minister's cabinet, made up of the MPs who hold significant power. Stephen Harper's last cabinet was made up of 39 members, 12 of whom (31 per cent) were women. Justin Trudeau named 15 women to his 31-person cabinet, giving women 48 per cent of the positions. Do you think

Justin Trudeau picked a cabinet meant not just to achieve gender balance but to reflect Canada's diversity overall. What are the benefits to having high-ranking political positions filled by people who reflect Canada's diversity? Why do you think that older white men would be the most likely to laugh at this cartoon?

that Justin Trudeau's move will have a significant impact on the role of women in Canadian politics?

Adding age to the picture, we can say that those who are just starting or who have just ended their careers often feel peripheral to the dominant culture. Other factors to consider are sexual orientation, level of education, and overall health (since those with disabilities or chronic medical conditions might feel outside the dominant culture in terms of access). To summarize, our portrait of Canada's dominant culture looks something like this: white, English-speaking, heterosexual, male university graduates of European background between the ages of 30 and 55, in good health, who own homes in middle-class neighbourhoods of cities in Ontario or Quebec. (I came *so* close—but I'm too old, and my Ontario town is too small for city status. How well do you fit the portrait of Canada's dominant culture?)

What do YOU think?

Television both reflects and contributes to our sense of culture. Pick a sitcom you're familiar with (it's probably American). In your opinion, does it reflect the dominant culture we've just described? What are the principal attitudes, concerns, and occupations of its main characters? What sexualities and ethnic backgrounds do they represent (and represent positively, not just as the subject of jokes, which can be a form of marginalizing people)? How much are the main characters like you?

Minority Cultures: Subcultures and Countercultures

Minority cultures are those that fall outside the cultural mainstream. These may be countercultures, which are groups that feel the power of the dominant culture and exist in opposition to it, or subcultures, which differ in some way from the dominant culture but don't directly oppose it. Subcultures are typically characterized by a more neutral cultural contrast than countercultures are. Examples include computer nerds, lawyers, sociologists, stamp collectors, and so on. A subculture, then, is defined in terms of the minor cultural differences possessed by certain groups organized around occupations or hobbies, engaged in no significant opposition to the dominant culture.

Countercultures are defined oppositionally. They are groups that reject elements of the dominant culture (for instance, clothing styles or sexual norms). Examples of counterculture range from the relatively harmless hippies of the 1960s and early 1970s to dangerous biker gangs like the Hells Angels that have flourished since the 1960s. "Alternative" was a watchword of the 1990s, used to describe a culture of music and fashion that defined itself in contrast to what was then the mainstream. Today we might use the word "indie," which first applied to artists who were independent of major media companies and now applies to anyone or anything that is independent of mainstream commercial culture.

A counterculture still in evidence today is that of the Goths. Descriptions of this counterculture abound on the Internet, from which the following portrait is summarized.

Quick Hits

Mind Traps in Understanding Culture

Try to avoid these common mind traps in understanding culture:

- thinking that "culture" refers only to high culture
- thinking that total agreement on what defines a culture can ever exist
- thinking that culture is synonymous with tradition and doesn't change over time

- thinking that "our" culture is contested whereas other cultures are comparably simple and fixed (for instance, the false but popular notion that Christians around the globe are quite different but that all Muslims, Hindus, Jews, Sikhs, or Buddhists essentially think alike).

What are Goths? Most people can summon up a rough image: dyed black (or, less often, blue) hair, dark clothes, with white makeup that contrasts sharply with clothing and hair colour. They may think of a fascination with death and with art—especially music and film—that reflects this fascination. But who are the people who belong to this counterculture?

First, they tend to be young. The Goth lifestyle is invented and reinvented by the youth cohort of the time. Some bloggers claim that there are three generations of Goths, each not so aware of its predecessors or reincarnations. The "generation gap" seems a perpetual feature. Second, they are typically white. There are Internet references to black and Asian Goths, but it appears their numbers are small. Third, they seem to come mostly from middle-class families.

Oral/Internet history places the origins of the Goth counterculture in the late 1970s. Goths of that period are associated with the look and music of bands such as The Cure and Siouxsie and the Banshees.

The opposition of Goths to dominant culture is expressed most clearly in their dress and overall appearance, but it goes beyond the visual. Goths of the 1980s rejected the yuppie world of financial self-indulgence and the conservative politics of Margaret Thatcher, Ronald Reagan, and, here at home, Brian Mulroney. They pursued a life concerned with less world-exploitive politics and with cultish small-market arts.

High Culture versus Popular Culture

High culture is the culture of the elite, a distinct minority. It is associated with theatre, opera, classical music and ballet, "serious" works of literary fiction and non-fiction, "artsy" films (note: *films*, not *movies*) that may be difficult to appreciate without having taken courses on the subject, and a "cultivated palate" for certain high-priced foods and alcoholic beverages. High culture is sometimes referred to as "elite culture," which Canadian sociologist Karen Anderson defines as follows:

> Elite culture is produced for and appreciated by a limited number of people with

Peter Steffen/AFP/Getty Images

LARPers don elaborate costumes to engage in live-action role play, re-enacting battles from history or fantasy. Subculture or counterculture?

The Point Is . . .

What Happens When a Youth Counterculture Ages?

What happens when a youth counterculture ages? Does it just disappear with the youth of the members? Or does it last as part of their lives into middle age?

Writing about British Goths, sociologist Paul Hodkinson (2011, 2013) offers some instructive answers to these questions. The Goths he studied entered the counterculture during the 1980s in their teens and early twenties. To a significant extent they were from white, middle-class families. Hodkinson characterizes the Goths as a "spectacular" counterculture, because of their ability to catch the attention of the media and the public generally with their unique appearance. (Hippies and punks are other often cited examples of spectacular countercultures.) Goths of the 1980s were known for their distinctive style of dress and makeup, their regular late-night clubbing and heavy drinking, and their social "transgressions" of casual sex and short-term relationships.

Hodkinson studied Goths as they aged, using participant observation at Goth events, observing Goth communication online, and doing in-depth interviews with 19 individuals between the ages of 27 and 50, both male and female. He noted that from the late 1990s,

> the previously very small number of older goths in the scene began to grow and, as a result of the coincidence of this with slower recruitment of youngsters, the average age of the scene rose, to the extent that some events now are thoroughly dominated by over-thirties. The goth scene therefore provides an example of a subculture dominated by "the same body of continuing participants" (Smith, 2009: p. 428), something which contrasts with the isolated older participants in otherwise adolescent cultures focused on in my other studies. . . . (Hodkinson, 2013: p. 1077)

As they aged the Goths followed dominant cultural practices by getting married and becoming parents (to "baby bats" or "gothlings"), the latter causing more of a withdrawal from the Goth scene by females than males. Aging Goths attended monthly festivals that included supervised children's activities and subscribed to online countercultural magazines and blogs that included discussions of Goth-themed baby outfits and children's clothes. When they did go out at night, they spent less time preparing their appearance, drank less, and came home sooner—and with their spouses, not with someone they had just met.

Philartphace/iStockphoto

Hodkinson's research suggests that most youths in a counterculture—Goths excepted—withdraw from the counterculture as they age. Why do you think this is so? Can you think of why Goths may differ in this regard?

specialized interests. It tends to be evaluated in terms of "universal" criteria of artistic merit and to be seen as a sign of prestige. Appreciation of elite culture usually entails a process of learning and the acquisition of specific tastes. (Anderson, 1996: p. 471)

French sociologist **Pierre Bourdieu** (1930–2002) coined the term cultural capital to refer to the knowledge and skills needed to acquire the sophisticated tastes that mark someone as a person of high culture. The more cultural capital you have, the "higher" your cultural class.

Popular culture, on the other hand, is the culture of the majority, particularly of those people who do not have power (the working class, the less educated, women, and racialized minorities). Serious academic discussion of popular culture has grown with the recent rise of cultural studies courses and programs. Cultural studies draws on both the social sciences (primarily sociology) and the humanities (primarily literature and media studies) to cast light on the significance of, and meanings expressed in,

popular culture, a topic previously neglected by most academics.

Popular Culture and Mass Culture

A crucial distinction exists between popular culture and mass culture. The two differ in terms of agency, the ability of "the people" to be creative or productive with what a colonial power, a dominant culture, or an instrument of mass media has given them. Sociologists disagree on how much agency people have. Those who believe that people take an active role in shaping the culture they consume (e.g. the clothing they buy, the music they listen to, the websites they visit, the TV shows and movies they watch, even the political views they subscribe to) use the term "popular culture" to describe the majority of those who fall outside the world of the cultural elite. Those who believe people have little or no agency in the culture they consume are more likely to use the term mass culture. They tend to believe that big companies (such as Walmart, McDonald's, Disney, and Apple) and powerful governments dictate what people buy, watch, value, and believe. Many see the

A counterculture, if it becomes popular, may have to reinvent itself or "push the envelope" to keep from going mainstream. What does this cartoon suggest about how and why culture is contested?

Telling It Like It Is
A Sociologist Goes to an Art Show

My wife and I attended a contemporary art exhibit at Toronto's downtown convention centre. The show was billed as "one of the most important art events in Canada" (www.arttoronto.ca). Although I liked the art, I could not help but see it—through the eyes of a sociologist—as an example of what is wrong with high culture as opposed to popular culture. What exactly did I see?

Let's start with "race." There were few people of colour there. A black woman with white sanitary gloves was cleaning up at the cafeteria; another was working the cash register. A Filipino woman swept, and a South Asian man was provided security services. No Caribbean, Filipino, or South Asian art was in sight. Despite the fact that there is a large Chinese community in Toronto, my sociologist's eye perceived almost no Chinese people there, and no Chinese art. The East Asian attendees were almost exclusively Japanese (although I did not see any Japanese art). There was one "Native Art" exhibit, but it was white-manned by a non-Native.

Ethnicity is less easy to see, although the names of the artists and the locations of the hosting galleries give some strong clues. I did not see any works by artists of Italian, Portuguese, or Greek ethnicity, although there are large Italian, Portuguese, and Greek communities in Toronto, and all have artists.

Age can be seen. The vast majority of people admiring the works on display were middle-aged. Several had children with them, but most did not. The relatively few young adults there had the hungry, desperate look of people who define themselves as artists but who have financial problems sufficient to make them question whether they could really afford to be at this show.

Class was also easy to see. Many people there wore expensive clothes and carried themselves with the elegance of a prosperous upbringing and long-term money. Older men were seen with significantly younger women. Price tags on the works ranged from between $1,000 and $3,000 to prices exceeding $20,000.

I did not try to guess the *sexual orientation* of the art patrons around us, though there were certainly pairs of men and pairs of women, some of them acting as couples. What was striking was that although there were many works depicting heterosexual love, I saw no art exploring homosexuality and just one piece of lesbian (which, to be honest, looked more like the stuff of male fantasy than an expression of lesbian desire).

Since rupturing my Achilles tendon some years ago I have a better sociological eye for *ableism*. There was no art by people from the Canadian branch of the Mouth and Foot Painting Artists, an organization representing some incredible artists whose work compares favourably with drawings and paintings created by people with complete use of their hands (see www.mfpacanada.com). This genre is often branded, unofficially, as "disabled art," which sets it apart from other works of art such as those on display at this exhibit.

High culture derives its prestige by being exclusive: it is meant to be enjoyed by those who can lay claim to a certain standard of wealth, education, and breeding. Popular culture is intended to be enjoyed by everyone, regardless of their upbringing, social class, and other factors. The website advertising the event called Toronto

one of North America's wealthiest cities as well as . . . one of the most diverse in the world. It is home to Canada's highest-income neighborhoods and boasts an engaged and supportive community of arts patrons and professionals. Cultural amenities abound in this stunningly multicultural metropolis, which claims a population of just over 6 million, making it the fifth largest city and the fourth largest economic centre in all of North America. (www.arttoronto.ca)

As if the other factors I saw weren't enough, the emphasis here on Toronto's wealth makes it clear that the event was designed for well-heeled members of the urban social elite, not the city's hoi polloi.

What do YOU think?

Why do you think there was so little diversity in the art on display and in those attending the show? Who do you think the sponsors were, and how would that affect the sociological nature of the audience?

Internet as a boon for popular culture, enabling people to get their stories, social commentaries, photos, and so on, seen by an enormous audience without any sponsorship by big companies. Critics see the Internet as an instrument of mindless escapism distracting people from real social issues and political manipulation by governments. These differing viewpoints highlight the difference between popular culture and mass culture.

One feature of mass culture is what French sociologist **Jean Baudrillard** (1929–2007) calls simulacra. Simulacra are stereotypical cultural images produced and reproduced like material goods or commodities by the media and sometimes by scholars. For example, the Inuit are often represented by simulacra of described practices (e.g. rubbing noses, abandoning elders, and wife-sharing) and physical objects (e.g. igloos, kayaks). These images tend to distort contemporary Inuit "reality." Consider the way the inukshuk, the Inuit stone figure, has become a Canadian cultural symbol, with models of these stone figures sold in tourist shops across the country. It has such cultural currency that it was incorporated into the logo for the 2010 Winter Olympics held in BC—a province with no Inuit community.

Baudrillard describes simulacra as being "hyperreal"—that is, likely to be considered more real than what actually exists or existed. He illustrates the principle with an analogy of a map, but we will consider a GPS system instead. Imagine you are driving down a country road on a winter's night. Your GPS system tells you to turn right ahead onto a major road that will lead you straight home, yet all your eyes see is a narrow dirt road covered in snow. If you follow that road and get stuck at a dead end, the GPS system was hyperreal to you: you believed the information it was giving you was more real than what your eyes detected. This information is thus a simulacrum.

When sociologists encourage their students to be critical of what the media present, they are hoping their students will be able to detect simulacra. In 2003, the United States and a coalition of allies (not including Canada) invaded Iraq to disarm the country of a large stockpile of weapons of mass destruction (WMDs) that the country supposedly possessed and was prepared to use against its adversaries in the West. This is a classic example of a simulacrum: though no evidence of the weapons was ever found, governments operated as though they actually existed. The weapons were hyperreal.

British sociologist John Fiske (2010) takes the popular culture position. He does not believe that people are brainless consumers of mass culture; rather, he believes that the power bloc—the political

---

Quick Hits

Are You Excluded from the Dominant Culture?

Here is a simple test.

		Yes	No
1.	Are political leaders (your prime minister, premier, local federal or provincial representative, mayor, etc.) like you in sex, religion, clothing style, language, and ethnic background?	❑	❑
2.	Do the homes portrayed in most television shows you watch look like yours?	❑	❑
3.	Do the leading characters in movies live lives like yours?	❑	❑
4.	Is your boss of the same sex, ethnicity, "race," and age as you?	❑	❑
5.	Do the people who get arrested on reality-based police shows look like you and your neighbours?	❑	❑
6.	Are people like you frequently made the subject of news stories for demonstrating or protesting something?	❑	❑
7.	Are there a lot of derogatory slang terms that refer to people like you?	❑	❑
8.	Are people like you described as a "special interest" group?	❑	❑
9.	Are people like you often told they're "too sensitive" or "too pushy"?	❑	❑
10.	Are you often asked, "Where do you come from?"	❑	❑

A "no" answer to questions 1–4 equals exclusion from the dominant culture; for questions 5–10, a "yes" answer equals exclusion from the dominant culture.

and cultural institutions with the greatest influence on society—merely supplies people with resources that they resist, evade, or turn to their own ends. He recognizes agency and warns about the dangers of sociologists presenting people as mere dupes of mass media.

An important distinction between the two positions involves the contrast, identified by de Certeau (1984), between *decipherment* and *reading*. Decipherment involves looking in a text for the definitive interpretation, for the purpose (conscious or unconscious) the culture industry had in mind in creating the text. For sociologists who believe that mass culture predominates, decipherment is about looking for the message that mass media impose on consumers, who are left without the opportunity to challenge it or reject it by substituting their own.

YOUR DAD WAS NOT A METROSEXUAL

He didn't do pilates. Moisturize. Or drink pink cocktails. Your Dad drank whisky cocktails. Made with Canadian Club. Served in a rocks glass. They tasted good. They were effortless. **DAMN RIGHT YOUR DAD DRANK IT**

Canadian Club® Blended Canadian Whisky. 40% Alc./Vol. ©2007 Canadian Club Import Company, Deerfield, IL.

Canadian Club.

Advertisers often promote simulacra in order to manufacture a need or desire for the products they're trying to sell. What simulacra are being presented here? How persuasive is the message?

Sociologists who believe that popular rather than mass culture predominates tend to use the term "reading." Reading is the process in which people treat what is provided by the culture industry as a resource, a text to be interpreted as they see fit, in ways not necessarily intended by the creators of the text. The sociological technique of reading involves analyzing the narratives of those using the text in this way.

Eric Michaels (1986) offers a good example of the difference between decipherment and reading in his description of how Australian Aborigines received the 1985 action adventure movie *Rambo: First Blood Part II*, starring Sylvester Stallone as John Rambo, a Vietnam War veteran who returns to North Vietnam and—in contravention of orders given to him by a senior officer—releases several American prisoners of war from a Soviet-run POW camp. At the time of the movie's release, there was still quite a bit of Cold War antagonism between the United States and the Soviet Union. A mass culture interpretation of the movie would be that it delivers a propaganda message about the triumph of good (the US and the capitalist West) over evil (the Soviet-led communist bloc). But the Australian Aborigines had their own reading of the film, as Michaels explains:

> [T]hey understood the major conflict to be that between Rambo, whom they saw as a representative of the Third World, and the white officer class—a set of meanings that were clearly relevant to their experience of white, postcolonial paternalism and that may well have been functional in helping them to make a resistant sense of their interracial relationships. . . . The Aborigines also produced tribal or kinship relations between Rambo and the prisoners he was rescuing that were more relevant to their social experience than any nationalistic

What do YOU think?

Reality TV shows like *America's Got Talent* and *American Idol* (and its Canadian spinoff) give off-the-street competitors the chance to realize the dream of achieving national celebrity (thanks to voter viewing). Do you think this is evidence of popular culture, or is the notion that the people are the real stars just a media manipulation?

relationships structured around the East–West axis. . . . (Fiske, 2010: p. 46)

Norms

Norms are rules or standards of behaviour that are expected of members of a group, society, or culture. There isn't always consensus concerning these standards: norms may be contested along the sociological lines of ethnicity, "race," gender, and age. A quick illustration: a student of mine once told me he remembered being embarrassed, as a child, when his grandmother refused to "pick up" after her poodle. Although stoop-and-scoop laws weren't yet in effect, it had become common custom, as far as the boy was aware. Yet his grandmother was completely unselfconscious, even as the neighbours eyed her and her poodle with annoyance. Many years later, when the boy, now a young man, was engaged to be married, he was reprimanded by his grandmother for failing to write out the invitations individually, by hand. "It is bad form," she told him, "to send *printed* invitations unless you are inviting more than one hundred guests." Coming from different generations, the student and his grandmother recognized different norms of behaviour.

Norms are expressed in a culture through various means, from ceremonies that reflect cultural mores or customs (a wedding, for example) to symbolic articles of dress (the white dress worn by the bride). In the following sections, we'll have a look at the different ways in which norms are expressed and enforced.

Sanctions

People react to how others follow or do not follow norms. If the reaction is one that supports the behaviour, it is called a positive sanction. It is a reward for "doing the right thing." Positive sanctions range from small gestures like a smile, a high five, or a supportive comment, to larger material rewards like a bonus for hard work on the job. A hockey player who gets into a fight is positively sanctioned by teammates at the bench banging their sticks against the boards, or by the cheering crowd.

A negative sanction is a reaction designed to tell offenders they have violated a norm. It could be anything from a glare, an eye roll, or a sarcastic quip to a parking ticket or the fine you pay at the library for an overdue book. When someone around me says, "Hey, look—it's Santa Claus," I know that behind the apparent joke is a negative sanction about my well-proportioned frame and my bushy grey beard.

Folkways, Mores, and Taboos

Folkways

William Graham Sumner (1840–1910) distinguished three kinds of norms based on how seriously they are respected and sanctioned. He used the term folkways for norms governing simple day-to-day matters. These are norms that you *should* not (as opposed to *must* not) violate. They are the least respected and most weakly sanctioned. The term "etiquette" can often be applied to folkways. George Costanza, on the TV show *Seinfeld*, continually violated folkways by, for instance, double-dipping chips at a party or by fetching a chocolate pastry out of the garbage.

Mores

Mores (pronounced like the eels—*morays*) are taken much more seriously than folkways. You *must* not violate them. Some mores—against rape, killing, vandalism, and most forms of stealing, for example—are enshrined in the criminal code as laws. Violation of some mores, even if they are not laws, will meet with shock or severe disapproval. Booing the national anthem of the visiting team prior to a sporting event is likely to cause offence among supporters of the visitors and even anger or embarrassment among fans of the home side. Mores are complicated and may be contested. Mores of cleanliness, for instance, are in the cultural eye of the beholder. In Britain, dogs are allowed in pubs; in Canada, they are not. This does not mean that bars in Canada are more sanitary than those in Britain. Differences in mores of cleanliness can lead to serious problems when, for instance, an overdeveloped Western sense of what is hygienic jeopardizes the health of a hospital patient (see the discussion of Hmong refugees on page 381 of Chapter 13, on medical sociology).

Like folkways, mores change over time. A young woman sporting a tattoo would once have been seen as violating the mores of acceptable behaviour for "a lady." Today, many women have tattoos and display them without arousing the kind of shock or condemnation generally produced when mores are violated.

Taboos

A taboo is a norm so deeply ingrained in our social consciousness that the mere thought or mention of it is enough to arouse disgust or revulsion. Cannibalism, incest, and child pornography immediately come to mind. Taboos affect our dietary habits. Eating dogs, cats, or other animals that might be considered family pets is taboo in North American culture. There are religious taboos surrounding the consumption of certain foods—pork by Jews and Muslims, beef by Hindus. Some cultures recognize gender taboos, such as those surrounding women who interfere with or attempt to partake in typical male activities. Like folkways and mores, taboos differ from culture to culture.

Culture Symbols

Symbols are cultural items that take on tremendous meaning within a culture or subculture of a society. They can be either tangible (i.e. physical) material objects (as illustrated in the narrative on page 81) or intangible, non-material objects, such as songs or even remembered events. Just as culture itself is contested, culture symbols are likely to be interpreted differently by people inside and outside of the culture they represent.

Symbols of nationality tend to take on tremendous cultural significance. Think of the maple leaf a Canadian tourist stitches to the backpack she wears when travelling in Europe. It's meant to stand not just for her country of origin but for a whole set of qualities that we like to think make up the Canadian cultural identity—courtesy, tolerance, knowledgeableness, peacefulness, and so on. To the European who sees and recognizes it as a symbol of Canadian cultural identity, the maple leaf might conjure up a very different set of qualities: our rejection of the Kyoto agreement on climate change, our tar sands, our seal hunt . . . Some of these are recent developments, illustrating another point: the cultural significance of symbols can change over time.

The Veil as a Symbol for Canadian Muslim Women

Few clothing symbols have a greater power to evoke emotions than the *niqab*, the veiled head covering worn by some Muslim women. To many in the West it is a symbol of patriarchal domination by religious extremists, similar in effect to the full-length, screen-faced *burqa* that many Afghan women wear and to the *chador* that Iranian women are forced by law to wear. In the lead-up to the 2015 federal election, Canadians debated whether the *niqab* aligned with our national cultural values. The issue came to the fore when a young woman, Zunera Ishaq, wanted to take her oath of Canadian citizenship while wearing the veil. The federal government under Conservative prime minister Stephen Harper attempted to deny her that right on the grounds that most Canadians would find it offensive. The Supreme Court overruled the government's motion, upholding Ms Ishaq's right to keep her face covered during the public ceremony. In October 2015, shortly before the election, she took her citizenship oath while wearing the veil.

It is important to understand why women of various cultures—especially in Canada—choose to wear the *niqab*. For this information there can be no better source than the community of Canadian women of Middle Eastern background who have considered the choice themselves. Some of them have provided the narratives that appear on pages 82–3. What stands out, as we read their views, is that for a significant number of women in Canada, as for those women in France who opposed a law that would ban the veil in French schools, the *niqab* is a matter of choice, not command.

The perspectives featured on pages 82–3. are part of a groundbreaking study carried out in Montreal by Iranian-Canadian anthropologist Homa Hoodfar (2003). The voices Hoodfar recorded speak compellingly of their choice to wear the veil as

What do YOU think?

For Americans, the cultural significance of their flag is firmly entrenched: it is the subject of their national anthem; in schools, they pledge allegiance to it; and many support a law that makes it illegal to burn or otherwise desecrate it. But, like the maple leaf, the stars and stripes symbolizes a whole set of cultural values that make up the national identity. What cultural values do you think the American flag suggests to someone in each of these cities?

- Vancouver, British Columbia
- Austin, Texas
- Tijuana, Mexico
- Tel Aviv, Israel
- Moscow, Russia
- Hong Kong, China
- Baghdad, Iraq

What does the stars and stripes mean to you?

The Point Is . . .

The Jackrocks Story: A Narrative about the Power of Symbols

In the fall of 1989, I travelled through rural Virginia on a short lecture tour, having been invited by staff and students of Southwest Virginia Community College who had attended a lecture of mine during their spring break. I spent the first night of my stay at the home of the college president. It was elegant, finely furnished, with everything in its place. While there, I noticed something that surprised me. In a glass case—the kind normally used to hold curios and *objets d'art*, such as glass and china figurines—I saw two 6-pointed objects, each one made of three nails. They reminded me of the jacks I had played with as a child, but bigger, and menacing. Why had these mean-looking items been placed on display?

The next night I stayed with a coal miner's family. There I learned about the dynamics of a months-long coal miner's strike in the one-industry area. I was taken on a tour of the strike centre, where bunk beds were being built to accommodate the families of striking workers who had been thrown out of their homes for failing to pay the rent. The people I met there were friendly, but the long strike was crushing their spirit.

The mining company was owned by people from outside the area—foreigners, in the eyes of the locals. The company owners had circumvented the picket lines by trucking the coal out at night, but striking miners in camouflage had found ways to thwart their efforts.

The next day, at the college, I spoke to a sociology class about symbols. Near the end of the class, I asked students to name some local symbols. One student shouted out "jackrocks." When I asked what "jackrocks" were, I got a description of the 6-pointed objects I had seen in the president's glass case, as well as a bag full of jackrocks handed to me by a student who went to his car to get them. I was told that one of the tactics used to keep the coal trucks from shipping out the coal was to toss these jackrocks underneath the tires. The jackrocks had become symbols of the miners' resistance. They appeared in store windows in the town nearest the mine, and I was given a pair of small, aluminum jackrock earrings. I then understood why the college president kept the two jackrocks in the glass case. He was from Florida, and therefore a "foreigner" to the area. By keeping the jackrocks in a place of honour, he was expressing solidarity with his students and their community.

What do YOU think?

1. What cultural significance did the jackrocks have for the local people of southwestern Virginia?
2. Why do you think the college president kept jackrocks in his glass case at home? Do you think he fully appreciated their significance?

a way of opposing restrictions placed on them (and not their brothers) as teenagers by parents concerned that their daughters would fall prey to the irreligious sex-, alcohol-, and drug-related behaviours of North American culture. Some of those interviewed saw the decision to wear the *niqab* as a step, together with Qur'anic study and banding together with Canadian Muslim women of different cultural backgrounds, down a path of opposition to some of the patriarchal mores of their specific cultures. In addition, taking the veil gave some women the opportunity to defend their faith against the ethnocentric ignorance of some of their fellow Canadians.

What do YOU think?

1. Could you sociologically predict which social characteristics—age, religion, sex, etc.—might make a person more likely or less likely to oppose the wearing of the *niqab* during an oath of Canadian citizenship?
2. Do you see the *niqab* as a symbol of personal choice, patriarchal oppression, religious honour, or something else? Do you find it offensive? How, if at all, do the narratives presented on pages 82–3 affect your view?

Telling It Like It Is

The Hijab as Worn by Young Canadian Muslim Women in Montreal

MorelSO/Thinkstock

The Narrative of a 19-Year-Old Palestinian-Canadian Woman

The veil has freed me from arguments and headaches. I always wanted to do many things that women normally do not do in my culture. I had thought living in Canada would give me that opportunity. But when I turned 14, my life changed. My parents started to limit my activities and even telephone conversations. My brothers were free to go and come as they pleased, but my sister and I were to be good Muslim girls. . . . Life became intolerable for me. The weekends were hell.

Then as a way out, I asked to go to Qur'anic classes on Saturdays. There I met with several veiled women of my age. . . . None of them seemed to face my problems. Some told me that since they took the veil, their parents know that they are not going to do

anything that goes against Muslim morality. The more I hung around with them, the more convinced I was that the veil is the answer to all Muslim girls' problems here in North America. Because parents seem to be relieved and assured that you are not going to do stupid things, and your community knows that you are acting like a Muslim woman, you are much freer. (cited in Hoodfar, 2003: pp. 20–1)

The Narrative of a 17-Year-Old Pakistani-Canadian Woman

Although we did not intermingle much with non–Indian Canadians, I very much felt at home and part of the wider society. This, however, changed as I got older and clearly my life was different than many girls in my class. I did not talk about boyfriends and did

not go out. I did not participate in extracurricular activities. Gradually, I began feeling isolated. Then my cousin and I decided together to wear the veil and made a pact to ignore people's comments; no matter how much hardship we suffered at school, we would keep our veils on. . . .

At first it was difficult. At school people joked and asked stupid questions, but after three months they took us more seriously and there was even a little bit of respect. We even got a little more respect when we talked about Islam in our classes, while before our teacher dismissed what we said if it didn't agree with her casual perceptions. (cited in Hoodfar, 2003: pp. 28–9)

The Narrative of Mona, an Egyptian-Canadian Woman

I would never have taken up the veil if I lived in Egypt. Not that I disagree with that, but I see it as part of the male imposition of rules. . . . The double standard frustrates me. But since the Gulf War, seeing how my veiled friends were treated, I made a vow to wear the veil to make a point about my Muslimness and Arabness. I am delighted when people ask me about my veil and Islam, because it gives me a chance to point out their prejudices concerning Muslims. (cited in Hoodfar, 2003: p. 30)

A Response to the Narratives by a Muslim Feminist

[The following was written by a 19-year-old university student in Alberta, who describes herself as a Muslim feminist (not a contradiction in terms). After reading the above narratives in a previous edition of this textbook, she felt compelled to comment.]
Hijab and the veil are religious decisions to be made between the person choosing to wear it and God. It is highly disrespectful to belittle the value of Hijab, making it to be something as simple as a political statement or a statement to your classmates or parents. If you're wearing Hijab simply so your parents can treat you the same as your brother, you are using a religious statement to combat culturally driven inequality (which, in fact, goes against Islam).

These responses made Hijab seem entirely misogynistic, when it is in fact the exact opposite. Compare it with the following. In almost any magazine, book, advertisement, or movie you encounter, women are overly sexualized. Women are used to sell products, and are constantly treated as no more than just eye candy. Magazines injected with unrealistic beauty standards tell you "HOW TO LOSE 10 INCHES OFF YOUR WAIST!" and "HOW TO BE THE SEXIEST WOMAN IN THE ROOM!"

In movies and TV shows, girls are constantly purchasing cosmetics and discussing weight loss, talking about boys, and competing with one another to impress boys. Everything about Western media values women according to appearance, sexualizing and exploiting us in every way possible, just to please the male-kind. From a young age, women are trained to prioritize our physical appearance so that we can "fit in" and be "normal."

When young women fail to meet these unfair beauty standards naturally, we see millions of dollars spent on cosmetics and cosmetic surgery. Money aside, we also find an increase in eating disorders (i.e. anorexia and bulimia) as well as mental disorders (i.e. depression and anxiety), resulting from a lack of self-worth and self-esteem, which can ultimately lead to drug abuse or suicide.

Now back to the topic about Hijab. I chose to wear Hijab to protect myself from all of that. Hijab and the veil create a barrier between the woman choosing to wear it and the rest of the world. It forces people to actually *listen* to what she has to say, rather than to pass judgments solely on her physical appearance. Hijab gives me the comfort and liberty of knowing that I'm being judged according to my intellect rather than my sexual appeal. I know that I can freely stroll down the street without feeling insecure because men are staring at my body or talking about it to others. Not that they should in the first place, but Hijab and the veil ensure that they don't have the opportunity.

Values

Values are the standards used by a culture to describe abstract qualities such as goodness, beauty, and justice, and to assess the behaviour of others. Values have long been a topic of great interest to sociologists. Max Weber's identification of the Protestant work ethic is one early example of a sociological study of values. Many others have followed since. But in spite of these studies, values remain difficult to understand and to represent accurately. What makes the issue especially puzzling is that the values that people claim to have are not always the ones they act upon. In other words, there is a discrepancy between the ideal culture that people believe in and the actual culture that really exists. Do we recognize, then, the value that is professed or the value that is reflected in human action? Is the person who preaches a value but fails to honour it in everyday life necessarily a hypocrite?

Canadian and American Values

Canadians regularly compare themselves with Americans on anything from foreign policy to curling prowess. Some Canadians like to define themselves by what an American is *not*, making statements like, "A Canadian is an unarmed American with proper health insurance." But how much do our two neighbouring societies really differ in their values?

Michael Adams, of the Environics Research Group, has been conducting and publishing opinion polls since the early 1980s. During the 1990s, he measured and tracked 100 "social values" among Canadians and Americans, including such things as acceptance of violence, obedience to authority, penchant for risk, and sexual permissiveness. He published the results of his work in *Fire and Ice: The United States, Canada and the Myth of Converging Values* (2003), in which he aimed to demonstrate that Canadians and Americans are becoming more different rather than more alike in their values. It certainly seemed so in 2003, when the American military was heading into Iraq and Canada was not, and when a modest majority of Canadians supported gay marriage and the liberalization of marijuana laws, which a majority opposed in the US.

Adams based his findings on data from Environics polls conducted in the US and Canada in 1992, 1996, and 2000. It's always important to look at the data critically. For instance, the polls invited respondents to "talk" about their values. But you will recall that there is often a difference between the values we profess and those we act upon. Another point: is the time period—from 1992 to 2000—long enough to produce evidence of what he calls "long-term shifts"? All of this data was gathered before the September 11 terrorist attacks, which occurred in 2001. Adams argued that the events of 9/11 would only make the differences he had identified greater.

There have been some changes since then. During the period in the study above, the United States had a conservative Republican administration led by George W. Bush, and Canada had a liberal Liberal administration headed by Jean Chrétien. However, from 2006 until 2015, Canada had a prime minister, Stephen Harper, with very conservative values, on par with those of American Republicans; in contrast, Americans elected a liberal Democratic leader and first-ever black president, Barack Obama. In a 2014 presentation at the Woodrow Wilson Center in Washington, DC, Adams asked whether Americans and Canadians were trading places.

The answer to Adams's rhetorical question was, no: he found that Canadians and Americans remained far apart on certain values (see Table 3.1). However, there were some surprising findings. Consider one of the value clusters Adams identified: patriarchy, or the acceptance of men in positions of political, cultural, and social power. One statement used to measure patriarchy was the following:

> "The father of the family must be master in his own home."

Respondents were asked whether they agreed with this statement.

Figure 3.1 shows the results over a 20-year period from 1992 to 2012. Note the increase in the difference after each four-year period from 1992 to 2004. During that time, even the ranges of the two countries did not intersect: in the 2000 poll, agreement with this statement among Canadian respondents ranged from a province-wide low of 15 per cent (in Quebec) to a high of 21 per cent (in the Prairie provinces), while agreement among US respondents ranged from 29 per cent in New England all the way to 71 per cent in the Deep South (Adams, 2003:

| Table 3.1 | Values on Which Canadians and Americans Differ the Most, 2012 |

Stronger in Canada	Stronger in the US
• flexible families	• national pride
• ecological concern	• fear and acceptance of violence
• cultural assimilation	• work ethic
	• spiritual quest
	• propriety
	• religiosity
	• patriarchy

Source: Adams, 2014.

p. 87). However, between 2004 and 2012, the margin between the two countries dropped back to 1992 levels. What do you think caused the change?

Here in 2016, as I'm writing this book, Canada has, once again, a Liberal prime minister, one who promises "sunny ways" and whose outlook on many social issues sets him in stark contrast to his Conservative predecessor. The United States is preparing for its own federal election, which will feature, as one of its candidates, a controversial demagogue who has claimed the Republican Party's nomination thanks largely to his regressive anti-immigration, anti–free trade stance and his "us versus them" rhetoric. Are Canadian and American values cyclical?

What do YOU think?

1. Adams has argued that American and Canadian social values are becoming less alike. How convincing do you find his argument?

2. If the difference is indeed growing, what do you think is the cause? What role do you think factors such as religion, politics, and the economy play in the difference?

3. An anonymous book reviewer on Amazon wrote that the real difference between Canadians and Americans is that Americans don't care what the difference is between Canadians and Americans. Why is this difference so important to Canadians?

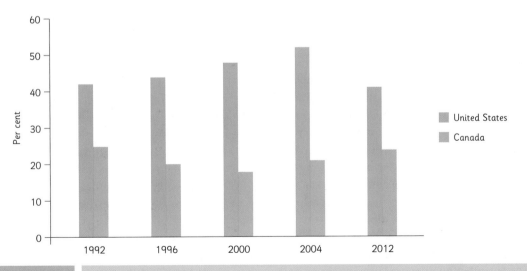

| Figure 3.1 | Percentage Agreeing with the Statement "The Father of the Family Must Be Master in His Own Home," US and Canada, 1992–2012 |

Source: Adams, 2014.

Even Canadian and American flags reflect different cultural values. The Canadian flag, handed down by the government in 1965, features a leaf that is not native to most of the country. First sewn by Betsy Ross, the American flag emerged as a powerful symbol during the American Revolution and is still the subject of the country's national anthem. Children in the US "pledge allegiance to the flag" at the beginning of the school day.

Ethnocentrism

Ethnocentrism occurs when someone holds up a culture (usually one's own) as the standard by which all cultures are to be judged. It follows a simple formula: all cultures like the gold-standard culture are good, praiseworthy, beautiful, moral, and modern; those that are not are bad, ugly, immoral, and primitive. Ethnocentrism can manifest itself in many forms, but it often entails declaring that there is only one right way (the way of the cultural model) to run a business, handle finances, or manage social policy.

Ethnocentrism is often the product of ignorance, something experienced by Hmong refugees who arrived in the United States from Southeast Asia during and after the Vietnam War. The Hmong were targeted in the US in part because of their supposed practice of stealing, killing, and eating dogs. Lack of evidence or truth did not deter an ethnocentric

public from spreading these stories about a "foreign" culture. The false stories followed particular themes, as Anne Fadiman explains in her book on Hmong Americans:

> [Rumored] methods of [dog] procurement vary. Some are coaxed home by Hmong children. Some were adopted from animal shelters. . . . Others are strays. The most common accusation is theft, often from backyards, sometimes leaving the head and collar as mute testimony to Rover's passing. . . . The dog is usually an expensive one, often owned by a doctor. The theft is observed, the license plate number is marked down. When the police check, the dog is already in some Hmong family's pot.
>
> The supposed proof varies. That fixture in the urban legend, the garbage man,

reports the presence of canine remains in Hmong garbage cans. Carcasses are seen hanging in the cellar by meter readers, salesmen, or whomever. Freezers are said to be full of frozen dogs. A bizarre touch is that the dogs are supposedly skinned alive to make them more tasty. (Fadiman, 1997: pp. 190–1)

On a larger scale, ethnocentrism has played a role in the colonizing efforts of powerful nations imposing their political, economic, and religious beliefs on the indigenous populations of lands they "discovered." The following discussion highlights how Canada's First Nations were forced by an ethnocentric government to abandon a traditional custom.

The Potlatch Act of 1884

The potlatch is a traditional ceremony of Northwest Coast Indigenous people. It often involves the acquisition or affirmation of hereditary names. During the ceremony, the host demonstrates his (the host is typically male) social, economic, and spiritual worthiness. An important aspect of the event is the telling, singing, and acting out of stories. In this way, potlatches affirm the possession of the stories, songs, dances, carved and painted images, masks, and musical instruments used by the hosting group to celebrate the cultural history of the name and those identified with it. These hereditary names carry more than just symbolic significance: they are connected with rights to fish, hunt, or forage for plants in particular territories, and with the responsibility to conserve the living entities in those areas. Potlatches thus serve to maintain the strength and social unity of the group.

Another important aspect of the potlatch is the giving away of gifts and possessions. One traditional way for a high-ranking man to prove he was worthy of his position was to give away many gifts. The hierarchical nature of Northwest Coast culture made this competitive, as those holding or aspiring to high rank gave away a great deal. The level of competition rose after European contact, because of the sudden availability of European manufactured goods, and because of the toll European diseases took on the people. The population of the Kwakiutl of Vancouver Island, for example, dropped from roughly 8,000 in 1835 to around 2,000 in 1885. When diseases decimated lineages entitled to important names, more distant relatives would vie for prestigious family names. In some cases, competition could become socially divisive, and there were even incidents in which property was destroyed as a show of wealth ("I am so rich that this property means nothing to me"). Such incidents appear to have been rare, but over-reported in the literature.

In 1884, the Canadian Government made the potlatch illegal with the following decree:

> Every Indian or other person who engages in or assists in celebrating the Indian festival known as the "Potlatch" . . . is guilty of a misdemeanour, and shall be liable to imprisonment for a term of not more than six nor less than two months in any gaol or other place of confinement, and any Indian or other person who encourages, either directly or indirectly, an Indian or Indians to get up such a festival or dance, or to celebrate the same, or who shall assist in the celebration of same, is guilty of a like offense, and shall be liable to the same punishment.

In 1921, 45 of the highest-ranking Kwakiutl were arrested. Twenty-two were sentenced to prison terms of two to three months. The people lost many sacred potlatch items that were taken as a condition for the release of community members arrested but not charged. The items became the property of the minister of Indian Affairs, who distributed them to art collectors and museums.

In 1951, the potlatch ban was repealed. But it wasn't until 1975 that the National Museum in Ottawa declared it would return the sacred items—provided they be kept in museums. The Royal Ontario Museum returned its items in 1988, and the National Museum of the American Indian in New York repatriated some of its holdings in 1993. Some items were never recovered.

Colonial ethnocentrism is not confined to the West, or to white people. When the Japanese seized control of its northern islands from the Ainu, the indigenous people there, they developed and implemented ethnocentric policies and laws similar to those enacted by the governments of Canada and the United States concerning their Aboriginal people.

Eurocentrism

Eurocentrism involves taking a broadly defined "European" (i.e. western and northern European, plus North American) position to address others, and assuming that the audience shares that position. It can be seen in historical references to the "known world"—i.e. the world as it was known by Europeans—and to Christopher Columbus "discovering," in 1492, continents that were already home to millions of people. It foregrounds discoveries and contributions that are Western, and backgrounds those that are not. Did you know that our standard numbering system is known (poorly) as the Hindu–Arabic system? Did you know that chocolate and vanilla, corn, squash and pumpkins, most beans, peppers, potatoes, tomatoes, and sunflowers were first grown by Aboriginal people? The Eurocentric perspective of many textbooks used in the West tends to champion advances made by people of European stock while downplaying or altogether ignoring important non-European developments such as these.

Cultural Globalization

Global studies expert Manfred Steger defines cultural globalization as "the intensification and expansion of cultural flows across the globe" (2003: p. 69). Our concern is with the one-way flow of culture from the West, or what we might call the "Americanization" of the world. Think of the factors. First of all, English has emerged as by far the most prominent language of science, of the Internet, and of other powerful media. Second, American movies and television are seen in almost every country in the world. But to label this "American" culture is perhaps giving it too broad a scope. It is just a small number of transnational companies—AT&T, AOL/Time Warner, Universal, Viacom, General Electric, and Walt Disney in the US, as well as the European companies Bertelsmann and Vivendi, and Sony in Japan—that control most of the media. Not only do these companies reap enormous dividends by exporting their respective brands of Western culture to consumers across the globe, but as Steger points out, they draw audiences abroad away from the culture of their own countries into a global "gossip market" that revolves around the "vacuous details of

the private lives of American celebrities like Britney Spears, Jennifer Lopez, Leonardo DiCaprio, and Kobe Bryant" (Steger, 2003: p. 77). We could update this list to include the Kardashians, Taylor Swift, Jay Z, and, I hate to say it, Canada's own Justin Bieber.

It's worth noting that interpretations of globalized items of Western culture are not necessarily the same abroad as they are in their countries of origin. The classic study of a cultural reading of a Western cultural item by a non-Western audience is described by American anthropologist Laura Bohannan in "Shakespeare in the Bush" (1966). In it she describes her experience of telling the story of *Hamlet* to the Tiv of West Africa, and the reading they put on it. The article concludes with the words of a Tiv elder. After admitting that he had enjoyed Bohannan's story, told "with very few mistakes," the elder said:

> Sometime . . . you must tell us some more stories of your country. We, who are elders, will instruct you in their true meaning, so that when you return to your own land your elders will see that you have not been sitting in the bush, but among those who know things and who have taught you wisdom. (Bohannan, 1966: p. 47)

Cultural Relativism

Cultural relativism is an approach to studying and understanding an aspect of another culture within its proper cultural context. Because of the *holistic* nature of culture—because a culture is a complex system in which everything is connected—no single cultural practice can be understood in isolation, outside of its social, historical, and environmental context. Just as you cannot understand a single part of a car without understanding the system of which it is a part, you cannot attempt to understand individual aspects of culture without looking at their cultural context.

Unlike what Spock used to say in the original *Star Trek* series, logic (as a pure entity) does *not* dictate. Logic is a cultural construct, and every society has its own cultural logic. Any explanation of a cultural practice or belief must in some way incorporate this logic. This is especially important in medicine. Western medicine is dominated by a kind

Going Global

Observing Cultural Globalization in Taiwan

The impact of cultural globalization struck me when I was visiting the Taipei night market in Taiwan. As I was shopping for clothes, I turned a corner and was jolted by the sudden appearance of a tall black man. As my mind and eyes adjusted, I realized that it was none other than Michael Jordan, decked out in his Chicago Bulls uniform, circa 1996. True, it was merely a life-sized cardboard cutout, used for promotional purposes, but it was a shock nevertheless.

A few days later, talking to a high school class in Taipei, I asked the students what their favourite sport was. I was expecting it to be baseball, given Taiwan's enviable international record in Little League baseball. I was surprised to hear most of them answer, "Basketball!"

I checked on some statistics, and I noticed something interesting. While Taiwan had been very successful in international Little League baseball at all age levels (9–12, 14–16, and 16–18) throughout the 1970s and 1980s, that success was not repeated from the mid-1990s, when Michael Jordan was at the pinnacle of his career and international fame, into the early twenty-first century, when Chinese centre Yao Ming made his debut with the Houston Rockets. The NBA has, for some time, been very aggressive in marketing its product around the globe. I wondered whether Taiwan's baseball program was a victim of cultural globalization? Was a significant aspect of Taiwanese culture being pushed aside through the marketing efforts of a commercially successful North American sports league?

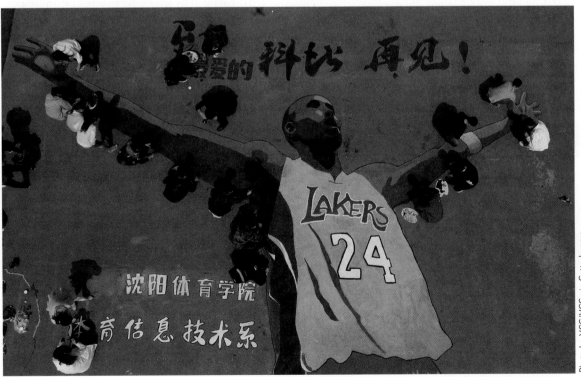

Photo by VCG/VCG via Getty Images

Students at Shenyang Sport University in China paint a portrait of NBA star Kobe Bryant on the eve of his retirement from professional basketball in 2016. Do you think that fifteen years from now there will be Chinese basketball players honoured the same way? Will there be NBA teams in Beijing and Shanghai? Will China have its own professional league to rival the NBA?

of ethnocentric logic that states that nothing worth knowing comes from non-Western traditions. Yet in order to cure or to heal, it's important to respond to the way the patient envisions the healing process. This point comes across with striking clarity in Anne Fadiman's study of Hmong refugees in America (1997), mentioned earlier in this chapter. The book describes the way American doctors and nurses failed to respect, among other things, the Hmong people's spiritual connections to medicine, the importance of encouraging their belief that a cure is available, and the role this belief plays in the curing process.

Cultural relativism is about not just how we *understand* cultural practices that are not our own but how we *judge* those practices. One prevailing viewpoint argues that individuals should not be judged by the practices of their culture. They have relatively little choice in what they do. After all, those living today no more invented those customs that you might find objectionable than you invented customs in Canadian culture that others may find strange. Consider the Maasai, an African people with a strong warrior tradition, who have a custom in which boys, at the onset of puberty, are circumcised. It is frightening and painful, but it is an important initiation ceremony: only once he has gone through the ceremony is a Maasai boy treated as a man and permitted to have sex with women. It is easy for Canadians to judge this custom negatively, to be critical of those who perpetuate what they consider a cruel and barbaric ritual. But is that right? The Maasai might identify as a sign of our cultural weakness the fact that most Canadian boys are never ritually transformed into men.

The doctrine of cultural relativism becomes problematic when studying historical practices and views that were once widespread but are now considered abhorrent and offensive. The city of Halifax has recently had to consider the appropriateness of honouring its founder, Edward Cornwallis, who, as governor of Nova Scotia, endorsed the use of violence to eliminate the colony's Mi'kmaq population in what some have called an act of genocide. In 2010, a new statue of women's rights activist Nellie McClung in Winnipeg touched off similar debates. While McClung was instrumental in winning Canadian women the right to vote and hold public office, she was also a proponent of eugenics (literally "good genes"), the movement to improve the population by sterilizing people with mental and physical disabilities, as well as people of "races" deemed "inferior." Not even Canada's first prime minister is safe: in 2016, the board of governors at Wilfrid Laurier University shelved a plan to erect on campus a statue of John A. Macdonald—and 21 other past prime ministers—after students and instructors protested the plan, citing in particular Macdonald's racist policies toward Indigenous people. The doctrine of cultural relativism suggests we should judge figures like Cornwallis, McClung, and Macdonald not by today's moral standards but by the standards of their own time; failing to do so is known as *presentism*. But can we really let bygones be bygones when those cultural practices are so repugnant? What do you think?

Cultural Relativism, Ethnocentrism, and Smell: Two Stories

Our senses—the way we perceive what is beautiful or ugly, pleasant or disgusting—are culturally conditioned. Think of female beauty. For many North Americans, the image that comes to mind is that of a skinny model with very white teeth. Do you think this is true in other cultures?

What about our sense of smelling "good" or "bad"? Part of how we smell is determined by the food we eat (e.g. dairy products, meat, garlic, curry), but there is more to it than that. Describing his experience working in the Peace Corps, an organization of volunteers working in developing countries, Tom Bissell noted how difficult he found it to share a bus in the central Asian country of Uzbekistan with people who were overdressed for the weather and, understandably, hot and sweaty. He observed:

> When I was in the Peace Corps, one of my least favorite things was when my fellow volunteers complained about Central Asian body odor. . . . But Gandhi probably smelled bad. Surely Abraham Lincoln smelled. William Shakespeare was, in all likelihood, rank. . . . Most certainly Jesus and Julius Caesar and the Buddha all smelled terrible. People have been smelly for the vast majority of human history. By gooping up our pheromonal reactors with dyed laboratory gels, could it be that we in the West

Telling It Like It Is

The Beauty Standard in Taiwan: A Case of Reverse Ethnocentrism

Reverse ethnocentrism involves assuming that a particular culture that is not one's own is better than one's own in some way. It sets an absolute standard that one's own culture does not or cannot match. In the United States, liberal Americans who blame their own country's cultural values and foreign policy for terrorist attacks on Americans at home and abroad are sometimes accused of reverse ethnocentrism (and anti-Americanism) by more conservative thinkers.

I experienced reverse ethnocentrism during a trip to Taiwan. It was a different world for me. The streets of Taipei, the capital, buzzed with the sound of scooters; small feral dogs roamed the sidewalks; rooftop gardens crowned many of the buildings with lush greenery; and everywhere my whiteness drew stares from the locals. A group of school kids in the museum pointed to me more often than to the exhibits.

Late one evening, my companions and I decided to go to the Shilin night market, where food and clothing are sold at hundreds of stalls. Weighing well over 200 pounds, I didn't find any cheap clothes, but that did not detract from the cultural experience of visiting the clothing vendors, being beckoned by entire families to come and buy from their family stall.

Among the strange things I saw, one in particular set my sociological spider senses tingling. After noting it once I began to look for it, and I saw it repeatedly: the mannequins in the clothing stalls were modelled after Europeans. I did not see one "Chinese" mannequin, either there or anywhere I went the entire week-and-a-half I spent in Taiwan.

What does a sociologist make of this? While I was in Taipei, I read an article in one of the English-language newspapers questioning whether the Taiwanese people admired the West too much. What I had found was an example. Mannequins, which we, as prospective customers, are meant to admire for their beauty and exquisite fashion sense, are in Taiwanese terms "not us." Beauty is "not us." I decided it couldn't be economics dictating this move, that these mannequins couldn't be spares from the Western market. They must have been made and bought for the domestic market.

Later I remembered a beautiful young Italian-Canadian woman, a former student of mine, who had worked in Japan as a model. She had remarked to me that a number of her colleagues in the Japanese modelling industry were white. I remembered reading about how, during the Vietnam War, some South Vietnamese prostitutes underwent eye operations on their epicanthic folds (the skin and fat tissue that makes most East Asian people distinctive) to make themselves look "more white." I thought of Japanese manga and anime characters with big eyes—Sailor Moon comes to mind.

Are these examples of "beauty is not us," of a prevailing belief that standards of beauty come from another culture, of reverse ethnocentrism? I think so, but some of my students do not agree with me (particularly the white students). What do you think?

What do YOU think?

1. Summarize the author's experience of reverse ethnocentrism in Taiwan. Do you agree that the prevalence of European mannequins in Taiwan is a sign of reverse ethnocentrism?
2. Do you think that Canadians sometimes subscribe to reverse ethnocentrism? Under what circumstances?

are to blame for our peculiar alienation? Might not the waft from another's armpit contain crucial bioerotic code? Could it be by obscuring such code we have confused otherwise very simple matters of attraction? (Bissell, 2003: p. 98)

In a very different setting, Emma LaRocque, a Métis writer, came to a similar conclusion:

> Several summers ago when I was intern-teaching on a northern reserve, one of the teachers told me how she "had to get used to" the smells of the children. She insisted it was not just stuffiness but a "peculiar odor." . . .
>
> Oddly enough, the "peculiar" smell was a redolent mixture of spruce, moose-hide, and woodsmoke. All the while this teacher was complaining about the smell of the children, the children reported a "strange" odor coming from the vicinity of some of the teachers and their chemical toilets. And it never seemed to occur to the teacher that she could be giving off odors.
>
> More to the point, both the teacher and the children attached value judgements to the unfamiliar odors. As a friend of mine noted, "to a person whose culture evidently prefers Chanel No. 5 or pine-scented aerosol cans, moosehide and woodsmoke can seem foreign." The converse is true, I might add. (LaRocque, 1975: p. 37)

As we have seen, ethnocentrism and cultural relativism are opposing ways of looking at cultures, both our own and those of others. Ethnocentrism is laden with negative judgement, while cultural relativism is characterized by a greater appreciation for context in understanding and evaluating culture. This is not to say that everything is relative, or that there are no universal standards. Practices such as female genital mutilation, the use of land mines and child soldiers, and the torture of political prisoners can be considered universally bad.

The point to take from this is that it's important to realize how easy it is to make an ethnocentric assessment of a different culture. It is important to try to understand why different cultures do what they do. And, while true appreciation of aspects of other cultures might not always be possible, it is worth the trip to take a few steps down that path.

Sociolinguistics

Sociolinguistics is the study of language as part of culture. Language exists at the centre of communication between individuals and between groups. It is a source both of understanding and of misunderstanding. It is also the main vehicle for transmitting culture, and a culture cannot be understood without some sense of the language(s) it uses and the way those languages fit with other aspects of culture. Sociolinguistics thus looks at language in relation

Going Global

Pioneer Global Village

I was taking some Indonesian science teachers on a bus trip to a few of the educational sites near my college in northwestern Toronto. We were going to Black Creek Pioneer Village, a reconstructed nineteenth-century settler community, where historical interpreters dressed in period costume demonstrate various aspects of pioneer life. As we approached the site, I was frantically searching my mind for points of connection that would make this part of the trip understandable.

I needn't have bothered. For as I entered the site with my Indonesian teachers, one loud voice suddenly piped up, "Hey, it's like *Little House on the Prairie*." That television show, based on the novels by Laura Ingalls Wilder and depicting life in the American West during the 1870s, had been shown from 1975 to 1982 in North America, but had lived on in reruns around the world—including Indonesia.

My visitor's ready reference to a classic American television show caught me by surprise, but then the American Midwest of the nineteenth century has no less to do with Indonesia than turn-of-the-twentieth-century Prince Edward Island has to do with Japan, where Lucy Maud Montgomery's heroine Anne of Green Gables flourishes as a cultural icon. Should we feel proud, as Canadians, that one of our literary figures has been embraced halfway around the globe, or unnerved that a piece of cultural property has been bought and transformed to serve the global marketplace?

to such sociological factors as "race," ethnicity, age, gender, and region.

Dialect as a Sociological Term

A dialect is a variety of a language, a version that is perhaps different from others in terms of pronunciation, vocabulary, and grammar. To the sociologist, the distinction between dialect and language is interesting because it can be as much a product of social factors as of linguistic ones. Dutch and German, for instance, are considered separate languages, although going strictly on linguistic criteria they could be called dialects of the same language. For some German speakers living near the Netherlands, Dutch is easier to understand than dialects of German spoken in Austria or Switzerland.

Dialects, unlike languages, are often evaluated according to whether they represent proper or improper, casual or formal, even funny or serious versions of a language. These judgements usually depend on the social status of the dialect's speakers. In Britain, the "Queen's English" is an upper-class dialect, more highly valued in written and formal communication than regional dialects like that of the city of Manchester. The latter is often heard spoken by characters of TV shows such as *Coronation Street*, where it signifies that the characters using it are "real people" rather than upper-class people with what are called BBC accents. A few years ago, a commercial for a Nissan SUV featured a voice-over spoken in a Newfoundland accent. The accent here is used to put the audience in a receptive mood by evoking the famed good nature and affability of the people of Newfoundland and Labrador. You would not hear that accent extolling the marketable features of a Lexus.

Linguistic Determinism and Relativity

The relationship between language and culture is usually discussed in terms of the Sapir–Whorf hypothesis, which posits the existence of linguistic determinism (or causation). The principle of linguistic determinism suggests that the way each of us views and understands the world is shaped by the language we speak. Like theories of biological or social determinism, the Sapir–Whorf hypothesis can be cast either as strongly or weakly deterministic—that

is, language can be seen to exert either a strong or a weak influence on a person's world view. I tend to favour a weak determinism: I believe that linguistic differences are a valid form of cultural relativism, that exact translation from one language into another is impossible, and that knowing the language of a people is important to grasping the ideas of a people.

Noun Classes and Gender

Consider linguistic determinism in the context of the following statement: the different noun classes that exist in a language can reinforce the beliefs its speakers have within their culture. English speakers in Canada have some awareness of difference in noun classes through the presence of gender exhibited by the Romance languages to which they are exposed (e.g. French, Italian, Portuguese, Spanish, and other languages based on Latin, the language of the Romans). Students struggling through French classes may wonder why every French noun has to be masculine or feminine. Why are the words for "tree" (*arbre*) and tree species masculine, while the parts of trees—roots, leaves, branches, bark, blossoms—are feminine?

While it does not have noun classes labelled as "masculine" or "feminine," English does have a certain degree of grammatically mandated gender, with our use of *he, him, his,* and *she, her, hers.* Take the following two sentences: *One of my sisters is called Ann. She is younger than I am, and her hair used to be the same colour as mine.* In the second sentence, the words "she" and "her" are grammatically necessary but do not add any new information. Am I assuming that you have forgotten the gender of my sister? We already know from the nouns "sister" and "Ann" that the person spoken about is female. The Indo-European languages—the family of languages that includes almost all the languages of Europe plus Farsi (Iranian) and the languages of Pakistan and northern India—all impose gender grammatically in some way.

Algonquian languages, which together make up the largest Aboriginal language family in Canada and the United States, have no grammatically mandated gender, in either the French or the English sense. They have no pronouns meaning "he" or "she." They are not alone in that respect. Almost every Canadian Indigenous language does not recognize gender grammatically. Does this mean that Algonquian speakers were traditionally more flexible about gender roles than their European contemporaries, that there was a greater degree of equality between the sexes? The latter was certainly true at the time of contact, but whether that can be related to the absence of grammatical gender in their language is difficult to determine.

It is worth noting that there is a movement to bring gender-neutral pronouns to English. In 2014, the Vancouver School Board agreed that students should have the right to be referred to by the pronoun of their choice, including the gender-neutral options *xe*, *xem*, and *xyr* (Brean, 2014). The decision was made to accommodate transgender, gender-fluid, and gender–non-conforming students for whom neither *he/him* nor *she/her* was felt to be appropriate. When assessing the validity of the Sapir–Whorf hypothesis, consider how you might feel as a transgender person repeatedly referred to as "him" or "her": how would you feel about yourself knowing that neither option adequately described you? Do you think that English will ever have gender-neutral singular pronouns?

A Final Thought

Sometimes the terms that a language *doesn't* have tells you something significant about the culture. I have worked with the Wendat (Huron) language for 40 years. I have noticed that it doesn't have terms for the following concepts:

- *guilt* or *innocence*
- *best* or *worst*
- *command* or *obey*.

What do you think might be the cultural implications of these "holes" in the Wendat language?

WRAP IT UP

Summary

Not only do cultures differ, but cultures are viewed and lived differently by people who occupy different social locations, based on gender, sexuality, "race," ethnicity, age, and so on. Similarly, although humans, as intensely social creatures, cannot live without culture, they can also feel oppressed by their culture, if their social location is not one of power and influence.

Remember, as well, that cultures are contested, that not everyone is in agreement concerning the rightness or goodness of every aspect of their mainstream culture. This is why there are minority versions that exist in contrast or opposition to the dominant culture. Subcultures tend to organize around preoccupations—we might call them hobbies or pastimes—not found within the dominant culture. Countercultures oppose the defining elements of the dominant culture, but there's something inherently attractive in a counterculture—people like to cast themselves as rebels—and so a counterculture sometimes must reinvent itself repeatedly to keep from becoming mainstream. Even high culture, which occupies a privileged position, is a minority culture, concerning itself with sophisticated pursuits that may be beyond the reaches of the masses. Which brings us to popular culture or mass culture: the label you use depends on whether or not you believe people create culture independent of the powerful and manipulative influence of large commercial interests.

THINK BACK

Questions for Critical Review

1. Differentiate the following:
   - high culture
   - mass culture
   - popular culture.

2. Differentiate the following:
    - dominant culture
    - subculture
    - counterculture.
3. Differentiate the following:
    - folkways
    - mores
    - taboos.
4. Identify and give examples of Eurocentrism and ethnocentrism.
5. Contrast the linguistic expectations of speakers of Algonquian and Indo-European languages.

READ ON

Suggested Print and Online Resources

Online

Anishinaabemowin

http://imp.lss.wisc.edu/~jrvalent/ais301/index.html
- This is an excellent introduction to the grammar and other key aspects of the Ojibwa language. Students can consider linguistic determinism as they enjoy an introduction to an Aboriginal language.

Cannabis Culture

www.cannabisculture.com
- This Vancouver-based online retailer and information site reflects the viewpoints of the marijuana counterculture, particularly in Canada. Students can consider the aspects that define it as a counter-culture at a time when recreational marijuana use is becoming a mainstream concern.

TED: Culture

www.ted.com/topics/culture
- Technology Entertainment Design, more commonly known as TED, is a non-profit organization dedicated (since 1984) to what it calls "ideas worth spreading." This page offers links to different TED talks on pop culture.

In Print

Sajida Sultana Alvi, Homa Hoodfar, & Sheila McDonough, eds (2003), *The Muslim Veil in North America: Issues and Debates* (Toronto: Canadian Scholars' Press).
- This insightful look into the cultural image of the *niqab* focuses especially on the North American (particularly Montreal) experience of the 1990s.

John Fiske (2010), *Understanding Popular Culture*, 2nd edn (London: Routledge).
- A classic sociological study of popular culture, recently updated.

Edward Said (1979), *Orientalism* (New York: Vintage Books).
- Said's landmark work is a Palestinian-American's influential study of how the Middle East has been misrepresented by Western scholars.

Socialization

The Gist

Reading this chapter will help you to . . .

- Outline and assess the basic ideas of Freud as they apply to sociology.
- Discuss the application of over-socialization to the concepts of Mead and Cooley.
- Discuss the similarities and differences between social determinism and biological determinism.
- Distinguish between agency and determinism.
- Explain the roles of various agents of socialization.
- Discuss critically the effects of television and movie violence.

Terms of the Trade

- agency
- agents of socialization
- autism spectrum disorder
- bar mitzvah
- bat mitzvah
- behaviourism
- behaviour modification
- branding
- confirmation
- culture and personality
- degradation ceremony
- desensitization theory
- determinism
- ego
- eros
- game stage

- generalized others
- generation gap
- habitus
- hurried child syndrome
- id
- internalize
- law of effect
- longitudinal study
- looking-glass self
- national character
- observational learning theory
- oversocialized
- peer group
- peer pressure
- play stage
- preparatory stage

- primary socialization
- psychoanalysis
- refrigerator mothers
- reproduction
- resocialization
- risk behaviour
- rite of passage
- role-taking
- secondary socialization
- significant others
- superego
- swaddling hypothesis
- thanatos
- total institution
- vision quest
- XYY males

Names to Know

- Bruno Bettelheim
- Pierre Bourdieu
- Charles Horton Cooley
- David Elkind
- Sigmund Freud

- Carol Gilligan
- John T. Hitchcock
- George Herbert Mead
- Ann Leigh Minturn
- Edward Thorndike

- John B. Watson
- Dennis H. Wrong

For Starters

The Canadian Press/Richard Buchan

Playing for Fun versus Playing to Win: A New Policy and Its Effect on Youth Sports as an Agent of Socialization

Organized sports have long been a way of socializing Canadian children. As well as promoting fitness through exercise, organized sports provide an environment for children to learn key values from their peers and from adults. These values include teamwork, co-operation, work ethic, practice, and even friendship. They also include competitiveness.

It is well known that when it comes to competitiveness, parents and coaches do not always model healthy behaviours. They may hurl abuse at players, officials, and even one another. I have seen riled-up parents shout, "Kill her! *Kill her!*" at a girls' house league hockey tournament. When fist fights break out in the stands, these anecdotal cases become news stories. When an isolated case of parental rage becomes a pattern of devastating abuse, someone may write a book about it, as former NHL player Patrick O'Sullivan (2015) did.

The perceived overemphasis on competition has caused some people to question the value of organized

sports as a socializing agent for children. As a result, some youth athletic associations in Canada have made the move to no-score sports. In 2013, the Ontario Soccer Association announced that it would stop keeping score in matches involving under-12 teams in its recreational, or "grassroots," leagues. A number of associations across the country followed suit, adopting the "festival" format and the philosophy of "No scores, no standings, no trophies" (OSA, 2015). The aim of no-score programs is to lower the stress associated with the pressure to win (see the discussion of hurried child syndrome later this chapter) and to focus instead on fostering skill and love of the game among child athletes.

The response has been predictable. Newspaper editorials supported by online comments warn that no-score sports will blunt the "natural" human trait of competitiveness and encourage young people to believe in a world with no winners and losers, setting them up for failure when they encounter "real world" hardships and adversity. They'll just keep score anyway, some critics argue. This is true. Kids, living in a culture that stresses "better" and "best," will "naturally" compete and measure themselves against their peers: this is an important part of their socialization into Canadian culture. They will do this with or without adults bellowing encouragement from the sidelines or the stands. Kids will know who the best and the worst teams are and whether their team is winning or losing; they will still have to learn how to take failure well, how to lose with pride, and how to win with grace. And while end-of-season participation awards can seem as meaningless as "Everyone's a winner" when you're 15 years old and in your tenth year of organized sports, they matter a great deal when you're 5 and earning your first trophy. My son once received an award in hockey not for first place

or MVP but for being the most improved player on his team. That gave him a sense of pride and showed that real achievement can be celebrated without keeping score.

What do YOU think?

1. What values did you learn from participating in youth competitive activities—chess club, gymnastics, tennis, baseball, video games? Who was it who reinforced those values: Your peers? Your parents? Your coaches? Someone else?
2. Do you think the no-score policy makes athletic programs more beneficial or less beneficial to young people? How would you design a sociological study to research the issue?

Introduction: Socialization Is a Learning Process

Socialization is an area of sociological study that brings the discipline close to psychology. The intersection of sociology and psychology is clear from the fact that a good number of the leading socialization theorists are psychologists. Socialization is a learning process, one that involves learning how to be a social person in a given society. It brings changes in an individual's sense of self. This applies both in the earliest socialization that an individual undergoes in childhood, generally known as primary socialization, and in socialization that occurs later in life, which is sometimes known as secondary socialization.

Determinism: Nature versus Nurture

Any discussion of socialization needs to cover the topics of *determinism versus free will* and *biological determinism versus social determinism*. When we speak of determinism, we are talking about the degree to which an individual's behaviour, attitudes, and other "personal" characteristics are *determined*, or caused, by a specific factor. There are "hard" and "soft" versions of determinism. Proponents of the

former claim that we are, in essence, programmed to think and act in a particular way, either by our biology or by our culture. Champions of the latter believe there is some room for free will or the exercise of agency in one's life. Agency involves personal choice above and beyond the call of nature or nurture.

Biological Determinism

Biological determinism ("nature" in the old "nature versus nurture" debate) states that the greater part of what we are is determined by our roughly 26,000 genes. Biological determinism has become a popular subject of discussion and debate in the mainstream media, owing in large part to the rise of human genetic research generally and, in particular, the Human Genome Project, which involves a painstaking count of the number of genes we have and investigation into what each of those genes singly or in combination code for (if anything).

Certain abilities seem to fall into the "nature" category. We all know of people who are "naturally good" at sports, music, art, and so on. However, we have to be very careful in making even tentative statements about biological determinism. A notorious research study into XYY males that began in 1962 provides a cautionary tale. The standard pattern of chromosomes in men is XY; the corresponding pattern for women is XX. During the 1960s, the atypical XYY chromosome pattern was found in some men studied in hospitals for dangerous, violent, or criminal patients with emotional/intellectual problems, first in England and then in the United States and Australia (see Jacobs et al., 1965; Price & Whatmore, 1967; Telfer, 1968). The "criminal gene" was hastily declared.

The problem was that the researchers had neglected to study non-criminals. When the study was extended to the general population, researchers discovered that roughly the same percentage of men studied (about 1 in 1,000) were XYY (Court Brown, 1968). There remain some well-documented associations of XYY males with above-average height, a tendency to have acne, and with somewhat more impulsive and anti-social behaviour and slightly lower intelligence, but there is no evidence to conclude that XYY males are genetically determined criminals.

Softer forms of biological determinism focus on predispositions that people have (for shyness, for aggressiveness, and so on). These findings tend to have a stronger foundation and are easier to support than the more sensational claims of hard determinism—the ones beginning "*We have found the gene for ____*"—that sometimes make the news. What we are comes from too complex a mixture of the social and the biological, even too complex a genetic mixture, for one gene to be an absolute determinant of behaviour or personality.

Social or Cultural Determinism: Behaviourism

Behaviourism is a school of thought in psychology that takes a strong cultural-determinist position. It emphasizes the power of learning ("nurture" in the "nature versus nurture" debate) in the development of behaviour. For the behaviourist, the social environment is the prime mover in the development of personality. Biology and agency count for little. One cautionary statement about this school of thought is that much of the research on which it is based involved non-human animals: Pavlov and his dogs, Thorndike and his cats, B.F. Skinner and his rats and pigeons. Critics say that the theory disallows the existence of choice, of agency, which even a dog, pigeon, or rat can be seen as possessing (e.g. try training a dachshund—personal experience).

One of the earliest principles of behaviourism is the law of effect, introduced by **Edward Thorndike** (1874–1949) in his book *Animal Intelligence* (1911). The law of effect has two parts. The first says that if you do something and it is rewarded, the likelihood of your doing it again increases. The rewarded behaviour is said to be "reinforced." On the other hand, according to the second part, if you do something and it is punished or ignored, then the likelihood of your doing it again decreases. It boils down to the idea of the carrot (reward) and the stick (punishment). Accordingly, if the screaming child in the grocery store lineup is given a chocolate bar to be quiet, the reward reinforces the screaming: expect it to happen again. If a student is ridiculed giving an answer, then he or she will never answer in that class again.

There are debates about what constitutes a reward for an individual, and about what behaviour is or is not being rewarded. For example, if you punish a child who is acting out at school by making her sit in the corner and the objectionable behaviour persists, could it be that she sees the "punishment" as a reward? Is she getting attention? Is that her goal? If you pick up a crying baby, does that teach him that he can get anything he wants by crying? Or does it reward communication, which, once he learns to speak, becomes words and not tears? Attempting to change someone's behaviour using this kind of approach is called behaviour modification. When you scold a dachshund for peeing on the floor and praise her for peeing on the lawn (*not* the steps leading *to* the lawn), you are attempting to practise behaviour modification. What the dachshund does is another matter; if she's like my dog Trudy, she may be highly resistant to behaviour modification, like a dachshund Jedi master—the Force is strong in her breed.

Hard social determinism claims that just about any behaviour can be taught and learned. A powerful expression of this view comes from **John B. Watson** (1878–1958), the founder of behaviourist psychology:

> Give me a dozen healthy infants, well-formed, and my own specified world to bring them up in and I'll guarantee to take any one at random and train him to become any type of specialist I might select—doctor, lawyer, artist, merchant-chief and yes, even beggar-man and thief, regardless of his talents, penchants, tendencies, abilities, vocations, and race of his ancestors. There is no such thing as an inheritance of capacity, talent, temperament, mental constitution and behavioral characteristics. (Watson, 1925: p. 82)

Sounds like it comes from a scary science fiction movie: *Attack of the Rat Psychologists*. Indeed, some of Watson's research methods were controversial. His most famous experiment, the "Little Albert" study (Watson & Rayner, 1920), involved conditioning fear of a white rat in an 11-month-old infant ("Little Albert" was the infant, not the rat). It is hardly surprising that someone who felt that manipulating humans was so easy would write popular books and articles on parenting, and eventually enter a career in advertising.

What do YOU think?

How much of your own behaviour do you think is influenced by your social environment—by friends, family, your charismatic sociology professor—and how much were you simply born with?

Sigmund Freud: Balancing the Biological and the Sociocultural

The theories of **Sigmund Freud** (1856–1939), father of psychoanalysis, consider socialization in terms of a balance of biological and social aspects of human personality. Freud believed the mind had three parts: the id, the superego, and the ego. Think of it as a team with three players. The id is motivated by two **i**nstinctive **d**rives that we are born with as part of our unconscious mind: they are *eros* and *thanatos*. Eros (related to the word "erotic") is the drive that tends to be stressed by Freud's fans and critics. It is a "life drive" that involves pleasure—particularly, but not exclusively, sexual pleasure. Thanatos, the less celebrated of the two drives, is the "death wish," an instinct for aggression and violence.

The superego, also part of the unconscious, is your conscience. It takes in the normative messages of right and wrong that your parents, family,

Joe Cicak/iStockphoto

Behaviourism asserts that behaviour is the product of stimulus and response: a lab rat will develop certain patterns of behaviour (say, pressing a lever in a cage) if it produces a particular reward (like a pellet of food) even some of the time. Do you believe that human behaviour is mostly conditioned the same way?

The Point Is...

Parrot Socialization

If John Watson could be called a "rat psychologist," I could be considered a "parrot sociologist." Our parrot room, or aviary, is home to eight birds that are fascinating to watch for the insights they yield into animal behaviour. I believe, like the classical behavioural psychologists, that an understanding of animal behaviour can help us to understand human behaviour. Consider this example.

Our Senegal parrot, Sam, is a rescue parrot, having survived in hideously dark, crowded but lonely living conditions for a year before we "saved" him and brought him home. At first, he was very anti-social—both with humans and with the other birds in

his flock. During his first week with us, he bit off the toe of Stanee, the highly maternal "mother" of the flock, and got into a brutal fight with Louis, Stanee's mate, bloodying the smaller bird on his beak and head.

Then Sam was socialized. Stanee, together with the "father" of our flock, Quigley (Louis is just the biological mate—it's a complicated love triangle), socialized him into the flock. The two of them did this by preening him, gently scratching the back of his neck (the way to a parrot's heart). Sam learned to approach them with his neck turned in anticipation. His fights with the others now are more displays than actual fights. He has been socialized into being less aggressive.

What do YOU think?

1. How might some of the theorists we've encountered so far interpret this situation? How, if at all, would your interpretation differ?
2. If a social animal (a dog, a parrot, a whale, etc.) does something that humans do also, what can it tell us about our behaviour? What part of that shared behaviour is biological, and what part is social?

friends, teachers, and other socializing agents give you, and *internalizes* them. In other words, it adopts them as a personal code of moral behaviour. Picture a caped crusader with a big "S" on her chest, saying "Don't hit your sister or want to have sex with your mother—that's wrong!"

In Freud's thinking, the id and superego often come to blows in conflict that could take years of psychotherapy to resolve. If one is too strong, the individual is either too unrestrained or too controlled. The ego, meanwhile, mediates between the conscious and unconscious while trying to make sense of what the individual self does and thinks. It can interpret well if individuals are aware of what is going on in their unconscious with information from dream analysis, talks about childhood, ink-blot tests, hypnosis, and "Freudian slips" ("Today, we'll be talking about Sigmund Fraud"). If the ego is weak or lacks self-awareness, there will be serious problems.

The Oversocialized View of Human Behaviour

Critics of social determinism argue that it is important not to view humans as merely passive recipients of socialization. Canadian sociologist **Dennis H. Wrong** (1961), for example, criticized what he called an oversocialized representation of people. Wrong argued that people do not completely conform to the lessons of their socialization, automatically doing what socializing agents dictate. Rather, they can elect to resist their socialization.

This was an important point to make at the end of the 1950s, a time of relatively great conformity to norms in North America. It remains important in the branding days of the twenty-first century, when advertisers try to socialize children at younger and younger ages into thinking that they can acquire social acceptance through branded products. It's also worth considering this point in terms of the debate, discussed in the last chapter, between proponents of mass culture (who see individuals as passive recipients of cultural messages) and of popular culture (who view individuals as having agency in interpreting culture).

Luis Aguiar, who teaches sociology at the Okanagan campus of the University of British Columbia, offers another view of the conflict between socialization and *agency*, the ability to influence the outcomes of one's life. Born in the Azores, off the coast of Portugal, Aguiar experienced the "working-class socialization" of his parents, who encouraged him to adopt a trade rather than pursue a postsecondary education. The idea of finding a "career" was incomprehensible to Aguiar's parents (Aguiar, 2001: pp. 187–8). They considered boys who preferred mental to physical work "sexually suspect"

and "unmanly." Aguiar's father even supplied him with examples of men who "became insane as a result of too much reading and studying" (180).

Ultimately Aguiar did go to university, demonstrating agency by overcoming his parents' attempts to socialize him into entering a trade. However, he was not unaffected by their efforts, which left him with feelings of guilt, since he could not, because of the length of his schooling, help provide for the family until relatively late in life:

> Today I still feel terribly guilty because of my selfish educational pursuits that deprived my parents from owning a home or car or having some higher level of comfort in their retirement years. My parents never complained about my lack of financial

The Point Is...

Cold Mothers Don't Cause Autism

The tendency to adopt an oversocialized view of certain behaviours has caused experts to ascribe biological conditions to faulty socialization, usually with the parents to blame. Male homosexuality was once commonly attributed to poor socialization involving a smothering, over-attentive mother and a weak or absent father. Joseph Nicolosi is a clinical psychologist who still holds this outdated view. In a 2002 handbook for parents, he warns that

> if a father wants his son to grow up straight, he has to break the mother–son bond that is proper to infancy but not in the boy's best interest afterward. In this way, the father has to be a model, demonstrating that it is possible for his son to maintain a loving relationship with this woman, his mom, while still maintaining his own independence. (Nicolosi & Nicolosi, 2002: p. 27)

Thankfully, not many clinical psychologists today subscribe to this oversocialized view.

Ineffective parenting and faulty socialization were

once also blamed for the behaviours associated with autism, now formally known as autism spectrum disorder, as it encompasses several different conditions. Autism is a complex neurological condition associated with social communication difficulties, repetitive or fixated behaviours, and sensory problems. No cause of autism has been discovered, though the condition appears to have a strong biological or genetic component. The influence of the effects of socialization is strongly contested. There was a time, though, when it was widely believed that so-called refrigerator mothers, described as women who were cold toward and withheld affection from their sons, were responsible: they had supposedly socialized their children into not expecting warmth from a parent. This oversocialized view developed in the 1940s, when autism was first identified as a specific disorder, and then expounded single-mindedly with great influence by child psychologist **Bruno Bettelheim** (1903–1990). Bettelheim's oversocialized explanation of autism has been rejected today, but two generations of women had to endure being blamed for the autism of their children: they were considered to be socializing their children improperly.

contribution to the family, but my sense is that they are extremely disappointed at not achieving the immigrant dream of owning their own home. To my mind, only immigrant students of working-class background feel this heavy load of class guilt. (Aguiar, 2001: p. 191)

Agents of Socialization

Luis Aguiar's parents were among his most influential agents of socialization, meaning the people who had a significant impact on his socialization. Many individuals, groups, and institutions can act as agents of socialization—and the list varies from person to person—but the following seven in particular are thought to hold sway when it comes to socialization:

- family
- peer group
- neighbourhood/community
- school
- mass media
- the legal system
- culture generally.

The impact of each of these agents is severely contested, both in the sociological literature and in the day-to-day conversations of people in society. In the following sections, we'll take a closer look at some of the debates.

Significant Other, Generalized Other, and Sense of Self

The American psychologist **George Herbert Mead**, whom we introduced as a symbolic interactionist in Chapter 1, saw all agents of socialization falling into one of two categories he named "significant other" and "generalized other." He believed that children develop their sense of self from being socialized by the "others" in their lives. They internalize norms and values they observe, incorporating them into their way of being.

Significant others are those key individuals—primarily parents, to a lesser degree older siblings and close friends—whom young children imitate and model themselves after. Picture a mother or father doing yardwork with a young child imitating the practice (for instance, clearing leaves with a toy

rake). Please note: your boyfriend/girlfriend, your spouse, or your partner is *not* your significant other. When people ask me to bring my significant other to a party, I inform them that my parents are dead. (I hope that somewhere Mead is chuckling.)

Later on, the child comes under sway of generalized others and begins to take into account the attitudes, viewpoints, and general expectations of the society she or he has been socialized into. Freud would say that during this period, the individual's superego internalizes the norms of society.

Mead also identified a developmental *sequence* for socialization, beginning with the preparatory stage, which involves more or less pure imitation. The next step is the play stage, where the child engages in role-taking, assuming the perspective of significant others and imagining what those others are thinking as they act. The third stage is the game stage, in which the child considers simultaneously the perspective of several roles. In terms of baseball, for example, this is when a child, fielding the ball at shortstop, might be able to consider what the runner and the first baseman are thinking and doing. She is aware that her role is different from the roles of other participants and understands how her role fits with those other roles.

This is a common image in North American culture, one you've likely seen in TV commercials or in a scene from a movie. Why aren't images of a mother and daughter shaving their legs or doing their makeup as common?

Significant and generalized others continue to exert strong socialization influences later on in the life of an individual, with significant consequences for the individual's self-concept. Mentors and other role models can become important significant others for the adolescent or adult individual. A generalized other may be a social group or "community" that has an impact on the individual's sense of self. Think of television ads. When an Old Navy commercial presents a group of young, attractive, and Old Navy–dressed people dancing and having a good time, the advertising agency is trying to tell you that this is what your cool, young community likes, and you should, too. Whenever a star athlete, the latest pop sensation, or any other celebrity is chosen to endorse a product, the marketing team behind the advertising is banking on the person being viewed as a significant other by the target market. Note, however, that when celebrity spokespeople transgress the moral norms of a society, they lose their marketability as role models. Tiger Woods was quickly shunned by his corporate sponsors after details of his extramarital affairs became public.

What do YOU think?

Think of a current celebrity endorsement that works (Jennifer Aniston promoting face cream, Beyoncé selling haircare products) or one that doesn't work (say, Matthew McConaughey shilling for Ford Lincoln). What makes the endorsement effective or ineffective? How much has to do with the celebrity's status as a significant other among the ad's target audience? Can a bad celebrity endorsement damage the credibility of the brand—or the celebrity?

Another symbolic interactionist, **Charles Horton Cooley** (1864–1929), put forth the idea of the looking-glass self. This is a self-image based on how a person thinks he or she is viewed by others. In Cooley's poetic words, "each to each a looking glass / Reflects the other that doth pass" (quoted in Marshall, 1998: p. 374). The looking-glass self has three components:

1) how you imagine you appear to others
2) how you imagine those others judge your appearance
3) how you feel as a result (proud, ashamed, self-confident, embarrassed).

The relationship between body image and self-esteem, especially in young women, illustrates this well. Harvard educational psychologist and respected feminist **Carol Gilligan** noted how the self-esteem of girls declines during their teenage years (Gilligan, 1990). Studies show that this happens more with girls and young women than with boys. The harsher standards of body type that we apply to women have rightfully been associated with this difference in self-esteem.

What do YOU think?

1. What do you think the impact of selfies might be on a teenager's looking-glass self?
2. You and your peers belong to the most photographed generation in history. Do you think this gives you a more fragile or a more robust self-image than that of past generations?

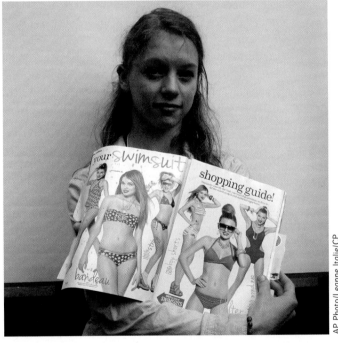

Julia Bluhm, 14, holds up a copy of *Seventeen* magazine as she leads a protest urging the magazine to publish one spread each issue of model photos that have not been photoshopped. In response, the magazine announced that it would never alter girls' faces or body shapes in its photos, and it now posts behind-the-scenes images on Tumblr. Has this change improved the representation of women in the magazine, or just reinforced a standard that most women can't live up to?

Family

The family is the first agent of socialization, and often the most powerful one. Significantly, just as families differ across cultures, so do the means and goals of families in socializing the child. Consider the narrative below, which is based on research done on the Rajput of Khalapur in northern India, carried out by **John T. Hitchcock** (1917–2001) and **Ann Leigh Minturn** (1928–1999) in the early

An Expert's POV

Telling It Like It Is

The Rajputs: Child-Rearing and Personality in a North Indian Village

Although Rajput infants will be picked up and attended to when they are hungry or fussing, for the most part they are left in their cots, wrapped up in blankets. . . . Except for anxieties about a baby's health, it is not the centre of attention. A baby receives attention mainly when it cries. At that time, someone will try to distract it, but when it becomes quiet, the interaction will stop. Adult interaction with babies is generally aimed at producing a cessation of response, rather than stimulation of it. Infants and children of all ages are not shown off to others. . . . Children are also not praised by their parents, who fear that this will "spoil" them and make them disobedient.

Rajput children . . . are never left alone, yet neither are they the centre of interest. The child learns that moodiness will not be tolerated. Few demands are put on Rajput children; they are not pressured or even encouraged to become self-reliant. Weaning, which generally occurs without trouble, takes place at two to three years; but if the mother does not become pregnant, a child may be nursed into its sixth year. There is no pressure for toilet training. . . . Babies are not pressured, or even encouraged to walk. They learn to walk when they are ready, and mothers say they see no reason to rush this. . . .

Village women do little to guide children's behaviour by explaining or reasoning with them. There is also little direct instruction to small children. Small children learn . . . the customs and values of the group through observation and imitation. In the first five years of life, the child moves very gradually from observer to participant in village and family life. . . .

[C]hildren are not encouraged in any way to participate in adult activities. The chores a child is given are mainly directed to helping the mother. . . . There is little feeling that children should be given chores on principle in order to train them in responsibility. . . . Rajput children take little initiative in solving problems by themselves. Instead, they are taught whom they can depend on for help in the web of social relations of kin group, caste, and village. . . . Although chores increase somewhat as the child gets older, it is not a Rajput custom to require children to work if adults can do it. Children are not praised for their work, and a child's inept attempt to do an adult job is belittled. Thus children are reluctant to undertake what they cannot do well.

—J.T. Hitchcock & A.L. Minturn

What do YOU think?

1. How would this be interpreted by a behaviourist?
2. What values are being taught with this form of socialization?
3. How does this compare with your upbringing?

1960s. Their work was part of a classic study of cross-cultural socialization, Beatrice Whiting's *Six Cultures: Studies of Child Rearing* (1963).

Culture and Personality

Some have argued that the impact of family socialization in its different forms has long been over-emphasized. During the first half of the twentieth century, sociology, anthropology and psychology were involved in the culture and personality school of thought. Proponents of this school attempted to identify and describe idealized personalities or "personality types" for different societies, and attach to each one a particular form of family socialization. During World War II and in the early years of the Cold War standoff between the West and the Soviet Union, the scope of these studies broadened to examine national character, the personality type of entire nations. These studies typically drew conclusions about how the primary socialization of child-raising was linked with a country's national character.

An example is *The People of Great Russia* (1949), in which Geoffrey Gorer and John Rickman proposed the swaddling hypothesis. They identified moodiness as a supposedly typical Russian character trait, citing extremes of controlled and out-of-control behaviour (for example, intense bouts of alcoholism), and attributed it to the fact that the country's people were tightly *swaddled*—as in "bundled up"—as infants. Theories like this that attempt to generalize about such large populations are extremely difficult to prove.

Studies attempting to link child socialization practices to national character could very well be sitting on the dusty shelf of old theories that no longer affect us if it weren't for a persistent preoccupation with trying to understand overarching personality traits of certain populations. Since the September 11 attacks on the United States and the rise of Daesh (the self-styled Islamic State), there has been a great deal of focus in the media and among Western political and military leaders on the "Arab mind." Raphael Patai's book of this very title, first published in 1973 and revamped in 1983, was reprinted in 2002, the year after the attacks, and again in 2014. Each edition has sold well. *The Arab Mind* currently enjoys considerable influence in upper military circles in the United States. It replicates the negative excesses

of the national character study publications, both by oversimplifying the psychological makeup of very sociologically diverse peoples and by tying that broad portrait to overgeneralized child-raising practices. As one critic wrote,

> It is hard to see how Patai's findings can apply equally to a Saudi prince and a Tunisian fisherman, to a Libyan Bedouin [a desert nomad] and a Kuwaiti commodities broker, to an Egyptian soldier and Moroccan "mulla," to a wealthy Palestinian businessman in Qatar and an impoverished Palestinian migrant-worker from Ghazzah, to a child who is growing up in the hills of Syria and the one doing so in coastal Yemen, to a woman who is an executive director of the Cairo museum and one who farms field in northern Iraq, to a Marxist in Aden and a Christian in Beirut, a "muadhdhin" in Marrakesh and a musician in Muscat, and so on. (https://crescent.icit-digital.org/articles/the-zionist-diatribe-underpinning-american-attitudes-towards-muslims-and-arabs))

Different cultures socialize their children differently, but no culture exhibits complete uniformity in its socialization practices. Think of how a practice like spanking can generate considerable debate and variety of viewpoints when a newsworthy incident raises it in the Canadian media. Remember the point made in Chapter 3: it is a common mistake to view one's own culture as complex and dynamic while viewing others as simple and fixed. All cultures have elements that are contested, and a population of over 200 million people cannot be reduced to a single set of personality traits or mindset.

Peer Group

An important agent of socialization is the peer group, a social group sharing key characteristics such as age, social position, and interests. The term is usually used to talk about children and adolescents.

The term peer pressure refers to the social force exerted on individuals by their peers to conform in behaviour, appearance, or externally demonstrated values (e.g. not appearing excited about something that isn't deemed acceptable or "cool"). Peer pressure is socialization in action.

A classic sociological study that argues for the influence of the adolescent peer group is Paul E. Willis's *Learning to Labor: How Working Class Kids Get Working Class Jobs* (1977). Willis studied the informal culture of a group of 12 teenage boys attending a working-class, all-male school in the industrial town of Hammertown, England. Willis wanted to know why working-class boys settled for labouring jobs rather than directing their energies to getting the kinds of jobs obtained by middle-class kids in their cohort. He believed the boys were not passive recipients, through socialization, of the informal working-class culture. Rather, he speculated that, as an act of minority-culture resistance to the dominant culture, they were active participants both in the creation of this culture, with its belief and values systems and rules of behaviour, and in socializing newcomers into the culture. Among the evidence Willis found to support his theory were vocalized disdain for and humour directed against more conformist middle-class peers, ridicule of the "effeminate" nature of the mind-centred work done in school and in offices, and denunciation of middle-class values in general. The minority-culture resistance also involved manipulating the classroom (by controlling attendance and the level of work done, for example) and educational figures of authority in ways that the youths would repeat in the "shop floor" environments of factories and warehouses and with the middle-management figures they encountered there. Their classroom behaviour prepared them for their future.

What do YOU think?

1. Do you think the power held by the Hammertown peer group was related more to the fact the students attended a single-gender school or to the fact they were from working-class families?
2. Do you think these individuals had as much agency as Willis claimed that they had? If not, then what sort of determinism were they subject to?

An Author's POV

Telling It Like It Is

Experiencing Peer Pressure

Growing up, everyone is exposed to peer pressure. How we respond to the powerful influence exerted by our peer group helps to mould us into the adults we become.

When I was 10, I had a small group of classmates I hung out with. I felt they were "cooler" than I was, so I was susceptible to peer pressure from them. I was up for pretty much any of their hijinks, even when I knew they weren't the wisest things to do. We never did anything seriously wrong. We begged candy from a local candy manufacturer and stole chocolate bars from the neighbourhood drug store. We played "chicken" with trains on the railroad tracks. We threw snowballs at passing cars. Peer pressure made me do things I knew were wrong and would never have done otherwise.

But it's important to recognize that, while leading us to do some pretty silly things, peer pressure plays a vital role in forging personality. Peer pressure hits us hardest when we're insecure adolescents striving for acceptance among people outside our immediate family. By encouraging a degree of conformity, peer pressure helps children develop friendships and find acceptance among others their own age, fostering both self-confidence and independence. I belonged to a class of smart kids culled from various schools in the district, and it was easy to feel separate, different. My classmates and I formed a close circle from which we all gained a sense of belonging. It also gave us a safe place to test norms and values. I don't (often) throw snowballs at passing cars anymore. And perhaps, by remembering these stories, I will be less likely to judge younger people who do similar things.

Community and Neighbourhood

Community and neighbourhood can be important agents in child socialization. It's one of the reasons parents debate whether they should live in the city or in a town or suburb outside the big city where they work. It's also why urban planners are concerned about creating mixed-class city neighbourhoods rather than ghettoizing the poor in government-assisted housing projects.

Studies during the late twentieth century showed that young people living outside large cities were at lower risk of becoming involved in crime, drug and alcohol abuse, and other risk behaviour. Risk behaviour can be defined as any lifestyle activity that places a person at increased probability of suffering negative consequences, such as illness, injury, death, or confinement in prison or some similar institution. Much of this research was carried out in the United States, although Arnett and Balle-Jensen (1993) performed a cross-cultural study of adolescents in the US and in Denmark. Their findings showed a correlation between risk behaviour and city size (1993). As the authors explained,

City size was related to adolescents' reports of sex without contraception, sex with someone known only casually, marijuana use, heavy marijuana use, shoplifting, vandalism, and cigarette dependency. For most types of risk behavior, adolescents in the larger city were more likely to report the risk behavior than adolescents in the smaller city. . . . (Arnett & Balle-Jensen, 1993: p. 1849)

More recent research suggests that rates of drug and alcohol use in rural areas of North America have caught up to and in some cases surpassed the rates in cities. A 2015 review of the literature for the Canadian Centre on Substance Abuse reports that "Among American youth, those living in a rural setting are more likely to report use of alcohol, compared to those living in urban areas," and that "The former group is also more likely to report heavy drinking on one occasion and risk behaviours, such as drinking and driving, or driving under the influence of illicit drugs" (McInnis, Young, et al., 2015: p. 4). Drawing on studies of Canadian students from across the country, the researchers found that students in rural

A row of mailboxes in an Ontario suburb collects litter and unwanted junk mail. If you were to pass by this area, would you assume anything about the neighbourhood based on this scene? Would the litter on the ground change your behaviour—for example, would it make you more likely to drop your own trash on the ground rather than waiting for an available recycling bin?

schools in Canada were more likely than students in urban schools to report alcohol use, heavy drinking, and driving while under the influence of alcohol or cannabis (McInnis, Young, et al., 2015: p. 17). There were no significant differences in rural and urban rates of using illicit or prescription drugs.

> ## What do YOU think?
>
> How might you account for the correlation between risk behaviour and type of community (big city, small city, rural)?

Mass Media

Questions about the role communication for the masses plays in socializing young people go back at least as far as the ancient Greek philosopher Plato, who felt that art (in his day, plays) aroused primal instincts, stimulating violence and lust. Plato's student Aristotle believed that violence depicted in art actually produced among those viewing it an experience of *catharsis*, a relief from hostile or violent emotions, leading to feelings of peace.

Does mass media today—through action movies that make heroes out of vicious criminals, video games that promote war and crime, and TV shows that glorify death and murder—socialize young people, especially adolescent males, into committing violence, or at least into being desensitized to violence and the pain of others? Or does it provide a safe outlet for pent-up hostile emotions? The two sides of this contentious debate are taken up by contemporary writers in the following excerpts. First, arguing for a link between media violence and criminal activity, are psychologists Brad Bushman and L. Rowell Huesmann:

> True, media violence is not likely to turn an otherwise fine child into a violent criminal. But, just as every cigarette one smokes increases a little bit the likelihood of a lung tumor someday, every violent show one watches increases just a little bit the likelihood of behaving more aggressively in some situation. (Bushman & Huesmann, 2001: p. 248)

Arguing for the other side is communications professor Jib Fowles, in *The Case for Television Violence*:

> Television is not a schoolhouse for criminal behavior. . . . Viewers turn to this light entertainment for relief, not for instruction. Video action exists, and is resorted to, to get material out of minds rather than to put things into them. . . . Television violence is good for people. (Fowles, 1999: pp. 53 and 118)

Having whetted your appetite for the debate, we'll take a closer look at how Huesmann and Fowles arrived at their views.

Huesmann's Longitudinal Studies

Huesmann's pioneering work on the effects of television violence on children involved the use of longitudinal studies, which examined data gathered on research subjects over an extended period. His first was a 22-year study of 856 youths in New York State. At the beginning of his study the participants were all in Grade 3, about 8 years of age. Huesmann followed up by interviewing them again when they were 19, and then again at 30 (Huesmann & Eron, 1986). Among male subjects, the relationship between viewing television violence and engaging in aggressive behaviour roughly 10 years later was both positive and highly significant—in other words, there was a link, and it was a strong one. These findings were consistent for males of different social classes, IQ scores, and levels of aggressiveness at the start age. When the male subjects were checked again at age 30, the relationship between violent television viewing and aggressive behaviour—both self-reported and as documented in criminal records—was just as strong.

Huesmann and his colleagues (2003) also studied 557 Chicago-area children from Grade 1 to Grade 4, beginning in 1977. Fifteen years later, they interviewed as many of them (and their spouses and friends) as they could, and also looked at public records and archival material. The researchers were able to gather reasonably complete data for 329—roughly 60 per cent—of the original research participants (153 men and 176 women, all then in their early twenties). The results of this study were similar to those of the earlier study, with the only difference being that the link between TV violence and aggressive behaviour was evident among women as well as among men. The researchers concluded their study as follows:

Overall, these results suggest that both males and females from all social strata and all levels of initial aggressiveness are placed at increased risk for the development of adult aggressive and violent behavior when they view a high and steady diet of violent TV shows in early childhood. (Huesmann et al., 2003: p. 218)

Huesmann proposed two theories to explain the data. One, observational learning theory, states that children acquire what he termed "aggressive scripts" for solving social problems through watching violence on television. The other, desensitization theory, states that increased exposure to television violence desensitizes or numbs the natural negative reaction to violence.

Fowles's Defence of Television Violence

Jib Fowles has argued that sociologists and others who condemn violence on television are really using TV violence as a pretext to tackle other issues: class, "race," gender, and generation. He calls television violence a "whipping boy, a stand-in for other clashes":

> The attack on television violence is, at least in part, an attack by the upper classes and their partisans on popular culture. In this interpretation, . . . the push to reform television is simply the latest manifestation of the struggle between the high and the low, the dominant and the dominated. (Fowles, 2001: p. 2)

Fowles draws upon the work of **Pierre Bourdieu** (1930–2002), a French thinker best known for his work on the connection between class and culture. Fowles applies two of Bourdieu's key concepts in particular: habitus and reproduction. Habitus (somewhat different in meaning from the English word "habits") is a wide-ranging set of socially acquired characteristics, including, for example, definitions of "manners" and "good taste," leisure pursuits, ways of walking, even whether or not you spit in public. Each social class has its own habitus,

david pearson/Alamy Stock Photo

Which is more likely: that this young man is becoming desensitized to violence, or that he is ridding himself of aggression?

Telling It Like It Is

Branding Consciousness, Selling Pretty

In an era in which feminism has made many legislative gains toward gender equity, and more women are entering into professional and non-traditional fields for their gender, the world of children's media seems unable or unwilling to keep up. Most toys are still marketed along strongly demarcated gender lines of

Tree Change Dolls/Sonia Singh

before

treechangedolls.com.au

after

Australian artist Sonia Singh takes girls' toys (such as the Bratz dolls, left) and repaints them to make them more realistic, makeup free, and more childlike (right). What do you think the impact of playing with the doll on the left versus the doll on the right would be on a child's understanding of "growing up"? Are toys like Bratz dolls harmless fun or roads to self-objectification?

its set of shared characteristics. Reproduction, in Bourdieu's definition, is the means by which classes, particularly the upper or dominant class, preserve status differences among classes. As Fowles phrases it, "the reproduction of habitus is the key work of a social class" (Fowles, 2001: p. 3).

Fowles's main point is that sociologists who condemn television violence are merely fighting proxy wars aimed at reproducing the habitus of the dominant class by condemning the habitus of the

What do YOU think?

1. Do you think that Fowles's arguments are valid? What other criticisms of mass media might be challenged using this kind of approach?

2. In a number of cities police forces put more officers on duty on nights when the latest instalment of The Fast and the Furious franchise is opening. Is this a statement about the socialization potential of these movies?

what constitutes femininity and masculinity. Through pervasive marketing campaigns of many different toy brands, girls are compelled to obsess, and enjoy obsessing about, clothes, makeup, shopping, boys, and babies. They are also given the message that to be physically attractive you must also be sexy.

Through product lines and advertising, the gender roles young girls are frequently and repeatedly labelled with include Diva, Princess, Angel, and Pop-Star. These roles are not usually seen by parents as part of gender socialization. Girls who are labelled as such are often seen by parents as sweet, cute, and girly; however, these roles embody and encourage traits such as vanity, self-centredness, and an "all about me" attitude, while encouraging, normalizing, and rewarding girls' preoccupation with their bodies over their minds.

Marketing toward young girls is not just stuck in the past; in many ways, it is worse than in the past. The Bratz doll emerged as a hypersexualized version of Barbie, Mattel upped the ante with "Lingerie Barbie," and there is an array of T-shirts that objectify and impose an adult sexuality on toddlers and young girls through slogans like "Future Trophy Wife," "Hot Tot," "Made You Look," and "Born to Shop." Costume stores feature many provocative costumes for pre-teen girls, one of which is "Major Flirt"—a provocative "military" uniform complete with high, black, leather-look boots with a platform heel, kilt-style miniskirt, and studded black leather belt and choker.

Everywhere they turn—family, toys, advertising, media, and school—girls learn that beauty, narrowly defined and sexualized, is of utmost importance. This definition of beauty is also dependent on the consumption of beauty aids and products. "Salon" and "spa" birthday parties aimed at little girls as young as three years old are gaining popularity, providing a venue for girls to indulge in a range of services from manicures and pedicures to full makeup and hair extensions. One website for such services (replete with descriptors such as "diva" and "little princess") suggests that such experiences "build confidence," a statement reflecting the sad reality of girls who are taught that their self-worth is dependent on validation they receive from others in response to their physical and sexual attractiveness.

—Angela Aujla

What do YOU think?

Between 2008 and 2014, the rate (per 100,000) of child pornography incidents in Canada rose from 3.68 to 11.31, while the rate of total sexual violations against children increased from 4.32 to 12.53 (Statistics Canada, CANSIM Table 252-0051). Social media play a part in the dramatic change; law enforcement agencies have also become better at detecting these crimes. What role do you think the "pornification" of girls' clothing (a term used by sociologist Danita Kagan) has played in making children more vulnerable to sexual predators?

dominated class. It is ironic that he uses Bourdieu's writing to do this, as Bourdieu (1996) was a severe critic of television.

Education

Education can be a powerful socializing agent. Schools often are the first source of information that children receive about social groups other than their own. Teachers, curriculums, textbooks, and the social experience of being in the classroom and in the playground all play a part. We will focus here on the role teachers play in the socializing function of education.

What we call the "social location" of the teacher—the teacher's gender, age, ethnicity, and so on—can have a powerful effect on the educational socialization of the student. The fact that the early years of schooling are dominated by women teachers will have different effects on female and male students. The fact that science and math courses in high school are usually taught by men and English courses by women will also have different effects on girls and boys. Being of the same ethnic background or "race" as the teacher can have a positive effect on a child's socialization experience, as Kristin Klopfenstein points out in her article "Beyond Test Scores: The Impact of Black Teacher Role Models on Rigorous Math-Taking." In the introduction to her article she notes that

> Poor [in terms of income] black students, amongst whom teachers are often the only college-educated people they know, are in particular need of role models who (a) are interested in their educational progress; (b) understand the school system as an institution [i.e. as being located in the middle class and more in "white culture" than in "black culture"]; and (c) actively encourage academic excellence and the pursuit of challenging curriculum. Culturally similar teachers may take more interest in mentoring black students and have more credibility with those students. Given the importance of a rigorous mathematics curriculum and that math is frequently a gate-keeper subject for black students [i.e. success in math determines whether or not they will advance to postsecondary education], same-race math teachers play a potentially vital role in preparing black students for their academic and working futures. (Klopfenstein, 2005: p. 416)

Klopfenstein looked for a correlation between having a black math teacher in grade 9 and the kinds of math courses a black student would take the following year. She found that black students who had had a black math teacher in Grade 9 were more likely to enrol in a more challenging math class in Grade 10. These students, she found, also had a greater chance of postsecondary entry and success than students who had not had a black math teacher.

The socialization effect of having black teachers does not end there. Klopfenstein quotes P.R. Kane and A.J. Orsini's assertion that "Teachers of color are important role models to white students, as they shape white students' images of what people of color can and do achieve" (Kane & Orsini, 2003: p. 10).

Though you probably didn't notice, the prevailing demographics of the teachers you had growing up—their age, sex, ethnic background, and so on—played a role in your socialization.

What do YOU think?

How do you think the social location of a teacher might affect a student's socialization? Give some examples. How do you think this might differ for male and female students, especially during the early years when, typically, most of the teachers are women?

Issues of Socialization

In the sections that follow, we will look closely at two issues of socialization, both involving adolescents and both involving a complex combination of agents of socialization.

Male Readers

Traditionally, school-aged boys do best in maths and sciences, while girls fare better in writing and reading. Sociologists and educators today recognize that this is partly a result of socialization: boys have always been encouraged more in the former area of study, girls in the latter. In fact, beyond a lack of encouragement, there has been outright discouragement, as girls struggling in the supposedly male subjects have often been told not to worry: "You aren't expected to do well in math," or "You won't need to know it."

A lot has been done to improve female performance in the "male preserve" of math, science, and technology (sometimes known as MST), including the institution of all-girl classes in these subjects and the conscious promotion of role models such as our first female astronaut, Roberta Bondar (there are five elementary schools named after her in Canada—four in her home province of Ontario and one in BC). On average, boys still tend to perform better in these areas, but the difference has been lessened. This lessening has not been as great when it comes to career choice (more on this in Chapter 9, on gender and sexuality).

The same cannot be said for male–female differences in performance when it comes to language arts, as a 1999 federal government report, based on studies done in 1994 and 1998, makes clear. The following is an excerpt:

> Girls score substantially higher than boys in language skills and this gender difference is already pronounced by the age of 13. Boys and girls do not differ in mathematics achievement at the age of 13; however a gender gap in favour of males, particularly in problem-solving skills, seems to emerge by the time students are in their last year of secondary schooling. . . . It appears nevertheless that any gender differences in numeracy are substantially smaller than such differences in literacy. Hence, with respect to skills attainment, by the end of secondary schooling, girls should be in a somewhat better competitive position than boys. (Thiessen & Nickerson, 1999: p. 3)

More recently, Canada's Council of Ministers of Education reported the following results from an international study of 15-year-old students carried out by the Organisation for Economic Co-operation and Development (OECD) as part of its Programme for International Student Assessment (PISA):

> As was the case in PISA 2000, girls performed significantly better than boys in PISA 2012 on the reading test in all countries and all provinces. On average across OECD countries, girls outperformed boys by 38 points in PISA 2012, while in Canada this difference was 35 points. This difference is much larger than the 10-point difference favouring boys in mathematics. At the provincial level, the gender gap favouring girls ranged from 26 points in British Columbia to 53 points in Newfoundland and Labrador. (Brochu, Deussing, Houme, & Chuy, 2013: p. 40)

This raises a number of questions. To what extent is socialization to blame for gender differences in learning? Which agents of socialization might be having the greatest effect? How might educators change their approach to socialization in order to diminish the gender differences in literacy skills?

Many education experts recognize that boys and girls have different learning styles, and this view

has led to experiments with single-sex classrooms and schools. However, the benefits of single-sex learning environments are difficult to assess. A 2012 commentary by members of the Canadian Council on Learning concluded that "the existing research on single-sex schooling is inconclusive and too tenuous to support a widespread move to single-sex classrooms or schools" (Ungerleider, Thompson, & Lavin, 2012). If classroom socialization is not the problem, what is? The commentary suggests that "Parents may play a role in the different performance levels achieved by boys and girls in math and reading," adding that "girls may be doing better in reading and boys may be doing better in math because of parents' own beliefs about boys' and girls' natural abilities. . . . Children absorb their parents' beliefs about their own abilities and then those beliefs become powerful determinants of their school success" (Ungerleider, Thompson, & Lavin, 2012).

What do YOU think?

Blaming the parents seems to be a recurring theme in our chapter on socialization. Do you think the criticism is fair when it comes to gender differences in classroom performance? What other socializing influences are at play? Which one do you think has the greatest bearing on academic performance?

"Hurried" Children

David Elkind studies culture as an agent of socialization. One of his interests is the negative effects on children whose lives have been over-programmed by their parents, with little free time built in for spontaneous play. On this topic, Elkind's tone is dire. "[The] traditional culture of childhood is fast disappearing," he warns. "In the past two decades alone, according to several studies, children have lost 12 hours of free time a week, and eight of those lost hours were once spent in unstructured play and outdoor pastimes" (Elkind, 2003).

Spontaneous play, Elkind argues, has been replaced by a programmed schedule of organized sports and extracurricular learning. Technology is partly to blame: digital communication enables us to do more, faster, giving us a false feeling that we can accomplish much more than we used to. We extend this push for accomplishment to our children, putting pressure on them to take part in more after-school activities, play more organized sports, do more homework, and learn languages and other academic subjects at an earlier age. All of this is part of what Elkind calls the hurried child syndrome, which causes kids to feel adult-like levels of stress and guilt. It also contributes to the sometimes crippling apprehension that postsecondary students feel about deadlines and their career—"I'm 21 and I don't know what I want to be." It doesn't help that television and the movies often present people in their twenties as being financially successful.

Elkind also worries about the role of technology in socializing children. For one thing, the modern child's comfort with new technology is creating a generation gap (a significant cultural difference, complete with an equally significant lack of understanding, between generations). As he explains:

> [D]igital youth has a greater facility with technology than their parents and other adults. As a result, there is a greater disconnect between parents and children today, and some adolescents have even less respect for the knowledge, skills and values of their elders than they did a generation ago. . . .
>
> Independence from parents and adults means greater dependence on peers for advice, guidance and support. The availability of cell phones and immediate access to friends through instant messaging has only exaggerated this trend and quite possibly worsened the divide between children and their parents. (Elkind, 2003)

On top of its role in creating a generation gap, today's digital culture, with its "many adult-created toys, games and amusements," is affecting childhood socialization in ways that may compromise personal autonomy and originality:

> Game Boys and other electronic games are so addictive they dissuade children from enjoying the traditional games. Yet spontaneous play allows children to use their imaginations, make and break rules, and socialize with each other to a greater extent than when they play digital games. While research shows that video games may improve visual motor coordination

and dexterity, there is no evidence that it improves higher level intellectual functioning. Digital children have fewer opportunities to nurture their autonomy and originality than those engaged in free play. (Elkind, 2003)

In a 2012 editorial, the *Globe and Mail* sounded a similar note of alarm:

> The loss of spontaneous play from children's lives is not quite complete. . . . But the situation is pretty dismal. . . .
>
> [C]hildren between grades 6 and 12 spend an average of 7 hours 48 minutes on various screens each day. Horrifying, if true. And not without risks, whether from the health problems associated with a sedentary life, cyberbullying or even pedophiles reaching through their screens. ("Editorial," 2012)

Parents reading this may be nodding in agreement, while younger readers will likely shake their heads. Can this debate be considered like Fowles's discussion of media violence: an attack of one generation, growing older and losing power, on the habitus of a younger generation?

Secondary Socialization and Resocialization

At the start of the chapter I touched on the difference between *primary socialization*, which occurs early in childhood, and *secondary socialization*, which occurs usually in adolescence and early adulthood. Secondary socialization also differs from primary socialization in that

a)   it typically involves a group that is smaller than society in general, such as a new school or a new neighbourhood; and
b)   it usually takes place outside of the family (unless it involves a "new" blended family with step-parents and step-siblings).

Secondary socialization involves learning life lessons from a different source—from classmates at school or teammates on the ice instead of from parents at home. What you learn during secondary socialization may contradict some of what you've learned in primary socialization. Any time you switch from one experience of socialization to another—whether as a child or an adult—you undergo resocialization. This is a process that typically involves both learning and unlearning. In its extreme form, the individual unlearns all of the behaviours, attitudes, and values that were appropriate to the previous social environment while learning those that make it possible to fit into the new situation.

Karen Armstrong describes her process of unlearning values in *Through the Narrow Gate* (1982). Armstrong was a teenager in the 1960s, when she joined a strict order of nuns in Britain. In the following passage she recollects what the Mother Superior said to her and others who had just joined the order as postulants:

> Novices and postulants are kept in a particularly strict seclusion. They may not speak at all to seculars [i.e. to those who are neither nuns nor priests]. If a secular speaks to you, you must never reply. It is only by severing yourself absolutely from the world that you can begin to shed some of its values. Again no novice or postulant may ever speak to the professed nuns unless she is working with them and those few necessary words are essential for the job. The professed are in contact with the world, and even that indirect contact might seriously damage your spiritual progress. . . .

The Point Is...

The Vision Quest: A Modern Indigenous Rite of Passage

A traditional rite of passage for Indigenous people is the vision quest, which once marked the passage from childhood to adulthood. After receiving months of informal instruction from elders, the individual would embark on a journey away from the home community to an isolated location. Then, he or she would fast for days, and possibly go without sleep, in the process of seeking a vision. A vision could be a song that comes to mind, or the appearance in dreams of an animal or other spirit who instructs the dreamer and initiates a connection with him or her that will continue until death.

More recently, adults have used the vision quest as a way of resocializing themselves with traditional ideals following a period of difficulty. The following is a generalized example of the Ojibwa vision quest as it has been practised recently in northeastern Ontario (Steckley & Rice, 1997: pp. 226–7). It begins in a sweat lodge, a dome-shaped structure built around overlapping willow poles, covered with skins or tarpaulins and used as a kind of sauna. The participants throw sacred tobacco on a fire to thank the Creator. They are told the story of how the sweat lodge came to the people from a little boy who was taught about healing from the seven grandfather spirits. Water is put onto the seven stones that represent those spirits. The Elder sings ceremonial songs.

After the sweat, the participants are led to their own small lodges, where they fast and meditate. The Elder visits them to ask about their spiritual experiences. The participants fast for three nights and four days. What they learn changes with each night:

> The first is described as the night of doubt, where participants pray but are uncertain about what will happen. Hunger is mitigated by a feeling of excitement. The second night is one of fear, sometimes known as the dark night of the soul. Participants realize that their bodies are beginning to weaken, and they may question their resolve. The third night is the night of the spirit. It is often said that if something meaningful is going to happen, it will occur between the beginning of the spirit night and when the fast is finished. (Steckley & Rice, 1997: pp. 226–7)

After the final sweat there is a feast with gift-giving to the Elder and to those who have assisted the individuals in their resocialization.

You have to be absolutely ruthless in your rejection of the world, you know, Sisters. So many of its attitudes, even in really good people, are permeated with selfish values that have nothing at all to do with the self-emptying love of God. You yourselves are riddled with these ideas; you can't help it—it's not your fault. (Armstrong, [1982]/2005: pp. 92–3)

Resocialization can be voluntary or involuntary. *Voluntary resocialization* occurs when someone starts school or moves to a new school, when someone begins a job with a new company, when someone retires from work, or when someone undergoes a religious conversion (which can also, in extreme circumstances, be involuntary, as with cults). Associated with this kind of resocialization is the rite of passage, which is a ritual marking a life change from one status to another, typically following some form of training. A wedding is a rite of passage; so is a funeral. Other examples include the Christian practices of baptism and confirmation, and the Jewish bar mitzvah (for boys) or bat mitzvah (for girls), when adolescents become "adults in the faith" after a period of instruction.

Involuntary resocialization occurred in First Nations residential schools, like the one in Shubenacadie discussed in the narrative on page 119, where the language, religion, and customs of Indigenous children were brutally beaten out of them. Other examples of involuntary resocialization include being drafted into military service, being put in prison, being committed to a psychiatric hospital, and being subjected to mandatory retirement. Goffman (1961) called institutions where involuntary resocialization takes place total institutions, as they regulate all aspects of an individual's life. A significant part of the unlearning process associated with involuntary resocialization is what has been termed a degradation ceremony, a kind of rite of passage where a person is stripped of his or her individuality. Hazing, whether of Grade 9 students, first-year college or university students, or rookies on amateur and professional sports teams, is a degradation ceremony in which being made to perform acts of minor (sometimes major) humiliation informs the initiates that they are in a new social world where they are mere beginners.

Sometimes voluntary and involuntary resocialization can occur together. Consider, for instance, programs for treating alcoholism or obesity, which begin with the sufferer's decision to change his or her lifestyle but then involve a strict and rigorous regime that is imposed for the duration of treatment.

Hazing as Resocialization

Hazing is a particular way of resocializing new members of some group or organization, such as a high school, a university fraternity, a sports team, or a military unit. It is like a test in which the initiate must demonstrate, by successfully undergoing a demeaning or uncomfortable experience, that he or she is "tough enough" to be a member. In sports, hazing typically involves some form of ritual humiliation of the rookies, imposed by the veterans, who as first-year members had to go through the same trial themselves. Usually this kind of hazing is fairly minor: male players might have to shave their heads, or wear women's clothing or dress like a chicken in a public place. Sometimes, however, it crosses the line in ways that can harm the individual being hazed, particularly when the activity involves nudity and sexualized activities. In 2005, sports hazing made national headlines when a member of the McGill University football team quit after he and other rookies were forced to participate in a hazing ritual: nude and gagged, they were made to bend over while being prodded up the backside with a broom. This was nothing less than sexual abuse. At around the same time, a 16-year-old rookie on the Windsor Spitfires of the Ontario Hockey League became the subject of media attention after refusing to go through a hazing ritual called the "sweat box." This entailed crowding, naked, with other rookies into the washroom at the back of the team bus, with the heat turned up high enough to make the participants perspire.

Traditionally hazing has been much more a male than a female activity. Establishing one's toughness has long been viewed as a manly thing to do. But this may be changing. In September 2009, the Carleton University's women's soccer team was suspended by the university for holding a rookie initiation party that ended up with a player becoming so drunk that she had to be rushed to hospital by ambulance. Interestingly, while the suspension made the national news, the ensuing decision to reduce the suspension to just two games did not.

Telling It Like It Is
Resocializing the Mi'kmaq

The Shubenacadie Indian Residential School operated for 45 years, beginning in the early 1920s, under the auspices of two Roman Catholic orders in the small Nova Scotian community of Shubenacadie. Mi'kmaq students at the school suffered terrible abuse at the hands of the staff, whose mission was to resocialize students by beating their traditional culture out of them—literally, if necessary. The abuse is illustrated graphically in the words of anthropologist and former student at the school Isabelle Knockwood, who provides the following account of a young Mi'kmaq girl caught speaking in her native language:

The nun came up from behind her and swung her around and began beating her up. . . . Then the Sister pinched her cheeks and her lips were drawn taut across her teeth and her eyes were wide with terror. . . . Then the nun picked the little girl clean off the floor by the ears or hair and the girl stood on her tiptoes with her feet dangling in the air. . . . The nun was yelling, "You bad, bad girl." Then she let go with one hand and continued slapping her in the mouth until her nose bled. (Knockwood, 1992: p. 97)

Resocialization at the Shubenacadie Indian Residential School. Notice that the boys have more freedom in what they can wear than the girls do. Why do you think that was so?

It's Opening Day 2016, and San Diego Padres pitcher Luis Perdomo takes to the field with his *Frozen* backpack, an accoutrement of his rookie hazing ritual. Hazing is common in professional sports. As a rite of passage, what are its benefits? What are the drawbacks? When does it cross the line?

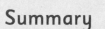

WRAP IT UP

Summary

Whether you're a lab rat or a domesticated parrot, a young teen buying her first bra, a rookie at training camp, or a first-year student at frosh week, everyone's undergone processes of socialization and resocialization. (To see what human life without socialization would be like, check out the 1970 film *The Wild Child*, based on the true story of a young boy who grew up entirely on his own in the wilds of France.) The people we are depends significantly on the agents of socialization we've grown up around—parents and family, educators, peer groups, culture, and the media. Sometimes these agents work together, but sometimes they send conflicting messages (you might have very different ideas about how to dress from your parents and your friends). How influential are these messages? Well, to a cultural determinist, who you are depends almost entirely on the messages you receive from your social environment. Others, though, like Dennis Wrong, believe we have the power to choose which messages we hear, that we have agency.

Postsecondary educators like the author of this book are heavily engaged in resocialization, in preparing students for careers, and for making them think critically about how they were and are being socialized. In fact, this chapter (and all the others) has been written in an effort to resocialize you. Did you notice? Do you think it worked?

THINK BACK

Questions for Critical Review

1. Outline the basic ideas of Freud as they relate to socialization.
2. Outline the basic ideas of Mead and Cooley as they apply to socialization.
3. Explain the differences between social determinism, biological determinism, and agency.
4. Identify at least five different agents of socialization and outline their roles.
5. Career, clothing, hobbies: do you believe each of these is more socially or more biologically determined?
6. Consider one or two situations in which you have been resocialized (for instance, starting a new school, moving to a new neighbourhood or city, entering or leaving an intense relationship). What did you have to learn? What did you have to unlearn?
7. In terms of socialization, what do you feel has been the impact of television, video games, movies, and the Internet on your life?
8. When was the last time you went through secondary socialization? What lessons did it entail?

READ ON

Suggested Print and Online Resources

Online

Social Psychology Network

http://Huesmann.socialpsychology.org
- Maintained by Wesleyan University professor Scott Plous, the Social Psychology Network is dedicated to psychological research and teaching. This page presents an overview of the work of Rowell Huesmann, with free access to some of his articles.

National Longitudinal Survey of Children and Youth

http://www23.statcan.gc.ca:81/imdb/p2SV.pl?Function=getSurvey&SDDS=4450&lang=en&db=imdb&adm=8&dis=2
- Launched in 1994 by Statistics Canada and Human Resources and Development Canada, the NLSCY is a long-term study of Canadian children designed to follow their development and well-being from birth to early adulthood.

The Hurried Child

www.youtube.com/watch?v=IOWbh8qqTGU
- David Elkind, who pioneered the concept of hurried child syndrome, talks about the importance of play in this YouTube video.

In Print

Karen Armstrong (2005), *Through the Narrow Gate, Revised: A Memoir of Spiritual Discovery* (New York: St Martin's Griffin).
- Karen Armstrong's recounting of her time inside a Catholic convent provides a window into religious training and spiritual life.

Ruth Benedict (1946), *The Chrysanthemum and the Sword* **(Boston: Houghton Mifflin); David Riesman (1950),** *The Lonely Crowd: A Study of the Changing American Character* **(New Haven, CT: Yale University).**
- These two books are classic examples of national character studies.

Sigmund Freud (1953), *On Sexuality: Three Essays on the Theory of Sexuality and Other Works* **(New York: Penguin).**
- This collection features three of Freud's key articles on sexuality, ranging in scope from sexual abnormality to puberty.

Isabelle Knockwood (2001), *Out of the Depths: The Experiences of Mi'kmaw Children at the Indian Residential School at Shubenacadie, Nova Scotia* **(Halifax: Fernwood Publishing).**
- Knockwood's work is an insightful ethnography on the residential school experience by one who survived the experience herself.

Laurie Kramer (2009, Winter), *Siblings as Agents of Socialization: New Directions for Child and Adolescent Development* **126 (Hoboken, NJ: Jossey-Bass).**
- A look at how brothers and sisters act as socializing agents in ways similar and different to those of parents, and as differing in different cultures and classes.

Shirley Steinberg, ed (2011), *Kinderculture: The Corporate Construction of Childhood*, **3rd edn (Boulder, CO: Westview Press).**
- An important look at how corporate marketing is socializing small children and teenagers.

Patrick O'Sullivan with Gare Joyce (2015), *Breaking Away: A Harrowing True Story of Resilience, Courage, and Triumph* **(Toronto: HarperCollins).**
- A former NHL player discusses growing up with an abusive hockey dad and how it affected his adolescence—a model of how not to socialize children.

Social Roles, Interaction, and Organization

5

The Gist

Reading this chapter will help you to . . .

- Understand what sociologists mean by the term *status*, and how ascribed and achieved statuses differ.
- Describe what it means to hold several statuses at once, and the complications that arise from this.
- Explain the relationship between status and role.
- Define role conflict, role exit, and role strain, and explain the effect these can have on an individual.
- Discuss the impact of bureaucracy and formal rationalization on the lives of Canadians.

Terms of the Trade

- achieved
- ascribed
- collectives
- control
- cosmology
- critical management studies
- definition of the situation
- disenchanted
- efficiency
- egalitarianism
- feminist organization
- formal rationalization (or rationality)
- formal social movement organizations
- interaction process analysis (IPA)

- McDonaldization
- marginalization
- master status
- organizational behaviour
- organizational culture
- organizational theory
- passing
- pecking order
- predictability
- quantification
- role
- role conflict
- role exit
- role set
- role strain
- scientific management

- service-provider organizations
- small groups
- social mobility
- social order
- social organization
- social segregation
- status
- status consistency
- status hierarchy
- status inconsistency
- status set
- substantive rationalization
- Taylorism
- team approach
- Thomas theorem

Names to Know

- Robert F. Bales
- Howard Becker
- Charles Horton Cooley
- Helen Rose Fuchs Ebaugh
- Sir Francis Galton
- Everett C. Hughes

- Georg Simmel
- Frederick W. Taylor
- Frederic M. Thrasher
- Max Weber

For Starters

A. Steckley

Learning to Be a Stepfather

In *David Copperfield*, Charles Dickens describes a truly evil stepfather for young David. That character was the model I hoped to avoid when I acquired the status of stepfather in the early 1990s, when I gained, through marriage, stepsons who were seven and eight. During my first years as stepfather I felt that of all the statuses I had, it caused me the most grief. I couldn't sort out what my responsibilities were. They weren't clearly defined. I wasn't "their dad," and yet I felt I was expected to take on the responsibilities that go along with being a father of sons.

I felt as though I was making up my job as stepfather as I went along. What do you do when a seven-year-old boy grasps your hand and walks with you in public? What do you do when a 10-year-old won't go out the front door because there's a bee outside? I wished there were a manual—*Stepfathering for Dummies*—I could consult. At first, I was anxious to win them over by acting like the uncle I already knew how to be—the one who spoils nephews and nieces with presents and crazy antics, then leaves Mom and Dad to deal with their rambunctious children inspired to reckless hijinks by my very physical humour. But I

didn't want to be like the stepfather I had once met whose stepson could get away with anything. I had stayed with this acquaintance's family for a few days, and the boy soon learned that I wasn't soft like his stepfather. When he wouldn't wash his face, as part of the routine I was asked to supervise, I took a cloth and gave him a good, hard scrub. Next time, he did it himself. But then, I wasn't emotionally attached to him or his mother. I had nothing to lose.

In this new relationship, I had to be more like a father: strict but fair. Not an easy path to take for a "live and let live" kind of guy. It was good that I loved sports, like they did. I went to all their hockey, baseball, and lacrosse games. I coached Rob in baseball, and drove Justin all over the countryside when he made the local rep baseball team.

I found that people are sometimes suspicious of stepfathers. When the school called or I went for parent–teacher interviews, I felt that my status was being judged. Sometimes after I'd explained the nature of my relationship to the boys, I perceived a certain knowing look in the eyes of teachers, principals, and office staff: a look that said, "Well *that* explains it."

Now that both boys are in their early thirties, I have become comfortable with my stepfather status. I refer to them as "my sons." When Rob had a near-fatal car accident and he asked me to drive him home when he was confined to a hospital bed, I was moved to tears. Justin's co-workers call me "Justin's dad." I'm happy with that. Although I know I made lots of mistakes, I feel I know what it means to have the status of "stepfather."

And perhaps I *can* write *Stepfathering for Dummies*.

What do YOU think?

1. Why is the status of stepfather a complicated one? What does this status entail?
2. Imagine the narrative the author's stepsons might write in response to this. Do you think they would have found the status of stepson just as complicated?
3. Are you involved in a godparent–godchild relationship? What do you think the expectations surrounding the status of godparent are?

Introduction: Why Sociologists Obsess over Status

Unlike some of the sociological concepts we've encountered so far, *status* is a term that probably has meaning for you already. You might think of it as something along the lines of high social standing, credibility, or a favourable reputation. In this sense, status is something you either have or don't have, something you can gain or lose. You might also think of the update you post to your favourite social networking site to give followers some insight into your condition, state of mind, or romantic relationships. In this sense, status is something singular that can change as often as you post to Facebook.

To a sociologist, status is something different. For one thing, status isn't something you either have or you don't: everyone has a status. In fact, everyone has *several* statuses that they hold at the same time. Moreover, while some statuses can change and be replaced, others do not change, or change very infrequently. I gained a status when I became a stepdad; that was over twenty years ago, and I still have that status.

Our statuses are vitally important to how we see ourselves and how others see us. When we interact with people, much of what goes on both in thoughts and in behaviour relates to the statuses we hold and the way we perform the *roles* attached to those statuses. The interaction may be relatively simple when the expectations are well understood by both parties. But if a status is more complex because the set of expectations attached to it is not well

established, the exchange may be more difficult, as with step-parents and stepchildren. Sometimes, too, the expectations associated with one status interfere with those of another, as we will see.

The sociological concept of status is important to understanding how people interact in pairs and in small groups. Later in the chapter we'll look at the social dynamics that exist in large groups and organizations. While statuses are social components that help establish us as successful humans, the principles at play in large social organizations can have the opposite effect, as we'll see.

Social Status

Status and role: it sounds like a quick order for lunch, but these two concepts are central to sociology. A status is a recognized social position that an individual occupies. It contributes to the individual's social identity by imposing responsibilities and expectations that establish the individual's relationships to others. You don't have just one status; in fact, you can have several at once—daughter, mother, wife, CEO, volunteer board member, soccer coach, and on and on. The collection of statuses you have is your status set. If you are a man, you could have the statuses of son, brother, uncle, teacher, drummer (for your band), neighbour, citizen, white person—all at the same time. These would make up your status set. We gain and lose statuses as we age, so we possess, however briefly, dozens of statuses throughout our lives.

One way of classifying our many statuses is to distinguish between statuses that are *achieved* and those that are *ascribed*. A status is considered achieved if you've entered into it at some stage of your life, but you weren't born into it. A professional position (assuming it's not a job in the family business), a role in a hobby or recreational activity, an academic standing ("college graduate"): all are achieved statuses. They assume some kind of personal ability, accomplishment, or voluntary act, although very few statuses are completely achieved (for instance, an accomplished drummer has *some* natural ability).

An ascribed status is one that you were born into ("female" or "male," "daughter" or "son," "sister" or "brother," etc.) or one you have entered into involuntarily ("teenager," "elderly person," "cancer survivor," "paraplegic"). Circumstances trump choice in ascribed statuses.

Some statuses can be both achieved and ascribed. The degree to which a status is achieved or ascribed often depends on how much social mobility exists. Consider a professional title: normally these are achieved. However, in a society with little social mobility, where a small ruling elite dominates, the statuses of lawyer, politician, doctor, professor, or rich business owner can be more ascribed than achieved. For a long while, it looked as though being

Darcie Bernhardt is the first Inuit person from Tuktoyaktuk to participate in the RCMP's Aboriginal Pre-Cadet Training Program. What statuses does she hold? Which are ascribed and which are achieved? How might they conflict?

born rich, white, and male was a prerequisite for attaining the status of president of the United States. On the other hand, while "race" is for the most part ascribed, people from a racialized group who want to avoid discrimination and whose appearance does not clearly put them into that group can sometimes successfully claim (or "achieve") dominant racial status. This process is known as passing. It is not unusual for Indigenous people in Canada to "pass" for white, or at least to try, particularly in big cities.

What do YOU think?

Does it matter if a status is ascribed or achieved? Consider the status "poor person." First, do you think this is an ascribed or an achieved status? Now imagine you're a politician responsible for drafting social welfare policies. How would your policy proposals differ depending on whether you considered being a poor person to be primarily an ascribed status or primarily an achieved status?

Sexual Orientation and Status: A Problem Area

Sexual orientation is primarily an ascribed status. Heterosexuality is natural for some, and homosexuality is natural for others. Others still feel naturally asexual, bisexual, demisexual, sapiosexual, and so on. There are those who believe that homosexuality is simply a "lifestyle choice," one that can be overcome with heavy doses of therapy (see Dr Joseph Nicolosi last chapter), drugs, religion, or conservative politics. Remember, homosexuality was against the law in Canada until 1969. The scholarly literature strongly argues that sexual orientation is a physical/psychological predisposition that may or may not be acted upon at some point. According to this definition, regardless of whether you live in a gay or lesbian relationship, you are homosexual if your sexual fantasies are overwhelmingly about people who are of the same sex as yourself.

Of course, sexual orientation is much more complicated than this. One problem with naming it as either an achieved or an ascribed status has to do with the way one's own sexuality is recognized by others. Someone who is gay but who marries into a heterosexual relationship because of social pressure would not be socially recognized as homosexual (this is another example of passing, defined in the section above). In terms of statuses, that would mean the status of sexual orientation is, at least partially, achieved because it is a lifestyle choice based on what society recognizes and how it exerts pressure to conform with the norm. Status, then, lies in what you do, not in what you feel; in this case, choice can trump circumstances.

Master Status

Everett C. Hughes (1897–1983) introduced the concept of master status in "Dilemmas and Contractions of Status" (1945), published when he worked at the University of Chicago. He applied the term in the context of "race" in the US:

> Membership in the Negro race, as defined in American mores and/or law, may be called a master status–determining trait. It tends to overpower, in most crucial situations, any other characteristics [i.e. statuses] which might run counter to it. (Hughes, 1945: p. 357)

The term master status signifies the status that dominates all of an individual's other statuses in most social contexts, and plays the greatest role in the formation of the individual's social identity. You can learn a lot about people by asking them what they consider their master status to be. Canadians, upon being introduced to someone, will often ask: "What do you do?" This implies that a person's occupation is his or her master status. It isn't always the case, though: ethnicity and gender can be master statuses, even when an individual doesn't want them to be. If you met Barack Obama at a dinner party (say you

crashed it) and asked him, "What do you do?", he would probably inform you, politely, of his status as president of the United States. Nevertheless, during his presidential campaign, his master status was that of a black man. For some conservative Americans, it still is.

Status Hierarchy

Statuses can be ranked from high to low based on prestige and power; this ranking is referred to as status hierarchy. For each of the basic social categories—gender, "race," ethnicity, age, class, sexual orientation, and physical ability—one status tends to be valued above the others. In Canadian society we rank male over female, white over black or brown, British heritage over eastern European and Asian, upper class over middle and working class, heterosexual over homosexual or bisexual, and able-bodied over disabled.

Applying the status hierarchy to age is complicated. Power is concentrated in the hands of those who are middle-aged, yet because we live in a society that promotes the cult of youth—the desire to look, act, and feel young—youth also has some prestige. The middle-aged often abuse their bodies, injecting poison (e.g. Botox) into their faces, undergoing facelifts, and fighting to hold onto their youthful appearance through fitness regimes and the masking effects of makeup. We could also call this a form of *passing*, as those who engage in such rejuvenating practices are trying to achieve higher status by "passing" for younger than they really are.

Status Inconsistency

Not all social statuses align in all people, creating a situation in which a person holds statuses that are ranked differently. This can result in social tension. You may find yourself with a high-ranking gender or ethnic status but a lower-ranking class status. You are a WASP (a white, Anglo-Saxon Protestant), but you're working-class.

Some people do seem to hold all the statuses favoured by society. Federal and provincial parliaments, for instance, tend to be clubhouses for people who are male, white, of British heritage, rich, heterosexual, and able-bodied: that is a winning status set, consisting of mostly ascribed statuses, that

What do YOU think?

1. Hughes called "black" a master status because in most interactions it was more significant than statuses based on sex, age, or other characteristics. Do you think that white can be an individual's master status? Why or why not?

2. Has there ever been a time in your life when your "race" or ethnicity was your master status? How did you know?

Our Stories

Normie Kwong and Statuses through Time

Norman Kwong (1929–2016) was born in Canada, six years after the Chinese Exclusion Act was passed. Though it did not stop Chinese immigration to Canada, the act required all Chinese people—even those born in the country—to register with the government. In this way, it gave Chinese Canadians a legal status different to that of other Canadians, a diminished one. The act was in place until 1947, when Normie Kwong was 18 years old. His master status as a child would have been Chinese-Canadian. Among his other statuses were son, brother, and student.

The year the act was repealed Kwong became a star junior football player. The next year, he began his professional football career, playing first for the Canadian Football League's Calgary Stampeders (1948–50) and then, after a trade to the team's fiercest rival, for the Edmonton Eskimos (1951–60). During this time, professional football player was his master status in a status set that also included Chinese-Canadian, husband, and father.

When he retired from football, Kwong became involved in sports management, both for the Calgary Stampeders and for the National Hockey League's Calgary Flames, a team he helped bring to the city and part-owned. This was but one of several business interests he was involved in during this time. It is hard to know what his master status was then, although Chinese-Canadian would still have been prominent.

From 2005 to 2010 Kwong served as lieutenant-governor of Alberta. His appointment was not surprising, given his high profile as an athlete and sports executive and his connections with the then-ruling provincial Conservative Party. This political position would have been his master status at the time. When we look at Norman Kwong's life, we can see that he held many different statuses, some ascribed and some achieved, as well as at least three different master statuses (Chinese-Canadian, professional football player, provincial lieutenant-governor).

Weekend Magazine/Louis Jaques/Library and Archives Canada/e002505702

CP Photo/Jeff McIntosh

Normie Kwong went from rights-restricted citizen to star football player (*left*) and then to provincial lieutenant-governor (*right*). What are some of the other statuses he held?

Quick Hits

Labelling Theory

Sociologist **Howard Becker** (b. 1928) developed labelling theory in the 1960s to explain the negative effects a label can have when applied to a group outside of the majority. Part of this theory states that when negative labels are attached to a status, a powerful master status can be created and internalized both by the individual and by others. The process is well portrayed in the following excerpt from a study of drug culture:

> [I]f people who are important to Billy call him a "druggie" this name becomes a powerful label that takes precedence over any other status positions Billy may occupy. Even if

Billy is also an above average biology major, an excellent musician, and a dependable and caring person, such factors become secondary because his primary status has been recast as a "druggie." Furthermore, once a powerful label is attached, it becomes much easier for the individual to uphold the image dictated by members of society, and simply to act out the role expected by significant others. (Hanson et al., 2009: p. 76)

A label like "druggie" thus becomes a master status that can follow a person for his or her entire life, despite efforts to change it.

gives anyone who holds it a significant life advantage. Likewise, there are a lot of black or Aboriginal women living at or below the poverty line, and who are lowly regarded. Status consistency is the result when all of the social status hierarchies line up; when they do not—when an individual is highly ranked in one status category but not in others—the condition is called status inconsistency. Aboriginal women who are cabinet ministers (such as Jody Wilson-Raybould) and white men born to wealth but working as Starbucks baristas are examples of status inconsistency.

Everett C. Hughes noticed that when people of "lower" status moved into occupations associated with more favoured statuses, they became targets of certain strategies others used to reduce the apparent inconsistency. One strategy was to modify the stereotype surrounding the lowly regarded status. This would cause upwardly mobile individuals to be alienated both from people sharing their low ascribed status and from people defined by the more highly regarded achieved status. Referring to sociological data gathered during his research for *French Canada in Transition* (1943), Hughes wrote:

> [I]n Quebec the idea that French-Canadians were good only for unskilled industrial work was followed by the notion

that they were especially good at certain kinds of skilled work but were not fit to repair machines or to supervise the work of others. In this series of modifications the structure of qualities expected for the most-favored positions remains intact. But the forces which make for mobility continue to create marginal people on new frontiers. (Hughes, 1945: p. 356–7)

This situation, where individuals live in a kind of limbo—partly in the old world of stereotypes and prejudices assigned to one status, partly in the new world of achieved occupational status—is embodied in the figure Robert E. Park called "marginal man." The male bias implied in the term is the main reason it's no longer used; however, it is historically important and preserved in the commonly used term marginalization, which refers to the process by which groups are assigned into categories that set them at or beyond the margins of the dominant society.

Another strategy that Hughes identified was social segregation, which he illustrated as follows:

> The woman lawyer may become a lawyer to women clients, or . . . may specialize in some kind of legal service in keeping with

The Point Is...

Status Inconsistency and Master Status: A Political Cartoon about Olivia Chow

Olivia Chow was born to middle-class parents in Hong Kong in 1957. When she was 13, she came to live in Toronto, where she earned a university degree and became an artist and a trustee on the Toronto District School Board. In 1988 she married Jack Layton, then a member of Toronto City Council. Chow's accomplishments are many. She has taught at college. She was a very popular city councillor in Toronto from 1991 to 2005, and a member of Parliament from 2006 until she resigned in 2014 to run for mayor of Toronto.

Despite holding the widely valued statuses of professional politician and middle class, Chow has faced opposition throughout her career, most of it targeting her lower-ranked statuses. A controversial cartoon that appeared in the *Toronto Sun* during her mayoral campaign brought together several strains of this opposition. The cartoon (which we were unable to reprint, but which is easily found online) shows Chow on a skateboard, dressed in olive drab and holding the coat of the recently deceased Jack Layton. Two of her statuses figure prominently in the cartoon. One is her Chinese-Canadian background. This is apparent in the exaggeration of the Chinese nature of her eyes (the epicanthic fold) and in her wearing the traditional uniform of the Communist Party of China, closely associated with Chinese Communist Party chairman Mao Tse-tung. This was to stress her otherness, her foreign nature, and her being the most left-leaning candidate. (Recall, however, that she was born in Hong Kong, not Communist China.) The other status that figures prominently in the cartoon is wife, a woman ranking lower than a man. In the cartoon she is standing on the coat to imply that she is "riding on the coattails" of her dead husband.

What do YOU think?

1. What does the story tell you about the sociological nature of politics in Canada?
2. Are "race" and sex considered important statuses in Canadian elections? Are they more important statuses than those surrounding ideology (left-wing, right-wing, conservative, liberal, socialist, and so on)?

woman's role as guardian of the home and of morals. Women physicians may find a place in those specialities of which only women and children have need. A female electrical engineer was urged by the dean of the school . . . to accept a job whose function was to give the "woman's angle" to design of household electrical appliances. The Negro professional man finds his clients among Negroes. The Negro sociologist generally studies race relations and teaches in a Negro college. (Hughes, 1945: p. 358)

In this way, social segregation is both the outcome of being marginalized as well as a strategy to deal with marginalization.

Social Roles

A role is a set of behaviours and attitudes associated with a particular status. Roles attached to a status may differ across cultures. For example, people holding the status of elder in traditional cultures of China and Africa and Aboriginal communities of North America are expected to have acquired a certain level of wisdom. The same expectations seldom exist in mainstream Canadian culture, where the status of elder has few positive role expectations attached to it; the status is more "old person" than it is elder. One reason that Western social scientists were slow to question the myth of Inuit elder abandonment—discussed in Chapter 1—is that Western culture lacked its own positively defined role of elder, making the myth much more credible in their eyes.

A given status may be associated with more than one role. Robert Merton (1949) developed the idea of the role set, which comprises all of the roles that are attached to a particular status. As professors, we have the role of teacher to our students, but we are also colleagues to our peers, employees to our schools, sometimes demanding children to our support staff, and of course, trouble-making underlings to our administrators. Students have a peer role with classmates in addition to their student role with instructors. To the college or university, they are paying customers.

Role Strain

Role strain develops when there is a conflict between roles within the role set of a particular status. For example, if a student complains to his instructor about a teacher in another class, the instructor is placed in a conflict between her role as educator, in which she has the student's best interests at heart, and her role as colleague, in which she must be loyal to the professor teaching the other class. Similarly, a student who catches a classmate cheating on an exam is at once a member of the academic community with a responsibility to report the offence and a member of the student body who wouldn't rat out a peer. Role strain can even affect a single role. Consider the parent who feels more at ease with one of his children than with the other but tries to balance his attentions between them. It can be a very difficult game to play.

Role Conflict

Another useful concept for understanding social tensions is role conflict. Role conflict occurs when a person is forced to reconcile incompatible expectations generated from two or more statuses he or she holds. If you are both a mother and a student, then you know all about role conflict. Imagine: it's the night before the big exam and you need to study—part of the set of behaviour expectations attached to being a college or university student; however, your daughter needs help with her homework, your son is ill, and your husband is out with friends watching the big game—he's been looking forward to it

Imagine trying to study for an exam during a shift at your part-time job. What role conflict do you think this student experiences?

Photo © Cindy Moser; used with permission

for weeks. You're on your own with the demands of conflicting statuses of mother and student. These clashing sets of expectations illustrate role conflict. Role conflict occurs when people turn down promotions because they do not want to move into a position where they might have to reprimand peers and friends who suddenly occupy a lower position within the organization.

Role Exit

Role exit is the process of disengaging from a role that has been central to one's identity, and attempting to establish a new role. **Helen Rose Fuchs Ebaugh** (an ex-nun turned sociologist) has studied role exit processes extensively. Her findings are summarized in *Becoming an Ex: The Process of Role Exit* (1988). According to Ebaugh, who wrote about not just ex-nuns but also ex-priests, ex-convicts, and recovering alcoholics, role exit involves shifting your master status. If you were forced to retire having always defined yourself by what you did ("I am a nurse"), you might feel uncomfortable when asked, "What do you do?" If you are a stay-at-home mother

The Point Is...

Dungeons & Dragons: Virtual and Real Status

Before video games, there was E. Gary Gygax's Dungeons & Dragons (or D&D), the first worldwide role-playing game. During the 1970s and 1980s it sold millions of copies as a pen-and-paper, sit-at-the-table game before it joined the computer world.

D&D was set in any one of a number of fantasy worlds populated by such creatures as elves, trolls, gnomes, dreaded orcs, and wyverns, all borrowed from Tolkien's *Lord of the Rings* and the fantasy works of Michael Moorcock, H.P. Lovecraft, and Roald Dahl. Players entered these worlds as sorcerers, knights, and holy warriors, their fate in encounters with various monsters or sealed passages determined by the roll of any one of a number of different dice. As for

the dungeons, they weren't jails but settings invented by the person acting as the "dungeon master" (the DM). You could call the DM a sort of referee, but for author Mark Barrowcliffe, "To call the DM a referee is a bit misleading. His role is nearer to that of a god. He creates a world, sets challenges for players' characters, and rewards or punishes them according to the wisdom of their actions" (2008: p. 32).

Barrowcliffe's *The Elfish Gene: Dungeons, Dragons and Growing Up Strange—A Memoir* (2009) is a good introduction to D&D as a sociological phenomenon. Barrowcliffe grew up in working-class England, and began playing D&D in 1976 at the age of 12. Explaining his fascination with the game, Barrowcliffe

D&D was played with dice and a map sketched on a sheet of graph paper, typically around the dining room table. How do you think that would affect the status formation of those who played? How might it differ from the experience of participants in today's online gaming community, who may never meet one another face to face?

Wikipedia

and your children grow up and move away, you have lost a very important purpose in your day-to-day life that is not easily replaced by being merely a wife (and grandmother might be far away in the future). If you are a father and your parental role is reduced because your ex-wife gains primary custody of the children, then becoming a part-time dad may feel like a role exit.

The role exit of married people who become single through separation, divorce, or death of a spouse is difficult, as it entails shifting from "we" to

"I." Previous relationships with friends and family change, and in the case of divorce, people take sides. Some people you've been close to might start avoiding you, treating your divorce like something contagious and you as a carrier of the "failed relationship" virus. On the other hand, others might begin to pay you more attention, and in ways you haven't been used to. As a "single," you are expected to be "out there" meeting other eligible singles. Role exit is something we all experience throughout our lives.

notes that he and his friends didn't aspire to their parents' simple and (from their perspective) dull lives, characterized by predictability and stability. Instead, they sought the kind of magic that was missing from their "real" world. They were, in Barrowcliffe's estimation, intelligent (particularly in the mathematical calculations necessary to be a successful player), but not necessarily school-smart. They certainly were not jocks or tough guys, and they weren't concerned with fashion or appearance.

What does D&D have to do with status and role? For a generation of adolescents—almost exclusively boys—their D&D characters formed a status that was recognized by other players, and that was as significant as traditional statuses such as son, brother, friend, and student. The roles played in Dungeons & Dragons were more engaging than those occupied in real life, though some real-life "truths" were learned through playing.

Players adopted their statuses from among a number of different character classes. Initially, these were simple: fighter (warrior), cleric (priest), and magic-user (wizard). As the game evolved, however, the number of character classes grew to include alchemists, assassins, berserkers, druids, ninjas, paladins, and female characters such as witches and the bizarrely sexual houris—"a cross between sorcerers and prostitutes" (Barrowcliffe,

2008: p. 227). By rolling dice and recording the results, players would determine the strength, magical ability, charisma, and intelligence of their characters, and they would speak and act as they imagined their characters would. According to Barrowcliffe:

> People . . . identified very strongly with their characters. . . . This is where it differs from a computer game. You can't reboot if your character is killed. In D&D if the character dies, he's dead, which . . . is a serious threat to his future. Losing a character that you've had for . . . years can be a major emotional experience. At fourteen years old it can be the first real grief you've known in your life. It's like having an imaginary friend but one you get to actually look at, that other people will discuss as if they're real and may even attempt to kill. (2008: p. 35)

The game socialized young males, giving them self-knowledge, opportunities to exercise creativity, and experience in the competitive world of adults. Just as important, it allowed them to invent for themselves an alternative status set, one that gave them the control to choose a number of statuses that are typically ascribed, like sex, age, and social position.

What do YOU think?

What lessons does participating in role-playing games produce? Does it matter that they are learned while playing out fictional rather than real statuses?

Studying Social Interaction in Small Groups

Status and role are important concepts in understanding individual identity-formation. The statuses we hold are crucial to how we see ourselves. They also lay the groundwork for interaction with others. A man walks into a bar (seriously). His statuses as male and customer establish certain expectations around the interaction he will have with the woman waiting

his table, who holds the statuses of female and server. Before either of them says a word to the other, we can predict how each one might act based on the statuses that each one holds in that situation. Statuses related to age and whether or not the customer is a "regular" will also have an effect: my own advancing age and my status as a long-term patron of my local pub affect the way I play the role of customer.

In small-group settings, statuses can be a valuable way to establish the pecking order, or who is in charge. It's not uncommon for criminal gangs to

Quick Hits

Pecking Order

In the 1920s, Norwegian zoologist and comparative psychologist Thorleif Schjelderup-Ebbe introduced a term that, when translated into English, became pecking order. It originally applied to chickens (hens in particular), with reference to who can get away with pecking whom. If no one pecks you (and you are a chicken), then you are at the top of the flock's social hierarchy, or pecking order.

have a hierarchy of statuses, ranging from president to associate, soldier, and wannabe. Each of these statuses carries its own set of roles, or expected behaviours. A gang member's status—be it official or unofficial—sets out his (usually his) responsibilities and the reporting structure: whom does he take orders from, and who answers to him?

The study of small-group interaction came early to sociology with the pioneering work of German sociologist **Georg Simmel** (1858–1918), who was among the first to narrow his focus to the daily, one-on-one social interactions of individuals. He was a microsociologist and a forerunner of the symbolic interactionists whom we met in Chapter 1. Others working in this tradition around the turn of the twentieth century include **Charles Horton Cooley** (1864–1929), whose concept of the looking-glass self we discussed last chapter, and **Frederic M. Thrasher** (1892–1962), whose classic study of gangs in Chicago, *The Gang: A Study of 1,313 Gangs in Chicago* (Thrasher, 1927) represents a study of group interaction rooted in fieldwork. He saw the gangs that he studied as small clusters of intense interaction socially separated from the larger world:

> An immigrant colony . . . is itself an isolated social world. . . . [T]he gang boy moves only in his own universe and other regions are clothed in . . . mystery. . . . [H]e knows little of the outside world. (1927)

Thrasher's ethnographic research on gangs and small-group interaction was carried on brilliantly in William Whyte's *Street Corner Society* (1955), which we considered in Chapter 2. The social interactions of North American gang worlds continues to be an area of study for sociologists, including Sudhir Venkatesh, whose *Gang Leader for a Day* (2008) is a "rogue sociologist's" look at New York street gangs,

and Humber College criminologist Mark Totten, author of *Nasty, Brutish and Short: The Lives of Gang Members in Canada* (2012) and *Gang Life: 10 of the Toughest Tell Their Stories* (2014).

Another key contribution to the study of small-group interaction—and another study of European immigrants who flooded to North America during the first two decades of the twentieth century—came from the symbolic interactionist William I. Thomas, whose monumental work with Polish sociologist Florian Znaniecki, *The Polish Peasant in Europe and America* (1918–20), illustrated the important part narratives play in defining situations. Thomas showed that the way people interpret their own lives was a sociological element well worth studying. As he expressed it, the "situations we define as real become real in their consequences" (Thomas, 1966: p. 301). This idea, which came to be known as the Thomas theorem, influenced other developments in symbolic interactionism, including a concept known as the definition of the situation. The term refers to the notion that different individuals will define a given situation differently and in contradictory ways, based on their own subjective experiences. For this reason, understanding how an individual defines a situation is crucial to understanding the individual's actions and responses to it.

A classic case of how different ways of defining a situation can lead to misunderstanding and mistrust surrounds the practice that Europeans referred to as "Indian giving." In traditional Indigenous culture, people would give gifts as statements that they wanted to strengthen the bonds between them. In the language of the trading people, the Wendat (Huron), the verb meaning "to trade" translates literally as "to give to each other." Accepting a gift was an important gesture: it was the first step in acknowledging and accepting the wish to strengthen bonds. Returning the favour was the second, equally important step: it confirmed the desire to establish friendly terms. From the European perspective, when a gift-giver expressed a desire for a return gift, it was looked upon as demanding and selfish.

During the 1950s, a Harvard research team headed by social psychologist **Robert F. Bales** (1916–2004) brought the study of small-group interaction to the laboratory. Bales and his colleagues developed a system of coding for social interaction in small groups, called interaction process analysis (IPA). It dealt initially with ways of determining whether groups and their members were task- or relationship-oriented. They later developed the methodology to identify patterns of behaviour such as dominant/submissive, friendly/unfriendly, and accepting of authority/non-accepting of authority.

Most sociologists today are not involved in studying small-group interaction, for several reasons. First, the work was very much the product of a structural-functional perspective, which has become a minority perspective in twenty-first-century sociology. Second, small-group studies at the time when they were popular seemed to lack a proper consideration of gender, "race," ethnicity, and other sociological factors that are now considered essential to any rigorous inquiry. Imagine how the dynamics of a group of women change when a man is part of the group. Imagine how the opportunities and strategies for leadership differ in a small group of women and a small group of men. And what if we were to bring "race" into the discussion? Third, many contemporary sociologists view the study of small groups—especially in a lab setting—as artificial.

Quick Hits

The Thomas Theorem and Arthur Kleinman's Eight Questions

The Thomas theorem has important implications in health care across cultures. Anne Fadiman's work on how Western medicine failed to properly address the situation of a young Hmong girl with epilepsy (see Chapter 13) concludes with a consideration of eight questions, first posed by Arthur Kleinman, that Western doctors should use in interactions with patients from non-Western cultures. Their purpose is to determine, from the point of view of the patient and her family, the definition of the healing situation and sickness in order to mitigate any problems that might arise around opposing situational definitions based on cultural differences:

1. What do you call your illness? What name does it have?
2. What do you think has caused the illness?
3. Why and when did it start?
4. What do you think the illness does? How does it work?
5. How severe is it? Will it have a short or long course?
6. What kind of treatment do you think the patient should receive? What are the most important results you hope she receives from this treatment?
7. What are the chief problems the illness has caused?
8. What do you fear most about the illness?

Studying Social Interaction in Large Groups: An Introduction to Social Organization

So far in this chapter we've looked at status and role and how these serve to structure one-on-one and small-group interactions. Whenever we look at individuals and small groups, we're taking a microsociological approach. For the remainder of the chapter we'll be moving from micro to macro as we look at social organization from a bird's eye view.

When we think of the term *social organization*, we might think of the way a society and its institutions—family, law, religion, polity, economy, and so on—are organized. What we seldom consider is that the basis for social organization, whether imagined or real, rests on a particular set of principles.

In the sociological literature, *social organization* is rarely defined, and when it is, it's often conflated (i.e. blended together and considered part of the same thing) with the terms *social structure* or *social institution*, as though they were all synonymous. They are not. While social institutions *are* social structures and *are* socially organized, social structures and social organization are *not* social institutions. So, what is social organization?

We can think of social organization as the social and cultural *principles* around which things are structured, ordered, and categorized. In this way, we are able to speak about the social organization of cultures, social institutions, or corporations. For example, a culture may be socially organized around the principle of egalitarianism (society based on equality), or it may be socially organized around the principle of hierarchy (a system with clear, well-defined ranks or levels). In either case, the culture may be further organized according to the specific form of egalitarian or hierarchical government that is in place. All of this is part of the culture's social organization.

Organizational Structure

Under the European system of feudalism, a person's allegiances were, in order, to God, to king, to the feudal lord, and then finally to country. As European societies moved from theocracies (religious states) to secular (non-religious) states, from monarchies to democracies, and from kingdoms to nation-states, the nation-state or country became the main locus of allegiance and loyalty. When we go to war, we fight for our country more than we fight for our religion or our leader. And in spite of the emotional feelings—pride, loyalty, sentimentality—that are aroused when we sing the national anthem or win an Olympic gold medal, "Canada" is an imaginary geopolitical space in which a diverse population is constructed as an "imaginary community" through symbols such as the anthem and flag. Canada is not a "natural" thing: it is a socially organized invention based on certain collectively shared principles. Culture, and the organizing principles culture is based on, imposes a structure that is seen as "natural." In this way, organizing principles are upheld by shared cultural beliefs and maintained through a network of social relations.

At the heart of organizing principles are the ways in which a culture produces knowledge about the world based on a particular cosmology. A cosmology is an account of the origin and ruling principles of the universe, especially the role of humans in relationship to non-humans (living and non-living). Cosmologies and corresponding myths are often seen as a high form of truth.

Aboriginal cosmologies are rooted in the belief that all matter, both inanimate and animate, is interdependent: everything is connected. They emphasize the interdependence of humans and nature. Judeo-Christian and Islamic cosmology emphasizes human dominion over nature as decreed by God. This cosmology, together with the emergence of modern science beginning in the Enlightenment, has helped establish "control over nature" as an important organizing principle of Western culture. Consider the fact that both sides of the climate change debate in some senses believe that humans control the environment. Those who deny climate change believe that humans can control the effects of manufacturing and waste disposal, whereas those who are concerned about global warming think that we are not controlling these effects well enough and must change our behaviour to minimize the impact.

The Study of Organizations

To recap: organizational principles are based on our knowledge or understanding of the world, which is informed by our cosmology. These principles

Maria Janicki/Alamy Stock Photo

What principles make up the social organization of your college or university? Democracy versus hierarchy (e.g. in administration–faculty and faculty–student interaction)? Freedom versus strict control of discussion and debate? Commercialism? Elitism versus access? How would you detect the presence and influence of these factors?

determine not just how our culture and society are organized but how other social bodies are organized, whether we're talking about social institutions like the family and education, or bureaucracies and corporations, or community-based organizations. What is important in the study of organizations is to distinguish both the level of organization and the level of analysis.

Interest in the sociological study of organizations picked up after Weber conducted his detailed work on bureaucracy, and again when the study of organizations filtered into the business sector and commerce degree programs that began to be offered at colleges and universities during the 1980s. The study of organizations shifted from the examination of social institutions to the examination of business corporations as a way to uncover more effective and efficient management practices. The result was an explosion of studies in the fields of organizational theory and organizational behaviour (see Mills & Simmons, 1995).

During the last twenty years, the study of organizational behaviour has expanded by integrating approaches from other disciplines. Anthropology, for instance, has contributed to the study of organizations through its understanding of corporations as communities in which an organizational culture, with "organizational rituals" and "symbolic acts," is an aspect of organizational dynamics. An *organizational ritual*, as defined by Islam and Zyphur (2009: p. 116), is "a form of social action in which a group's values and identity are publicly demonstrated or enacted in a stylized manner, within the context of a specific occasion or event." TV shows such as *The Office* and the comic strip *Dilbert* make fun of organizational rituals such as the office Christmas party, employee-of-the-month awards, "town hall" meetings, the company picnic, and the charity golf tournament—events intended to project a specific identity the organization wants to convey. An anthropologist (or sociologist) may also study the informal organization of a company to determine how decisions are made or how information actually flows—processes that may not quite follow the mandated, formal structure of the organization itself.

What do YOU think?

1. Can you think of any rituals, events, or symbolic acts that reflect the organizational culture where you have worked or where you go to school?
2. Do you think that "work outings" or holiday gift exchanges are an important part of the organizational culture of a business? Does the size of a company make a difference in the answer to this question?

With the spread of globalization, there has been increased study of cross-cultural organizations, which are of particular interest to businesses and those who study organizational behaviour. In the 1980s, organizational structures based on models derived from the productive corporate culture of Japan were implemented in North America. They failed, however, in part because they did not account for the organizational principles of Japanese culture, which are more collectivist than the individualist organizational principles favoured in Canada and the US. Organizational structures based on a *collective* model, in which employees work in teams, did not have the same success when applied to the competitive individualism found in North American business culture and society generally.

Much of the increase in organizational studies has been fuelled by Western capital, invested by companies in an effort to find ways to increase profits by managing employee behaviour and practices more efficiently. This has led to questions about the ethics of controlling worker behaviour, not to mention the inherent ethnocentric and capitalist assumptions in organizational theory given the context of global culture. These critiques have fostered the growth of critical management studies, which challenge traditional theories of management. Mills and Simmons (1995), for example, have challenged the assumptions of mainstream accounts of organization. They point out that there is little in the literature of organizational theory and behaviour that deals with "race," ethnicity, class, or gender, despite the high participation rates of women and people of colour in the labour force. They also note that there is too little attention given to the impact organizations have on the social and psychic life of individuals and groups affected by organizations. Despite the demonstrated link between organizational life and lack of self-esteem, a sense of powerlessness, segregated work life, stress, physical injury, pay inequality, sexual harassment, and racism, standard organizational theory and behaviour studies continue to ignore it (Mills & Simmons, 1995).

Feminist Organizations

Organizational structure and process have been a major focus for the contemporary women's movement. Whether the structure is based on networks and coalitions or at the level of individual organizations, feminists have always been concerned with the form of the organizations they create. In some instances, feminists have developed organizational forms that differ from mainstream forms as an expression of feminist politics. Because of their political and symbolic importance, issues surrounding organizational structure like the internal distribution of power and control, the division of labour, and decision-making rules can make it difficult for feminist coalitions to maintain their organizational cohesion.

Feminist organizations are generally organized around principles different to those found in traditional patriarchal organizations based on hierarchy. Carol Mueller (1995) identified three different models that typify feminist organizations:

1) formal social movement organizations, which are professionalized, bureaucratic, and inclusive, and which make few demands of their members (examples include organizations dedicated to basic women's rights)
2) small groups or collectives, which are organized informally, and which require large commitments of time, loyalty, and material resources from its members (examples include women's publishing houses)
3) service-provider organizations, which combine elements of both formal and small-group organizations (examples include organizations dedicated to specific women's rights, such as providing counselling services and protection to victims of domestic abuse).

Mueller found that these organizational forms varied in the degree to which they practised typical feminist organizational principles, such as inclusivity and democratic participation. She also found these forms combined in a variety of structural configurations ranging from coalitions to complex social movement communities.

Mills and Simmons (1995) believe that feminism has had a growing presence in organizational theory, where it challenges the male domination of organizations and calls attention to the absence of gender analysis in organizational theory.

The Point Is . . .

Feminist Organization at Work

The Teaching Support Staff Union (TSSU) represents teaching assistants, tutor markers, and sessional instructors at Vancouver's Simon Fraser University. Certified in 1978, the TSSU began as Local 6 of the Association of University and College Employees (AUCE). AUCE was a feminist trade union that developed out of the Vancouver Women's Caucus in the late 1960s and early 1970s. The feminist roots of the TSSU make it strikingly different from more conventional unions. From its start, the AUCE rejected the traditional form of organization found elsewhere in the Canadian union movement, which tends to be based on hierarchical structure and centralization. It successfully organized large numbers of women working in underpaid positions, mostly as clerical and teaching support staff. But since AUCE's inception, all of the AUCE locals, with the exception of Local 6, joined larger, more mainstream unions, such as the Canadian Union of Public Employees (CUPE); Local 6, now the TSSU, has continued to maintain its independent status.

The TSSU today is no longer affiliated with any other larger union or umbrella organization. All of its decisions come from the general membership. There are three salaried officers who are part of the larger executive committee and who handle the day-to-day operation of the union. The officers, as well as all members of the executive committee, are also members of the union itself, an arrangement that ensures that executives are in touch with issues of concern

to the broader TSSU membership. Executive positions come up for re-election annually, and no member is allowed to occupy a position for more than two years consecutively. This practice encourages skills development among the general membership and prevents the concentration of knowledge in the hands of a few members. The executive meets every two weeks, and meetings are open to all TSSU members.

General meetings (GMs) of the membership take place three times every semester, and a minimum of 20 members must be present before decisions can be made. The membership has control of union resources and must approve the annual budget, financial statements, and most expenditures of the union. Committees and executive members make regular reports to the GM, guided by the motions put forward at these meetings. Any member can bring forward a motion at a GM. The TSSU provides child care subsidies so that members with young children can attend the regular meetings and events.

The TSSU maintains a global vision. It actively fights for labour rights and social justice locally, nationally, and internationally. The TSSU has supported CUPE's University Bargaining Sector, the BC Teachers' Federation, and other striking teachers from Hamilton, Ontario, to Oaxaca, Mexico. They have initiated a Social Justice Committee to expand the scope of the union's advocacy, with a mission to fight the root causes of injustice, inequality, and poverty.

What do YOU think?

Go to the TSSU's website and look at the union's list of accomplishments: www.tssu.ca/about/our-accomplishments/. In what way do you think these reflect the TSSU's status as a feminist organization?

Bureaucracy

The Origins of Bureaucracy

As Israeli-American Amitai Etzioni pointed out, "organizations [and bureaucracies] are not a modern invention" (1964: p. 1). Bureaucracies arose out of the formation of states and writing systems some 5,000 years ago.

As empires emerged and grew, administrative bureaucracies expanded at a pace to match imperial expansion. In Han Dynasty China (fifth century BCE), the bureaucratic system developed out of Confucius's concern with creating social stability, which required a system of administrators to ensure good governance. Administrators were appointed based on the merit of examinations (i.e. written tests). What became known as the imperial examination system continued in China until the early twentieth century.

The term "bureaucracy" originated in eighteenth-century France and comes from the word *bureau*, meaning "writing desk"—in other words, the place where officials work. The cumbersome processes of bureaucracies are sometimes referred to as "red tape," which dates back to nineteenth-century Britain, when government officials used red tape to tie up official documents until they were needed. Red tape, then, refers to the slow procedures associated with acquiring and dispensing bureaucratic information. Most of us have encountered bureaucratic red tape in our federal, provincial, or municipal agencies—when applying to replace a lost passport or driver's licence, for instance—but this is not confined to government agencies. Many private companies, including banks, cable companies, Internet providers, maybe even your college or university admissions office, are known for their red tape. As we will see, despite their inefficiencies and the difficulties in changing bureaucratic organization to meet individual and societal needs, bureaucracies are necessary for the successful functioning of complex societies.

Bureaucracy and Formal Rationalization

Max Weber's extensive work on bureaucracy is still frequently cited today. It was part of his larger study of the process of rationalization, specifically, his examination of formal rationalization (or rationality). "Rationalization" is a term frequently heard in business reports, where it is used as a euphemism for firing workers and cutting jobs in an effort to reduce costs and become more efficient. This is an example of formal rationalization, which, according to Weber, has four basic elements:

xijian/iStockphoto

iPhone: check. Fitbit: check. Were he alive today, what would Weber say about rationalizing technologies that keep us connected, on time, and on pace at all times?

- efficiency
- quantification
- predictability
- control.

We will look at the implications of these terms in the section on McDonaldization.

Formal rationalization, with its emphasis on forms, differs from other models of rationalization, like substantive rationalization, which involves the substance of values and ethical norms. Organizations governed by substantive rationalization are constantly asking themselves, *are we reflecting our values?* By contrast, organizations governed by formal rationalization tend to ask, *have we instituted the most efficient or predictable forms in our organization?* Take, for example, Indigenous organizations. Democracy, spirituality, and respect for elders are all important values among Indigenous people. Forms that reflect those values are open meetings, where anyone can speak and be listened to, and prayers spoken by elders. How do you think Indigenous organizations

at opposite ends of the substantive rationalization–formal rationalization spectrum would act?

Weber was critical of both formal rationalization and bureaucracy, arguing that the former led to the "irrationality of rationality" and that the latter was dehumanizing by nature. Workers within the rational, bureaucratic organization of various companies and political bodies came to be viewed as "cogs in the wheel," reminded frequently that they could always be replaced. You may feel similar effects even when you're not part of the bureaucracy but are confronted by the impersonal nature of its public face. When you're told, "Your call is important to us," you know that it isn't (see Laura Penny's *Your Call is Important to Us: The Truth About Bullshit*, 2005). These examples speak to the dehumanizing feelings we experience daily through our interactions with bureaucratic organizations.

The "irrationality of rationality" involves the "disenchantment of the world," an important concept in Weber's writing. Weber believed that with the increase in formal rationalization, the West

Going Global

Economic Globalization and Formal Rationalization

One of the pillars of economic globalization is a belief in liberalizing trade by reducing or eliminating protective tariffs. The view that poor countries of the developing world will abandon inefficient industries that have been supported by protective tariffs in favour of more productive industries is heavily influenced by the principles of formal rationalization. But as Joseph E. Stiglitz argues in *Globalization and Its Discontents* (2003), policies designed to enhance a country's income by forcing resources from less to more productive uses often fail in countries where, because of conditions imposed by global loan-granting agencies like the International Monetary Fund (IMF), those human and capital resources are altogether lost through diminished productivity and job loss:

> It is easy to destroy jobs, and this is often the immediate impact of trade liberalization, as inefficient industries close down

under pressure from international competition. IMF ideology holds that new, more productive jobs will be created as the old, inefficient jobs that have been created behind protectionist walls are eliminated. But that is simply not the case. . . . It takes capital and entrepreneurship to create new firms and jobs, and in developing countries there is often a shortage of the latter, due to lack of education, and of the former, due to lack of bank financing. The IMF in many countries has made matters worse, because its austerity programs often also entailed such high interest rates . . . that job and enterprise creation would have been an impossibility even in a good economic environment such as the United States. The necessary capital for growth is simply too costly. (Stiglitz, 2003: pp. 59–60) was becoming increasingly disenchanted—lacking in magic, fantasy, and mystery—which could only lead to further alienation on the part of individuals. Enchantment is a quality that cannot be efficient, quantified, predicted, or controlled. Disney's "Magic Kingdom," for instance, is anything but magical: it is a rationalized system of pre-packaged enchantment commodities—there are to be no surprises. Weber worried and warned about the oncoming danger of the "iron cage of rationality," meaning a world in which every aspect of life is controlled by the formal rationalization of bureaucracy, a world dehumanized and over-controlled.

The Evolution of Formal Rationalization

The Industrial Revolution, which occurred in the late eighteenth and early nineteenth centuries, was the starting point for the development of formal rationalization. **Francis Galton** (1822–1911), considered the father of modern statistical analysis, was a pioneer in developing methods to measure the capabilities and productivity of individuals. He had a natural love of numbers and made formal rationalization a part of his everyday life. An example: he spent many hours getting the quantities (temperature, volume, etc.) just right for the "perfect" pot of tea (he was English, after all).

Along these same lines, **Frederick W. Taylor** (1856–1915) developed the practice he referred to as scientific management. Based on "time-and-motion" studies, scientific management (later known as Taylorism) was designed to discover the *one best way* of doing any given job. Taylor and his team of "efficiency experts" studied the time, methods, and tools required for a proficient worker to do a particular job. His objective was to eliminate wasteful

Norm Betts/Bloomberg via Getty Images

Do you think you would be happier performing one task in the assembly of twenty vehicles or several tasks in the assembly of five? The first approach reflects formal rationalization principles such as maintaining quotas. The second reflects the substantive rationalization principle of worker ownership of the work and the product. Why do you think some instructors feel as though their college or university endorses the first of these two approaches to education?

or "inefficient" (i.e. slow, non-productive) motions or movements. Frank Gilbreth, a follower of Taylor's, undertook an intensive study of a bricklayer's job and reputedly reduced the number of motions involved in laying a brick from 18 to just 5. Assembly line work also used Taylor's methods to the maximum efficiency, though Henry Ford is credited with making the assembly line an industry standard.

One of the weaknesses of Taylorism/scientific management is that it didn't allow the individual worker to develop a broad set of skills, because he or she was asked to perform a single set of actions over and over again. Workers often became alienated from their work, with little sense that they had anything to do with the overall manufactured product.

Taylorism, slightly modified, was still practised in North America during the 1980s and 1990s. At that time, the success of Japanese auto manufacturing prompted North American businesses to implement "non-Tayloristic" Japanese business practices in their training sessions. Among these practices was the team approach, which incorporated worker input and fostered the idea that workers could be involved in several stages of the manufacturing process, generating a greater sense of product ownership. (If you thought this might be an instance of substantive rationalization, you'd be right.) This approach was first adopted by car manufacturer Saturn, which, until the downturn in the automotive sector in 2008, was very successful, in large part because it managed to reduce the sense of alienation among its workers.

The McDonaldization of the World

George Ritzer, in *The McDonaldization of Society* (2004), draws on Weber's concept of formal rationalization in his conception of McDonaldization. McDonaldization is similar to "Disneyfication," "Walmartitis," and "Microsoftening"—in Ritzer's words, "the process by which the [rationalizing] principles of the fast-food restaurant are coming to dominate more and more sectors of American society as well as the rest of the world" (2004: p. 1).

Ritzer applies the four fundamental elements of Weber's formal rationalization—efficiency, quantification, predictability, and control—to his

examination of contemporary fast-food restaurants. To see how McDonaldization is affecting other areas of everyday life, let's apply his theory to the world of postsecondary education.

Efficiency relates to the streamlined movement in time and effort of people and things. This efficiency is achieved mainly by breaking up larger organizational tasks into smaller, repeated tasks performed by individuals who are separated from each other by a division of labour. Smaller tasks are often performed later by machines rather than by people. It should be noted that efficiency has different meanings in the different layers of a social organization. What is efficient for a college administrator might not be efficient for a college professor (for example, the former finds efficiency in the networking of printers, rather than allowing the prof to use his own little printer and not wait in line when print requests are heavy—personal experience here). And being efficient in this way is not the same as being *effective*, although it's possible for a process to be both efficient and effective. Think of the potential differences between being an efficient teacher—one who teaches quickly and articulates a great number of concepts—and an effective teacher—one who successfully communicates to students all or almost all that is taught. A teacher can be one or the other, both, or none of the above. At college and university, the multiple-choice test is a classic example of bureaucratic efficiency: questions are often provided by the textbook's publisher, and they can be marked quickly using a computer. But are they the most effective means of promoting and testing learning? Would you be surprised that the author of this textbook never uses multiple-choice questions?

Second, formal rationalization in bureaucracy involves the *quantification* of as many elements as possible. The efficiency, or "success," of the process is measured by the completion of a large number of quantifiable tasks. For instance, the success of call centres is primarily measured by how many calls are handled rather than how many clients are actually satisfied. When educational administrators pressure instructors to quantify the type and exact percentage of tests on a course syllabus, this is a type of formal rationalization—the logic being that if courses are equally quantified, then students are equally served. With bureaucratic education, administrators and instructors can quantify the number and length of interactions between students and professors through computer platforms that monitor such things as the number of e-mails and the number and length of "chats." In the classroom, instructors can monitor students by having them use electronic clickers to respond to questions, which is an attempt to counteract the impersonal nature of large, "efficient" lectures with increased and quantifiable electronic interaction.

Next, *predictability* means that administrators, workers, and clients all know what to expect from employees, underlings, colleagues, and companies; this is the "uniformity of rules." A Big Mac in

Ivana Katz

McDonald's Canada recently introduced an option to "build your own burger," meaning you no longer have to peel the pickles off your Quarter Pounder™. Is this a move away from the four pillars of formal rationalization—efficiency, quantification, predictability, and control—that for decades have guaranteed that your experience is the same in any McDonald's restaurant anywhere in the world? Or is it more of a symbolic move in one small area of the process?

Moscow is the same as a Big Mac in Calgary. You can wake up in a Holiday Inn anywhere in the world and not know where you are until you look out the window. Hollywood, too, is all about predictability—if you've seen one Will Ferrell movie, you've seen them all. With the advent of rationalized, bureaucratic education, teachers are replaceable in the delivery of predictable, pre-packaged courses, and creative, innovative input is minimal. Students who have already taken a course can tell others almost exactly what to expect and what will be taught. Pre-packaged online courses cut down on the time spent planning lessons, thus making class prep more "efficient," leading to what might be called the "silicon cage" of rationalization. However, in a recent lecture, culture critic Henry Giroux (currently director of the McMaster Centre for Research in the Public Interest and a distinguished visiting professor at Ryerson) noted that it is the value of the indeterminate in education—in effect, the value of the unpredictable—and the free-flowing "don't know where this is going" instructor–class discussion that makes for an inspiring classroom experience. This creative process, however, is lost through formal rationalization and the imposition of predictability.

Finally, *control*, for Ritzer, is always hierarchical. He characterizes the hierarchical division of labour in the following passage:

> Bureaucracies emphasize control over people through the replacement of human judgment with the dictates of rules, regulations, and structures. Employees are controlled by the division of labor, which allocates to each office a limited number of well-defined tasks. Incumbents must do the tasks, and no others, in the manner prescribed by the organization. They may not, in most cases, devise idiosyncratic ways of doing those tasks. Furthermore, by making few, if any, judgments, people begin to resemble human robots or computers. (2004: p. 27)

This control is exercised over both workers and clients. People who work at McDonald's are taught exactly what they have to do, while customers have

Telling It Like It Is

Little Boxes: Mass-Produced Suburban Communities

After the end of World War II, which marked the start of North America's "baby boom," there was a fairly severe housing shortage in both Canada and the United States. One response was the development of mass-produced suburban communities. The first and standard-setting effort in this regard was the series of "Levittowns" built in the eastern US. Between 1947 and 1951, Levitt and Sons built 17,447 houses on Long Island, New York, creating an instant community of about 75,000 people. This model would soon be reproduced in Pennsylvania and then New Jersey. The company began by building warehouses for their supplies, their own workshops for wood and plumbing manufacture, and gravel and cement plants. Ritzer describes the rationalization of the house-building process in the following excerpt:

> The actual construction of each house followed a series of rigidly defined and rationalized steps. For example, in constructing the wall framework, the workers did no measuring or cutting; each piece had been cut to fit. The siding for a wall consisted of 73 large sheets of Colorbestos, replacing the former requirement of 570 small shingles. All houses were painted under high pressure, using the same two-tone scheme—green on ivory. . . . The result, of course, was a large number of nearly identical houses produced quickly at low cost. (Ritzer, 2004: p. 36)

The owners of the construction company knew that their employees did not enjoy many of the intrinsic rewards experienced by skilled independent tradespeople, but they felt that the *extrinsic* rewards of money would make up for that:

> The same man does the same thing every day, despite the psychologists. It is boring; it is bad; but the reward of the green stuff seems to alleviate the boredom of the work. (A. Levitt, 1952, quoted in Ritzer, 2004: pp. 35–6)

This kind of rationalized uniformity can come at the cost of oppression of minoritized people. In the case of Levittown, the covenants (agreements signed by homeowners with the developer) included racial segregation. Blacks were not allowed. The story of how one family "conspired" to bring a black family into Levittown, and how it was resisted, sometimes violently, by neighbours and social organizations illustrates this (see Kushner, 2009). This leads to the question: Does extreme rationalization of organization lead automatically to social oppression?

In the Toronto area, the suburb of Don Mills, constructed during the early 1950s, became known as Toronto's "first planned community." I grew up there beginning in 1956. It had the city's first shopping centre, the first Country Style doughnut shop, and the first Shoppers Drug Mart. As a teenager, I was a "plaza boy"—a term for someone who spent his leisure hours hanging around the mall. Famous Canadians from this community include comedian Rick Green (of *The Red Green Show*), "Martha" of the 1980s band Martha and the Muffins, and singer and writer Dan Hill. It also produced an outstanding Canadian sociologist: Neil Guppy. And yours truly, of course.

What do YOU think?

Think of a suburb you're familiar with. What aspects of it do you think reflect formal rationalization or "McDonaldization"? Do you think these qualities are beneficial or not?

their selection controlled by the menu board. Even the uncomfortable seating is part of the process, helping to control how long customers stay in the restaurant. We can see the formally rationalized, bureaucratic package at its most extreme in the following overview of material from a 1958 copy of the McDonald's operations manual, cited in John F. Love's *McDonald's: Behind the Arches* (1986):

> It told operations *exactly* how to draw milk shakes, grill hamburgers, and fry potatoes. It specified *precise* cooking times for all products and temperature settings for all equipment. It fixed *standard* portions on every food item, down to the *quarter ounce* of onions placed on each hamburger patty and the *thirty-two slices per pound* of cheese. It specified that french fries be cut at *nine thirty-seconds of an inch* thick. And it defined quality *controls* that were unique to food service, including the disposal of meat and potato products that were held more than *ten minutes* in a serving bin. (quoted in Ritzer, 2004: p. 38)

As with people who have only ever eaten French fries from McDonald's, never real "chips" cut and prepared on site, students experiencing today's increasingly bureaucratized education might become less able to judge the quality of what they are receiving.

Social Order through Social Organization

Social organization and social stability are fundamental aspects of the human condition. We couldn't really dispense of all social organization without falling into chaos. However, the foundational principles and forms of organization themselves can have a profound effect on society and the lives of individuals, and so they deserve to be critically examined and questioned.

As we have seen, social organization impacts everything from the environment (through our relationship with nature) to the places where we work, study, and live, where the dehumanizing effects of formal rationalization sometimes prevail. Large, bureaucratized organizations, instead of serving the needs and interests of people, often dictate our values and interactions (think of your most recent shopping experience at a mall or big box store). And the perils of bureaucracy and formal rationalization that Weber warned of long ago have only gotten worse, if we use Ritzer's work on McDonaldization as an indicator. The inefficiency of efficiency seems to dominate organizations from the military and businesses to hospitals and postsecondary institutions. Red tape, long lineups, quantity over quality, apathy, and even violent reactions (going "postal," road rage, fighting with the registrar's office or school board) have become the norm both within and outside of organizations and bureaucracies. In short, we need the social order that organizational structures promote, but there is evidence that bureaucracy has lost sight of the "greater good" of a greater number and a broader world. Through a perversion of means and ends, in which the means become ends in and of themselves, organizational bureaucracies become increasingly self-serving, behaving as though they were self-sustaining communities with no meaningful positive social connections to the other citizens of the planet.

WRAP IT UP

Summary

While there is a lot to learn in this chapter, a lot of terminology to remember, I would stress one basic thing. There is more choice involved in both social interaction and social organization than what might seem to be "out there." Often that choice is between oppressive forms that have been practised over years and less oppressive, and more empowering, ways that have been little tried, or that have come from groups outside the mainstream. The oppressive forms are not as "natural" as they may seem.

It is important to see that much of the frustration that we feel on a daily basis flows from the fact that we lead complicated lives. This complication arises from the increasing array of statuses we have and the many roles (including virtual roles we maintain online) that we perform at the same time. Think of the way our master statuses change as we go through life. Shifts are not easy. At the same time, we all deal with large organizations—banks, service providers, the local motor vehicle office—that often frustrate us with their lack of flexibility and human contact. Studying organizational behaviour, as we have done in this chapter, should, hopefully, enable you to see these personal frustrations through the lens of the sociological imagination. Don't take it personally—it's not just your call that isn't important to them, but everybody's.

THINK BACK

Questions for Critical Review

1. Why and how might the status of stepmother be more complicated and difficult than that of stepfather?
2. Do you think men or women are more likely to have virtual statuses? Why?
3. Is gender an achieved or ascribed status? What about sexuality? (Consider returning to this question after you've read Chapter 9, on gender and sexuality, to see if your perspective has changed at all.)
4. Why can it be said that, generally speaking, the larger the organization, the less well it serves the needs of its customers/clients/students?
5. Take a social organization that you are part of—a family, business, religious organization, or school. How do formal and substantive rationalization influence these organizations?
6. What do you see as the positive and negative effects of increased bureaucratization?

READ ON

Suggested Print and Online Resources

Online

Maysoon Zayid: I Got 99 Problems . . . Palsy Is Just One
www.youtube.com/watch?v=buRLc2eWGPQ

- In this 15-minute TED talk, Maysoon Zayid, an Arab-American comedian with cerebral palsy, promises that "if there was an oppression Olympics, I'd win the gold medal." Watch the talk and see if you can trace her evolving statuses. Which would you say is now her master status?

TSSU

www.tssu.ca

- The website of the Teaching Support Staff Union at Simon Fraser University shows how the organization works and reviews some of its accomplishments. The TSSU is a good example of a feminist service-provider organization; its "bargaining road map" (www.tssu.ca/2012/05/30/bargaining-road-map/), from the spring 2012 contract negotiations, is a playful graphic illustrating the collective bargaining process.

Paperland: The Bureaucrat Observed

www.nfb.ca/film/paperland

- Students may enjoy this one-hour 1979 National Film Board documentary by Donald Brittain, which criticizes "the absurdities of bureaucratic behaviour . . . with humour and irreverence." The film targets the originators of bureaucratic practices, not those tasked with implementing them.

In Print

Mark Barrowcliffe (2009), *The Elfish Gene: Dungeons, Dragons and Growing Up Strange* (New York: Soho).

- This memoir of how a British man spent his youth playing Dungeons & Dragons provides some insights into socialization, virtual status, and interactive role-playing games before the age of the Internet.

Amitai Etzioni (1975), *A Comparative Analysis of Complex Organizations*, rev. edn (New York: Free Press).

- In this landmark text, sociologist Amitai Etzioni examines a wide range of social organizations, from prisons, hospitals, and schools to communes, churches, and businesses.

Robert Kanigel (2005), *The One Best Way: Frederick Winslow Taylor and the Enigma of Efficiency*, paperback edn (Cambridge, MA: MIT Press).

- This readable introduction to Taylor's life and ideas gives a good account of the effects of Taylorism.

Laura Penny (2006), *Your Call Is Important to Us: The Truth About Bullshit*, reprint edn (New York: Broadway Books).

- Penny's work is a refreshing look at how corporate behaviour says one thing but really means another.

George Ritzer (2014), *The McDonaldization of Society*, 8th edn (Thousand Oaks, CA: Sage); John F. Love (1995), *McDonald's: Behind the Arches*, rev. edn (Toronto: Bantam).

- Ritzer's work is a classic and readable study of how the means and methods of McDonald's are reproduced in many areas of our lives. Read it in conjunction with John F. Love's history of the fast-food burger empire.

Deviance

The Gist

Reading this chapter will help you to . . .

- Avoid some of the leading misunderstandings of the term *deviant*.
- Distinguish between *overt* and *covert* characteristics of deviance.
- Discuss the reasons that deviance is sometimes associated with ethnicity, culture, "race," gender, sexual orientation, disability, and class.
- Discuss the contested nature of deviance.

Terms of the Trade

- American dream
- assimilation
- bodily stigma
- conflict deviance
- contested
- corporate crimes
- covert characteristics
- criminology
- delinquent subculture
- deviance
- dominant culture
- essentialism
- heteronormative
- ideology of fag
- impression management

- labelling theory
- marked term
- misogyny
- moral entrepreneur
- moral panic
- moral stigma
- multiculturalism
- negative sanctions
- non-utilitarian
- normalized
- norms
- occupational crimes
- Other
- overt characteristics
- patriarchal construct

- positive sanctions
- racializing deviance
- racial profiling
- sanctions
- social constructionism
- social resources
- status frustration
- stigma
- strain theory
- subcultural theory
- subculture
- tribal stigma
- unmarked term
- white-collar crime

Names to Know

- Howard Becker
- Albert Cohen
- E. Franklin Frazier
- Erving Goffman

- Robert K. Merton
- D. Kim Rossmo
- Edwin Sutherland

For Starters

© John Steckley

Gordon Dias, 1985–2001

If deviance involves acting against the values of a society, then perhaps suicide is the ultimate act of deviance. It takes the gift society values most—life—and withdraws all value from it. Explaining this act of deviance has been a part of sociology since Durkheim's *Suicide* was published in 1897.

It has been over a decade since my nephew, Gordon Dias, committed suicide at the age of 16. He hanged himself from a tree in front of a local high school. As a sociologist, and as his uncle, I struggle to understand why he did this.

Gordon was a young, single man. This made him part of the social group most prone to suicide. He was on the margins of society in several ways. He was the youngest of three children, a child whose brother and sister demanded attention by their achievements. His older brother was the first-born grandchild and nephew on both sides of the family, a position that brought ready attention. His older sister is simply brilliant, a very hard act to follow. Both now have graduate degrees. In my earliest memory of Gordon talking, he is straining to be heard above his siblings.

He was a person of colour, the product of a mixed South Asian and Caucasian marriage, living in the very white city of London, Ontario. He was very close to his South Asian grandmother—so much so that when he left home for a while, he went to live with her. It could not have been easy in that city to have made that choice.

Gordon was artistic. It is not easy for a young man to express himself artistically in our culture, not without presenting some counterbalancing signs of macho behaviour. Perhaps that's one reason why he sought the social company he did. According to my sister and brother-in-law, he had been spending time with guys who regularly got into trouble. This eventually got him suspended from school. Zero-tolerance policies don't leave a lot of time for even temporary allegiances with groups of kids who act out. At some level, zero-tolerance is simply intolerance. For him, I guess, that was the final piece of the puzzle, and the picture he was left with led him to suicide.

Suicide is a personal act. Yet it's an act that reflects the society that alienates the victim, usually for being an outsider, deviant.

Introduction: What Is Deviance?

Many people, when they hear the word *deviance*, think of behaviour that is immoral, illegal, perverse, or just "wrong." But deviance is better thought of as a neutral term. It simply means "straying from the norm or the usual." It does not mean that the deviant—the one engaging in deviance—is necessarily bad, criminal, perverted, "sick," or inferior in any way. The word is based on the Latin root *-via-*, meaning "path." To deviate is simply to go off the common path.

When looking at deviant behaviour it's also useful to distinguish between the overt characteristics of deviance—the actions or qualities taken as explicitly violating the cultural norm—and the covert characteristics, the unstated qualities that might make a particular group a target for sanctions. Covert characteristics can include age, ethnic background, "race," sexual orientation, degree of ableism and sex. In an example presented on pages 162–3, the *overt* characteristics of the young people associated with "zoot suit" culture include their clothing, hairstyle, music, and dance style—fashions that violated the cultural norm. The *covert* characteristics are age (the youths were mostly teens) and ethnicity/"race" (they were mostly Latino or African-American).

Deviance, then, comes down to how we define "the norm." It's also about *who* defines the norm, and the power of those who share the norm to define it and treat others as inferior or dangerous. And we must recognize that just as the norm changes—over time and across cultures—so does deviance.

When we invoke "the norm," we're usually referring to what we defined in Chapter 3 as the dominant culture. As you read through the different

Some would call this deviance, while others see it as art. What other forms of art might be considered deviant?

Quick Hits

Getting Deviance Straight

- Deviant just means *different from the norm, the usual.*
- Deviant *does not mean bad, wrong, perverted, sick, or inferior* in any way.
- Deviant is a category that *changes with time, place, and culture.*
- Deviance is about *relative quantity*, not quality.
- Definitions of deviance often *reflect power.*

sections of this chapter, keep in mind the dominant culture in Canada is white, English-speaking, of European heritage, Christian, male, middle-class, middle-aged, urban, heterosexual, able-bodied and without visible signs of mental/emotional difference. To a certain extent it is true that to differ from the dominant culture is to be deviant. That doesn't make it wrong.

Another term to revisit here is subculture. This is a group existing within a larger culture and possessing beliefs or interests at variance with those of the dominant culture. Subculture is the focal point of one of two early theories of deviance that we'll examine later in detail.

Conflict Deviance

Deviance Is Contested across Cultures

What gets labelled "deviant" differs from culture to culture. Consider tattoos, for example. In mainstream Western culture, tattoos have traditionally been associated negatively with certain marginalized groups considered deviant. These groups include prisoners, sailors, prostitutes, and performers in circus sideshows (once known as "freak shows"). But around the world, tattooing has been a longstanding and highly respected practice in many cultures, including the Aboriginal people of Australia, the Austronesian peoples of the Pacific Islands (e.g. the Maori of New Zealand, Hawaiians, and Fijians), and Canada's Inuit, who long saw it as an important coming-of-age ritual. Among some of these cultures the practice died out during generations of colonial oppression. Ashleigh Gaul (2014) describes how, in the North, tattooing the face of

young women went from being "a widespread rite of passage and a source of Inuit pride to a mark of shamanism in a Christianized community." The practice there has recently undergone a revival sparked by young Indigenous people and cross-cultural contact with interested young people of dominant Western cultures. Tattooing in the North is now a way to communicate messages about who the young people are and what they want to be, both a link to the past and a way to display how "modern" they are.

Tattoos make for a good study in the realm of deviance, highlighting three key ideas. First, deviance differs across cultures: what one culture defines

John Burridge

Alethea Arnaquq-Baril is a director of the documentary Tunniit: Retracing the Lines of Inuit Tattoos, *about the lost art of Inuit facial tattoos. How are her tattoos both a link to the past and to modernity?*

as deviant may be considered a venerable practice in another. Second, deviance changes over time. In the North, tattooing was a respectable practice for generations before becoming a cultural taboo; in mainstream Western culture, tattoos have now become so popular that they are no longer seen as deviant. In fact, we may have hit "peak tattoo": when your mom offers to take you for matching mother–daughter tats, the practice loses some of the value it once held as an act of rebellion. Third, deviance is contested: whether something is or is not considered deviant can become a source of conflict among people within a community. This can have unfortunate social consequences when a dominant culture condemns as deviant the practices of a minority culture and, by extension, the minority culture itself.

Deviance Is Contested within Cultures

Definitions of deviance differ not only *across* but *within* cultures. It is true that the culture defines deviance—that deviance is essentially a social or cultural construct—but it is important to remember that there is seldom total or even near total agreement within a culture as to what is deviant. Deviance, like other elements in a culture, can be contested: not everyone agrees.

When deviance is contested, we have a situation known as conflict deviance. Conflict deviance is a disagreement among groups over whether or not something is deviant. It may be a sign that a practice long condemned as deviant is gaining wider acceptance in mainstream culture. Consider marijuana use, for example. In Canada, marijuana was made a prohibited substance in the 1920s. Those who flouted the law were cast as deviant: they faced public condemnation and arrests by police. During the late twentieth century, efforts to have marijuana possession and use decriminalized made cannabis a focal point of conflict deviance. In 2001, the government made it legal to possess small amounts of marijuana for medicinal purposes. In 2012, a Canadian Community Health Survey suggested that 3.4 million people aged 15 and older had used marijuana at least once in the previous year, a finding that

The Point Is...

Deviance Can Have Rules

Deviance is not always a random violation of norms. It can be carefully signified by symbols and gestures set out in "the rules," which may be written or unwritten.

I discovered this during the 1980s, when I was sharpening my writing skills and supplementing my income by penning articles about my sociological insights for local newspapers and magazines. I had an idea to write a piece on men who wear earrings.

The prevailing style of dress for young men in the 1980s was very conservative. The trend was known as "preppy," and it was characterized by polo shirts in pastel shades of pink or green tucked into khaki trousers, with an argyle sweater draped over the shoulders like a cape (don't ask me why). Preppies were clean-cut: there were no hipster beards, and even stubble was an odd choice (until it was popularized in the show *Miami Vice*). Anyone with a tattoo was assumed to be a sailor on shore leave or a "skinhead," a member of the anti-preppy set inspired by British punk rock bands like The Clash. For a man to wear a single stud earring was an act deeply imbued with deviance.

My choice of newspaper topic was deeply personal: I was thinking of getting an ear piercing myself. When I turned 40, between marriages and living on my own, I did just that. But first I had to learn the rules. I had known for years that it was left ear pierced = drug dealer, right ear pierced = gay. The hypothesis I adopted for my article was that the vast majority, perhaps all, of the men I observed with pierced ears would have them on the left side. Sure enough, over the months that I observed men with pierced ears, I saw that rule followed religiously. I took note of over 100 men wearing earrings, and all of them had the earring on the left ear. A few had earrings in the right ear as well, but the showier of the earrings (they never matched) was always on the left side. So when I had my own ears pierced, I followed the convention so that my act of deviance would be interpreted correctly.

went a long way toward changing public perceptions and normalizing the practice. Debates over whether possession of small amounts of marijuana for recreational use should be legalized entered the mainstream in 2015, when the Liberal Party of Canada made legalizing recreational cannabis use a campaign issue. By the time you're reading this, it is possible that smoking up has become legal in Canada, though there will be many who still condemn the practice, meaning that it is still a subject of conflict deviance.

Prostitution is another issue of conflict deviance. Prior to 2013, it was illegal in Canada to own or operate a brothel, act as a pimp or agent for a prostitute, or sell sexual services in a public place; prostitution itself—the exchange of money for sex—was not technically illegal. In 2013, after Canadian sex workers challenged the constitutionality of the legislation, the Supreme Court struck down Canada's prostitution laws, arguing that they created dangerous conditions for prostitutes: in the court's view, the laws "prevent[ed] people engaged in a risky— but legal—activity from taking steps to protect themselves from the risks" (Canada *v* Bedford, 2013). The ban on brothels and pimping had been in place to protect women from being exploited by third parties, but it made work more dangerous for prostitutes, who were otherwise forced to fend for themselves. With the ruling, the government had one year to introduce a new law, which it did in 2014. The Protection of Communities and Exploited Persons Act made it legal to advertise one's services and solicit in public, but it made the purchase of sex illegal. Criminalizing the "johns" who buy sexual services reflects the government's view that sex work is deviant and should be abolished "to the greatest extent possible" (Canada, Department of Justice, 2014).

What do YOU think?

The prostitution debate pits those who think it victimizes prostitutes and should be abolished against those who see sex work as a legitimate (and lucrative) trade that should be made as safe as possible. Where do you stand on the issue?

KatarzynaBialasiewicz/iStockphoto

Feminist critics of pornography say it degrades women and encourages sexual violence. "Pro-sex" feminists argue that by validating women's sexuality, some sexually explicit materials (characterized as "ethical pornography") can be empowering. Assess pornography as an issue of conflict deviance. Can there ever be "ethical" porn?

Deviance Can Change

Definitions of deviance within a culture change over time, as the examples of tattoos, marijuana use, and prostitution show. Consider another example: trophy hunting.

Trophy hunting, or big-game hunting, is the practice of hunting large animals for sport. Some of the animals may be predatory (lions, tigers, cougars, etc.); others (e.g. antelope) simply produce impressive trophies. Trophy hunting is a practice strongly associated with well-respected figures in American life, including president Theodore Roosevelt (1858–1919) and the writer Ernest Hemingway (1899–1961), and it was once a common and acceptable practice among the well-to-do in North America to display in one's den or living room the spoils of hunting: fur rugs, ivory tusks, heads on walls, or antlers that could be "scored" or "rated" according to how many points they had.

Trophy hunting remains popular today, and it is a big tourist business: people will pay thousands of dollars to travel to sites in Africa and the Middle East for the chance to hunt wild game for sport. However, the case of Cecil the lion should serve as a warning to would-be big-game hunters that those who engage in the practice are increasingly likely to be seen as deviant. Cecil was a lion who made his home in a national park in Zimbabwe until he was killed by an American hunter in 2015. The incident made international news and sent animal rights activists and conservationists to social media to decry the killing of the park's beloved attraction. The hunter, who had a permit, was not charged with any offence, but he became the target of hate mail, threats, and angry protests at his home and business in the US.

What do YOU think?

What has caused perceptions of big-game hunting to change, so that what was once seen as a brave and noble activity is now seen as a deviant pastime?

Social Constructionism versus Essentialism

One of the reasons deviance is contested has to do with the differing viewpoints of social constructionism and essentialism. Social constructionism puts forward the idea that certain elements of social life—including deviance, but also gender, "race," and other social characteristics—are not natural but artificial, created by society or culture. Essentialism, on the other hand, argues that there is something "natural," "true," "universal" and therefore "objectively determined" about these aspects of social life.

When we look at any given social element, we can see that each of these two viewpoints applies to some degree. Alcoholism, for instance, is a physical condition, so it has something of an essence or essential nature, but whom we label an alcoholic and how we as a society perceive an alcoholic (i.e. as someone who is morally weak or as someone with a medical or mental health problem) is a social construct, one that will vary from society to society.

The interplay between social constructionism and essentialism receives excellent treatment from **Erving Goffman** in his study of stigma and deviance, *Stigma: Notes on the Management of Spoiled Identity* (1963). A stigma is a human attribute that is seen to discredit an individual's social identity. It might be used to label the individual or group as deviant. Goffman identified three types of *stigmata* (the plural of *stigma*):

- bodily stigmata
- moral stigmata
- tribal stigmata.

He defined them in the following way:

> First there are abominations of the body—the various physical deformities. Next there are blemishes of individual character perceived as weak will, domineering or unnatural passions, treacherous and rigid beliefs, and dishonesty, these being inferred from a known record of, for example, mental disorder, imprisonment, addiction, alcoholism, homosexuality, unemployment, suicidal attempts, and radical political behavior. Finally there are the tribal stigma of race, nation, and religion, these being stigma that can be transmitted through lineages and equally contaminate all members of a family. (Goffman, 1963: p. 4)

According to this definition, bodily stigmata exist physically, putting them within the essentialist framework. And yet, definitions of "deformed" can be and often are socially constructed: think of

Canada's Mennonites are known for their belief in adult baptism, their commitment to non-violence, and the modest everyday fashion worn by the group's conservative members, all of which keep them outside of the cultural mainstream. Which type of stigma is demonstrated here? Would you consider it socially constructed or essentialist?

Debra Wiseberg/iStockphoto

descriptions such as "too fat" or "too thin." People in a variety of societies "deform" their bodies to look beautiful according to social standards—for instance, by engaging in extreme dieting and exercising, by piercing their bodies, or, in certain cultures, by putting boards on their children's heads to give them a sloping forehead, all to achieve socially constructed standards of beauty and avoid certain bodily stigmata associated with deviance. People who hear voices and see what is not physically present may be considered religious visionaries in some cultures, but they may be thought to require a medical diagnosis in others, where the tendency to experience visions is constructed as a moral stigma. Racializing groups based on their ethnicity or religion is another social process, one that gives rise to tribal stigmata: national identity is a social construct open to change over time, and a religion given privilege and respect in one society is very likely to be cast as deviant in another.

In this textbook, we have adopted a view of deviance that is more social-constructionist than essentialist. Following Howard Becker's classic work *Outsiders* (1963), we will tend not to speak of deviance as being inherently "bad," conformity to a norm being inherently "good." Instead, we will generally follow the rule that

social groups create deviance by making the rules, whose infraction constitutes

What do YOU think?

A trend on Facebook a few years ago had people posting pictures of young female cancer patients who had lost their hair because of chemotherapy. Facebook members were asked whether they considered these girls and women "beautiful." Was this an attempt to change the bodily stigma of having no hair, as well as the more powerful bodily stigma of having cancer? Do you think this could change the norm concerning female beauty and the way people sometimes avert their eyes from cancer patients?

deviance, and by applying those rules to particular people and labelling them as outsiders. . . . Deviance is *not a quality* of the act the person commits, but rather a consequence of the application by others of rules and sanctions to an "offender." (Becker, 1963: pp. 8–10)

The Other

An important concept in the sociological analysis of deviance is "the Other," or "Otherness." Difficult to define and even harder to use, it intersects with such concepts as ethnocentrism, colonialism, stereotyping, essentialism, and prejudice.

The Other is an image constructed by the dominant culture to characterize subcultures, or by a colonizing nation to describe the colonized. When the United States took over Haiti (between 1915 and 1934), Hollywood and the Catholic Church helped to make deviant the indigenous religion of the Haitians by casting it as "Other." Voodoo, which combines elements of Catholic ritual with traditional African magical and religious rites, became an example of how Haitians deviated from "civilized" norms. Along with sympathy and aid for Haiti following the January 2010 earthquake came criticism of Haitians, mostly in the conservative media, for their "fatalistic" or "superstitious" views and adherence to voodoo, which, some critics argued, made the people incapable of helping themselves. The "Other" label, once applied, can be extremely difficult to erase.

The image created of the Other can be mysterious, mystical, or mildly dangerous, but somehow it is ultimately inferior. Edward Said, in his discussion of Orientalism, characterizes the West's treatment of the Middle East as the creation of an Other. The dominant culture in Canada typically defines "Indigenous" as Other. English Canada has portrayed French Canada the same way. In "slacker movies" written and directed by men and aimed at underachieving, socially inept, young white men, "woman" is constructed as an Other.

Deviant behaviour, once it has been associated with Otherness, is often subject to negative sanctions or punishment. But should deviant behaviour be punished? Certain acts of deviance, those that fall under our criminal justice system, are considered illegal and have sanctions attached, ranging from a judge's warning to fines and jail time for more serious offences. But remember that deviance is not synonymous with criminality: it simply means anything outside the norm. Young people trying to establish their independence and individuality will often breach societal norms when it comes to fashion and style of dress. This can make them targets of the negative sanction of *bullying*—aggressive behaviour that includes shaming, ridiculing, physical attacks, and generally having unwanted attention drawn to their Otherness. Should this kind of deviance be punished?

Children with allergies can be considered deviant: they differ from the norm and form a distinct minority of the population of children. Although school boards are increasingly making efforts to accommodate their difference (e.g. by prohibiting classmates from bringing peanut-contaminated products and certain other foods to school in their lunches), these measures draw attention to the Otherness of children with allergies and can actually increase the potential for the negative sanction of bullying. An article in the *Annals of Allergy, Asthma & Immunology* (Lieberman et al., 2010) reported the results of an American study in which 353 questionnaires were completed by parents of food-allergic children and by food-allergic teenagers and adults. Twenty-four per cent of the survey subjects reported having been "bullied, teased, or harassed" because of their allergy. Of the reported incidents, 82 per cent had occurred at school, and 80 per cent had been perpetrated by classmates. Disturbingly, 21 per cent of the respondents reported having been bullied by teachers or other school staff. Also surprising is that the greater part (57 per cent) of the reported incidents were physical: victims were touched with the allergen, had it thrown or waved at them, or had their food deliberately contaminated with the substance.

What do YOU think?

1. Why do you think children with food allergies are bullied?
2. What positive sanctions may reinforce the bullying behaviour or legitimize it in the eyes of the bullies? How might this be changed?
3. What do you think is the effect of this being a relatively new phenomenon that the parents of today's children did not have as an issue when they were children?

The Point Is...

The "Zoot Suit Riots" of the Early 1940s: Clothes and Ethnicity as Deviant

An instructive case of deviance labelling and sanctioning surrounds the "Zoot Suit Riots" that occurred in June 1943 in Los Angeles, California. The targets were racialized groups—young African-American and Latino men—who made convenient scapegoats for wartime tension.

In the early 1940s, Los Angeles was undergoing rapid change. The city's population was growing, and its demographics were changing. Large numbers of Mexicans and African Americans were coming to the city. Teenagers made up a large share of the population, as older men and women had gone off to join the war effort. With a surplus of well-paying jobs left available by older brothers and sisters drafted into the military, the young people who remained made money that they were able to spend on music and clothes. These teens—black and Latino males in particular—adopted a unique style of dress, a distinctive haircut (the "duck tail," also known as the "duck's ass," or DA), and a musical style that were countercultural. The music was jazz, rooted in

the African-American experience and only slowly gaining general acceptance in the United States. The dancing (the jitterbug) was more sexual than dancing of the 1930s. The clothing was the zoot suit: a jacket with broad shoulders and narrow waist, ballooned pants with "reet pleats," "pegged cuffs," and striking designs. Zoot-suit culture swaggered with a distinctive bold strut and posing stance, and distinguished itself from the older set with new slang words unknown to parents and other adults.

How did the zoot suit get labelled as deviant? The main media vehicle was the comic strip *Li'l Abner*, by Al Capp. In a time before television, comic strips were a major part of popular media. *Li'l Abner*, with maybe 50 million readers a day, was one of the most popular strips of the time. It's difficult to overstate its influence.

Al Capp identified the zoot suit as a target for his negative sanctioning humour. From 11 April to 23 May 1943, the strip presented the story of "Zoot-Suit Yokum," an invention of US clothing manufacturers bent

UCLA/Library Special Collections/Charles E. Young Research Library

Los Angeles police detain a group of kids in their zoot suits, under suspicion of being part of the riots of 1943. Do these zoot-suiters look like troublemakers to you?

ENTIRE NATION GRIPPED BY ZOOT-SUIT MANIA!!

FROM MAINE TO CALIFORNIA A FANATICAL TYPE OF HERO WORSHIP HAS ENGULFED THIS ONCE CONSERVATIVE NATION. THE OBJECT OF ALL THIS ADULATION IS "ZOOT-SUIT YOKUM" WHO HAS, UPON INNUMERABLE OCCASIONS, RUSHED TO SCENES OF DISASTER ALL OVER THE COUNTRY—AND, WITH INCREDIBLE, FOOLHARDY COURAGE, PERFORMED AMAZING FEATS OF STRENGTH AND HEROISM. NATURALLY, "ZOOT-SUIT YOKUM" HAS BECOME THE IDOL OF ALL RED-BLOODED YOUNG AMERICANS—AND THIS IDOL-WORSHIP HAS LED MILLIONS OF MEN TO IMITATE HIS PECULIAR COSTUME, KNOWN AS THE "ZOOT SUIT." CLOTHING STORES REPORT THAT THERE HAS BEEN A MAD RUSH TO BUY "ZOOT SUITS"— WHILE THE REGULAR MEN'S CLOTHING MARKET HAS HIT ITS WORST SLUMP IN ONE HUNDRED YEARS.

ZOOT-SUIT YOKUM

on taking over the country politically and economically. In Capp's strip, these industrialists had conspired to create a national folk hero, who would popularize their zoot suits by performing feats of bravery clad in this signature costume. The triumph of conservative clothiers was proclaimed in the third frame of the 19 May strip, which displayed the mock headline: "GOVERNOR ISSUES ORDER BANNING ZOOT-SUIT WEARERS!!" (Mazón, 1984: p. 35).

Beyond the pages of dailies carrying the *Li'l Abner* comic strip hostility emerged between mainstream society and the zoot-suit counterculture. One LA newspaper ran a piece on how to "de-zoot" a zoot-suiter: "Grab a zooter. Take off his pants and frock coat and tear them up or burn them. Trim the 'Argentine ducktail' that goes with the screwy costume" (Mazón, 1984: p. 76). Whether it was intended with humour or not, instructions for the negative sanctioning of zoot-suiters were carried out by people opposed to the counterculture.

The conflict reached a climax in early June 1943, when thousands of young white men—soldiers, marines, and sailors on weekend leave from nearby military installations—launched a campaign to rid Los Angeles of zoot-suiters by capturing them, buzzing their hair down in a military style, and tearing or burning their clothing. Historian Mauricio Mazón describes the extent of the riots and police intervention:

They were not about zoot-suiters rioting, and they were not, in any conventional sense of the word, "riots." No one was killed. No one sustained massive injuries. Property damage was slight. No major or minor judicial decisions stemmed from the riots. There was no pattern to arrests. Convictions were few and highly discretionary. (Mazón, 1984: p. 1)

The conflict lasted just under a week, and was brought to an end with two acts. First, the military reined in their troops. More significantly, on 9 June, Los Angeles City Council issued the following ban:

NOW, THEREFORE, BE IT RESOLVED, that the City Council by Resolution find that wearing of Zoot Suits constitutes a public nuisance and does hereby instruct the City Attorney to prepare an ordinance declaring same a nuisance and prohibit the wearing of Zoot Suits with reet pleats within the city limits of Los Angeles. (Mazón, 1984: p. 75)

This, the culmination of a series of increasingly explicit and punitive sanctions, shows how humour with a social edge and a large audience can be used against a particular group.

What do YOU think?

1. Why do you think the zoot-suiters were targeted?
2. Can you think of any parallels between zoot-suiters of the 1940s and any group today?

Deviance and the Moral Panic

When deviance or the Other is sensationalized in the media, it can become the source of a moral panic. A moral panic is a campaign designed to arouse concern over an issue or a group. The issue at the heart of a moral panic is typically something very small that has been exaggerated so that it seems like a significant threat to social order; in some cases, the issue has been fabricated entirely. To use a phrase I learned in my first sociology class, the moral panic is about a problem that is more apparent than real; it is, to use Baudrillard's term introduced in Chapter 3, hyperreal. Finally, it is volatile: it rises and falls quickly in the public eye and consciousness. The Russian communist threat to Canada, which was a major concern of *Sun* media writers during the time of the Cold War, has pretty much completely disappeared.

A moral panic is spearheaded by a moral entrepreneur—someone who has something to gain from public fear around the issue. The term was coined by Becker (1963) to describe a person who tries to convince others of the need to take action around a social problem that he or she has defined. The

moral entrepreneur could be a journalist sensationalizing an issue as clickbait, or an activist trying to draw supporters to a cause, or a politician hoping to advance a policy agenda. The moral entrepreneur often has a recommended course of action that is disproportionate to the actual threat, the proverbial hammer to kill a fly.

A recent Canadian example of a moral panic, discussed in Chapter 3, concerns Zunera Ishaq, a Muslim woman who fought to wear her *niqab* while taking the oath of Canadian citizenship in 2015. In its efforts to uphold the ban on covering the face during citizenship ceremonies, the federal Conservative government created a moral panic, calling it "offensive" that anyone should want to "hide their identity at a time when they are committing to join the Canadian family" (Quan, 2015). In fact, Ishaq removed her *niqab* before an official, in private, prior to the ceremony to confirm her identity. In this case, the moral panic was socially constructed for political gain, although it would appear to have failed. An older Canadian example of a moral panic is described in the Our Stories feature presented on page 165.

INCANADA, YOU'RE WAY **MORE LIKELY TO BE KILLED BY A MOOSE** THAN BY A TERROR PLOT.

▶ Don't let politicians manipulate you.

Take action @ you.leadnow.ca/p/reject-fear

leadnow.ca

What "moral panic" is this campaign trying to debunk? Who is the moral entrepreneur?

"Race" and Deviance: To Be Non-white Is Deviant

To racialize deviance is to link minority ethnic groups—particularly visible minorities—with certain forms of deviance, and to treat these groups differently because of that connection. We see this in movies and television shows that portray all Italians as being involved in organized crime, and news reports that link young black men with gangs and gun violence. We see it when a person of Middle Eastern background is suspected of being a terrorist. Muslims who wear the *niqab* are seen as deviant for concealing their faces. Part of racializing deviance is making ethnic background a covert characteristic of deviance, as though all people of a particular ethnic group are involved in the same supposedly deviant behaviour.

Despite the public promotion in Canada of multiculturalism—the set of policies and practices designed to encourage respect for cultural differences—the pressure to assimilate (i.e. become culturally the same as the dominant culture) is

Our Stories

Black Candle, Yellow Scare: Racializing Deviance and Moral Panic

In the 1920s, Canada experienced a moral panic around racialized deviance. The "race" was Chinese Canadians, and one of the people who gave fuel to the panic was Emily Murphy. Journalist, activist, and self-taught legal expert, born of a prominent and wealthy Ontario family, Murphy was a gender heroine of first-wave feminism. In 1916 she became the first woman magistrate in the British Empire. She would later play a role in the historic "Persons Case" (1928), which ended when the British Privy Council overturned a Supreme Court ruling that women were not "persons" eligible to hold public office.

In 1922, Murphy published *The Black Candle*, a collection of her articles, many of which had originally appeared in *Maclean's* magazine. Murphy's four books of personal sketches, written under the pen name "Janey Canuck," were well known when she published *The Black Candle* to expose the insidious details of the Canadian drug trade. The collection cast Chinese Canadians as the main villains in the trafficking of illegal drugs—particularly opium, heroin, and cocaine—although blacks were also singled out for censure. The main theme was that Chinese men—those bachelors who, because of the restrictive head tax on Chinese immigrants, could not be reunited with their wives or find companionship among women "of their own race"—were corrupting white women through drug dealing, "ruining them" and making them accomplices in their dealing. The following excerpt from a chapter titled "Girls as Pedlars" is typical:

> Much has been said, of late, concerning the entrapping of girls by Chinamen in order to secure their services as pedlars of narcotics. The importance of the subject is one which warrants our closest scrutiny: also, it is one we dare not evade, however painful its consideration. (Murphy, [1922]/1973: p. 233)

Murphy believed that the "yellow races" would use the drug trade to take over the Anglo-Saxon world, and she warned North American readers to be wary of these "visitors":

> Still, it behooves the people in Canada and the United States, to consider the desirability of these visitors . . . and to say whether or not we shall be *"at home"* to them for the future. A visitor may be polite, patient, persevering, . . .but if he carries poisoned lollypops in his pocket and feeds them to our children, it might seem wise to put him out.
>
> It is hardly credible that the average Chinese pedlar has any definite idea in his mind of bringing about the downfall of the white race, his swaying motive being probably that of greed, but in the hands of his superiors, he may become a powerful instrument to this very end. . . .
>
> Naturally, the aliens are silent on the subject, but an addict who died this year in British Columbia . . . used to relate how the Chinese pedlars taunted him with their superiority at being able to sell the dope without using it, and by telling him how the yellow race would rule the world. They were too wise, they urged, to attempt to win in battle but would win by wits; would strike at the white race through "dope" and when the time was ripe would command the world. (Murphy, [1922]/1973: pp. 187–9)

As a moral entrepreneur, Emily Murphy was a success. *The Black Candle* had a huge impact on the perception of the drug trade and on drug legislation in Canada. Chapter XXIII, "Marahuana—A New Menace," was the first work in Canada to discuss cannabis use. It contained a lot of damning half-truths and anecdotes but nevertheless led to the enactment of laws governing the sale and use of marijuana in Canada.

persistent. Immigrants who have experienced the embarrassment of having Canadians stumble over their names—sometimes deliberately for supposed comic effect (as when Don Cherry knowingly mispronounces French and Russian names)—may feel pressure to anglicize their names to make themselves more "Canadian."

Racial profiling is one way in which deviance is racialized. Ontario's Human Rights Commission defines racial profiling as

> any action undertaken for reasons of safety, security or public protection that relies on stereotypes about race, colour, ethnicity, ancestry, religion, or place of origin rather than on reasonable suspicion, to single out an individual for greater scrutiny or different treatment. (OHRC, 2003: p. 6)

The report notes that racial profiling can arise from a combination of these factors, and that age and gender may also "influence the experience of profiling."

Racial profiling assumes that visible characteristics of an individual can be used to predict engagement in illegal activity. This is not the same as criminal profiling, which "relies on actual behaviour or on information about suspected activity by someone who meets the description of a specific individual." As we saw with the example of bullying above, racial profiling uses a person's Otherness as grounds to single the individual out for different treatment, often involving some sort of sanction.

Racial profiling can occur in a variety of contexts involving various agents and individuals. Examples include incidents involving

- law enforcement personnel, such as police and border control agents;
- security personnel, such as private security guards;
- employers, for example, in conducting security clearances of staff;
- landlords, for example, when a property owner assumes that certain applicants or tenants will be involved in criminal or other illegal activity;
- service providers, for instance, a taxi driver who refuses to stop at night for certain people; and
- the criminal justice system, such as courts.

Racial profiling is commonly associated with *carding*, a police intelligence-gathering procedure in which officers stop, question, and document people when no offence is being committed. Individuals may be carded during police street checks or "community engagement" initiatives, carried out in neighbourhoods with high rates of crime. The practice has come under criticism from human rights groups, who argue that it targets mainly black youths, Indigenous people, and other racialized groups. And it can provoke a response that becomes an excuse for arrest.

Crossing the Border While Black: A Case of Racial Profiling

When I was completing my Education doctorate I took a course on community college leadership. It was a high-powered group, including faculty, middle administrators, and presidents of three colleges. As part of the course, we went on a cross-border field trip to tour Monroe Community College in Rochester, New York. It was the summer before 9/11, so "homeland security" was not the issue it would shortly become.

The car I was in was driven by one of the administrators, who was white, as were the passengers. I looked like an extra in a Cheech and Chong movie—scruffy and disreputable—but the others looked polished and upstanding. We passed through customs with no problem. Few words were exchanged with the border guards. The same was true for the other white travellers in our convoy: no delays, no problems.

There was one exception. One of our cars carried two black passengers. One of the men was an upper-level administrator, well dressed and distinguished-looking, from the Caribbean. The other was a faculty member, younger, also well dressed, articulate, with an American accent. They were stopped and asked to get out of the car. The trunk of the car was searched carefully. They were not treated with the respect usually given to people of their social class. It took them over half an hour to cross the border. They were guilty of crossing the border while black.

What do YOU think?

Read again the OHRC's definition of racial profiling. Do you believe that racial profiling is undertaken only "for reasons of safety, security, or public protection"?

The Yellow Envelope Story: A Case of Racializing Deviance

People are sometimes taken aback by my appearance. For one thing, I am a big man. I have a bushy grey beard that is probably older than you are. I am bald. I dress for comfort, not "for success." Imagine me as Santa's hippie biker gang brother.

In terms of my appearance, then, I am deviant. Usually I am considered a relatively harmless deviant, but not on this day in June 2015 at Toronto's Pearson Airport. My wife, Angie, and I were going to Oklahoma to teach children of the Wyandotte their ancestral language and to act out some traditional stories. This is precisely what we told the border guard who asked what the purpose of our trip was. We didn't anticipate any problems.

I have already described my appearance as an oversized, over-aged beatnik. At the time I was wearing a Native Pride baseball cap. And I have described the purpose of my trip. With my dark colouring, I have several times been mistaken for being an Aboriginal person. Taken together, these elements made me a threat. We were given a yellow envelope and directed to Secondary Inspection. We had no good idea what that meant.

When we walked into the room, signs prohibiting the use of cellphones and similar devices, I handed the yellow envelope to a border guard sitting at a computer, who instructed us to sit down. We waited. After about 45 minutes of nothing happening, I went up to talk to one of the guards. He answered my inquiry with one of his own: "Are you an American citizen?"

"No," I replied. He told me to sit down and wait for my "case" to come up. We repeated this exchange several times.

Eventually, a man who appeared to be the head of border security came to talk to us. I stood up when he approached me, and he advised me to sit down.

"I prefer to speak to people eye-to-eye," I told him. In hindsight this was foolish.

"You are not going to the United States today," he informed us. Moments later, a young and enforcement-hungry local police officer advised us that if we did not leave in five minutes, we would be arrested. Fortunately for us, he was followed by an older and wiser officer who led us out and told us that we should rebook our flight for early the next morning. He said that sometimes people waited as long as six hours in the Secondary Inspection room. We thanked him for his kind help.

Early the next day we re-entered the airport. When we put our passports up to the scanning machine, the photo of my passport had a big cross over it. We were redirected to the Secondary Inspection room, but we were there for only 10 minutes when the border guard called my name. "Bad day, yesterday?" he asked.

"Airports stress me out," I said. He told us we were free to go.

Three months later we went down to Oklahoma again. The cross again appeared on my passport, but we were not handed the yellow envelope this time. In June 2016, head down, quiet and wearing no confrontational baseball caps (instructions from Angie), I went through the border check without any problems. And the deviant-marking cross had been removed from the scan of my passport.

What do YOU think?

1. Why was the author labelled as deviant?
2. Does this appear to be a case of racializing deviance? Is it a case of moral panic?

Gender and Deviance: To Be Female Is Deviant

Feminist sociologists teach us that in a patriarchal society (one dominated by men), what is "male" is treated as normal, while what is "female" is treated as Other and seen as inherently deviant. Male values are normalized (i.e. made to seem normal, right, and good), through customs, laws, and culture production. Two related concepts are important here: misogyny and patriarchal construct. Misogyny means literally "hating women." In a patriarchal or male-dominated society, images of women are often constructed in ways that contain and reflect misogyny. Patriarchal construct refers to social conditions considered or structured in a way that favours men and boys over women and girls. Think, for example, of highly prized and well-paying jobs—corporate lawyer, investment banker, emergency room doctor—that have been constructed so that the job-holder is forced to place family in a distant second place to employment. This gives advantages

Oleksandr Rupeta/Alamy Stock Photo

This "women only" subway car in Tehran, Iran, exists with the officially declared purpose of protecting riders from sexual harassment. Is separating women—treating them as "Other"—the best way to crack down on groping and other sexual attacks?

to men, who in Canadian society are expected to fulfill fewer domestic and child-rearing duties than women are.

Casting women as deviant is not new. Take the witch-hunts waged in Europe and, later on, in colonial America from about the fourteenth to the seventeenth centuries. The women identified as witches were tried and, if found guilty, executed. Here we have a good example of moral panic surrounding deviance that was entirely fictitious. While some of those tried may have committed criminal acts, their alleged powers and connections with Satan were not real. Why were they believed to be involved in dark magic? The vast majority of those accused were women (the figure usually cited is 85 per cent). The word "witch" itself is closely associated with women, conjuring up negative images of pointed black hats, warty faces with pointed noses, and flying broomsticks: bad clothes, bad looks, and bad use of a female-associated cleaning implement. In a patriarchal society, this image of deviance is very much associated with femaleness, its opposite—normalcy—with maleness.

In the eighteenth and nineteenth centuries, European doctors and psychotherapists used a diagnosis of "female hysteria" to account for natural emotional states that, in women, were considered unacceptable or deviant (see Scull, 2009). Excessive emotionality, restlessness, and sexual desire were among the symptoms of the supposed neurological disorders. Much like accusations of witchcraft (only with less severe punishment), the diagnosis of hysteria was used to account for and sanction behaviour that was considered deviant because it occurred in women.

"Fallen Women": Sexual Deviance as Gendered

The double standard that has long applied to male and female sexual activity is evidence that deviance can be gendered. The Magdalene asylums serve as a case in point.

Magdalene asylums existed in Ireland, Australia, and North America from the eighteenth to the late twentieth century. Their stated purpose was to house "fallen women": prostitutes and unmarried women who were sexually active, but also women deemed by the Church to be at risk of being led astray. This includes very attractive and "feeble-minded" women who might be easily talked into unmarried sex. Moral purity was the Church-imposed standard for women, one that was to be preserved at all costs. Anything short of that standard constituted deviance. As a result, many women were incarcerated against their will, and with no formal trial. They were stripped of their rights and their children. It seems hardly worth noting that men were not held to the same standard.

In Ireland, it is believed that up to 30,000 women were incarcerated because they were unmarried and either were or could become sexually active (G. Smith, 1998). They were held in institutions commonly known as Magdalene laundries, because the inmates were required to perform the hard physical labour of washing clothes (this was well before there were washing machines). The women laundered the uniforms of other prisoners, priests, and nuns, and this enabled the institutions to be financially self-supporting. When not working, the women were forced to spend long periods of time praying, or at least remaining silent. They could not leave. The doors to the outside were locked, and there were iron gates. Nuns acted as prison guards. The last Magdalene laundry was closed there in 1996.

Being *Incorrigible*: Gendered Deviance in Ontario

Canada has its own history of gendered deviance. From 1913 to 1964, thousands of women in Ontario were put into reformatories under the Female Refuges Act. Among the "offences" for which young women would be placed in these institutions was being sexually active outside of marriage. This kind of behaviour and the women guilty of it were branded "incorrigible."

In 1939, Velma Demerson, 18 years old and white, became sexually involved with a Chinese man. They intended to get married. When she became pregnant, her parents reported to the authorities that she was "incorrigible." Velma was arrested and sent to a "home" for young girls, then to the Andrew Mercer Reformatory for Women, Canada's first prison for women (16 and over), in operation from 1872 to 1969. She was confined to a cell that was seven feet long and four feet wide, one bare light bulb, a cot, a cold-water tap, and a basin. A covered enamel pail was provided for use as a toilet (Demerson, 2004: p. 5).

Class and Deviance: To Be Poor Is Deviant

Poverty can be considered a covert characteristic of deviance. Marginally illicit activities like overindulgence in alcohol are more likely to be considered deviant in poor people than in middle-class or "rich" people. Jeffrey Reiman, in *The Rich Get Richer and the Poor Get Prison: Ideology, Class, and Criminal Justice*, argues that the criminal justice system has a distinct class bias. This bias appears in the way we define what constitutes a crime, and in our processes of arrest, trial, and sentencing. Each step shows bias against the poor. As Reiman explains:

> [T]he criminal justice system keeps before the public . . . the distorted image that crime is primarily the work of the poor. The value of this to those in positions of power is that it deflects the discontented and potential hostility of Middle America [the American middle class] away from the classes above them and toward the classes below them. . . . [I]t not only explains our dismal failure to make a significant dent in crime but also explains why the criminal justice system functions in a way that is biased against the poor at every stage from arrest to conviction. Indeed, even at the earlier stage, when crimes are defined in law, the system primarily concentrates on the predatory acts of the poor and tends to exclude or deemphasize the equally or more dangerous predatory acts of those who are well off. (Reiman, 1998: p. 4)

This is how behaviours associated with poverty and criminality become synonymous with deviance while criminal activity associated with wealth and celebrity is often labelled "good business." Martha

Stewart, media star and founder of a business empire aimed at aspiring home decorators and entertainers, was convicted of contempt of court for lying under oath during a probe into alleged insider trading, and yet she received a standing ovation from a mostly supportive public and press following a hearing at which she was sentenced to five months in prison.

Class bias is at the centre of what is known in the literature as the *"schools-to-prison" hypothesis*: the idea that in schools located in poorer, often racialized neighbourhoods, there is a biased application of practices such as "zero-tolerance," which creates a misleading perception of higher crime rates. Greater rates of suspension and expulsion, higher numbers of random locker and student searches, and tough anti-violence measures like the installation of metal detectors, the hiring of security guards, and even periodic police raids characterize the schools in these poorer neighbourhoods, but these measures are greatly out of proportion to the amount of violence and crime actually occurring at the schools. As we will see shortly in the discussion of labelling theory, when you treat people like they're potential criminals, they are more likely to actually become criminals.

While most of the literature relates to the American situation, the schools-to-prison hypothesis applies in urban Canada as well. In a 2009 Toronto *Star* article, "Suspended Sentences: Forging a School-to-Prison Pipeline?", authors Sandro Contenta and Jim Rankin reported that Ontario's Safe Schools Act, in force from 2001 to 2008, produced startlingly high numbers of suspensions and expulsions. The *Star*'s analysis, which examined school suspension rates for 2007–8 alongside sentences and postal code data for inmates in Ontario provincial jails, showed that the highest rates of suspension tended to be in those areas that also had the highest rates of incarceration. This is a positive correlation, which suggests that punishing youths from the city's poorest neighbourhoods with zero-tolerance measures reinforces the higher incarceration rate in those areas.

"But wait," I can hear you say; "Isn't it possible that low-income neighbourhoods naturally produce crime, and that greater rates of true crime, not increased levels of scrutiny or harsher application of zero-tolerance policies, are responsible for higher incarceration rates corresponding to these neighbourhoods?"

Indeed, lower-class people are overrepresented in the statistics on criminal convictions and admission to prison. That means that per population they are more often convicted and admitted to prison than are middle- and upper-class people, and this contributes to the idea that lower-class people are criminally deviant. However, a closer look at the statistics helps us see why they do not give us an accurate picture of the lower classes.

"Lower class" is a designation that is often established by looking solely at recorded income, but it covers a broad and far from homogeneous set of individuals. Some are part of the working class, who labour for long hours with little financial reward. Others are on welfare. These two subgroups of the lower class are probably not significantly more involved in criminal activity than are middle-class or upper-class people. In fact, it's a separate subgroup, representing a small minority of the lower class, that is responsible for a high percentage of the crimes. These people are lumped together with the first two groups statistically because of their low reported income, giving a misleading forensic picture of the working poor.

Another reason for the overrepresentation of the lower class in crime statistics has to do with *social resources*. In this context, *social resources* refers to knowledge of the law and legal system, the ability to afford a good lawyer, influential social connections, and capacity to present oneself in a way that is deemed "respectable." Lower-class individuals generally have access to fewer social resources than middle- and upper-class people do, and this makes them more likely to be convicted of charges people from the wealthier classes might be able to avoid. Tepperman and Rosenberg explain the importance of social resources:

> Social resources help people avoid labelling and punishment by the police and courts. For example, in assault or property-damage cases, the police and courts try to interpret behaviour and assess blame before taking any action. They are less likely to label people with more resources as "criminal" or "delinquent" and more likely to label them "alcoholic" or "mentally ill" for having committed a criminal act. (Tepperman & Rosenberg, 1998: p. 118)

The authors make use of Goffman's concept of *impression management*, which they define as "the control of personal information flow to manipulate how other people see and treat you" (Tepperman & Rosenberg, 1998: p. 118). The upper classes are better at managing impressions than are people who belong to the lower class. Therefore, they conclude,

> Official rule-enforcers (including police and judges, but also social workers, psychiatrists and the whole correctional and treatment establishment) define as serious the deviant acts in which poor people engage. On the other hand, they tend to "define away" the deviant acts of rich people as signs of illness, not crime. They are more likely to consider those actions morally blameless. (Tepperman & Rosenberg, 1998: pp. 118–19)

Sexual Orientation and Deviance: To Be Gay Is Deviant

Homosexuality is still defined as deviant across the world, although not in every culture. This particular social construction of deviance does differ among cultures in terms of how and what kind of social sanctions are applied. At the beginning of 2003, sexual activity between consenting adult homosexuals was still against the law in 13 US states (Alabama, Florida, Idaho, Kansas, Louisiana, Michigan, Mississippi, Missouri, North Carolina, South Carolina, Texas, Utah, and Virginia). In June of that year, in the case *Lawrence vs Texas*, the Supreme Court voted 6–3 against the constitutionality of the Texas law. That ruling effectively

Punishment for homosexual acts
- Homosexual acts can be punished by death
- Homosexual acts are illegal

Relatively neutral
- Homosexual acts are legal

Recognition of same-sex unions
- Same-sex marriage is allowed
- Same-sex marriage is allowed in some jurisdictions
- Civil unions are legal

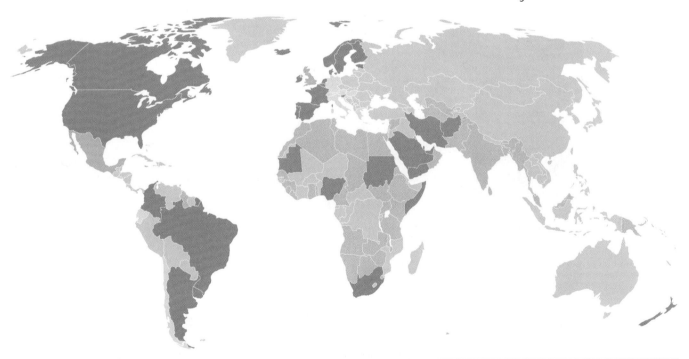

Figure 6.1   Legal Status of Homosexuality Worldwide, 2016

Source: Cameron & Berkowitz, 2016.

rendered anti-homosexuality laws in the other 12 jurisdictions unconstitutional also. This was a big step, to be sure, and as of 2015, same-sex marriage is recognized in all American jurisdictions. However, the June 2016 mass shooting at Pulse, a gay bar in Orlando, Florida, is evidence that homosexuality remains an issue of conflict deviance in North America.

The Point Is...

The Criminalization of Sexuality

Even though rights for lesbian, gay, bisexual, transgender, two-spirited, and queer/questioning people (LGBTTQ) in Canada are some of the most progressive in the world, the laws regarding sexual activity and sexual regulation continue to reflect a heteronormative bias. In Canada, acts of sodomy and buggery (which comprise any sexual activity that does not lead to procreation, such as oral sex and anal sex) were punishable by death until 1869. In 1892, any homosexual activity by men was deemed "gross indecency" under criminal law. And in 1948 and 1961, changes to the criminal code branded those who engaged in homosexual sexual activity as "criminal sexual psychopaths" and "dangerous sexual offenders," who could be charged with an indeterminate prison sentence. In the mid-1960s, just over 50 years ago, George Klippert, after being charged and convicted of gay sexual activity, was labelled a dangerous sexual offender and sentenced to life in prison.

Today, Canadian law does not prohibit anal sex if it is between consenting parties over the age of 18 and provided there are no more than two people present. However, for all non-anal sex, the age of consent is 16 regardless of the sexuality of the participants. While both homosexuals and heterosexuals engage in sodomy and anal sex, there remains a legal double standard that continues to target gay male sexual activity over heterosexual sexual activity (Kinsman, 1995).

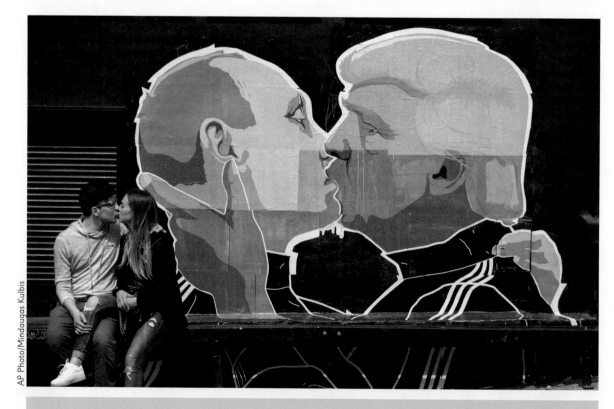

AP Photo/Mindaugas Kulbis

Why do you think certain kinds of sexual activity between consenting participants continue to be criminalized?

Around the world, homosexuality remains illegal in over 60 countries, with penalties ranging from flogging and imprisonment to death (see Figure 6.1). The countries with the most severe penalties for homosexuality are Islamic countries of Africa and the Middle East where Sharia law is practised.

In communities where homosexuality is regarded as deviant, whether or not it is illegal, negative sanctions can have a powerful influence. In Canada, young men can influence the attitudes of other young men by sanctioning behaviour perceived as effeminate or even just immature or silly with statements like, "Don't be so gay." This practice, promoting what is sometimes referred to as the ideology of fag, is a way of influencing people, especially young males, to behave according to gender role expectations.

It is interesting to note that the attitude toward homosexuality as deviant is, on a global scale, stricter concerning men than women. There are several countries in the world in which only male homosexuality is condemned (e.g. Jamaica and Uzbekistan).

Disability and Deviance: To Be Disabled Is Deviant

Society, as we have seen, punishes deviance with negative sanctions, and offers positive sanctions to those who adjust their behaviour to fall in line with the mainstream. A negative sanction can be fairly mild—a rude hand gesture from a fellow driver who didn't appreciate your sudden lane change—but we also have an institutionalized criminal justice system that exists, in part, to punish those who have been judged as deviant according to the laws of a certain jurisdiction. Punishment typically involves restriction of freedoms (e.g. of movement and residence) and an effort to diminish the independence and self-respect of the deviant.

A reasonable sociological question to ask is whether society punishes disabled people for their disability. For example, do the ways in which we design and build houses (with steps to the front porch and narrow interior stairways), public buildings (with revolving doors), sidewalks (without sloping edges to meet the road), public transport (cramped buses too small in which to manoeuvre a wheelchair) and shelving in grocery stores essentially punish—by limiting freedom, independence, and self-respect—those who cannot walk? (An

injury recently deprived me of the ability to walk for a three-month period that was as illuminating as it was terrifying.)

When it comes to "punishing" disability by failing to accommodate differences in physical ability, the sanction is typically an act of omission. It's not that disabled people have been singled out; it's actually that they haven't been taken into account at all. But there are many cases in which people with disabilities have been targeted because of their difference. A vivid example is Alberta's Sexual Sterilization Act, which was in effect from 1928 until 1972. The act was a product of the *eugenics* (literally "good genes") movement, which promoted the science of using controlled breeding to improve the population by increasing the occurrence of favourable heritable characteristics and limiting the reproduction of unfavourable ones. Essentially, the Alberta policy was designed to enact measures that would make it physically impossible for people deemed "mentally inferior" to reproduce.

It also punished racial and ethnic deviants. Many of those targeted were Aboriginal people and immigrants from eastern Europe, making this an example of how racial and cultural difference, cast as deviance, has been punished. But the act was also principally against people living with mental disabilities. The signal case in this regard is that of Leilani Muir.

In 1955, Leilani Muir was confined at what was then called the Provincial Training School for Mental Defectives (later the Michener Centre). At the age of 14 she had taken an IQ test (one reflecting a number of biases concerning class, culture, and ways of evaluating intelligence) and had scored 64, earning her the official designation of "moron." ("Normal" intelligence is confirmed by any score around 100.) In 1989, Muir would take another test and score a "normal range" 87. By then it was too late. Following the earlier test she was informed that she would be taken into surgery to have her appendix removed; instead, at the age of 14, she had her fallopian tubes destroyed. This was the negative sanction for Leilani Muir's mental difference. In 1996, the Alberta government admitted she had been wrongfully sterilized and agreed to a court-appointed settlement of $740,280.

Lennard J. Davis is a leading figure in the sociological study of disability. In his article "Constructing Normalcy," he writes:

To understand the disabled body, one must return to the concept of the norm, the normal body. So much of writing about disability has focused on the disabled person as the object of study, just as the study of race has focused on the person of color. But as with recent scholarship on race, which has turned its attention to whiteness, I would like to focus not so much on the construction of disability as on the construction of normalcy. I do this because the "problem" of the disabled is not the person with disabilities; the problem is the way that normalcy is constructed to create the "problem" of the disabled person. (Davis, 2006: p. 3)

The politics of disability involves promoting respect for difference, as opposed to just respecting the "normal." For example, proud and politically active members of the Deaf community have represented cochlear implants (surgically implanted electronic devices that assist the deaf in sensing sound) as an attempt to "normalize" people with hearing disabilities while disrespecting Deaf culture, with its long history of using (and respect for) sign language. Deafness, they argue, is merely a difference in ability and not a disadvantage to be corrected.

We all have different sets of mental and physical abilities; the world does not divide easily into those who are disabled and those who are not. Davis's point is that the social problem of disability is actually created by those people (typically able-bodied people) who view and treat those with a different set of abilities as "Other." There is often a sense of pride and entitlement that goes with being "normal" rather than "deviant" in the context of ability. Even if it isn't mean-spirited, it shows through in even the courteous and respectful communication that may characterize interactions with those who are "differently abled." A good example of a situation in which a difference in ability is turned into the "problem" of disability is presented in the following student narrative about an incident that took place in a bookstore at Yorkdale Mall in Toronto:

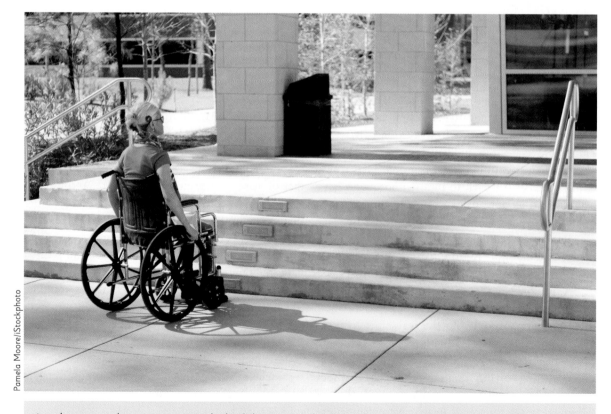

Pamela Moore/iStockphoto

In what ways does society punish disability? Does the failure to better accommodate people with disabilities arise simply from carelessness, or can it be taken as a negative sanction of disability?

I was browsing cookbooks with my dear friend Pearl, making innocuous chit-chat and the like, when all of a sudden we are interrupted by a middle-aged soccer Mom. I assumed she wanted something standard-issue like help finding a book . . . WRONG.

"Excuse me. Are you her helper? How much do they pay you to tow her about?"

Pearl shuffled awkwardly formulating a response, while I sit with eyes blurring and feeling the sting of a slap across my cheek.

"Um, no. I'm her friend. Didn't know payment was involved but . . ."

"Oh, my, this is embarrassing. Just, I've never seen one of them out before and my son is heavily autistic. We're looking for some in-home help."

She then just walked away without contrition or even meeting my eyes once she figured we could not help her. (Mirela Todorovic)

Criminal Deviance

Over the course of this chapter we have seen examples of how people in power have sanctioned deviant behaviour by making it illegal. Zoot-suiters, *niqab*-wearing Muslims, "fallen women," and homosexuals have all been persecuted under the law for deviant behaviour that places them outside of the mainstream.

Of course, while deviance and crime are not synonymous, deviance does encompass criminal behaviour. A growing area of sociology is criminology. You would get no marks on a test for defining criminology simply as the study of crime. In fact, criminology involves the sociological (and psychological) study of crime in terms of such key elements as causation, prevention, management or control, and the statistical patterning amongst certain groups and geographical areas. When I taught sociology to students in the Police Foundations program, I opened my first class with the criminological statement that I had much (perhaps most) of the sociological profile of a serial killer: I am male, white, middle-class, and highly intelligent, and I am deviant in a number of ways (I have a big beard, don't own a cellphone, own nine parrots, and make fun of

skinny white men in suits who drive black BMWs). This gets their attention. The point is, criminology is about studying patterns in criminal behaviour to learn more about how we can predict and prevent (or at least control) crime.

A leading Canadian criminologist is **D. Kim Rossmo**, who was involved with police in investigating the high-profile serial killer Robert Pickton. He is the first police officer in Canada to receive a doctorate in criminology, and an innovator in using statistical methodologies in what is called geographic profiling, which involves the study of locations where certain crimes are committed, or where people "disappear." In *Geographic Profiling* (1999), Rossmo relates the ways in which the methodology can be used by police services:

> Geographic profiling can be used as the basis for several investigative strategies, including suspect and tip prioritization, address-based searches of police record systems, patrol saturation and surveillance, neighbourhood canvasses and searches, DNA screening prioritization, Department of Motor Vehicle searches, postal or zip code prioritization, and information request mailouts. (Rossmo, 1999: p. 2)

He applied these techniques to his study of the deaths and disappearance of a number of women, most of them Aboriginal, who were involved in drug use and the sex trade in Vancouver's Downtown Eastside. He rightfully predicted that police should be looking for a serial killer who spent a lot of time in the area. A great example of the kind of insights his approach can yield is in his article "Place, Space and Police Investigations: Hunting Serial Violent Criminals" (1995).

Three Theories of Criminal Deviance

Strain Theory: Robert K. Merton

Early sociological theorist **Robert K. Merton** developed strain theory (1938) to explain why, in his opinion, some individuals "chose" to be criminally deviant. The "strain" Merton identified was a disconnect between society's culturally defined goals and the uneven distribution of the means necessary to achieve those goals. Merton was describing a situation in which social reality—the real-life circumstances of some individuals—inhibits the attainment of "the American dream." The American dream is essentially success, however you choose to define it (e.g. fame, wealth, or social prestige), mythologized as an opportunity that any American citizen, regardless of background or circumstances, can seize provided he or she is willing to put in the hard work to get it. Merton was aware that the dream of success is most readily available to those who possess upper- and middle-class resources (wealth, expensive postsecondary education, and social connections). When those without these resources find themselves prevented from achieving society's culturally achieved goals, they turn, according to Merton, to criminal deviance.

Subcultural Theory: Albert Cohen

Albert Cohen developed subcultural theory in an effort to challenge some aspects of Merton's work and refine others. He was also building on foundations laid by Frederic Thrasher in his studies of gangs (mentioned last chapter) and by **E. Franklin Frazier** (1894–1962), who had carried out some pioneering studies of African Americans living in Chicago.

Cohen's study of teenage gangs (1955) presents a model of what he called the delinquent subculture, made up of young, lower-class males suffering from a status frustration. Failing to succeed in middle-class institutions, especially school, they become socialized into an oppositional subculture that inverts the values of the school. For example, the youths he studied engaged in delinquent stealing that was primarily non-utilitarian—in other words, the objects weren't stolen because they were needed for survival but because the act of stealing was respected within the delinquent subculture. Cohen stressed that becoming a member of the delinquent subculture is like becoming a member of any culture. It does not depend on the psychology of the individual, nor is the subculture invented or created by the individual. When members of the delinquent subculture grow up and leave the gang (to join adult gangs or mainstream society), the subculture persists. Cohen asserted that

> delinquency is neither an inborn disposition nor something the child has contrived by himself; that children *learn* to

become delinquents by becoming members of groups in which delinquent conduct is already established and "the thing to do"; and that a child need not be "different" from other children, that he need not have any twists or defects of personality or intelligence in order to become a delinquent. (Cohen, 1955: pp. 11–12)

We can use Cohen's model to review other ideas presented earlier in the textbook. First, the norms of the delinquent subculture—the rules or expectations of behaviour—would be different, at least in part, from those of the dominant culture. The difference, according to Cohen, comes from the inverting of norms. In Cohen's words, "The delinquent's conduct is right, by the standards of his subculture, precisely *because* it is wrong by the norms of the larger culture" (Cohen, 1955: p. 28). Likewise, there is an inverting of the sanctions, the reactions to the behaviour of the individuals. The negative sanctions of non-gang members—negative reactions to their behaviour—can be seen as positive sanctions from the delinquent gang's perspective, and vice versa.

Labelling Theory: Howard Becker

One weakness of subcultural theory is that it stresses subcultural values as developed in opposition to mainstream society. The theory is only partially useful, and generally inadequate, to address social situations in which subcultural values, beliefs, and practices considered deviant by mainstream society in fact flow from the history and traditional culture of the people involved. Consider the way Indigenous people in Canada are often cast as deviant. You could not argue that most of their cultural differences have been consciously shaped to oppose the culture of mainstream Canadian society. Certain aspects of their situation might be better explained by **Howard Becker**'s labelling theory.

Becker theorized that labels applied to individuals and groups outside the mainstream become internalized both by those cast as deviant and by the majority group. Take the image of the "Indian drunk." Cree playwright Tomson Highway described it as "our national image":

> That is the first and only way most white people see Indians. . . . In fact, the average white Canadian has seen that visual more

frequently than they've seen a beaver. To my mind, you might as well put an Indian drunk on the Canadian nickel. (as quoted in York, 1990: p. 191)

Yet when an image like this gets applied to an individual and becomes a master status, dominating all other statuses, it may eventually become internalized.

A few facts should be presented here. One is that Indigenous people, in greater percentages than any other group in Canada other than Muslims, abstain entirely from alcohol: they do not drink. According to the 2012 Aboriginal Peoples Survey, 26 per cent of First Nations people aged 15 and over had not consumed alcohol in the previous 12 months, versus just 21 per cent of the total Canadian population (Rotenberg, 2016: p. 9). Second, Indigenous people who drink are more likely to be *binge drinkers* (i.e. people who have five or more drinks at a time). Third, there is no conclusive evidence that

Aboriginal people have lower tolerance of alcohol than other racialized groups. What effect do you think the image of the "Indian drunk" has on the first two statistics presented in this paragraph?

Another criticism of strain theory and sub-cultural theory is that while both have been used productively to address deviance in what can be termed "male culture," the research in this area falls short when applied to "female culture."

What do YOU think?

We tend to think of gangs as male, but girls and young women also band together in groups that could be considered deviant subcultures. A recent Ontario study of 9,288 students from grades 7–12 found that girls were more likely (at 28 per cent) to be cyber-bullied than were boys (15 per cent; see Canadian Press, 2012). Can Cohen's theory help to explain why girls "gang up" on other girls in this way?

John MacDougall/AFP/Getty Images

In 2015 Volkswagen made headlines for being caught with software in their vehicles that lied about its vehicles' emissions, in order to pass American standards without actually changing their emissions. Who is held responsible when an entire company has been lying since 2005 (when the software was first created)? Should white-collar crime, with its wider-ranging impacts, be more harshly prosecuted, or should people be excused for just following orders?

White-Collar Crime

In a speech to the American Sociological Society in 1939, criminologist **Edwin Sutherland** (1883–1950) introduced the term white-collar crime. He defined it as "crime committed by a person of respectability and high social status in the course of his occupation" (1949: p. 9). His article "White-Collar Criminality" was published the next year in the *American Sociological Review* (Sutherland, 1940). He later published a book on the subject (Sutherland, 1949).

Sutherland's work was an important step in the sociological study of criminology. Previous work had focused on the poor and the crimes they committed, creating at the very least a biased sample. But Sutherland's definition is not flawless. Associating certain kinds of criminal behaviour with a particular class reflects a class bias and a misleading view of the situation. After all, you don't have to be a person of "high social status" to commit identity theft (making copies of bank or charge cards), which tends to be included in the category of white-collar crime. The implication in Sutherland's original definition is that only people of the higher classes are capable of planning and carrying out crimes that are essentially non-violent. In this way it fails to recognize that industrial accidents caused by unsafe working conditions that are allowed to exist by a negligent owner are in a real sense crimes of violence. Even the term itself reflects this class bias: the addition of the qualifier ("white-collar") to the word "crime" suggests that most crime, ordinary crime, is not committed by people of "high social status," in much the same way that the term "white trash" carries the implication that it is unusual for whites to be "trash," unlike people of other ethnic backgrounds.

More recent works have refined the definition of white-collar crime to remove the class bias associated with Sutherland's original definition. Clinard and Quinney (1973) went further, breaking white-collar crime into two categories by distinguishing between what they called occupational crimes and corporate crimes. They defined the former as "offenses committed by individuals for themselves in the course of their occupations [and] offenses by employers against their employees" (1973: p. 188). The latter include "offenses committed by corporate officials for their corporation and the offenses of the corporation itself" (1973: p. 188). The difference is one of beneficiaries and victims: occupational crimes benefit the individual at the expense of other individuals who work for the company; corporate crimes benefit the corporation and its executives at the expense of other companies and the general public. This latter definition, by placing less emphasis on the individual, hones in on the negative aspects of corporate culture and the way that individuals and corporations work together to commit illegal acts against consumers and the common public.

In the spring of 2001, energy giant Enron, the seventh largest company in the United States, announced that it was declaring bankruptcy. This had devastating effects not just on the company's employees and shareholders but on the US economy as a whole. And it was only a taste of things to come, as the failure and collapse of several key financial agencies in the US between 2008 and 2010 would later contribute to a major worldwide economic downturn. The creative legal financing and letter-but-not-principle-of-the-law accounting schemes of the executives involved in the Enron affair, taken together with the multimillion-dollar salaries and perks they were paying themselves,

Table 6.1	Occupational and Corporate Crimes
Occupational Crimes	**Corporate Crimes**
sexual harassment	industrial accidents (sometimes called corporate manslaughter)
embezzlement	pollution
pilfering	price-fixing
expense account fraud	bribery
tax evasion	misleading advertising

constitute white-collar crime of both varieties. Their crimes were occupational in that they took from the economic viability of the company, causing its bankruptcy; they also caused the personal bankruptcy and economic hardship of thousands of employees by encouraging them to sink their life savings into Enron stock. At the same time, their crimes were corporate in that they had a profound negative impact on the American economy (particularly the financial sector) and were a major cause of the energy crisis that occurred in California.

It would be wrong to think smugly that this kind of crime is far more common in the US than in Canada, where, we like to think, we are more conservative and financially secure. It is happening and in Canada as well, as is recorded by PriceWaterhouseCooper:

> Thirty-six percent of Canadian organizations said they were hit by white-collar crime, compared with 37 percent globally. The Canadian figure is up from 32 percent in 2011, but significantly lower than in mid-2000s, when the response rate to a similar survey was more than 50 percent.
>
> "While Canada sits below the global average, the threats from economic crime continue to evolve," said Steven Henderson, national forensic service leader at PwC in Canada.

More often than not—at 61 percent of reported crimes—the perpetrator is someone inside the organization. The typical internal fraudster is middle-aged, university- or college-educated, in a middle management job, and with at least 10 years of service.

The four most common crimes in Canada are theft of assets (58 percent of reported crimes), fraud in the procurement process (33 percent), accounting fraud (22 percent) and cybercrime (22 percent). Nearly half of Canadian organizations surveyed said the risk from computer crime has increased. (McKenna, 2014)

What do YOU think?

Those who study linguistics distinguish between **marked** and **unmarked terms**. The unmarked term is the usual or standard one, while the marked term has a label added to it to distinguish it from the common term. "Field hockey" (as opposed to the usual brand of hockey played in Canada), "light beer," "white chocolate," and "decaffeinated coffee" are all marked terms. "White-collar crime" is another example. By distinguishing this variety of upper-class criminal activity, are we implying that most crime is committed by the lower or working class?

WRAP IT UP

Summary

Deviance can be examined from one of two positions: essentialism and social constructionism. This chapter has taken a social-constructionist perspective, reflecting the belief that deviance is not natural but is socially constructed, artificial, and something that can vary from culture to culture and can change over time. What's more, the social construction of what is considered deviant is often contested or challenged within a culture. There is a power element found in deviance, with those who hold power in society getting to define what is deviant and what is "normal." The dominant culture's definition of deviance (in North America, a predominantly white, male, English-speaking, middle-aged, middle-class, and ableist definition) can override the definitions of deviance that come from people less powerful in the same society. People may be classified and treated as deviant not because of their behaviour but because of their ready identification as belonging to a group outside of what makes up the dominant culture. Once branded as deviant, these groups may find themselves the targets of social sanctions designed to punish members of minority cultures and people with "alternative" lifestyles.

THINK BACK

Questions for Critical Review

1. Describe, with examples, what is meant by the term "deviant." Is deviance always bad for society?
2. Outline how deviance can be associated with ethnicity, culture, "race," gender, sexual orientation, disability, and class.
3. Michel Foucault said that "the guilty person is only one of the targets of punishment. For punishment is directed above all at others, at all the potentially guilty." What do you think he meant by that?
4. Explain, with examples, what "conflict deviance" is.
5. Give some examples of "white-collar crime." What would be the opposite of white-collar crime? How would these two types of crime differ?

READ ON

Suggested Print and Online Resources

Online

Cohen's Subcultural Theory
http://compass.port.ac.uk/UoP/file/9127b0f2-dd6d-4cd7-8ef9-5368b13bfd3c/1/Subcultural_theory_IMSLRN
.zip/page_02.htm
- The University of Portsmouth's page on Cohen's subcultural theory includes discussion, examples, and activities.

critcrim.org: Critical Criminology Information and Resources
www.critcrim.org
- Affiliated with the American Society of Criminology, this site provides a forum for organizations and individuals who are working to critically analyze, and change, the American justice system.

The SocioWeb: Criminality and Deviance
www.socioweb.com/directory/sociology-topics/criminology-and-social-deviance
- The SocioWeb is a guide to sociology resources on the Internet. This page gives links to websites covering topics in criminology and deviance.

Track Two: Enough Is Enough
https://www.youtube.com/watch?v=iN4_8eurids
- In February 1981, Toronto Police raided four gay bathhouses, making over 250 arrests. This documentary sheds light on how "deviant" sexuality was criminalized in the 1980s and became a source of moral panic, while at the same time sparking a backlash that gave rise to the city's Gay Pride movement.

In Print

James William Coleman (2002), *The Criminal Elite: Understanding White-Collar Crime*, 5th edn (New York: Worth Publishers).
- Coleman's work offers an in-depth analysis of how white-collar crime affects society, and an evaluation of the legal remedies.

Sandro Contenta & Jim Rankin (2009, June 6), "Suspended Sentences: Forging a School-to-Prison Pipeline?" *Toronto Star*.
- A readable news feature on class and criminal deviance.

Velma Demerson (2004), *Incorrigible* (Waterloo: Wilfrid Laurier University Press).
- An autobiography of a white woman who was incarcerated for having sex with a Chinese man.

Claudia Malacrida (2015), *A Special Hell: Institutional Life in Alberta's Eugenic Years* (Toronto: University of Toronto Press); Leilani Muir (2014), *A Whisper Past: Childless After Eugenic Sterilization in Alberta* (Calgary: Friesen Press).
- Malacrida's work is a powerful account of the Michener Centre, where people were imprisoned for being deemed "mental defectives." It may be read in conjunction with the memoir of Leilani Muir, who was sterilized under Alberta's eugenics program.

Jeffrey Reiman & Paul Leighton (2012), *The Rich Get Richer and the Poor Get Prison: Ideology, Class, and Criminal Justice*, 10th edn (New York: Taylor & Francis).
- Reiman's timeless work, with updates by Paul Leighton, gives an excellent look at how class and deviance go hand in hand.

Kim Rossmo (1995), "Place, Space, and Police Investigations: Hunting Serial Violent Criminals", pp. 217–35 in D. Weisburd & J.E. Eck (eds), *Crime and Place* (New York: Criminal and Justice Theory).
- Rossmo provides a fascinating account of environmental criminology, the study of how the environment contributes to crime.

Andrew Scull (2009), *Hysteria: The Disturbing History* (Oxford: Oxford University Press).
- Scull offers a sometimes funny, always readable, and overall instructive sociological history of how women's "emotional and mental disturbance" was diagnosed during the eighteen and nineteenth centuries.

John Steckley (2011), *Learning from the Past: Five Cases of Aboriginal Justice* (Whitby, ON: de Sitter Publications).
- This short work outlines what constitutes the deviance of being Aboriginal through five notorious cases.

PART THREE

Social Difference

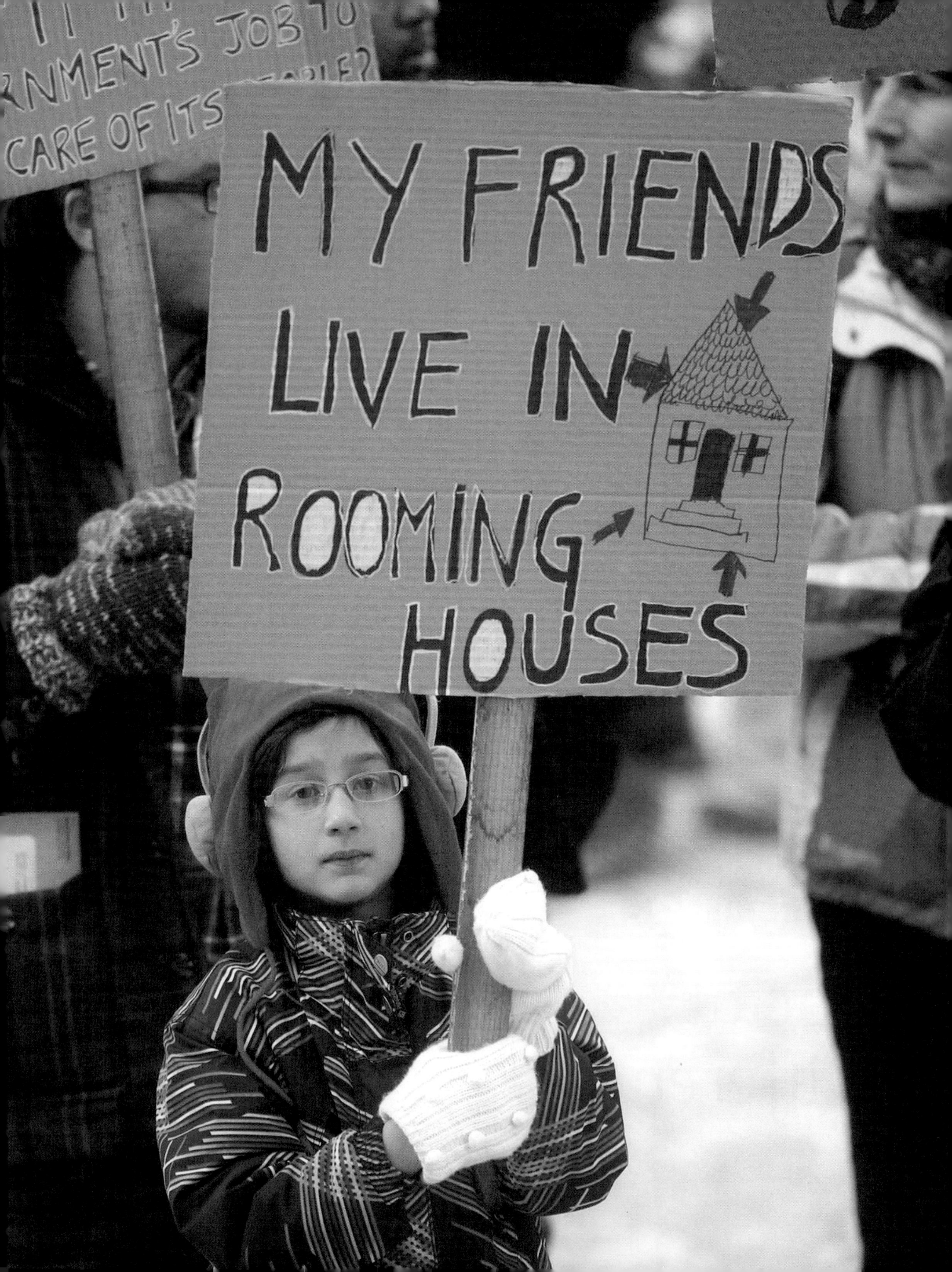
MY FRIENDS
LIVE IN
ROOMING
HOUSES
CARE OF ITS

Social Inequality

The Gist

Reading this chapter will help you to . . .

- Differentiate between "class" and "strata."
- Discuss liberal ideology critically.
- Distinguish between a Marxist notion of class and one that includes a middle class.
- Discuss the current and possible future state of food banks in Canada.
- Critically discuss social inequality in terms of quintiles.

Terms of the Trade

- American dream
- aristocrats
- blaming the victim
- bourgeoisie
- capital
- capitalists
- class
- class consciousness
- class reductionism
- corporate identity
- counter-ideology
- dominant capitalist class
- dominant ideology

- false consciousness
- food bank
- hegemony
- Highland Clearances
- ideology
- liberal ideology
- living wage
- lumpenproletariat
- means of production
- middle class
- mobility sports
- organic identity
- peasants

- petty (or petite) bourgeoisie
- professionalization
- proletariat
- quintiles
- relational
- social inequality
- social mobility
- strata
- trickle-down theory
- workers
- working class

Names to Know

- Herbert Brown Ames
- Friedrich Engels
- Antonio Gramsci

- Colin McKay
- Thomas Malthus
- Karl Marx

- C. Wright Mills
- Adam Smith
- Max Weber

For Starters

The Canadian Press/Adrian Wyld

A Picture of Poverty in Canada's Backyard

Situated on the west coast of James Bay in Ontario's far north, the Cree community of Attawapiskat gained international attention in October 2011, when the leaders of Attawapiskat First Nation declared a state of emergency, citing inadequate housing and poor sanitation. It was not the first time the community had resorted to this measure. In May 2008, hundreds of residents had been evacuated from their tents, trailers, and shelters because of serious flood conditions. And yet, in the fall of 2011, the media seized on stories of poverty and overcrowded, substandard housing as though they were new developments, while politicians claimed to have had no idea how bad the situation was.

How bad was it? You can read statistics about lack of housing, but to me, this account tells the story much more vividly:

> In a one-room, tented shack where Lisa Kiokee-Linklater is watching television with her two toddlers, two mattresses lie on the floor. Each is a bed for three. Mould is creeping across one mattress even though Ms Kiokee-Linklater just bought it last summer. It cost her $1,000.

There is no running water, no bathroom, and cold comes through the uninsulated floor. There is little room for her four children to play. The broiling cast-iron wood stove that takes up one corner of the room represents a burn hazard and eliminates the notion of the rambunctious play that is the norm for most young kids.

Moving into the tent was Ms Kiokee-Linklater's choice. It seemed a step up from her previous home next door, where she shared a single bathroom with 20 other people until it became too much for her and her growing family.

> "It's kind of better, yeah," she said. . . . "But during the winter, it's hard. I cut back on the baths because it is so cold." (Scoffield, 2011)

A situation like that doesn't just develop overnight. Nor is it quickly resolved. A year later, Attawapiskat chief Theresa Spence began a hunger strike to draw attention to the desperate circumstances of her own community and others across the country. The reaction in Ottawa and in the media focused on the alleged mishandling of funds in her community, a "red herring" that distracted the public from the real issue—the desperate state of Indigenous housing in Canada. Then in April 2016, Attawapiskat again declared a state of emergency, this time because of an eight-month-long epidemic of suicide attempts. In one month alone, 28 people in the community of 2,000 tried to kill themselves (Rutherford, 2016). The crisis was acute among young people suffering from bullying, sexual abuse, drug and alcohol addiction, and the dismal prospects they face in a town where jobs, housing, and even drinkable water are in short supply. Once again, politicians expressed shock at how grave the situation had become, as if it had happened overnight.

The plight of the residents of Attawapiskat is thrown into sharp relief by the success of its wealthy neighbour, the international mining giant De Beers. Since the summer of 2008, De Beers has been working a diamond mine in the James Bay Lowlands, less than 100 kilometres away from the Attawapiskat settlement. The operation has not been good for local wetlands and wildlife.

I learned about Attawapiskat close to 20 years ago, when I edited *Only God Can Own the Land* (2003), a book that speaks about how extensively the Attawapiskat Cree used their land—for food, for clothing, for building supplies—before the diamonds were found. Based on extensive fieldwork by author Bryan Cummins, the book provides an uplifting account of the community's success in spite of exploitative commercial enterprises and negligent governments.

So what happened? Different answers come from different groups. Provincial and federal government officials point fingers at one another for failing to notice and address the horrifying conditions, while the conservative media play "blame the victim" for the overcrowded housing and lack of jobs—after all, the community was receiving financial compensation from both the government and De Beers, so surely those funds were squandered, right? Some locals recount that the mining development brought a sudden influx of outsiders, who brought, acquired, and spent big money during their short stay in Cree country, creating short-term jobs for the locals and giving a tantalizing taste of what could be. But short-term wealth brings trouble, too—corruption, alcohol, drugs.

Neither causes nor solutions are easy to identify. Poverty wherever it exists—in a northern Indigenous community, a drought-stricken farming region, a once prosperous Atlantic fishing village, a rundown urban neighbourhood—is a complex problem. There is rarely one cause, never one solution. It is the sociologist's job to look at each situation critically to identify causes and possible remedies. To use the terminology of the first chapter, we need a mix of critical, policy, and public sociology.

A few years ago the CBC profiled an entrepreneur in Sudbury who was starting up a company in which new immigrants would be taught how to polish and cut diamonds and other gems. I wondered why that work didn't immediately go to the people of Attawapiskat. The land that bears the diamonds also bears thousands of years of their history. A community that was once a model of social equality is now a poster child for social inequality in Canada. It could have been avoided.

Introduction: Is Social Inequality Inevitable?

For there will never cease to be poor in the land. Therefore I command you, "You shall open wide your hand to your brother, to the needy and to the poor, in your land." (*English Standard Version Bible*, Deuteronomy 15:11)

The disposition to admire, and almost to worship, the rich and the powerful, and to despise, or at least, to neglect persons of poor and mean condition . . . is . . . the great and most universal cause of the corruption of our moral sentiments. (Adam Smith, *The Theory of Moral Sentiments*, [1759]/1976)

The study of social inequality has long been a part of the sociological tradition. You could argue that modern sociology evolved from the writings of eighteenth-century economists such as **Adam Smith** (1723–1790) and **Thomas Malthus** (1766–1834). Smith, quoted above, was an early proponent of laissez-faire economics, the idea that governments should not try to manage or interfere in the so-called free market. To those who believe in laissez-faire economics, "interference" does not include the financial incentives and tax benefits that governments pay to big businesses; that kind of interference is okay. To critics of laissez-faire economics, there is no such thing as a "free" market when it is dominated by corporations with near-monopolistic power.

Smith was optimistic that a market free of government interference would raise standards of living for everyone, though he might have agreed with the idea that there will always be at least some "poor in the land." Malthus wasn't nearly as optimistic about the chances of the poor. He warned that dramatic population growth would inevitably lead to a scarcity of food and other resources. He warned that famine, disease, and war would "naturally" limit population growth unless other measures, including birth control and celibacy, were adopted.

Is poverty really inevitable? Is it the best we can do to offer a hand to "the needy and the poor"? I like to think that most sociologists would say no to both questions. The political philosopher **Karl Marx** (1818–1883), whose writings we'll get to in a moment, certainly didn't see inequality as inevitable—and he was prepared to do something about it. Perhaps that's why he is often seen as one of the founders of sociology. But it would be wrong to suggest that all sociologists share his view. Indeed, few areas are more contentious in the sociological, economic, and political study of societies than the study of social inequality, the long-term existence of significant differences in access to goods and services among social groups.

Inevitable or not, social inequality is a function of many factors, only some of which we will cover in this chapter. Ethnicity, "race," and gender are discussed in their own chapters, but they all have an impact on the economic status of an individual or family. This chapter will focus mainly on two related concepts, class and stratification, beginning with an introduction to the writings of Karl Marx. There is a special language involved in interpreting Marx. I apologize in advance for the large number of bold terms you will find bearing down on you as you read the following sections.

Marx and Weber: Historical Approaches to the Study of Social Class

The main term used to talk about social inequality is *class*, the definition of which has been the subject of much debate since Karl Marx popularized the term. Near the beginning of *The Communist Manifesto* (1848), Marx and his co-author, **Friedrich Engels** (1820–1895), give us some clues about their understanding of class:

> The history of all hitherto existing society is the history of class struggles. Freeman and slave, patrician and plebian, lord and serf, guild-master and journeyman, in a word, oppressor and oppressed, stood in constant opposition to one another, carried on an uninterrupted, now hidden, now open fight, a fight that each time ended, either in a revolutionary reconstitution of society at large, or in the common ruin of the contending classes. . . .
>
> The modern bourgeois society that has sprouted from the ruins of feudal society has not done away with class antagonisms. It has but established new classes, new conditions of oppression, new forms of struggle in place of the old ones.
>
> Our epoch, the epoch of the bourgeoisie, possesses, however, this distinct feature: it has simplified class antagonisms. Society as a whole is more and more splitting up into two great hostile camps, into two great classes directly facing each other—bourgeoisie and proletariat.

"Opposition," "fight," "antagonism," "hostile camps"—if you gleaned anything from these paragraphs, you will understand that Marx saw society as divided into two groups embroiled in a bitter rivalry. That sets the tone for much of what he says about the distribution of wealth in society.

Class, as Marx described it, is relational: it reflects a relationship to what he called the means of production—the resources needed to produce goods (and hence, wealth). In the pre-industrial Europe that Marx studied, the chief means of production was land. Wealth was produced by growing food crops and raising livestock. Once Europe began to become industrialized during the nineteenth century, when Marx and Engels lived, the means of production became capital, the money needed to build factories, purchase raw materials, and pay labourers to turn those raw materials into manufactured products. In spite of the fact he devoted an entire book (*Das Kapital*) to the topic, the precise meaning of Marx's term "capital" has been contested. We define it here as the funds and properties necessary for typically large-scale manufacturing and trading.

For Marx, there were only two possible relationships to the means of production: either you owned them or you worked for those who did. In pre-industrial Europe, the owners were called aristocrats and the workers, peasants. Marx called the owners of capital in industrial-era Europe capitalists; he referred to the members of this class collectively as the bourgeoisie. The class of workers, which succeeded the peasant class of the industrial era, made up the proletariat. Marx identified various sub-classes—the petty (or petite) bourgeoisie, made up of small-time owners with little capital, and the lumpenproletariat, the small-time criminals, beggars, and unemployed—but these terms do not have the significance of his two primary classes, the "two great hostile camps" referred to in the final sentence of the passage quoted above.

Marx's Historical Context

If you wonder at Marx's black-and-white view of society, remember the conditions he saw, and the context in which he lived. Britain was operating according to the laissez-faire market practices advocated by Adam Smith and others, in which business was supposed to take care of itself without any interference from

Atmotu Images/Alamy Stock Photo

Marx and Engels, along with the Marxist Soviet premier Vladimir Lenin, watch over a neighbourhood in Laos. Laos remains one of the last strongholds of communism in the world today. What about these images of dead, white, European men do you think resonates with Laotians?

government. The Factory Act of 1833, which targeted primarily the booming textile mills of Britain, was considered radical at the time. The mill-owning bourgeoisie claimed it interfered with the "natural course" of business by "severely" limiting the hours that people were allowed to work. Factory owners complained that the act would ruin them financially, even drive them out of business. (Similar complaints are made in twenty-first–century Canada, when moves are made to raise the minimum wage or increase employer contributions to the Canada Pension Plan.) The Factory Act specified that the working day was to start no earlier than 5:30 a.m. and end no later than 8:30 p.m. It included these additional provisions:

- "[N]o person under eighteen years of age shall [work] between half-past eight in the evening and half-past five in the morning, in any cotton, woollen, worsted, hemp, flax, tow, linen or silk mill. . . ."
- "[N]o person under the age of eighteen shall be employed in any such mill . . . more than twelve hours in . . . one day, nor more than sixty-nine hours in . . . one week. . . ."
- "It shall not be lawful . . . to employ in any factory . . . as aforesaid, except in mills for the manufacture of silk, any child who shall not have completed his or her ninth year."
- "It shall not be lawful for any person to employ . . . in any factory . . . for longer than forty-eight hours in one week, nor for longer than nine hours in one day, any child who shall not have completed his or her eleventh year. . . ."
- "Every child restricted to the performance of forty-eight hours of labour in any one week shall attend some school." (*Statutes of the Realm*, 3 & 4 William IV, c. 103)

Such "liberal" rules as these would not apply to adults.

Class as a Social Identity

Another characteristic of class in Marx's view is that it has a corporate (or organic) identity as a real social group. There is a shared sense of common purpose among members of each class. One key aspect of this is class consciousness, an awareness of what

is in the best interests of one's class. Marx believed that the owner class always possesses class consciousness, always knows what is in its best interests, and attempts to shape society in a way that promotes those interests. Witness the Highland Clearances that occurred in Scotland in the late eighteenth and early nineteenth centuries. Land-owning aristocrats, recognizing the increasing value of wool to the rapidly industrializing textile industry, began evicting tenant farmers from their estates to make room for sheep. The clearances caused extreme hardship among the evicted "crofters," whose families had been on the land for generations. Many were forced to emigrate, notably to North America. The aristocrats knew that evicting the crofters would benefit them, and them alone.

The worker class, on the other hand, does not always have such an awareness. On the contrary, it often has false consciousness, the belief that something is in its best interests when it is not. Marx believed that the proletariat's false consciousness kept them from waging open revolt against a system that was not working in their favour. Factors that could contribute to false consciousness include religion ("God made you poor and your boss rich") and patriotism ("It is better to be exploited by a Canadian bank than an American one"). False consciousness also occurs in societies that are divided by ethnicity or "race."

The Tutsi people of Rwanda provide a good example of false consciousness. When Rwanda (together with neighbouring Burundi) was a colony of Belgium, the Belgians gave this numerical minority (representing about 13 per cent of Rwanda's population) power over the numerically dominant (roughly 85 per cent) Hutu. The Tutsi suddenly enjoyed more power than they had possessed prior to colonization. But it was only a handful of the Tutsi who held such power. The majority of the Tutsi people were exploited by the Tutsi elite, whom they could not challenge because the elite would play the "common ethnicity" card to demand their loyalty. The exploited Tutsi had class interests in common with the Hutu, who had become the most exploited group in the country during the Tutsi rise to power. However, the two groups did not recognize the class interests they had in common. That false consciousness prevented the two exploited groups from forming a mutually beneficial alliance capable of grabbing a share of power and wealth from the Tutsi elite, and their Belgian masters. The situation later repeated itself in the reverse following the overthrow of the Tutsi monarchy by the Hutu people in 1962. Many Hutu, impoverished and under the thumb of the newly ruling Hutu elite, thought of all Tutsi as former feudal exploiters, even though many had never been any richer than the Hutu. We'll examine Rwanda's ethnic conflict further in the next chapter.

Weber's Critique of Marx

Another early sociologist to look at social inequality was **Max Weber**, whom you encountered in the opening chapter. Weber didn't quite agree with Marx's theory of class relations, and though the two men were not contemporaries (it is sometimes said that Weber engaged in a theoretical discussion with Marx's ghost), their views on the subject are frequently compared and contrasted. (Hint: the topic makes a good essay question on exams.)

Like Marx, Weber viewed society as divided into different economic classes, but he believed that Marx's materialist approach was too simplistic, that there was more to social inequality than just who owned the means of production. In particular, Weber stressed three elements—*wealth*, *prestige*, and *power*—as contributing to social inequality. For Weber, wealth, or material resources, includes not just factories and other property involved directly in making money but also properties that are highly respected by members of the society in question: in Western society, the flashy car, the expensive house, the trophy spouse, the winning good looks you seem to find so often among Super Bowl quarterbacks. Prestige is the degree of respect with which individuals, their socially valued possessions, and their master statuses are viewed by the majority of people in a society. Prestige can be turned into various forms of social power, which is usually defined as the ability of individuals or groups to achieve their goals despite the opposition of others.

One example of a person embodying (literally!) wealth, prestige, and power is Arnold Schwarzenegger. As a young man, his wealth was his good looks and muscular body, which earned him prestige as a bodybuilder (then his master status) and winner of the Mr Universe competition. The respect accorded him for his physical appearance enabled Arnie to change careers and become an actor, which brought him further prestige. This he turned into real social and political power, first by

Pedro Castellano/iStockphoto

This young man owns two gas-powered lawnmowers and, with the help of his buddy Jake (whom he pays $18 an hour) operates his own small landscaping business. Assess his class position from both a Marxist and a Weberian perspective.

marrying a Kennedy relative (more prestige) and then by being elected governor of California in 2004. He followed a course laid out by an earlier governor of California, Ronald Reagan, who parlayed his prestige as an actor, ultimately, into presidency of the United States. From a Weberian perspective, what is important is that Schwarzenegger's membership in the dominant social class was not about controlling the means of production in a Marxist sense.

Using Class to Study Social Inequality Today

There are some problems with applying a traditional Marxist interpretation of class to contemporary societies in countries such as Canada. For one thing, there are many people who, as employees of big businesses (bank presidents, corporate lawyers, hospital administrators, high-ranking government bureaucrats, professional hockey players, and college administrators), would belong to Marx's class of "workers," even though their incomes put them in the top 1 per cent, on a par with the wealthiest of capitalists. Likewise, there are farmers, owners of small retail stores, and other small business operators who have incomes and levels of control that are more like those of workers. And unlike Marx, who was concerned with the binary opposition of the bourgeoisie and proletariat, we can argue for the existence of a very large middle group with some sense of itself as a class.

Within the Canadian context, we can amend Marx's class paradigm by arguing that there are essentially three different classes in this country. Following Curtis, Grabb, and Guppy (1999), these would be the following:

1) a dominant capitalist class that is "composed mainly of those who own or control large-scale production"; this would include the presidents and CEOs of large businesses (including universities), who may not own their companies but who are paid handsomely for running them.

2) a middle class that is "a mixed . . . middle category of small-scale business people, educated professional-technical or administrative personnel, and various salaried employees or wage-earners possessing some certifiable credentials, training, or skills." This group would include small business entrepreneurs, teachers and nurses, academic researchers, and those who have been able to translate a postsecondary degree into a modest but respectable office or skilled trade job.

3) a working class or proletariat, "made up of people who lack resources or capacities apart from their own labour power": people in construction or manufacturing, retail employees, and others in the service industry. (Curtis, Grabb, & Guppy, 1999: p. ix)

Class Divisions and Popular Sport

There is a strong connection between class and sport at both the professional and recreational level. The traditional association of sports like golf and tennis with the wealthy classes has been reinforced through the prohibitive cost of—and prestige surrounding—membership at golf and tennis clubs. Weber would probably recognize a membership at an exclusive Vancouver golf club as a form of wealth. Compare

that with membership in a bowling league, where players enjoy a sport generally seen as having more of a working-class appeal. Marketers and advertisers involved in professional sports often exploit these associations to attract a particular fan base to their sport, in spite of the fact that most professional athletes earn lucrative salaries that put them in the top 1 per cent.

Sports that offer people from poorer socio-economic backgrounds the chance to reap large financial rewards as professional athletes can be called mobility sports. Any sport that is cheap to play (with low costs for equipment and enrolment in organized competition), in which opportunities to play and "be discovered" are readily available to people of all classes, and that provides middle- to upper-class incomes for the select few that "make it" can be considered a mobility sport. Historically, boxing has done that. It provides young men raised in poor and sometimes violent circumstances an alternative to "the mean streets." Professional boxers rarely come from the middle class. Taking boxing's place today, both in popularity and in prestige, is mixed martial arts and its professional embodiment, UFC, or Ultimate Fighting Championship. UFC has developed a loyal and increasingly mainstream fan base rooted in lower- and middle-class North America. During the last 25 years, basketball has been a mobility sport for young black men in North America. Across the world, particularly in developing countries, soccer also provides mobility for the poor, especially the racialized poor.

Hockey in Canada: Mobility Sport or Elitist Sport?

Canadian hockey lore is filled with stories of poor young men from farming communities in the West or mining towns in the East rising from poverty and obscurity to achieve celebrity status playing in the NHL. Gordie Howe, who passed away recently at the

pumkinpie/Alamy Stock Photo

A youth in Cochin, India, wears the soccer jersey of his hero, Lionel Messi, ranked second on Forbes's list of wealthiest athletes in 2016 with an income of $81.4 million (Forbes, 2016). What would it take for this youth to follow in Messi's footsteps? Is "the beautiful game" also the world's greatest mobility sport?

age of 88, was born in 1928 and was one of nine children raised on a failing farm in Depression-era Floral, Saskatchewan; he became a superstar, arguably (among older fans) the greatest player ever. Johnny Bucyk (born in 1935), who grew up in a rough neighbourhood of north Edmonton, the son of Ukrainian immigrants, recalls learning to play hockey with "road apples," without sticks, pads, or skates:

> I can remember playing street hockey when I was a kid, maybe seven or eight years old. In those days you couldn't afford to buy hockey sticks, nobody in our group could. I was from a poor family and I really didn't know what it was to own a hockey stick, so I didn't care. I played a lot of street hockey and we used brooms for sticks. We couldn't afford pucks either, so we'd follow the milk wagon which was pulled by a couple of horses, waiting until the horses did their job, dropping a good hunk of manure. Usually it would be a cold day, anytime between the start of October through the end of April, and we'd let it freeze up solid.

> We'd use it as a hockey puck. . . . I didn't get my first pair of skates until I was about 10 years old. It was a pair of my older brother Bill's, which he outgrew. (Quoted in Lowe, Fischler, & Fischler, 1988: pp. 43–4)

Bucyk played in the National Hockey League from 1956 to 1978, most of that time with the Boston Bruins. He was the fifth NHL player to score 50 goals in a season, and was inducted into the Hockey Hall of Fame in 1981.

Players like Howe and Bucyk earned decent livings playing hockey, though they came nowhere near the earnings of players today. They grew up at a time when the cost of playing organized hockey was relatively low. Over the last 20 years, the costs associated with raising a potential professional hockey player have risen astronomically. Beyond the price tag for the latest equipment and league fees, a player who shows skill enough to play for a rep or select team will incur travel costs and increased rink fees (for practices and for games). During the first decade of the twenty-first century, players in the elite Greater Toronto Hockey League paid between $500 and $1,600 in annual dues; the range today is nearly double. The rise in costs is a feature of the professionalization of elite minor hockey, which now depends heavily on professional coaches and trainers.

The trend is evident not just in other sports but in activities such as music, drama, and dance. It reflects in part the diminishing role of schools in extracurricular activities. School boards facing tight budgets may be forced to cut dedicated gym and music teachers, leaving athletic and arts programs starving for staff and funding. It also reflects changing middle- and upper-class expectations concerning extracurricular

Quick Hits

Minor Hockey, Major Cash

The cost of outfitting a child for hockey in 2017 depends on what level the child is at, where you shop, and how much you're willing to pay. Below are two extremes based on the new equipment a 10-year-old might typically wear to play forward or defence (goalie equipment is even more expensive).

	Department Store	Speciality Store
helmet	$44.99	$219.99
cage/mask	34.99	39.99
mouth guard	19.99	29.99
neck guard	18.99	44.99
long underwear	58.99	138.99
shoulder pads	49.99	159.99
elbow pads	27.99	74.99
gloves	44.99	119.99
pants	64.99	209.99
jockstrap/jill	39.99	44.99
shin pads	37.99	84.99
skates	64.99	699.99
skate guards	8.99	12.99
stick	(wood) 19.99	(composite) 249.00
hockey bag	49.00	79.00
TOTAL	**$586.86**	**$2,209.87**

Other basic costs

- average registration for boys' or girls' house league: $650
- average registration for boys' or girls' competitive league: $2,500–$3,000
- ice time for extra practices
- power-skating lessons
- summer hockey schools
- gas, food, and accommodations for "away" games and out-of-town tournaments
- skate sharpening

Why gear is dear

- **Long shopping list.** No other team sport requires as much gear.
- **Small market.** The number of hockey players worldwide is relatively small compared to players of soccer, baseball, and basketball, so hockey equipment is not mass produced on the same scale as athletic shoes or baseball gloves, which affects pricing.
- **NHL influence.** For kids, the peer group isn't as important as the professionals, which means they are drawn to the most expensive products on the shelves.

Source: Ormsby, 2007; Rutherford, 2009.

What do YOU think?

1. Do you think that hockey in Canada can still be seen as a mobility sport or has it become solely an elitist sport? What arguments can be made for the two different positions?
2. How could you conduct a sociological study to determine which position is more true?
3. Do you think that banning expensive composite sticks for players under 12 would make hockey more of an access sport?

activities, as parents indulge in the dream that, with sufficient funds, their children may one day become highly paid professionals. Many lower-class families cannot afford the same experience for their children, giving middle- and upper-class families a distinct advantage and making various sports—hockey in this case—much less of a mobility sport.

Class Reductionism

Class reductionism occurs when a sociologist studying a situation attributes all forms of oppression to class, downplaying the impact of "race," ethnicity, gender, age, and sexual orientation. Social scientists in the former Soviet Union were guilty of class reductionism when they justified Russian oppression of Indigenous people in Siberia in the name of class revolution against the indigenous bourgeoisie. In the pre-industrial world of these peoples, there was no bourgeoisie. There were usually just herders who had more or fewer animals (yaks, camels, horses, etc.). Calling those with more animals the "bourgeoisie" and using that as a justification for trying to get rid of private ownership of livestock was a serious distortion of Marx's analysis, and a good example of class reductionism.

Albert Memmi, one of the founders of anti-colonialism theory, argued against class reductionism in colonial studies in his classic work *The Colonizer and the Colonized* (1957):

> To observe the life of the colonizer and the colonized is to discover rapidly that the daily humiliations of the colonized, his objective subjugation, are not merely economic. Even the poorest colonizer thought himself to be—and actually was—superior to the colonized. This too was part of colonial privilege. The Marxist discovery of the importance of the economy in all oppressive relationships is not to the point. This relationship has other characteristics which I believe I have discovered in the colonial relationship. (Memmi, [1957]/1991: p. xii)

The failings of class reductionism are shared by anyone who reduces oppression to a single factor or fails to examine all relevant factors. This includes paying insufficient attention to the voices of the people affected. Edgar Dosman, in a study of Indigenous people in Saskatoon carried out in 1968–9, rarely included Indigenous voices. When he did, it was usually to criticize a comment or the individual quoted. He stressed the significance of class divisions over the unifying experience of "race" among urban Indigenous people, misleadingly dividing them into categories he labelled "aristocracy," "bourgeoisie," and "welfare and anomic." In so doing, he disqualified the leaders in the urban Indigenous community from legitimately articulating a position worthy of sociological consideration.

Dosman criticized two contemporary Indigenous leaders: Métis academic Howard Adams and Cree politician Harold Cardinal, two authors of influential works published around the time of Dosman's study (Adams in 1975 and Cardinal in 1969 and 1977). Dosman described Adams's work as being "too flowery and intellectual for the native people" (Dosman, 1972: p. 162). He formed this opinion without asking Indigenous people of all "classes" what they thought of Adams (a well-respected figure in First Nations circles). In the same study he dismissed a comment of Cardinal's with the terse remark, "What, however, does that mean in the real world?" (Dosman, 1972: p. 183). He was not prepared to respect Cardinal's standpoint.

Social Stratification: An Alternative Approach to Social Inequality

The class structure that Marx introduced remains a useful way to talk about social inequality, but it is imprecise. For example, many North Americans identify as middle-class, which makes sense: no matter how comfortable you are, there will always be others with more and less than what you have, and what you have never seems like enough—that puts you in the middle, right? Politicians exploit this when they pledge to help the middle class: most voters see themselves as likely beneficiaries of those promises.

The trouble comes when we try to define what it means to be middle-class. Definitions vary so much that it can be hard to know who belongs. Does it have to do with what you own or what you earn? Is it more nuanced than that? A CBC article from 2015 quotes Scott Brison, federal member of Parliament and, at the time, finance critic for the Liberal Party, as saying the middle class includes "the broadest swath of

Canadians whose working income gives them the capacity to provide decent housing, quality of life, and a good education for their families, while saving for retirement" (Blatchford, 2015). But how do we define "decent"? Wouldn't it be better if we could *quantify*, or measure, what it means to be middle-class?

That brings us to social stratification. When we talk about social stratification, we're borrowing a geological term to describe society as though it were divided into a series of layers. In geology, a stratum is a single level or layer of rock made up of tiny particles deposited together; if you look at a cross-section of sedimentary rock, you will be able to see the different strata and note the differences.

In sociology, a stratum is a level to which people belong depending on their social status, education, or income. It's usually each of a number of equal groups into which a population has been divided for comparison. Strata are used as units of analysis in stratified sampling, an approach to statistical research in which a sample is drawn from each stratum or level of the population rather than drawn at random from the whole population. This produces a more representative sample for analysis.

Most studies of social stratification in Canada divide the population into quintiles for analysis. A quintile is one of five equal groups into which a population is divided according to the distribution of values of a particular variable; each one represents 20 per cent of the population. Let's say that we wanted to divide the population into quintiles according to household (family) income. Grattan (2003) offers a good explanation of how we arrive at our quintiles:

Imagine that all families are placed in a line, a family's place being determined by its income level. The poorest family is placed at the front of the line, followed by the next poorest, and so on, until the last family, with the highest income, is placed at the end. Next, the line is split into five equal groups. The first group, or quintile, is composed of the first 20 per cent of the line. Obviously, this group will consist of the poorest people. The next group consists of the next 20 per cent. A similar process occurs in selecting the third, fourth, and fifth groups. The fifth group, of course, comprises those families with the highest incomes. (Grattan, 2003: pp. 64–5)

Figure 7.1 shows what you would find if you conducted that very procedure using Canadian families and their 2013 household incomes. This gives us a basis for our definition of "middle-class." We could define it narrowly as any family in the middle quintile—meaning the middle 20 per cent of Canadians—or more broadly as any family in the middle three quintiles, representing 60 per cent of Canadian families. Politicians prefer the latter of these two definitions, which gives them the largest group of "middle-class voters" to pitch their promises to. But consider this: is it realistic to treat the middle three quintiles as a single group when their household incomes range from a meagre $38,750 all the way to $125,000?

Quintiles are useful for comparative purposes, both across time periods and across countries. Table 7.1 divides the populations of five countries into quintiles. Each quintile represents 20 per cent of the county's population. For each country, the table shows what percentage of the national income is earned by the members of each quintile. For instance, if we look at Canada, we can see that the middle 20 per cent of the population—the third quintile—earned 17.2 per cent of the total after-tax income earned by all Canadian families in 2000; that's down from 19.0 per cent a decade earlier.

Keep in mind that if the total income for all families were distributed equally, each of the five quintiles would earn 20 per cent of the country's total income. Because income is not distributed

Quintile	Household Income Range
Top 20%	$125,010 and above
Upper-middle 20%	$88,075 to $125,009
Middle 20%	$61,929 to $88,074
Lower-middle 20%	$38,755 to $61,928
Bottom 20%	$0 to $38,754

Figure 7.1 Stratification of Canadian Households[a] by Income, 2013[b]

[a] Estimates for 2013 were compiled by *MoneySense* magazine based on Statistics Canada 2011 data.
[b] A household is any family of two or more people.
Source: Data from Hodges & Brown, 2015.

equally, the highest quintile will always have the highest share of income, well above 20 per cent; the lowest quintile will always have the smallest share of income, well below 20 per cent. The narrower the gap between the highest and lowest quintiles, the greater the equality. So, another way of calculating income inequality involves the ratio between the top and bottom quintiles. In 1990, Canada's top quintile earned 34.8 per cent of all income, while the bottom quintile earned 7.7 per cent. The ratio is 34.8 to 7.7 or 4.52 to 1. Figure 7.2 shows the ratios between high and low quintile in each country for all three years. Remember: the lower the number, the greater the equality.

Table 7.1	Distribution of After-Tax Income by Quintile for Five Western Countries, 1990–2000					
		1st (lowest)	**2nd**	**3rd**	**4th**	**5th (highest)**
Canada	1990	7.7%	**13.7%**	**19.0%**	**24.8%**	34.8%
	1995	7.5	12.9	17.3	23.0	39.2
	2000	7.2	12.7	17.2	23.0	39.9
France	1990	7.3%	12.7%	17.1%	22.7%	40.2%
	1995	8.0	13.0	17.0	23.0	38.0
	2000	9.0	13.0	17.0	23.0	37.0
Netherlands	1990	7.9%	13.6%	18.1	23.6	36.8
	1995	8.5	13.6	17.8	23.1	36.8
	2000	**9.4**	14.6	17.3	23.1	36.2
Great Britain	1990	7.6%	12.2%	16.8%	22.8%	40.7%
	1995	7.4	12.3	16.6	22.7	41.3
	2000	7.7	12.5	16.6	22.4	41.2
United States	1990	3.9%	9.6%	15.9%	24.0	46.6%
	1995	3.7	9.1	15.2	23.3	48.7
	2000	3.6	8.9	14.9	23.0	**49.6**

Note: **Bold** is used to denote the highest figure in each column; *italics* are used to denote the lowest figure in each column.

Source: Ortiz & Cummins, 2011, Annex 2.

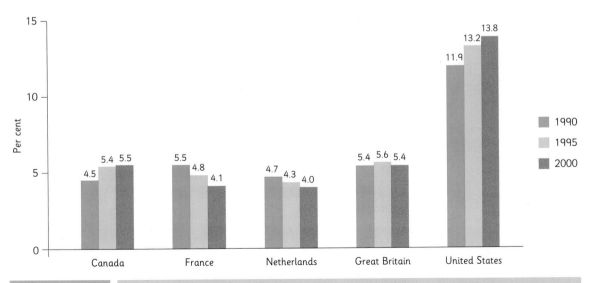

| Figure 7.2 | Measuring Income Inequality for Five Countries Using the Ratio of Highest to Lowest Quintiles, 1990–2000 |

Figure 7.2 shows us several things:

1) The United States began and ended the decade with the least income equality.
2) France showed the greatest improvement in income equality over the decade, but by 2000, income equality was greatest in the Netherlands.
3) Canada had the greatest income equality of the five countries in 1990 but developed less equality during the 10-year period, with the lowest three figures all going down and the top quintile going up.

In 2011, the ratio between the highest and lowest income quintiles in Canada was nearly the same (5.4 per cent) as it was in 2000 (5.5 per cent). Table 7.2 shows the 2011 distribution of after-tax income by quintile for all provinces. See if you can predict, based on the data, which provinces will have the greatest and least income equality. You can confirm your prediction by referring to Figure 7.3, which shows the high-to-low quintile ratios for Canada and the 10 provinces, in order of highest to lowest equality.

Let's return to our question about Canada's middle class. Table 7.3 shows that the gap in after-tax

Table 7.2	Distribution of After-Tax Income by Quintile for Canada and Provinces, 2011				
	1st (lowest)	2nd	3rd	4th	5th
CANADA	7.3	12.5	17.2	23.3	39.7
British Columbia	6.9	12.5	17.6	23.8	39.2
Alberta	7.4	12.2	16.8	22.4	**41.2**
Saskatchewan	7.5	13.0	**18.0**	23.8	37.7
Manitoba	8.0	13.2	17.8	23.4	37.6
Ontario	7.2	12.5	17.2	23.5	39.6
Quebec	8.0	13.0	17.4	23.3	38.2
New Brunswick	7.9	13.1	17.7	23.7	37.6
Nova Scotia	**8.2**	**13.3**	17.9	23.8	36.6
Prince Edward Island	7.9	12.9	17.7	23.6	38.0
Newfoundland and Labrador	7.4	*11.9*	16.5	**23.9**	40.2

Note: **Bold** is used to denote the highest figure in each column; *italics* are used to denote the lowest figure in each column.

Source: Statistics Canada CANSIM Table 202-0703, www5.statcan.gc.ca/cansim/a47

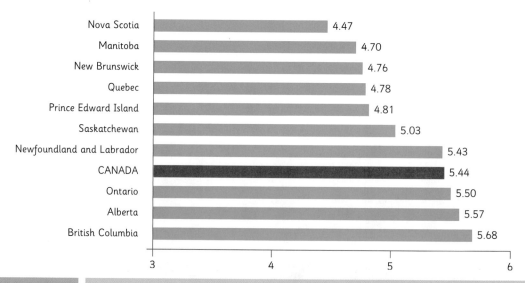

Figure 7.3	Income Inequality, Canada and Provinces, Using the Ratio of Highest to Lowest After-Tax Income Quintiles, 2011

Table 7.3	Change in Total After-Tax Income, Highest, Middle, and Lowest Quintiles, 1996–2011				
	Difference from Highest Quintile ($)				**Increase in After-Tax Income 1996–2011 (%)**
	1996	**2001**	**2006**	**2011**	
Highest quintile	—	—	—	—	37.9
Middle quintile	60,700	79,400	82,400	89,500	27.1
Lowest quintile	92,600	115,300	119,600	128,700	33.3

Source: Statistics Canada CANSIM Table 202-0703, www5.statcan.gc.ca/cansim/a47.

income between the highest-earning 20 per cent of families and the middle 20 per cent of families is growing. (The gap between the highest and lowest quintiles is growing even more.) Moreover, between 1996 and 2011, the average income for the middle quintile grew by just 27.1 per cent compared to 37.9 per cent for the highest quintile. Average income in the lowest quintile grew by 33.3 per cent, a better growth rate than that of the middle quintile but not enough to keep pace with Canada's highest earners.

What do YOU think?

Based on the data presented in Table 7.3, how would you describe the health of Canada's middle class? Was it better off or worse off in 2011 than it was in 1996?

Ideology: Explaining Social Inequality

Dominant Ideology and Counter-Ideology

When political economists write and speak about social inequality, their arguments and ideas are typically shaped by their ideology. An ideology is a set of beliefs about society and the people in it, usually forming the basis of a particular economic or political theory. A dominant ideology is the set of beliefs put forward by, and generally supportive of, society's dominant culture and/or classes. In Marxist terms, it reflects the class consciousness of the ruling class and is used to defend or justify the status quo. The trickle-down theory is a dominant ideology in North America. It states that if you allow the rich the freedom to generate wealth, others in society will benefit: new jobs will be created, more money will

be spent on consumer goods, and a good part of the generated wealth will eventually find its way into the hands of members of the middle and lower classes. American author and historian William Blum described it as "the principle that the poor, who must subsist on table scraps dropped by the rich, can best be served by giving the rich bigger meals" (Blum, 2003: p. 20). As a dominant ideology, trickle-down economic theory is used to justify policies that favour wealthy business owners. These policies include government subsidies for certain industries and low corporate taxes and other incentives for businesses that promise to "invest" in Canada by setting up offices and factories here. Canada has greater subsidies and lower corporate taxes than do the less trickle-down–based economies of Norway and Iceland.

A counter-ideology is one that offers a critique of the dominant ideology, challenging its justice and its universal applicability to society. People promoting a counter-ideology are typically looking to create significant social change. Classical Marxism, which predicted the overthrow of the capitalist classes by the proletariat, is an obvious example of a counter-ideology. The Occupy movement, though it did not have a well-defined set of objectives, is another example. Its basic premise, that 99 per cent of the world's wealth is concentrated in the hands of 1 per cent of the world's population and must be subject to greater taxes in order to be distributed more equitably, challenged the dominant ideology of trickle-down theory. The 2011–12 Montreal student protests represented a counter-ideology. The largest student group, CLASSE, demanded that universities cut research programs (which, they argued, benefited private interests) and advertising with an aim to making college and university tuition-free (Bruemmer & Dougherty, 2012). A counter-ideology is developing among contemporary Indigenous

Our Stories

Early Studies in Canadian Social Stratification

Sociology in Canada began as the study of social stratification. This can be seen through examining the work of two Canadian sociology pioneers: Herbert Brown Ames and Colin McKay.

Herbert Brown Ames:
A Businessman's Sociology

During the last half of the nineteenth century, the population of Montreal grew fourfold to over 270,000. With this growth came social problems—poverty, unemployment, homelessness. This led **Herbert Brown Ames** (1863–1954) to engage in Canada's first comprehensive urban sociological study, designed to promote the construction of affordable housing for the working-class people of Montreal's west end.

Ames had inherited a prosperous business that guaranteed him a lifetime of financial stability. But he wanted more than to earn easy money. He wanted to improve the city of his birth. He became involved in municipal and federal politics, and he engaged in ambitious sociological research. In 1896, he and his research team went door to door to canvass the inhabitants of an area he called "the city below the hill." The study was very detailed. Ames's fascination with statistics is sometimes overwhelming. At the time of the study his approach was unique. He was possibly the first person in Canada to speak of family size not in round numbers but with decimals, saying the average size of families he studied was "4.90 people," 1.41 of whom worked for wages and 1.64 being children under 16. He was keenly aware that this level of precision was key to achieving the most suitable remedy for the housing problem:

> Should the time come when capital shall be ready to be invested in the erection of improved industrial dwellings, it is evident that for its intelligent expenditure, in this or that locality, definite knowledge must be in hand as to the personnel and composition of the average family of the section selected. The number and size of the rooms to be provided, in the improved dwelling for the average family, will depend not only upon the size of the family, but also upon its composition, since the larger the proportion of the adult or school-child element the more the amount of space and air that will need to be allowed.
>
> To make a success of this work of improvement we can afford to allow no facts to be overlooked. (Ames, [1897]/1972: p. 30)

Ames's plan was to have old, inadequate housing torn down, and have business leaders finance construction of new housing. He led by example, bankrolling the construction of model apartments for 39 families. Unfortunately, but predictably, others refused to follow his lead.

We can argue that Ames was naive. We can be amused by the powerful rhetoric he invoked to declare his determination to get rid of the 5,800 outhouses he reckoned there were in the city ("That the privy pit is a danger to public health and morals needs no demonstration, and yet in 'the city below the hill' *more than half the households* are dependent entirely upon such accommodation" [Ames, [1897]/1972: p. 45]). But we must admire Ames for his concern for the lives of the working class.

Colin McKay: A Worker's Sociology

Nova Scotian **Colin McKay** (1876–1939) was described by Ian McKay (an unrelated namesake) as "a working-class intellectual who exemplified a widespread enthusiasm for radical sociology in turn-of-the-century Canada," and who, "drawing upon theories of Karl Marx and Herbert Spencer, . . . developed [his] own critical understanding of capitalist development" (I. McKay, 1998: p. 390). Colin McKay was a self-educated man, who worked as a merchant seaman, soldier, labour organizer, and journalist. At 24, he spent a short time in jail for "defaming the reputation of a cigar factory proprietor notorious for mistreating children [workers] and discriminating against trade unionists" (I. McKay, 1998: p. 401).

McKay was a prodigious writer, contributing at least 952 articles and letters-to-the-editor to union publications such as the *Canadian Railway Employees Monthly*, the *Canadian Unionist, Eastern Labor News, Butler's Journal, Cotton's Weekly, Le Monde Ouvrier, Citizen and Country*, and *Western Clarion*. The scope of his work is revealed in a few selected titles:

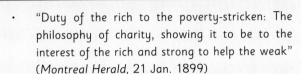

- "Duty of the rich to the poverty-stricken: The philosophy of charity, showing it to be to the interest of the rich and strong to help the weak" (*Montreal Herald*, 21 Jan. 1899)
- "The small business man. How the capitalist system annihilates self-earned private property and reduces the small business man to the economic category of the worker" (*Eastern Labor News*, 8 June 1912)
- "The crime of low wages" (*Labor World / Le Monde Ouvrier*, 18 April 1925).

As part of a vigorous working-class press with considerable influence, Colin McKay was widely acknowledged as one of Canadian labour's leading intellectuals. It is likely that McKay's writings . . . in the 1930s were reaching thousands of working-class readers in at least four major journals. . . . (I. McKay, 1998: p. 415)

Ian McKay suggests that with the death of Colin McKay and the greater institutionalization (or departmentalization) of sociology, there was loss as well as gain. The drive of well-read working-class radicals such as McKay is sorely missed in assisting the efforts of Canadian sociologists to make a difference in the social inequality of their country.

© McCord Museum

In the early twentieth century, the more successful members of Montreal's working class moved to new homes in the suburbs, leaving poorer citizens to take up residence in abandoned houses like this one. Can you see why Ames was concerned about living conditions in "the city below the hill"?

© Brian Jungen and Cattriona Jeffries Gallery

Prototype for New Understanding #23 (2005), by Vancouver Indigenous artist Brian Jungen. What do you think the message of this artwork is? What ideology could it be critiquing?

people in Canada, who are drawing on traditional values and who are critical of the capitalist/materialist society that has oppressed them. The social change they are promoting may be taking place within the Indigenous community, but it is not without influence in mainstream society also.

Liberal Ideology

Liberal ideology is a dominant ideology that views the individual as a more or less independent player on the sociological scene. It reflects a belief in a great deal of social mobility—the ability of individuals to move (generally upward) from one class, or stratum, to another—and minimizes criticism of social inequality. According to liberal ideology, people who are successful are so because they have justly earned that success and not because they have benefited

from the social privileges of "race," ethnicity, class, or gender. The American dream—the belief that anyone can "make it" if he or she is willing to work really hard for it—reflects liberal ideology. Failure to achieve the American dream (resulting in the "American nightmare" of poverty) is likewise placed solely on the individual. William Ryan referred to this as blaming the victim, assigning individuals more or less complete responsibility for events or circumstances that have broader social causes, such as the quality of a person's upbringing and education or a lack of the resources and social connections that help a person secure a well-paying job. Other examples of blaming the victim include the following arguments:

- People become alcoholics because they lack willpower; no biological factors of genetic predisposition or sociological factors of racial or ethnic stereotypes or systematic oppression need be considered.

- People receiving employment insurance are on welfare because they don't have a strong work ethic, not because they come from poor families with the odds of success stacked against them.
- Criminals offend and reoffend because they have a "criminal mind," not because "the street" offered them the best chance to escape a socioeconomically disadvantaged position.

C. Wright Mills critiqued American liberal ideology in two influential studies of the middle and upper classes, *White Collar* (1951) and *The Power Elite* (1956). The excerpt below, from the former book, contains some of that criticism as he discusses how the upper class perpetuates its own power:

The recent social history of American capitalism does not reveal any distinct break in the continuity of the higher capitalist class.... [I]n the economy as in the political order, there has been a remarkable continuity of interests, vested in the types of higher economic men who guard and advance them. The main drift of the upper classes, composed of several consistent trends, points unambiguously to the continuation of a world that is quite congenial to the continuation of the corporate rich....

The propertied class, in the age of corporate property, has become a corporate rich, and in becoming corporate has consolidated its power.... Its members have become self-conscious in terms of the corporate world they represent. As men of status they have secured their privileges and prerogatives in the most stable private institutions of American society. They are a corporate rich because they depend directly, as well as indirectly, for their money, their privileges, their securities, their advantages, their powers on the world of the big corporations. (Quoted in Horowitz, 1971: pp. 82–3)

Hegemony

Antonio Gramsci (1891–1937) was a critic of the dominant ideology. The Italian-born political theorist and activist was a co-founder and leader of the Italian Communist party and an opponent of Fascist dictator Benito Mussolini. Jailed in November 1926, he remained a political prisoner for nearly 10 years. During that time he developed the concept of hegemony.

Gramsci used hegemony to mean non-coercive methods of maintaining power. He believed that the ruling classes relied on something more than their military and police forces to keep society running smoothly while quietly oppressing the masses. In her study of Gramsci, Kate Crehan defines hegemony as all the ways by which "the power relations underpinning various forms of inequality are produced and reproduced" (Crehan, 2002: p. 104).

Hegemony can take many forms. It is expressed in the reproduction and celebration of the idea that the path to prosperity is available to everyone equally, and that inequality exists not because of problems in "the system" but because some people are willing to work harder than others. Hegemony can also be seen in the rampant materialism of people waiting in long lines for the latest iPhone or other tech gadget considered a must for those who want to keep up with changing trends.

Recalling the case of Attawapiskat, we can consider then prime minister Stephen Harper's response as an instance of hegemony. He sent in an auditor to examine the community's finances. He thereby shifted blame *onto* the people and the handling of their money by the chief and council, and *off of* the inadequate measures taken by the federal and provincial governments and the exploitative practices of the powerful mining company. That exercise of hegemony worked, as the government managed to avoid any serious backlash for failing to avert a crisis that had been building for years.

Even an introductory sociology textbook could become an instrument of hegemony. Say its author portrayed Canadian society as though there were no destructive social splits based on "race," ethnicity, gender, ability, and class—in other words, as though there were none of the social divisions that create and sustain social inequality. In this sense the textbook would be playing a part in maintaining the power of the ruling classes by suggesting that there were no problems of social inequality that needed to be addressed.

Poverty and Excess: The Real Effects of Social Inequality

So far in this chapter we have looked at how social inequality is talked about by theorists, how it is measured by economists, and how it is sometimes explained or justified by policy-makers. In the final section of this chapter we will look at some of the ways social inequality affects society.

Canada's Haves and Have-Nots: The Extremes of the Social Inequality Spectrum

Studying social inequality is often about looking at the extremes. In this section we'll take a broader look at extremes of social inequality by looking first at food bank use and then at the contrast between the top 100 earners and where they stand in relation to the average Canadian earner.

Food Banks

Changing Rates of Food Bank Use

One indicator of the social inequality that exists in Canada comes from statistics concerning the

---

Quick Hits

"Jobs Increase by 12,000"—But Look beyond the Headlines

In October 2015, various media outlets reported the latest Statistics Canada job figures showing that in the month of September, the number of jobs in Canada increased by 12,000. It sounded like good news. However, you would have been misled by this if you hadn't read the whole article or seen the whole report on television. Here are the relevant statistics for your appraisal of the situation:

- **full-time jobs:** dropped by 62,000
- **part-time jobs:** increased by 74,000
- **self-employed jobs:** increased by 31,000
- **public-sector jobs:** decreased by 29,000
- **private-sector jobs:** increased by 16,000
- **unemployment rate:** increased by 0.1% to 7.1%.

What do YOU think?

1. How is the 12,000 statistic true but misleading?
2. What does the increase in self-employed jobs tell you? Is it a positive or negative change (or a bit of both)?
3. Why would it be useful to compare the statistics for this September with data for other Septembers?

use of food banks. A food bank, as defined by the Canadian Association of Food Banks (now Food Banks Canada) is a "central warehouse or clearing house, registered as a non-profit organization for the purpose of collecting, storing and distributing food, free of charge, directly or through front line agencies which may also provide meals to the hungry" (Food Banks Canada, 2004). Food Banks Canada is a national charitable organization that supports provincial agencies and community groups dedicated to fighting hunger. Each year the organization issues *HungerCount*, a report on national food bank use. The statistics presented in the report are generated from a survey distributed annually in March to food banks across the country, so *HungerCount* provides a good snapshot of food bank use that can be tracked from year to year, serving as an indicator of how Canada's neediest citizens are faring. Note that *HungerCount* covers just one aspect of efforts to relieve hunger in Canada: it does not include the efforts of other free food providers such as soup kitchens, shelters, and breakfast programs for schoolchildren.

In March 2015, food banks in Canada helped 852,137 people. That figure is 26 per cent higher than the total in March 2008, when 675,735 received help from food banks (Food Banks Canada, 2015). When considering that dramatic increase, it is important to keep in mind that graphs of statistics seldom rise or fall in a straight line; they will typically do both over a significant period of time. We need to look at what happened over that seven-year interval to produce a 26 per cent increase in food bank use.

In 2009, a short recession began in North America, which caused an increase in food bank use all over the country. In 2010, Alberta and Ontario had more people visit food banks than ever before: 59,311 Albertans and 402,056 Ontarians received help from food banks in 2010; however, by 2014, those figures had fallen to 49,766 and 374,698, respectively.

The peak year for food bank use in Canada was 2012, when 872,379 individuals visited food banks in March; that figure is 20,000 more than the number of people who used food banks in March 2015 (Food Banks Canada, 2015). But from 2013 to 2014, four provinces—Ontario, New Brunswick, Nova Scotia, and PEI—saw their number of March food bank visitors drop. Ontario, New Brunswick, and PEI, joined by Saskatchewan and Newfoundland and Labrador, saw additional declines in food bank use

from 2014 to 2015. In fact, only one province saw its number of food bank visitors increase by more than 4.0 per cent from March 2014 to March 2015: Alberta experienced a whopping 23.4 per cent increase in the number of people served by food banks from 2014 to 2015 (Food Banks Canada, 2015). This can be largely attributed to a sudden drop in oil prices in mid-2014, which caused a downturn in the economy, leading to a loss of employment for many who made their living in the province's oil and gas industry.

All of this is to say that the number of food bank visitors in Canada varies from year to year and from province to province, and it is important to look at the factors, many of them regional, that produce these fluctuations. Overall, there is no denying that food bank use in Canada is on the rise. I will leave you with a final statistic to consider: in 2014, the number of first-time food bank users was 87,533—that is more than 10 per cent of all food bank visitors. This is one reason to believe the increased need for food banks will continue over the long term, unless something changes drastically.

What do YOU think?

1. As you have just seen, you could arrive at very different impressions by looking at changing rates of food bank use from 2012 to 2015 versus 2008 to 2015. If you were a sociologist critical of the federal government, which set of data would you use? What if you were a cabinet minister of the federal government or a sociologist working for the conservative Fraser Institute?
2. In 2014, just before Thanksgiving, Walmart Canada had their first national food drive, in which customers could donate some of the food they had just bought to help the needy. According to an online report (Simon, 2014), a good number of Walmart employees in the United States have to resort to food banks, so we expect that this fact is also true in Canada. Do you think it is reasonable to say that Walmart was enlisting the aid of their customers in supporting their low-paid workers? What should they do?

Who Uses Food Banks?

Who do you think the typical food bank user is? Some of the details might surprise you. First, just

4.4 per cent of food bank users are homeless, a category that includes those living temporarily with family or friends. Roughly 66.5 per cent of them pay market rent, while 22 per cent live in subsidized housing. The remaining 7 per cent own their own homes (Food Banks Canada, 2015: p. 17).

Looking at household structure, close to 55 per cent of food bank users were families, whether single-parent families (22.9 per cent), two-parent families (20.6 per cent), or couples without children (10.9 per cent). The remaining 45.6 per cent of food bank visitors were single people. Children (under 18) make up nearly 36 per cent of those helped by food banks, while seniors (65 and over) make up 5 per cent (Food Banks Canada, 2015: p. 17).

Principal sources of income for these households, in decreasing order, were social assistance (46.3 per cent), disability-related income (18.3 per cent), current or recent work (11.6 per cent), pensions (7.1 per cent), and employment insurance (4.0 per

The Point Is...

Detroit: The Black Face of Poverty in the United States

Detroit has long been the poster city for urban poverty in the United States. There are several reasons for the homelessness and derelict housing that characterize the city's downtown. One is the decline of the automotive industry. The birthplace of the Ford Motor Company and the Model-T, Detroit was so synonymous with car and truck manufacturing that it earned the nickname Motor City. It was also home to a flourishing music scene that launched the careers of Diana Ross, Stevie Wonder, Marvin Gaye, Smokey Robinson,

Table 7.4	Motor City Math: A Reversal of Fortune		
	1970	**2015**	**Change (Percentage)**
City Population	1,500,000	677,116	–815,201 (–54%)
Jobs	735,000	346,500	–388,500 (–54%)
Since 1972 . . .			
Decline in manufacturing	80%		
Decline in retail establishments	78%		
Debt obligations at 2013 filing	$18 billion		
Abandoned structures	78,000		

Sources: *Toronto Star*, December 13, 2014, IN3, from *Detroit: A Biography*, Scott Martelle, and *Detroit City is the Place to Be: The Afterlife of an American Metropolis*, Bloomberg Brief, *Washington Post*.

Table 7.5	Black and White in Detroit, Michigan, and the United States		
	Detroit	**Michigan**	**United States**
White population (2010)	10.6%	78.9%	72.4%
Black population (2010)	82.7%	14.2%	12.6%
Per capita income (2009–14)	$14,984	$26,143	$28,555
Median household income (2009–14)	$26,095	$49,087	$53,482
Percentage of population in poverty	39.8%	16.2%	14.8%

Sources: United States Census Bureau, Quick Facts, http://quickfacts.census.gov/qfd/states/26/2622000.html.

cent) (Food Banks Canada, 2015: p. 17). The "Other" category (12.7 per cent) likely includes spousal support payments and student loans.

For their 2011 report, Food Banks Canada surveyed users on other variables that gave some insight into the social location of food bank users. There was relative gender balance among food bank users, 47 per cent of whom were women, compared with the 53 per cent who were men. In terms of ethnicity, 10 per cent of users self-identified as First Nation, Métis, or Inuit, slightly less than the 11 per cent who were recent immigrants or refugees (their numbers rose to 18.5 per cent in large cities). Then there were the college and university students: 4 per cent.

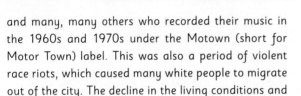

What do YOU think?

Do you think that use of food banks will increase or decrease significantly in the future?

and many, many others who recorded their music in the 1960s and 1970s under the Motown (short for Motor Town) label. This was also a period of violent race riots, which caused many white people to migrate out of the city. The decline in the living conditions and earnings of the people since that time is well documented. In 2013, the city filed for bankruptcy.

A study of social inequality in Detroit warrants an intersectional approach that considers both class and "race." It is both one of the blackest and one of the poorest big cities in the United States. The tables below look at the figures for Detroit, Michigan, and the United States generally.

Robin Buckson/Detroit News via AP

Students from Westside Christian Academy serve the homeless at Mount Lebanon Strathmoor Church in Detroit. Why do you think so many black people remained in Detroit's downtown as white people were moving into the city's suburbs and beyond?

Canada's "1 per cent"

In the fall of 2011, protesters in cities around the world joined the Occupy movement to draw attention to the fact that 1 per cent of the world's population controlled 99 per cent of the world's wealth. Does the ratio apply in Canada?

On 3 January 2012, Canadians beginning their work year learned that by noon that day, each of the top 100 chief executive officers (CEOs) in Canada had already earned as much as the average Canadian would make in an entire year ("Canada's Top CEOs", 2012). The report, prepared by the non-profit Canadian Centre for Policy Alternatives, was based on figures from 2010, when the average Canadian was earning $44,300 per year, while the average annual salary for the top 100 CEOs was $8.4 million. These CEOs include the heads of well-known companies including Canadian Tire, Rona, Air Canada, Loblaws, Rogers, Shaw, Telus, and Cineplex (no wonder the popcorn is so expensive) as well as a significant number of oil and mining companies and the "big six" banks.

Reports like this are meant to shock us by sensationalizing a situation we all know exists. Issued in the early days of the calendar year—a notoriously slow time for news—they play well in the media. As students of sociology, we have to look at the statistics critically. Here, then, is some context. The figure cited as the average salary of the top 100 Canadian CEOs in 2010—$8.4 million—represents an increase of 27 per cent over the previous year, while the average Canadian salary went up by 1.1 per cent from 2009 to 2010 (Flavelle, 2012). Another way of looking at the situation: the highest salary of a Canadian CEO in 2010 was 189 times that of the average wage earner in 2010. Compare this with the situation in 1998, when the best-paid CEO made 105 times what the average Canadian earned, and in 1995, when the wealthiest CEO's salary was 85 times that of the average Canadian (Flavelle, 2012). This suggests that social inequality in Canada is growing, not diminishing.

Social Inequality and Education

Participation Rates

Postsecondary education can be a major avenue of social mobility, offering people from lower-class

---

Quick Hits

A Living Wage

Social activists and sociologists who study poverty often argue about the need for what they call a **living wage**. It is a vague term, but it generally represents a target above the existing minimum wage, which is considered too low for the "working poor" to live on. People paid minimum wage often have to use food banks, especially if they can find only part-time work and if they are supporting or helping to support a family. You could safely say that anyone using a food bank is not paid a living wage.

As a sociologist in training, how would you calculate a living wage? The Vancouver-based Living Wage for Families Campaign uses the Market Basket Measure, which we examined in Chapter 2. As you'll recall, the MBM is based on the cost of a standard set of goods required to support an individual or family, and it is adjusted to account for regional variations in the cost of housing, food, and other necessities. A visit to the organization's website (www.livingwageforfamilies. ca) provides living wages for 21 municipalities in southern BC and Vancouver Island. Vancouver and Victoria have among the highest hourly living wages ($20.64/hr and $20.02/hr, respectively), because of the high cost of rent in BC's two largest metropolitan centres. However, the highest living wage is in the small city of Powell River ($21.30), where the scarcity of affordable child care makes the cost of living greater.

As of September 2016, the minimum wage in BC is $10.85. It is set to rise to $11.25 in September 2017. If you are a migrant worker employed by one of BC's many farms, your pay is based on what you can harvest by hand, ranging from 16.3¢ per pound for Brussels sprouts to 39.6¢ per pound for blueberries (plus they taste better). According to the Living Wage for Families Campaign, the lowest living wage in the province is $16.28 in the Fraser Valley.

families the opportunity to secure jobs paying middle- or upper-class salaries. But if postsecondary education becomes so expensive that low-income students either cannot attend college or university or leave because of crippling student debt, then this avenue for mobility is blocked.

In Canada, college tuition costs less and is therefore more accessible than university education. Look at the figures in Table 7.6. Do you think the data point to something of a class system in postsecondary education?

Tuition Fees and University Education

Tuition fees for university education rose significantly during the 1990s, and have continued to climb, albeit less dramatically, since the start of the twenty-first century. Consider that the average undergraduate tuition fee in Canada has increased from $4,400 in the 2006–7 academic year to $6,191 in 2015–16, an increase of 40 per cent (Statistics Canada CANSIM

Table 477-0077). Students in Ontario (53 per cent), Saskatchewan (44 per cent), and Quebec (45 per cent) have faced the steepest tuition increase over that period, although Quebec's tuitions remain among the lowest in Canada. A drop in federal and provincial funding for postsecondary education has been a major factor contributing to the increase.

There are significant regional differences in tuition costs for both undergraduate and graduate students (see Figure 7.4). Ontario has the highest average tuition costs, at $7,868 for undergraduate students and $8,971 for graduate students. This should not be surprising as Ontario's provincial government spends less per postsecondary student than any other province. New Brunswick, Nova Scotia, and Saskatchewan are other provinces with undergraduate tuition fees above the Canadian average, while higher-than-average graduate fees are charged in Nova Scotia and British Columbia. The lowest tuitions, for both graduate and undergraduate

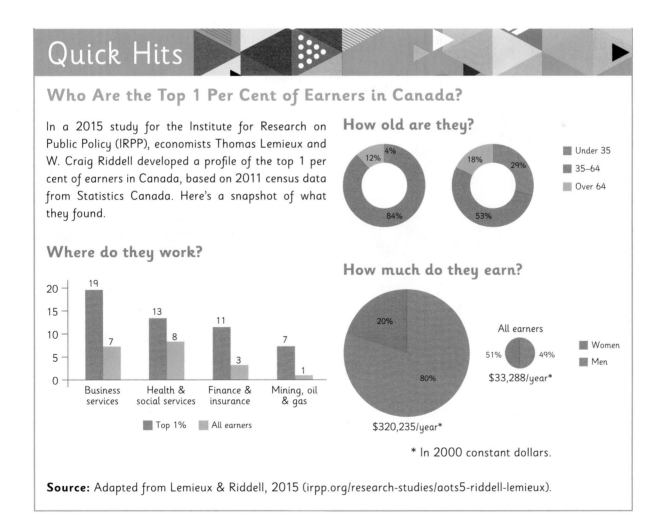

Quick Hits

Who Are the Top 1 Per Cent of Earners in Canada?

In a 2015 study for the Institute for Research on Public Policy (IRPP), economists Thomas Lemieux and W. Craig Riddell developed a profile of the top 1 per cent of earners in Canada, based on 2011 census data from Statistics Canada. Here's a snapshot of what they found.

How old are they?

- Under 35
- 35–64
- Over 64

4% / 12% / 84%

18% / 29% / 53%

Where do they work?

Business services: Top 1% = 19, All earners = 7
Health & social services: Top 1% = 13, All earners = 8
Finance & insurance: Top 1% = 11, All earners = 3
Mining, oil & gas: Top 1% = 7, All earners = 1

■ Top 1%   ■ All earners

How much do they earn?

20% / 80%
$320,235/year*

All earners
51% / 49%
$33,288/year*

■ Women
■ Men

* In 2000 constant dollars.

Source: Adapted from Lemieux & Riddell, 2015 (irpp.org/research-studies/aots5-riddell-lemieux).

Table 7.6	University and College Participation in Canada, by Parental Income, 2001	
Parents' Income ($)	**Attending University (%)**	**Attending College (%)**
Less than 25,000	19.5	29.4
25,000–50,000	23.3	36.5
50,000–75,000	25.0	38.2
75,000–100,000	38.2	38.1
More than 100,000	45.6	38.1
Overall	30.0	35.4

Source: Based on data from www.statcan.gc.ca/pub/11f0019m/11f0019m2005243-eng.pdf

students, are found in Newfoundland and Labrador and in Quebec, where the fees are below the average by several thousand (see Figure 7.4).

Of course, what you pay depends on not just *where* you're studying but *what* you're studying. The so-called "professional schools" of dentistry, medicine, pharmacy, and law have the highest average fees across the country, scoring $18,934, $13,416, $11,723, and $10,983, respectively, in 2015–16 (Statistics Canada CANSIM Table 477-0021). Needless

Chris Schmidt/iStockphoto

What quintile are the families of these university students most likely to be in? How would that change if this were a college library instead of a university library?

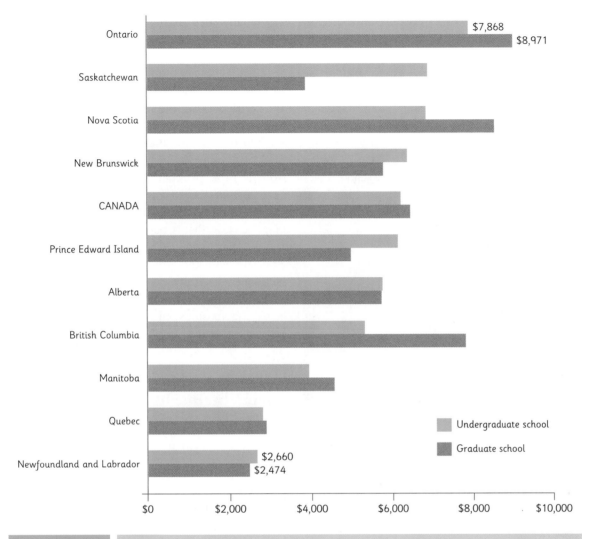

Figure 7.4 Average Undergraduate and Graduate Tuition Fees for Canadian Full-Time Students, by Province, 2015–16

Source: Statistics Canada CANSIM Table 477-0077.

to say, this has affected who goes to the professional schools. A study undertaken in 2004 by the five law schools in Ontario (where the tuition is highest) found that their schools were attended by "more students from affluent homes headed by parents with a university education: two-thirds of law students come from the top 40 per cent of the family income distribution and about 10 per cent from the bottom 40 per cent of the distribution" (King, Warren, & Miklas, 2004).

The situation at professional schools changed dramatically after 1997, when tuition fees were

What do YOU think?

In 2012, the province with one of the lowest average tuitions (by a large margin), Quebec, saw massive student unrest concerning a proposed tuition increase, yet the province with the highest tuition, Ontario, had no student response to this strike. Why do you think that is?

deregulated (i.e. government controls on what the universities could charge were withdrawn). The law school study reported that between 1997 and 2004 there was "an increase of 4.7 per cent in the proportion of law students' parents who earn incomes in the top 40 per cent of the average family income distribution for Canada and a decrease in the proportion of students whose parents earn incomes in the middle 20 per cent of the distribution" (King, Warren, & Miklas, 2004). And, as with postsecondary tuition fees generally, there is a regional disparity in the cost of attending a professional school. Table 7.7 shows the average cost of attending dentistry school, medical school, and law school in the nine provinces where these programs are available for 2015–16, presented in order of most to least expensive.

What do YOU think?

Higher tuition fees are a barrier to social mobility. Universities charging higher fees for professional schools usually justify the costs as a way of generating the revenue needed to attract "star professors" and (for schools of medicine and dentistry) to purchase better equipment. Is it reasonable to say there's nothing wrong with the education of students from poorer families attending cheaper universities?

Finally there is the issue of student debt. A Statistics Canada report on the impact of student loans, based on three different surveys conducted between 1995 and 2005, noted that over that 10-year period, the proportion of students graduating with outstanding debts rose from 49 per cent to 57 per cent, while the average debt rose from $15,200 to $18,800, and the percentage of those graduating with at least $25,000 of debt climbed from 17 to 27 per cent (Statistics Canada CANSIM Table 477-0021).

We can see, then, that postsecondary education and class (that is, parental income) relate to one another, particularly when it comes to university, especially with the professional schools. The province in which the student lives is a factor, again especially with the professional schools, with Ontario being the most expensive and Quebec the least expensive province for university education.

Dentistry as an Indicator of Social Inequality

Dentistry is a good indicator of the amount of social inequality that exists in Canada. Put quite

Table 7.7	Average Tuition Fees for Full-Time Canadian Students in Dentistry, Medicine, and Law, 2015–16		
	Dentistry ($)	Medicine ($)	Law ($)
Ontario	34,400	23,770	15,479
Saskatchewan	32,960	15,840	12,255
Nova Scotia	19,168	17,180	13,692
Alberta	20,184	13,328	11,372
Manitoba	19,832	8,084	9,483
BC	27,111	17,066	10,014
New Brunswick	N/A	N/A	8,693
Newfoundland and Labrador	N/A	6,250	N/A
Quebec	3,345	2,936	2,716
Canada	**20,156**	**13,409**	**10,928**

Note: The averages presented for Quebec and Nova Scotia take into account the different fees charged in these provinces to "in province" and "out of province" Canadian students.

Source: Statistics Canada CANSIM Table 477-0021.

Quick Hits

Student Employment and Economic Meltdown

In May 2009, 18.3 per cent of students aged 20–24 who intended to go back to college or university in the fall were unemployed. This figure was up from 15.4 per cent a year earlier, in May 2008.

That means that over the course of a year, roughly 59,000 full-time summer jobs were lost (www.statcan.gc.ca/subjects-sujets/labour-travail/lf-epa/lfs-epa-eng.htm).

What do YOU think?

What do you think the impact of this greater unemployment was on student life in colleges and universities in the 2009–10 academic year?

simply, the rich are much better served by dentistry than are the poor. This can be seen in two main ways: in access to the job of dentist and in access to dental work.

We have already seen the cost of becoming a dentist in the seven provinces with dental schools (Table 7.7: see p. 212). It is clear, based on these numbers, that outside of Quebec, you have to have access to a great deal of money if you want to become a dentist.

According to the Canadian Dental Association (2016a), in 1997 there was one dentist for every 1,850 Canadians, roughly; by 2013, there was one dentist for about every 1,650 Canadians. This trend of improving population-to-dentist ratios is seen in every province in Canada. The most favourable ratio is in British Columbia, where there is one dentist for roughly every 1,500 British Columbians. The worst ratio is in Newfoundland and Labrador, where there is presently a dentist for every 2,750 residents of the province.

Overall, these statistics are good, and they point to better access to dentists across the country. However, having a dentist in your neighbourhood benefits you only if you can afford the services. Unlike medicine, dentistry is not greatly supported by public funding, and this contributes to significant class differences in access to dental care. Consider that in 2010 Canadian governments, on average, subsidized just 4.9 per cent of dental costs, a slight decrease from the previous year's figure (CDA, 2016b).

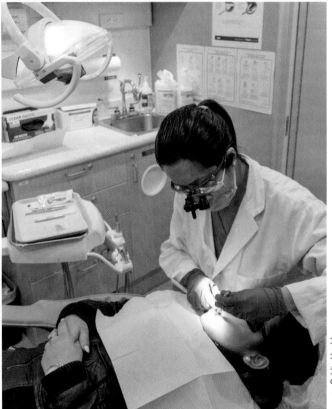

Toronto Public Health

A teen gets dental care inside a bus, courtesy of Toronto Public Health's mobile dental unit. Have you been to the dentist in the past six months? If so, did you consider it a privilege? If not, were there barriers preventing you from going (or do you just hate the dentist)?

Government funding of dental care is highest in the territories; among provinces, the greatest government contribution to dental costs (14.3 per cent) is in Saskatchewan, the home of socialized medicine and a long history of NDP governments. In Ontario, the government covers just 1.3 per cent of dental costs (CDA, 2016b). If we look at this in an international context (Table 7.8), we see that Canada ranks well behind Japan, the Scandinavian countries, New Zealand and Australia, and even the United States in this regard.

While Canadians, of the 10 countries examined in Table 7.8, spend the second-highest amount per capita on dental health (much of it presumably on not-strictly-necessary services such as "improving your smile"), they have the second-smallest percentage coming from public funding. It should be noted that of the high amount spent on dental work in Canada, 62.6 per cent comes from employer-based insurance, and 31.9 per cent comes purely from personal finances. The 5.4 per cent coming from public funding is typically for some form of emergency dental work. If you or someone in your household has a job with good employee benefits, you will likely have most of your necessary dental costs covered. However, the jobs that come with good employee benefits are typically professional jobs associated with higher incomes. As Figure 7.5 shows, families in the lowest income quintile are the most likely to put off trips to the dentist because of the cost. Looking at this generally, if I am poor with bad teeth, I would like to live in Norway or Sweden; I would not want to live in Canada or the United States.

What do YOU think?

1. If you were to engage in the sociology of dentistry, how would you study it?
2. Every academic article I have ever read on the sociology of dentistry has been written by a dentist, a doctor, a nurse, or an association of dental or medical workers—not a sociologist. Why do you think that is? How would an article written by a sociologist be different?

Table 7.8	Total Per Capita Dental Expenditures and Public Funding, Select OECD Countries, 2009

Country	Mean Per Capita Expenditures (US$)	Public Contributions to Total Dental Expenditures	
		Per Capita (US$)	Percentage
United States	333.30	31.60	9.5
Canada	**300.50**	**16.30**	**5.4**
Sweden	275.80	113.00	41.0
Norway	266.80	71.70	26.9
Australia	241.10	59.30	24.6
Finland	192.10	85.10	44.3
Denmark	182.20	34.60	19.0
Japan	170.60	130.60	76.6
Spain	152.40	2.30	1.5
New Zealand	96.90	33.20	34.3

Note: All figures are expressed in US dollars.

Source: Ramraj, Weitzner, Figueiredo, & Quiñez, 2014: Table 5.

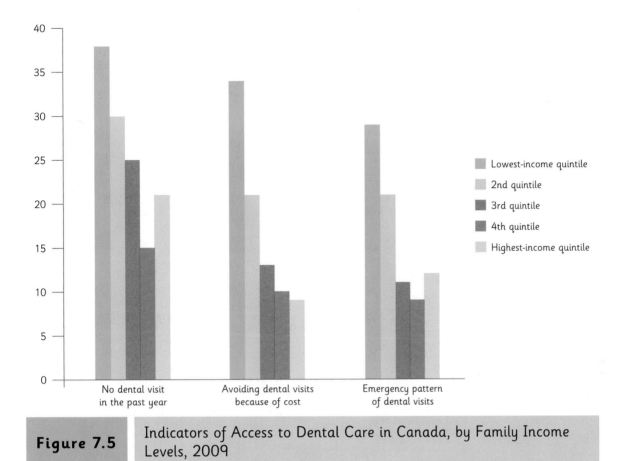

| Figure 7.5 | Indicators of Access to Dental Care in Canada, by Family Income Levels, 2009 |

Source: Canadian Academy of Health Sciences, 2014: p. 17, Fig. 2.7.

WRAP IT UP

Summary

In this chapter, we looked at social inequality from the perspective of two classical theorists, Karl Marx and Max Weber, as well as through the eyes of two early twentieth-century Canadian sociologists, Herbert Brown Ames and Colin McKay, who were engaged in investigating very specific situations.

Social inequality seems less unjust when there are good avenues for mobility, which might give someone from a lower class a decent chance to climb the socioeconomic ladder. We looked closely at two of these avenues: sports (particularly hockey, which admittedly benefits just a tiny proportion of our population, making it a pipe dream for many hockey dads and moms) and postsecondary education, which is more accessible, though perhaps not as accessible as it should be. The rising costs of hockey have helped one of our national sports creep into the elitist category, while the rising costs and student debts that come with a college or university education bring challenges of their own (as if you were unaware of them!).

The chapter also offered a look at emblems of the extremes of social inequality in Canada: food banks, whose users don't easily fit into the stereotype of the homeless and the income-less, and the CEOs of some of our best-known companies.

THINK BACK

Questions for Critical Review

1. Distinguish between a Marxist notion of class and a system that includes a middle class.
2. Differentiate between "class" and "strata."
3. Identify what quintiles are and demonstrate how they are used.
4. Identify what liberal ideology is. Who supports it, and on what grounds? Who opposes it, and on what grounds?
5. Imagine that you have been asked to study trends in the use of food banks in Canada and put forward recommendations to help reduce Canadians' reliance on them. Which of the following policies would you recommend, and why?

    a)   issue food stamps or coupons to low-income families, and reduce social assistance payments accordingly

    b)   implement a "living wage" to replace the minimum wage

    c)   increase the age of retirement

    d)   increase family allowance cheques

    e)   crack down on employment insurance fraud to ensure there is more money in the system for deserving families

    f)   increase the availability of low-cost housing

    g)   implement free or minimal-cost daycare

    h)   subject EI recipients to drug testing and provide counselling services as necessary

    i)   create incentives for businesses to hire and train unemployed people

    j)   make postsecondary education free

    k)   write your own: _____.

READ ON

Suggested Print and Online Resources

Online

Walmart's Hunger Games: How America's Largest Employer and Richest Family Worsen the Hunger Crisis

www.eatdrinkpolitics.com/wp-content/uploads/Walmarts_Hunger_Games_Report.pdf

  ·   This seven-page report argues that Walmart "builds their wealth off of workers' inability to afford food," by underpaying their employees and then redeeming the food stamps their low-paid workers rely on.

Is the Cost Keeping Kids out of Minor Hockey? Absolutely, Players and Parents Say

www.cbc.ca/sports/hockey/ourgame/story/2009/01/16/hockey-costs-too-much.html

  ·   This feature article on the CBC's website gives an informative, journalistic look at the high price of hockey in Canada, which may be to blame for falling minor hockey registration numbers.

Canadian Council on Social Development

www.ccsd.ca

  ·   The CCSD is dedicated to exploring issues of social inequality, especially poverty, with an aim to influencing social policy. The website provides current news stories and recent reports prepared by the CCSD.

Food Banks Canada
www.foodbankscanada.ca
- On its website Food Banks Canada documents the hunger problems of the poor in Canada and proposes policy solutions. Its annual report, *HungerCount*, gives details of the organization's activities and findings on a yearly basis.

Canadian Centre for Policy Alternatives
www.policyalternatives.ca
- The Canadian Centre for Policy Alternatives is an independent, left-wing research institute that studies inequality and creates policies addressing that inequality.

Living Wage for Families Campaign
www.livingwageforfamilies.ca
- Visit this website for more information on how the BC-based organization calculates its living wage for different metropolitan centres and why a living wage is important.

In Print

Patrizia Albanese (2009), *Child Poverty in Canada* (Toronto: Oxford).
- An important work by a Canadian sociologist on theories of, and possible solutions to, child poverty in Canada.

Zygmunt Bauman (2011), *Collateral Damage: Social Inequalities in a Global Age* (Malden, MA: Polity Press).
- A readable look by a prolific sociology author about how contemporary society is producing an underclass of disposable people.

Ed Grabb & Neil Guppy, eds (2008), *Social Inequality in Canada*, 5th edn (Toronto: Pearson).
- An insightful collection of articles, edited (and with some articles written) by two leading Canadian sociologists studying social inequality in Canada.

Bryan D. Cummins (2003), *Only God Can Own the Land*, Canadian Ethnography Series Vol. 1. (Toronto: Pearson).
- This book looks at how the life of the Attawapiskat Cree has changed since diamond exploration and mining began in Ontario's north.

"Race" and Ethnicity

The Gist

Reading this chapter will help you to . . .

- Discuss the extent to which "race," ethnicity, and gender are social constructs.
- Distinguish between different forms of racism.
- Explain four "mind traps" associated with studying blacks in Canada.
- Demonstrate how, historically, Canadian laws can be said to be racist.
- Contrast the social inequality in Quebec before and after the Quiet Revolution.
- Explain how the ethnic conflict in Rwanda was socially constructed by colonialism.
- Distinguish between the different legal entities that make up Indigenous people in Canada.
- Discuss the racialization of positions in professional sports.

Terms of the Trade

- anti-colonialism
- colonialism
- cultural mosaic
- discrimination
- dual colonialism
- epiphenomenal
- essentialism
- ethnic class
- ethnic entrepreneurs
- friendly racism
- indirect rule
- institutional racism
- instrumentalism
- interlocking matrix of domination
- internal colonialism
- intersectionality theory
- Inuit
- master narrative
- melting pot
- Métis
- minoritized
- polite racism
- postcolonialism
- prejudice
- primordialism
- racial bigotry
- racialization
- refugees
- registered Indian
- scrip
- smiling racism
- social constructivism
- systemic racism
- vertical mosaic
- visible minorities

Names to Know

- Patricia Hill Collins
- Kimberlé Crenshaw
- W.E.B. Du Bois
- Franz Fanon
- Daniel G. Hill
- Everett C. Hughes
- Albert Memmi
- John Porter

For Starters

csakisti/iStockphoto

Refugees

In 2015, a regional humanitarian crisis sparked by the civil war in Syria became an international emergency as citizens displaced by the fighting left their homes to seek refuge abroad in numbers not seen since the Second World War. With European countries struggling to process and integrate the staggering number of asylum-seekers, countries further from the crisis were asked to receive **refugees**.

Here in Canada the question of how best to help Syrian refugees became a hot item in the lead-up to the October federal election. How many *should* we take in given our recent military activity in the area, which may have contributed to the crisis? Did the refugees deserve full Canadian rights to health care and welfare? There was resistance among some conservative-minded Canadians to the idea of welcoming non-Christian refugees lest they be terrorists; it became a moral panic when some government officials tried to politicize the issue. Others turned the matter into an either/or question: support *either* homeless veterans *or* refugees; provide humanitarian relief *either* to neglected Indigenous communities at home *or* to asylum-seekers from halfway around the world. I saw that one a lot on Facebook.

Many Canadians supported the idea of bringing Syrians to Canada. The number of private sponsors willing to house, feed, educate, and generally support the newcomers outstripped the government's ability to process applicants. Many did so while proudly claiming that we are a nation of refugees. To give true sociological meaning to that statement, we need to hear people's stories.

The Steckleys were Mennonites who had once lived in Switzerland. They were not well received there as they would not serve in the army. In the eighteenth century they fled to Pennsylvania. Later, they came north to southern Ontario, beginning in the 1780s, I believe because they had heard stories of cheap land. Others would follow a century later to settle on the Prairies. There is still a vibrant Mennonite community in these parts, just as there are Amish communities in the US.

During the War of 1812 in North America, between British, Canadians, and First Nations allies on one side, and the Americans on the other, the British government encouraged African-American slaves to leave the US and come to Canada, where they would be "free" citizens. Roughly 2,000 came to Nova Scotia and New Brunswick, but they were not welcomed with open arms by white people in the area (Whitfield, 2004). They were free but oppressed. The story of Viola Desmond presented later in this chapter should give you a feel for that.

I remember as a child hearing of the Hungarian refugees, or DPs, as these "displaced persons" were called then. Hungary had revolted against the Soviet Union in 1956, and the country was soon overrun by Russian soldiers. Some 200,000 people left as refugees, and Canada received 37,500 of them (Canada, 2015). Frank Palmay was seven years old when he and his four-year-old brother came to Canada as refugees in 1956. After spending a week in a refugee camp in Austria, the Palmays learned that only two countries were accepting Hungarian refugees without quotas: Canada and Venezuela. Palmay writes:

> I am forever grateful my parents chose Canada.
>
> Canada processed our application in less than a week. Medicals were waived. Canada paid for a flight to London. . . . We were taken to Liverpool, where we boarded the *Empress of Britain*, arriving in St John on Dec. 13. . . . [T]he Canadian government had chartered the whole ship for transporting the refugees. (Palmay, 2015)

Once they were in Canada, the family was provided with accommodation, which had been paid for before they arrived, and money to get started. Palmay's father was able to gain employment and eventually return to engineering, his profession.

In 1975, another Cold War conflict, the Vietnam War, ended in triumph for the communist North, which led to a massive refugee exodus from South Vietnam. I remember seeing news stories and pictures of the "boat people," Vietnamese refugees who had escaped in small boats, often not to survive. In 1978, the Canadian government passed the Immigration Act, which first defined refugees as a distinct class of immigrant, with different admission criteria. The government promised to sponsor one refugee for every refugee sponsored privately. The peak time for Vietnamese refugees to come to Canada was 1979–80, when Canadians received some 60,000 refugees from Vietnam and the neighbouring countries of Cambodia and Laos (Canada, 2015).

What do YOU think?

1. How were these four groups—Mennonites, African Americans, Hungarians, and Vietnamese—treated differently as refugees in Canada? How do you explain the differences?
2. What do you think is Canada's responsibility to the Syrian refugees?

Introduction to "Race": Why the Scare Quotes?

The term "race" was first applied to humans during European colonial expansion in the sixteenth and seventeenth centuries. Use of the term has long reflected beliefs about biological superiority and inferiority in the context of colonial power. It does not always follow the formulas *lighter skin = good* and *darker skin = bad*. Russian racism was directed at white Siberian communities speaking languages related to Finnish and Hungarian. Japanese governments and citizens have long exhibited racism toward the indigenous Ainu. The Chinese government has long established racist practices against Tibetans and the Muslim Uighurs. However, white supremacy—involving discrimination against anyone not of western European ethnic background—has been the prevailing pattern since people began discussing humans in terms of different "races."

Why do we often put quotation marks around "race"? Races do not exist as clear biological entities among humans. When early scientists tried to divide humans into three "races"—Caucasian, Mongoloid, and Negroid—there were always peoples, such as the Ainu of Japan or the Aborigines of Australia, left over. Differences *within* supposed races often outnumbered those *between* races. "Negroid" people included both the tallest and shortest people in the world, and people of greatly varying skin colour and build. Human biologists and physical anthropologists have for over 60 years established there is but one human species, one race, albeit one that displays variation among its members—rather like *Ursus americanus*, the black bear, which can be black, cinnamon brown, and even white (the "spirit bears" of British Columbia).

Ann Ronan Picture Library/HIP/The Image Works

A late nineteenth-century artist's representation of the five "human races": (clockwise from top left) American, Malayan, Mongolian, Ethiopian, and Caucasian. What role do you think politics and religion might have played in scientific efforts to prove the existence of different races during the eighteenth and nineteenth centuries?

Racialization is a social process in which human groups are viewed and judged as essentially different in terms of their intellect, morality, values, and their innate worth because of perceived differences in physical appearance or cultural heritage. In this chapter we will examine some of the contexts in which this process plays out, and the effects it creates.

Racialization in Canada

Indigenous People in Canada

Evidence of racialization in Canada exists in the way Indigenous people are treated. The racialization of the Aboriginal population of the Americas began in the sixteenth century in Europe, with a discussion of whether or not these people were human

and had souls. To western Europeans, they were an "Other" that needed to be explained. Racialization formed part of that explanation. A few facts from the sociological profile of Indigenous people in Canada will illustrate.

First, Indigenous people have been living in what is now Canada for at least 14,000 years. The first Europeans (the Norse or Viking explorers) visited Canada's eastern shores roughly 1,000 years ago (leaving shortly thereafter). We can say that roughly 93 per cent of Canadian history is Indigenous alone.

Yet as Métis writer Emma LaRocque aptly describes, sociologically, Indigenous people have been studied primarily as social problems:

> Several years ago in a sociology class on social problems, I recall wondering if anyone else was poor, because the professor repeatedly referred to Native people as statistical examples of poverty. . . . Not for one moment would I make light of the ugly effects of poverty. But if classroom groups must talk about Indians and poverty, then they must also point out the ways in which Native people are operating on this cancer. To be sure, the operations are always struggles and sometimes failures, but each new operation is faced with more experience, more skill, more confidence and more success. (LaRocque, 1993: p. 212)

Another factor contributing to the racialization of Indigenous people is the fact that their voices have barely been heard in the sociological study of their people (Steckley, 2003). As Indigenous people have only recently been able to take advantage of graduate-level work in Canadian universities, and as sociology has been tainted as an outsider-privileged research area, it will be a while yet before more Indigenous voices speak loudly in Canadian sociology.

Indigenous, or Aboriginal, people are defined by a complex system of legal statuses that separates them from non-Indigenous people, and from each other. The main designations, as defined in Canadian legislation, are

- registered Indian;
- Bill C-31 Indian;
- band member;

- reserve resident;
- treaty Indian (a category with its own sub-divisions, as each treaty is different);
- Métis; and
- Eskimo.

The legal differences come from the Indian Act, which is administered by the federal Department of Indian Affairs (now called Indigenous and Northern Affairs). Passed in 1876, the Indian Act enshrined a sexist definition of "Indian" as any man of "Indian blood" reputed to belong to a particular band, any child of such a man, or any woman married to such a man. A man kept his status no matter whom he married, but a woman, if she married someone not legally an Indian, lost her status, and her children would share that fate. A non-Indian woman could gain Indian status by marrying an Indian man. This discriminatory law was in force until 1985, when Bill C-31 was passed, enabling people who had lost their Indian status through marriage or through the marriage of their mother to apply to be reinstated.

Inuit (from a word in their language meaning "people"; the singular is "Inuk") differ from "Indians," having been in Canada for a shorter time—somewhere between 5,000 and 10,000 years. It was not until 1939, when the federal government wanted to assert territorial claims in the Arctic, that Canada officially took responsibility for the Inuit. Each Inuk was given a metal disc with a number that was to be used as a token of his or her status. Today, about 60 per cent of Inuit have disc numbers. The lives of the Northern Indigenous population changed on 1 April 1999, when the territory of Nunavut ("Our Land") came into being. More than 80 per cent of Nunavut's 37,000 residents are Inuit. They own 18 per cent of the land, have subsurface rights to oil, gas, and other minerals for about 2 per cent of Nunavut, and will receive royalties from the extraction of those minerals from the rest of the territory. They do not require a licence to hunt or fish to meet their basic needs.

The term Métis is used in two ways. It is commonly used, often with a lowercase *m*, to refer to anyone of mixed Indigenous and non-Indigenous heritage. With an uppercase *M* it usually refers to the descendants of French fur traders and Cree women. Starting in the late eighteenth century, the Métis developed a culture that brought together European and First Nations elements. Over time, they achieved a sense of solidarity from their shared legal struggles with the Hudson's Bay Company (HBC) over the HBC's trade monopoly. The HBC owned most of the Prairies and about half of present-day Canada,

Quick Hits

Which Terms to Use and Avoid When Discussing Indigenous People

When sociologists talk about Indigenous people living in Canada, they are referring to the earliest inhabitants of this land and their descendants. The Canadian government recognizes three distinct groups of Indigenous people: First Nations, Métis, and Inuit.

While it is appropriate to speak of Indigenous people *in* Canada, you should try to avoid the expressions "Indigenous Canadians," since not all Indigenous people embrace Canadian citizenship, and "Canada's Indigenous people," which reinforces centuries of paternalistic treatment by Canadian governments. "People" is used when referring to a group of individuals or the entire Indigenous community; "peoples" is used only when referring to distinct groups (as in, *the Gitksan, Nisga'a, and other Indigenous peoples*). "Aboriginal," when used as an adjective, is an acceptable synonym

for "Indigenous," but it is becoming less common since Canada officially adopted the UN's Declaration on the Rights of Indigenous Peoples in May 2016. Do not use "Aboriginal" as a noun (as in "Aboriginals living in Canada").

Although it is embedded in the Indian Act, the word "Indian" has gradually given way to "First Nations," just as "Eskimo" has been replaced by "Inuit." Wherever possible, use the self-defined name of the community you're discussing instead of more general terms (e.g. *a Mi'kmaq woman*, instead of *a First Nations woman* or *an Indigenous woman*). Keep in mind that most of the names that identify specific Indigenous peoples in history books are not the people's names for themselves (e.g. "Huron" rather than "Wendat").

thanks to a 1670 charter granted by the English King Charles II, who knew little about the land. In 1867, the HBC negotiated the sale of most of its lands to the federal government, which, with no regard for Métis land rights, set up a colony in Manitoba. In 1869, led by 25-year-old, college-educated Louis Riel, the Métis achieved a military takeover, setting up an independent government to negotiate with Ottawa. The Manitoba Act of 1870 established the province and recognized the rights of the Métis. The Métis were given scrips, certificates declaring that the bearer could receive payment in land, cash, or goods. But government officials and land speculators swindled the Métis out of their land, buying up the scrips for next to nothing. Most Métis moved west. In 1885, with western expansion again threatening their rights to the land, the Métis, led again by Louis Riel, made a stand in Saskatchewan. Canadian forces attacked and defeated them. Riel was hanged for treason.

The Métis settled in a patchwork of rural prairie communities and nearly disappeared altogether. But during the 1930s, Alberta Métis pushed for the creation of communal settlements similar to First Nations reserves. In 1938, eleven Métis "colonies" were formed (eight remain). These colonies carry some political rights, making them like rural municipalities. However, they do not have rights to the royalties for oil and gas extracted from their land. Beyond the colonies, the Métis are represented by the Métis National Council and provincial organizations in Ontario and the Western provinces.

In the 2011 census 451,795 people identified themselves as Métis, part of a growing increase over the last 10 years (see Figure 8.1 and Figure 8.2). Alberta has the highest Métis population of any province (96,865), and Winnipeg the highest city figure (46,325) (Statistics Canada, 2013d: pp. 12–13). The most likely reason for this increase is a heightened tendency to self-identify as Métis.

Beware of statements that involve the idea that the government is "giving too much" to Indigenous people. In fact, the government is returning to the people what is owed. Here is an example. The Nawash, or Cape Croker, Anishinabe community in 1898 had $385,124.94 in the bank, money paid for land they had sold to the federal government. Yet they were never granted possession of that money, and had access only to some of the interest earned on the total. Even that was safeguarded by the local Indian agent, who had almost absolute power over the community and its money.

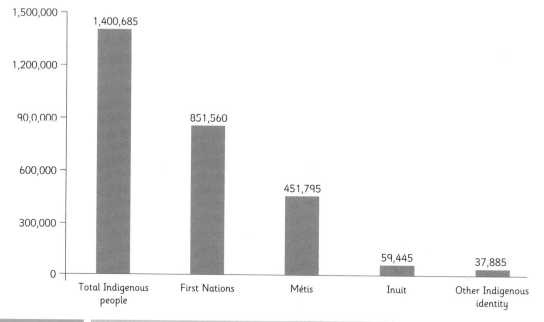

| **Figure 8.1** | Indigenous Population in Canada by Identity Group, 2011 |

Source: Statistics Canada, 2015a: p. 6, Chart 2.

Photo by Evan Agostini/Invision/AP

No wonder the Métis population is on the rise: from the runway to the summer music festival, going native has become cool. For those seeking what Tuck and Yang (2012) describe as a "move to innocence," Métis ancestry is ripe for appropriation because it is perceived to be harder to disprove than First Nations official status. What's wrong with donning a ceremonial headdress in kinship with Canada's earliest inhabitants? No, seriously, what is wrong with it?

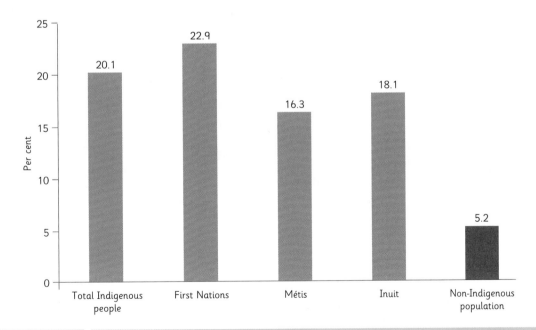

| **Figure 8.2** | Increase in Indigenous Population in Canada by Identity Group, 2006–11 |

Source: Statistics Canada, 2015a: p. 7, Chart 3.

Blacks in Canada

Black communities have existed in Nova Scotia since the British Proclamation of 1779 offered freedom to slaves who left their American masters to fight on the British side in the American Revolution. As you read in the chapter's introductory narrative, more came north in the first half of the nineteenth century. They were offered significantly less land and fewer opportunities than white immigrants were,

Our Stories

Viola Desmond: Canada's Rosa Parks

As with Indigenous people in Canada, it does not help to view black people only in terms of problems such as overrepresentation in the prison system and in homicide statistics. Canada's school systems recognize Black History Month in February, but too often it is the stories of African Americans that are taught, even though Canada has its own black civil rights heroes. Viola Desmond is one.

Viola Desmond (1914–1965) grew up in a well-respected, middle-class black family in Halifax, Nova Scotia. Inspired by her father, a successful independent businessman, she aspired to open a beauty parlour in her home town. Unable to train as a beautician in Halifax—very few schools accepted black students—she went to Montreal and then to the US to pursue her education. When she returned to Halifax she established a hair salon, a beauty school, and her own line of beauty products.

On a fall evening in 1946, as she was travelling on business to Sydney, her car broke down in the town of New Glasgow. Since she would have to wait several hours for repairs, she thought she would take in a movie at New Glasgow's Roseland Theatre. She bought a ticket and proceeded to a seat on the main floor. After taking her seat, she was advised that her ticket entitled her to sit in the balcony, not on the main floor, where seating was more expensive. She offered to pay the difference but was informed that she would not be permitted to sit on the main floor; she soon became aware that blacks were expected to sit in the balcony, and that the main floor was reserved for whites. When she refused to surrender her seat, she was forcibly taken out of the theatre and held in jail overnight to await her trial the next day.

Desmond was charged with fraud for attempting to take a seat on the main floor without paying the 1¢ tax charged for the more expensive seating. Even though she had offered to make up the difference and

Why do you think Viola Desmond's story of refusing to give up her seat in the Roseland Theatre is not as well known as that of Rosa Parks's refusal to move to the back of the bus?

had been refused, she lost the case and was fined $26. The case was later appealed to the Supreme Court of Nova Scotia, where Desmond's conviction was upheld. She eventually left Nova Scotia for Montreal and, later, New York, where she died at the age of 50. Segregation in Nova Scotia was legally ended in 1954, and Desmond was issued an official apology and pardon by the government of her home province in 2010.

Source: Robson & Caplan, 2010; Bingham, 2013; Nova Scotia Communities, Culture, and Heritage, 2015.

and they endured incredible hardship and prejudice. Despite having been in Canada for more than 200 years, Nova Scotian blacks are treated as an anomaly when they travel west in Canada; "But where are you really from?" is a question they are often asked.

The black population of Canada has declined several times. In 1792, nearly 1,200 black Loyalists left for the new African colony of Sierra Leone. Many more returned to the United States following the Civil War. Between 1871 and 1911 there was a slow decline in the black population in Canada, from 21,500 to 16,900, and after a brief resurgence a further drop, from 22,200 to 18,000, between 1941 and 1951. The black population in Canada began to increase consistently in the 1970s, when the population rose from 34,400 in 1971 to 239,500 by the end of the decade (Milan & Tran, 2004: p. 3).

According to the 2011 National Household Survey, 945,665 people who identified as black were living in Canada in 2011, an increase of 161,870 from 2006 (Statistics Canada, 2013a: p. 15). Over 40 per cent of black Canadians were living in Toronto, where visible minorities make up 47 per cent of the city's population (Statistics Canada, 2013a: p. 16). Montreal, where blacks make up the largest visible-minority group, had the second-largest black community in Canada, thanks to recent immigration from former French colonies such as Haiti, Rwanda, Chad, and Cameroon. These numbers may underrepresent the actual number of African-heritage people in Canada: according to a 1997 study out of McGill University (Torczyner, Boxhill, Mulder, & James, 1997), many immigrants from countries where the colour bar does not play the role that it does in North America will list an ethnicity based on the language they speak (French or English) or the country of their birth rather than the colour of their skin (Clarke, 1997).

Despite their long history in this country, particularly in Atlantic Canada and southern Ontario, black people are often viewed and treated as relative newcomers. Canadians can be smug about our role in helping slaves escape the American South during the eighteenth and nineteenth centuries, even though slavery was also practised in pre-Confederation

According to the 2011 National Household Survey, 1 in 5 Canadians is a member of a visible minority. What makes someone a "visible minority"? Who in this photo would count? The term is used in federal legislation, but what does it say about us that we distinguish between visible minorities and other ethnic minorities?

Sergeibach/Dreamstime.com

Canada, and many freed American slaves were treated with hostility and contempt upon their arrival here. Black people today continue to be racialized by mainstream Canadian society, which views them as "Other." Black people are greatly over-represented in our prisons: from 2005 to 2015, the black inmate population grew by 69 per cent (versus 10 per cent for the inmate population overall), and the rate of incarceration for black people is three times their rate of representation in society, according to Canada's correctional investigator, Howard Sapers (2015). There is evidence—difficult to obtain because Canada does not keep race-specific crime data—that while blacks may be overrepresented in some forms of violent crime, they are also victims of bias in policing and the administration of criminal justice (Owusu-Bempah & Wortley, 2014).

Sociologists have studied the underlying causes of crime in predominantly black neighbourhoods—poverty, lack of employment opportunities, absence of strong male role models, the attraction of gangs as fostering a sense of belonging—but too little has been done to address these factors. The situation has sparked a resurgence of black rights activism led by organizations such as Black Lives Matter, which aims to "dismantle all forms of anti-black racism, liberate blackness, . . . [and] affirm black existence" (http://blacklivesmatter.ca/about/).

Mind Traps in the Study of Blacks in Canada

There are several "mind traps"—misconceptions or unsubstantiated generalizations—that you must

Telling It Like It Is

The Skin I'm In: Being Interrogated by Police—All Because I'm Black

When I was 22, I decided to move to Toronto. . . . In Toronto, I thought I could escape bigotry and profiling, and just blend into the crowd. By then, I had been stopped, questioned, and followed by the police so many times I began to expect it. In Toronto, I saw diversity in the streets, in shops, on public transit. The idea that I might be singled out because of my race seemed ludicrous. My illusions were shattered immediately. . . .

I was carded for the first time in 2007. I was walking my bike on the sidewalk on Bathurst Street just south of Queen. I was only steps from my apartment when a police officer exited his car and approached me. "It's illegal to ride your bike on the sidewalk," he informed me. "I know, officer, that's why I'm walking it," I replied edgily. Then the cop asked me for ID. After sitting in front of the computer inside his car for a few minutes, the officer returned nonchalantly and said, "Okay, you're all set." I wanted to tell him off, but thought better of it and went home. I still don't know what he saw when he ran my name.

Over the next seven years, I was carded at least a dozen times. One summer evening in 2008, two friends and I were stopped while walking at night in a laneway just north of my apartment, only a few hundred metres from where I was carded the first time. Two officers approached in their cruiser, briefly turning on their siren to get our attention. Once they got out of the car, they asked us what we were doing. "We're just walking, bro," I said. The cops immediately asked all of us to produce identification. While one officer took our drivers' licences back to his car, the other got on his radio. I heard him say the word "supervisor," and my stomach turned. Within 60 seconds, a second cruiser, marked S2, arrived in the laneway, and the senior officer at the wheel got out to join his colleagues.

The officer who had radioed for backup returned and asked us to empty our pockets. As the supervisor watched, the radio officer approached us one at a time, took our change and wallets and inspected them. He was extremely calm, as if he was thoroughly accustomed to this routine. "I'm going to search each of you now to make sure you didn't miss anything," he explained. I knew it was my legal right to refuse, but I couldn't muster the courage to object. The search officer avoid when studying the history and culture of black people in Canada. Here are four:

- Canada's black population consists mostly of recently arrived immigrants.
- Canada's black community has a relatively short history.
- The majority of black people living in and coming to Toronto are from Jamaica.
- A black student who receives a post-secondary education has just as good a chance of succeeding in Canada as a non-black student.

Roughly 45 per cent of Canada's black population was born in this country (Statistics Canada, 2013a: p. 17). The tendency of Torontonians (whose city is home to nearly half of Canada's black population) to think of all black immigrants as "Jamaicans" is also flawed. Of the roughly 195,200 black immigrants who came to Canada between 2001 and 2011, only 10 per cent came from Jamaica; 15 per cent came from French-speaking Haiti (settling mostly in Montreal), while 20 per cent came from Nigeria (10 per cent), Ethiopia (6 per cent), and Somalia (4 per cent). An immigrant from Nigeria brings with her a cultural heritage very different to someone arriving from, say, Trinidad.

Education does not produce the same benefits among black people that it does among others. In 2011, Canadian-born black people between the ages of 25 and 64 were slightly more likely than other Canadian-born citizens to be university graduates (24 per cent, compared with the national average of

A Black Canadian's POV

approached me first. "Before I search you, I want you to tell me if I'm going to find anything you shouldn't have," he said gravely. "I don't have anything," I replied, my legs trembling so violently I thought they'd give out from under me. The officer patted down my pockets, my pant legs, my jacket, my underarms. He then repeated the search with my two friends, asking each of them before touching them if he would find anything. One of my friends spoke up: "I have a weed pipe in my back pocket, but there's nothing in it." The officer took the pipe and walked with the supervisor to the car with the officer who had taken our ID. As the policemen huddled for what felt like an hour, my friend apologized. "It's not your fault," I replied. I cursed myself for choosing that route rather than staying on Queen Street, where hundreds of people would have been walking. Here, we had no witnesses.

When the officers finally came back, they returned the pipe to my friend. "Are any of you currently wanted on an outstanding warrant?" asked the search officer. We all said no. "Okay, guys, have a good night," he said. I was still too scared to move, and apparently my friends were too; we just stood there and looked at the cops for a second. "You can go," the officer assured us. I made sure not to look back for fear they'd interpret some outstanding guilt on my part. I was certain that the police had just documented my name along with the names of my friends, one of whom was carrying a pipe for smoking an illegal substance. This information would be permanently on my record.

After years of being stopped by police, I've started to internalize their scrutiny. I've doubted myself, wondered if I've actually done something to provoke them. Once you're accused enough times, you begin to assume your own guilt, to stand in for your oppressor. It's exhausting to have to justify your freedoms in a supposedly free society. I don't talk about race for attention or personal gain. I would much rather write about sports or theatre or music than carding and incarceration. But I talk about race to survive. If I diminish the role my skin colour plays in my life, and in the lives of all racialized people, I can't change anything.

—Desmond Cole

What do YOU think?

What effect has carding had on the writer of this narrative? What effect do think these interactions have on police?

22 per cent) and to have a college diploma (26 per cent, compared with 23 per cent). However, the average income of Canadian-born black people was substantially lower than the average for all Canadian-born citizens ($31,899 versus $40,650). Some analysts have tried to "explain away" this discrepancy by arguing that the majority of working black citizens are relatively young, earning the lower incomes typical of younger workers. Yet when the income of Canadian-born blacks is age-standardized to overcome the statistical bias, the result is an annual income of $34,400—still significantly lower than the national average.

> ## What do YOU think?
>
> 1. How do you account for the prevalence of the four "mind traps" noted above?
> 2. Why do you think black university graduates earn considerably less than other graduates do?

Racism

Four Elements of Racism

Racism can be understood as the product of four linked elements. The first is *racialization*, the construction of certain groups of people as different and biologically superior or inferior. This fosters ideas of relative worth and quality, which leads to prejudice, the "pre-judgement" of others on the basis of their group membership. The third element is discrimination, which involves individuals treated differently—rewarded or punished—based on their group membership. Finally, there is *power*, manifested when institutionalized advantages are regularly handed to one or more groups over others. Tatum touches on the importance of power in this equation:

> People of color are not racist because they do not systematically benefit from racism. And equally important, there is no systematic cultural and institutional support or sanction for the racial bigotry of people of color. In my view, reserving the term *racist* only for behaviors committed by Whites in the context of a White-dominated society is a way of acknowledging the ever-present power differential afforded Whites by the culture and institutions that make up the system of advantage and continue to reinforce notions of White superiority. (Tatum, 2003: p. 10)

Without power, non-white people in Canada can be prejudiced, but not racist. They can perform discriminatory acts, but they cannot be racist without institutional, structural, ideological, and historical support. Certainly this is true of systemic racism, which by definition involves power.

There are different kinds of racism. Racial bigotry is the open, conscious expression of racist views by an individual. When racist practices, rules, and laws become institutionalized, then we have systemic (or institutional) racism. The Chinese Exclusion Act (1923–47), which prohibited the immigration of Chinese people from China and other countries, is an example of systemic racism. Canada's residential school system, aimed at suppressing Indigenous culture, is another example.

Sometimes, racism can be subtle, hidden in a way behind a smile or words that seem friendly to the perpetrator. This is called friendly (or polite or smiling) racism. Henry Martey Codjoe provides an example:

> The realtor who showed our house to prospective buyers quietly hinted that if I wanted my house to sell quickly, I would have to remove all traces of anything that indicated that Blacks had lived in the house: no family pictures, no African art or crafts, everything Black or African must go, and we must be out of the house before he showed the house to prospective buyers. He would call and let us know. No matter what we were doing, we must leave. One time we were late in getting out and we ended up hiding in our minivan in the garage. When he showed the garage, we ducked. It was a shameful and degrading experience. The house sold, but my wife and I never did meet the family that bought it. (Codjoe, 2001: p. 286)

A common form of friendly racism is the *microaggression*, a casual remark or gesture that reflects

Quick Hits

Racism

Racism is the product of four linked elements:

- racialization
- prejudice
- discrimination
- power.

Different kinds of racism include

- racial bigotry,
- systemic (institutional) racism, and
- friendly (polite/smiling) racism.

---

racial prejudice and causes offence. Most microaggressions aren't intended as insults; they may even be misguided compliments or attempts at conversation. Even so, they are offensive. Though the comments may be spoken without any intent to cause insult or self-consciousness, they are hurtful because they reflect the speaker's awareness of racial difference and preconceptions based solely on the visible racial characteristics of the person addressed. A good example of a microaggression is contained in the title of a book by Ojibwa writer Drew Hayden Taylor, who called his 1996 collection of essays, *Funny, You Don't Look Like One: Tales of a Blue-Eyed Ojibway*. Here are some remarks that are considered microaggression:

- Where are you really from?
- What are you?
- I never think of you as black.
- You're really pretty for a . . .
- But you sound white.

What do YOU think?

1. Should we be concerned about microaggression when so much overt, intentional racism still exists?
2. Are people today too sensitive about "race"?

Master Narratives and Buried Knowledge

In the master narratives that countries construct about themselves, which get repeated in textbooks and in the stories people tell about their country,

racism is often downplayed or altogether omitted. Stories about the mistreatment of minorities, stories that make the dominant culture or their ancestors look bad, are often excluded. For example, the master narrative of early Canadian history describes how First Nations people co-operated with Europeans to make the fur trade successful, by obtaining the furs, teaching Europeans how to use canoes and snowshoes, and providing the Europeans with new foods (such as pemmican and corn). This "official" version of the story often appears in elementary and middle-school textbooks. It overlooks the exploitation and social destruction that occurred when Europeans introduced alcohol into the fur trade. To use Michel Foucault's terminology, that story becomes "buried knowledge."

Canada's master narrative depicts a country that is more multicultural than the United States. While there is evidence to support this, the master narrative does not include some buried knowledge about the history of certain racial groups in Canada. The following three stories are part of that buried knowledge.

1. Defending the Women: An Act to Prevent the Employment of Female Labour

The head tax of $500 imposed on Chinese immigrants beginning in 1903 (a sizeable increase on the $50 tax levied in 1885) had a dramatic effect on Chinese immigration to Canada. For the overwhelmingly male population of Chinese immigrants who had already settled in Canada, it meant the chances of marrying a Chinese woman were greatly reduced. Many Chinese-Canadian men were forced to lead a bachelor's life. This made them a threat to white women in the eyes of some European Canadians.

This prejudice brought about Saskatchewan's Act to Prevent the Employment of Female Labour in Certain Capacities on 5 March 1912. It declared that:

> No person shall employ in any capacity any white woman or girl or permit any white woman or girl to reside or lodge in or to work in or, save as a *bona fide* customer in a public apartment thereof only, to frequent any restaurant, laundry or other place of business

or amusement owned, kept or managed by any Japanese, Chinaman or other Oriental person. (Quoted in Backhouse, 1999: p. 136)

In May 1912, Quong Wing was convicted and fined for employing two white women in his restaurant. His appeals to the supreme courts of Saskatchewan and Canada failed.

In 1924 in Regina, restaurant owner Yee Clun challenged the law. He had strong personal support

Quick Hits

"Race"-Based Hate Crime in Canada

A hate crime is one that is motivated by prejudice (e.g. based on "race," religion, sex, or sexual orientation). According to a 2015 Statistics Canada report, half of the 1,167 hate crimes reported to police in 2013 were motivated by hatred toward "race" or ethnicity, and the majority of those (255 incidents) targeted the black community (Allen, 2015). The greater

part of the criminal activity motivated by hatred of "race" (56 per cent) was non-violent, most of it falling under the heading "mischief," which can include, for example, graffiti painted in a public place. Overall, hate crimes declined by 17 per cent from 2012 to 2013, but bear in mind that two-thirds of all hate crimes go unreported (Dauvergne & Brennan, 2011).

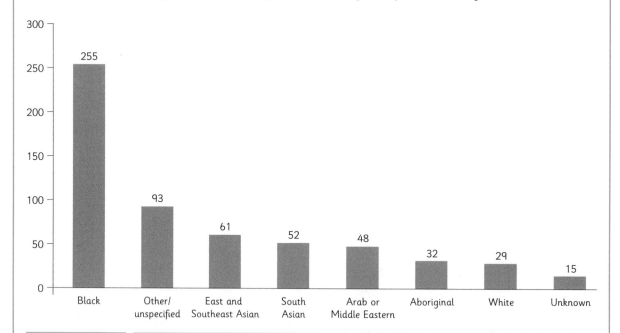

Figure 8.3   Number of Police-Reported Hate Crimes Motivated by "Race" or Ethnicity by Victim Group, Canada, 2013

Note: "Other/unspecified" includes motivations based on "race" or ethnicity not otherwise stated (e.g. Latin American, South American) as well as hate crimes that target more than one "race" or ethnic group (such as immigrants generally).

Source: Allen, 2015: p. 14, Chart 7.

in the city from members of both the Chinese and the non-Chinese communities. But local newspapers were spreading poorly researched stories of Chinese men bringing opium into Saskatchewan and turning white women into "drug fiends." Clun won the case in court but found his efforts foiled by the Saskatchewan Legislature, which passed another statute authorizing any municipal council to revoke the court ruling. The act was not repealed until 1969.

2. Punished for Success: Japanese-Canadian Fishers

In 1919, the Federal Department of Marine and Fisheries responded to growing concern that Japanese-Canadian gill net salmon fishers were "taking over" at the expense of white Canadian fishers. In the words of Port Alberni MP Major R.J. Burde, reported in the Victoria *Colonist* on 22 May 1920, "they have become so arrogant in their feeling of security that many white settlers are reaching the limit of tolerance" (quoted in Adachi, 1976: p. 105). The government then drastically reduced the number of licences that Japanese-Canadian fishers could obtain (see Figure 8.4).

In just three years, white fishers gained 493 licences, an increase of 33.5 per cent; Indigenous fishers gained 215 (up 20.8 per cent). Japanese-Canadian fishers, by contrast, lost 974 licences, a drop of 48.9 per cent. Japanese-Canadian fishers in the north Skeena area were even prohibited from using power boats between 1925 and 1930.

3. Not Wanted on the Voyage: The *Komagata Maru*

Most of the first South Asians to come to Canada were Sikhs, who had been given special status by the British as soldiers and police serving imperial purposes throughout the world. In 1904 they began to arrive in small numbers, many of them settling in Port Moody, east of Vancouver. By 1906, those small numbers had increased considerably, with as many as 5,000 Sikhs entering the country between 1905 and 1908 (Johnston, 1989: p. 5; Burnet & Palmer, 1988: p. 31). They were young men, most of them single, though a good number had wives back in India. They arrived in British Columbia at a time when there was a shortage of labourers willing to work in the sawmills, on the roads, and in the bush cutting wood and clearing land. Some were greeted with a measure of respect, as many were British army veterans, and they soon earned a reputation for working hard for low

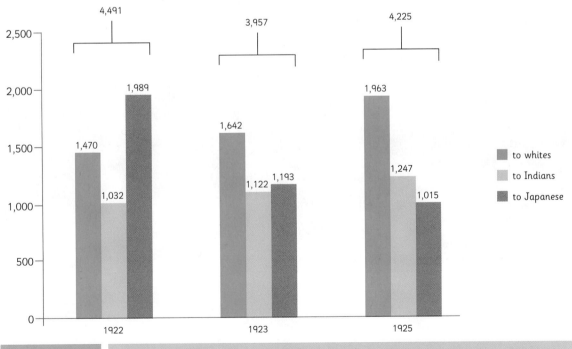

Figure 8.4   Salmon Gill Net Licences Issued, 1922–25

Source: *Report on Oriental Activities within the Province*, British Columbia Archives NW 305.895R425.

wages. An October 1906 report in the Vancouver *Daily Province* quoted one employer as saying, "I would have White labourers of course if I can get them. . . . But I would rather give employment to these old soldiers who have helped fight for the British Empire than entire aliens."

Telling It Like It Is

Two White Guys Playing Catch: Racialized Positions in Sports

If you are a fan of professional football, you have watched this scene countless times: a white guy (the centre), flanked by four white guys (offensive guards and tackles), snaps the ball to another white guy (the quarterback), whom all five white guys try to protect. This white guy looks up, sees that there are some white but probably more black guys coming after him, and so hands the ball off to a black guy (the running back), who gets tackled by the onrushing black guys. If the running back is stopped before advancing 10 yards, another white guy might come in to try to kick a field goal.

Racialized positions—player positions identified with particular racialized groups—exist in North American professional sports. The two most racialized positions in professional football are place-kicker and running back. The former is exclusively white. A well-researched sports blog indicates that since 1966—the beginning of the National Football League's modern era—there have been just five black place-kickers in a league where 60 per cent of the players are black (Matthews, [2011]/2016). Why? Some say it is because many kickers come to the sport from playing soccer,

Tom Brady and Brandon Bolden play the positions of quarterback and running back for the New England Patriots. Can you guess which of them plays which position?

Photo by Jim Rogash/Getty Images

BC's natural resources–based economy has long fluctuated between periods of wild success, with employers happy to hire anyone willing to work hard, and short periods of unemployment, in which newcomers are seen as taking jobs from whites. It wasn't long before the initial acceptance of the hard-working

An Author's POV

which traditionally has not been played by many black athletes in North America (although this is changing).

In contrast, running backs are nearly all black. A few explanations have been proposed. First, a number of players who broke the colour bar in American football were running backs: Jim Brown, Gale Sayers, and the now infamous O.J. Simpson paved the way for Walter Payton, Marcus Allen, Emmitt Smith, and LaDainian Tomlinson. A list of the 25 greatest running backs could easily not feature a single white player. Precedent and role modelling helped establish a stereotype around the running back position (as they did, perhaps, with white place-kickers).

Prejudice has also played a role. Some black running backs took up the position only after they were told they would never make it to the NFL as a quarterback, a position of authority once reserved for white players. (Others, such as Chuck Ealey and Warren Moon, came north to play quarterback in the Canadian Football League.) Worth noting: there are strict rules in place to protect quarterbacks and kickers; there are no rules designed to protect running backs specifically. Also worth noting: the average NFL playing career is 3.3 seasons. Kickers (4.87 seasons) and quarterbacks (4.44 seasons) have the longest average careers, while running backs (2.57) have the shortest (Statistica.com).

A similar situation exists in Major League Baseball. Most of the game involves "two white guys playing catch." At the start of the 2016 season, there were just 14 African-American pitchers, representing 3.1 per cent of all MLB pitchers (Nightengale, 2016). Canadian

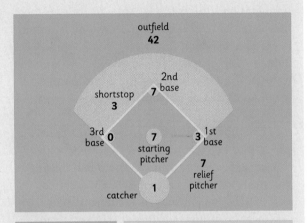

Figure 8.5 African-American Players on MLB Rosters at the Start of the 2016 Season, by Position

Russell Martin, whose father is black, is currently the league's only black catcher. Pitcher and catcher are, like the quarterback in football, positions of authority and have long been white. Outfielders tend to be black (see Figure 8.5), as the first "Negro" players to break the colour bar and be stars were outfielders: Jackie Robinson, Willie Mays, and Hank Aaron. Latino players dominate the middle infield positions—shortstop and second base—as the first Latino player to star in professional baseball was Luis Aparicio, a shortshop.

What do YOU think?

1. How and why are racialized positions established in professional sport? Can you think of other examples not discussed here?
2. What is the broader sociological significance of the findings discussed in this box?

Sikh immigrants was undermined by a growing unease over their rise in numbers. The local press fuelled the simmering discord with stories about the unfamiliar cultural practices of these "Hindus" (as South Asians collectively were called, regardless of their religion). "Hindus Cover Dead Bodies with Butter" announced a headline in the *Daily Province* in October 1906 (quoted in Johnston, 1989: p. 3).

Amid a growing moral panic, Vancouver police began taking Sikh immigrants directly from the immigration shed to the BC interior to keep them out of the city. In spite of the deplorable accommodations in which they were placed—some were housed in an abandoned cannery with no running water and little electricity—the Sikhs showed tremendous resilience, as Johnston records:

> Two thousand had arrived during the latter half of 1906. By the end of December, with the exception of some 300 who had taken steamers for Seattle and San Francisco, all but fifty or sixty had found employment in British Columbia, most of them in saw mills. The authorities would gladly have deported any convicted of vagrancy, but there were few such cases; those who were out of work were looked after by their companions, and . . . none became a public charge. (Johnston, 1989: p. 3)

Facing pressure from both white British Columbians disconcerted by the influx of Sikh immigrants and British government officials in India who wanted to curtail emigration, the Canadian government responded with clever discrimination. They passed a law requiring that all Asian immigrants entering Canada possess at least $200—a large sum for people who typically earned about 10 to 20 cents a day. They also prohibited the landing of any immigrant arriving directly from any point outside of India—significant because most Sikhs were making the journey from Punjab province by way of Hong Kong—while pressuring steamship companies not to provide India-to-Canada service or to sell tickets to Canada from Indian ports. These measures brought Sikh immigration to a halt. Unable to bring their wives and families over, denied the right to vote or hold public office, and facing open discrimination, Canada's Sikh population became discouraged.

Opposition to Sikh immigration continued to grow. In December 1913, the *Daily Province* claimed that the "Hindu problem" had assumed "a most serious and menacing aspect" (Johnston, 1989: p. 22), even though only 39 Sikhs had entered the area that year. The following spring, the Japanese steamship *Komagata Maru* left Yokohama, Japan, headed for Canada. Rented by a 55-year-old Sikh, Bhai Gurdit Singh, the ship contained 376 passengers: 340 Sikhs, 24 Muslims, and 12 Hindus. News of the ship's approach was announced in headlines such as "BOAT LOADS OF HINDUS ON WAY TO VANCOUVER" and "HINDU INVASION OF CANADA" in the BC dailies. When the ship reached Vancouver, on 23 May 1914, the local South Asian community was ready with lawyers, funds, and food to assist the passengers. Local immigration officials, politicians, and vigilante groups were also ready. For about two months, the ship's passengers were forced to endure legal battles and severe shortages of food and water. Finally, on 23 July 1914, the *Komagata Maru* was forced to leave. Only 24 passengers were permitted to enter Canada.

On 26 September, as the ship approached Calcutta, the remaining passengers were told that they would be put on a special train taking them to the Punjab area. A riot ensued. Twenty of the passengers were killed; others were imprisoned or became fugitives.

Little changed afterward. After 1918, a few of the men were able to bring over to Canada their long absent wives and children, but most could not afford such an expense. By 1941, there were no more than 1,500 South Asians in Canada. Most were men, many aged between 50 and 65. Only when India was granted its independence from British imperial control in 1947 were South Asians given the vote and full citizenship status.

Ethnicity

Everyone belongs to at least one ethnic group. But understanding ethnicity is not just a matter of collecting social traits—language, clothing, religion, foods, and so on—and applying the appropriate ethnic label. This would not help us understand conflict between closely related ethnic groups, nor would it help us understand why "ethnic pride" surfaces in certain times and situations, and not during others.

Quick Hits

Who Has the Right to Vote?

1867   Confederation: Canadian federal and provincial vote is given only to white men with property.

1875   Chinese are denied the provincial vote in British Columbia.

1885   "Indians" west of Ontario are denied the vote; eastern "Indian" males are given the vote only if they own land separate from the reserve and have made at least $150 worth of improvements. Chinese are denied the federal vote.

1895   Japanese are denied the provincial vote in BC.

1898   "Indian" males east of Manitoba are denied the federal vote regardless of property.
        White males without property are given the vote federally and provincially.

1907   South Asians are denied the federal vote.

1908   Chinese are denied the provincial vote in Saskatchewan.

1917   People born in "enemy countries" (i.e. Ukrainians) are denied the vote.
        Japanese-Canadian war veterans are promised the federal vote.

1931   Japanese-Canadian war veterans receive the federal vote.

1947   Chinese and South Asians get the federal vote and the provincial vote in British Columbia.

1948   Japanese Canadians get the federal vote.

1949   "Indians" are given the provincial vote in British Columbia and Newfoundland.
        Japanese Canadians get the provincial vote in British Columbia.

1951   Chinese are granted the provincial vote in Saskatchewan.

1952   "Indians" get the provincial vote in Manitoba.

1954   "Indians" get the provincial vote in Ontario.

1960   "Indians" get the federal vote, and also get the territorial and provincial vote in Yukon, Northwest Territories, and Saskatchewan.

1963   "Indians" get the provincial vote in New Brunswick and Nova Scotia.

1965   "Indians" get the provincial vote in Alberta.

1969   "Indians" get the provincial vote in Quebec.

There are various ways of theorizing ethnicity. This discussion will focus on five approaches. Political sociologists often divide theoretical approaches to ethnicity into three categories: *social constructivism*, *instrumentalism*, and *primordialism*. Wsevolod W. Isajiw, in *Understanding Diversity: Ethnicity and Race in the Canadian Context*, discusses primordialism in relation to the *epiphenomenal approach*, which is helpful to consider here as well. To this list I will add one more approach, *postcolonialism*, because it is essential to understanding ethnicity in the context of the case study I am about to present.

One of the most savage and destructive ethnic conflicts of recent times—and it is ongoing in the Democratic Republic of the Congo—involves rival Hutu and Tutsi tribes in Rwanda and neighbouring Burundi. The history of Rwanda since it gained independence in 1962 has been punctuated by uprisings of the disenfranchised Hutu majority against the ruling Tutsi elite, which have brought about the deaths of hundreds of thousands of civilians in both groups. The violence reached a bloody peak during the spring and summer of 1994, when Hutu military forces massacred between 500,000 and 1,000,000 of the Tutsi minority, sending more than a million destitute Hutu civilians, fearing reprisals from the surviving Tutsi population, fleeing to refugee camps in neighbouring Zaire (now the Congo) and Tanzania. It is easy to dismiss the conflict as just another instance of tribal violence in Africa, but this is far from the truth. What happened presents a challenge of interpretation that can be facilitated by looking at it through the lens of various theories of ethnicity.

Primordialism

Primordialism, or essentialism, is the view that every ethnic group is made up of a "laundry list" of traits that have been carried down from the past to the present with little or no change. Adopting this view uncritically leads to believing that the tribal conflicts in Africa have a deep history that existed

Our Stories

A Minoritizing Episode: Canada's Ukrainians and World War I

In August 1914, shortly after the start of World War I, a group of Canadians was **minoritized** through the War Measures Act, which would be used as an instrument of discrimination against Japanese Canadians nearly 30 years later.

As with different South Asian ethnic groups lumped together as "Hindoos," this minoritized group had its natural, chosen identity ignored by most Canadians, who assigned them a different, "alien" identity. Like Indigenous people in both world wars, members of this minoritized group sometimes had to change their names and lie about their identity to pass as Canadian to enlist in the army. And like the Chinese, South Asians, Indigenous people, and women of their time, many were denied the federal vote. During the First World War they were put into concentration camps, like the Japanese were during World War II.

Surprisingly, the members of this group were white.

Britain and its allies, including Canada, were fighting Germany and the decrepit Austro-Hungarian Empire. The latter was home to a people who thought of themselves as Ukrainians by nationality, even though their official citizenship was Austrian. Canada's War Measures Act led to the internment of 8,579 people labelled "enemy aliens" in 24 camps across the country. More than 5,000 of them were Ukrainians. Another 80,000—most of them Ukrainians—

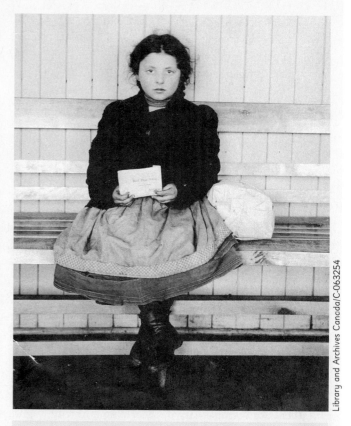

A young "Galician" immigrant in Saint John, NB, in May 1905. Ukrainians began to settle in Canada during the 1890s; today, in spite of the discriminatory and dispiriting measures they endured during World War I, Canada's Ukrainian population is among the highest in the world outside of Ukraine and Russia.

had to register as "enemy aliens." More than 10,000 Ukrainians enlisted in the Canadian military, some by faking their names and identities to conceal their ethnicity. This included Filip Konoval, one of only 83 Canadians to be awarded the prestigious Victoria Cross.

Those who spent time in internment camps worked hard, developing Banff National Park, logging, working in mines and in steel mills. One hundred and seven internees died. Tuberculosis killed 26, pneumonia, 22. Six were shot to death trying to escape camp; three committed suicide. An undetermined number died due to unsafe working conditions. One hundred and six were sent to mental institutions, all but three of whom were eventually deported. Running the camps cost Canadian taxpayers $3.2 million.

The effects of the discrimination did not end with the war. Some of the land, valuables, and money possessed by Ukrainian Canadians and confiscated by the Canadian government "disappeared." Internment and suspicion killed the spirit of many who had been keen to contribute to the growth of Canada, who had nurtured high hopes for their new home.

long before colonialism, and that these conflicts are reignited only once the "stabilizing influence" of the colonial power has left. It does not allow for conflicts to arise during colonization. It absolves colonial powers of any blame for regional conflicts.

Primordialism presents a static, as opposed to a dynamic, view of culture. In this view, culture does not seem to change from the inside; change such as "modernization" is ascribed primarily or entirely to outside forces. Primordialism is a functionalist theory, displaying one of the weaknesses of functionalism: that it poorly explains conflict.

Postcolonialism

Colonialism is the economic and political exploitation of a weaker country or people by a stronger one. Typically—historically—it involves the domination by a European state of an African, Asian, or American people; however, it is not limited to this. The Chinese have exercised and continue to wield colonial control over Tibetans and Uighurs. Internal colonialism is colonialism of one people by another within a single country. The history of Canada involves the internal colonialism of Indigenous peoples by European settlers and their governments.

Postcolonialism (or anti-colonialism) is a theoretical framework that analyzes the destructive impact colonialism has on both the colonizer and the colonized. It was first developed by writers such as **Franz Fanon** (1925–1961) and **Albert Memmi** (b. 1920) to examine French colonies in North Africa and their fight for independence from France. Fanon, born in the French West Indian colony of Martinique, was radicalized by his experience as a black intellectual in France and by his work as a doctor and psychiatrist in Algeria during the fight for independence there. His influential works *Black Skin, White Masks* (1952) and *The Wretched of the Earth* (1961) deal with the psychological effects of colonization and have inspired considerable sociological study. Albert Memmi was a Jew born in predominately Muslim Tunisia, which gained its independence in 1956 (six years before neighbouring Algeria). His *The Colonizer and the Colonized* (1957) demonstrated how the two groups negatively conditioned each other, and how no party could be "neutral" in the relationship between the two.

Postcolonial theory, as it applies to ethnicity, involves identifying colonialism as a factor in the development or escalation of conflict between ethnic groups. In Canada, for example, postcolonial theory can significantly explain the increasing conflict between the Wendat (Huron) and Haudenosaunee (Iroquois) during the 1640s in terms of the former group's connections with the French and the latter's ties with the English. In the African context, it is usefully applied to study situations involving the concept of indirect rule, a governance policy in which a European nation uses the members of a particular ethnic group as its intermediaries in ruling African territory.

One problem with postcolonialism as a theory is that it can attribute every negative change in a colonized area to outside forces. It does not leave much room for the agency of one or more of the colonized groups. A corrective perspective is provided by dual colonialism theory, which is the idea that under a colonial regime, the most oppressed groups suffer both at the hands of the colonizing outsider group and at the hands of a local group that is given privilege and power by the outsiders. Catharine Newbury applies this idea well in her discussion of Rwanda in *Cohesion of Oppression* (1988).

Primordialism, Postcolonialism, and Rwanda

As you read the following description of ethnic conflict in Rwanda, consider how well the theories of primordialism and postcolonialism apply.

In Rwanda, three main ethnic groups are currently recognized: Hutu, Tutsi, and Twa. Numerically, the Hutu are by far the dominant group. The 1956 census lists 83 per cent of the population as Hutu, with 16 per cent Tutsi and 1 per cent Twa (Newbury, 1993: p. 3). Yet from at least the eighteenth century

What do YOU think?

When Western researchers during the colonial period studied the people of Rwanda and Burundi, their main question seemed to have been "How are the Hutu and Tutsi different?" How would the results of their research been different if they gave equal weight to the question, "How are the two peoples the same or similar?"

onwards, the Tutsi have been the group with the most power. If we consider a list of typical "ethnic traits"—including physical attributes, language, religion, kinship structure, occupation, and economic circumstances—we gain some interesting findings about Rwanda prior to colonization.

Physical Appearance

Tutsi and Hutu tended to differ *on average* in their physical appearance. The former were typically portrayed as being taller and thinner than the latter, with longer and thinner faces. One study (Chrétien, 1997) found that the Tutsi averaged 1.75 metres in height, the Hutu 1.66 metres. We must note that before and during the colonial period, intermarriage was not uncommon. The physical differences combined with the fact that the Tutsi appear to have come later to Rwanda than the Hutu led colonial administrators and social scientists to draw otherwise unfounded conclusions about the Tutsi being a "superior, conquering race." This helped justify European colonial support of the Tutsi elite.

Occupation

The Tutsi were, in the pre-colonial period, primarily pastoralists. They herded cattle. The Hutu, on the other hand, were primarily agriculturalists, growing crops. The division was not absolute: some Hutu, particularly those heading up the richer lineages, herded cattle, and some Tutsi were agriculturalists. Passing from one group to the other was not uncommon. But during the colonial period, the more powerful Tutsi took advantage of their enhanced privileges to gain a greater share of the cattle.

Language

The people of Rwanda all speak the same language, with regional dialect variants. The language, belonging to the Bantu language family, was likely spoken in Rwanda before the Tutsi moved into the area (probably from Ethiopia).

Religion

In terms of religion, the Tutsi and Hutu did not differ historically, and during the colonial period most were converted to Christianity by Catholic missionaries. However, religion would, through the education system, come to have a powerful effect on the development of a strong sense of ethnicity in

Rwanda by entrenching the ethnic-based class system that placed the Tutsi at the top and the Hutu at the bottom. Established in 1932 and recognized as the best school in Rwanda, the Groupe Scolaire played a part in promoting class and ethnic divisions, as Newbury explains. One goal of this school was to create a "new social class,"

> and in accordance with this goal . . . very few Hutu were admitted; indeed, after World War II *the school even had a minimum height requirement for admission.* Graduates of the Groupe Scolaire considered themselves superior to other educated Rwandans, . . . and their diplomas were accorded greater value by the Belgian [colonial] administration. Thus, in theory because of their professional qualifications but in reality because they were overwhelmingly drawn from among the families of Tutsi chiefs, the graduates of the Groupe Scolaire enjoyed the benefits of both the "traditional" economic structures, and of the higher status jobs and better pay available in the "modern" sector. (Newbury, 1993: p. 116; emphasis added)

Identity

Prior to the colonial period, Rwandan sense of identity was derived mainly from lineage, clan, chiefdom, or kingdom, and from a general sense of being Rwandan. Among the kin groups, the two that were of the greatest significance were lineage and clan. Lineage heads were important figures, and a person's primary identity came from lineage. Clan was less important, but a single clan could include members of all three Rwandan ethnic groups.

Under colonialism, lineage heads lost power, being replaced by centrally appointed chiefs who were overwhelmingly Tutsi. The previously often blurred lines of distinction between Tutsi and Hutu became strengthened, their importance reinforced by the fact that Rwandan citizens now had to carry identification cards with "Hutu," "Tutsi," or "Twa" written on them.

The growing central authority of the king during the colonial period also helped enhance the status of the Tutsi. The colonial administration and the Tutsi elite collaborated to take away the more diverse traditional government forms through which the Hutu in particular could play one authority against another into a more simplified and powerful system. A system of taxes payable either in money or with labour was developed and exploited, with colonial support, by unscrupulous Tutsi chiefs who took advantage of free labour from Hutu civilians.

Altogether we see a situation that is not well explained by primordialism but which fits well with dual colonialism theory. How do other theories fit into this situation?

Ethnicity as Epiphenomenal

The word "epiphenomenal" describes a secondary effect or phenomenon that arises from, but does not causally influence, a separate phenomenon. Marx was the first to apply it in a sociological context. He believed that economic structure was the main causal factor in society, and everything else was epiphenomenal, or non-causal.

Epiphenomenal theory suggests that any ethnic conflict is really just a byproduct of the struggle between economic classes. Thus, the strife in Rwanda stems from a situation in which the country's rich and powerful (the Tutsi elite) were exploiting its poor (the Hutu and the poorer Tutsi). Ethnicity was just a smokescreen, a false consciousness that made it impossible for poorer Hutu and Tutsi with shared class interests to overcome their oppression by the Tutsi elite. This lasted through the 1950s, when Hutu of all classes shared what Newbury termed a "cohesion of oppression," until 1962, when the country became independent and witnessed a social revolution that replaced the Tutsi elite with a Hutu one. The Hutu elite used the pretense of the idea that "rule by Hutu is automatically democratic" to gain broader Hutu support. There is a measure of truth in the epiphenomenal explanation, yet it fails to fully account for why the poor identified with the rich.

Instrumentalism

Traditionally presented in direct opposition to primordialism and compatible with the epiphenomenal approach is instrumentalism, which focuses on

Rwanda today. Would you say that this person is most likely Hutu or Tutsi?

Guenter Guni/iStockphoto

emerging ethnicity rather than on long-established ethnic characteristics. It acknowledges that elites can mobilize others who identify with them ethnically. Ethnic identification and action come from a competition for scarce resources for and by the elite. In Newbury's words, ethnic groups are created or transformed when

> groups gain self-awareness (become "self-conscious communities") largely as the result of the activities of leaders who

mobilize ethnic followings in order to compete more effectively. Improved communications and the spread of writing are important in this process; so is "ethnic learning," where groups develop ethnic awareness as a result of seeing others using ethnic solidarities to compete. The state is important, instrumentalists suggest, as an arena in which competition between these groups occurs (the state controls many of the scarce resources over which elites are

Telling It Like It Is
Disney Is Destructive

As a multinational enterprise, Disney may appear to function solely as an innocent purveyor of entertainment to young children, but it is vital to recognize that:

> media conglomerates such as Disney are not merely producing harmless entertainment, disinterested news stories, and unlimited access to the information age; nor are they removed from the realm of power, politics and ideology (Giroux, 2001: 4).

Disney subtly reinforces racist ideas in several of its animated movies. Black people are depicted as crows (e.g. Jim Crow in *Dumbo*). In the animated movie *Tarzan*, Disney completely eliminates black people's presence in Africa. In *The Jungle Book*, monkeys (like King Louise), who are supposed to be representative of black people, sing about wanting to be like the other men—white men. Latinos are represented as hyenas and chihuahuas (including Shenzim, Banzai, and Ed in *The Lion King*, and the often-angry Tito in *Oliver and Company*). East Asians are portrayed as cunning and dishonest in their role of Siamese cats in *Lady and the Tramp*. Arabs are shown as barbaric in *Aladdin*. Think of the following lyrics to the song "Arabian Nights": "I come from a land from a faraway place . . . where they cut off your ear if they don't like your face; it's barbaric—but hey, it's home!"

All of this teaches children of colour from different cultures around the world that they are mischievous, badly behaved, and "animalistic," and should view white culture as ideal. Simultaneously, this teaches white children to view people of colour with fear and contempt. As a result, children who are not white may view themselves from "primitive" perspectives rather than from dominant or powerful positions that Disney producers grant to white characters.

Disney reinforces what Peggy McIntosh (1989) refers to as "white privilege" in which "whites are taught to think of their lives as a morally neutral, normative, and average, also an ideal . . ." (McIntosh, 1989: p. 10). McIntosh states that white privilege operates and is sustained through its pervasiveness that is both taken for granted as "normal" and, also, made to seem invisible. Disney's flawed representation of people of colour and constant depiction of white characters in positions of power function as manifestations of white privilege. The fact that children watch these images continuously is part of how white privilege is continually reproduced.

Disney's influence on what we see is profound, and consequently, what we do *not* see. As a result, Disney's narrow scope of racial and ethnic characters limits access to a range of representations about people of various races and ethnicities.

—Lia Gladstone

competing), and also because government policies can significantly affect the strategies chosen by ethnic leaders. (Newbury, 1993: p. 15)

Elite members who mobilize ethnicity for personal gain are called ethnic entrepreneurs. The classic example of ethnic entrepreneurship is Adolf Hitler's construction and manipulation of the German "Aryan race." An instrumentalist approach better explains how a frustrated Hutu leadership could invoke the injustice of Tutsi elite oppression to draw poorer Hutu into their political parties and their acts of revolution.

Social Constructivism

Social constructivism is the view that ethnicity is constructed by individuals for varying social purposes. Instrumentalism can be considered a partly formed version of social constructivism in that it shows how ethnicity is constructed by the elite.

A Sociologist's POV

A Chinese girl gets a Princess makeover at the recently opened Disney Resort in Shanghai, China. Is there anything wrong with wanting to look like a white Disney princess? Is there a risk this girl may someday seek out makeup products, or even surgeries, to make herself look "more white"?

AP Photo/Ng Han Guan

However, it suffers as a theory of ethnicity and ethnic action by overstating the influence and impact of the elite. It generally fails to attribute the non-elite members any agency, any power to choose and act without being manipulated. A social constructivist theory of ethnicity would look to the motivations of the broader group.

The social-constructivist approach makes sense in the case of Rwanda, where it helps to explain why the general rural population of the Hutu became so thoroughly engaged in driving off and killing local Tutsi. Rwanda was, for most of the twentieth century, a very crowded land, with many people, particularly Hutu, becoming regularly malnourished because their farms were insufficient for their needs. Unlike in the nineteenth century, when there was considerably more space and people could move to new land in difficult situations, during the twentieth century people suffered through various famines and cattle diseases while the country's rise in population shrank farm size.

What do YOU think?

Marie Beatrice Umutesi is a Hutu sociologist who experienced the horrifying conditions of the UN-neglected refugee camps in Zaire, an experience she recorded in *Surviving the Slaughter: The Ordeal of a Rwandan Refugee in Zaire* (2004). She does not condemn the Tutsi in her book. What types of insights can her work lend to the sociology of Rwanda?

Summary

What happened in Rwanda and Burundi? We can say that prior to colonialism, the experience of being a member of an ethnic group was not a major part of the day-to-day lives of most Rwandans: it did not exert an influence on people's sense of identity the way that lineage, region, and sometimes individual chiefdom or kingdom did. Under the Belgians, a dual colonialism developed in which Europeans and elite Tutsi collaborated to put social, economic, and political substance to an increasingly rigid ethnic divide between Hutu and Tutsi. And when Belgian rule ended in 1962, the common oppression experienced by Hutu of all classes led to a social revolution in which the majority Hutu overthrew their oppressors, only to set up an ethnic dictatorship of their

own. Ethnic violence was a not surprising effect, and an easily fanned racial hatred, combined with a powerful need for land, led in 1994 to the massacre of the Tutsi and neutral Hutu.

That was not the end of the story. Tutsi from Rwanda and Burundi persuaded the Ugandan army to capture control of the two countries, driving Hutu refugees west into Zaire (now Congo), where fighting continues. It helped that the new Ugandan president was Tutsi.

Ethnicity in Canada: Classic Studies

Ethnic Class: English and French in Quebec

When **Everett C. Hughes** (1897–1983) joined the sociology department at McGill in 1927, the focus of his research became the "ethnic division of labour" between the English, who held positions of power, and the French, who occupied the lowest rung of the employment ladder. This was an injustice he wished to correct.

Hughes studied the small industrial city of Drummondville, his work summarized in *French Canada in Transition* ([1943]/1963). In the book he talks about two principal kinds of industries he found there. First, there were small, local, French-Canadian–run industries, which "do not make the town grow but proliferate and grow with it" (Hughes, 1963: p. 47). Second, were *"nos grandes industries."* The top 9 of these 11 "big industries" had headquarters in Montreal, England, or the United States. Their managers were Americans, English Canadians, and British nationals. In 1937, the largest of these industries, a textile company, employed 389 "English and Others" and 2,337 French workers. The former group occupied 24 of the 25 positions above the foreman level and 57 of the 82 foreman's jobs. The vast majority of French-Canadian employees (1,882) worked on the "factory floor," where they were involved directly in production (Hughes, 1963: p. 55).

In a mid-century study of intergenerational (father to son) occupational mobility, Yves de Jocas and Guy Rocher (1957) found that anglophones in Quebec cities scored much higher than francophones (11.8 per cent versus 3.2 per cent) in the occupational category they called "professional, proprietor, manager." The discrepancy among their sons was even greater (17.3 per cent versus 6.8 per cent; Langlois, 1999: p. 73). This suggested that the ethnic division of labour was increasing. French-Canadian sociologists Jacques Dofny and Marcel Rioux (1962) labelled this separation as ethnic class, in which people of a particular ethnicity belong predominantly to one class.

The balance shifted somewhat during the Quiet Revolution of the 1960s. The Quiet Revolution is the name given to a set of actions and policies that, together, represented an attempt by a growing educated, skilled, and French urban middle class to overthrow three social bodies that restricted the people:

1) the English-dominated large businesses
2) the Union Nationale, a provincial political party that exerted great conservative control through the rurally supported premier Maurice Duplessis (1936–9 and 1944–59)
3) the Catholic Church, which had a firm grip on education, the press, even the unions.

In large measure, the decreased inequality between French and English was brought about by provincial policies and practices, designed in part by sociologists, enacted as part of a concerted effort to make French Canadians "maîtres chez nous" ("masters in our own house").

John Porter and the Vertical Mosaic

The best-known book of Canadian sociology is *The Vertical Mosaic: An Analysis of Social Class and Power in Canada* (1965) by **John Porter** (1921–1979). The title derives from the often-stated notion that Canadian society more closely resembles a "cultural mosaic" than a "melting pot." A mosaic is ceramic artwork made of many tiles that lend different colours to the picture. The term cultural mosaic applies to societies in which individual ethnic, cultural, and religious groups are able to maintain separate identities. The opposite model is the melting pot, where immigrating ethnic and religious groups are encouraged/forced to assimilate into their new society. The term is typically used to describe American society.

Porter's vertical mosaic refers to a hierarchy of higher and lower ethnic, cultural, and religious groups. Speaking with the metaphor of the mosaic,

Porter found that the different tiles were stacked one above the other, with the tiles representing white Anglo-Saxon Protestants on top.

Landmarks in the Sociological Study of "Race"

As presented earlier, standpoint theory suggests that the perspective sociological researchers bring to their work is strongly influenced by their social location, their perspective as it is shaped by gender, age, ethnicity, sexual orientation, and other social characteristics. This does not mean that sociologists should study only "their own people." But pioneers in the sociological study of specific groups—women, for instance, or black people—are often those who belong to the group themselves. They bring unique and valuable insights to the study. In this section we will look at the work of W.E.B Du Bois, Daniel Hill, Kimberlé Crenshaw, and Patricia Hill Collins.

W.E.B. Du Bois: First Black Sociologist

W.E.B. Du Bois (1868–1963) was the first African-American sociologist. He researched and wrote about the major problems concerning Africans, both those living in the United States and those living elsewhere. He was a "pan-Africanist," one who sees the connection between the oppression or success of Africans and that of their descendants around the world.

Du Bois's sociology had an applied perspective to it. He was one of the founders of the NAACP (the National Association for the Advancement of Colored People). He used his position as editor-in-chief of their magazine, *Crisis*, to advocate for such causes as opening up training schools for black military officers and initiating legal action against white people who lynched African Americans. He was a prolific writer, producing several landmark studies, including *The Suppression of the African Slave Trade in America* (1896); his comprehensive study of Philadelphia's black slums, *The Philadelphia Negro* (1896); *The Souls of Black Folks* (1903); *Black Reconstruction* (1935); and *Dusk of Dawn* (1940). The following captures his oratorical power and sense of fairness:

[I]t is the duty of black men to judge the South discriminatingly. The present generation of Southerners are not responsible for the past, and they should not be blindly hated or blamed for it. . . . The South is not "solid"; it is a land in the ferment of social change, wherein forces of all kinds are fighting for supremacy; and to praise the ill the South is today perpetuating is just as wrong as to condemn the good. Discriminating and broad-minded criticism is what the South needs—needs it for the sake of her own white sons and daughters, and for the insurance of robust, healthy mental and moral development.

Today even the attitude of the Southern whites toward the blacks is not . . . in all cases the same; the ignorant Southerner hates the Negro, the workingmen fear his competition, the money-makers wish to use him as a laborer, some of the educated see a menace in his upward development, while others . . . wish to help him to rise. National opinion has enabled this last class to maintain the Negro common schools, and to protect the Negro partially in property, life, and limb. Through the pressure of the money-makers, the Negro is in danger of being reduced to semi-slavery . . . ; the workingmen, and those of the educated who fear the Negro, have united to disfranchise him . . . while the passions of the ignorant are easily aroused to lynch and abuse any black man. To praise this intricate whirl of thought and prejudice is nonsense; to inveigh indiscriminately against "the South" is unjust. . . . (Du Bois, 1903)

Daniel G. Hill: First Black Canadian Sociologist

Although he was not born in Canada, **Daniel G. Hill** (1923–2003) is considered the first black Canadian sociologist.

Hill studied sociology at the University of Toronto, receiving his MA in 1951 and his PhD in 1960. His primary writings include *Negroes*

in Toronto: A Sociological Study of a Minority Group (1960) and *The Freedom Seekers: Blacks in Early Canada* (1981). But it is mainly in applied work that Hill's sociology is expressed. He was a researcher for the Social Planning Council of Metropolitan Toronto (1955–8), executive secretary of the North York Social Planning Council (1958–60), and assistant director of the Alcoholism and Drug Addiction Research Foundation (1960). In 1962, Hill became the first full-time director of the Ontario Human Rights Commission, and 10 years later, he became Ontario Human Rights Commissioner. He formed his own human rights consulting firm in 1973, working at various times for the Metropolitan Police Service, the Canadian Labour Congress, and the government of British Columbia. From 1984 to 1989, he served as Ontario's ombudsman, fielding complaints from citizens concerning their treatment by provincial government agencies. In 1999 he was made a Member of the Order of Canada.

What do YOU think?

1. Do you think it is more likely that a black Canadian sociologist would get involved in human rights work than a white Canadian sociologist would? Why?
2. How do you balance the need to ensure that minoritized groups are well represented in citizens' groups against the perception that a black or Asian committee member is a token appointment, hired simply to give the group the appearance of diversity? What kind of appointment does Hill seem like to you?

Crenshaw, Collins, and Intersectionality Theory: Tracking "Race" and Gender

Intersectionality is an important word in current sociological research. It refers to the way different social factors—"race" and ethnicity, gender, sexual orientation, class, age, and disability—combine to shape the experience of a minoritized group. It recognizes that, for instance, the discrimination and prejudice experienced by a young black woman is different from that experienced by a young white woman or a young black man.

"The Ombudsman of Ontario: At Your Service" [n.d.] (Archives, Ontario, F 2130-4-4-8)

[*left*] In his work as director of the Ontario Human Rights Commission and, later, as ombudsman of Ontario, Daniel Hill reached out to Ontarians of all ethnic and cultural backgrounds. The pamphlet shown here testifies to the importance he placed on the accessibility of his position to all provincial citizens. [*top*] Daniel G. Hill, ombudsman of Ontario, *circa* 1985.

Intersectionality theory was first developed by **Kimberlé Crenshaw,** and then elaborated shortly thereafter by critical sociologist **Patricia Hill Collins** in *Black Feminist Thought: Knowledge, Consciousness and the Politics of Empowerment* (1990). Intersectionality theory argues against the notion, promoted by early white liberal feminists, that the experience of being "female" is basically the same for all women. It states that gender is experienced differently, with unique forms of oppression when combined with negatively valued social locations, such as certain minoritized ethnicities (e.g. African-American, Hispanic, Indigenous, and South Asian). Gender-based stereotypes, when combined with racial prejudice, create an interlocking matrix of domination significantly more powerful and oppressive than gender alone.

In Canada, the interlocking matrix of domination has been experienced painfully by many Indigenous women. Amnesty International maintains an online forum devoted to the issue of violence against Indigenous women in Canada. It chronicles the experience of families whose sisters and daughters have gone missing, likely murdered,

over the past 30 years, and calls for better policing and greater funding for organizations that help First Nations women and girls. The following are two passages from the website (www.amnesty.ca/our-work/campaigns/no-more-stolen-sisters):

> There's still a double standard when it comes to Aboriginal women and girls. When is the government going to take action to make sure that every case of missing and murdered Aboriginal women and girls is thoroughly investigated? (Laurie Odjick, whose 16-year-old daughter disappeared in September 2008)

> Refusing to keep track of the numbers of our sisters and daughters who have been murdered or gone missing is just another way of ignoring the trouble. (Gwenda Yuzippi, whose 19-year-old daughter was murdered)

The federal government is currently preparing to hold a national inquiry into murdered and missing Indigenous women, something that activists have been demanding for several years.

Al Dunlop/Toronto Star via Getty Images

People take part in a march for missing and murdered Indigenous women on Parliament Hill in Ottawa. The federal government has agreed to hold a national inquiry into violence against Indigenous women, years after activists began calling for such a measure. Why do you think there has been such resistance?

WRAP IT UP

Summary

There are no human "races." From a sociological standpoint, "race" (or, rather, racialization) is a social process that reflects the ways in which people of different ethnic background are treated, and have been treated over time, by institutions such as our provincial and federal justice systems, our legislative bodies, our schools, and the media. It's also about how we view one another.

Racism is also a process, one that not only appears in personal biases and discrimination but is institution-alized in society as a whole. It's not just about the "rotten apples": the whole orchard smells. Racism certainly exists at the individual level, but it requires the support of social institutions to perpetuate itself. Fortunately, social support can be withdrawn from the features of institutions that maintain the level of racism. The apple trees can be pruned, and new trees planted and encouraged to grow.

THINK BACK

Questions for Critical Review

1. Discuss the extent to which "race" and ethnicity are social constructs.
2. It is sometimes said that white people are "invisible" in Canada. What do you think this means?
3. How is institutional, or systemic, racism different from other forms of discrimination?
4. What groups have been discriminated against by voting laws in Canada?
5. How did the Quiet Revolution change the social position of francophones in Quebec?
6. How were Ukrainians minoritized during World War I? What effect do you think that had on their participation in Canadian society for the period that immediately followed? Why do you think that stories of this minoritization are not better known in Canada?

READ ON

Suggested Print and Online Resources

Online

Stolen Sisters: No More Indigenous Women Lost to Violence
www.amnesty.ca/our-work/campaigns/no-more-stolen-sisters
- Amnesty International's "Stolen Sisters" page is an important source of documentation of the missing and murdered Indigenous women who otherwise remain invisible to mainstream Canadian society.

Settlers Claiming Métis Heritage Because They Just Feel More Indigenous
http://rabble.ca/blogs/bloggers/apihtawikosisan/2015/03/settlers-claiming-métis-heritage-because-they-just-feel-more-
- Rabble blogger Âpihtawikosisân explains why some non–Indigenous Canadians, especially in Quebec, are laying claim to Métis ancestry—and why it's wrong.

The Skin I'm In: I've Been Interrogated by Police More than 50 Times—All Because I'm Black
http://torontolife.com/city/life/skin-im-ive-interrogated-police-50-times-im-black/
- This is the full text of Desmond Cole's article excerpted in the narrative box on pages 228–9, which appeared in an April 2015 issue of *Toronto Life* magazine.

Canadian Race Relations Foundation / Fondation Canadienne des Relations Raciales
www.crr.ca
- This government-created agency is dedicated to fighting racism in Canada. The website has information on current research, diversity education and training, and anti-racism programs, as well as an extensive catalogue of resources.

Metropolis: Enhancing Policy through Research
www.canada.metropolis.net
- The Metropolis project is an integrated network involved in comparative research and public policy discussions regarding diversity and the immigrant experience in cities both in Canada and around the world.

Adjusting to Canada: From ABCs to -40 Degrees
www.cbc.ca/archives/entry/adjusting-to-canada-from-abcs-to-40-degrees
- The CBC online archives contain interviews with Vietnamese refugees taken in 1981, a few years after they had come to Canada, to hear about their experiences.

In Print

Kay J. Anderson (1991), *Vancouver's Chinatown: Racial Discourse in Canada, 1875–1980* (Montreal: McGill–Queens).
- A classic study of how "Chinese" and "Chinatown" have been expressed in the Vancouver area over a little more than a century.

Richard Brignall (2010), *China Clipper: Pro Football's First Chinese-Canadian Player, Normie Kwong* (Toronto: James Lorimer and Company).
- This tells the story of the challenges faced by Normie Kwong, the first Chinese-Canadian player in the Canadian Football League.

Agnes Calliste & George J. Sefa Dei, eds (2000), *Anti-racist Feminism: Critical Race and Gender Studies* (Halifax: Fernwood).
- A collection of readings on the intersection of gender and "race," edited by two leading anti-racist theorists.

Jael Ealey Richardson (2012), *The Stone Thrower: A Daughter's Lessons, a Father's Life* (Toronto: Thomas Allen).
- The story of how a black, wildly successful US college quarterback, Chuck Ealey, was kept from entering the NFL and ended up in the CFL.

Wanda Robson & Ronald Caplain (2010), *Sister to Courage: Stories from the World of Viola Desmond, Canada's Rosa Parks* (Wreck Cove, NS: Breton Books).
- Viola Desmond's sister, author and educator Wanda Robson, has done much to keep her sister's story alive since Viola's death at the young age of 50. This is Wanda's account of Viola's story.

Gender and Sexuality

The Gist

Reading this chapter will help you to . . .

- Explain the difference between sex and gender.
- Contrast the effects of biological and sociological influences on the gender.
- Explain what is meant by the "gendering" and "feminization" of work.
- State the differences among the four masculinities outlined in the section on male daycare workers.
- Compare the four different categories of feminism outlined in this chapter.
- Talk about the stereotyping involved in the intersection of female gender and minoritized ethnicity/ "race."

Terms of the Trade

- *bakla*
- bisexual
- *boyat*
- cisgender
- complicit masculinity
- Dragon Lady
- essentialist feminism
- feminization
- gay
- gender
- gendered
- gender role
- hegemonic masculinity
- heterosexual
- homosexual
- ideology of fag
- Indian Princess
- intersex
- lesbian
- LGBTTQ
- liberal feminism
- Lotus Blossom Baby
- marginalized masculinity
- metrosexual
- mismatch
- pay equity
- postmodernist feminism
- purple collar
- queer
- queer theory
- queer value
- sex
- sexuality
- socialist feminism
- squaw
- subordinate masculinity
- tabula rasa
- transgender
- transsexual

Names to Know

- Judith Butler
- Henrietta Muir Edwards
- The Famous Five
- Beatrice Kachuck
- Nellie McClung
- Louise McKinney
- Emily Murphy
- Ann Oakley
- Irene Parlby

For Starters

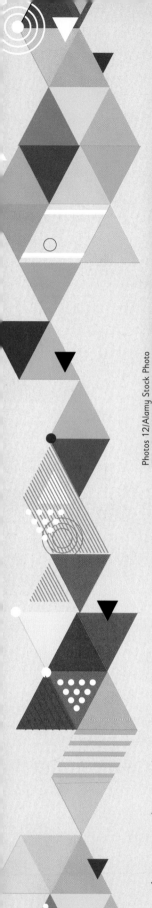

What It Means to Be a Man

How flexible are we concerning gender roles?

Most of us like to think we're very flexible, both in the way we act and in the way we perceive others. But I have to be honest. Although I feel "secure in my masculinity," as they say, there are a number of things I—a Toronto-bred white man in my mid-sixties—will not do because they're inconsistent with my own sense of being male, and with the sense of maleness I wish to project for others. For instance, I will not . . .

- use an umbrella (in part from having lived in Newfoundland, where a "real man" is not afraid of getting wet)
- use a hair dryer (despite having really long hair—it seems effeminate to me to blow my hair around like I'm in a shampoo commercial)
- use one of those convenient book and file carriers on wheels—the ones that remind me of a flight attendant's suitcase (a man should carry a brief-case or a backpack)
- wear clothes that are yellow, orange, or pink (high-school classmates of mine wearing those colours were given a hard time concerning their masculinity)
- use a snow blower instead of a shovel (real men aren't afraid of heaving snow); the same goes for

leaf blowers (rakes are easy to operate: skinny end up, wide end down)
- spend longer than five minutes getting dressed or 15 minutes in any one clothing store
- clip favourite recipes from a magazine (male cooking involves fast frying, barbecuing, or nuking in a microwave)
- shake hands in a "wimpy way" (a Canadian man is still judged by how strong his handshake is; I don't make a contest of it—as some do—but I try to meet a minimum standard)
- wear cologne or body spray (women should smell good; men should try not to smell bad)
- colour my hair (or my beard)
- use the word "lovely" without being sarcastic
- have a manicure or a pedicure.

It's important to note that this list reflects the standpoint of an old white man who grew up in Canada. I'd like male readers who are younger and of different "races," ethnicities, and sexual orientation to think about this list. Do you share my inflexibility on these issues? Be honest. What other things will you not do out of male pride? Women readers can set us straight. Would you be bothered or impressed if you knew the young man sitting next to you has weekly manicures?

I was once interviewed about my sense of fashion for a student newspaper. I referred to myself as a "rural-sexual" (because I live in a small town—it had nothing to do with livestock). Now, of course, I am referred to as "lumbersexual" because of my big beard. I was having fun with the term **metrosexual**. This term appears to have very different definitions, depending on whether a man or a woman uses it. While both male and female students can identify celebrities who can be classed as metrosexual, they are not in total agreement about what it means. It may, as some suggest, refer to "a man who takes care of himself," but for a woman that typically refers to serious mirror and clothing store time, while for a man, it often suggests working out. It still seems an uncomfortable label for many men, for whom, I suspect, "metrosexual" sounds too much like a euphemism for "gay."

Now comes the critical perspective. Why do we feel the way we do? And how flexible are gender roles in Canadian culture? Here are two other scenarios to consider:

1. How would you feel if your son took an interest in figure skating? One of my nephews, when he first learned to skate, became interested in figure skating. He took lessons for two years before he eventually quit, in large part because his father

didn't encourage him. To give my brother-in-law credit, he never made fun of the sport, but I don't think he gave his budding figure skater the kind of support he might have given a budding hockey player.

2. What's your reaction to women who box or who play rugby? Is your reaction more negative than it is toward female figure skaters or tennis players?

Compare notes on the topics above with your classmates. You're likely to find a fair bit of disagreement. That's because as inflexible as we might be when it comes to how we see gender, we all see gender differently.

> ## What do YOU think?
>
> 1. Do you think that you are relatively flexible or rigid concerning gender roles? What would your friends say about your answer?
> 2. What socializing influences (e.g. family, friends, and media) have conditioned your view of gender roles, either positively or negatively?
> 3. How long do you think it will be before young men are comfortable identifying as "metrosexual"? Will differing male and female definitions of the term come closer together?

Introduction: Sex and Gender—What's the Difference?

Gender is a highly contested area within sociology. Sociologists theorizing about gender and gender roles differ sharply, particularly on the degree to which gender is determined by either culture or biology. The absolute duality (male–female) of gender has for some time been contested. Not surprisingly, the greatest part of the critical work on gender has been carried out by women, reflecting the (now) obvious fact that before the women's movement of the 1960s and 1970s, male sociologists had done an inadequate job on the subject.

Gender is different from *sex*. British sociologist **Ann Oakley** formally distinguished the two when she stated that sex refers to "the biological division into male and female," while gender refers to "the

parallel and socially unequal division into femininity and masculinity" (Oakley, 1972). *Gender*, then, is a sociological term that refers to the roles and characteristics society assigns to women and men. It typically carries with it notions of men's and women's inequality. *Sex* refers to anatomical or biological characteristics of women and men. We could say that sex is what you're born with, but gender is about how you see yourself and how you choose to live your life.

Another key term is gender role. This is a set of attitudes and expectations concerning behaviour that relates to being male or female. Think of a gender role as being similar to a movie role. It is a part we're assigned at birth, based on our sex. How we play it reflects what we understand about what it means to act as either a female or a male.

Gender roles differ across cultures, both in content—in the specific expectations society holds for each gender—and in the severity or permissiveness with which society treats those whose behaviour contravenes the expectations for their gender.

In this chapter we will be looking at sex and gender. Most of this chapter concerns the way society views the gender categories "male" and "female," and how we—with considerable variation—interpret and live out our roles as "men," "women," and categories in between.

Sex, Gender, and Sexuality: A Primer

Sex refers to the differences between the categories *male* and *female*, based on biology. Gender refers to the social expectations that surround these biological categories. Sex categories are fairly absolute; gender categories are not: they can be fluid, and most sociologists today see gender as a continuum extending from femininity to masculinity with considerable variation in between.

Sexuality refers to feelings of sexual desire and attraction and how these are expressed; like gender, sexuality can be fluid and often changes over time.

- A heterosexual, or "straight," person is sexually attracted to people of the opposite sex.
- A homosexual is sexually attracted to people of the same sex; gay and queer are, today, accepted synonyms. A lesbian is a female homosexual.
- A bisexual is sexually attracted (equally or unequally) to people of both sexes. The once common notion that bisexuals are really gays and lesbians who are in denial because of social pressure is a myth (see Rosario, Scrimshaw, Hunter, & Braun, 2006).

Gay, straight, and bi are but three shades of the sexuality spectrum, and a growing list of terms are gaining currency to describe other hues of sexual preference. These include "asexual" (no sexual attraction), "demisexual" (sexual attraction only once an emotional bond is formed), "pansexual" (attraction to those of all sexes), and "sapiosexual" (attraction to people of high intelligence).

A transgender person is someone whose identity and behaviour do not conform to the gender role associated with the individual's biological sex. For example, a person born biologically female may feel little connection to the gender role associated with

being a woman. A transsexual is someone with the physical characteristics of one sex and a persistent desire to belong to the other. Transsexuals feel they have been born into the wrong body and may pursue sex reassignment therapy or surgery to change their biological sex. The opposite of transgender is cisgender (or "cis") for someone who strongly identifies with the gender role associated with their biological sex.

An intersex person is someone born with both male and female sexual characteristics. It is a biological condition that may produce in an individual an atypical combination of male and female chromosomes or both male and female genitals or secondary sexual characteristics. An intersex person may undergo sex assignment surgery either in childhood or in adulthood.

The abbreviation LGBTTQ (lesbian, gay, bisexual, transgender, two-spirit, queer/questioning) is an all-encompassing term for anyone who is not heterosexual and/or cisgender. An "I" is sometimes added to denote intersex people, and "2S" may be added for two-spirit people (see p. 280 later in this chapter).

As the case studies that follow show, gender is a powerful concept that can overcome biology, socialization, and pressure to conform.

Case Studies in the Relationship between Sex and Gender

David Reimer: Assigning Gender

In May 2004, 38-year-old David Reimer of Winnipeg committed suicide. His decision to take his life was likely influenced by his separation from his wife, the loss of his job, and the suicide death of his twin brother two years earlier. But there is a deeper cause to examine. David was the victim of a childhood medical accident that was compounded by an unsuccessful social experiment in assigning gender.

As infants, David and his brother were both circumcised electronically using an experimental method. During David's circumcision, too much electricity was applied, and his penis was damaged beyond repair. Desperate for a solution, David's parents consulted numerous specialists. Popular at the time was behaviourism, the psychological school of thought that emphasizes the power of socialization (nurture) over biology (nature). It was held in high

The Point Is...

The Lumbersexual: Reclaiming Traditional Masculinity?

The second decade of the twenty-first century will be remembered for the rise of the "lumbersexual," a trend in men's fashion characterized by a full but neatly trimmed beard, a plaid shirt or jacket (sometimes known as a "Kenora dinner jacket"), and a strategic scruffiness of hair. (I almost qualify, but my beard and hair are too long, and I only wear "lumberjackets" in the winter.)

What is interesting is that it is a largely urban phenomenon—a rugged, rural look adopted by city dwellers—with no lumberjack lifestyle to go with the fashion (although I have heard of recently opened establishments where friends or co-workers can engage in the manly art of axe-throwing as a social activity). American journalist Denver Hicks (2014) suggests that "lumbersexuality" is a way of reclaiming elements of traditional masculinity at a time when other elements of traditional masculinity are "threatened."

regard by some feminist psychologists (both male and female) as it supported the notion that gender and gender roles were not "natural" but taught. In its extreme version, behaviourism advanced the theory that each of us starts out as a tabula rasa, or blank slate, on which our social environment "writes" our gender. A proponent of this school, psychologist Dr John Money was one of the specialists contacted by David's parents. He persuaded them to have David castrated and given female hormones; their child, renamed "Brenda," would be raised as a girl.

In articles that made the case famous, Money claimed that David was adapting successfully to his new gender, socially taught and hormonally enhanced. But his view of the situation was based more on wishes than on facts. In *As Nature Made Him*, John Colapinto shows that David's childhood was highly conflicted. He felt male, not female. He didn't like wearing dresses, and he preferred roughhousing with boys to the company and play of girls his age.

He wasn't told he had been born male until he was 13, when his parents, under pressure from Dr Money, approached him about allowing surgeons to create a vagina. David rebelled and several times attempted suicide. He abandoned his female identity and sought out surgery to have his male sex restored. He later married and had stepchildren, but the effects of both the accident and the social experiment never left him.

David Reimer's tragic case illustrates that while gender is a social construct, it has a strong biological component. It also shows, as recent research confirms (Kruijver et al., 2000), that gender has a neurological component in addition to the biological features of genitals and hormones: the brain helps to shape our gender. It also clearly demonstrates the dangers of allowing social theory to impose itself into unthinking social practice.

What do YOU think?

1. In what way(s) can we say that David Reimer was neurologically male? How could we argue that he was not a gender "tabula rasa"?
2. How could we study individuals to determine the extent to which their gender roles are natural versus taught/learned?
3. In what ways, if at all, do you feel that you have resisted gender socialization? Were you successful in your resistance?

What do YOU think?

1. Is traditional masculinity really under attack? If so, by what (or whom)?
2. Can lumbersexuality be seen as a reaction against the rise of metrosexuality?

Storm: Choosing Neutral

In May 2011, a Toronto couple made headlines around the world when they announced that they would not be disclosing to family or friends the biological sex of their newborn. Having raised two children who were sometimes teased for failing to conform to gender stereotypes, the couple wanted their third child, Storm, to grow up without the pressure to conform to the expectations of a particular gender role.

Two-and-a-half years later, a Toronto *Star* story reported that Storm, who was still being raised gender-neutral, would sometimes say, "I am a girl," and sometimes, "I am a boy" (Poisson, 2013). In 2016, the family disclosed that Storm, then five years old, had chosen to be referred to as "she" (Botelho-Urbanski, 2016).

What do YOU think?

Given that contemporary Canadian society sets clear boundaries between the sexes, is it possible for parents to raise their children relatively free of gender scripts? Is there a point, do you think, when sex and society take over?

Caster Semenya: Measuring Gender

Caster Semenya is a two-time Olympic medallist, having won the silver medal in the women's 800 metre final at the 2012 Summer Olympics in London and a gold medal in the 2016 Rio Olympics. But in 2009–10, she missed an entire year of competition while the International Association of Athletics Federations (IAAF), track and field's official governing body, investigated claims that Semenya's body produced testosterone in levels far greater than those found in most women. Results of the "gender verification test" were leaked to the media, which sensationalized her condition and turned a situation that had been kept private into a source of controversy and criticism. "World athletics is in crisis over the gender of Caster Semenya after tests revealed the South African world champion has male sex organs and no womb or ovaries," read one article in London's *Daily Telegraph* (Hurst, 2009).

Bernard Weil/Toronto Star via Getty Images

Storm (*centre*) with her family in 2016. Do you think that more parents will opt for a gender-neutral approach to raising their children?

Semenya was cleared to compete, but in April 2011, the IAAF established new gender verification guidelines based on a maximum level of testosterone an athlete may possess in order to compete as a woman. The limit forced some intersex athletes to take treatments to reduce their testosterone levels to allowable standards. The rule was put on hold in 2015, making intersex athletes identifying as female free to compete in events for women regardless of their testosterone levels.

What do YOU think?

1. Should intersex athletes be free to compete as women or men regardless of their hormone levels?

2. What is the effect, do you think, of subjecting an intersex person to a test to verify their gender? Can gender be measured?

3. Intersex characters have appeared in recent popular fiction, including Japanese manga and Jeffrey Eugenides's 2002 novel *Middlesex*. The fascination goes all the way back to a character from Greek mythology, Hermaphroditus, who was physically joined with his lover, Salmacis, in one body that retained the characteristics of both sexes. Why do you think there is contemporary interest in this condition?

Raising the Profile of Transgender People

In 2015, Caitlyn Jenner brought the experience of transgender people into public consciousness. An American track and field hero, gold medallist at the 1976 Montreal Summer Olympics, and member of the extended Kardashian clan, Jenner was a well-known public figure when she announced her status as a transgender woman in a television interview in April 2015. She was featured on the cover of *Vanity Fair* two months later, and her transition was documented in an eight-episode miniseries.

Jenner is now the world's best-known transgender woman, but she is not the first public figure to raise awareness around the rights of transgender people. Jenna Talackova, a Vancouver-born transgender woman and model, fought for and won the right to compete in the 2012 Miss Universe Canada pageant after initially being disqualified because she was born male. Thomas Beatie, a transgender man legally married to a woman, made headlines in 2007, when he became pregnant through artificial insemination—his female reproductive organs had not then been removed. Six years later, his male identity was challenged by an Arizona judge presiding over his divorce proceedings, who ruled that because Beatie was able to carry and bear children, he could not, in the eyes of the court, be considered a man. This rendered his marriage invalid in a state that did not then recognize same-sex marriage. The ruling was overturned by the Arizona Appeals Court in 2014.

While stories such as these have helped shine a light on a community that has long been misunderstood, the cases of Jenner and Talackova in particular have glamorized an experience that has caused discrimination, social exclusion, and depression among others who lack the same degree of public support. A 2015 study by researchers at the University of Western Ontario reports that as many as 43 per cent of transgender people in North America and Europe have attempted suicide (Bauer, Scheim, Pyne, Tavers, & Hammond, 2015). The team found that the risk of suicide drops with increased social and parental support, reductions in transphobia, and greater access to transition treatments and surgeries, which are not available in all provinces and which can be costly in provinces where only some surgeries are covered by health insurance.

Trans people make up a minority of the LGBTTQ population. They may experience discrimination within the medical system, where they face reluctance by doctors to make the necessary referral for surgery and reluctance by surgeons to operate (Ubelacker, 2015). In May 2016, Canada's only surgery clinic exclusively for trans people, located in Montreal, was targeted in an arson attack carried out by a man armed with a machete. The attack caused extensive damage and forced the clinic to close temporarily, putting off several scheduled surgeries. As Brightwell (2016) reports, the incident was underreported in the mainstream media and did not receive extensive coverage on social media, even among the LGBTTQ community. Later the same month, the federal government introduced legislation to extend the rights of transgender Canadians by adding gender identity and gender expression to existing laws against discrimination and hate speech. The legislation would make it easier

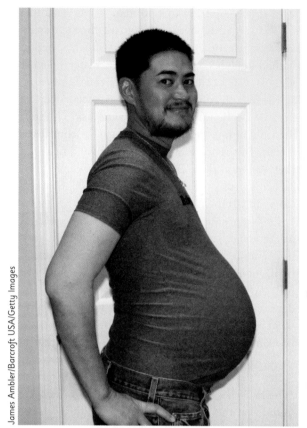

[Left] Thomas Beatie, the "pregnant man." What does his case tell you about the relationship between biological sex and gender? [Right] Jenna Talackova appeared in the 2012 Miss Universe Canada pageant after initially being disqualified because she was born male. Do you think it was right to allow her to compete in the women-only competition?

to prosecute attacks such as the one on the Centre Métropolitain de Chirurgie as hate crimes.

Feminism and Gender Theory: Four Categories

As noted in Chapter 1, much of the critical work on gender theory has been carried out by feminist sociologists. We saw, in that introductory chapter, that some scholars have traced the evolution of feminism through a series of "waves," each one distinguished by a different set of objectives. That is one way of viewing a dynamic movement and theoretical framework that has exerted tremendous influence on the growth of sociology. In this section, we will take a different approach, looking at four different strains of feminist theory and how each one approaches the study of gender. I borrow here from the excellent

work of **Beatrice Kachuck** ([1995]/2003), who divides the diverse range of feminist theories into the following categories:

- liberal feminism
- essentialist feminism
- socialist feminism
- postmodernist feminism.

Liberal Feminism

Liberal feminism, as Kachuck explains, is about securing equal rights for women in all phases of public life, including access to the same education, jobs, and pay that men receive. It is associated with the fight for pay equity, the guarantee that women in traditionally female-dominated industries (nursing, child care, library science, for instance) receive compensation similar to the salaries of those working in

Going Global

Purple-Collar Workers in the Philippines: Is That a Woman or a Man on the Other End of the Phone?

Since the start of the twenty-first century the Philippines has seen a rapid growth in global call centres. Between 2000 and 2010 the number of Filipinos employed as call centre operators skyrocketed from roughly 2,000 to 400,000. A byproduct of that growth is the emergence of an occupational niche for transgender women.

The finding comes from a study by Emmanuel David, who interviewed 39 trans women and two trans men between 2009 and 2012 (David, 2015). Twenty-eight of these "purple-collar workers," ranging in age from 19 to 35, held university degrees, while the rest had done at least some college. David refers to the call centre work as **purple-collar** labour, distinguishing it from the "blue-collar" work associated with skilled and unskilled trades, "pink-collar" work associated with female-defined or -oriented jobs, and "white-collar" office work. As David explains it, purple-collar work involves

> structural and interactional conditions experienced by transgender women workers in the labor market. Structurally, the concept refers to transgender workers' spatial location in particular work sites. The purple-collar workforce can be both densely clustered in a particular industry and systematically dispersed, vertically and/or horizontally, within particular workplaces. Interactionally, the purple-collar concept theorizes how transgender women employees' micro-interactional work is characterized by specific systems of rewards, responsibilities, and penalties. (David, 2015)

The term "systematically dispersed" refers to the fact that the trans women workers are not working together in one group, but are spread out over all of the worksites in "patterned inclusions" (David, 2015). This is how trans women produce what David calls **queer value** for the industry. Work at the call centre is repetitive and boring, especially for educated young people. The operators frequently have to deal with nasty remarks from potential customers in the West. The trans women keep it light: they make co-workers happier by being entertaining or upbeat while they all work, acting as a "social lubricant" to keep the call centre operating productively. In this way, trans women are performing "value-producing emotional labour" and providing "queer value" to their employer.

The entertainer's role is associated with what are called *bakla* in Tagalog (the national language of the Philippines). *Bakla* cannot be directly translated into "gay" or "transsexual" in English—there are too many different cultural strings of meaning. Jobs typically associated with *bakla* are hairstylist, beautician, designer, club entertainer, wedding planner, and sex worker. The trans women in the call centres "play the role" of bakla. They regularly lighten the mood, fulfilling expectations of the role that are both implicit and explicit. For example, apart from being expected to lighten the mood on a day-to-day basis, the trans call centre workers participate in ball gown and makeup contests that occur several times yearly, in "team-building" social events designed to help "foster productivity, ease workplace tensions, and boost employee morale" (David, 2015).

The trans call centre workers occupy a class apart from the typical *bakla*. They are educated and fluent in English, and they have a job that pays fairly well for the Philippines, although it is less than 15 per cent of what call centre workers are paid in the United States. While they are willing to follow the bakla stereotype to a certain degree, they recognize that there are only a few chances for upward mobility, and they have to meet a certain level of professionalism if they want to be truly successful at the job. This can create an atmosphere of competition that limits group solidarity, the kind of class consciousness that Marx talked about.

What do YOU think?

How does the "queer value" of the purple-collar workers both help and hurt their professional aspirations (i.e. their chances of being promoted to management positions)?

comparable (in terms of educational qualifications required, hours worked, and social value) professions typically dominated by men. Think of it this way: if we value our children so much, why do we pay so little to those in primary and early childhood education, who play such an important role in the social and educational development of our children? Feminist liberalism is credited with securing benefits for women on maternity leave, including the rights to claim employment insurance and to return to the same or an equivalent job in the same company after a fixed period of time (up to a year in Canada).

Criticism of liberal feminism and its view of gender roles centres around the idea that it universalizes the position of white, middle-class, heterosexual, cisgender Western women. It fails to recognize that the social location of this category of women enables them to receive benefits not as available to other women. White, middle-class women in Europe and North America are the main beneficiaries of the gains that feminist liberalism has obtained. It has been far less successful in promoting the interests of women who differ in class, "race," ethnicity, sexual orientation, and nationality.

Essentialist Feminism

Liberal feminism argues that gender is an artificial social construct that has been used to assign men and women different roles, rights, and opportunities based on perceived differences in intellect. It argues that men and women possess the same intellectual capabilities and should therefore be treated equally. Essentialist feminism differs by arguing that women and men are essentially different in the way they think. Men, for example, see the world in terms of competition and opposition to others, and they have created a social order based on "paradigms of dominance and subordination" (Kachuck, 2003); women, in contrast, view the world in terms of unities. Women's "maternal thinking" (Ruddick, 1989) naturally gives women social norms and a sense of morality that (most) men do not possess. This morality is negatively valued in a *patriarchal* society (i.e. one dominated by and favouring male roles, views, and ideas).

Kachuck presents the criticisms of the essentialist approach in terms of what other Western feminists think and also in terms of what feminists in India

have to say. In the eyes of the first, she writes, feminist essentialism has the following shortcomings:

- it universalizes women, assuming erroneously that all women experience gender alike
- it confuses natural instincts with strategies that women have devised for coping with the demands of a patriarchal society
- it encourages us to see women "as social housekeepers in worlds that men build" (Kachuck, 2003: p. 66).

She adds that feminists in India have their own concerns about essentialist feminism:

Indian feminists deplore assumptions of women's inherent caring function as an ideology that impedes their full human development. Thus, essays on education critique practices that socialize girls for dedication to family service. . . . This puts them [Indian feminists] in opposition to calls for women's devotion to families as their national identity. (Kachuck, 2003: p. 66)

In sum, then, while essentialist feminism speaks constructively about the potential for women's differences from men to be positively valued, it can fall into the trap of generalizing from the Western model—a trap that Western social scientists have often fallen into.

Socialist Feminism

Kachuck explains that socialist feminists "revise their Marxism so as to account for gender, something that Marx ignored. They want sexuality and gender relations included in analyses of society" (2003: p. 67). According to this school of thought, there is insight to be gained from looking at the intersections of oppression between class and gender. The struggles faced by, and resources available to, lower-class women can be different from those of middle- and upper-class women, and feminist socialism is useful in identifying these. Still, there is the danger that "race," ethnicity, ableism, and sexual orientation get overlooked in the focus on class. Black women in North America face some of the same difficulties of prejudice and stereotyping regardless of whether they come from the upper or lower classes.

Postmodernist Feminism

Postmodernist feminism takes the strongest social-constructionist position, a position almost diametrically opposed to that of essentialist feminism. Social constructionism, which we encountered in Chapter 6, is the idea that there is no natural basis for social identities based on gender, ethnicity, "race," and so on. Some postmodernists even contest the widely held view that all women are biologically *all female*, and all men are *all male*. From this perspective, it is impossible to form an objective, scientific, universally relevant explanation of what it means to be male or female. For this reason, postmodernist feminists refer to women more as subjects than as objects of sociological study, allowing the perspective of the women studied to guide their research. Standpoint theory is an important aspect of this category of feminism.

Another methodology that fits within the broad-ranging perspective of postmodernist feminism is queer theory, first articulated in the book *Gender Trouble* (1990) by **Judith Butler**. Queer theory first rejected the idea that male and female genders are natural binary opposites. It also disputes the idea that gender identity is connected to some biological "essence," arguing instead that gender identity is related to the dramatic effect of a gender performance. Gender is seen not as one of two categories—male and female—but as a continuum with male and female at the extremes; individuals act, or perform, more one way or another along the continuum at different times and in different situations.

Cultural configurations and norms of gender keep us from playing out a broader variety of gender performances. In this sense, gender performances are restricted by sanctions. Consider the gender performance of a male athlete crying in public, as he apologizes for having failed a drug test or having cheated on his wife. The monologue by a late-night comedian/talk-show host or the between-period comments by a former-coach-turned-pundit provide opportunities for negative sanctions concerning that kind of gender performance. Professional sport—in fact, sport in general—because it is a prominent theatre for gender performance, is a breeding ground for

negative sanctions. In hockey, refusing to drop the gloves against a taunting opponent and donning a protective visor are just two actions that could incur negative sanctions drawn from what is known as the ideology of fag. This is a set of beliefs and sanctions invoked throughout society to keep people in line. If you violate a gender role, you *must* be gay. The negative way in which this accusation is presented makes it a very powerful sanction.

Kachuck's main criticism of feminist postmodernism is that it leads to no conclusions. It merely problematizes other people's conclusions and generates no solid criteria for judging better or worse positions, but satisfies itself with "constructing a 'feminine' space where intellectuals aggressively play out tentative ideas" (Kachuck, 2003: p. 81).

Gendered Occupation and Education

Certain jobs, as well as the college and university programs preparing people to work in those jobs, are considered gendered. That means two things. First, one sex will be prevalent among the people employed in certain kinds of work or among the students in a particular program. Second, as Sargent puts it, "the work itself is typically imbued with gendered meanings and defined in gendered terms" (Sargent, 2005). What this means is that, for example, the gendered profession of nursing is described with words like "caring" and "nurturing" that are typically associated with women; nursing is thus characterized as a natural offshoot of the mother role. By contrast, the job of police officer (still often called "policeman") is described in terms of "toughness" and the "brotherhood" of officers.

Gendered Jobs

In 2001, men outnumbered women by a ratio of at least 3 to 1 in the following occupations categorized by Statistics Canada:

- the primary industries of forestry, fishing, mining, and oil and gas
- utilities
- construction
- transportation and warehousing.

Telling It Like It Is
Gender Roles and Being Lesbian

People in my life in the past have tended to believe that because I am a lesbian, I automatically have more male-specific interests, and that I do not enjoy typical girl-oriented activities. Shortly after I told my brother, he invited me to a football game, stating, "you like football now don't you?" Although he was joking at the time, this is a typical comment often made to me. Although I may enjoy fixing things around the house, my partner is a sports fanatic, and while I like to sew and knit, she enjoys cooking and romantic comedies. The gender stereotyping, which is exactly what this comes down to, even goes so far as to include the style of clothes I wear. I remember one time that I went into work wearing a baseball cap, although I usually do not wear a hat to work, as I find it unprofessional. This particular day I was coming from school and in a rush. Immediately after entering work I began to hear comments and mutters from my co-workers. It seemed that in their eyes because I was wearing a hat, I was portraying a male characteristic. They assumed that being a lesbian is the closest thing to being a male.

There is a significant difference between sexual orientation and gender identity. All of the gay people that I know, including myself, are very happy with their sex. They just happen to be attracted to the same sex as well. I am proud to be a woman. I enjoy it and would not want to change it.

For one reason or another people with little understanding of the gay population seem to need definite clarification of "who's the man and who's the woman," a question that I have been asked on too many occasions to count. In many gay relationships there are no specific roles, and each individual's identity is not masculine or feminine, but it slides on a continuum. It is ridiculous to assume that there is a male and female figure in the relationship. If I wanted a male–female partnership, I wouldn't be gay.

Many people believe that gay people, male or female, are involved in a sexual scene full of promiscuity, voyeurism, and *ménages à trois*. This is evidenced by the number of people that have made suggestive comments to me about non-committed casual sexual encounters. Although these beliefs are positive in one aspect as they break down the very untrue opinion that women cannot have the high sex drive that men are more known for, it also reflects a larger belief that being in a gay relationship is all about the sex. This leads people to believe that gay people do not commit and take part in stable, settled relationships. I remember talking with my father once about the relationship I was in and he responded, "It's alright if that's what you want, but it's unfortunate because those relationships don't last; they just don't settle." Ironically, I must say that gay relationships in fact have very little to do with sex. As a heterosexual relationship has many dimensions, so does the homosexual one, encompassing all one's needs such as emotional support, companionship,

In the prestigious occupational fields of "professional, scientific and technical services," men outnumbered women by 14 per cent; in the administrative category of "business, building, and other support services," men outnumbered women by 10 per cent.

By comparison, women outnumbered men in the following categories:

- finance, insurance, real estate, and leasing
- educational services
- accommodation and food services
- health care and social assistance.

In the last of these categories, the dominance was more than 4 to 1.

The most recent data come from the 2011 National Household Survey and show that little changed from 2001 to 2011. In fact, since 1991, the top three jobs for young Canadian women with a

the sharing of values and spirituality, and of course, physical attraction does play its role as well. I once saw an advertisement that mocked this expectation of such extravagant sex lives. The poster was in a bookstore located in a gay community. The caption read: "What do lesbians do in bed?" and the picture had two women in bed wearing flannel pajamas, one watching television and the other reading a book. I saw this as an accurate portrayal and a clever way to challenge this opinion.

Hero Images Inc./Alamy Stock Photo

Do you think this couple spends a lot of time worrying which of them is "being the man" at any given moment?

university degree have consistently been (1) elementary school or kindergarten teacher (9.8 per cent), (2) registered nurse (6.1 per cent), and (3) secondary school teacher (4.8 per cent). In 2011, 20 per cent of 25- to 34-year-old women with university degrees were employed in one of these three jobs (Uppal & LaRochelle-Côté, 2014).

Tables 9.1 and 9.2 show the top 10 jobs for young women and men, respectively. While there are some occupations that appear in the top 10 for both women and men, particularly among degree-holders, the list of jobs held by women is dominated by positions in health care, education, social service, and customer service. The list of jobs held by men shows a greater share of roles associated with computer technology, engineering, and trades. Sociology students need to look at what might cause these gender specializations to occur. A place to start would be postsecondary education, where men and women typically take different routes.

Table 9.1	Top 10 Occupations for Women Aged 25–34, with and without a University Degree, 2011

Occupation	Percentage
With a University Degree	
Elementary school/kindergarten teacher	9.8
Registered nurse	6.1
Secondary school teacher	4.8
Financial auditor/accountant	3.0
General office clerk	2.1
Administrative officer	1.9
Community/social service worker	1.8
Retail salesperson/sales clerk	1.8
Social worker	1.7
Postsecondary teaching/research assistant	1.7
Without a University Degree	
Retail salesperson/sales clerk	4.4
Early childhood educator	4.3
General office clerk	4.2
Cashier	2.7
Retail trade manager	2.6
Food and beverage server	2.6
Nursing aide/orderly/patient service associate	2.5
Customer service/information clerk	2.4
Administrative officer	2.4
Receptionist/switchboard operator	2.3

Note: *Occupations in italics* appear in both Table 9.1 and Table 9.2.
Source: Uppal & LaRochelle-Côté, 2014, Table 1 & Table 3.

Table 9.2	Top 10 Occupations for Men Aged 25–34, with and without a University Degree, 2011

Occupation	Percentage
With a University Degree	
Computer programmer/interactive media developer	3.6
Financial auditor/accountant	3.5
Secondary school teacher	3.4
Information systems analyst/consultant	2.9
Elementary/secondary school teacher	2.4
Postsecondary teaching/research assistant	2.4
Mechanical engineer	2.1
Retail salesperson/sales clerk	2.1
Civil engineer	1.9
Sales, marketing, & advertising manager	1.8
Without a University Degree	
Retail salesperson/sales clerk	3.3
Carpenter	2.7
Truck driver	2.7
Car, truck, & bus mechanic/service technician	2.4
Retail trade manager	2.4
Construction trades helper/labourer	2.3
Material handler	2.2
Electrician	1.8
Cook	1.6
Welder/machine operator	1.6

Note: *Occupations in italics* appear in both Table 9.1 and Table 9.2.
Source: Uppal & LaRochelle-Côté, 2014, Table 2 & Table 4.

What do YOU think?

1. In 1991, 2001, and 2011, the most common jobs for women with degrees were schoolteacher and nurse. Do you think this will be the case again in 2021? Why or why not?

2. To what extent do the jobs in Tables 9.1 and 9.2 reflect gender stereotypes? Do you think gender stereotypes reinforce these patterns?

3. Many of the jobs in Table 9.1 involve engaging the public, whether as clients, patients, customers, or students. Compare these jobs with those in Table 9.2, many of which are relatively solitary. What do you think is the significance of that?

What Keeps Women from Taking Science- and Math-Related Courses?

When applied to college and university programs, the acronym STEM stands for science, technology, engineering, mathematics and computer science. These are programs where the enrolment is typically dominated by men. It was traditionally thought that male intelligence and skills were "naturally" geared to these subjects, with the implication that female intelligence and skills "naturally" lay, well, somewhere else. A recent study by Statistics Canada's Darcy Hango (PhD in sociology) tested the validity of this belief.

Quick Hits

The Wage Gap in Canada

There is still a gap in the wages that men and women earn in Canada, though it appears to be shrinking. Consider Table 9.3 below. Note that all dollar amounts are expressed in 2010 constant dollars; this means that any increases from 1981 to 2011 are not a result of inflation, which has already been factored in and adjusted for.

Table 9.3 Real Hourly Wages* of Men and Women Aged 17–64 Employed Full-Time, 1981–2011

	Median Hourly Wage				Average Hourly Wage			
Year	Men	Women	Gap	Ratio	Men	Women	Gap	Ratio
1981	$21.81	$15.72	$5.46	0.721	$22.55	$17.38	$5.17	0.771
1990	21.86	16.35	5.51	0.748	23.31	18.03	5.28	0.774
2001	21.53	17.71	3.82	0.823	23.68	19.43	4.25	0.821
2011	22.27	19.37	2.90	0.870	25.03	21.85	3.18	0.873
Change from 1981 to 2011								
	+$1.09	+$3.65	−$2.56	+0.149	+$2.48	+$4.47	−$1.99	+0.102

Change in Pre-tax Yearly Income (40 hours x 52 weeks, with 2 weeks of paid vacation)

	+$2,267.20	+$7,392.00	−$5,124.80		+$5,158.40	+$9,297.60	−$4,139.20	

* Expressed in 2010 constant dollars.

Note: The ratio is calculated by dividing women's wage by men's wage.

Source: Adapted from Morissette, Pico, & Lu, 2013: p. 12, Table 1.

What do YOU think?

1. Based on this table, would you say there has been significant improvement for women's pay since 1981?
2. Which set of statistics was most meaningful to you in answering question 1?
3. Which of these two possibilities seems most realistic to you:
   a) That women's wages will catch up to men's wages, and the two figures will remain more or less even?
   b) That women's wages will peak at a certain level below men's wages?

Hango (2013) used data from the 2011 National Household Survey (NHS) to assemble findings on university graduates aged 25 to 34. He noted that women made up 39 per cent of those who had graduated from university with a STEM degree, and 66 per cent of those who had graduated with a non-STEM degree. In other words, women make up less than half of those who complete STEM programs at university but more than half of those who graduate in all other fields. Within STEM, women actually make up the majority of those in science and technology programs (59 per cent), but they account for only 30 per cent of those with degrees in mathematics and computer science and just 23 per cent of those with engineering degrees (Hango, 2013; see Figure 9.1).

Another interesting finding concerns the job prospects for men and women graduating with degrees in science, technology, and engineering. Hango found that the unemployment rates for young

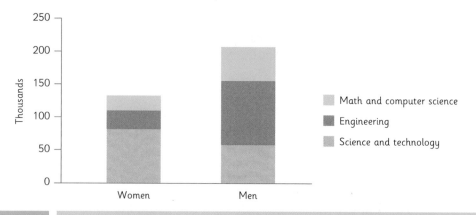

| **Figure 9.1** | Number of Male and Female STEM University Graduates Aged 25–34, by Program, 2011 |

Source: Hango, 2013: p. 2, Chart 1.

men and women graduating with non-STEM degrees in 2011 were about the same: 5.5 per cent for men and 5.7 per cent for women. However, the unemployment rate for male STEM graduates was nearly a point lower than that (4.7 per cent), while the unemployment rate for women with STEM degrees was over a point higher (7.0 per cent) than the non-STEM rate. The gender difference was greatest for those completing programs in math and computer science, where the unemployment rate was 8.5 per cent for women and

4.2 per cent for men (Hango, 2013: p. 3). Only among students of technology was the unemployment rate lower for women than for men (3.4 per cent versus 6.7 per cent; Hango, 2013: p. 3).

Hango also looked at the rate of "employment mismatch." Formerly referred to as the "under-employment rate," the mismatch rate calculates the percentage of university graduates in jobs requiring a high school diploma or less—jobs, in other words, for which that expensive university education is not

Toronto's Ryerson University came under flak when it was reported that its engineering students were forced to crawl through slush in their underwear as part of a hazing ritual. How do social expectations of women conflict with this controversial rite of passage? If you are a woman, would it make you think twice about applying to one of the country's engineering schools?

required. Women STEM graduates had a much higher employment mismatch rate than their male counterparts (18.3 per cent versus 11.8 per cent). Women with degrees in mathematics and computer engineering had a mismatch rate of 22.4 per cent, compared with just 10.1 per cent for men. The only STEM field in which women had the lower mismatch rate was technology (20.5 per cent versus 23.5 per cent for men); that happens to be the STEM field associated with the lowest average pay. Incidentally, the mismatch rate among those with non-STEM degrees was lower for women than for men (18.5 per cent versus 22.2 per cent). Figure 9.2 provides a summary of Hango's findings.

The pay difference is predictable. Hango found that women STEM graduates earn less than men regardless of their program of study. Overall, the median pay for women with STEM degrees was $53,200, compared with $62,300 for men. (see Table 9.4).

Back to the question at the start of this section: are male students naturally better at math, and does this explain their greater participation rate in university STEM programs? Hango looked for the answer in longitudinal data on mathematical ability gathered from the Youth in Transition Survey and the Programme for International Student Assessment (YITS–PISA). The study was started in 2000 with a sample of 15-year-olds, who were interviewed every two years until they were 25. (The study was *longitudinal* because it looked at the individuals over a *long* period of time.) Significantly, 40 per cent of the men who went straight into university after high school entered a STEM program, while only 20 per cent of women did (Hango, 2013). Women were much more likely to enter programs in the social sciences.

Among both men and women, the students who entered STEM programs were those with the highest PISA test scores in mathematics. What was interesting, Hango found, was that "women with *higher* scores were less likely to choose a STEM university program than men with *lower* scores (23% versus 39%)" (Hango, 2013: p. 5). Specifically, of the students scoring high in mathematical proficiency in the PISA test, only 23.2 per cent of women but 45.7 per cent of men went into STEM programs. Of those with low PISA scores, 38.5 per cent of men and just 15.3 per cent of women entered university programs in science, technology, engineering, and math. These findings, based on PISA scores, were supported by data based on high school math marks. While students with higher marks were generally more likely to choose STEM programs, male students at every mark range were more likely than female students to opt for STEM programs (Hango, 2013: p. 6). Girls who had scored at least 90 per cent in math in grades 9 and 10 were less likely to choose a STEM program than boys with marks in the 80 to 89 per cent range.

Another factor Hango considered was self-perception of mathematical ability: students were asked to rate their proficiency in math from excellent to poor (can't count above 10 without taking your shoes off). There was a strong correlation between

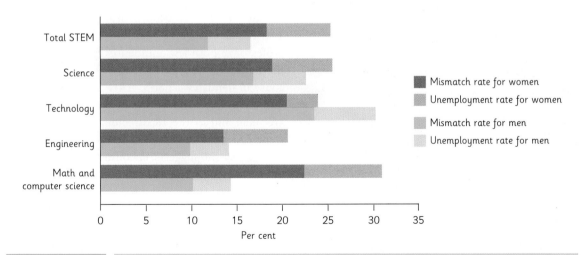

| **Figure 9.2** | Rates of Unemployment and Employment Mismatch among Male and Female STEM Graduates, by Program, 2011 |

Source: Hango, 2013: p. 3, Table 1.

Table 9.4	Median Salaries of STEM Program Graduates Aged 25–34, by Sex and Field of Study, 2011		
	Women	**Men**	**Difference**
Total STEM	$53,200	$62,300	$9,100
Science	49,100	55,300	6,200
Technology	49,700	54,600	4,900
Engineering	61,100	66,300	5,200
Math & computer science	54,900	60,800	5,900

Source: Hango, 2013: p. 3, Table 1.

an individual's perception of his or her ability in math and the likelihood that the individual would choose a STEM program. However, male students with a high perception of their math skills were more likely to choose a STEM program than women with an equally high perception of their own skills (66 per cent versus 47 per cent). Among students who rated their ability as "good," 36 per cent of boys and just 15 per cent of girls chose a STEM program.

Overall, Hango concludes that the gender gap in science, technology, engineering, and math programs is unrelated to differences in both actual and perceived mathematical ability, even when such factors as whether or not the student was born in Canada are taken into account. "This suggests," he writes, "that the gender difference in the selection of a STEM program at university is due to other, unobserved, factors that go beyond academic achievement, parental interactions and influence, and immigration status" (Hango, 2013: p. 7).

What do YOU think?

1. Why are women with higher math scores and perceptions of their ability choosing not to take STEM programs?
2. Why are men with lower levels of math proficiency and perception of their ability opting for STEM programs?
3. What role do you think socialization—by parents, teachers, guidance counsellors, peers, and the media—plays in these decisions?
4. Is it a problem that women with high math scores are entering the social sciences instead of the "hard" sciences? Is this a situation that needs to be "fixed"?

Gender and Dentistry

Dentistry, at both the academic and the professional level, is undergoing a changing gender dynamic. That change has brought tension, resistance, sexism, and bullying, all in evidence recently at Dalhousie University in Halifax, when a scandal involving the university's dentistry school came to light. Male students at the school had set up a Facebook forum where they discussed "hate sex," fantasized about the rape of female classmates, and denigrated women who aspired to be more than "chefs, housekeepers, babysitters, etc." (Halsall, 2015). The group, ironically, called themselves the "Class of DDS 2015 Gentlemen"; their comments were steeped in misogyny, sexism, and homophobia, and a task force set up to investigate the matter found that these elements were widespread throughout the school (Halsall, 2015).

In a *Globe and Mail* article published shortly after the scandal broke, Joan Rush, a former adjunct professor of both law and dentistry at UBC, said we should not be surprised to learn of harassment and abuse in dentistry schools. After all, she explained, "the deans of all 10 faculties of dentistry in Canada are men, and of the 18 directors of the Canadian Dental Association, only one is a woman." This lack of diversity, she suggests, encourages a sense of entitlement among white male students and a disregard for others aspiring to enter the profession.

One of the difficulties involved is the changing gender face of dentistry. The vast majority of Canadian dentists over the age of 45 are male; a small majority of practising dentists under 30 are female (Canadian Dental Association, 2016c). The dentistry faculty at Dalhousie is predominantly male. The higher up the authority ladder you go, the greater the ratio of men to women, so that the positions at the top, occupied by those with the greatest tenure and experience, are almost all held by men. For those men at the top, the school has a gender profile that is very different to the one they experienced when they were students and when they started teaching. The boys' club atmosphere will gradually disappear, but in the meantime, change can be threatening.

The university and the department have issued statements that reflect the view that the issue is about a few "rotten apples." But sociologists do not believe that most social problems come from rotten apples: it is the state of the orchard we have to look at. The nearby fields that are other university departments could be similarly fertile ground for the chauvinism and abuse that were rampant at Dalhousie; even the huge farm that is Canada could be the source of the problem.

It is interesting to note that while the majority of dentists in Canada are male, the role of dental hygienist—normally seen as subordinate to that of dentist—is dominated by women. In 2011, a staggering 98.1 per cent of dental hygienists, dental therapists, and dental nurses were women, two-thirds of them under the age of 44 (Service Canada, 2015). What bearing could that have on misogyny within the dentistry community?

What do YOU think?

1. Citing the lack of diversity "at the top," Rush comments that the misogyny and discrimination at Dalhousie "have been carefully taught." Can we say that part of the problem is the way that male dental students have been socialized into the profession by male dentistry professors?

2. Do you ever read the comments on an online news article? A popular response to stories on the Dalhousie scandal was that the public reaction was sexist: people would not have been offended by sexually charged comments appearing in a Facebook forum for "Dentistry School Ladies." What important points about gender are these posters missing?

Feminization of Occupations

The feminization of an occupational sphere occurs when a particular job, profession, or industry comes to be dominated by or predominantly associated with women. Since the start of World War I, when women began to work outside the home in greater numbers, many occupations have become feminized, including bank teller and secretary (now financial services adviser and administrative assistant, respectively), but job feminization was occurring well before that, as the first of the two examples below describes. Typically, the feminization of an industry works to the disadvantage of those involved in it, who earn lower salaries with less job protection and fewer benefits than those enjoyed by workers outside the feminized occupational sphere.

Women's Work During the Eighteenth-Century "Gin Craze" in London

Beginning around 1720 there was a sudden rise in the sale and consumption of gin in London, England, that lasted until the middle of the century. The liquor was sold not just in bars but in the streets, from wheelbarrows and baskets, in alleyway stalls, in shady one-room gin shops, and from boats floating on the Thames River.

Anyone selling gin without a licence was operating illegally. This was the case for the majority of the thousands of women involved in the gin trade, who couldn't afford the expensive licence. They operated at great risk, and were primary targets of the Gin Acts, which were passed chiefly to restrict the selling of gin to bars owned predominantly by middle-class men. Women were more likely than men to be arrested, and were more likely to be put in prison if convicted.

Why take the chance? At the time, thousands of young women were immigrating to London from Scotland, Ireland, and rural England, looking for jobs and for husbands. The quality and availability of both turned out to be greatly lacking. So why sell gin? Historian Jessica Warner gives three reasons:

> [I]t required little or no capital; it did not require membership in a professional organization; and it was one of the few occupations from which women were not effectively or explicitly excluded. It was, in other words, a means of economic survival. (Warner, 2002: p. 51)

The Gin Acts often pitted women against women. Enforcement depended heavily on the accusations of paid informants, half of whom were women. Warner describes the harsh economics involved:

Consider the options of a young woman newly arrived in London in 1737 or 1738. She could work for a year as a maid and earn £5 in addition to receiving room and board, or she could inform against one gin-seller, and upon securing a conviction collect a reward of £5. There were two ways to make money, one hard, the other easy, and many people naturally chose the latter. Most did so only once, collecting their reward and then attempting to hide as best they could. (Warner, 2002: p. 137)

This could be called danger pay, as informers were not well liked.

What do YOU think?

Did the feminization of the gin trade in eighteenth-century London benefit women or harm them? What alternatives might have been available to female immigrants to London who chose not to get involved in selling gin illegally?

Women's Clerical Work in Canada, 1891–1971

The early twentieth century saw the spectacular increase in the number of clerical workers in the Canadian labour force. It also saw the feminization of the position, along with the degradation of the role, as measured in terms of wages, skill level, and opportunity for promotion. How all three trends—growth, feminization, and degradation—mesh together is a story that gives insight on both the past and the present.

Clerical work was traditionally a man's job. The male bookkeeper's varied duties required a lot of what we now call multitasking. As companies grew in size, there was much more clerical work that needed to be done, and businesses moved toward a more "rationalized" and "efficient" approach to task management, according to the principles of scientific management (or Taylorism, discussed in Chapter 5). The result was a kind of assembly-line office work, in which several clerical workers were engaged in the rapid performance of repeated simple tasks, with little variety and few opportunities to move up in the company. The growing belief (based on assumptions about women's limited capabilities) that this was ideal

work for women, who were supposed to be wives and mothers first and labourers second, was reinforced by discrimination that offered them few alternatives. The thinking of the time is illustrated in the following passage from a book called *Office Management, Principles and Practice*, published in 1925 by William Henry Leffingwell, a proponent of applying scientific management to the office:

A woman is to be preferred for the secretarial position for she is not averse to doing minor tasks, work involving the handling of petty details, which would irk and irritate ambitious young men, who usually feel that the work they are doing is of no importance if it can be performed by some person with a lower salary. Most such men are also anxious to get ahead and to be promoted from position to position, and consequently if there is much work of a detail character to be done, and they are expected to perform it, they will not remain satisfied and will probably seek a position elsewhere. (Leffingwell, 1925: p. 116)

This job transformation got a big push during World War I (1914–18), when women entered the workforce to replace men who had gone overseas to serve in Europe. During this time the number of clerical workers in Canada jumped by 113,148—around half of them women. At the Bank of Nova Scotia's regional offices in Ontario, the percentage of clerks who were women jumped from 8.5 per cent in 1911 to 40.7 per cent in 1916. Although, overall, the number of women clerical workers in Canada fell slightly when the men returned from the war, the figure remained high and steadily grew, as Table 9.5 shows.

What do YOU think?

1. Where in Canada can you see evidence of the feminization of work today? What effect do you think the feminization of these workplaces has on the employees working there?

2. Is there any evidence of a reverse trend that we might call the "masculinization" of work, in which a particular type of employment dominated by men acquires greater prestige and, of course, greater pay?

| Table 9.5 | The Feminization of Clerical Workers in Canada, 1891–1971 |

Year	Total Clerical Workers	Women Clerical Workers	
		Number	Percentage
1891	133,017	4,710	14.3
1901	57,231	12,660	22.1
1911	103,543	33,723	32.6
1921	216,691	90,577	41.8
1931	260,674	117,637	45.1
1941	303,655	152,216	50.1
1951	563,093	319,183	56.7
1961	818,912	503,660	61.5
1971	1,310,910	903,395	68.9

Being a Gender Minority in a Gendered Occupation

When individuals find themselves in gendered jobs and they are of the minority sex, it can have a profound effect on their gender performance at work.

Paul Sargent (2005) discusses the phenomenon in his look at men in early childhood education (which, for Sargent's purposes, includes the lower grades of primary school as well as the daycare profession, where most ECE teaching jobs are found). Sargent incorporates Raewyn Connell's (1995) four performances of

jo unruh/iStockphoto

Does this ECE's hands-off celebration of a toddler's achievement look natural to you? Why do you think we're so suspicious of men who want to be daycare workers? What societal influences have conditioned our suspicion?

Our Stories

The Famous Five and the "Persons" Case

The "**Famous Five**" is the name given to five Canadians who fought for equal rights for women during the first half of the twentieth century. They are **Henrietta Muir Edwards** (1849–1931), **Nellie McClung** (1873–1951), **Louise McKinney** (1868–1931), **Emily Murphy** (1868–1933), and **Irene Parlby** (1868–1965). Among their distinguished achievements is their successful campaign to have women awarded the status of "persons" under British and Canadian law.

When Emily Murphy, in 1916, was named the first woman police magistrate in Alberta, her appointment was challenged on the grounds that women were not "persons" under the British North America (BNA) Act, which had officially created the Dominion of Canada in 1867. It was understood, when the BNA Act was written, that "persons" meant "men," for women were not allowed to vote or to hold public office. In 1917, the Supreme Court of Alberta ruled that women were, in fact, "persons" in that province. Emily Murphy thus became the first woman magistrate in the British Empire. In order to advance the cause of women aspiring to hold public office at the federal level, she then had her name put forward as a candidate for the Canadian Senate, only to have the Conservative prime minister Robert Borden, invoking the BNA Act and its reference to "persons," reject her bid.

In the years that followed, the fight to have women in the Senate was taken up by women's groups across the country. In 1927, Murphy and the other members of the Famous Five, all of them prominent women's rights activists in Alberta, petitioned the Supreme Court of Canada with this question: *Does the word "persons" in Section 24, of The British North America Act, 1867, include female persons?* The Court answered that it did not. There were no women in the British House of Lords, so the notion of female members in the Canadian Senate was easily dismissed. The Famous Five took their case to a higher court of appeal: the Judicial Committee of the Privy Council in Britain. On 18 October 1929, the Lord Chancellor of the Privy Council, announcing the judicial committee's decision, ruled that "women are persons . . . and may become Members of the Senate of Canada." The committee stated "that the exclusion of women from all public offices is a relic of days more barbarous than ours. And to those who would ask why the word 'persons' should include females, the obvious answer is, why should it not?"

The following year, 1930, Montreal-born Cairine Wilson (1885–1962) became the first woman appointed to the Senate of Canada.

---

masculinity—essentially, four ways Connell identified in which men act out gender roles. These are

1) hegemonic masculinity;
2) subordinate masculinity;
3) marginalized masculinity; and
4) complicit masculinity.

Sargent explains them this way:

> Hegemonic masculine practices are those that serve to normalize and naturalize men's dominance and women's subordination. Subordinate masculinities are those behaviors and presentations of self that could threaten the legitimacy of hegemonic masculinity. Gay men, effeminate men, and men who eschew competition or traditional definitions of success are examples frequently cited. . . . These men are vulnerable to being abused and ridiculed by others. Marginalized masculinities represent the adaptation of masculinities to such issues as race and class. For example, a Black man may enjoy certain privileges that stem from success as a small business owner, yet still find himself unable to hail a cab. . . . Finally, complicit masculinities are those that do not embody hegemonic processes *per se*, but benefit from the ways in which hegemonic masculinities construct the gender order and local gender regimes. (Sargent, 2005)

Library and Archives Canada, PA-030212

In her popular writing, Nellie McClung often drew her readers' attention to the hard-working reality of farm women. During the early 1920s, she was a member of the Legislative Assembly in Alberta.

Quick Hits

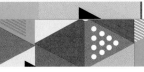

Women and Canadian Politics

1867 Canadian federal and provincial vote given only to white men with property.

1916 Women in Manitoba, Saskatchewan, and Alberta get the provincial vote.

1917 World War I nurses and the female relatives of soldiers get the federal vote.
Women in British Columbia and Ontario get the provincial vote.

1918 Women in Canada get the federal vote.
Women in Nova Scotia get the provincial vote.

1918 First woman provincial cabinet minister (Mary Ellen Smith, BC).

1919 Women in New Brunswick get the provincial vote.

1921 First woman federal cabinet minister (Mary Ellen Smith).

1922 Women in Prince Edward Island get the provincial vote.

1925 Women in the British colony of Newfoundland get the vote.

1930 First woman senator in Canada (Cairine Wilson).

1940 Women in Quebec get the provincial vote.

1951 First woman mayor in Canada (Charlotte Whitten, Ottawa).
First Nations women allowed to vote and run for office in band councils.

1954 First Indigenous woman elected band chief (Elsie Knott, Curve Lake First Nation, ON).

1991 First woman provincial premier (Rita Johnson, BC).
First woman territorial premier (Nelly Cournoyea, NT).

1993 First woman prime minister (Kim Campbell).

2008 Number of women premiers in Canada: 1 (NU).

2013 Number of women premiers in Canada: 6 (NU, NL, BC, AB, QC, ON).

2016 Number of women premiers in Canada: 3 (BC, AB, ON).

Sargent argues that men who work in early childhood education are caught up in a conflict between performing a *subordinate masculinity* (for example, by being "nurturing"), which would make them good at their job, and engaging in more stereotypical masculinity performances, which are imposed on them by the gendered nature of the job. Examples of male gender images involved in this context are "homosexual–pedophile" and "man as disciplinarian." Male ECE teachers are not allowed the caring physical contact that female teachers are encouraged to have. As one male teacher explains, "Women's laps are places of love. Men's are places of danger" (Sargent, 2005). This stems from the popularly reproduced image of the homosexual–pedophile, which mistakenly conflates two different

sexualities. As a result, male teachers are reduced to less threatening performances of complicit masculinity, which include "high fives" and handshakes rather than hugs, and rewarding children with prizes and names written on the board rather than physical contact. This can be demoralizing for the male early childhood educator. As one male teacher wrote , "I sometimes feel really inadequate when I watch the kids draped all over the women and all I'm doing is keeping them busy, handing out trinkets, or slapping high fives" (Sargent, 2005).

The "man as disciplinarian" gender image also restricts the performance of male gender roles in the ECE environment. Because it is assumed that men more naturally perform discipline, they are assigned greater responsibility for monitoring the behaviour of "problem kids." Classrooms occupied by male teachers then become seen as sites of discipline. No matter what the particular male's natural inclinations or teaching styles are—whether or not they are more nurturing or "female-defined"—these teachers are forced to conform to a masculinity performance that reinforces male authoritarian stereotypes.

Telling It Like It Is

On-the-Job Training: Making the Right Impression in a Male-Defined Business

I was on my very first job as a criminologist. I had gone through years of school to learn theories, statistics, research methods—everything that I *thought* was necessary before going out into the field.

I had been hired as a research assistant to make observations and conduct interviews at a law enforcement conference. This was the first time that I was actually going to be around the law enforcement community. I was eager to make a good impression on my new colleagues.

I got to the conference a bit early and waited for the rest of the research team to arrive for our scheduled meeting. We were meeting near the entrance of the venue, where most people would be entering and exiting the premises. It was quite early, and not many people were around.

A gentleman came up and introduced himself to me as a fellow conference attendee. We chatted for a minute or so before I noticed that he was staring at the ring on my finger. Next thing I knew, he was asking me questions about whether or not I was happy in my relationship. That's when I realized that this man was not being kind or professional—he was hitting on me!

I made it very clear that I was only at the conference as a researcher, and then excused myself from the conversation. Just then, someone from my team walked through the door and I quickly went over to say hello.

I was a little thrown by the whole incident at first. While it might not seem like a big deal, I want you to consider this: imagine that you are a brand-new graduate from your field of study—who happens to be a woman. You have been given an opportunity to begin your career. On your very first day, instead of being met with professionalism, you are met with sexist attitudes that see every woman as "available".

How did I deal with this? I had brushed it off by the time the rest of the team arrived and was ready to get back to work.

As the conference continued, I started to hear that other women (researchers, attendees, and keynote speakers alike) were having similar experiences. Law enforcement is a male-dominated field. At least 70 per cent of the people at this conference were men; women stood out.

I discussed my concerns with my supervisor and learned that my experiences were not atypical of the experiences of women criminologists. My supervisor was a wonderful source of information and support. I quickly learned how to react appropriately to inappropriateness. There's a fine line between a reaction that will enable you to work with people who have just offended you, and putting up walls that get in the way of your research objectives.

Over the years, I have informally gathered similar stories from other women in the field.

I do not want to paint a picture of the male law enforcement community as predators. Most of the people at the conference (men and women) were there to learn and share ideas with other professionals. However, there were a few people who made one thing very clear: the professional world is not a completely level playing field—not yet anyway. Being a woman does matter.

—Rhea Adhopia

What do YOU think?

How was the author of this narrative essentially sanctioned for being deviant?

Men in early childhood education are expected to want to move into occupational positions more in keeping or complicit with male hegemony: administrative positions in ECE organizations and higher grades or the principal's office in elementary schools. Sargent's study did not verify this trend, but it could be argued that a longitudinal approach, looking at male teachers' careers over time, would yield evidence of men "moving up" in the system. We might find, too, that this kind of trend is as much or more the product of the gendered nature of the organizations as of the individuals' actual intent.

What do YOU think?

In some ways it's easier to examine the impact on men of working in a female-gendered occupation because it is much less common than the reverse: women working in male-dominated occupations. Think of three jobs defined as male. For each one, think of how the masculinized nature of the job might affect a female worker's gender performance.

"Race" and Gender: Intersecting Oppression

As we saw in Chapter 8, on "race" and ethnicity, "race" and gender often intersect to amplify oppression. Racial prejudice and discrimination can often reinforce gender bias, and vice versa. In some cases, opposing gender/"race" stereotypes can affect an oppressed group, as in the case of Asian women, described below.

Opposing Gender/"Race" Stereotypes

There is a tendency to stereotype visible minority women into two extremes, an example of the intersectionality referred to in an earlier chapter. Renee Tajima (1989) writes about how an East Asian woman may be stereotyped either as the Lotus Blossom Baby or as the Dragon Lady. In Tania Das Gupta's words, the former stereotype "encompasses the images of the China doll, the geisha girl and shy Polynesian beauty. The latter includes prostitutes and 'devious madams'" (Das Gupta, 1996: p. 27).

Black women also face discrimination on the basis of opposing "race"/gender stereotypes. Das Gupta describes the double image as follows:

On the one hand there was the slow, de-sexed, "cow-like" mammy, evolved into the "Aunt Jemima figure"—familiar to many from older boxes of pancake mix—a servile and contented image which brings together gender and race ideologies. On the other

Photo by Ezra Shaw/Getty Images

University of Waterloo professor Naila Keleta-Mae calls "Formation," the debut track of Beyoncé's 2016 visual album Lemonade, "a complex meditation on female blackness, . . . one that is ambitious, spiritual, decisive, sexual, capitalist, loving, and communal" (2016). Yet critics say that as the most powerful woman in the American music industry, Beyoncé occupies a position of privilege that puts her out of touch with what life is like for most black women in North America. Does her social standing enhance or diminish her status as a hero of black American feminism?

hand, there was the sexual objectification of Black women's bodies, or body parts to be more exact. (Das Gupta, 1996: p. 27)

The sexually objectified black woman is a familiar figure in music videos. White stars such as Miley Cyrus and Taylor Swift have been criticized for both objectifying and dehumanizing their black female back-up dancers in their videos and on stage.

The Indian Princess and the Squaw

Indigenous women have long been subject to the opposing gender/"race" stereotypes of the "Indian princess" and the "squaw." In the United States, the Indian princess is a heroine at the heart of the American master narrative of how their country was built. She is the beautiful Disneyfied Pocahontas saving handsome John Smith from death, in the process abandoning her people to serve the interests of the incoming colonial power. She is Sacajawea, the Shoshone woman who aided the Lewis and Clark expedition from 1804 to 1806, helping to open up the West to "civilization" and the eventual reservation entrapment of her people.

The Indian princess is not part of the master narrative of Canada. Still, she is found here and there in Canadian history. Emily Pauline Johnson, popular Mohawk writer at the turn of the twentieth century, was billed as "The Mohawk Princess" to audiences in North America and Britain, for whom she performed her poetry. Catharine Sutton, a heroic Ojibwa woman of the nineteenth century, is known in Owen Sound, Ontario, as "the Indian Princess" (Steckley, 1999).

While the stereotype of the Indian princess has been used as a metaphor for the supposed open-armed acceptance by North American Native people of European colonizers, the squaw is a figure that has been used by white writers (including American presidents Thomas Jefferson and Theodore Roosevelt) to characterize Indigenous people as savages, providing ample justification for white colonial dominance (Smits, 1982). The image summarizes the impressions of Aboriginal culture as brutal and barbaric, with lazy, abusive Indigenous men overworking and generally mistreating their wives, sisters, mothers, and daughters. It has contributed to the disproportionately high number of Aboriginal women in Canada who are counted as missing or murdered.

Gender and Immigration

There have been several instances in Canadian history when only the men or the women of a particular ethnic group were permitted or encouraged to immigrate. We have seen, in Chapter 8, that Chinese and South Asian women were effectively blocked from entering Canada for significant parts of the twentieth century. Later in the century, women from the Philippines were encouraged to immigrate to fill labour shortages in certain feminized occupations. However, their immigration was subject to strict conditions, and they faced hardships upon their arrival.

Filipino immigration to Canada is distinctive in that it allowed women to become the "pioneers." They made the journey before their husbands and other male family members, sending most of their money, together with care packages of bargain-hunted goods, back home to their families and sponsored relatives and provided them with a place to stay. There have been two periods of Filipino immigration to Canada. The first brought nurses, mostly women, while the second brought nannies, who suffer more from the intersectionality of gender and "race" than did the earlier generation of Filipino immigrants.

In 1981, the Canadian government instituted its Foreign Domestic Movement Program (FDMP) to address the growing need for in-house child care that was created as more women began working outside the home. In 1992, the FDMP was replaced by the more restrictive Live-In Caregiver Program, which required selected immigrants to commit to 24 months of domestic work within a three-year period, during which time they were also required to "live in" with the family. Nannies came mainly from the Philippines, Jamaica, and Britain. Filipino nannies dominated the figures, the percentage of domestics coming from the Philippines rising between 1982 and 1990 from 10.6 per cent to 50.5 per cent. This trend occurred not just in Canada but in Hong Kong, Singapore, Saudi Arabia, Britain, and the United States. The political and economic unrest that surrounded the fall of the corrupt Marcos government made the Philippines a place many wanted to leave.

The women of the second period of Filipino immigration were older than their compatriots who had migrated earlier: those aged 30–34 predominated, with those aged 25–29 and 35–39 forming smaller but roughly equal groups, and those aged 20–24 and 50–54 sharing about the same low

Going Global

Boyat and Deviant Gender Performance in the Arab World

In Arab countries such as Qatar and the United Arab Emirates, there is an emerging pattern of deviant behaviour that cuts across gender and ethnic lines. It involves young women who adopt a masculine style of dress, including baggy jeans or military pants, aviator shades, heavy watches and other jewellery, combat boots or running shoes, and so on; many of the women keep their hair cut short. A woman dressed this way wouldn't look out of place in North America, but in many parts of the Arab world women in public customarily wear a *burqa* or *abaya*, a full-length, loose-fitting robe that covers the whole body from the shoulders down.

The women are known as *boyat* (singular *boyah*), an Arabic word akin to "tomboy" and sometimes translated as "transsexual." But the behaviour is not sexual. It is more a deviant way of acting out and exploring gender. Dressed in their male "disguise," *boyat* seem able to talk and act more aggressively and independently than they could dressed as women. The women involved consider their behaviour a way of life, not just a frivolous game. They find an important kind of solidarity with other women engaged in the same behaviour (see "Cross about Cross-Dressing," 2010; "Defying Gender Expectations," 2009; Naidoo, 2011).

What are the factors influencing the *boyat* phenomenon? Globalization has played a role, by exposing girls in Middle Eastern countries to images of women acting more independently than women in the Arab world are traditionally permitted to do. Social media allow *boyat* to communicate with one another anonymously, and get together online without being seen. There are also links between the *boyat* phenomenon and higher education. A college or university education prolongs the period of unmarried youth for young women. Like-minded *boyat* gathering together in women's colleges and campuses like those of the UAE's Higher Colleges of Technology are less likely to arouse suspicion with their behaviour. In such settings, their increasing number makes them the majority, putting them in a position to poke fun at and even bully their more conservative female peers.

In most settings, *boyat* remain a minority, and deviant behaviour is met with negative sanctions. Some opponents of the *boyat* phenomenon have attempted to medicalize the "problem" by proposing rehabilitation therapy and medicine. In some jurisdictions, cross-dressing has been made illegal.

Wisky/Dreamstime.com

What do YOU think?

1. Read additional accounts of the *boyat* phenomenon listed at the end of this chapter. Do you think this is just a social fad, or will it continue for, say, more than 10 years? Could it be a stepping stone to more independence in gender expression in Arab countries?

2. How would you compare the governmental and general institutional treatment of *boyat* to the twentieth-century reaction to homosexuality and lesbianism in the West (e.g. arrests, gay bashing, and prescribed courses of treatment)?

Quick Hits

"Two-Spirit People" and "Manly-Hearted Women": Alternative Gender Roles among North American Aboriginal People

North American Indigenous people have traditionally had an enlightened view of gender variability. One example is the two-spirit person, or *berdache*, who is either a man who occasionally dresses as a woman and takes part in some domestic activities traditionally associated with women, or a woman who engages in hunting and warfare and takes on leadership roles. In traditional Aboriginal culture two-spirit people were not seen as abnormal but were, rather, respected and recognized as making up a legitimate "third gender" (Roscoe, 1998).

Another example is the *Ninauposkitzipxpe*, or "manly-hearted women," found among the Peigan and described in the following passage by anthropologist Alice Kehoe:

> About a third of elderly (sixty years or older) North Piegan women in 1939, and a few younger women, were considered manly-hearted. . . . Such women owned property, were good managers and usually effective workers, were forthright and assertive in public, in their homes, and as sexual partners, and were active in religious rituals. They were called "manly-hearted" because boldness, aggressiveness, and a drive to amass property and social power are held to be ideal traits for men. . . . [T]he manly-hearted woman is admired as well as feared by both men and women. (Kehoe, 1995: p. 115)

Photo by John H. Fouch, 1877. Courtesy of Dr. James Brust.

This stereoview photograph, taken in 1877, shows "Squaw Jim" (*left*), a two-spirit person of the Crow Nation. How does the term *two-spirit person* compare to *transgender*? How do we in Canadian society tend to characterize women who are bold, aggressive, and career-oriented? Do we think of them as positively as the traditional Blackfoot did?

percentage. It was more difficult for this generation of Filipino immigrants. They were better educated than immigrating British and Jamaican nannies: among those receiving authorization for temporary employment as nannies between 1982 and 1990, 8 per cent held bachelor's degrees, 7 per cent had at least some university education, 17 per cent had some trade and technology training, and 12 per cent had other non-university training. Working as nannies made these women grossly underemployed, as sociologist Anita Beltran Chen argues (1998). Yet only domestic work could bring them to Canada.

As women, as visible minorities, and as temporary and poorly paid employees subject to few industrial controls, the women were vulnerable to exploitation and physical, emotional, and sexual abuse. Those who had been trained in a specific field such as nursing also had to fight losing their skills through disuse. Between 15 and 20 per cent were married and had to endure separation from their husbands and, often, children. Those who were single returned a large portion (estimates vary around 75 per cent) of their income to their family back home, holding on to little money to look after themselves. They are restricted by the stereotypes of "race" and gender that treat Asian women as caregivers, overlooking skills that might make them productive in other areas of Western society

WRAP IT UP

Summary

We have seen that gender and sex are different. You are born with a sex: typically male or female, although intersex people may be born with both male and female sexual organs. Your gender is socially constructed to a significant extent. It may not fit neatly into the binary categories "male" and "female" but may sit somewhere between these two points. The social construction of gender applies not just in obvious areas such as clothing and colours, but in occupations as well. You need be neither a woman nor a feminist to recognize that the feminization of an occupation—making it unrewarding in terms of pay, power, and social status—helps to create inequality between men and women. This inequality, reflected in pay ratio and in the greater likelihood of women working part time, is changing very little. As sociologists, we need to investigate why this is so, and look for ways to address the inequity. We also must ask ourselves whether the separate paths that men and women take in postsecondary education lead to social inequality or just difference, an issue we considered in Chapter 4, on socialization.

THINK BACK

Questions for Critical Review

1. Explain, in your own words, the difference between sex and gender.
2. What does it mean to say that gender is socially constructed to a significant extent?
3. Do you think there are still common stereotypes in North America surrounding those who transgress gendered work roles (e.g. the male nurse, the woman construction worker)? If so, do you think they can be changed? What would it take?
4. Describe how gender and ethnicity intersect to create stereotypes about women of different ethnic backgrounds.
5. How do you think gender-based immigration (i.e. with immigrants of one sex entering the country in much greater numbers than the other) affects the settling experiences of different groups, such as Filipinos?
6. Do you think that the ideology of fag is used to keep men, more than women, in line with gender norms? If so, why do you think that would be?
7. To what extent can a man really be considered a feminist? How would that define his role as a sociologist?

READ ON

Suggested Print and Online Resources

Online

"Cross about Cross-Dressing: Is It a Wicked Western Habit that Should be Stopped?"
www.economist.com/node/15403091

"Shedding Light on the 'Boyat' Phenomenon: Conference Separates Fact from Fiction on the Issue."
http://gulfnews.com/news/uae/general/shedding-light-on-the-boyat-phenomenon-1.796816

- The *Economist* article provides an account of the "debate about fashion in Qatar," and looks at both sides of the issue of cross-dressing and *boyat* in the Middle East. The second article, from GulfNews. com, reviews a conference on the topic that was held at the Sharjah Women's College in the United Arab Emirates.

"Converging Gender Roles"

www.statcan.gc.ca/pub/75-001-x/10706/9268-eng.htm

- Katherine Marshall's article, from Statistics Canada's *Perspectives on Labour and Income*, offers a stats-based view of the extent to which gender roles may be converging in Canada.

"The 'Genderless Baby' Who Caused a Storm of Controversy"

www.thestar.com/news/article/1105515--the-genderless-baby-who-caused-a-storm-of-controversy-in-2011

"Remember Storm? We Check In on the Baby Being Raised Gender Neutral"

www.thestar.com/life/parent/2013/11/15/remember_storm_we_check_in_on_the_baby_being_raised_genderneutral.html

"Baby Storm Five Years Later: Preschooler on Top of the World"

www.thestar.com/news/gta/2016/07/11/baby-storm-five-years-later-preschooler-on-top-of-the-world.html

- These Toronto *Star* articles look at the life of Baby Storm from the eve of the infant's first birthday to the start of preschool.

The Gender Book

www.thegenderbook.com

- Four Texans set out to create an illustrated guide to gender that would be accessible to children but of equal interest to adults. The website includes resources and some of the colourful hand-drawn illustrations found in the book itself (published in 2014), which is available for order through the website.

Transgender Woman Says Community Faces Employment Discrimination

www.ctvnews.ca/canada/transgender-woman-says-community-faces-employment-discrimination-1.1985731?

- A news item on the CTV website discusses the difficulties that transgender women are having in the business world, particularly regarding being underpaid and not being able to get jobs for which they are qualified.

In Print

Judith Butler (1990), *Gender Trouble: Feminism and the Subversion of Identity* (New York: Routledge).

- Butler's pioneering work launched the study of queer theory.

John Colapinto (2000), *As Nature Made Him* (New York: Harper).

- Colapinto provides the definitive account of David Reimer's life and tragic death.

Andrea Medovarski & Brenda Cranney, eds (2006), *Canadian Women Studies: An Introductory Reader*, 2nd edn (Toronto: INANNA).

- This volume combines an introduction to feminist thought in general with an insightful survey of feminist theory in Canada.

Maureen G. Reed (2008), "Reproducing the Gender Order in Canadian Forestry: The Role of Statistical Representation," *Scandinavian Journal of Forestry* (23, 1: pp. 78–91).

- This article looks at how and why the number of women engaged in forestry is not increasing significantly.

PART FOUR

Social
Institutions

▲ Dinodia Photo/Getty Images

Family

10

The Gist

Reading this chapter will help you to . . .

- Characterize the diversity of the Canadian family.
- Explain the ways that family in Quebec is different from family in the rest of Canada.
- Discuss eight major changes taking place in the family today.
- Identify the different forms that conjugal roles can take.
- Describe the varying impacts of endogamy on different racial and ethnic groups in Canada.
- Identify how immigration patterns can affect family development.
- Outline and comment on the argument that Indigenous families were "under attack" during the twentieth century in Canada.

Terms of the Trade

- Bott hypothesis
- cluttered nest
- cohabiting union
- common-law union
- companionate conjugal roles
- complementary conjugal roles
- complex household
- conjugal roles
- crude marriage rate
- disabled family
- double burden
- double ghetto
- empty nest
- endogamy
- eugenics
- exogamy
- extended family
- fecundity
- gender strategy
- general intelligence
- genocide
- intelligences
- joint conjugal roles
- marital roles
- master status
- matrilineal
- nuclear family
- occupational segregation
- polygamy
- polygyny
- replacement rate
- residential schools
- scientific classism
- scientific racism
- second shift
- segregated conjugal roles
- simple household
- Sixties Scoop
- total fertility rate
- work interruptions

Names to Know

- Rod Beaujot
- Elizabeth Bott
- Ann Duffy
- Nancy Mandell
- M. Reza Nakhaie

◀ Photo by George Rose/Getty Images

For Starters

Johan Ordonez/AFP/Getty Images

Can I Blame It All on My Parents?

You probably know someone who blames their family for all of their problems—the inability to find meaningful relationships, financial success, a fulfilling career, and so on. It's a common theme among stand-up comics and sitcom writers, who have mined the "dysfunctional family" as a source of humorous material. It is a therapy prescribed by some psychoanalysts who draw on Freud's notion that we all harbour a volatile mix of love and anger toward our parents that we need to bring into consciousness. Rooted in mainstream psychology of the late twentieth century, this idea gave a veneer of legitimacy to pop psychologists who turned blaming the family into a daytime and late-night television phenomenon known as the tabloid talk show, which flourished under hosts such as Jerry Springer and Maury Povich, who encouraged guests to confront their family members in episodes that often ended in onstage fist fights and chair-throwing. While these shows may have mocked conventional family dynamics in a setting contrived to create drama, the raw emotion at the heart of many episodes was real.

Family-blaming is not restricted to trash TV and online psychology forums. Consider the anger of the following lines written by acclaimed British poet Philip Larkin (1922–1985) in the poem "This Be the Verse":

They fuck you up, your mum and dad.
    They may not mean to, but they do.
They fill you with the faults they had
    And add some extra, just for you.

But they were fucked up in their turn
    By fools in old-style hats and coats,
Who half the time were soppy-stern
    And half at one another's throats.

Man hands on misery to man.
    It deepens like a coastal shelf.
Get out as early as you can,
    And don't have any kids yourself. (1971)

Of course, "getting out" is one thing; escaping your upbringing is quite another. We can see Larkin's poem as a very cynical take on socialization, the process of learning the values and standards of behaviour required to become members of the society to which we belong. As we saw in Chapter 4, socialization comes first through interactions with one's closest family members, and it leaves an impression that can last a lifetime.

Incidentally, this is a short poem I wrote in response to Larkin:

Larkin never married,
> But he did know how to rhyme.

He maintained non-committal relations
> With three women at the same time.

Larkin fed his family misery
> To readers down the years;

I'm glad he didn't have any kids himself
> To pass down all his fears. (2015)

Because as much as we may at times want to blame our families, we have to recognize the value that families bring in shaping responsible citizens of a society that functions harmoniously and advances over time.

Ultimately, you can't run away from your family. You're better off understanding how your family made you who you are and how the family as an institution gives shape to society. By the end of this chapter, you should have some ideas.

What do YOU think?

1. What negative aspects of family was Larkin describing? In what ways is his poem a cynical interpretation of the process of primary socialization?
2. Are you optimistic or pessimistic about your future family life as husband or wife, mother or father? Why, sociologically, do you think that is?
3. Do you have married uncles and aunts who have chosen not to have children? If so, why do you think that they didn't?

Introduction: Family Is Diverse

The opening line of Russian novelist Leo Tolstoy's tragic romantic novel *Anna Karenina* reads: "Happy families are all alike; every unhappy family is unhappy in its own way." I disagree. Happy families, functional families, and good families exist in many forms, and are alike only in their success at serving basic purposes, such as providing emotional support for family members, taking care of elders, and raising the next generation. In most other respects, happy families are diverse. But Tolstoy and even Larkin were right in one regard: there are many ways to screw up family.

It would be misleading to say that one family form is demonstrably better than any other for its members. And yet conservative media are filled with judgemental remarks about contemporary family forms. Even traditional sociology is not free from this bias. If you were presented with the terms nuclear family (which includes a parent or parents and children) and extended family (which might include, in addition, grandparents, aunts, uncles, and cousins), you might be led to believe that the former is "normal" and the other some kind of deviation from the regular model. This is not the case. For some cultures, historical and current, using the word "family" to mean parents and children alone would be as odd as using the term "body" to refer just to the heart.

The Wendat (Huron) language of the seventeenth century had no terms for "nuclear" or "extended" family. The common way for the Wendat to refer to family was through the noun root -*hwatsir*-, meaning "matrilineage," or the verb root -*yentio*-, meaning "to belong to a matrilineal clan." Matrilineage is the line of descendants that follows the mother's line. A woman, her sisters and brothers, and their mother would belong to the same matrilineage. The longhouses that the people lived in would usually be dominated by one matrilineage, with married sisters and their husbands and children forming the nucleus of the people living in one house. Thus, the most common term for "family" in Wendat referred to what we would probably brand with the term "extended family."

More useful than "nuclear family" and "extended family" are terms proposed by Frances Goldscheider and Regina Bures in their study of intergenerational living arrangements in America. They favour the terms "simple household" and "complex household." A simple household consists of unrelated (by blood) adults with or without children. Conversely, a complex household includes "two or more adults who are related but not married to each other and hence could reasonably be expected to live separately" (2003). A simple household tends to consist of a single adult or married adults living with or without children. Probably the most common form of complex household in Canada today is one in which adult children live at home with a parent or parents. My household is complex: my wife and I live on the

Catherine Yeulet/iStockphoto

Would you call this a typical Canadian family? How many families do you know that look like this? Does yours?

Quick Hits

What Is a Census Family?

For the purpose of collecting census data, Statistics Canada defines a family as any of the following:

- a married couple, with or without children, living together in the same dwelling;
- a common-law couple, with or without children, living together in the same dwelling; or
- a lone parent (single, separated, married, or divorced) with at least one child, living together in the same dwelling.

The first two of these are considered *couple families*. The couple may be same-sex or opposite-sex. A situation in which a child or children live with their grandparents but not their parents is also considered a census family.

In addition to this definition, a couple with children is considered an *intact family* when all of the children are the biological or adopted children of both parents.

A couple family in which at least one child is the biological or adopted child of one parent only is a *stepfamily*. In a *simple stepfamily*, all of the children are the biological or adopted children of one parent only. In a *complex stepfamily*,

- there is at least one child of both parents and at least one child of only one parent;
- there is a least one child of each parent; or
- there is at least one child of both parents and at least one child of each parent.

Source: Statistics Canada, 2016a: note 1; www.statcan.gc.ca/eng/concepts/definitions/c-fam.

Going Global

What Is Your Family Name? A Story of Diversity

Patronymics are family names or surnames derived from a father's given name. Common British names such as Johnson, Peterson, and Jackson are patronymics, as are Scottish and Irish names beginning with Mac- or Mc- (meaning "son of"): Macdonald, McAndrews. "Ben" in Hebrew names and "Bin" or "Ibn" in Arabic names are similar. Russian features separate patronymics for sons and daughters: for example, Mikhailovich means "son of Mikhail," while Mikhailovna means "daughter of Mikhail."

Icelandic culture also features a separate patronymic to represent the father–daughter relationship. If Jon's son and daughter are named, respectively, Olaf and Katrin, they are known as Olaf Jonsson and Katrin Jonsdottir. There is also the option to use *matronymics*, based on the mother's name. This would come into play especially if a mother and/or a child wanted to sever ties with the father. For example, if Olaf and Katrin wanted to do this and their mother's name was Bryndis, they would be called Olaf Bryndisarson and Katrin Bryndisardottir.

There is an Icelandic movie, *Bjarnfreðarson* (2009), in which the male title character is made fun of for having a "woman's name," the product of the feminist stance of his mother and his own dislike of his father. Note that if you wanted to call someone in Iceland, their telephone books are organized by first name.

In some Spanish-speaking societies, it's conventional to use one's father's surname followed by one's mother's surname. The current (2016) president of Mexico is Enrique Peña Nieto, who uses both his father's surname (Peña) and his mother's (Nieto).

Contact with other cultures influences prevailing naming conventions. For instance, there are also people in Iceland who have surnames that sound more like the sort of surname you would hear in Canada, without any patronymic or matronymic construction. At the same time, it is becoming increasingly common in North America to give children the surnames of both parents in order to preserve the mother's as well as the father's family name.

main floor, with our youngest son and his wife living in the furnished basement. (This does not even count the nine parrots who live in the aviary that used to be our living room.)

When sociologists talk of a family's diversity, they may mean one of two things. Some mean "diversity" in the sense that there are different family structures: dual-earner, single-earner/two-parent, lone-parent. I use "diversity" here and throughout this text in a broader sense that includes not just differences in structure but also cultural differences in the roles performed by each member. The discussion of the family in Quebec later in this chapter highlights this broader sense of diversity.

Nine Changes in the Canadian Family

There are a number of changes occurring in the makeup and behaviour of Canadian families today. In a number of these areas where change is occurring,

families in Quebec are leading the way. This is not to say that they are "further ahead" in some kind of modernist progressive model, but that they offer the clearest evidence of certain general trends.

1. The marriage rate is decreasing while the cohabitation rate is rising.

A quick look at crude marriage rates will tell a sociologist whether more or fewer people are getting married these days. The crude marriage rate is the number of marriages per 1,000 people in a population. "Crude" refers to the fact that no statistical wizardry has been used to "refine" the rate (to use an oil analogy). It doesn't mean that marriage itself is crude. Since the population keeps rising, the crude marriage rate will give a better indication of trends than the overall number of marriages taken alone. If the number of marriages were the same for 2002 and 2012, the actual rate of marriage would be decreasing, since the population overall is rising. A sociologist would conclude that fewer people were getting married.

The crude marriage rate has fluctuated over the years. In 1920, it was relatively low at 6.1 per 1,000 people. Many young men (married and single) had died during World War I and the Spanish flu epidemic that followed it. When I think of that statistic, I think of two of my great aunts who were young then—Aunt Nell the nurse, Aunt Margaret the teacher. They were gifted, intelligent women adored by the children and grandchildren of their married brothers. Neither of them ever married.

The marriage rate rose to a peak of 11.2 marriages per 1,000 people in 1946, representing a post–World War II marriage boom that would precede (and contribute to) the post-war baby boom (Statistics Canada, 2011b: Chart 6).

After dropping a little in the years that followed, the marriage rate remained fairly high over the next three decades, peaking at 9.0 in 1972 and hovering around 8.0 for the rest of the decade (Statistics Canada, 2011b: Chart 6). That was just before a recession hit. Since then, the rate has dropped steadily, to 5.5 in 1995 and 4.7 in 2001. After that, a directly comparable figure became harder to obtain, as laws allowing same-sex marriage were

Our Stories

The Crestwood Heights Family

Between 1948 and 1953, sociologists John Seeley, Alexander Sim, and Elizabeth Loosley studied a white, upper-middle-class neighbourhood in North Toronto, which they nicknamed "Crestwood Heights." The following is a brief introduction to their chapter on the family:

> The family of Crestwood Heights . . . consists of father, mother, and two (rarely more) children. The children are healthy, physically well developed, attractively dressed, and poised as to outward behavior. The mother, assured in manner, is as like an illustration from *Vogue* or *Harper's Bazaar* as financial means and physical appearance will allow. The father, well tailored, more or less successful in radiating an impression of prosperity and power, rounds out the family group.
>
> This small family unit is both lone and love-based. It is, more often than not, formed by the marriage of two persons from unrelated and often unacquainted families . . . who are assumed to have chosen each other because they are "in love." Other reasons for the choice (perpetuation of property within one family, the linking of business or professional interest, an unadorned urge to upward social mobility and so on), even if influential, could not reputably be admitted as grounds for marriage.
>
> This family unit is not embedded in any extended kinship system. The newly formed family is frequently isolated geographically and often socially from the parental families. It is expected that the bride and groom will maintain a separate dwelling removed by varying degrees of distance from that of each set of parents. . . . The isolation of each family acts to decrease the ability of the family to transmit traditional patterns of behavior, which might otherwise be absorbed from close contact with, for instance, grandparents. The absence of kinship bonds also tends to concentrate the emotional life of the family upon a few individuals. . . . (Seeley, Sim, & Loosely, 1956: pp. 159–60)

What do YOU think?

1. How many families do you know that conform to the Crestwood Heights model? In what ways is it a "good" or a "bad" model?
2. In what respects does your own family differ, if at all, from the description given here? In what respects does it resemble this model?

© Scott Griessel/Dreamstime.com

Compare this photo with the one on page 288. Is this family any less typical of the families you know? What factors in our culture might lead us to view one family as more conventional than another?

passed in 2003 in British Columbia and Ontario, and two years later in the rest of Canada. BC and Ontario were, not surprisingly, the only two provinces in which the rate of marriages increased in 2003. By 2008, the crude marriage rate in Canada was 4.4 per 1,000 population, having fallen below 4.5 for the first time in history. The highest provincial rate was 6.8 in PEI, the lowest was Quebec, with 2.9. Quebec, in fact, was the only province under the national rate, accompanied only by the three territories. Following a review of their practices in 2008, Statistics Canada announced in 2011 that it would no longer be tracking annual marriage and divorce rates, owing to the cost of collecting these data and the difficulty, given the changing nature of marital relationships (Grant, 2011).

Fewer *marriages* does not mean fewer *couples*. The number of common-law (or cohabiting) unions has risen since 1980. Precise figures are difficult to track, since society doesn't ritually mark the beginning of common-law relationships the way it records marriages. Still, we do know that the percentage of all couples living in common-law or cohabiting unions rose from 0.7 per cent in 1976 to 20.0 per cent as of 2011, and that between 2006 and 2011, the number of common-law couples rose by 13.9 per cent, which is more than four times the 3.1 per cent increase in the number of married couples (Statistics Canada, 2012a: p. 3). Figure 10.1 provides a snapshot of Canadians 18 and over by marital status.

The cohabitation rate in the United States is always lower than in Canada; for instance, in 2001 the American cohabitation rate of 8.2 per cent was barely half the Canadian rate of 16.0 for the same year. Can you think of why that is? Here's a hint: in 2011, the proportion of census families that included a common-law couple was 16.7 per cent for all of Canada; Quebec, with a cohabitation rate of 31.5 per cent, skews the Canadian figures considerably (the province with the next highest cohabitation rate was New Brunswick, at just 16.0 per cent) (Statistics Canada, 2012: p. 6). Figure 10.2 shows the ratio of Canadians living in common-law unions to married Canadians by province for 2015. As you can see,

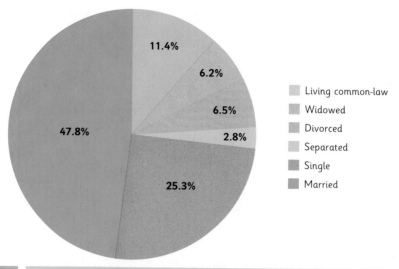

| **Figure 10.1** | Marital Status of Canadians Aged 18 and Over, 2015 |

Source: Statistics Canada CANSIM Table 051-0042.

Quebec is the only province where the proportion of cohabiting unions is above the national average.

A number of questions can be addressed concerning cohabiting couples. Is cohabitation replacing marriage? So far the answer is a tentative no. Despite the dramatic increase in the number of common-law couples since 2006, married couples still make up the predominant family structure in Canada by a wide margin (67.0 per cent, compared with just 16.7 per cent for common-law couples) (Statistics Canada, 2012: pp. 5–6). Does cohabitation benefit men more than women? Do you think your answer to this question is affected by your sex? Do you think men and women view cohabitation differently (i.e. as an alternative to marriage versus a trial marriage)? How does cohabitation, compared with marriage, affect children? These are questions sociologists today are asking.

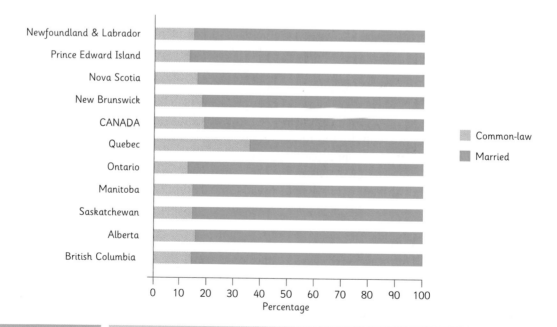

| **Figure 10.2** | Ratio of Married People to Cohabiting People by Province, 2015 |

Source: Statistics Canada CANSIM Table 051-0042.

2. The age of first marriage is rising.

The average age of first marriage in Canada has risen steadily since the early 1970s, but as Figure 10.3 shows, it wasn't until the 1990s that the figures really began to climb.

Questions arise. Has this figure peaked, or will it continue to climb? What has contributed to the rise since the 1990s? (Note that, unfortunately, we don't have data on first-marriage ages after 2008, so we have to speculate.)

It's worth noting that the averages differ from province to province. In 2004, the lowest average age of first marriage was in Saskatchewan, where it was 27.0 for women and 29.3 for men; the same year in Quebec, the figures were 33.0 and 31.9, respectively.

What do YOU think?

Having just paid a small fortune for our son's wedding, I am left wondering—sociologically, not parentally—why it is that "middle-class" weddings have become increasingly expensive over the last decade or so. Is it the influence of the shows noted in the caption to the photo on page 294? Is it related to the decline in the religious aspect of weddings? Does it have to do with the need to put on a big show in order to make it worthwhile for family members attending from far away? What do you think?

3. There are more divorces overall, but the rate is falling.

Analyzing divorce statistics can be complicated. If you ask a group of people whether they think the divorce rate is rising or falling, they would probably say that it's going up. This is not the case. The rate has jumped on several occasions over brief periods of time, but we can account for these, in part, by looking at changes to the legislation surrounding divorce.

In 1961, there were 6,563 divorces in Canada, producing a divorce rate of 36.0 per 100,000 population. In 1968, the grounds for divorce were expanded in most of Canada: no longer was adultery the sole grounds for divorce. From 1968 to 1969, the divorce rate shot up from 54.8 per 100,000 to 124.5. Remember that the average age of first marriage was at an all-time low in the 1960s. This is significant as there is an inverse correlation between age at first marriage and the likelihood of divorce (i.e. the younger the couple, the greater the chance the marriage will end in divorce).

By 1982, the number of divorces had peaked at a rate of roughly 280 per 100,000 population. Then in 1985, the Divorce Act was changed again, allowing "marital breakdown" as legitimate grounds for divorce. By 1987, the numbers had peaked again, this time producing a rate of 363.75 divorces per 100,000 (see Figure 10.4). (My divorce was in 1988,

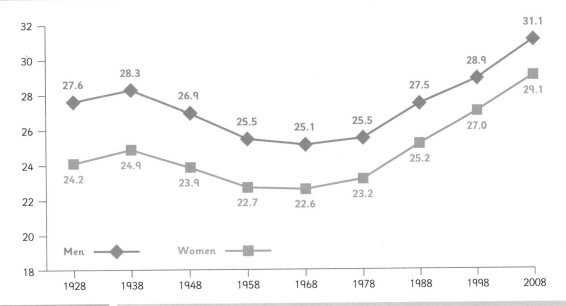

| **Figure 10.3** | Average Age at First Marriage by Sex, Canada, 1928–2008 |

Source: Based on Human Resources and Skills Development Canada, *Indicators of Well-Being in Canada: Family Life—Marriage*, www4.hrsdc.gc.ca/.3ndic.1t.4r@-eng.jsp?iid=78

Victor de Jesus/UNP

Shows like *Say Yes to the Dress* and *My Big Fat Gypsy Wedding* celebrate the commercial and secular aspects of the modern wedding ceremony. But even stripped of its religious significance, the wedding remains for many people an important rite of passage that distinguishes marriage from living together in an important way. To you, how important is the institution of marriage? In what ways does it differ from living together? How much do you think your answer is influenced by factors such as your age, your sex, and your sexual orientation?

not contributing to the record.) By 2002, the numbers were back down to mid-1970s levels: a total of 70,155 divorces for a rate of 223.7.

As with other marriage data, Statistics Canada stopped collecting regular information on divorces after 2003. However, Mary Bess Kelly, for a 2012 Statistics Canada *Juristat* article, collected data on the number of divorce cases initiated in a sample of six provinces and territories (Ontario, Nova Scotia, BC, Nunavut, Yukon, and Northwest Territories). She reported that the number of cases fell by 8 per cent between 2006 and 2011, decreasing each year (Kelly, 2012). That's good news for marriage, right?

Not necessarily. Although it's possible that some married couples are staying together longer, it could also be that because a greater proportion of couples are living common-law, fewer couples require formal divorces when their relationships end. But consider

this also: we know that the average age of first marriage in 2008 was roughly 30. Those people would have been 9 years old in 1987, when divorce was at an all-time high in Canada. What effect do you think it might have on your commitment to marriage if you grew up in a household that experienced marital discord and breakup? Without more detailed data, we can only speculate.

4. More women are having children in their thirties.

In 2010, the average age of a woman giving birth in Canada surpassed 30, a figure not seen since the 1930s (Statistics Canada, 2016b: Chart 1). This signifies that the number of women in their thirties giving birth is increasing. Not only that: the number of women in their thirties giving birth *for the first time* is also increasing. In 1987, 4 per cent of women

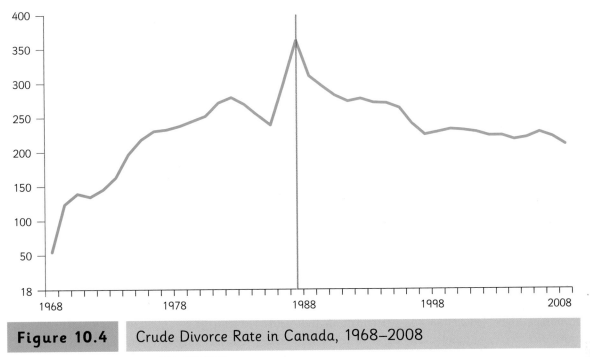

| **Figure 10.4** | Crude Divorce Rate in Canada, 1968–2008 |

Source: Statistics Canada CANSIM Table 053-0002.

who gave birth for the first time were aged 35 and older; by 2011, the percentage had tripled to 12 per cent. Over the same period, the percentage of first-time mothers who were over 30 increased from 15 per cent to 28 per cent.

Another way of looking at this is by considering what proportion of all births were to women aged 30 and older. As the table here shows, just under one-fifth of all births in 1975 were to women over 30; by 2012, over half (53 per cent) of all births were to women over 30.

	Percentage of All Births by Women over 30					**Change**
Year	1975	1985	1995	2005	2010	
Percentage	19.2	27.8	42.5	48.9	51.2	+32.0%

Source: Statistics Canada CANSIM Table 102-4503.

At the other end of the scale, births to mothers in their teens, we see a sharply contrasting profile. From 1991 to 2011, the proportion of births to young women under 20 decreased to just 3.6 per cent. While not the sole reason for the decrease, improved access to abortions since 1988, when the Supreme Court struck down Canada's anti-abortion laws, has certainly played a role in the decrease in teen child-bearing.

	Percentage of All Births by Teens					**Change**
Year	1991	1996	2001	2006	2011	
Percentage	6.0	5.9	4.9	4.1	3.6	−2.4%

Source: Statistics Canada CANSIM Table 102-4503.

There are significant regional differences in teen pregnancy today. In 2011, Quebec and British Columbia had the lowest percentages of births to mothers in their teens, at 2.5 per cent and 2.6 per cent, respectively (Milan, 2013: p. 7). The provinces with the highest percentages of births to young women under 20 were Saskatchewan (8.1 per cent) and Manitoba (8.0 per cent). Nunavut was an extreme outlier with a rate of 20.8 per cent (Milan, 2013: p. 7). The provincial/territorial differences roughly correlate with differences among urban and rural populations. Canadian regions with the highest percentages of rural residents have the greatest number of teenage mothers. Is this coincidence, or do you think that living in a rural community is a causal factor in teen pregnancy? What other factors might be involved?

An interesting set of statistics related to this is the average age of mother at the birth of her first child, which has a different profile:

	Average Age of Mother at Birth of First Child							
Year	1945	1955	1965	1975	1985	1995	2005	2010
Age	25.2	24.1	23.5	24.3	25.5	26.3	28.0	28.4

Source: Statistics Canada, 2016b: Chart 1.

Plotting the average age of the first-time mother in Canada shows a steady drop from the mid-1940s to the mid-1960s, followed by a gradual climb that hasn't yet stopped (see Figure 10.5). It's no coincidence that the shape of this graph is nearly identical to the line in Figure 10.3, depicting the average age at first marriage. Following a decade of economic depression, the Second World War (1939–45) caused young people to delay marriage and child-bearing until soldiers returned home in the mid-1940s. The age of first marriage and first birth fell from that time until the 1960s, when the women began to pursue higher education and participate in the workforce in greater numbers. At the same time, the sexual revolution changed social attitudes that had frowned upon sex before marriage and the use of contraception. The war had caused families to delay marriage and child-bearing out of necessity; the sixties brought new freedoms that enabled couples to delay marriage and child-bearing by choice.

In 2011, the age-specific fertility rates were relatively close for women in their early forties (10.3 births per 1,000 women) and those in their late teens (12.6). In the late 1990s, the fertility rate for women in their early forties was roughly one-quarter that of women in their late teens. Historically, the age-specific fertility rate for young women aged 15 to 19 was high throughout the late 1940s all the way to the 1960s. In 1959—the peak of the baby boom—it was 59.7 births per 1,000 women, about 4.5 times the 2011 rate for this age group. In general, the period throughout the 1980s to the present has seen the lowest fertility rates for young women in the data observed since 1926. While at its highest level in 2011 (10.3 births per 1,000 women), since 1970, the age-specific fertility rate for women in their early forties was about five times as high in 1926 (50.6) as it was in 2011 (Milan, 2013).

An important factor to consider when looking at delays in child-bearing is fecundity, the physical ability to conceive. This ability changes during a woman's fourth decade. Estimates are that 91 per cent of women at the age of 30 are physically able to become pregnant. This drops to 77 per cent for

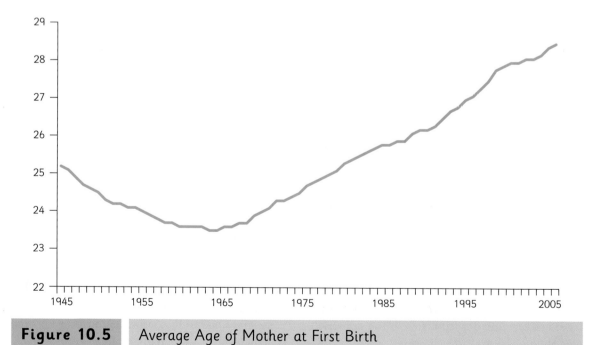

Figure 10.5   Average Age of Mother at First Birth

Source: Statistics Canada, 2016b: Chart 2.

women aged 35 and just 53 per cent of women at 40 (Rajulton, Balakrisnhan, & Ravanera, 1990). Do you think the fact that more women are waiting longer to have their first child may be lowering the *total fertility rate*?

5. The number of children per family has dropped below the "replacement rate."
The total fertility rate is an estimate of the average number of children that a cohort of women between the ages of 15 and 49 will have in their lifetime if current factors remain constant during their reproductive years. It's a projection, in other words, based on current fertility rates, even though we know that these actual rates will change.

Figure 10.6 shows the total fertility rate for select years between 1921 and 2015. In 2002 the total fertility rate in Canada bottomed out at 1.51. How does that compare with the rate for other countries? Rates for the 100 most populous countries in the world in 2014 ranged from 2.22 to 6.89, with 9 of the top 10 fertility rates being in Africa. Those countries with fertility rates below Canada's include eastern European countries, such as the Czech Republic (1.43) and Georgia (1.77); some Mediterranean countries, including Italy (1.42), Greece (1.41), and Portugal (1.52); and several East Asian countries—Singapore (0.80), Hong Kong (1.17), Japan (1.40), South Korea (1.25), and Taiwan (1.11). In each of these countries, the population is

The Point Is . . .

Does Having a Disabled Family Member Mean Having a Disabled Family?

A lasting image of the 2010 Vancouver Winter Olympics is of Alexandre Bilodeau getting a hug from his older brother, Frederic, who has cerebral palsy, after Alex won the first gold medal of the games for Canada. Alex told reporters, "My brother is my inspiration—he taught me so many things in my life." The story was inspiring, but how common is a story like that?

Wayne Hower examined the extent to which the family of a person with a disability becomes, itself, disabled in *Does a Disabled Child = a Disabled Family?* (spoiler alert: his answer was no). Once the politically correct substitute for earlier terms like "handicapped" and "crippled," *disabled* has now itself become a target for those who find it an inappropriate way to characterize someone who might function at a high level in many areas of life. But Hower chose it deliberately, and a sociologist can shed some light on why he might have done so.

In Chapter 5 we examined the nature of a person's master status, a trait that, according to Everett C. Hughes, "tends to overpower, in most crucial situations, any other characteristics" (Hughes, 1945: p. 357). For many people, disability can be an unshakable master status that consistently overshadows or diminishes other statuses and accomplishments (older brother, musician, computer programmer, younger

sister, mother, or friend). Being viewed primarily as "disabled"—as imperfect—can have a huge effect on the way one is treated by others.

Disability is also a master status that can extend beyond the individual to the individual's family. It is clear from his comments that Hower himself feels the sting of any sanction directed at his daughter, who has a developmental delay: "We have been asked to leave a church in which the pastor has a special education degree, and we have been turned down by a household name organization that works with the disabled in Dallas, Texas" (Hower, 2006: p. 3). The disabled family, like the disabled individual, becomes treated as Other. The role of caregiver, too, can become a master status for a parent who becomes, above all else, primarily responsible for a child with a disability. The adoption of the caregiver master status can lead the parent to neglect other children and the spouse, while blocking others from sharing the caregiver's role.

Alex Bilodeau's comments about Frederic suggest that he sees him very much as older brother and teacher—statuses that are not qualified or diminished by his cerebral palsy. But is the healthy attitude of other family members toward an individual with a disability enough to help the unit avoid the designation "disabled family"?

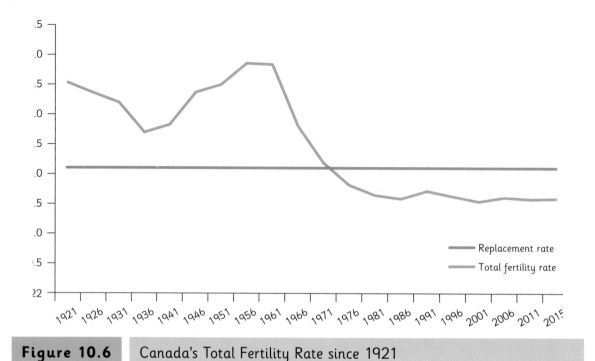

Figure 10.6   Canada's Total Fertility Rate since 1921

Source: Adapted from Beaujot (2000)

expected to fall. Why do you think their fertility rates are so low? Is it just economics (national and family), or is some pessimistic sense of the future involved as well?

Consider the following. Of women born between 1927 and 1931, 31.0 per cent had five or more children. Compare that with women born between 1952 and 1956, of whom just 1.3 per cent had five or more children. Among the latter group, 38.3 per cent had just two children, and 33.7 per cent had one child or no children, meaning that a total of 72.0 per cent of women born in 1952–6 had two children or fewer, compared with 42.7 per cent of women born in 1927–31.

Figure 10.6 also shows the replacement rate, the number of children that the average woman must bear if the overall population is to continue at the same level. The replacement rate is 2.1, meaning that 2.1 children must be born for every woman in a population aged 15–49 in order for the population to hold constant. As Figure 10.6 shows, it's been almost 50 years since Canada had a total fertility rate above the replacement rate.

So what does a country do when its national fertility rate is below the replacement rate? Canada makes up for its low fertility rate with high levels of immigration. Take note, however, that immigrants from countries with higher fertility rates soon begin to reproduce at a rate consistent with the fertility rate here in this country. Are there ways to boost the fertility rate? Would government incentives (such as those offered in Quebec) help to offset the cost of having and raising children? Would a system of universal, publicly funded daycare, similar to what exists in Quebec, change things significantly? Recent studies in the US suggest that women are willing to have more children when their husbands are willing to take a greater share of responsibility for child care and general housework. How significant a factor do you think that could be?

6. There are more couples without children than with.

Related to the decline in the total fertility rate is this statistic: the proportion of couples living *with* children has been surpassed by the proportion of couples living *without* children. In 2001, couples with children made up 43.6 per cent of all census families, while couples without children accounted for 40.3 per cent. In 2006, the proportion of childless couples topped the share of couples with children for the first time (42.7 per cent versus 41.4 per cent), and by 2011, the gap had spread considerably (44.5 per cent versus 39.2 per cent).

We have to be careful not to jump to hasty conclusions. This is just a 10-year trend, which is pretty short, by demographers' standards. The 2016 census could easily show a reversal (data from the 2016 census will only start to be released in 2017). Still, it's worth asking: are these figures explained by the fact that women are waiting longer to have their first child? Or do they have more to do with the fact that Canada's overall population is aging, which means there are more older couples whose grown-up children have left home? If you're thinking the latter, consider the following.

7. Children are leaving home at a later age.

The term cluttered nest is sometimes used to describe the phenomenon in which adult children continue to live at home with their parents (the opposite, empty nest, describes a household in which children have moved out to live on their own). In 1981, 33.6 per cent of women aged 20–24 and 51.4 per cent of men of the same age were living with a parent or parents; by 1996, those figures had risen to 50.4 per cent and 64.3 per cent, respectively (Beaujot, 2000: p. 98). And between 1981 and 2011, the percentage of adults aged 20–29 living with parents rose from 26.9 per cent to 42.3 per cent (Rennie, 2012).

Causation is easy to establish. First, it takes more time and education nowadays to establish a career. Some adults living with parents are "boomerang kids," who have returned home after going away to college or university, prior to setting up on their own. Second, there is the higher cost of living, including rising housing prices, and a number of costs that earlier generations didn't have to face. (As a child, I never had to pay for wifi.) With couples marrying later and later in life, it takes that much longer to set up a dual-earner household, the only model that is financially viable for some people who want to move out of their parents' home.

8. There are more lone-parent families.

The number of lone-parent families in Canada has been increasing since 1966 (which followed a 35-year period of decrease from 13.6 per cent during the Depression year of 1931). In 1966, 8.2 per cent of

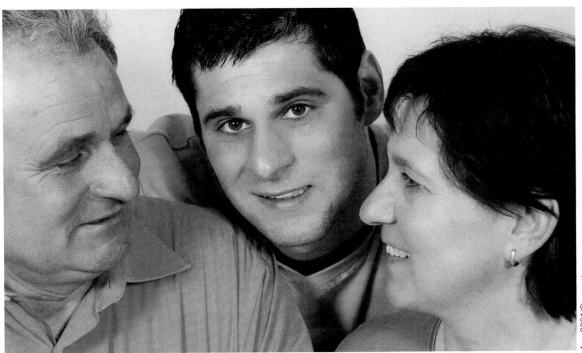

Does it surprise you that young men (20–29) are more likely than young women to be living at home with their parents? Why do you think this is the case?

all families were lone-parent families; since then, the figure has risen steadily, to 12.7 per cent in 1986, 14.5 in 1996, 15.7 in 2001, 15.9 in 2006, and 16.3 in 2011 (Statistics Canada, 2012a: p. 5).

People often speculate about the negative effects on children of living in lone-parent households, particularly with regard to school dropout rates and criminal activity. The critics need to be cautious here, though, as most lone-parent households began as two-parent households. It is hard to determine whether unfavourable conditions existing in the pre-divorce or pre-separation family—an abusive parent perhaps, or parental fighting—could have been the real cause of a child's crime or truancy. You can't just blame the lone-parent situation.

There is, however, a strong connection between lone-parent families and poverty, especially where the mother is the family head. Beaujot (2000: p. 348) compared child poverty rates among lone-parent households for various countries before and after taxes have been deducted and transfer payments (social assistance) distributed. The countries include Canada, the United States, Australia, Israel, and a number of European nations, all studied over a 10-year period from 1982 to 1992.

Before taxes and transfer payments, Canada had the sixth highest rate of child poverty in lone-parent households, with a 1991 pre–transfer payment rate of 68.2. However, Canada moves up to third on the list when the after-tax-and-transfer totals are considered. Canada, with a poverty rate in lone-parent households of 50.2 per cent, falls behind only the US (59.5 per cent) and Australia (56.2). This suggests that Canada is not doing enough—less than the other countries studied—to help children living in poverty in lone-parent families. What do you think can be done to change this?

9. There are more people living alone.

In 1996, Beaujot (2000: p. 117) reported, 12 per cent of the entire Canadian population aged 15 and over were living alone; the rate was highest for those over 85 (48 per cent), and lowest for those younger than 55 (10 per cent). By 2011, the overall percentage of Canadians living alone had climbed to 13.5 per cent (Statistics Canada, 2012a: p. 3).

A Statistics Canada publication offers an interesting comparison. In an examination of the changing percentages for 1-person and 5+-person households, the authors note:

> In 2006, there were three times as many one-person households as households with five or more people. Of the 12.4 million private households, 27% were one-person households, while 9% were large households of five or more people.
>
> In 1941, 6% of houses were comprised of one person, while 38% were comprised of five or more people. (Statistics Canada, 2009)

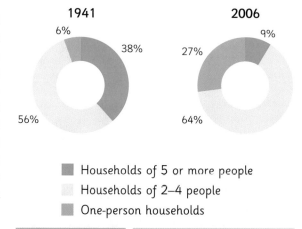

- ■ Households of 5 or more people
- ■ Households of 2–4 people
- ■ One-person households

Figure 10.7   Households in Canada, 1941 and 2006

Our Stories

Rod Beaujot and Delayed Life Transitions

In "Delayed Life Transitions: Trends and Implications," University of Western Ontario demographer **Rod Beaujot** linked together some of the trends discussed in this section as part of a phenomenon he calls *delayed life transitions*.

We go through a number of major life transitions in our lifetime—getting a full-time job, moving out to live on our own, getting married, having children, retiring, and so on. During the prosperous socioeconomic times of the 1950s, 1960s, and early 1970s, people went through what we could call "sped-up life transitions,"

making these major life changes at a relatively young age. The situation has changed considerably, as Beaujot observes, and people today are making these transitions later and later in life.

Several questions arise here. To what extent is our current speed of life transition "delayed," and to what extent is it simply "normal"? What are the implications for today's generation of college and university students of having parents who went through life transitions at a much more advanced speed, perhaps at a rate that was "less normal" than now?

Family in Quebec

By just about every statistical measure the family in Quebec is sociologically distinct from the family in other parts of Canada. For example, consider that in 2005, Quebec was the province with

- *the highest cohabitation rate*: 33.95 per cent of all couples, almost twice the next highest rate in Canada (New Brunswick, at 17.1 per cent);
- *the lowest marriage rate*: 2.9 per 100,000, significantly lower than the next lowest rate (Ontario and Manitoba, tied at 4.9);
- *the highest divorce rate*: 69.2 per 100 marriages, ahead of Ontario's rate of 46.7; and
- *the highest number of divorces* among couples married less than 30 years, with 61.0 per 100 marriages (Ontario's rate of 43.1 was the next highest).

In 2005—the last year that Statistics Canada provided this information—Quebec led all provinces with an abortion rate of 7.6 per 1,000 women, or 372.5 per 1,000 live births (trailing only Northwest Territories in the latter statistic). In 2011, Quebec was the province with the greatest number of total births by single (never married) women. By percentage (58.5 per cent), the province trailed only Nunavut (New Brunswick was the next closest province at 47.5 per cent). At the start of the century Quebec also had the greatest percentage of births to women who were divorced (2.1 per cent in 2002), but has since dropped to sixth place (1.2 per cent in 2011). Why might this one ranking have changed?

Another feature unique to Quebec is the province-wide support for same-sex marriage (see Table 10.1). In a poll conducted among 10,015 Canadian adults in August 2003, residents of Quebec showed the greatest support for changing the legal definition of marriage. In March 2004, it became the

Table 10.1	Support for Changing the Definition of Marriage to Include Same-Sex Unions, by Region, 2003		
	Agree Somewhat (%)	**Agree Strongly (%)**	**Total (%)**
Quebec	**36**	**25**	**61**
British Columbia	26	25	51
Atlantic Provinces	19	26	45
Ontario	19	23	42
Prairies	16	17	33

Source: TNS Canadian Facts, www.tns-cf.com/news/03.09.05-samesex-charts.pdf, 2003. The study was conducted by TNS Canadian Facts (formerly NFO CFgroup), one of Canada's leading full-service marketing, opinion and social research organizations.

third province (following Ontario and BC) to legally recognize same-sex marriage.

In social statistician Reginald Bibby's 1995 Project Canada survey, Quebec had the highest rate of approval for premarital and extramarital sex (Bibby, 1995: p. 76), with 88 per cent supporting the former (compared with 82 per cent, the next highest, in BC) and 24 per cent supporting the latter (compared with 14 per cent, the next highest, in the Prairies).

Quebec residents have also shown a difference when it comes to parenting, as indicated by a *Globe and Mail*/CTV poll of 648 Canadian parents conducted by Ipsos-Reid and published in the *Globe and Mail* on 10 April 2004. The poll noted the following results:

Percentage of parents who said they spanked their children for disciplinary reasons:	
Alberta	60
British Columbia	52
Saskatchewan/Manitoba	46
Ontario	45
Atlantic Provinces	42
Quebec	22

Percentage of parents who agreed that using flashcards at an early age makes kids smarter:	
British Columbia	71
Saskatchewan/Manitoba	67
Alberta	63
Ontario	60
Atlantic Provinces	57
Quebec	25

What should we make of this? First, it is noteworthy that a number of the statistical indicators discussed show a major change from the situation in Quebec prior to the Quiet Revolution of the 1960s. Take divorce. Prior to 1968, if you were living in Quebec and you wanted a divorce, you had to seek it through the federal Parliament. A growing separation from the Catholic Church has been cited as a possible explanation for the rising divorce rate. Yet in the 2001 census—the last year that religious affiliation was broken out by province—Quebec had a low rate of residents declaring they had "no religion"

(a rate of 5.8 per cent, compared with the national average of 16.5 per cent). Of course, being affiliated with the Church and being influenced by it can be two different matters. The Catholic Church considers suicide a sin, but Quebec, the most Catholic province, has the highest suicide rate in Canada, especially among men. In 2007, the age-standardized suicide rate for Quebec males was 20.7 per 100,000, compared with approximately 13 per cent in British Columbia, Nova Scotia, and Ontario.

Can we say that family life is falling apart in Quebec? After all, in 2011, Quebec had the highest rate of one-person households—about 32 per cent. But a more likely interpretation is that Quebec went through more rapid modernization and outright change during the last 40 years than any other province. The falling away of old structures does not mean the falling apart of the institutions. Québécois are perhaps best seen as reinventing family as they are reinventing other institutions—political, religious, and educational.

Conjugal Roles

Conjugal (or marital) roles are the distinctive roles of the husband and wife that result from the division of labour within the family. The first important sociological study done on this subject was a 1957 work called *Family and Social Networks*, by Canadian/British social scientist **Elizabeth Bott**. Bott characterized conjugal roles as being either segregated—in which tasks, interests, and activities are clearly different—or joint, in which many tasks, interests, and activities are shared. These ideas came to be known as the Bott hypothesis. Her study was set against a backdrop in which men were primarily responsible for the financial support of the family, while women were primarily responsible for the housework and child care. This was 1957, remember—how much do you think that situation has changed?

Earning and Caring: Changes in Conjugal Roles

In 2000, Rod Beaujot published *Earning and Caring in Canadian Families* (2000). He wanted to study how conjugal roles were changing from a situation in which they were more or less *complementary* to one in which they were *companionate*. Complementary

Telling It Like It Is

Telling Your Family You're Gay

Growing up in the small town of Whitby, Ontario, I never felt the negative effects of discrimination. I am an English-speaking, Caucasian female and had never been a part of a minority group, in any sense of the word. At the age of 21, this changed and I became aware of how easily people are judged. I am a lesbian, and from the moment I became open about my sexual preferences, I felt first-hand what it feels like to be viewed based solely on one aspect of your life, and not as an entire person. When meeting someone new in my life it was as though I was wearing a sign on my forehead reading, "I am gay," and it was perceived as "I am gay . . . that is everything you need to know about me." Once I divulge this information, almost instantly people form opinions on who I am as a person and who I should be. They develop expectations that quite often are illogical and unrealistic. By writing a paper such as this one, I am being given the opportunity to address a few of these numerous stereotypes and prejudiced beliefs. Hopefully, I can educate some to stop these beliefs from spreading.

From my experience, the original thought that people tend to have when finding out that I am gay is that it is simply a phase I am going through, a time of experimentation and rebellious behaviour. My brother's reaction was as such. He believed that it was just a phase and that it would pass. He continued to express this for an entire year after I had told him. He realizes otherwise now. . . . When telling my mother . . . , I was shocked to hear her initial reaction to what I had told her. After a moment or two of silence, she . . . said, "But I thought you wanted to get married and have kids one day." The thought of these dreams possibly fading away is what seemed to unsettle her the most. I found two things wrong and rather presumptuous about this statement. To begin with, the idea that a woman must want/need a husband and children to live a fulfilling life is old-fashioned and a step backward from the times we live in today. I figure, why can't a woman who is independent and who has a satisfying career be considered to lead a successful, happy life, despite the fact that she has no family to raise. Furthermore, my mother was correct in assuming that I did want a family, but it was not the family that she had in mind. Marriage and children are a large part of my future plans, and, with adoption, and artificial insemination, this is a very feasible option for lesbian couples. Simply because a woman falls in love with another woman, it does not mean that she didn't grow up with the same desire for nurturing children and caring for a home and family that a lot of heterosexual girls do.

---

roles (like Bott's model of *segregated roles*) cast men primarily as earners or breadwinners, doing paid work, with women involved primarily in the unpaid work of child care and housework. In companionate relationships (like Bott's *joint* relationship) the roles overlap.

Beaujot recognized that the shift from complementary/segregated conjugal roles to companionate/joint roles is far from complete. But he also stated that complete overlap was not necessarily possible, nor even desirable. Gender roles are different to a significant extent because men and women are different biologically. There is, however, a point at which we may be able to say that a basic fairness or justice has been reached. We are far from that point. As Beaujot documents, married women do more total work per day than married men do, even though married women are more likely to do part-time paid work. Married women, especially the mothers of small children, do much more *unpaid* work than married men do. And while women have caught up to men in their participation in the workforce, men have not gone as far in taking on new roles at home. This has created an imbalance in conjugal roles, where women take on what some sociologists have called a "double burden" or "second shift" (Hochschild & Machung, 1989). Canadian sociologists Pat Armstrong and Hugh Armstrong ([1978]/2010) used the term double ghetto to describe the marginalization working women experience in the workplace and in the home. The difficulty of correcting this imbalance in households with small children has led some women to conclude, pessimistically, that "childlessness is the easiest route to equality" (Beaujot, 2002).

In 1995, sociologist **M. Reza Nakhaie** published "Housework in Canada: The National Picture," a summary of his study demonstrating that gender was a greater factor than either relative income or amount of available time in determining how much housework an individual did. The author's most striking discovery concerned the relationship between gender, hours of paid work, and share of the housework. Nakhaie found an inverse relationship between the hours of paid work a man does and the size of his share of the housework: the more paid hours he has, the smaller his share of the housework. However, the same is not true for women. A direct relationship seems to exist over a particular number of hours of work: an increase over 30 in a woman's hours of paid work per week correlated to an *increase* in her contribution to housework.

What does your reaction to this image tell you about our perception of the gender roles handed down by society?

The key to correcting the gender imbalance is to recognize that gender roles are not carved in stone. Rather, they are products of what Arlie Hochschild terms a gender strategy, which is "a plan of action through which a person tries to solve problems at hand, given the cultural notions of gender at play" (Hochschild & Machung, 1989: p. 15). These "problems at hand" include the fact that small children have to be taken care of. From the studies that Beaujot cites, it is clear that the typical strategy for infant care is for the mother to take time off, then to work part-time as the infant matures toward school age, eventually to try to go back to full-time work.

The responsibility for care of children is the main reason that married women are much more likely to work part time than are married/unmarried men or unmarried women. It is also the cause of what Beaujot calls the occupational segregation of men and women. Women choose occupations in fields such as education and health care, which have the greatest flexibility in terms of child care–related work interruptions (which include staying home to care for a sick child or taking a longer-term leave to care for a newborn). Beaujot presents something of a chicken-and-egg scenario: women seek out jobs in employment areas that offer greater flexibility, but part of the reason these jobs offer greater flexibility is that they are dominated by women. Do you think that as women enter traditionally male-dominated occupations in larger numbers, a similar flexibility will develop?

The Ethnic Factor in Conjugal Roles

One weakness of Beaujot's work is that he ignores the role of ethnocultural factors in the gendered division of household labour. A classic study of conjugal roles among North American immigrant groups is Sathi Dasgupta's "Conjugal Roles and Social Network in Indian Immigrant Families: Bott Revisited" (1992). Although the article was written over 25 years ago about South Asian immigrants in the United States, its findings have relevance to the situation in Canada today.

Dasgupta studied 25 couples and found that *segregated* conjugal roles dominated. The men were invariably the primary breadwinners and made virtually all major decisions affecting the household, while the women, with few exceptions, were full-time homemakers and primary caretakers of the children. Interestingly, however, there were aspects of joint conjugal roles among the immigrant families that would not be nearly as well accepted back in India. These include joint discussion of the children's education and of the couple's social life (with joint leisure activities the norm).

Change will come, as immigrants to North America adopt a more "Western" approach to dividing conjugal roles, but the ethnic factor still must be considered in any study of gender roles in the Canadian family.

Marrying "In" and Marrying "Out"

Endogamy is an anthropological term that means "marrying within." It refers to marrying someone of the same ethnic, religious, or cultural group as oneself. The opposite of endogamy, marrying *outside* of one's group, is exogamy.

Support for exogamy, once quite low in Canada, is increasing, according to findings published by Bibby (see Table 10.2). However, I believe that this set of statistics gives a picture that is more positive than it is real. It seems more an expression of ideal culture than an indication of probable practice.

Do you think Dasgupta's findings on the separation of conjugal roles among Indian families are applicable in Canada today? To what extent is the "ethnic factor" still at play?

| Table 10.2 | Canadians' Approval of Intergroup Marriage (%), 1975–2015 |

	1975	1980	1985	1990	1995	2000	2005	2015
Whites and Aboriginal people	75	80	83	84	84	91	93	95
Whites and Asians	66	75	78	82	83	90	93	95
Whites and East Indians/ Pakistanis	58	66	72	77	80	87	91	92
Whites and blacks	57	64	72	79	81	88	92	94
Any other kinds of racial or cultural mixed unions	—	—	—	—	—	—	—	93
Protestants and Catholics	86	88	89	90	92	93	95	—
Protestants and Jews	80	84	84	86	90	91	93	—
Roman Catholics and Jews	78	81	82	85	89	91	92	—
Christians and people of other world faiths	—	—	—	—	—	90	90	89

Source: Reginald W. Bibby, Project Canada Survey Series.

Telling It Like It Is

Italian Families and Conjugal Roles: Four Generations

When I think of the topic of gender in an Italian family, I laugh. The struggles between what it means to be male and what it means to be female arise so very often in my family, at every dinner and almost every conversation. The discussions are always split between the three generations because my grandmother lives with my parents and she never misses an opportunity to include her views. The eldest generation undeniably believes that the female's role in life is to be a complement to her husband; everything she does is based on his needs and his demands. All domestic duties and child-rearing except for punishment are her responsibility. Working outside the home is secondary to household work. The husband makes all decisions, although she can make suggestions. It is the male's responsibility to take care of the family financially.

My parents (second generation) feel similarly, the main difference being that the father should be very involved with the children, not solely in areas concerning punishment. Where my grandmother would discourage my father from helping around the house, my mother would welcome the help though not demand nor expect it. In this generation, family decisions are made together; however, household duties are still very divided, even with my mother working full time

outside the home. For the female, postsecondary education and career are second to marriage and family. The main female role in life is keeping a clean house, cooking good homemade food, and keeping everyone happy and healthy. The main male role is to keep the food on the table by providing the family with its main source of income.

The third generation around the dinner table changed things a little. This generation in my family consists of my husband and I, the middle brother and his wife, and the "baby brother." Most of us are in agreement that gender roles in the new Italian family have changed. No longer is the female solely responsible for all household duties. Husbands cook, clean, and change diapers, something my father had never done even with having three children! The females have postsecondary education and careers and are not a complement to their husbands, but an equal.

I also grew up with a huge double standard that affected me immensely in all areas of my life. It goes something like this: "This is what boys can do and this is what girls cannot do" (my father's infamous words). Boys can play all day and not help their mothers (girls can't), boys can fight and play rough (girls can't), boys have to do well in school (girls don't have to), boys can

After all, according to data from the 2011 National Household Survey, only 4.6 per cent of all married and common-law couples in Canada were mixed unions (Statistics Canada, 2014: p. 4). Table 10.5 shows which visible minority groups in Canada are most likely to form mixed unions.

For all of the visible minority groups shown in Table 10.3, only people of Japanese ancestry are more likely to form a mixed union; the majority of people in all other groups—including the two largest visible minority groups in Canada, South Asians and Chinese—marry or cohabit within their own group.

Bear in mind that this survey includes people born outside of Canada, who might have been

married when they immigrated. Couples made up of people born in the same country overwhelmingly form non-mixed unions, and this is particularly the case for people born in the same country outside of Canada: 94 per cent of those couples were non-mixed. By comparison, 75 per cent of couples where both people were born in Canada were non-mixed (Statistics Canada, 2014: p. 5).

Remember, too, that at different times in its history, Canada has weighted the immigration of certain groups in favour of one sex (consider the pattern of early immigration among Filipino women, discussed in Chapter 9). What influence could factors like these have on the data?

go out whenever they want (girls can't), boys have to play sports (girls don't have to), boys can stay out late (girls have to come home early).

"This is what girls must do and this is what boys do not have to do." Girls must cook and clean (boys do not), girls must learn the traditions (boys do not), girls must be good always (boys do not), girls must stay home to take care of the family (boys do not), girls must not be left alone with their boyfriends (boys can live with their girlfriends). I fought with my younger brothers fairly consistently growing up. The words, "that is not fair" were spoken often. I disliked one of my brothers for years. It was not until he got a family of his own that we began to grow closer together. We even talked about the jealousy we felt for one another over different family issues and how the double standards we grew up with had a great deal to do with it.

My family's views on gender have had a great impact on my life. It has carved me into the woman I am today. Much to my parents' chagrin, I cannot cook. I hate housecleaning, run away from tradition whenever I can. I am constantly in school working on a career, and even though I am married, I frequently go out with my friends and stay out late! Being married has been difficult at times also. I always have an intense instinct to run from the gender roles that surround me, and yet I realize that in many circumstances they are needed to preserve peace in a family. I now have many concerns for my daughter. I know she will not be faced with an obvious double standard, as I do not have any sons and I am fully aware that being completely opposite of the Martha Stewart–like woman is not anything to be proud of. Something in the middle would be nice. Since little girls are greatly influenced by their mothers, I know I must be really careful to set a positive female role in our family. I truly hope the difference for my daughter will be the ability for her to choose the woman she wants to be instead of madly running away from what I demand her to become.

—Alina Mucci

What do YOU think?

1. What kind of narrative do you think the writer's brothers would write about conjugal roles, based on their upbringing?
2. Do you foresee any gender role conflict concerning the writer and her daughter?

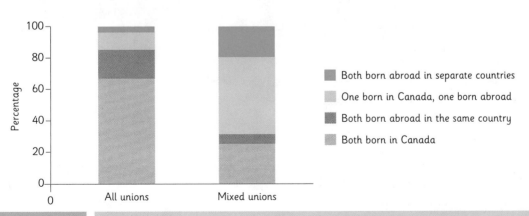

Figure 10.8   Composition of Canadian Unions and Canadian Mixed Unions, 2011

Source: Statistics Canada, 2014: p. 4.

Table 10.3	Mixed Couples by Visible Minority Group, 2011			
Visible Minority Group	**Number of Couples**	**Mixed Unions (%)**		**Non-mixed Unions (%)**
South Asian	407,510	13.0		87.0
Chinese	351,640	19.4		80.6
Black	167,950	40.2		59.8
Filipino	155,700	29.8		70.2
Latin American	112,265	48.2		51.8
Arab	94,315	25.4		74.6
Southeast Asian	74,560	21.9		78.1
West Asian	51,300	19.5		80.5
Korean	41,370	22.5		77.5
Japanese	32,820	78.8		21.3
Multiple visible minorities	40,415	65.9		35.1
Other visible minority	27,215	52.4		47.6
All visible minorities	**1,557,060**	**27.0**		**73.0**

Note: A mixed couple is any common-law or marital relationship comprising one spouse or partner who is a member of a visible minority group and one who is not, as well as couples comprising two members of different visible minority groups.

Source: Statistics Canada, 2014.

Based on findings from the 2006 census, Milan, Maheux, and Chui (2010) report that people in mixed unions "were younger, did better socio-economically, and were more likely to live in large CMAs [census metropolitan areas]" than non-mixed couples. How could you account for these facts?

Family and Ethnicity

As we saw in Chapter 8, on "race" and ethnicity, there is a history in Canada of federal government policies designed to deprive racialized minorities of family. The prohibitively expensive head tax levied on immigrants from China and South Asia in the late nineteenth and early twentieth centuries made it impossible in many cases for married couples or their families to reunite in Canada. Canadian sociologists **Nancy Mandell** and **Ann Duffy**, in *Canadian Families: Diversity, Conflict, and Change* (1995), noted a similar connection between government immigration policy and the denial of family for black women, claiming:

> [I]t has been a policy of the government not to encourage the possibility of developing families among women of colour who came as domestic workers. Thus, their status as "single" and as "temporary" is deliberately organized by immigration policies. (1995: p. 157).

The policy they refer to was initiated in 1910–11, during one of the country's greatest periods of immigration. About 100 black women from the Caribbean islands of Guadeloupe came to Canada to work as domestic servants, but when authorities discovered that many of the women were not as "unattached" as they had claimed to be—many had children they had been forced to leave behind—the women were sent back.

Between 1955 and 1967, a number of women from the Caribbean—primarily Jamaica—were allowed to come to Canada to work as domestics. They had to be young, of "good character," and single (in other words, not married or in a common-law relationship). They were given the status of landed immigrants, but they could not seek other work until they had served at least a year of domestic duty. Roughly 300 Caribbean women came to Canada each year between 1955 and 1960, the number rising to about 1,000 a year during the 1960s (Bolaria & Li, 1985: p. 178). Many of them agreed to work as domestics, even though they were trained as teachers or secretaries. Many, in order to be "single," left family behind, all because it was the only way they could enter the country.

Naturally, those immigrants who had left husbands and children in the Caribbean wanted to sponsor their families to join them in Canada, but their efforts were blocked by immigration officials. In 1976, seven Jamaican women applied to sponsor their children to come to Canada. They were ordered to be deported for having failed to report their children on their applications to come to Canada (Leah & Morgan, 1979). After an intense legal struggle, the seven women won their appeals and were allowed to stay in Canada.

Attacks on the Indigenous Family

Immigrant families are not the only ones affected by restrictive Canadian legislation. The Indigenous family has long been a target of federal policy. The following passage describes how, during the early twentieth century, an Indian Agent used the Blackfoot community's need for food rations as a tool to ensure the people remained monogamous:

> [I]n my last report, I expressed thankfulness that there had been no plural marriages during the preceding year. That report was barely out of my hand when I learned that three members of the band were dissatisfied with one wife each and had taken another. I immediately directed that the rations of these families be withheld until such time as they saw fit to obey the rules in this respect. One family missed one ration, and then decided that it was better to abide by the rules. The other two families held out for several rations, and then they succumbed and put away wife No. 2. (Dosman, 1972: pp. 52–3)

This incident, in which food rations were withheld to control marriage choices, is not atypical of the kind

Telling It Like It Is

The Religious Factor in Conjugal Roles: Polygamy and the Case of Bountiful, BC

In the aptly named commune village of Bountiful, British Columbia, **polygamy** (many marriages) or **polygyny** (many wives) is practised by the leaders of the Fundamentalist Church of Latter Day Saints, an offshoot of the Mormon Church. The commune has attracted attention and criticism, stemming mainly from reports of forced and underage marriage and the abuse of women and children. There have also been attempts to enforce Canada's anti-polygamy laws on the commune, the most recent coming in 2011.

The following quotations are taken from the testimony of a woman in her forties, given in a BC Supreme Court case examining the constitutionality of Canada's laws against plural marriages. The mother of nine children married one of the leaders when she was 16; her husband was already married to her older sister. She herself has nearly 30 siblings; her father had five wives. The woman is well educated, with six years of postsecondary training in nursing, elder care, and midwifery.

> I did not know him well; I knew he was in good standing in the church. . . .
>
> He (my father) told me, "You do not have to marry him if you don't want to." I felt good about him, and I married him. My sister wife and I have lived at times in the same home, we've lived in different homes. I feel that we are both very committed in having a good relationship with each other. . . .
>
> I feel my husband really supported me through my years of education and he really has been a life-long friend to me, as well as watched my children when I went to school. . . .
>
> I believe that there's so many people in mainstream society that make so many assumptions about us that we are treated with bias and prejudice, and that affects my everyday life. If I wanted to go anywhere and get any sort of counselling in mainstream society, I feel like I would not be accepted. . . .
>
> My beliefs are that living plural marriage isn't for everyone. . . . ("Plural Wife Describes Life in Bountiful Commune", 2011)

In November 2011, BC Supreme Court Chief Justice Robert Bauman ruled that the ban against polygamy was constitutional, even though it violated the religious freedom of this group. Protecting the rights of the women and the children, he ruled, was of greater importance than protecting the religious freedom of the commune's residents.

of treatment Native families suffered at the hands of government agents.

It's important to note that actions like this were often products of well-meaning agencies and their representatives. With the benefit of modern perspective, we can see just how misguided and racist these policies were. The following section looks closely at three policies aimed at controlling Indigenous families. In some cases, as we will see, the same strategies have targeted other groups that governments have felt they needed to manage, including certain cultural and ethnic groups as well as people with physical or mental disabilities.

Residential Schools

Among the institutionalized instruments of control devised to manage the lives of Canada's Indigenous populations, the system of residential schools tops the list for the devastating effects it has had on Indigenous families. Officially started in 1910 but existing in "industrial" and "boarding" schools established before then in the nineteenth century, the residential school program was created with the almost explicit objective of keeping Indigenous children away from the supposedly harmful influences of their parents and their home communities.

Students play an afternoon game of basketball at Bountiful Elementary-Secondary School. What relationship between these women does the photo appear to convey?

What do YOU think?

1. If you had been a government lawyer, what kinds of questions would you have asked the witness quoted in the narrative above? What concerns would you have voiced about plural marriage?
2. Do you think that individuals who are legally polygamous (i.e. their marriages were performed legally in another country) should be allowed to immigrate to Canada? What conditions might you put on their immigration?

Families were ripped apart as parents reluctantly signed over legal guardianship of their children to school principals, then watched their children leave for the state- and church-run boarding schools, where they would live for most, if not all, of the year. Parents were discouraged from visiting. Those who did were closely monitored. Brothers and sisters were kept apart, sometimes not seeing each other for months on end. Many families were never reunited.

Historian J.R. Miller tells the story of a Cree woman who went to a residential school that was 19 kilometres from her reserve. For hours on end, she would stand at the corner of a fence that surrounded the school property:

She would put her hand through the fence, because that meant she was closer to her home and family by the length of her arm and watch for her parents. She would say to herself, "the next black horse that comes along" will be drawing her parents' wagon on a visit. Disappointment only led to repetitions of the childlike incantation, a wish and a prayer that never seemed to come true. (Miller, 1996: p. 338–9)

Physical, emotional, and sexual abuse by residential school employees demoralized the students. And as those who have been abused so often become abusers, many Indigenous children grew up to bring the abuse they learned at school to their home communities.

Sexual Sterilization

In its definition of genocide, the United Nations includes attempts to destroy a people by imposing measures designed to prevent births within the group. This describes certain policies aimed at Canada's Indigenous population during much of the twentieth century. For instance, in 1928, the government of Alberta passed the Sexual Sterilization Act, with the intent of sterilizing "mental defectives" so that their "bad genes" would not be passed on. The act reflects the early twentieth-century belief in eugenics, the flawed notion that a single gene responsible for intelligence was absent in "stupid people," who would be capable of having only "stupid children"—in other words, children inheriting their parents' genetically defective intellect. We know now that there is a complex relationship between genetics and the various aptitudes that make up the biological potential known as intelligence. It is more accurate to say that we have intelligences of various kinds and levels (e.g. I have a talent for writing, but I am inept in drawing). This complexity makes the degree to which intelligence is inherited uncertain. We just don't know.

Eugenics has rightly been called scientific racism, as it was used to justify prejudices based on the supposed genetic inferiority or "feeble-mindedness" of certain immigrant groups to North America—particularly those from eastern Europe—as well as of black people and Indigenous people. Since it was used to support prejudice against the poor, it is also an instrument of scientific classism. The traditional yardstick for measuring intelligence is the intelligence quotient (IQ) test. This test has been rightfully criticized for its bias against people representing certain language and culture groups. The test also perpetuates the myth that we have a general intelligence to which a single number can be assigned.

During the history of Alberta's Sexual Sterilization Act, which lasted from 1928 to 1972, 2,832 people were sterilized, most of them women.

Sterilizations of Métis and First Nations people account for a disproportionately high number of the total, an estimated 25 per cent (roughly 10 times their percentage of the total population). Eastern European immigrants (Ukrainians, Russians, etc.)—people whose English language skills and cultural capital were low—were also represented in high numbers in the sterilized group.

British Columbia passed an act similar to Alberta's Sexual Sterilization Act in 1933, the same year that the notorious Law for the Prevention of Genetically Diseased Offspring was passed in Nazi Germany. Recently there have been accusations that, following both racial and religious prejudice, hundreds of non-Christian Indigenous people were sterilized by a United Church missionary doctor in a church-run hospital in the BC coastal community of Bella Bella, and that a good number of young Indigenous women made pregnant by residential school staff, clergy, and visiting officials were coerced into having abortions (see Truth Commission, 2001: pp. 12–13).

The Sixties Scoop

The United Nations' definition of genocide also includes attempts to destroy a people by forcibly transferring children of the group to another group. This characterizes what has been referred to as the Sixties Scoop, a program, beginning in the 1960s, of removing large numbers of Aboriginal children from their families, their communities, and the Indigenous world. Children could be taken from their families by government-affiliated agencies for a variety of reasons: some were children of parents judged to be alcoholics, some were newborns needing hospital care taken to the nearest city (and in many cases never returned), some were living in homes considered crowded or substandard. In 1964, the number of children of all backgrounds removed from their families was 4,228; roughly 34 per cent of those (1,446) were Indigenous children.

Between 1971 and 1981 in Manitoba, where Indigenous families were hardest hit, over 3,400 Indigenous children were removed from their homes. Many were taken from the province, and more than 1,000 of them were sent to the United States, where American child welfare agencies could get as much as $4,000 for each child placed. The province later launched an investigation into the practice, led by

Justice Edwin Kimelman. In his summary of the investigation, *No Quiet Place* (1985), he stated:

> [C]ultural genocide has been taking place in a systematic routine manner. One gets an image of children stacked in foster homes as used cars are stacked on corner lots, just waiting for the right "buyer" to stroll by. (cited in Fournier & Crey, 1997: p. 88)

But statistics and judges' reports do not give a real sense of the suffering caused. The following statement comes from a research report on the emotional return of children to their families, communities, and people:

> I was sixteen years old when my daughter was taken from me. My partner at the time was drinking and at eighteen he went to prison. I had no way of looking after her and felt very alone. The social worker told me that my daughter would be better off with a "nice, normal family." I thought that I would at least be able to visit her sometimes, but she was placed in Pennsylvania and we did not meet her again until she

© Joseph Tisiga

First Nation artist Joseph Tisiga's painting *With Friends* "re-imagines the moment of my mother's removal from her birth family by authorities as a child of the 'sixties scoop'" (www.our-story.ca/winners/arts/3083:with-friends). Can you interpret it? What might the image of the tall white man in the hall mean to an Indigenous person who was "scooped" as a child?

was 20 years old. I took a bus to Windsor and that is where we met. I was alone and scared. She looked just like me when I was twenty, but with a very different attitude. She had suffered sexual abuse in her adopted home and she blamed it on me. She had a little girl of her own, but she would not let me meet her. I wish there was someone who could help us get past this pain. (Budgell, 1999: p. 6)

WRAP IT UP

Summary

Family in Canada today is a diverse and complex form, and long has been so. This diversity expresses itself in family size, structure, age of marriage and of having children, qualifications for family membership, in who is and is not considered eligible for marriage into the family, in the expectations and practices of gender roles, and in the relationship between children (of all ages) and their parents. And this diversity works—the "good" family takes many forms. Why is there such diversity in the history, present, and, doubtless, the future of the Canadian family? The main reason is that family adapts: it evolves in the sense that it is flexible enough to change to best fit changing social circumstances.

THINK BACK

Questions for Critical Review

1. Describe the diversity of the Canadian family, both historically and today.
2. Describe how family in Quebec is different from family in the rest of Canada. Give some examples and some possible explanations. What is the significance of Quebec's difference when it comes to family?
3. Outline nine major changes taking place in the Canadian family today.
4. Identify the different forms that conjugal roles can take.
5. Outline the measures used to place Canadian Indigenous families "under attack" during the twentieth century.

READ ON

Suggested Print and Online Resources

Online

Marriage & Family Processes

www.trinity.edu/~mkearl/family.html

- Michael Kearl's website provides useful material on the study of the American family, including information on the cultural factors that shape family structures and data on Americans' relationship preferences.

Stats & Facts—Families: A Canadian Profile

www.ccsd.ca/factsheets/family

- Maintained by the Canadian Council on Social Development, this website provides data on the distribution of families by type across Canada, on single-parent families, and on marriage and divorce rates.

The Vanier Institute of the Family

www.vanierinstitute.ca
- This Ottawa-based organization researches and publishes on issues affecting the Canadian family. You can read their recent publications on such topics as family vacations, the changing role of fathers, and young people who become responsible for the care of older family members.

Stolen Children

www.youtube.com/watch?v=vdR9HcmiXLA
- This CBC story features interviews with survivors of Canada's residential school system.

In Print

Rod Beaujot (2000), *Earning and Caring in Canadian Families* **(Peterborough: Broadview Press).**
- One of this country's preeminent social demographers, Rod Beaujot, draws sociological conclusions about the Canadian family based on an analysis of statistical data.

Elizabeth Bott (1957), *Family and Social Networks: Roles, Norms, and External Relationships in Ordinary Urban Families* **(London, UK: Tavistock).**
- This classic work introduced and developed much of the terminology and ideas used by social scientists studying the sociology of the family today.

Wayne Hower (2006), *Does a Disabled Child = a Disabled Family?* **(Authorhouse).**
- This is a self-published work that combines the author's personal experience raising a disabled child with an academic and professional approach.

Nancy Mandell & Ann Duffy (2011), *Canadian Families: Diversity, Conflict, and Change,* **3rd edn (Toronto: Thompson Nelson).**
- This edited collection features articles that outline a number of ways in which family operates in Canada.

Karen Stote (2015). *Sterilization of Indigenous Women: An Act of Genocide* **(Black Point, NS: Fernwood Publishing).**
- This book delves into the hidden history of the forced sexual sterilization of Indigenous women in Canada.

Religion

The Gist

Reading this chapter will help you to . . .

- Outline Émile Durkheim's sociological approach to religion.
- Discuss the relationship between organized religion and gender roles.
- Talk about how the sociological profile of religion is changing in Canada.
- Analyze the relationship between organized religion and family.
- Describe the impact of religion on the lives of Hutterites in Canada.
- Detail the impact of Christian religious colonialism upon the Indigenous people of Canada.
- Discuss the banning of religious symbols in France.

Terms of the Trade

- Abrahamic religions
- age group
- agency
- aid evangelism
- androcentrism
- Catholic-Traditionalist
- cohort
- collective consciousness
- false consciousness
- haram

- hegemony
- Islamophobia
- jihad
- jihad-i-akbar
- jihad-i-asghar
- liberation theology
- misogynistic
- moral community
- neotraditionalism
- operational definition

- Orientalism
- phantom aid
- profane
- Protestant (work) ethic
- sacred
- social Darwinist
- social gospel
- tied aid
- totem
- ummaic jihad

Names to Know

- Marie Battiste
- Émile Durkheim
- Margaret Humphreys
- Mir Zohair Husain

- Mary-Ann Kirkby
- Haroon Siddiqui
- Max Weber

For Starters

Haidar Hamdani/AFP/Getty Images

The Christmas Rant

Starting around mid-November, the annual Christmas rant begins. A Christian Facebook friend of mine from the southern US (she asks people not only to like but to type "Amen" for some of her posts) has fired the first shot. It began something like this:

> We are not allowed to say "Merry Christmas" to people anymore—just "Happy Holidays" or "Season's Greetings." We can't even have Christmas parties anymore, just "holiday" parties.

From there the rant goes on, concerning how the United States is a Christian country and how she, as a Christian, should be able to say "Merry Christmas" if she wants to.

I both agree and disagree with what she has to say. I was raised as a Christian in what I thought of as a Christian country. People such as this friend have said "Merry Christmas" all their lives, not usually meaning it in any religious way, just invoking the happiness that Christmas has long meant to them. I have never said "Happy Holidays" to anyone, and certainly not "Season's Greetings" (I often feel like replying, "Hello, Winter!").

Then the sociologist in me comes to life. Canada is a Christian country, but it is also a Muslim, Jewish, Jainist, Sikh, Hindu, Buddhist, and Baha'i country. Not everyone in Canada has grown up with the cultural tradition of celebrating Christmas. If someone greets me with "Merry Christmas," I say it right back to them. If I know that a person is Christian, I might be the first to use the greeting. Otherwise, I don't say it. If I remember that it is Diwali, the Hindu Festival of Lights (held either in October or November, as its date is based on the Hindu calendar), then I might greet someone I know is Hindu, Sikh, Jain, or Buddhist with a reference to the special day. If I know that someone is Jewish, I might (if I think of it) greet the person with "Happy Hanukkah" (though again, because its date is based on the Hebrew calendar, this holiday could take place in November or December). Muslims celebrate two Eids: Eid al-Adha and Eid al-Fitr. I have no idea what a proper greeting might be, but this won't be an issue for some time, as these dates, based on the Islamic lunar calendar, shift by approximately 11 days every year and won't take place in December again until 2034. I try not to eat in front of a Muslim during Ramadan, when Muslims are supposed to refrain from eating from sun-up to sundown. In other words, I compromise within my knowledge, rather than assuming that everyone shares my religious and cultural experience.

Back to my Facebook friend. If you are to have a sociological imagination, you cannot blame the individual in cases such as this. Instead, you have to look at what the various media and social institutions—the education system, the family, and, in this case, organized religion—teach.

The "war on Christmas" has been loudly declared a problem for years by certain media outlets and churches. Americans are much more prone than Canadians are to feel threatened by Muslims. Stephen Harper found that out in the election of 2015, when he tried (and failed) to encourage moral panic over a woman attending the Canadian citizenship ceremony in her *niqab*. A year later, Donald Trump tried (and succeeded) to encourage moral panic over Muslim visitors in the US, as part of his strategy to become the Republican Party's presidential nominee. I am not excusing or justifying that misplaced sense of threat. I am just trying to explain societal phenomena, the job of a sociologist.

As you will learn from the rest of this chapter, Canada does not have a long history of tolerance and respect for people of other religions. Huguenots (French Protestants) were banned from entering Catholic New France for decades in colonial Canada of the seventeenth and eighteenth centuries. Quebec citizens of the twenty-first century faced a proposed ban on "overt and conspicuous" religious symbols in all public-sector workplaces. The federal government prohibited First Nations from practising the Potlatch and the Sun Dance from the late nineteenth century to 1951.

Why is religious tolerance so hard to come by? Because true tolerance of difference requires us to rethink long-held beliefs and behaviours, and that kind of change can be painful.

What do YOU think?

1. What is your response to the "Christmas rant"? Do you expect to hear the rant for years to come?
2. How do you think that the provincial governments and workplaces should deal with questions of religious holidays other than Christian ones?

Introduction: The Sociocultural Elements of Religion

One of the earliest sociological insights into religion came from the Greek philosopher Aristotle:

> All people say that the gods also had a king because they themselves had kings either formerly or now; for men create the gods after their own image, not only with regard to form, but also with regard to their manner of life. (*Politics*, i.2.7)

Aristotle was suggesting that a society with a powerful king would likely have in its religion a commanding authority figure. And, a less hierarchical society would likely have a spiritual society of gods that is more egalitarian, in their relationships both with one another and with human beings. People are likely to use the same language they use to describe human relationships to describe their relationship with their god or gods. In this way, according to Aristotle, the gods we worship are a mirror, reflecting our own social structure. Aristotle, it's worth noting, spent over 20 years in Athens, the birthplace of democracy, where the Greeks worshipped a host of gods who, according to their mythology, would frequently interact with humans and be influenced by them.

You can see something of Aristotle's insight by comparing the religious and social practices of the seventeenth-century French Jesuit priests and the Wendat (Huron) people among whom they lived and did missionary work. The Jesuits had a powerful king and an omnipotent God. The language they used when speaking of either political or spiritual figures was one of great authority, with frequent reference to "masters" and to commanding and obeying. By contrast, the Wendat nation had formed as an alliance of four member nations, or tribes. Each of the separate nations had a tribal leader who could recommend actions but not give orders. The Wendat word used to refer to the leader can be translated as "we cause him to be a principle to imitate"—in essence, "him whom we see as our role model." There were no words in Wendat that meant "order" or "command." As for religion, the Wendat recognized a series of spiritual figures, including Yaatayentsik, the first woman on earth, who had fallen from the sky, and her twin grandsons, Ioskeha and Tawiskaron, who had transformed the earth. These and other spirits did not *command* people; rather, they *inspired* them through visions, or else they plagued them with curses.

This does not suggest that the Wendat, or other societies without strong political hierarchy, had no sense of a creator or god above all other gods. It simply means that the relationship between people and spirits was more in line with the relatively egalitarian relationships between humans.

By the late nineteenth century, this idea of the link between social and spiritual relationships became set in a social Darwinist, or evolutionary, model. According to this model, the most "primitive" people had pesky spirits; "barbarians" had playful or nasty but ultimately impotent gods. Only "civilized" people had a Supreme Ruler. This way of thinking justified policies aimed at converting heathens in the colonies to Christianity. The methods used were often anything but civilized, as survivors of Canada's residential school system can attest.

What do YOU think?

How do you think a social Darwinist would have characterized the gods and level of civilization of the seventeenth-century Wendat?

Religion and Class Intersect

Religion and class intersect. If you are an Anglican in Canada, your income is likely to be higher than if you are a Catholic or a Baptist, and certainly higher than if you are a Pentecostal. Why so? One explanation is the Protestant (work) ethic. This theory, touched on in Chapter 1, was developed by **Max Weber** to explain the rise of modern capitalism. Weber was familiar with the Protestant belief in a predestined "elect" who would be saved during the second coming of Christ. A person demonstrated membership in this elect group by achieving material success through hard work. According to Weber, this religious/cultural influence spurred people to accumulate wealth, making this set of values, associated with Protestantism, a key factor in the rise of capitalism. Were he alive today, Weber might argue that the Protestant work ethic survives in the general prosperity of some religious groups over others.

But this is only part of the story. The Anglican Church (the Church of England) is a socially conservative church with a long historical connection to power in Canada. One of the issues that led to the 1837–8 rebellions in what are now Ontario and Quebec was the set of privileges that the Anglican Church enjoyed in British North America (e.g. having land specially reserved for their use or sale, called "clergy reserves"). The official wording was "for the support and maintenance of a Protestant clergy," but it was understood that "Protestant" in this context meant "Anglican only."

Class and "race" aligned with religion. The Methodist Church attracted small-scale farmers and Aboriginal people. The Baptist Church long welcomed members of Canada's black community, particularly in the Maritimes, as well as white people with lower-than-average income. The Pentecostal Church is likewise racialized, and has a connection to poor people living in rural areas. The Catholic Church has been home to minoritized groups that have experienced discrimination. The earliest Catholics were French, who, living within a British colony, historically did not have the power that the English did. During the nineteenth century, many poor Catholic Irish immigrants came to Canada, only to find "No Irish Need Apply" on signs for jobs in Toronto. Subsequent periods of immigration brought Italians, Croatians, Poles, Hungarians, and other working-class groups whose presence affected the class standing of Catholics in Canada.

According to Karl Marx, religion generally functions as an instrument of hegemony. It serves the interests of the ruling class by dissuading oppressed members of the working class from organizing around their own class-based self-interests to challenge the inequality of society. Religion helped instill a false consciousness, Marx's term for the workers' belief that the class-based hierarchy—in which they occupied the lowest position— was justified and to their advantage. Religion, in Marx's critical view, made members of the lower class believe that God had planned society to be the way it was, and that by toiling away under oppressive conditions, they were really acting in the best interests of their class and would find their rewards ultimately in the "next life." A classic example of how religion supported the class system comes from the hymn "All Things Bright and Beautiful":

> The rich man in his castle,
> The poor man at his gate.
> God made them high or lowly
> And ordered their estate. . . .

That last line means that God determined the appropriate positions within the class system for the poor and the rich. The message: don't revolt against a God-determined social order, no matter how oppressive!

Yet religion can bear a "radical possibility," an ability to bring about positive social change. This is exemplified in Canada by the social gospel movement and the progressive politics of J.S. Woodsworth, Stanley Knowles, and Tommy Douglas. They were trained as ministers and became involved in the development of "radical" policies, such as socialized medicine and pensions that dramatically improved the lives of working-class people. That same Christian spirit of helping those in need is not just a fact of the past. It can be seen today in the strong, swift response of Canadian religious communities to the plight of Syrian refugees coming to Canada. Refugee sponsorship is strong in many Christian denominations, and was especially important in 2015, when the federal government under Stephen Harper was lagging behind church initiatives and public opinion on the matter.

Durkheim and the Elementary Forms of Religious Life

Although he was not particularly religious, **Émile Durkheim** (1858–1917) has profoundly affected how sociologists view religion. His father and grandfather were both rabbis, yet he heard no religious call. His great work on religion is *Les formes élémentaires de la vie religieuse: Le système totémique en Australie*, published in 1912. In 1915 it was published in English as *The Elementary Forms of the Religious Life*.

Durkheim took sociology into areas where at first glance it did not seem to belong, including suicide (surely the realm of psychology) and religion (certainly the realm of theology). Both suicide and religion were seen as being firmly rooted in the individual, not in the group or society, and there was strong resistance to his ideas among people studying psychology and religion at the time.

Durkheim's aim was to identify the basic elements of religion. He believed he could do this by studying the religion of the most basic society then being discussed by social scientists: the Aborigines

of Australia. Through this study he hoped to develop a sociological model applicable to all religions.

What Is Religion?

Here is how Durkheim defined religion:

> A religion is a unified system of beliefs and practices relative to sacred things, that is to say, things set apart and forbidden—beliefs and practices which unite into one single moral community called a Church, all those who adhere to them. (Durkheim, [1912]/1995: p. 44)

As Fields puts it, Durkheim's view was that "religion is social, social, social" (Fields, 1995: p. xxxiv). In using the term moral community, Durkheim was recognizing that religious groups are "made up of individuals who have mutually recognized and recognizable identities that set them, cognitively and normatively, on shared human terrain" (Fields, 1995: p. xxxiv). It's clear from this how dramatically Durkheim deviated from his contemporaries, who considered religion something experienced by the individual rather than the larger community.

Three Key Elements of Religion

There are three key elements in Durkheim's analysis of religion. The first is the equation *god = society*. Durkheim formulated this idea in the context of the totems of the Australian Aborigines.

Totem is a word that came into English in the late eighteenth century from the language of the Anishinabe or Ojibwa people. Its origin is the word *ndotem*, meaning "my clan" in Ojibwa. When Anishinabe people introduce themselves in formal situations, they often follow the statement of their name by saying something such as *waawaashkesh ndotem*, meaning "deer is my clan." In this way, they are telling something about their identity and who they are.

Edward Benton-Banai, a respected Anishinabe elder and author of *The Mishomis Book: The Voice of the Ojibway*, identified seven original clans of the Anishinabe (Benton-Banai, 1988: pp. 75–7). Traditionally, he explains, each clan was associated with a specific function and certain ideal characteristics of clan members. These characteristics connect with the clan's totem animal (see Table 11.1). The carved totem poles found on the Pacific coast of North America have images that represent different clans connected to the villages where the poles were erected.

Having some sense of what *totem* means, we can look at Durkheim's famous explanation of the *god = society* equation:

> [The totem] . . . symbolizes two different . . . things. [I]t is the outward and visible form of . . . the totemic principle or god; and . . . it is also the symbol of a particular society that is called the clan. It is . . . the sign by which each clan is distinguished from the others, the visible mark of its distinctiveness, and a mark that is borne by everything that in any way belongs to the clan: men, animals, and things. *Thus if the totem is the symbol of both the god and the society, is this not because the god and the society are one and the same?* How could the emblem of the group have taken the form of that quasi-divinity if the group and the divinity were two distinct realities? Thus the god of the clan, the totemic principle, can be none other than the clan itself, but the clan transfigured and imagined in the physical form of the plant or animal that serves as totem. (Durkheim, [1912]/1995: p. 208)

A totem, then, is a symbolic representation both of a god and of the society that reveres it. Another way of looking at it is that societies fashion deities represented as having characteristics like the people themselves. These characteristics are then projected back onto both the culture and the individuals. The god and the people are one and the same.

What do YOU think?

Consider the totemic principle equating god and society. Do you think this is similar to the connection of the cross, Christ, and Christians?

Totem pole Baburns/Dreamstime.com

The images in this totem pole are culturally stylized versions of the totem animals of clans of the artist's First Nation. What impression do you think these totem poles made on the Christian missionaries arriving in villages on the Pacific coast? What impression do they make on you?

Table 11.1	Clans and Totems of the Anishinabe
Clan/Totem	**Associated Characteristics**
Crane Clan Loon Clan	leadership, chieftainship
Fish Clan	mediation, settling disputes; philosophy
Bear Clan	protecting the community; medicinal plants
Marten Clan	warfare and war strategy
Deer Clan	poetry
Bird Clan	spiritual leadership

Source: Benton-Banai (1988)

Collective Consciousness and the Sacred and Profane

Durkheim focused primarily on the group experiences and rituals of people belonging to a particular religion. These sacred experiences foster what Durkheim called a collective consciousness. In Muslim countries, the cry of the Muzzin (the religious caller) over the loudspeaker calling the faithful to early morning prayer, followed by the collective deep bowing of people who are similarly dressed, is a compelling example of collective religious experience.

Durkheim distinguished between experiences, acts, and objects that are *sacred* and those that are *profane*. Sacred objects and acts are set apart from more ordinary (profane) ones as being positively regarded, holy, and therefore deserving of reverence or respect. Sacred objects include prayer beads, crosses, flags, and items in the medicine bundle of an Aboriginal shaman; sacred acts include prayer, some Aboriginal dances, and keeping kosher. But

Durkheim used the term *sacred* also for that which is forbidden or taboo. The Arabic term used in Islam, haram, applies here. Canadian writer **Haroon Siddiqui**, in *Being Muslim*, lists the following prohibited objects and practices:

Haram Foods: Pork and its by-products, carnivorous animals (those that tear their food apart with claws, such as lions), almost all reptiles and insects, animals that died before being properly slaughtered, blood, and all alcoholic or intoxicating drinks.

Haram Lifestyle: Gambling, including lotteries; all drugs that cause intoxication, alter sensory perception (hallucinogens) or affect one's ability to reason and make sound judgments; and paying and accepting interest. (Siddiqui, 2006: p. 80)

Durkheim argued that objects were not sacred by nature, but acquired the status socially.

© Hikrcn/Dreamstime

Muslims pray at a mosque in Turkey. How do you think this kind of communal prayer generates a sense of collective consciousness?

The Kandariya Mahadeva temple, a Hindu holy site at Khajuraho, in Madhya Pradesh, India. Close inspection reveals its erotic reliefs. Sacred or profane?

Durkheim's Study of Religion and Suicide

In his 1897 study of suicide, Durkheim stated that Protestants committed suicide more often than Catholics did. He explained the difference by arguing that Protestants were less connected to society than Catholics were. The implication was that being Catholic made a person less likely to die from suicide.

I have used this point without questioning it in earlier versions of this textbook, but not this one! The reason I have stopped merely citing it unquestioned is that Durkheim's social fact concerning Catholic and Protestant suicides has recently been challenged. Van Poppel and Day assert that the operational definition for suicide was different for the two groups: Catholics, they argue, were much less likely to count "sudden deaths" and "deaths from ill-defined or unspecified causes" as suicides than Protestants were (Van Poppel & Day, 1996: p. 500). The reason, they propose, is that in the Catholic Church suicide is considered a mortal sin, meaning that (until relatively recently) a person dying by suicide could not be buried with religious rites in a Catholic graveyard. The suggestion was that either doctors were reluctant to pronounce an unexplained Catholic death a suicide or they covered up some suicides; either way, Catholic suicides were systematically underreported. This viewpoint is not without critics (see e.g. van Tubergen, te Grotenhuis, & Ultee, 2005), but if true, it would throw into question Durkheim's assertion about the protective effects of being Catholic in France in his day.

Canadian Society and Religion

Trends

The last year that religion was included in the Canadian census was 2001. Canadians were invited to indicate their religious affiliation in the 2011 National Household Survey (NHS), which (temporarily) replaced the mandatory long-form census that Statistics Canada issues every five years. While the census and the NHS are not directly comparable, we can draw some conclusions by examining data from the 2001 census and the 2011 NHS. Table 11.2 summarizes some of these data.

Trends worth noting are the categories that show the greatest increase and decrease. According to the 2001 census, the categories with the largest increases by percentage from 1991 to 2001 were Pagan (281.2 per cent), Muslim (128.9), "Other Christian" (121.1), Serbian Orthodox (109.5), Hindu (89.3), Sikh (88.8), and Buddhist (83.8). Table 11.2 shows that many of these trends continued from 2001 to 2011.

Several points are worth observing. First, Canada is not "going Pagan." The respondents giving that answer are going from a low number to another low number. That is one reason why a good sociologist—professional or student—does not rely on percentage alone when looking at change. Raw numbers themselves are also important.

Immigration from South Asia is a major factor in the increase of Muslims (primarily from Pakistan), Hindus, and Sikhs shown in Table 11.2. War refugees have increased the numbers for some religions, notably Islam (from Somalia and parts of the Middle East). The growth of Canada's Tibetan population, owing to China's oppression of Tibet, correlates with the increased number of Buddhists.

The number of "Other Christians not included elsewhere" has risen in part because of West Indians joining local independent churches in relatively large numbers. However, the category also includes people who identify simply as "Christian" without specifying a particular denomination. In other words, they may celebrate Christmas and Easter and haven't given up their belief in God, but they don't identify with or attend a particular church outside of weddings and funerals. People who don't accept the supernatural premise of Christianity but who have a nostalgia for Christian traditions and ceremonies are sometimes known as "secular Christians." It's fair to assume that secular Christians make up a good share of the "Other Christians" category.

The second-largest group in Table 11.2, accounting for close to one-quarter of all Canadians, belongs to those claiming no religious affiliation at all. We can speculate on the reasons why this category grew by over 60 per cent between 2001 and 2011.

One explanation is that the demands of work and family life have left many people without the time to participate in organized religion. The emergence of social media has played a role as well. Have you ever lost four hours of your day turning on your laptop to quickly check your Facebook account? I have. Facebook didn't exist in 2001.

| Table 11.2 | Canadians' Religious Affiliation, 2001–11 |

Religion	2001		2011		10-Year Change (%)
	Number	**Percentage**	**Number**	**Percentage**	
Catholic	12,936,905	43.6	12,810,705	40.0	−0.01
Protestant	8,654,850	29.2	7,265,780	22.1	−19.1
Christian Orthodox	479,620	1.6	550,690	1.7	+14.8
Other Christian[1]	780,450	2.6	1,475,575	4.5	+89.0
Muslim	579,640	2.0	1,053,945	3.2	+81.8
Hindu	297,200	1.0	497,960	1.1	+67.6
Sikh	278,410	0.9	454,965	1.4	+63.4
Buddhist	300,345	1.0	366,830	1.1	+22.1
Jewish	329,995	1.1	329,500	1.0	−0.002
Eastern Religions[2]	37,550	0.1	35,185	0.1	−6.7
Other religions[3]	63,975	0.2	160,590	0.5	+51.0
No religious affiliation[4]	4,900,090	16.2	7,850,605	24.0	+60.2

Notes:

1. Includes those who indicated just "Christian" and those who indicated Christian religions not included elsewhere, including Born-again Christian, Apostolic, Messianic Jew (whose faith includes elements of Christianity and Judaism), Hutterite, etc.

2. Includes Baha'i, Eckankar, Jains, Shinto, Taoist, Zoroastrian, and Eastern religions not identified elsewhere.

3. Includes Aboriginal spirituality, Pagan, Wicca, Unity, New Thought, Pantheist, Scientology, Rastafarian, New Age, Gnostic, Satanist, etc.

4. Includes Agnostic, Atheist, Humanist, and No religion, and other responses, such as Darwinism, etc.

Source: Statistics Canada, 2011 National Household Survey, cat. no. 99-010-X2011032; Statistics Canada, 2001 Census of Population, cat. no. 95F0450XCB2001005.

This, though, would explain only why attendance at churches, synagogues, mosques, and other places of worship has decreased. It does not explain why people in greater numbers are denying any religious affiliation.

We could speculate that Canadians have become disillusioned with religion because of its central role in many wars and conflicts; it is hard to view religion as a force for peace when it is used as a pretext for attacks on others. In recent years, organized religion in North America has been linked to child sexual abuse and, in Canada, to the residential school system where so many young Indigenous people suffered. These affairs have a high media profile and could play a role in turning people off of religion.

It is possible, too, that organized religion, conservative by nature and steeped in centuries of tradition, has lost followers because it has trouble keeping up with the pace of change in a socially progressive country such as Canada. Some churches are still wrestling with same-sex marriage and equal employment opportunities for women long after gay marriage and the ability of women to lead the world's largest companies and most powerful governments have ceased to be topics of controversy in mainstream society.

Finally, in Canada today it is more socially acceptable than it was even a generation ago to admit to having no religious affiliation. Many Canadians of your grandparents' age, regardless of how deep their faith ran, would have been reluctant to identify as atheists for fear of the social backlash that such a bold declaration of non-faith might attract.

The decreases in percentage are also important sociologically. Over the 10-year period, the proportion of Canadians identifying as Catholic fell by 3.6 per cent, from 43.6 per cent to 40.0 per cent. The share of Protestants in Canada fell even further, from 29.2 per cent in 2001 to 22.1 per cent in 2011. One correlation to observe is religious affiliation and age (see Table 11.3). While over 8 out of 10 Canadians aged 65 and over identified as Christian

| Table 11.3 | Canadians' Religious Affiliation by Age Group, 2011 |

Religion	Under 15 n = 5,592,800	15–24 n = 4,324,065	25–54 n = 14,044,940	55–64 n = 4,338,980	65 and Over n = 4,551,535
Christian	60.3	61.8	64.3	75.4	82.5
Muslim	5.2	3.8	3.4	1.6	1.0
Jewish	1.0	1.0	0.8	1.2	1.3
Buddhist	0.8	1.1	1.3	1.2	0.9
Hindu	1.9	1.6	1.7	1.1	0.8
Sikh	1.8	1.4	1.4	1.0	1.0
Other religions	0.6	0.6	0.7	0.6	0.4
No religious affiliation	28.3	28.7	26.4	17.9	11.9

Note: Figures for 2011 are estimates based on the results of the 2011 National Household Survey, which was distributed to approximately 4.5 million Canadian households.

Source: Statistics Canada, 2011 National Household Survey, cat. no. 99-010-X2011032

in 2011, just 6 out of 10 Canadians aged 24 and under did so. We see Muslims and those without religious affiliation concentrated primarily in the younger age groups, offering a possible look at what the future holds. Lack of immigration is also a factor in the decreases. In 2001, the Presbyterian population had the highest median age (46.0) and the largest 10-year decrease in percentage (35.6 per cent). Presbyterianism has a long history in Canada, but it is connected with Scotland, no longer a major source of Canadian immigration. The decrease would be even sharper were it not for immigration from Korea, which was long a major Presbyterian mission. Several other Protestant denominations—the Anglican Church chief among them—have connections to other parts of Britain that, like Scotland, have declined as sources of immigration to this country.

What do YOU think?

1. Which religions do you think will continue to show significant increases or declines? Are there any religions you think may show a reversal of the 2001–2011 trend? Why?

2. Why do you think the percentage of Canadians claiming no religious affiliation jumped by over 60 per cent between 2001 and 2011? Do you think the share of Canadians claiming no religious affiliation will level off or continue to grow?

Age Group versus Cohort

Statistical studies consistently demonstrate that teens and those in their early twenties are less religious than older people are. The danger with looking at such studies in isolation is that they may be taken to mean that overall levels of participation in religion are falling, that as these young people age, there will be significantly fewer religious people in Canada. The mistake is in automatically seeing an age group difference (i.e. a consistent difference between old and young) and assuming it is a cohort difference (i.e. a difference between people born in two different periods). Young people may not attend church because they are too busy. They may reject religion if they feel it has been forced upon them by their parents. However, they may take up religion later in life—for instance, when they reach marrying age and want a church wedding, or when they become older and turn to a local church as a way to become more involved in the community, through charity work or through a church-based organization. When they are old, they might sense their mortality and need religious answers.

Having said that, it is worth looking at Table 11.3 to see which religions are strongest in different age groups. We can predict that the religious groups with higher concentrations in the lowest age groups are the ones that are likely to grow. The populations that stand out in this regard are Muslim, Hindu, and Sikh. At the other end of the spectrum are

Canada's Jewish population showed the least amount of change between 2001 and 2011. That could change, however, as a recent rise in anti-Semitism in France has made Canada—and Quebec, in particular—a destination for emigrating French Jews.

the Christian churches: they still have the highest overall numbers, but those numbers are highest in the oldest age categories, and much smaller in the youngest age categories. Still, for every Muslim in Canada today, there are roughly 21 people who identify as Christian. How much do you think that ratio will change over the next 10 years?

Religion and the Family

Religion and the Marginalized Family

Religion is often applauded for promoting "family values." Usually it does. Revisiting Merton's three kinds of function from Chapter 1, we could reasonably identify "strengthening the family" as a manifest (i.e. intended and recognized) or latent (largely unintended and unrecognized) function of religion. Yet there have been times when family and religion have stood in opposition, particularly when a certain kind of family situation has been negatively valued by state officials armed with religion.

In nineteenth-century Ireland, the Catholic Church established institutions to "rehabilitate" prostitutes and unmarried mothers. They were called "Magdalene asylums" (referencing Mary Magdalene, the classic "fallen woman" of the Bible) or sometimes "Magdalene laundries," since the women were often forced into hard labour laundering clothes to earn money for the institution. Many unwed mothers had their children taken away and put up for adoption. Magdalene asylums were established throughout Ireland and Britain, and Canada, some surviving until the late twentieth century (see J.M. Smith, 2007).

In Canada, thousands of Indigenous children were sent to church-run residential schools throughout most of the twentieth century. Consider the conditions:

> Children were taken from their parents and extended families for periods of time that often lasted the entire school year, even when the residential schools were located in the students' own communities. Parental visits, when they were permitted, were typically closely monitored in a special "visiting room." Brothers and sisters were often kept apart in strict sexual separation, meaning that siblings in many cases could communicate with each other only by waving from one building to another or through secretly arranged meetings. (Steckley & Cummins, 2008: p. 194)

Residential schools had a strong detrimental effect on Aboriginal parenting skills. Raised under the strict and often abusive authority of underpaid, underqualified, and poorly screened teachers and administrators, described by historian J.R. Miller as the "devoted and the deviant" (1996: p. 321), three generations of Indigenous parents had only these harsh role models on which to base their own parenting.

Imports from Britain

In *Empty Cradles*, British social worker **Margaret Humphreys** describes how thousands of British children—the vast majority born to parents who were either poor or socially marginalized as single parents—were shipped to Australia to live in church-run orphanages. Certainly, some of these children benefited from their change in circumstances. Yet as Humphreys relates, many of the children were told that their parents were dead, and were subjected to the same hard labour and abuse that Indigenous children experienced in Canadian residential schools. The following questions come from a woman who was shipped out to Australia when she was eight:

> Do you think I've got any family? Cousins, anybody. I'm not fussy. Anybody. They told me that my parents were dead. Do you think that's true? . . . I don't know anything about myself. Until I married, I didn't even have a birth certificate. I felt ashamed . . . Can you find out why they sent me? What did I do wrong? . . . (Humphreys, 1995: p. 14)

Humphreys collected a story of a five-year-old girl who had long, curly, blonde hair when she entered the Catholic orphanage named Goodwood:

> After being at Goodwood a few days, she packed all her possessions in a bag and ran down the drive in her nightie. The nuns followed her and dragged her back. The next morning, all the girls were made to line up in the yard and watch her being punished. . . . Two of the nuns held the little girl down, while another started cutting off her hair with garden shears. . . .
>
> When they had finished, there was just an inch or two of hair left on her head. "God wants her punished more than that," one of the nuns said, and she produced a pair of secateurs [small pruning shears]. She started cutting again and didn't stop until the young girl's hair was gone completely and her scalp was bloody with cuts. (Humphreys, 1995: p. 125)

In looking at the treatment of British and Irish orphans and Canadian Indigenous children, we can see common themes that characterize this conflict between religion and family:

- the marginalized (in terms of "race," class, and sexual behaviour) backgrounds of the families from which the children were taken
- the statistically deviant choice made by religious workers such as missionaries, priests, and nuns to opt for "religious life" over "normal" family life in their own society
- the strict hierarchical nature of religion operating in institutions such as religious orders, residential schools, and church-run orphanages
- the strict codes of discipline associated with religious-based institutions

- the ease with which religious concepts such as "sin" can be associated with negative judgement and used to justify harsh punishment.

Hutterites: Religion and Family

The preceding sections illustrate situations in which religion and family come into conflict, with damaging results. In contrast is the strong positive connection between religion and family found in Canada's Hutterite communities. In 2001, the last year for which we have such detailed census data, the Hutterites were the Canadian religious group with the youngest median age (22.2). Children aged 0–14 made up 37 per cent of their population, while young people aged 0–24 made up 54 per cent—well over half—of their total population. The Hutterites'

A Historian's POV

Telling It Like It Is

The Minister's Role in a Hutterite Community

The following passage comes from a study of the Hutterite community of Pincher Creek, Alberta, published by historian David Flint in 1975.

[The] minister . . . is the single most important member of the community. Not only does he attend to the spiritual needs of the colony, but his advice is often asked on everything from when the pigs should be marketed to the price that should be charged for eggs. He is the colony leader, and his election is the most vital decision the colony makes in affecting its future nature. . . .

Hutterites expect the minister . . . to set standards and demand conformity, and to guard the traditions and values of their religion, and they readily obey him. If the minister is easy-going about slight deviations in dress, the colony will reflect his attitude. On one new colony there was not yet a minister in residence. Dress became sloppy— women went around in summer without kerchiefs and shoes and socks. When asked about this, one embarrassed man replied, "When the cat's away, the mice will play." He admitted that there was laxity and confessed that this would change when the minister arrived. . . .

In the week-by-week, year-by-year operation of the colony, group consensus and Sunday-evening meetings play a vital role in maintaining solidarity and discipline. It is an accepted practice to bring pressure to bear on those adults who do not conform to the will of the community. It is considered ethical and necessary to report an individual's misdoings to the colony meeting, and this is accepted for the common good and in recognition of the weakness of human nature. Usually the minister will first caution any person who is stretching the colony regulations too far— for instance by showing too much interest in photographs or pictures (considered to be vain), by being overly concerned with one's flower garden (over-watering taxes the limited water supply), or by frequent outbursts of anger. If change is not evident in the person's behaviour, then the preacher and the elders will decide on a punishment. The commonly accepted practice is to have the guilty party stand during church service, or kneel in front of the entire congregation and confess guilt, or sit with the children. . . . In cases of minor transgressions against colony rules, the minister, as the elected official responsible for maintaining colony discipline, needs deep human understanding to know when and where to draw the line.

—David Flint (1975)

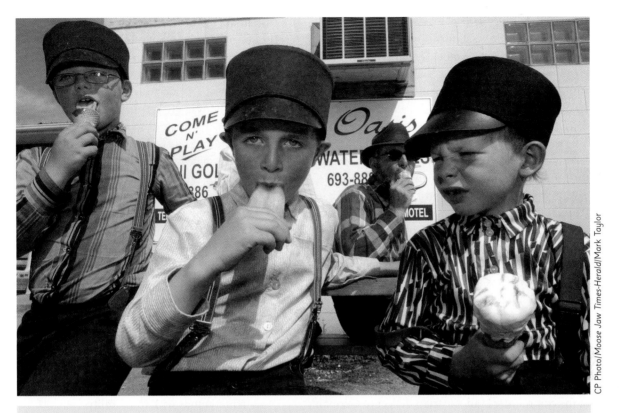

Three boys from the Hutterite colony near Moose Jaw cool off with some frozen treats after apple pick-ing. More than a third of Canadian Hutterites are below the age of 15. Do you think this means their population is on the rise?

CP Photo/Moose Jaw Times-Herald/Mark Taylor

fertility rate, despite declining somewhat in recent decades, approaches the maximum fertility rate possible for a single community and is famous in the sociological literature (see Nonaka, Miura, & Peter, 1993). The high fertility rate is attributed to several sociological factors, including:

- cultural/religious norms opposing contra-ception
- farming as the main industry, requir-ing a large population of strong, young farmhands
- the practice of communal living, which ensures that child care, a shared responsib-ility, is always available.

The Hutterites are named after Jacob Hutter, the leader of a radical Christian movement started dur-ing the 1520s and 1530s. Along with Mennonites, they were part of the Anabaptist religious move-ment, which advocated that baptism should be administered only to believing adults. What made them radicals? They opposed the class linkages between the established church, the state, and the rich. They were also pacifists, adhering strictly to the commandment *Thou shalt not kill.* Their belief that people should be baptized as adults, when they're old enough to make a mature choice, ran counter to the rules of the Catholic Church and the law in Austria, where the Hutterites first formed. Hutter was tor-tured and killed for his ideas.

The Hutterites were driven from one European country after another until they immigrated to the United States during the 1870s. In 1889, the Canadian government, wanting sturdy farmers to exploit the agricultural potential of the Prairies, offered them exemption from military service if they moved to Canada. During the First World War, many Hutterite communities, fearing persecution in the US, moved to Canada.

The social organization of the Canadian Hutterites involves three communal groups (called

"Leuts," meaning "people"): Lehrerleut, Dariusleut, and Schmiedeleut. Each forms a moral community in Durkheim's sense. The Lehrerleut and Dariusleut are found mainly in Alberta, Saskatchewan, and BC, while the Schmiedeleut are in Manitoba. The differences between them are slight, a measure of how conservative or liberal each is.

The three groups exist among roughly 300 farming colonies in Canada, each comprising 60 to 150 people who share a "community of goods," except for small personal possessions. They have frequently encountered opposition to their communal farming practices from other farmers and, in the past, also from provincial governments. The Hutterite system gave them several advantages over single-family farms. By pooling their resources, they could amass greater funds for equipment and supplies, and secure large contracts for their agricultural products, supplied by a large, well-trained, and comparatively cheap workforce.

Other characteristics separate the Hutterites from the general population. The primary language of the community is an Austrian dialect of German, which is taught in schools along with a more widely used German dialect and English. They live an austere and conservative lifestyle. They wear dark clothing—black headscarves with white polka dots, long-sleeved blouses and dresses, and long skirts (never pants) for the women. They are not permitted televisions, radios, snowmobiles (for recreational rather than work use), jewellery, makeup, dancing, or swimming (nakedness is an issue). They have a strong sense of spiritual superiority over the mainstream that appears in such phrases as the following, posted on churches: "Whoever cannot give up his private property as well as his own self-will cannot become a disciple and follower of Christ. The ungodly go each their own egotistical way of greed and profit. To such we should not be conformed" (Kirkby, 2007: p. 5).

Religion and Gender

Organized world religions are generally characterized by patriarchal power structures. Women tend to have subordinate roles that marginalize their participation. During the second wave of feminism in the 1960s and early 1970s, women in North America and western Europe became increasingly critical of Christian practices. They viewed Christianity's embedded patriarchy as an influential cultural factor in the reproduction of gender inequality. Consider, they said, just a few examples from the Bible:

- "Man" was created in God's image, while "woman" was created from spare parts (a rib, we are told) to be his companion. (Male and female humans have the same number of ribs.)
- The first woman, Eve, is blamed for having all humans banished from the paradise Eden after she succumbed to temptation by eating an apple supplied to her by the devil.
- The most memorable female characters in the Bible are associated with sin and destruction; among them are Mary Magdalene, who is customarily identified as a prostitute; Delilah, who brought about Samson's downfall; and Jezebel, who was denounced for introducing the worship of rival gods into Israel, and whose name is synonymous with immorality.

Add to these points the Christian tradition of a wife's obedience, subservience, and even belonging to her husband, and you have some powerful examples that inform, transmit, and reproduce patriarchal structures of inequality, including androcentrism (from *andro* meaning "man") and sexism. This same patriarchal inequality is blamed for numerous instances of women's oppression in society, from the denial of voting privileges and work opportunities to sexual objectification and male violence. In this sense, Christianity—in fact, all Abrahamic religions (including Islam and Judaism)—has much to answer for from a feminist perspective.

Gender Construction among the Hutterites

Mary-Ann Kirkby's *I Am Hutterite* (2007) gives a good sense of life lived as a Hutterite girl growing up in the 1960s. As in other strong religious societies, gender roles were (and continue to be) clearly delimited. Girls and women cook, sew, and take care of children and aging elders. Girls between the ages of 11 and 14 may be chosen by a new mother to take on the role of *Luckela* ("baby holder") for the first year of the child's life. It is a society in which the "community raises a child," though "community" in this case means "female community." If a woman in her prime child-bearing years is pregnant and finds the care of her toddler difficult, that child can be shared out for a while to another mother in the community.

Boys and men, meanwhile, learn their traditional roles of raising crops, managing livestock, running and repairing engines, and exercising primary decision-making for the colony. The minister guides the *Stübel*, or men's meeting, to make community decisions.

The connection between male authority and strong religion, aided by the absence of alternative models of authority from mainstream society, can foster dictatorial patriarchal power. Kirkby describes how such power was exercised in her colony:

> In spiritual terms, [the Head Minister] . . . was "shepherd of the flock," providing doctrinal guidance, administering discipline, and settling disagreements. He was . . . involved in every aspect of community life. No purchase was made without his knowledge or the approval of the council which he headed. . . .
>
> If you were out of favour with him, he had the authority to prevent you from leaving the colony to go to the doctor, to town on business, or for a Sunday visit. [His] . . . sweeping powers were enough to keep most of the men in line and agreeable, but his political manoeuvrings did not impress my father. He often found himself . . . at odds with [the minister's] . . . tactics. (Kirkby, 2007: pp. 62–3)

Women Priests in the Anglican Church

The Church of England or Anglican Church (in the US, the Episcopal Church) is the largest Protestant denomination in the world, with an estimated membership of between 76 and 84 million. Over the past half-century the battle for women to take on the orders of deacons, priests, and bishops has been long, hard, and accompanied by very emotional dialogue that has at times seriously divided the Church. Of the 38 individual provinces that make up the Anglican Church, the first two to be permitted to ordain female priests were the United States and Canada, in 1976. In Canada, on 30 November 1976, six women were ordained almost simultaneously (so that no one would be considered the first), in four different dioceses.

The situation in the United States is not as clear. While the General Convention passed a resolution stating that "no one shall be denied access" to ordination into the three orders (deacons, priests, bishops) on the basis of their sex, another resolution protects bishops who oppose women priests in their dioceses. As late as 2004, there were still three (of one hundred) dioceses whose bishops would not allow the ordination of women. Bishop Jack Iker, of Fort Worth, Texas, expressed his resistance:

> Are we a culturally conditioned church, trying to keep up with the times, and changing practices and teachings to conform with the times, or are we a part of the historic biblical church of the ages? (Iker, 2003)

The bishop's rhetorical question raises a conundrum that is central to organized religion today: how to preserve time-honoured values that are central to the church while remaining relevant to a society with changing values and practices.

It wasn't until 1998, when the Japanese province voted to ordain women priests, that most Anglican provinces accepted female clergy. The "mother church" in England began permitting ordination of women only in 1993, four years after the first female bishop was ordained, in New Zealand. The first female Anglican bishop in Canada was Victoria Matthews, who was consecrated in 1994. She had been made a deacon in 1979 and a priest the next year.

In 1998, the thirteenth Lambeth Conference, a convention of Anglican bishops worldwide held every 10 years, was attended by 11 women bishops, all of whom had been ordained as priests between 1978 and 1984. In the words of Katie Sherrod, a champion of acceptance within the American Episcopal Church:

> Nearly all can tell tales of painful marginalization, even, in a few cases, of being spat upon, shouted at, verbally abused. . . .

With each bishop, however, such tales are told only rarely and then reluctantly, and usually, only to illustrate how much progress has been made. (Sherrod, 1998)

As of 2016, only half of the 44 Anglican provinces allowed the consecration of women bishops, with just 9 actually having one. When Victoria Matthews was consecrated in 1994, Canada became one of the first provinces to have a woman bishop. England itself did not have a woman bishop until 2015. Parishes that have reluctantly accepted women bishops have what are termed "flying bishops," men who can step in as needed to serve in place of the woman bishop.

The resistance to women holding positions of authority within the Church is not restricted to Anglicans. It remains the official position of the Roman Catholic Church and of some fundamentalist Christian groups in Canada and the US (e.g. the Southern Baptists) that women should not be ordained.

Why is there such opposition? Much of it comes back to Christianity's embedded patriarchy, which is extremely difficult to overcome in an institution that derives much of its meaning from its history and traditions. Many Church leaders still justify their opposition to the ordination of women on the grounds that Jesus had no female disciples. Of course, in the patriarchal culture in which Jesus lived, there would have been strong social opposition to his having female disciples. He was revolutionary enough in his respectful treatment of women. And he had women followers who dedicated their lives to learning from him, with his approval (see his attitude toward Mary, sister of Martha, in Luke 10: 38–42).

The negative attitude of the disciple Paul, as expressed in his letters to the Corinthians, is another reason given for opposing women in authority, and reflects the cultural attitude toward women at that time:

As in all the churches of the saints, the women should keep silence in the churches.

Presbitera ARCWP

Despite the threat of immediate, automatic excommunication upon the act, around 180 women have now been ordained as Catholic priests. Can a religion that bars women from positions of authority represent all of its members equally?

For they are not permitted to speak, but should be subordinate, as even the law says. If there is anything they desire to know, let them ask their husbands at home. For it is shameful for a woman to speak in church. (1 Cor. 14: 33–35)

A similar attitude is expressed in Paul's correspondence with Timothy:

Let a woman learn in silence with all submissiveness. I permit no woman to teach or to have authority over men; she is to keep silent. For Adam was formed first, then Eve; and Adam was not deceived, but the woman was deceived and became a transgressor. Yet woman will be saved through bearing children, if she continues in faith and love and holiness, with modesty. (1 Tim. 2: 11–15)

Paul's historical role was to take the ideas of Jesus and organize them into a structure. That the role itself was patriarchal reflects the culture of his upbringing and experience.

What do YOU think?

1. Do you think that Paul's statements were (to use Bishop Iker's phrase) "culturally conditioned"?
2. Why do you think that the "innovations" of female priests and bishops came not from the centre of the Anglican Church in England (where the church head, the Archbishop of Canterbury, is housed) but from the fringe or periphery areas of New Zealand, Africa, and North America?
3. What should the role of sociological analysis be in discussing the position of women in the social structure of religions in Canada?

Quick Hits

The Myth about Islam and Women

While it can be argued that there is a tendency in all countries where organized religion is strong for women to be oppressed, the countries of the Middle East, where Islam is the dominant religion, have been singled out as especially oppressive and **misogynistic**. It is part of a generalized and uncritical targeting of Islam by the conservative Western media, a targeting that is related to deeper Eurocentric cultural beliefs that reproduce **Orientalism** and **Islamophobia**. When examining Islam and the rights of women, it is important to separate those anti-female practices that are specifically Muslim from those practices that happen to occur in Muslim countries but are not supported by the faith. The following list draws on Haroon Siddiqui's book *Being Muslim* (2006):

- The practice of honour killings (killing female relatives for alleged sexual misconduct that brings dishonour upon the family) in countries such as Pakistan, Turkey, and Jordan is *not* an Islamic tradition.
- The practice of female genital cutting (FGC) in North and Central Africa is *not* condoned by Islam. (At the First Islamic Ministerial Conference on The Child, held in Morocco in 2005, FGC was condemned as un-Islamic.)
- The number of cases of polygyny (one man having more than one wife) in Muslim families in Western and Muslim countries is greatly exaggerated. Most Muslim marriages involve couples.
- Most Muslim women around the world do not wear a hijab or head-covering. (Siddiqui, 2006: pp. 96–125).

What do YOU think?

What do you think contributes to the distorted view that prevails in the West of the way women are treated under Islamic law and tradition?

Banning Burkini, Headscarves, and Other Conspicuous Religious Symbols

In 1905 the government of France passed a law separating church and state. It stated that the government would not officially recognize or fund any religion. In the 1980s, questions arose concerning how the law related to children wearing signs of their religion: Christian students wearing crosses, Jewish boys wearing yarmulkes (kippahs), Sikh boys wearing turbans, and Muslim girls wearing headscarves. The debate centred on two competing principles:

During the beach volleyball competition at the 2016 Summer Olympics in Rio de Janeiro, some Muslim women donned body-covering burkinis, challenging the norms of a sport where women are expected to put their bodies on full display. Are both of these athletes conforming to the patriarchal gender expectations of their respective cultures? Is either one really free to dress as she pleases?

Yasuyoshi Chiba/AFP/Getty Images

freedom of expression and laïcité, or secularism of the French state. When in 1989 three girls were expelled from a school near Paris for refusing to take off their headscarves, the official government opinion was that the school's punishment was too extreme, violating the students' freedom of expression. Supporters of the school's actions argued the opposite, claiming that allowing the girls to wear their headscarves was in essence upholding the oppressive demands of a patriarchal religious culture that prohibits women from revealing more than the face in public. The debate concerning the right to ban headscarves came up several times during the 1990s, with no clear resolution.

In 2003, the French government set up an investigative committee (we would call it a royal commission in Canada). The committee recommended drawing a distinction between "conspicuous" religious symbols—headscarves and veils, yarmulkes and turbans—and "discreet" symbols, including small crosses, Stars of David, and hansa or hands of Fatima (daughter of Mohammed), the latter used both by Muslims and Jews. In 2004, the wearing of conspicuous symbols in schools was banned under a law that was passed by a large majority and supported by most people in France, including teachers. Interestingly, the French Archbishop of Marseilles and the Archbishop of Canterbury—the head of the Church of England—opposed the law, which applied not just to France but to its territorial possessions abroad. A few universities attempted to implement such a ban but were not successful.

Debates around secularism and freedom of expression in France continue. Controversy erupted in 2016, when several towns on the French Riviera imposed bans on the "burkini," a full body-covering swimsuit worn especially by Muslim women. The mayor of Cannes, the first town to pass the ban, did not use the emancipation of women as a justification for the policy; instead, he characterized the burkini as "a symbol of Islamist extremism" (Poirier, 2016). A French court that upheld the ban adopted a similar view. In its ruling, the court invoked recent high-profile terrorist attacks in the country, stating:

> In the context of a state of emergency and after recent Islamist attacks in France, the conspicuous display of religious signs, in this instance in the shape beachwear, is susceptible to create or increase tensions

and risk affecting public order. (quoted in Poirier, 2016)

The burkini, in other words, is seen as being not merely a form of dress that allows beach-going Muslim women to comply with Islamic code regarding modesty of appearance but a symbol of violent religious extremism.

Canada has had its own debates around the display of conspicuous religious symbols. In 2007, a nine-year-old girl was kicked out of a soccer tournament in Quebec for wearing a headscarf. The soccer association cited FIFA, the Fédération Internationale de Football Association, in defending its decision. In December 2011, the federal government banned the wearing of the face-covering *niqab* for new citizens taking the oath of Canadian citizenship; the law was eventually overturned, but not before sparking bitter debates about the right to religious freedom versus the expectation that newcomers to Canada should renounce the traditions of their homeland if they clash with Canadian mainstream cultural values such as a woman's right to reveal her face in public. In 2013, Quebec's Parti Québécois government proposed a law similar to the law in France, which would have banned the wearing of all conspicuous religious symbols in public-sector workplaces, including not just government offices but hospitals, government-run daycares, and public schools. The bill failed to pass before the PQ was defeated by the Liberals in the 2014 provincial election.

What do YOU think?

1. "Conspicuous symbols of religion" include turbans and yarmulkes—head coverings for men—and yet the debate always seems to centre on clothing worn by Muslim women. Why do you think that is the case?
2. Why do you think the Parti Québécois attempted to pass a law like the one in France?
3. Canada has a relatively recent tradition of defending the practices of religious minorities. Should that tradition be upheld even when a religious practice clashes with mainstream cultural values?
4. Where should we draw the line between defending the freedom of religious expression and promoting secularism, or the separation of church and state?

Religion and Social Change

Religion has been a primary agent of change throughout history. Both the emergence and spread of new religions—like Islam—and the loss of native religions have brought about and reflected significant social and cultural change. Examples already touched on include the Protestant ethic, which influenced cultural normative structures, and the European missionary movement, which was used to convert and subjugate populations as part of the broader aims of colonialism. And while religion has been used to submit populations to the will of authority, it has been used to emancipate populations as well. Take figures such as Mahatma Gandhi, Mother Teresa, Martin Luther King, Malcolm X, Desmond Tutu, and the aforementioned Canadians Stanley Knowles, J.S. Woodsworth, and Tommy Douglas. All of them were instrumental in using religion as a point of social change for the purposes of social justice. Marx, you will recall, claimed that religion pacifies people and stifles movements for change, as it encourages citizens to put up with their worldly hardships because of the promise of a better life in heaven. However, religion was a driving force behind anti-colonial liberation movements, anti-racism and anti-discrimination movements, struggles against poverty, and democratic reform throughout the nineteenth and twentieth centuries.

Christian Religious Colonialism and Its Impact among Indigenous People in Canada

When missionaries brought Christianity to Indigenous people, their actions were an integral part of colonization, designed to make the people more like Europeans, not just in beliefs but in other social areas such as gender roles (see Karen Anderson's *Chain Her by One Foot*) and in their obedience to political authority. But the people also had agency. They were not merely victims of colonially imposed religions. As Native prophets reacted to the new world of Christian beliefs and ensuing political turmoil, they began to promote innovative religious beliefs. The early nineteenth-century Seneca prophet Handsome Lake (*c.* 1735–1815) combined elements of traditional belief with what his people had learned from Quakers who had spent time among the Seneca. The Code of Handsome Lake combined traditional aspects of the Great Law of Peace, which had brought the initially five nations (Mohawk, Oneida, Onondaga, Cayuga, and Seneca) of the Iroquois together into one confederacy, with Quaker elements such as a strong opposition to witchcraft, sexual promiscuity, and gambling.

Indigenous people developed new forms of Christianity by integrating European-based religion into their own belief system and practices. In many instances, these adapted forms of Christianity

The Point Is...

Jihad: A Misunderstood Term

A religious practice wrongly connected with terrorism in the Arabic world is jihad. Movies, websites, 24-hour news channels, radio call-in shows, and even dictionaries and encyclopedias often lead us to believe that *jihad* means "holy war." Yet if you look in English copies of the Qur'an, the Muslim holy book, you will find the Arabic word translated as "struggle, striving, endeavour." The following is a description of jihad taken from the Qur'an:

> Those who believe, and emigrate
> And strive with might
> And main, in Allah's cause
> With their goods and their persons,
> Have the highest rank
> In the sight of Allah:
> They are the people
> Who will achieve (salvation). (9: 20)

There are three types of jihad: personal, community, and martial. In his insightful book *Global Islamic Politics*, **Mir Zohair Husain** explains them in the following way:

> The personal jihad or jihad-i-akbar, is the greatest jihad. It represents the perpetual struggle required of all Muslims to purge their baser instincts. Greed, racism, hedonism, jealousy, revenge, hypocrisy, lying, cheating, and calumny [false and malicious accusation] must each be driven from the soul by waging jihad-i-akbar, warring against one's lower nature and leading a virtuous life. . . .
>
> Likewise, ummaic jihad addresses wrongs within the community of Muslims, whether by the written word or by the spoken word. Ummaic jihad represents the nonviolent struggle for freedom, justice and truth within the dar-al-Islam [Muslim world]. . . .
>
> Martial or violent jihad is referred to in Islam as jihad-i-asghar (lit., the smaller, lower, or lesser jihad). Martial jihad ideally represents a struggle against aggressors who are not practicing Muslims. . . . Martial jihad should be used to protect and to promote the integrity of Islam and to defend the umma [community] against hostile unbelievers, whether they are invading armies or un-Islamic internal despots. (Husain, 1995: pp. 37–8)

Muslim college students asked for examples of jihad in their lives have answered with the following:

- donating money to a charity rather than spending it on yourself
- studying for an exam rather than watching television
- working hard at a job you don't like because your family needs the money
- avoiding temptation in all forms (similar to Christian avoidance of the seven deadly sins).

What do YOU think?

Describe in your own words how the three types of jihad differ. Why do you think non-martial forms of jihad are not well known outside the Muslim world?

enabled the people to preserve or return to the cohesiveness of Durkheim's moral community that had existed in pre-contact times. In *"Ta'n Teli-ktlamsitasit* ('Ways of Believing'): Mi'kmaw Religion in Eskasoni, Nova Scotia" (2002), Angela Robinson used the term Catholic-Traditionalists to refer to Mi'kmaq who adopted Catholicism but incorporated traditional elements into their religious practices (2002: p. 143). Mi'kmaq scholar **Marie Battiste** (1997) offers the following description of how her people claimed Catholicism as their own to give strength to their community:

> In 1610 the Mi'kmaq people entered into a compact with the Holy Roman Empire when our Chief Membertou and 140 others were first baptized. While our alliance with the Church was more political than spiritual, it was solidified in daily rituals when the French priest Father Antoine Maillard learned Mi'kmaq and began addressing the spiritual questions of the people.... Following the expulsion of the French priests [by the English] . . . [the] Mi'kmaq people held to their strong spiritual rituals in the Catholic Church by conducting their own services. They had prayer leaders who led Sunday prayers, baptized children, accepted promises of marriage, and provided last rites for the dying. . . . These Catholic rituals continue today in many communities, and elders still play an important role in them, although a priest in the community offers the primary services. (Battiste, 1997: pp. 157–8)

During the late nineteenth and early twentieth centuries Christian missionaries, along with federal officials in Canada and the US, took aim at important Aboriginal ceremonies that were conducted, in part, to nourish a strong, cohesive sense of community. These ceremonies were the heart and soul of "religious

The Canadian Press/Andrew Vaughan

Actors re-enact the first baptism of an Indigenous person in Canada, Henri Membertou, during celebrations of the 400-year anniversary of the event. In what ways have the Mi'kmaq community reclaimed this moment of colonialism?

Telling It Like It Is

The Golden Compass and Religious Censorship

Back in 2008, I saw the television premiere of *The Golden Compass*, based on the first novel of Philip Pullman's best-selling *His Dark Materials* trilogy. I knew that a sequel had been planned, so I did a search to find out when it was scheduled to come out. It wasn't. The movie had been the target of a strong religious-based boycott in the US, which had limited its American profits to just $70 million, although it had grossed a solid $300 million worldwide. The reason for the religious opposition to the movie was that the "bad guys" in the film, the evil Magisterium, were suspected to have been modelled on the Catholic Church and its hierarchical organization. I didn't pick up on that in the film, but then I wasn't looking for it—all I saw was a big evil, over-controlling administration (something I see a lot of places—not that I'm paranoid). The books, I've been told, are fiercely anti-religion and anti–church establishment. The author is both a declared atheist and a social anarchist.

If my reading of the religious criticism is correct, it is not so much that the movie supports an atheistic or anti-Christian position, but that it poses a threat to children who, if they enjoy the movie, will want to read the books and in turn may be turned off of religion to a life of atheism. I am of two minds about the boycott. I hate that the sequel will not appear because of religious opposition to the original. However, it is a democratic right to boycott a film, and I could not oppose that action without being a hypocrite. I, too, read into the meanings of movies that I don't like—such as *The Fast and the Furious* franchise and all the bloody *Saw* films—and consider the damaging effects such movies may have on young people. I'm concerned about the mindless Disney movies, which I fear will turn little girls into pouty, pink-clad princesses. Is there any real difference between my stance and the position taken by opponents of *The Golden Compass*?

In my mind, the difference is that *The Golden Compass*, and the books it is based on, encourage young people to think. It encourages people to challenge convention and, hopefully, be creative and original in the worlds they create as adults. Religion is often, in my opinion, overly concerned with conformity and blindly following the paths of the past. I believe that a rich religious life involves addressing the big questions of life, and perhaps answering them. The movies I don't like don't encourage people to really think at all.

---

competition" for missionaries, and a form of resistance to political domination for the government officials. The Sun Dance, the main ceremony for Indigenous groups living on the Prairies, is one example. "Sun Dance" is an English term. The Blackfoot, who live in southern Alberta, termed the ceremony *Okan*, after the pole at the centre of the ceremony. The Okan was initiated, sponsored, and presided over by a woman:

> The decision to hold a Sun Dance was made by a pure woman . . . who had a male relative in danger of losing his life. A husband might be ill or a son may not have returned from a raid. The woman made a public vow that if the person's life was spared, she would sponsor a Sun Dance. Then, if her prayer was

answered, she began preparations for the summer festival. (Dempsey, 1995: p. 392)

Montana governor John Rickard, speaking in 1894, captured the essence of Christian culture's attitude toward non-Christian religious practices:

> Investigation . . . convinces me that it is not only inhuman and brutalizing, unnatural and indecent, and therefore abhorrent to Christian civilization, but that its aims and purposes are a menace to the peace and welfare of communities. My information . . . leads me to regard the proposed exhibition as wholly inconsistent with Christian civilization. (Quoted in Dusenberry, 1998: p. 219)

Modern Nativity

While, overall, religious observance is on the decline in the West, Christmas is one institution of religion that manages to keep pace with the times and never goes out of fashion. Why do you think that is? How do you think Canadians will be celebrating Christmas 20 years from now?

One aspect of the ceremony gave Canadian government officials an excuse for issuing a complete ban on the Sun Dance in 1895. Sometimes, as a spiritual offering, young men inserted leather thongs through their chest or back muscles, attaching the other end either to a pole or to the skull of a buffalo. They would then dance until the thongs ripped free—a painful process. Section 114 of the Indian Act was amended to include a provision making it an indictable offence to take part in any ceremony "of which the wounding or mutilation of the dead or living body of any human being or animal forms a part or is a feature." Technically, this would have made the "mortification of the flesh" (self-flagellation, or whipping oneself) illegal, even though it was associated with Christian religious dedication and was practised throughout most of Christianity's history (and is still practised in parts of Latin America and the Philippines). Little Bear, a Cree leader who had moved with his band to Montana, is reported to have stated that he was willing to remove that part of the ceremony in the spirit of getting along with colonial authorities (Dusenberry, 1998: p. 220). However, the entire ceremony was deemed "uncivilized," prompting this response by one Blackfoot:

We know that there is nothing injurious to our people in the Sun-dance. . . . It has been our custom, during many years, to assemble once every summer for this festival. . . . We fast and pray that we may be able to lead good lives and to act more kindly towards each other.

I do not understand why the white men desire to put an end to our religious ceremonials. What harm can they do our people? If they deprive us of our religion, we will have nothing left, for we know of no other that can take its place. (Quoted in McClintock, 1910: p. 378)

The ceremony continued to be held in secret. Participants who were discovered were arrested. The Sun Dance did not return publicly in Canada until 1951. However, the damage to traditional religious beliefs had already taken its toll. The ceremony never recovered its former prominence.

More recently, religious revival among Indigenous people has gained popularity. Termed neotraditionalism, it involves the reinterpretation of traditional beliefs and practices in ways

342 PART FOUR | Social Institutions

that incorporate elements unique to one's own culture and others borrowed from Native cultures elsewhere. The sweat lodge, the drum, and the medicine wheel are examples of elements used in neo-traditionalist practice. The recovery of traditional customs has been very important in helping Indigenous people find and strengthen their identity. Neo-traditionalist practices are often used in the rehabilitation of people in prison or in treatment for substance abuse.

The Missionary Position

The primary role of missionaries is to change people, to make them leave the religious path they are on and walk a new one, one that often bears the mark of a different culture. But it is also important that missionaries exemplify the values that are at the core of the religion they represent, particularly the principle of charity. Here the sociologist asks whether the two aims clash. Can there be role strain between conversion and charity?

The practice of sending missionaries into developing countries in need of financial assistance is sometimes called aid evangelism. The financial assistance is a kind of tied aid—money that comes with strings attached. Often when countries in the developed world (including Canada) spend money on aid, it is given with the condition that the people receiving the assistance must spend at least some of the money on products and services that come from the donor country. Another term for this is phantom aid, which captures the idea that the aid is not real but rather a form of investment.

So, do religious-based aid workers and the religious communities that sponsor them sometimes see aid as a form of investment in conversion? Aid evangelism has taken various forms over the last few decades. Some American fundamentalist groups delivered thousands of 70-pound food packages to starving people in Iraq. The packages were covered with biblical verses written in Arabic. Following the disastrous tsunami that hit southern Asia in December 2004, the 2,000-member Antioch Community Church, based in Waco, Texas, sent "aid workers" to Sri Lanka to stage children's plays about Jesus and hold Christian prayer services for those suffering from the devastating effects of the flood. Sri Lanka is primarily a Buddhist country,

though Hinduism and Islam are also practised; the Christian element is small. Backlash to perceived aid evangelism caused vandalism and threats to local Christian groups, even to the point of attacking the offices of the Christian aid agency World Vision, which had no connection with the questionable missionary practices. In Indonesia, the world's largest Muslim country, the government blocked the move of American religious-based aid agency World Help to settle 50 Muslim children from the flooded Aceh province to a Christian orphanage, as they suspected that conversion was the cost of the aid.

What do YOU think?

What do you think is the motivation behind attacks on Christian aid agencies and government intervention against Christian charity?

Liberation Theology

Liberation theology is a progressive school of Catholic thought that advocates social justice for the poor. It takes as its model the life of Jesus as being politically opposed to privilege. It resembles the social gospel movement put forward by Protestant ministers of the late nineteenth and early twentieth centuries, except that it is rooted almost exclusively in the Catholic Church, particularly in Latin America, and especially among members of the Jesuit and Maryknoll religious orders. Liberation theology opposes the oppression of the poor by the corrupt, ruling class in developing and underdeveloped countries. Its proponents emphasize social practices that improve the situation for the poor. These practices are devised based on input received from the poor, not from the rich who, historically, have supported the "monarchic and pyramidic" system of hierarchical authority of the Catholic Church (Russell, 2001). There has been strong opposition from conservatives within the hierarchy of the Catholic Church, particularly those bishops in Latin American countries who had been appointed from the elite class. Marxist advocates for the poor argue that these bishops are conscious of their own class interests, and act upon these interests over those of the poor.

BrazilPhotos.com/Alamy Stock Photo

A small outdoor mass for landless workers at a Christian base community in the Amazon of Brazil. Compare the photo of Muslims praying in Turkey (p. 323). Do you think this setting is better suited to what Durkheim called the collective consciousness of religious experience?

The Sandinista National Liberation Front (known by its Spanish initials FSLN) was a Marxist revolutionary group in Nicaragua that began in the 1960s and overthrew the US-backed right-wing dictator Anastasio Samosa in 1979. The Sandinistas stayed in political power until 1990 despite an ongoing battle with the counter-insurgency Contras, who were backed by the American Central Intelligence Agency. The Sandinistas supported priests who worked to benefit the poor. The Catholic hierarchy in Nicaragua had supported the dictatorship of Samosa. In an official statement made in 1950, Nicaragua's conservative bishops said:

> [A]ll authority comes from God. God is the Author of all that exists, and from the Author comes Authority; [faithful Catholics] should remember that when they obey the Political Authority, they do not dishonor themselves, but rather they

act in a way that basically constitutes obeisance to God. (Quoted in Gilbert, 1988: p. 131)

Priests working with the poor and who believed in liberation theology became members of the FSLN. When the Sandinistas came to power, some priests took political office but were quickly reprimanded by Pope John Paul II and the Vatican hierarchy. One such priest was Father Miguel D'Escoto, who became the foreign minister for the Nicaraguan government. In 2008, he was elected president of the General Assembly of the United Nations.

Brazil is the largest Catholic country in the world, with well over 130 million people, yet it has a chronic shortage of priests. It has been estimated that in Latin America, there is one priest for every 7,000 Catholics, versus one for every 880 in the United States (Russell, 2001). One strategy to overcome this shortage supported and implemented by liberation theologians is the establishment of "base communities," numbering as many as about 75,000 in Brazil alone (Russell, 2001). Within the base communities, which average 10 to 30 members each, the focus is on shared religious instruction and prayer as well as communal self-help. Though local priests provide guidance to community leaders, the principal focus of the groups is on relating the lessons of the Bible to the day-to-day activities of their members, whether they are urbanites, slum-dwellers, or rural *campesinos*.

At a typical base community in the town of Campos Eliseos, 14 miles northwest of Rio de Janeiro, 30 local residents meet every Friday night in a cinderblock home to read the Bible and discuss their problems. Antonio Joinhas, a 44-year-old railroad signalman, relates how one study session inspired a local public health centre:

> After reading how one biblical community helped another to overcome a problem, we decided to work together too. We all supplied the manpower and raised money for materials from the community. Now we've got a health center, and it came from the Bible. (Quoted in Russell, 2001)

WRAP IT UP

Summary

Religions touch the spiritual and address human needs that are universal. These aspects of religion are, for the most part, outside the critical eye of sociology. However, religions have social organizations and practices that are well within the domain of the sociologist. They are intimately linked with other aspects of society—hierarchy, gender roles, and colonialism, to name just a few—that sociologists regularly analyze. From that link comes the very critical approach that I have brought to this chapter.

Some readers might think that I have gone too far in praising and defending Islam while criticizing Christianity. That is a legitimate impression, but it is not what I set out to do. What I have tried to do is to highlight the social benefits of organized religion while casting a light on some of areas of sociological concern, such as religious intolerance and the abuse of power. In Canada, Islam is often a target of ignorant and intolerant views, while Christian values and practices that are socially beneficial in most contexts have been used on some occasions as instruments of power by government and religious officials (even well-meaning ones). A critical sociology textbook written in a country where Islam, Buddhism, Judaism, or Hinduism are abused as tools of power (and that happens) would offer a different perspective by taking a closer critical look at the abuse of power within those religions.

THINK BACK

Questions for Critical Review

1. What social tension exists between hierarchy and egalitarianism in organized religion?
2. What would a feminist critique of organized religion look like?
3. What is the relationship between religion and colonialism?
4. Why do you think there is such a misunderstanding about the Muslim faith in the West?
5. Why are many sociologists critical of organized religion?
6. Summarize the arguments for and against a law banning the wearing of conspicuous religious symbols in public. Which of these arguments do you find compelling?

READ ON

Suggested Print and Online Resources

Online

The Immanent Frame: Secularism, Religion, and the Public Sphere

http://blogs.ssrc.org/tif/category/sociology-of-religion

- Founded in conjunction with the Social Science Research Council's program on religion and the public sphere, this site provides intelligently written blogs and useful articles on the sociology of religion, contributed by specialists representing a range of disciplines.

Marx, Weber and Durkheim on Religion

www.jeramyt.org/papers/sociology-of-religion.html

- Jeramy Townsley's very useful (and often plagiarized) article compares the three main sociological theorists of religion.

The Sociological Study of Religion

http://hirr.hartsem.edu/sociology/about_the_field.html

- Maintained by the Hartford Institute for Religion Research, this site presents a good overview of topics and current researchers in the sociological study of religion.

In Print

Timothy J. Gianotti, Jr (2011), *In the Light of a Blessed Tree: Illuminations of Islamic Belief, Practice, and History* **(Eugene, OR: Wipf & Stock).**

- This is an excellent, readable work explaining the basic beliefs and practices of Islam.

Margaret Humphreys (1995), *Empty Cradles: A Shameful Secret, a Miscarriage of Justice, and a Woman Who Wouldn't Give Up* **(London: Corgi Books).**

- This book introduces the reader to the story of over 150,000 English children from marginalized families, who were deported to Australian orphanages and similar institutions.

Isabelle Knockwood (2001), *Out of the Depths: The Experiences of Mi'kmaw Children at the Indian Residential School in Shubenacadie, Nova Scotia* **(Halifax: Fernwood Publishing).**

- This classic work by a First Nation writer examines life at a residential school for Mi'kmaq children.

Haroon Siddiqui (2006), *Being Muslim* **(Toronto: Groundwood Books).**

- This well-written work is designed to inform non-Muslim readers on what Islam is and is not about.

Education

The Gist

Reading this chapter will help you to . . .

- Outline the advantages and disadvantages of "streaming" (or "tracking") in elementary and secondary education.
- Discuss the positive and negative effects on postsecondary education of becoming reliant on (a) adjunct instructors, (b) online education, and (c) corporate sponsorship of research and infrastructure.
- State your view, from a sociologist's standpoint, of plagiarism occurring today in postsecondary institutions.
- Assess the social value of having schools run by and for marginalized groups such as Indigenous and African-Canadian students.
- Discuss how education can reproduce the class structure of society.

Terms of the Trade

- access without mobility
- adjunct professor
- alienation
- assimilation
- commodification
- credentialism
- critical education
- cultural reproduction theory
- cultures of education
- disqualified knowledges
- docile body
- Eurocentric

- examination
- Great White Man
- hidden curriculum
- hierarchical observation
- human capital thesis
- institution
- institutional racism
- instrumental education
- intellectual property
- latent dysfunction
- latent function
- legitimization of inequality

- McJob
- meritocratic
- monoculturalism
- normalizing judgement
- plagiarism
- relative deprivation
- reproduction (of the social structure)
- role models
- social distance
- tracking
- underemployment

Names to Know

- Jean Anyon
- Michel Foucault
- Jeannie Oakes
- Stephen Schecter

For Starters

Radius/All Canada Photos

The Academic Underclass: Take a Good Look at Your Professor

Take a good look at your sociology professor or TA—right now, while she or he isn't looking. Is she relatively young? Does she always seem to be running late, to be hurrying in or out, to be distracted before and after class? Does your prof also teach at another school? Does the department secretary know who you're speaking about when you say your instructor's name?

If your instructor is teaching an intro soc course, chances are he's been hired only for a session, a semester, or a year. He probably isn't a full-time, tenured member of the department. He likely falls into the category of "contract faculty" or "sessional staff." Or maybe he's an "adjunct professor," which sounds a bit loftier but still means that he's teaching courses and students—particularly intro courses—that permanent staff members don't want to teach. My *Canadian Oxford Dictionary* defines *adjunct* as "an assistant or a subordinate person, esp. one with a temporary appointment only."

In other words, the person teaching you may be fully qualified but an academic nomad, part of a growing postsecondary underclass that get paid less for teaching you than full-timers do. Their growing presence is an important change taking place in education today. In this chapter we'll look at what else is changing, and why—and, most important, how it's affecting students and society today.

What do YOU think?

1. Do you think you can tell the difference between a full-time professor and an adjunct? Do you know what percentage of your instructors fit the latter category?
2. What are some of the positive and negative aspects of being taught by an adjunct professor?

Introduction: Education as a Social Institution

To a sociologist, the social institution of education is important because of the multiple influences it has on everything from socialization and status formation to social order and economic productivity. When we refer to the institution of education, we're referring to an enduring set of ideas about education and how it can be used to accomplish goals that are deemed important to society. Education is an extremely powerful tool for promoting ideas among impressionable young people. Children spend more time at school than they do with their parents.

Education has a significant impact on the socialization of children and young adults. At school, behaviours are modified, skills for future employment are taught, social interaction and conflict are negotiated, and notions of social reality are defined. Structures of inequality such as classism, sexism, heterosexism, and racism are usually verbally discouraged even as they may be reproduced in actions taken by school boards, school officials, and teachers. Schools prepare children to be productive and obedient citizens. How children do in school plays a large role in determining their potential social acceptability and mobility.

The Rise of Public Education in Canada

Before the Industrial Revolution in Europe and North America there was little interest in educating the masses. But beginning with the rise of industrial capitalism, companies started to demand more from their labour force. Specifically, as industry became more complex, it required a more disciplined, trainable, and literate workforce that would be more economically productive. Industrialization and public education, then, became interdependent in the same way that labour is dependent on capital and capital on labour.

In Canada, education was seen as an important means of achieving economic modernization as early as 1846. That's when education reformer Egerton Ryerson (after whom Ryerson University is named) began promoting the idea of a school system that would be universal, free, and compulsory. According to Canadian sociologist **Stephen Schecter** (1977), Ryerson's public education model was not simply a method of producing social *order* but one that procured social *control* by subverting potential social conflict and animosity from incoming Irish labourers forced to leave their country during the potato famine of the 1840s. Speaking of the unskilled Irish Catholic migrants, Ryerson warned: "the physical disease and death which have accompanied their influx among us may be the precursor of the worst pestilence of social insubordination and disorder" (Schecter, 1977: p. 373). Education could avert the threat of discontent from these "alien" labourers by assimilating them into the dominant Protestant culture.

Schecter (1977) argues that compulsory, state-run education legitimized and acted to support social inequality, as it was premised on centralization and uniformity—instruments of social control to be used on the emerging working class. To ensure the uniformity of education—from textbooks to teachers—provincial boards were established to act as executive bodies to set up and maintain large systems of "normal schools" (the old and sociologically significant name for teacher's colleges). School boards were able to enforce codes of discipline and enact hierarchical authority relations that placed both students and parents in positions subordinate to school officials, including the teachers. Such practices served to a significant extent to subordinate the working class and to punish those who were "other than normal" (i.e. deviant).

How was compulsory education used as an instrument of social subordination? Consider the way education was used to rank and sort children in ways that were extremely destructive to those deemed "inferior." University of Lethbridge sociology professor Claudia Malacrida studied Alberta's Michener Centre, where many children were forcibly detained for being labelled "feeble-minded," a technical term based on questionable science of the time. In her study *A Special Hell: Institutional Life in Alberta's Eugenic Years* (2015), she identifies three ways in which children of different intellectual abilities were sorted out of the mainstream:

1) through truancy laws punishing those who did not come to class

2) through tests and curricula that standardized expectations of educational success

3) through "health" testing conducted via medical and psychological examinations (Malacrida, 2015: pp. 11–12).

Once sorted out of the regular system, these children were institutionalized in places such as the Michener Centre. There, most of their freedoms or rights (including their reproductive rights) were taken away. Their education (deemed "vocational") consisted mainly of forced labour that often served the financial needs of the institutions, a situation very similar to that of the residential schools that housed Indigenous children.

It may sound cynical to suggest that the state-run school system was born of a need to discipline the growing labour force and legitimize the social order. Bear in mind, though, that in the latter half of the nineteenth century, when public education systems were established, social reformers were warning of the civil disorder that might result from an unhappy working class. The public education system put a check on social conflict by reinforcing class divisions.

Post-war Expansion and the Human Capital Thesis

The Canadian economy after World War II required a workforce that was better educated than before, fuelling an expansion of colleges and universities across Canada to match the economic boom that peaked during the 1960s. Government officials may have loudly championed the expansion of postsecondary institutions as increasing access to education to all classes, but historians Newson and Buchbinder (1988) maintain that economic considerations were the driving force.

The perceived relationship between the expansion of education and economic growth is part of the human capital thesis, which asserts that just as industrial societies invest in factories and equipment to attain greater efficiency, so they invest in schools to enhance the knowledge and skills of their workers. When applied to social inequality, the human capital thesis is used to argue that marginalized groups earn less money than dominant groups because they possess less human capital in the form of education, skill, and experience.

Since the early 1970s, decreases in the taxes charged to corporations (but not to individuals) have contributed to cuts in governmental funding for postsecondary institutions. This has allowed the corporate sector to form stronger ties with cash-hungry colleges and universities that, in return for corporate finance, have made concessions to corporate capital. We see this most in increased advertising on campus, visible everywhere but in the classrooms (coming soon?). Academic research has become more closely tied to corporate agendas and control, especially in such areas as medical/pharmaceutical and agricultural product research. How long, I wonder, before your nutrition science class is brought to you by Gatorade?

Models of Public Education in Canada

The Assimilation Model

Education in Canada has historically been based on a monocultural model that emphasizes assimilation into the dominant culture. English Canada was viewed as a white Protestant nation. It was seen as natural that people arriving from outside this dominant culture would need to assimilate in order to fit in. The flaw in the assimilation model is that it failed to recognize that racial bias and discrimination—both inside and outside the school system—make the level playing field on which the assimilation model is premised virtually impossible. According to Henry and Tator (2006), the emphasis on monoculturalism (the promotion of just one culture) as opposed to multiculturalism formed a pervasive ideology that "influenced the training of educators, the practices of teaching, the content and context of learning, the hiring and promotion practices of boards, and the cultural values and norms underpinning all areas of school life" (Henry & Tator, 2006: p. 213). Students were expected to simply leave their cultural, religious, and ethnic identities at the door.

The assimilationist approach continues to influence Canadian public education, as sociologists George Dei and Agnes Calliste observe (Dei, 1996; Dei & Calliste, 2000). The experience begins in primary school and continues throughout secondary and postsecondary education, where literature courses are often really courses in *English* literature,

York University Schulich School of Business, Hyderabad India Campus

In 2014, York University's Schulich School of Business opened an international campus in Hyderabad, India. Whose history, values, and culture do you think are being taught at this school? Is it a form of academic colonialism?

which typically does not include works translated from other languages. Under these circumstances, English literature is really English cultural studies, representing the only 10 to 15 per cent of Canada's population that is of British ancestry. Implicit in this is the notion that British culture is superior, the only one worth learning.

Multicultural Education

Canada's federal government implemented its official policy of multiculturalism in 1971 to preserve and promote cultural diversity, while removing the barriers that had denied certain groups full participation within Canadian society. With a new objective of creating a learning environment that would respect all learners, school boards launched initiatives to study and celebrate the lifestyles, traditions, and histories of diverse cultures (Henry & Tator, 2006). These initiatives were based on three fundamental assumptions drawn from a study of multicultural education in six countries:

1) Learning about one's culture would improve educational achievement.

2) Learning about one's culture would promote quality of opportunity.

3) Learning about other cultures would reduce prejudice and discrimination.

Problems developed. Teachers often had little knowledge of the cultures they were presenting. Classroom focus tended to favour a museum approach that overlooked the complexity and vitality of these different cultures (Dei, 1996). Educators would focus on historical material and the "exotic" aspects of different cultures—food, festivals, and folklore. They would omit the values and beliefs that were fundamental to shaping a particular cultural identity (Dei, 1996).

Anti-racism and Anti-oppression Education

Henry and Tator (2006: pp. 213–14) argue that a glaring weakness of multicultural education is its failure to acknowledge that racism is systemic in Canadian society. While the superficial aspects of "other" cultures were being studied, the problem of racial inequality was being ignored.

Our Stories

The Great White Man Story of History

Library and Archives Canada, Acc. No. 1950-69-1

How do images like this support the Great White Man version of history? Who is left out of this image?

A product of our monocultural education is the **Great White Man** story of history, which celebrates the accomplishments of men of British descent—our "Founding Fathers"—over the contributions of women, Indigenous people, and immigrants from outside of Britain. A recent example of this narrative came in the form of a flyer I received from a local Conservative member of Parliament. In keeping with how Canadian history is often taught, the flyer describes the Canadian Pacific Railway, which joined Eastern Canada to British Columbia, as "Sir John A.'s Railway," drawing a link between our first prime minister (a white male Conservative) and the origin of the transnational railroad. A more multicultural approach would have mentioned the roughly 17,000 Chinese immigrants who helped build the mountainous stretch of the railway through BC. They worked for $1.00 a day and had to pay for their own food and camping/cooking gear. Their white co-workers did not have to pay for their equipment and were paid between $1.50 and $2.50 per day. The Chinese labourers were tasked with the more difficult and dangerous work of blasting the tunnels and clearing and grading the roadbed. Many died. I would say they made greater contributions and sacrifices than the Great White Man who was prime minister at the time. It was not just one Great White Man's creation.

What do YOU think?

What would you say are the biggest obstacles (e.g. gaps in teacher training, lack of source materials, lack of political will) to designing and implementing a public school curriculum that reflects the diversity of Canadian students while tackling racism in a meaningful way? How might these obstacles be overcome?

Students sit with their teacher during the opening assembly at Canada's first Africentric public school, which opened in Toronto in September 2009. Three years later, the city's first Africentric high school opened. Is it realistic to expect schools to cover all cultures in equal depth, or are ethnocentric schools the only answer for students who feel left out of the mainstream curriculum?

Anti-racism and anti-oppression education is meant to eliminate institutional and individual barriers to equity. It is intended to create a classroom environment where

- stereotypes and racist ideas can be exposed;
- sources of information can be critically examined;
- alternative and missing information can be provided;
- students can become equipped to look critically at the accuracy of the information they receive; and
- the reasons for the continued unequal social status of different groups can be explored.

The aim of this model is to change institutional policies and practices, as well as individual attitudes and behaviours that reproduce social inequality.

Anti-racism and anti-oppression education first appeared in Canada in the 1980s, when some school boards introduced new policies including changes to teacher education, new criteria for reviewing and evaluating the practices of educators, greater analysis of teacher placement procedures, employment equity strategies, and resource and curriculum development (Henry & Tator, 2006). The policy has seen gains and setbacks. As Henry and Tator explain:

> While lip service is paid to . . . ensure equality of opportunity for all students in the classroom, in reality, individuals, organizations, and institutions are far more committed to maintaining the status quo, that is, the cultural hegemony of the dominant culture with which most educators identify. (Henry & Tator, 2006: p. 223)

Topics in the Sociology of Education

The Hidden Curriculum

The hidden curriculum is a hot topic in the sociology of education, though its definition varies depending upon the specific issue being discussed and the vantage point of the sociologist doing the discussing. Essentially, it consists of the unstated or unofficial goals of the education system. We can look at the hidden curriculum in terms of Robert Merton's concepts of latent functions and latent dysfunctions, defined in Chapter 1. A sociologist adopting a structural-functionalist view might say that the hidden curriculum performs a latent

A Sociologist's POV

Telling It Like It Is

Eurocentric Curriculum and the University

Despite Canada's multicultural character and state-legislated multicultural policy, a **Eurocentric** curriculum still dominates our institutions of "higher learning." Such a curriculum offers a narrow view of the world even though there is a wealth of literature about non-European cultures by non-European academics. These works are not inferior to those of Europeans. They are integral to the attainment of a fuller, more encompassing education in which knowledge and ideas are derived from a wider, culturally diverse range of sources and perspectives. They are particularly useful in dispelling the racist assumptions and myths placed upon "others" by Western society.

In their inadequate attempts to be more inclusive, many of the professors I have encountered take a "just add and stir" approach to the inclusion of Native people, women, and "otherized" groups, which simply does not work. Just as they are treated as asides or special interest groups in society at large, women, Native people, and ethnic groups are often merely added on to Week 13 readings—if they are included at all. It was not until I experienced a course taught by a progressive, culturally sensitive anthropology professor who incorporated a multitude of perspectives that I became aware of the partial and limited view of the world to which I had previously been subjected. Those who perpetuate the mainstream academic curriculum seem to have fallen into a state of historical amnesia, whereby the contributions and, indeed, the very presence of non-Europeans

have been omitted from Canadian history. Though Chinese, Japanese, and Indian immigrants arrived in Canada at the same time as most European immigrants, one could pass through the entire school system from kindergarten to university without being aware of the fact. Many students emerge from the school system rightfully well versed in the works of Shakespeare, Plato, and Marx, but how many learned about the cultural genocide of Native peoples, or slavery in Canada?

I am concerned that the exclusion from postsecondary curricula of minority groups, their perspectives, and their writings perpetuates a view of the world taken through a Eurocentric lens. This exclusion is also dangerous because it may lead some students to believe that since little is studied from "other" cultures, then perhaps those cultures have nothing of benefit to offer, or else they are inferior to European thought.

The courses I found the most valuable and educational were those that, though not designated as courses specifically about multiculturalism, or Native people, still managed to incorporate a variety of cultural perspectives into the readings, films, and seminars. A culturally diverse curriculum and alternative critical forms of pedagogy can also have a positive effect on the academic achievement of minority students, whose experiences and interests are not validated but are typically marginalized or excluded from the existing curriculum.

—A.R. Aujla, 1996

What do YOU think?

This narrative was written in 1996, roughly 20 years ago. In your experience, how much has changed?

function by teaching the norms of society—the value of work, or the need to respect authority and to use one's time efficiently. A conflict sociologist might argue that the hidden curriculum reproduces the class system, hindering class mobility and therefore performing a latent *dys*function.

Cultural Reproduction Theory

Jeannie Oakes and the Hidden Curriculum of Tracking

Does the education system, as part of its hidden curriculum, really reproduce class divisions, as our conflict sociologist might argue? **Jeannie Oakes** (2005) put this idea, known as cultural reproduction theory, to the test in an influential study of tracking (or "streaming") in junior and senior high schools in the United States. Oakes defined tracking as "the process whereby students are divided into categories so that they can be assigned in groups to various kinds of classes" (Oakes, 2005: p. 3). Both classes and students are ranked according to different levels of aptitude and projected outcomes, such as whether or not students are expected to pursue a postsecondary degree. Oakes studied 297 classrooms in 25 schools in the late 1970s and early 1980s. Her work demonstrated that perceived ability is reflected through a lens of class, "race," and ethnicity. She also showed that lower tracks often offer lower quality of education than the higher tracks do. As a consequence, the American tracking system reproduces inequality.

Oakes argued that the disproportionate representation of lower-class and non-white students in the lower track reflects the cultural biases of testing and the prejudices of counsellors and teachers. The inferior quality of lower-track education came partly from the reduced expectations for students in the lower track. Lower-track English courses emphasized basic punctuation and form-filling as opposed to creating writing and studying great works of literature. Lower-track math courses emphasized basic computational skills rather than problem solving, critical thinking, and abstract logic. Lower-track vocational courses focused on clerical skills, not the managerial and financial skills taught in the higher-track courses.

Another important finding relates to differences in classroom time spent on instruction and learning activities versus administrative routines and discipline. The average amounts of classroom time spent on instruction in English and math courses in the higher track were 82 per cent and 77 per cent, respectively; the comparable figures for lower-track time were 71 per cent and 63 per cent.

From a cultural reproduction standpoint, it is also important to look at relationship differences between teachers and students, among students, and between students and the institution generally. Samuel Bowles and Harold Gintis point to the "close correspondence between the social relationships which govern personal interaction in the work place and the social relationships of the educational system" (1976: p. 12). In other words, in terms of social relationships, the education system trains students in the lower track to become lower-class workers. Oakes summarized their position as follows:

> These [lower-class] workers will be subordinate to external control and alienated from the institutions but willing to conform to the needs of the work place, to a large extent because of the way they were treated in school. . . . Bowles and Gintis suggest that the absence of close interpersonal relationships is characteristic of both lower-class work environments and classroom environments for lower-class children. In contrast, upper- and middle-class students, destined for upper-status and middle-level positions in the economic hierarchy, are more likely to experience social relationships and interactions that promote active involvement, affiliation with others, and the internalization of rules and behavioral standards. Self-regulation is the goal here rather than the coercive authority and control seen as appropriate for the lower class. (Oakes, 2005: pp. 119–20)

Oakes found that teachers were more punitive in lower-track classes, while higher-track classes fostered more trusting teacher–student relationships. She wrote, "[t]rust, cooperation, and even good will among students were far less characteristic of low-track classes than of high. More student time and energy were spent in hostile and disruptive interchanges in these classes" (2005: p. 132).

Key to cultural reproduction theory is the legitimization of inequality. If students accept that their

The Point Is...

Discipline, Punishment, and Evaluation

Discipline often forms part of the hidden curriculum. In primary school, discipline is focused on the body, restricting movement, impeding interaction, and normalizing confinement. Children are encouraged to use their "inside voices," to raise their hands before they speak or ask permission to go to the bathroom, to sit quietly in their seats, to keep their hands to themselves, to line up, and to be punctual. Secondary school continues to encourage physical discipline, and stresses a disciplining of the mind.

Common at all levels of education is the external and internal "routinization" of the individual. Punishment is enacted if the rules are not followed: a "time-out," a trip to the principal's office, a detention, or a poor mark on a report card. Grades are sanctions, designed to either negatively or positively reinforce norms.

While discipline can be enabling as well as inhibiting—many young students require and indeed thrive on a formalized structure of rules and routines—much of the discipline within the public school system can be considered repressive. This involves the mind as well as body. Children are naturally curious. Curiosity is the basis for asking questions, which is essential in the process of learning. Educators may learn at teacher's college that there are no "stupid questions," but when they have to stick to a strict schedule and a state-mandated curriculum, and when they are under pressure to see their students succeed on province-wide standardized tests that are used to measure the achievements of individual schools and teachers, they

may respond negatively to student questions that deviate from the prescribed lesson plan. By the time they reach college and university, students have often lost much of their curiosity. Postsecondary students, too, rarely ask questions with respect to ideas (other than "Is this on the exam?").

In many respects, public education creates what **Michel Foucault** termed the docile body, a group that has been conditioned, through a specific set of procedures and practices, to behave precisely the way administrators want it to (Foucault, 1977). Docile bodies are produced through three forms of disciplinary control:

1. hierarchical observation;
2. normalizing judgement;
3. the examination.

With hierarchical observation people are controlled through observation and surveillance. While Foucault used prisons as an example, the principle applies as well to schools and offices, places where our movements and activities are under constant surveillance within a setting based on hierarchical configurations. Educational institutions are based on a hierarchical structure in which authority figures observe and scrutinize the behaviour of students. For Foucault, hierarchical observation works on the psychology of observed individuals as much as it governs their specific movements. When people feel that they are always being watched, it induces in them an

differential tracking placement is fair, this legitimizes the inequality reproduced by the education system. Oakes found that "students in low-track classes tended to be saying that school's all right, but I'm not so good. In contrast, students in high-track classes were feeling pretty good about both their schools *and* themselves" (2005: pp. 143–4).

Overall, Oakes believes that with the deep class, ethnic, and racial distinctions existing in mainstream American society, a tracking system can only reproduce inequality. She argues for more of a common curriculum shared by all students, and for more mixing of students of different ability levels.

What do YOU think?

1. The strongest opposition to de-tracking comes from those involved with education of the "gifted." Why do you think they are more opposed to de-tracking than those involved with low-track education?

2. Imagine that you're the principal of a high school that is considering a tracking or streaming program. Come up with a list of pros and cons. How might your list change depending on such social factors as the class, ethnicity, and overall demographics of your school?

AP Photo/Hazleton Standard-Speaker/Ellen F. O'Connell

Kindergarten students pass through a metal detector at an elementary school in Pennsylvania. Some public schools in Ontario have been considering metal detectors after high-profile knife and gun crimes on school premises. Does this create a safe and secure environment or a "docile" one?

awareness of their permanent visibility, enhancing the power of the authority (Foucault, 1977: p. 172).

Normalizing judgement is another instrument of disciplinary control producing docile bodies. Individuals are judged not on the intrinsic rightness or wrongness of their actions but on how their actions rank when compared with the performance of others. Children are ranked at school, schools are ranked against one another, provincial education is ranked, and the level of education among countries is ranked. Ranking is a cultural artifact that we in Western society take for granted. Normalizing judgement is a pervasive means of control because regardless of how one succeeds, a higher level of achievement is always deemed possible.

The **examination** combines hierarchical observation with normalizing judgement. Foucault described it

as "a normalizing gaze [that] establishes over individuals a visibility through which one differentiates them and judges them" (1977: p. 184). It is, for him, the locus of power and knowledge, because it combines both "the deployment of force and the establishment of truth" (1977: p. 184). Test scores are documented and recorded, and provide detailed information about the individuals examined. Based on these records, various categories, averages, and norms are formulated by those in control, and these become the basis of knowledge. Power remains invisible, while those constructed as deviant become highly visible: those students with the thickest files are scrutinized by scores of anonymous, invisible functionaries (Foucault, 1977: p. 189). Deviance reflects difference from the norm. Both Lisa and Bart Simpson have the thickest files at school, but for different reasons.

Jean Anyon: Cultural Reproduction Theory in Five New Jersey Schools

An important aspect of cultural reproduction theory is the reproduction of the social structure, whereby the education system and other institutions help upper-class children grow up to be upper-class adults, middle-class children become middle-class adults, and so on. A useful study of this is **Jean Anyon**'s "Social Class and the Hidden Curriculum of Work" (1980), based on an ethnographic study of five elementary schools in New Jersey she carried out in 1978–9. Two of the schools she identified as

working-class. Here, most of the fathers had semi-skilled or unskilled jobs (assembly line work, auto repair or assembly, maintenance work); 15 per cent of the fathers were unemployed, and less than 30 per cent of the mothers worked. According to Anyon, school work in these schools consists of

following the steps of a procedure. The procedure is usually mechanical, involving rote behavior [i.e. drilled memorization] and very little decision making or choice. The teachers rarely explain why the work is being assigned, how it might connect

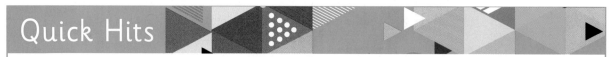

Quick Hits

Student Examples from Oakes's Study

What is the most important thing you have learned or done so far in the class (in terms of subject matter)?

Answers from the high track

- "We've talked about stocks/bonds and the stock market and about business in the USA." – student in junior high vocational education
- "Learned to analyze famous writings by famous people, and we have learned to understand people's different viewpoints on general ideas." – student in junior high English
- "The most important thing is the way other countries and places govern themselves economically, socially, and politically. Also different philosophers and their theories on government and man and how their theories relate to us and now." – student in junior high social studies

Answers from the low track

- "Learns to fill out checks and other banking business." – student in junior high English
- "to spell words you don't know, to fill out things where you get a job." – student in junior high English
- "I learned that English is boring." – student in senior high English

Source: Oakes, 2005: pp. 68–71.

---

to other assignments, or what the idea is that lies behind the procedure or gives it coherence and perhaps meaning or significance. . . . Most of the rules regarding work are designations of what the children are to do; the rules are steps to follow. . . . The children are usually told to copy the steps as notes. These notes are to be studied. Work is often evaluated not according to whether it is right or wrong but according to whether the children followed the right steps. (Anyon, 1980)

Students at a third school, identified as middle-class, had parents working in skilled, well-paid trades (such as carpentry, plumbing, or electrical work), working as professionals (firefighting, teaching, accounting, etc.), or owning small businesses. School work here focused on "getting the right answer":

One must follow the directions in order to get the right answers, but the directions often call for some figuring, some choice, some decision making. For example, the children must figure out by themselves

what the directions ask them to do and how to get the answer: what do you do first, second, and perhaps third? Answers are usually found in books or by listening to the teacher. Answers are usually words, sentences, numbers, or facts and dates; one writes them on paper, and one should be neat. Answers must be given in the right order, and one cannot make them up. (Anyon, 1980)

A fourth school, identified as "affluent professional," had students whose parents were employed as corporate lawyers, engineers, and advertising executives. At this school, the work involved

. . . creative activity carried out independently. The students are continually asked to express and apply ideas and concepts. Work involves individual thought and expressiveness, expansion and illustration of ideas, and choice of appropriate method and material. . . . The products of work in this class are often written stories, editorials, and essays, or representations of ideas in mural, graph, or craft form. The products of work should not be like anybody else's and should show individuality. . . . One's product is usually evaluated for the quality of its expression and for the appropriateness of its conception to the task. (Anyon, 1980)

The fifth school Anyon called "executive elite," as most of the students' fathers held positions as presidents and vice-presidents of major corporations (it was 1979, so many mothers would not have been working). In this school, work involved

. . . developing one's analytical intellectual powers. Children are continually asked to reason through a problem, to produce intellectual products that are both logically sound and of top academic quality. A primary goal of thought is to conceptualize rules by which elements may fit together in systems and then to apply these rules in solving a problem. (Anyon, 1980)

If there were a sociology class offered at this school level, daily activities in each category might look like this:

working-class school	copying down and memorizing the instructor's notes from the board
middle-class school	reading the textbook and finding the right answer
affluent professional school	finding information on an assigned topic and writing it up in one's own words
executive elite school	analyzing social systems and looking for strengths and weaknesses

Homework and Its Sociological Effects

Sociologists study homework to gauge the extent to which homework helps to reproduce class structure. Children raised by educated, middle- and upper middle–class parents have a number of advantages with respect to homework. Their parents are typically better able to understand teacher instructions and so are in a better position to help their children (sometimes doing the entire project themselves). The children of better-off parents tend to live in larger homes, where they have a quiet, dedicated space for doing homework, access to sophisticated computer software and high-speed Internet access, a colour printer, and other aids to completing their

Quick Hits

Social Mobility: Meritocracy versus Cultural Reproduction

During the 1960s, John Porter wrote:

No society in the modern period can afford to ignore the ability which lies in the lower social strata. Whatever may be said about average intelligence and social class, the fact remains that in absolute numbers there is more of the highly intelligent in lower classes than in the higher. If the principles of efficiency and equality are to be upheld, Canada must be prepared to put a great deal more money into education and educational research than it has. . . . Without such policies, intergenerational continuity of class will remain [and] mobility deprivation will continue. (in Helmes-Hayes, 2010: pp. 137–8)

There are two fundamentally opposing positions concerning education and social mobility. One is that education is meritocratic: academic performance reflects natural ability (i.e. merit), and the system provides mobility for those lower-class and minoritized students who work hard to succeed. Cultural reproduction theory, by contrast, argues that the education system reproduces and reinforces the inequality of the surrounding society. Which one do you think presents the more accurate statement about education in Canada as you have experienced it?

work. As a result, the more a course depends on homework as opposed to class work, the more it favours children from middle- and upper middle–class households.

The amount of homework a child receives can also have a profound effect on family life. In 2008, Linda Cameron and Lee Bartel published the findings of a study on the impact of homework on Canadian households. Their research was based on an online questionnaire completed by over 1,000 parents, the vast majority of them from Ontario. Of the 10 main conclusions drawn from the qualitative part of the questionnaire, two related to family life. The first was that homework "reduces family time":

> Homework is often seen as an incursion on what should be discretionary family time. . . . One parent stated it this way: "My children are in the educational institution for 6.5 hours per day. I feel this should be sufficient time to complete any school-related tasks. I am with them for significantly less time and would prefer to use this time engaging in activities to promote our relationship and increase bonding in order to reduce their stress levels." Consequently, parents often expressed feelings of resentment toward homework and the effect it has on family balance. (Cameron & Bartel, 2008: p. 53)

The second finding related to family life was that homework "affects family relationships." According to the authors, homework was found to be "a primary source of arguments, power struggles, and disruptive to building a strong family." In the words of one respondent cited by the report's authors, "Fights over homework with my children are common and very upsetting" (Cameron & Bartel, 2008: p. 54).

What do YOU think?

If you were the principal of an elementary school, what reasons might you give for "banning homework"? What reasons would you give for taking the opposite position?

Issues in Indigenous Education

The Politics of Representation in Textbooks

Textbooks form an important and influential part of education, and yet they remain an under-studied topic in the sociology of education. For my doctoral dissertation, I examined the representation of Indigenous people in 77 Canadian introductory sociology textbooks. What I discovered was a serious and progressive lack of Aboriginal voice. Indigenous writers were not represented as a significant source of information on their own people. In Michel Foucault's terminology, theirs were disqualified knowledges—"knowledges that have been disqualified as inadequate to their task" (Foucault, 1980: p. 82). Foucault might have argued that Indigenous writers were not included because they were not scientific or objective enough for the writers of sociology textbooks. Yet their viewpoints offer a legitimate alternative to standard sociology knowledge.

Early Canadian introductory sociology textbooks entailed collections of readings. As sociologists were not studying Indigenous people then, contributions written about Indigenous people were typically authored by outsiders to sociology, including Inuit leader Abraham Okpik, Ojibwa author Wilfred Pelletier, and Cree politician and scholar Harold Cardinal. When sociologists began studying Indigenous people in urban settings in the early 1970s, the Aboriginal voice was lost from sociology textbooks: the only coverage of Indigenous people came from non-Indigenous sociology writers. It is coming back, but slowly.

Credentialism

Credentialism often blocks Indigenous people's attempts to improve education. It is the practice of valuing credentials—degrees, diplomas, certificates—over actual knowledge and ability in the hiring and promotion of staff. In many Indigenous communities, elders are deeply involved in educating children and young adults. However, elders do not typically carry paper credentials; their qualification comes primarily from community recognition and valuing of their knowledge. Elders are recognized in Aboriginal communities as being experts in traditional knowledge, such as hunting, fishing, spirituality, healing, child care, and crafts. Most teachers coming from non-Indigenous communities are not familiar with elders because the role of elder is not assigned significant status in mainstream Canadian society.

Best Practices in British Columbia

Sociological discussions of Indigenous people's education tend to focus on the horrific stories of the residential schools, and the poor academic performance of Aboriginal students since. An alternative perspective comes from a report published by the C.D. Howe Institute (Richards, Hove, & Afolabi, 2008). Summarizing the results of a study that examined Aboriginal student performance in non-Aboriginal public schools, the authors identified five "best practices" that are key to the success of Indigenous students:

1) collaboration between school district personnel at all levels and local Indigenous communities
2) commitment by administrators and teachers to incorporating Aboriginal content into the curriculum
3) creation of influential positions (such as full-time teachers and school trustees) dedicated to Indigenous education
4) relationship building between Indigenous and non-Indigenous communities in the district
5) willingness of school district authorities to share responsibility for making decisions with Indigenous communities.

Interviews revealed that non-Aboriginal teachers often presented obstacles to Aboriginal involvement in their classrooms. While it is easy to say that personal racism is involved, sociologists look primarily for institutional barriers. The Canadian

Joe Bryska/Winnipeg Free Press

If there were 10 points that everyone in the Canadian education system should learn about Indigenous people what would they be? Examples could include the fact that more than 93 per cent of the human history of the land that is now Canada is Indigenous history alone. Another point could be the source language and meaning of such place names as Canada, Quebec, Ontario, Manitoba, Saskatchewan, Yukon, Nunavut, Ottawa, Toronto, Winnipeg, Saskatoon, and Kootenay. What else?

education system teaches very little about Indigenous people. Most Canadian teachers are ill prepared to work with an Aboriginal curriculum—they are poorly acquainted with Indigenous history, language, and culture generally because they are products of a school system that has failed to adequately cover these subjects. For example, a 2015 report by the advocacy group People for Education found that only 29 per cent of elementary schools in Ontario and 47 per cent of the province's secondary schools offered training on Aboriginal issues to teachers (Casey, 2015). The result is a self-perpetuating form of institutional racism.

What do YOU think?

What obstacles might there be to adopting the best practices referred to in this study?

Issues in Postsecondary Education

Long-Term Adjunct Instructors: An Educational Underclass

The growing ranks of long-term adjunct instructors in postsecondary institutions is the product of several economic and social factors, including the increasing number of postsecondary students, the reduction of government investment in postsecondary education, the increasing levels of private corporate funding, and the rising influence of a corporate culture that regards education just like any other business. The trend of turning full-time teaching positions into long-term adjunct posts is not unlike contracting out skilled jobs to avoid having to grant the benefits or long-term commitment that come with full-time work.

Names for this class of education workers differ. They are commonly referred to as adjunct professors, but they may also be called "sessionals," "contract staff," or "part-time instructors" (a misleading term, since many put in more hours than full-time instructors do). In Canada, the term "adjunct" is used to refer specifically to an experienced instructor who, because of seniority, is the first in line to take the courses full-time instructors can't or don't want to take on. Contract teaching used to be a first step

on the path toward a full-time job or a tenure-track position. Now that path is narrower and longer.

Ghosts in the Classroom: Stories of College Adjunct Faculty—and the Price We All Pay, edited by Michael Dubson, is a collection of narratives written by adjunct professors at American colleges and universities. Almost all of the contributors are English instructors—not surprising, given that many of them teach writing for a living, and English departments are large, with lots of temporary work for adjuncts. There is a lot of competition for jobs in this area, illustrated in the writers' frequent use of the phrase "dime a dozen" to refer to their competitive position. One of the topics raised repeatedly is the low pay, which is especially tough to swallow given that salaries for full-time staff are well over double what adjunct instructors are paid. One of the collection's contributors speaks eloquently of the sense of relative deprivation felt by many adjuncts:

> If I teach eight courses in an academic year, I make approximately $16,000. They [full-time instructors] teach eight to ten courses during an academic year and make, on the average, $40,000. I must horde my money and pinch my pennies for I must live on it during the semester breaks. Full-time teachers get paid all year long, whether they work or not.
>
> Because the pay is so poor, . . . I must string together collections of adjunct course assignments from several different schools. I have taught six, seven, eight classes a semester at three or four different schools. . . . I have worked other jobs and taught on the side. I have split my time between teaching four or five courses, a full-time load, and another job. (M. Theodore Swift, cited in Dubson, 2001: pp. 2–3)

Many contributors to the collection comment on their working conditions, which might involve sharing a desk (or not even having a desk) and having restricted use of facilities and equipment like the departmental photocopiers. Jody Lannen Brady's description is typical:

> I shared a dingy office with twenty other instructors, and some semesters I was lucky

Quick Hits

Gay–Straight Alliances: The Politics of the Schoolhouse

Jim Wells/Calgary Sun/QMI Agency

In 2015, the Progressive Conservative government of Alberta passed a law making it illegal for school boards or administrators to prevent students from setting up gay–straight alliances (GSAs) on school property. The move was applauded by anti-bullying activists and students, who had, prior to the law, been forced to hold GSA meetings outside of their schools. A recent study of Grade 8–12 students in BC suggests that GSAs help reduce "suicidal ideation" (i.e. thinking about suicide) and suicide attempts, as well as the experience of discrimination not only among sexual minority youth but among heterosexual youth who do not conform to normative gender-based behaviour (Saewyc, Konishi, Rose, & Homma, 2014). Nevertheless, the legislation faced stiff opposition from some parents and administrators of faith-based schools, particularly officials in the publicly funded Catholic school system who believe GSAs are too political and promote a lifestyle that is inconsistent with Catholic teachings.

The debate in some ways mirrored the controversy sparked when the Ontario provincial government introduced its new sex ed curriculum in 2015. Designed to teach students about diversity in sexual orientation and gender expression at an earlier age, the curriculum was initially opposed by some Catholic school educators who believed that parts of the curriculum did not align with Catholic values.

Catholic schools in Alberta and Ontario are part of the separate school system that exists in some provinces to protect religious minorities from discrimination by allowing them to direct their taxes to supporting faith-based elementary and secondary schools.

What do YOU think?

1. Should a Catholic school be forced to allow its students to set up a gay–straight alliance on school property when opposition to homosexuality is a key tenet of the Catholic Church?
2. What role can sociologists play in a controversy such as the one described here?

to find a chair to perch on during my office hours. I often met with students in the hallway because it was quieter than the office. I had one file cabinet drawer I could call my own, but I hauled all my papers and books back and forth from home to office and back each day because I couldn't work in the office, never knowing how many times I would have to jump up and answer the phone, and if I would have a desk to sit at. (in Dubson, 2001: p. 147)

What might surprise full-time professors is the extent to which the adjunct instructors feel they are engaged in a "class war" with full-timers. Two excerpts illustrate the point:

At one college, I share office space one day a week with one of the full-time instructors. He put a sign with my name by the door as a sort of welcoming gesture. The next week, the secretary of the English Department wrote me a note. Two of the full-time teachers were in a fury at the arrogance of my putting up a nameplate. (Gale, in Dubson, 2001: p. 13)

Once, in a heated personal discussion with a full-time colleague, she blurted out, "Who the hell do you think you are? You're only an adjunct here!" (Werner, in Dubson, 2001: p. 37)

Strained relations with colleagues are compounded by trying relationships with the students. Student evaluations are more important to the employment status of adjuncts than they are to the positions of full-time staff members. A poor evaluation won't get a full-timer fired, but it could cause an adjunct not to be hired back once the contract has ended. One writer explains:

If I have poor course evaluations, I will be out. . . . If my students complain about me, legitimately or otherwise, I will be out. If a full-time faculty member faces any of this, he or she will be supported, worked with, helped. Full-time tenured faculty may not even be evaluated, and . . . if their students complain about them, nothing affecting their employment or job security will be done. (Swift, in Dubson, 2001: p. 3)

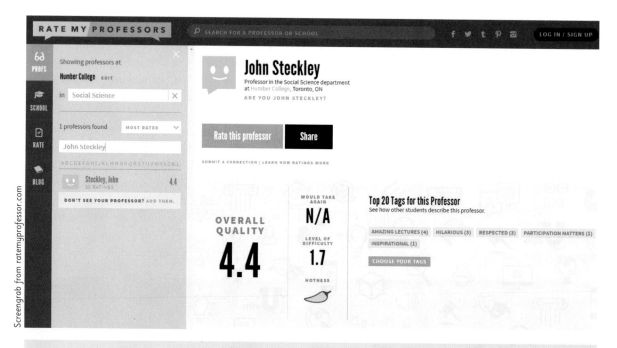

Screengrab from ratemyprofessor.com

Have you been to this site? What do you think are some of the consequences of rating your instructors online? How are these consequences different for adjuncts and full-time professors?

It should not be surprising that adjunct professors have been organizing. The kinds of conditions described above were a flashpoint in the strike by graduate student tutorial assistants and part-time instructors at York University in 2014–15.

Online Teaching: A Critical Sociological Approach

During the late 1990s and early 2000s, there was a push throughout North American colleges and universities to offer dramatically more online courses, even to the point of offering online diplomas and degrees, in some cases through "virtual" colleges based entirely online. This was driven by technological improvements, certainly, and by a desire to make education more accessible. But it was also spurred by cuts to postsecondary education funding. The online movement was hyped with the allure of change as progress, and played well to the susceptibility of educators to changes in intellectual

fashion. It was also driven by private organizations specializing in delivering educational packages over the Internet, who coined or co-opted sexy terms like "advanced learning" and "open learning," in spite of their yet unproven ability to provide education that is either more advanced or more open. They invest heavily in hosting or attending "educational" conferences (popular perks among postsecondary instructors), where they offer product demonstrations, aided by their "pet" instructors.

The success of online education providers has come at a time when many colleges and universities, feeling the financial pinch, have turned to the private sector as a partial solution to an underfunded public system. The boosters of online education are more often administrators and education companies looking for the government dollars that flow to public institutions rather than actual instructors, though the latter group does include believers. Student demand for these courses is more unsupported myth than documented fact.

The Point Is . . .

Online Education: A New Spin on a Failed Idea?

Historian David Noble (2002) reminds us that a movement similar to the online education movement happened from the 1880s to the 1930s, when correspondence courses, which enabled students to receive lessons and submit their work by mail (yes, mail!), became popular. The movement began with independent, privately run schools, before the universities, fearing competition and eager to benefit from a relatively easy source of profit, got involved. People marketing the correspondence courses used a language familiar to educators today: they promoted the ability to reach "non-traditional students" with the promise of "working on your own time." However, postsecondary administrators saw correspondence courses primarily as a good source of profit with relatively low overhead costs. Tuition was paid up front and was non-refundable, yet the dropout rate was high, the majority of students never completing their courses. Noble refers to this as "drop-out money." At the same time, the faculty involved were underpaid, receiving between 25 and 35 cents a lesson. By the 1930s, the institutions

involved were sharply criticized for being "diploma mills" that served up an inferior education.

The factors that sparked the establishment of correspondence courses in the late nineteenth century are similar to the ones that have created a favourable environment for the growth of online education today:

- the rise of *credentialism* (setting value on credentials such as certificates and diplomas)
- funding cuts, which prompt universities and colleges to seek out new sources of revenue
- the development of private training companies
- the rapid development of information technology (then, of course, advances in mail delivery services).

Noble sees online courses as suffering from the same flaws that plagued correspondence courses: profit considered over education, poorly paid staff with very little job security, and, on average, an inferior education when measured against its in-class equivalent.

In postsecondary education, a magic word is *access*. Online courses promise access to education for those who would find it difficult to attend college or university otherwise, the so-called "non-traditional students" (a group that supposedly includes working parents, who have traditionally made good use of night-school courses). As we have seen, access without mobility can readily reproduce the class system, while seeming to improve the lot of the more marginalized social groups.

From a sociological standpoint, how do online courses differ from in-class courses? Before addressing this question, it's worth noting that another flawed feature of many a North American university is the large lecture hall, which shares some weaknesses with online courses. The teacher–student relationship that is possible in smaller classes is replaced by a student's relationship with a teaching assistant (or TA), someone who may be at the university only temporarily and is paid significantly less than a full-time, tenured lecturer. This arrangement that features massive classes supported by smaller tutorials is, like the online movement, driven by the perceived economics of postsecondary education. When I talk in this chapter about in-class teaching, I am referring to classes held in the more intimate classroom setting, not the lecture hall or theatre.

Critics of the online movement (including me) fear that it is driven mainly by economics rather than access to education. Interestingly, though, the savings supposedly achieved by online education may be more apparent than real: acquiring and upgrading expensive technical equipment combined with hiring additional technical and administrative staff can drastically reduce the profit margin.

When boosting revenue becomes the main objective, it leads to the commodification of education. Noble (2002) describes this as

> the disintegration and distillation of the educational experience into discrete, reified, and ultimately saleable things or packages of things. In the first step toward commodification, attention is shifted from the experience of the people involved in the educational process to the production and inventorying of an assortment of "course materials"; syllabi, lectures, lessons, exams. . . . [T]hese common instruments

of instruction barely reflect what actually takes place in the educational experience, and lend an illusion of order and predictability to what is, at its best, an essentially unscripted and undetermined process. Second, these fragments are removed or "alienated" from their original context, the actual educational process itself, and from their producers, the teachers, and are assembled as "courses," which take on an existence independent of and apart from those who created and gave flesh to them. (Noble, 2002: p. 3)

Important here is the Marxist concept of alienation, which entails the separation between people and the work that they are paid to do. People working on assembly lines are disconnected from what they do. The workers have no say in what they do or how they do it. Chefs with signature dishes are closely connected with their work; people working the chip fryer at McDonald's are not. In a similar way, instructors can become disconnected from their intellectual property when it is used as part of an online course. Noble elaborates:

> Once faculty put their course material online, . . . the knowledge and course design skill embodied in that material is taken out of their possession. . . . The administration is now in a position to hire . . . cheaper workers to deliver the technologically prepackaged course. It also allows the administration . . . to peddle the course elsewhere without the original designer's involvement or even knowledge, much less financial interest. The buyers of this packaged commodity, meanwhile, . . . are able thereby to contract out . . . the work of their own employees and thus reduce their reliance upon their in-house teaching staff. (Noble, 1998)

Alienation involves the hierarchical control of a product, in which the boss has ultimate say in how it is developed, used, and distributed. With online courses, the potential for administrative monitoring and control increases. Instructors can be more closely supervised through the educational products they have supplied for the course's web-site. Online courses also allow administrators to measure instructor interactions with students: how often are instructors logging on? How responsive are they to students' online questions? This kind of supervision is also possible with course components offered by means of packaged Web products such as Blackboard.

Online universities are staffed with relatively few full-time instructors and many "tutors." Professors fear that this is the face of the future: part-time and limited-time contract staff dominating over full-time teachers. The following statement from Meritus University, which opened its virtual doors in September 2008, shows that they indeed have something to fear:

> While others established academic programs around tradition and tenure, Apollo has built programs in conjunction with the needs of business and industry—effectively translating those needs into clear and transparent learning objectives.

In its first semester, Meritus University had just four full-time teaching staff. In 2011, it closed its virtual doors.

The online delivery of education depends, like many exploitative systems, on getting workers to do more than they are paid for, relying on dedicated teachers who improve a bad situation with their talent and their labour. But some teachers "work to rule," calculating exactly how much work they have to do to get paid and do no more.

So what about the students? These courses suffer from significant dropout rates. Students who succeed are typically highly motivated, disciplined people, who get through despite the flaws inherent

william87/iStockphoto

Coursera is an education provider that has partnered up with several big North American universities—including the University of Toronto and the University of British Columbia—to offer "massive open online courses" ("MOOCs")—interactive online courses that are essentially free. Is free online learning the way of the future? What are the pros and cons of teaching in a chatroom rather than a classroom? Do you think they are more likely to be taught by adjunct or full-time staff? How do you think professors feel about this development?

in the method of delivery. Their good marks represent triumphs of individuals over systems.

Online education lends itself more to instrumental education, where courses are narrowly directed to a limited set of tasks, than to critical education, which involves analysis of ideas and, ideally, classroom discussion. With online courses, as the information flow is more one-directional than in the classroom, more controlled by the curriculum than by student–teacher interaction, students have less input into how the course proceeds. Their instructors have less input as well, since they are typically part-timers, vulnerable to administrative control.

Some worry that a two-tiered, two-class system will develop, with the middle and upper classes attending in-class institutions ("bricks and mortar" universities), preparing for jobs that will maintain their family's class standing, while those "attending" the digital institutions ("click universities") will be lower-class students and others for whom regular college or university attendance is financially impossible (including, for instance, single mothers and other working parents). They will receive lower-cost virtual vocational training that will lead them to lower-level, lower-paying service jobs. These are the people most likely to suffer, academically as well as socially, from the isolation that comes with online courses, the ones who would most benefit from in-class discussions. The system would then reproduce rather than challenge the class system.

What do YOU think?

1. What arguments would supporters of online education mount to combat the arguments given here?
2. Why might a sociology instructor be more critical of online education than an instructor from another discipline (business, for example)?
3. How could you do research that would test the effectiveness or ineffectiveness of online education?

Do You Want Fries with That Degree?

Students joke about the McJob—the low-paying, unskilled service job—they might get with their degree once they've graduated. The term refers to underemployment, which can have two meanings relevant to this discussion:

- involuntary part-time work for people seeking full-time employment
- low-wage, low-skill employment for people with valuable skills, experience, or academic credentials.

Statistics Canada defines "underemployed" as "seeking full-time work but finding only part-time work." The category does not include those who have been unable to work full-time for health or other personal reasons, nor does it acknowledge the problem of an over-skilled workforce. Underemployment is the result of several factors, including

- the rate of unemployment;
- regional disparity (lack of employment opportunities and resources like training and child care in economically depressed communities); and
- discrimination based on ethnicity, gender, disability, or lack of "appropriate" credentials.

How does this apply to postsecondary students? Those who hold high-quality skills and academic credentials become underemployed when there is low marketplace demand. The demographic bulge caused by the baby boomers means that access to employment is cut off for those newly entering the workforce, many of whom may be better qualified than their predecessors. For example, I received my college job with an MA. My replacement when I retired required a PhD.

During the 1990s, universities produced 1.2 million graduates, but only 600,000 jobs requiring university-level credentials were created during that same period. Currently, there are about one million students in the postsecondary system. If job creation remains the same as it did in the 1990s, then several hundred thousand graduates each year will be pursuing fewer than 100,000 job openings. This could effectively increase the structural underemployment rate from the 50 per cent level found in the 1980s and 1990s to 75 per cent.

In the case of new college and university graduates, underemployment can result from a lack of practical experience, even for those who have technical training in a specific field. As a result, recent graduates may be forced to work in low-paying or part-time jobs until they find work in their field. Canadian studies conducted between 1982 and 2004 suggest that while postsecondary education attainment has increased for various occupational classes, so too has the underemployment rate for those same occupational classes. The same research also shows that the rate of underemployment is greater than the underqualified rate. In 2004, 45 per cent of those aged 18–24 saw themselves as being overqualified for their jobs as opposed to 22 per cent of those 40 and over (Livingstone, 2004).

Among the solutions proposed to reduce underemployment are government-imposed restrictions on enrolment in postsecondary courses and programs with low labour market demand, although they often produce people who could make a significant contribution to the economy of the country. However, the university system would be unable to support such a proposal, as it would reduce student enrolment and, therefore, revenues.

The Sociology of Plagiarism

Ask any professor about the problems of teaching at a postsecondary institution, and plagiarism will be mentioned. This is particularly true of instructors teaching courses in the social sciences and the humanities—courses with a heavy grade component based on essay writing.

Carol Thompson defines plagiarism as "the wholesale copying of another's work or the collaging of several papers (or Web sites) via the Internet" (2006). Basically it involves passing off someone else's ideas or work as your own. The ideas and words

CP Photo/Andrew Vaughan

A university graduate takes his job search to the streets of Halifax. Should governments be allowed to cap enrolment in disciplines with low labour market demand? Or is up to the student to find the educational path most likely to lead to meaningful employment? What's your plan to avoid underemployment after graduation?

aren't yours, and the sources of those ideas and words aren't properly identified or even mentioned.

Thompson adopts a sociological approach to address why plagiarism has become such a common phenomenon. She emphasizes the influence of role models, asserting that students have the very patterns of behaviour they're warned not to fall into modelled for them by professors, school administrators, famous writers and academics, and politicians. More influential could be parents, who have often helped students in writing and assembling their projects in high school, and who may get involved in their children's postsecondary work as well. The idea that the work submitted does not have to have been prepared entirely on one's own could stem from that experience of having received help from parents.

Plagiarism has spawned two booming industries. One is the essay industry, selling students ready-composed or, for a higher fee, customized papers. These companies are not engaged in anything that is technically against the law, although the means they sometimes use to obtain papers do involve theft of academic property. Copyright laws are fuzzy about academic work. The fact that there are numerous companies of this kind out there, set up to accept your credit card number or payment via PayPal, might make the practice seem legitimate.

The industry can benefit graduate students, who are often desperate for money. They are trained to write academic papers. By selling their services to Web-based essay providers, they are capitalizing on their hard-earned skills in an industry in which these skills are valued.

Another group that profits from plagiarism are businesses such as Turnitin and iThenticate, which sell their services to colleges and universities with the claim that they can catch the plagiarizers. They expand their database with every postsecondary institution that pays for their services. You have to wonder how many people working on this side of the business once worked on the other side, like hackers who become computer security specialists.

A potential social factor in the willingness to plagiarize is social distance. If you know your instructors and they recognize you by name or by sight, then you are less likely to submit a plagiarized essay, since it would be like cheating a friend. However, if your professor is just a blurry face at the front of a crowded lecture theatre, or an even more

anonymous presence online, the social distance is far greater. Plagiarism might be like stealing from a large corporation. It appears to be a "victimless crime," since there is no identifiable injured party. This would make for interesting sociological research: is there more plagiarism in lower-level courses than in upper-level courses (where the classes are smaller and less likely to be offered online)? Is it more common in larger institutions than in smaller ones?

Cultures of Education

It is also worth considering plagiarism in terms of cultures of education. In mainstream Western culture there is a tendency to emphasize the individual's competition with others. This emphasis is made stronger when, for instance, a large first-year course is known to allow a fixed number of students to graduate with A's, or is marked on a bell curve. This makes these precious marks more valuable by artificially putting them in limited supply.

Other cultures put a greater emphasis on the group. Indigenous students, for example, have traditionally not wanted to be singled out in class. They whisper answers to peers who have been asked to reply to teacher questions, so that there will be no embarrassment for a classmate who doesn't know the answer. Research has shown that they are typically more likely to share answers on tests, the same way they would help their family members and friends. The cultural value of sharing is higher than in mainstream Canadian culture.

The Western culture of education emphasizes putting what you say "in your own words." There are cultural traditions in which "repeating the words of the master" is more valued than personalizing an answer. When international students come to Canada, they are unlikely to have been told about how education in Canada follows a model that may differ from the model used in their country of origin.

Another influential aspect of the Western culture of education is the increasingly corporate nature of postsecondary institutions, where students are viewed as customers (or "stakeholders"—a hideous term). Students may feel that it is their right as consumers to appeal grades or to sue over disappointing marks. As long as school administrators feel that their institutions are competing for students, they may be reluctant to cultivate an unfavourable reputation by aggressively pursuing plagiarizers, risking bad publicity. And with the increased level of credentialism—the emphasis on "getting the piece of paper"—rather than on learning, students may act more like customers than like learners.

The corporate culture of the postsecondary institution is also expressed and experienced internally, within the institution, and can have an influence on how plagiarism is treated and judged. Departments where students write a lot of essays (sociology, anthropology, history, literature, philosophy, and so on) are more involved in providing electives to students who are studying in different programs than in training majors in their fields of study. Pressure can be brought to bear on a department's administrator by administrators of the students' programs to "just let my student pass," rather than doggedly pursuing cases of plagiarism. The competition for students goes on within colleges and universities, as different departments attempt to draw students to take their electives. A popular course gains status for the department and can be used to justify new hires and a higher budget. A course with a high rate of catching plagiarism offenders is not popular. The increased use of temporary, sessional, or adjunct professors, who don't want to "rock the boat" also weakens the impulse to take a firm stand against plagiarism. They want to be seen as "team players" so that they will get rehired. Finally, as Thompson notes, when it comes to plagiarism, word gets around. Those schools that have a clear policy of dealing strictly with plagiarism have fewer instances of the offence. Where people often "get away" with it, student culture might simply become supportive of plagiarism.

What do YOU think?

1. Why do you think that plagiarism is on the rise at postsecondary institutions in Canada?
2. Do you accept the idea that students should always be encouraged to put things "in their own words"?

The Canadian Press Images/Maclean's Magazine/Andrew Tolson

Ever been tempted by an ad like this? What about the advertising makes the service seem morally legitimate and socially acceptable?

WRAP IT UP

Summary

We live in a time in which there are a number of important choices to make concerning the future of our education system. The sociology of education can help make those choices truly informed and democratic. At base, the most important issue is whether the Canadian education system—from primary school all the way up to our postsecondary institutions—is fundamentally meritocratic or whether it serves more to reproduce the class system and cultural privileges of the culturally dominant. At the elementary and secondary level, we need to ensure the suitability of the curriculum so that marginalized peoples get to read and hear about people like themselves. The effects of "streaming" (or "tracking") must be seriously studied. At the postsecondary level, we need to look critically at such practices as the increasing dependence on adjuncts, on corporate sponsorship, and on online education, in order to uncover the potential harm as well as benefits that they may bring.

THINK BACK

Questions for Critical Review

1. Summarize the factors that contribute to the growing problem of plagiarism. Which factors make plagiarism possible? Which ones encourage it? Are there any factors that legitimize it? Is it really the problem we think it is? If so, how would you address it? Consider factors outside of education, such as online music sharing and music sampling: do we live in a society where originality and authorship are less valued than they once were?

2. What do you see as the connection between the rise in online education and the growing reliance on adjunct professors? Are they both symptoms of the same factors? Which ones?

3. Have you experienced being "overqualified" for a job? Was it possible for you to "take the job seriously," as a less qualified worker might be able to do?

4. What evidence of corporate sponsorship exists on your college or university campus? What buildings are named after recognizable companies? What businesses have been granted the right to set up shop on the premises? What do you think are the drawbacks to corporate sponsorship of postsecondary education (including research grants)? Do they outweigh the benefits, including lower tuition costs?

READ ON

Suggested Print and Online Resources

Online

"In Defense of the Traditional Classroom: An Argument Against the Move to Online Classes"
www.articlemyriad.com/argument-traditional-classroom-online/
*   This online article defends the value of the traditional classroom. To better understand the other side of the argument, have a look at university webpages defending the move to Coursera, like the following, from UBC: http://ctlt.ubc.ca/2012/09/27/ubc-to-offer-free-online-courses-through-coursera/.

People for Education

www.peopleforeducation.ca

- This parent-led and parent-focused guide to educational issues in Ontario offers news and views, as well as research reports and survey findings. It includes a separate tab devoted to Indigenous education.

Stop Homework

http:/stophomework.com

- This website, initiated by one of the authors of *The Case Against Homework*, has become a discussion forum for parents and students concerned about homework.

In Print

Jamie Brownlee (2015), *Academia Inc: How Corporatization Is Transforming Canadian Universities* (Black Point, NS: Fernwood Publishing).

- This is the first comprehensive look at corporatization as it affects Canadian universities.

James Côté & Anton Allahar (2011), *Lowering Higher Education: The Rise of Corporate Universities and the Fall of Liberal Education* (Toronto: University of Toronto).

- This work, from two University of Western Ontario sociologists, looks at the effects on education of universities forming closer ties with large corporations.

George Dei & Agnes Calliste (2000), *Power, Knowledge and Anti-racism Education: A Critical Reader* (Halifax: Fernwood Publishing).

- An informative collection of readings on what anti-racism education entails.

Michael Dubson, ed. (2001), *Ghosts in the Classroom: Stories of College Adjunct Faculty—and the Price We All Pay* (Boston: Camel's Back Books).

- This book uses the first-hand accounts of adjunct professors to present the experiences and perspectives of the educational underclass.

Jeannie Oakes (2005), *Keeping Track: How Schools Structure Inequality*, 2nd edn (New Haven, CT: Yale).

- A classic critique of the cultural reproduction function of tracking or streaming students.

John Richards, Jennifer Hove, & Kemi Afolabi (2008), *Understanding the Aboriginal/Non-Aboriginal Gap in Student Performance: Lessons from British Columbia* (Toronto: C.D. Howe Institute).

- A useful guide to strategies used to improve Aboriginal education.

Health and Medicine

The Gist

Reading this chapter will help you to . . .

- Explain what is meant by the terms "sick role" and "social course of disease."
- Outline the various aspects of biomedicine, and contrast them with alternative medical practices, such as those found among Chinese healers and Indigenous people.
- Discuss how the process of medicalization takes place.
- Articulate the different views surrounding the accreditation of immigrant doctors.
- Provide an overview of Ivan Illich's critique of modern medicine.
- Discuss the relationship between medicine and "race."
- Discuss the relationship between medicine and gender.

Terms of the Trade

- absolutist
- alternative medicine
- Big Pharma
- biomedicine
- brain drain
- clinical iatrogenesis
- commodification
- complementary medicine
- critical sociology
- cultural iatrogenesis
- cultures of medicine
- iatrogenesis
- inverse care law
- medicalization
- medical sociology
- patient role
- policy sociology
- posttraumatic stress disorder
- psychoneuroimmunology
- racialized
- radical monopoly
- reductionist
- sick role
- social course (of disease)
- social iatrogenesis

Names to Know

- Dr Julian Tudor Hart
- Ivan Illich
- Talcott Parsons

For Starters

JackF/Thinkstock

Men's Pain and Women's Pain
Contributed by Jelena Ristic

Both my brother and I have sustained injuries serious enough to land us in the emergency room. His were from a snowboarding accident, mine from a chiropractic adjustment gone terribly wrong. Our symptoms were identical: unbearably excruciating pain that left us unable to bend, with weakness down one leg and back pain that felt like we were being electrocuted and burned with hot pokers at the same time.

Once we entered the ER doors (separately, I should add) the similarities ended.

As soon as I proved I could wiggle my toes I was sent home without any diagnostic tests having been performed, but with a script for Percocet and Valium. I was told to find myself a physiotherapist. To treat what? Completely undiagnosed pain. I returned to emerge 15 times over the next six months suicidal with pain. Not once was an MRI or CAT scan offered.

Conversely, my brother was immediately attended to, offered a wheelchair, and fast-tracked for an MRI scan. He was promptly referred to a neurosurgeon. Within a couple of weeks he had a diagnosis (he had stretched his sciatic nerve) and advice. Nothing could be offered but pain management and the hope that within a few years it would heal and the pain would subside. He was instructed to take it easy and avoid any kind of exercise, including physiotherapy. It was disappointing news, but at least it was news; he knew what he was up against. It took two years for the nerve to heal. There is still pain, but it is tolerable, and my brother is able to go to the gym, skate, and snowboard.

In my case, I had no clue where my pain was coming from. Every time I returned to the ER it was with not just excruciating pain but increasing anxiety. I also was starting to exhibit muscle atrophy at my back hip and down my leg. I could barely walk 10 steps at a time. It took six months for me to get an EMG done; it came back normal. No other tests were offered.

In the meantime, hospital staff had begun to view my frequent anxiety-ridden visits to the ER as a form of attention-seeking behaviour or mental illness. I was finally committed to the mental health ward, where for two weeks I kept begging for imaging, ultrasound, MRI, or CAT scan. Finally a doctor agreed to "humour" me with an MRI of my hip, where I had the worst pain, severe cracking sounds, and weakness. However, the same doctor, after consulting with a surgeon, changed the referral to an MRI of my back. The test results came back showing no damage. I changed doctors and finally, almost a year after the start of the pain, got an MRI of my hip, which showed severely torn tendons, a labral tear, and cartilage damage. The doctor also ordered a second EMG because she didn't believe the first EMG had been done properly, given that I had visible muscle atrophy. This time the test showed evidence of nerve damage.

When a man enters the emergency room complaining of intolerable pain, it is taken seriously. When a woman comes in with the same symptoms, she must be exaggerating her pain. Ultimately, her anxiety and tears are chalked up to mental and emotional weakness. I was rudely yelled at and told, "Stop crying!" by paramedics and doctors, as if the tears rolling down my cheeks somehow made my description of symptoms indecipherable or untrustworthy. And the more I was rejected, the more I cried, fulfilling the image of a weak weeping woman not to be believed.

It has been three years, and I am still disabled. Why did my brother get prompt attention and care while I did not? My only explanation is that he is a man, and I am a woman. Society seems to believe that men can tolerate much more pain than women can, so their complaints need to be taken very seriously, while a woman's can be dismissed as exaggeration or unchecked emotion.

What do YOU think?

1. Does this story follow a pattern that you have seen or experienced?
2. Why do you think that women's pain might be treated differently from men's pain?

Introduction: The Social Side of Medicine

Medical sociology is based on the view that medical practices and beliefs are intensely social. A large part of medical sociology involves policy sociology, which is about generating sociological data to help governments and health professionals develop the policies that drive health care in this country. Thus, we can say that one of the principal aims of medical sociology is to improve the delivery of health services through sociologically informed research. Critical sociology contributes significantly as well, especially when the focus shifts to the practices of multinational pharmaceutical companies, medical schools (particularly when they raise their fees), and privately run, for-profit clinics and hospitals.

Healing is achieved through social means, so it's natural that sociology has a lot to contribute to our understanding of the field of medicine. "Race," gender, ethnicity, age, and class—all social factors—can greatly affect an individual's experience of the medical professions. How? Let's say you're a middle-aged woman living outside the city, suffering from intensely sore feet. You go to your family doctor. She was born in Sri Lanka and educated in Britain, having moved to Canada just five years ago. She can't find a cause for your ailment, so she recommends a number of specialists. Which specialists she recommends will depend on her professional social network, the circle of people she knows and trusts. This network depends on such social factors as the location of her practice (outside the city) and the level of status she has as a doctor (itself possibly determined by how long she has been practising and the degree to which she has been politically active in medical associations). Religion can be a factor, since certain hospitals are governed by specific religious groups. Her sex might be a factor, as men are still more prominent in medicine than women are.

Compare this scenario with that of a very successful businessperson with a prominent white male doctor who has hospital privileges at one of the best hospitals in a large city. Your doctor has been head of the provincial medical association and is often asked to present papers at medical conferences. Imagine how his professional social network might differ from that of the doctor discussed in the preceding paragraph, and how your treatment might differ as a result.

This is just one illustration of why sociology cannot be ignored when it comes to health, an idea I hope to reinforce over the course of this chapter with many more examples. Now you can just sit back and say, "Ah!"

The Sick Role

American sociologist **Talcott Parsons** (1902–1979) came up with perhaps the first medical sociology term when, in *The Social System* (1951), he developed the concept of the sick (or patient) role. Like other sociological roles, he argued, being sick came with certain expectations—four, to be exact. In his thinking, two relate to what the sick person can expect from society, two to what society should expect of the sick person. The four expectations are as follows:

1) The person engaged in the sick role should expect to be granted "exemption from normal social responsibilities." In other words, a sick patient should not be expected to have to work, either at home or in the workplace, while he or she recovers.
2) The patient should expect to be "taken care of" rather than having to take care of him- or herself.
3) The patient is socially obligated to try to "get well" rather than remain in the undesirable state of being ill.
4) The sick person is socially obligated to "seek technically competent help" (in other words, the help of a qualified health professional).

The sick role, according to Parsons, gives the individual licence to be temporarily "deviant" with regards to the first two expectations, provided that he or she acts in accordance with the second two.

Parsons was a structural-functionalist sociologist. Structural functionalism presumes a social uniformity of experience that conflict or critical sociologists would challenge. Ask yourself this: is the sick role the same for everybody? The first challenge to the uniformity of the structural-functionalist

model came quickly. In 1954, Earl Koos wrote *The Health of Regionville: What the People Thought and Did About It*. It was based on research he had carried out between 1946 and 1950 on differences in what people thought and did about their health depending on their class. He learned that people in higher occupational groups were better able to afford to play the sick role, a privilege less available to those of lower occupational groups.

Similar arguments against the uniformity of the sick role can be made based on gender, "race," and age. Society has different expectations for a mother than for a father. When children are sick, the mother is typically expected to take time off work to look after them. And who is *least* likely to be allowed to play the sick role if the whole family gets sick? We can also look at people with chronic illnesses or disabilities. Are they to be considered permanently "deviant" according to Parsons's model?

It is hard to defend the universal applicability of Parsons's model of the sick role. In part, this is because the model changes over time. Ivan Emke

This worker has just been injured on the job. According to the sick role, what actions is he expected to perform? Now assume he has a family dependent on his income, and his job is part time (meaning he is only paid for the hours he works). Why might he opt out of the social contract that goes along with the sick role?

(2002) has proposed that in Canada at the turn of the twenty-first century, the sick role carries five new expectations. Two of these are central. The first is that "patients in the New Economy are responsible for their own illnesses." Emke's point is that instead of looking at social and environmental causes of sickness (pollution, unsafe working and living conditions, stress through overworking, economic insecurity, and social disruption), we've become inclined to blame individual "choices" (smoking, drinking, not belonging to a health club, not making time for exercise, eating the wrong foods). Emke notes that the bulk of cancer information then provided in ads and public health materials focused on individual risk factors rather than those presented by society, such as polluting industries and weak anti-pollution laws. This lowers society's sense that everyone is equally entitled to free health care. Do we feel less sympathetic to smokers with lung cancer? You can see how those who buy into this expectation might use the underlying argument to justify charging user fees for some medical services.

The second new expectation is really a conflation of two expectations Emke identified: "the patient in the new economy is instructed to tread lightly on the system" and "patients in the new economy are not to be trusted." We could recast it, a little less subtly, as "patients are assumed to be abusing the system" (see the narrative at the start of the chapter). Emke raises this belief in connection with a public education campaign to encourage people to use as few medical services as they can. He cites a 1994 pilot project by the Conservative Ontario government designed to encourage residents of London to stop going to their family doctor for relatively minor complaints. No research had been done to see whether people were actually "abusing" the system. The assumption underlying the project was that escalating health care costs can be attributed significantly to a large number of "unnecessary" visits to family doctors. Perhaps rising health care costs are more the result of building huge technology-intensive hospitals that are less cost-effective than having a greater number of small-town and community-based medical centres. Perhaps nurses, who make less than doctors do, should be permitted to perform basic medical procedures (stitching wounds, for example) that doctors are normally responsible for, so that the same work can be done at lower cost.

KatarzynaBialasiewicz/iStockphoto

Do you believe that people who smoke are fully entitled to free health care? What about people who eat too much junk food? People who engage in dangerous recreational activities? People who play video games all day?

What do YOU think?

1. How do you think factors such as gender and ethnicity affect the universality of Parsons's sick role?
2. Have you seen evidence of the trends Emke identified in Canadian health care?
3. Who do you think abuses our health care system most: patients? Doctors? Hospital administrators? Governments? Pharmaceutical companies? Industries that cause pollution?

The Social Course of Disease

A medical breakthrough of the nineteenth century was the realization that every disease has a natural course it goes through, a lifespan during which you

Our Stories

The Social Course of Tuberculosis among the Inuit

The "race" or ethnicity of a patient is a sociological factor that can affect the social course of a disease. Witness the treatment of Inuit with tuberculosis. In 1949, new antibiotics, combined with improved sanitation, screening, and treatment, helped reduce the tuberculosis rate in Canada to about 33 deaths per 100,000, down from 165 per 100,000 in 1908. But at the same time, the rate among the Inuit population in Canada was rising dramatically, peaking at an alarming 569 per 100,000 (then highest in the world) in 1952. In that year, there were 54 deaths among the roughly 10,000 people who make up the Inuit population in Canada.

The high rate of TB among Canada's Inuit was caused by a number of factors. First, the severe cold of the Arctic—though not cold enough to kill the *tuberculosis bacillus*—made the Inuit especially susceptible to respiratory problems. The intimate closeness of the Inuit in their igloos facilitated the spread of TB from one family member to another. A more significant cause was the increasing contact with people from southern Canada. Pat Grygier explains that

> as the Inuit adapted to accommodate the desires of the newcomers, trapping to exchange furs for store goods or working for the RCMP or on military construction sites for cash, their highly nutritious fresh-meat or fish diet and their warm caribou-skin clothing were gradually exchanged for a diet largely of white flour, lard, tea, jam, and canned goods, and for much less warm southern

clothing. When the caribou declined or the pattern of migration changed (possibly as a result of the incursions of military and mining into the North), malnutrition occurred. (Grygier, 1994: p. 55)

Inuit TB sufferers were treated differently from other Canadians. At the time, the standard treatment for tuberculosis involved a period of confinement—from six months to two years—in a hospital or sanatorium. These were not built in the Arctic, so the Inuit with tuberculosis were brought (or, more accurately, taken, since many were reluctant to leave their homes) to southern Canada. Grygier eloquently describes what happened once health professionals brought north by ship had conducted their patient examinations:

> When the doctors had made their final decision on whether an individual should go to hospital for treatment or stay in the North, the evacuees were sent down to the Inuit quarters in the prow of the ship and the rest were sent ashore. The evacuees were not allowed to go ashore to collect belongings, to say goodbye, or to make arrangements for their families or goods. If a mother was judged sick but her children were not infected, the children (sometimes including unweaned babies) were given to an Inuk woman going ashore. Fathers had no chance to arrange for someone to hunt for food for their families or to look after their dogs

catch the disease, suffer through it, and gradually get well (or sicker, in some cases). It depends on the virus or bacterium, and the way the human body reacts to it. Think of a cold. Doctors can prescribe medicine to help alleviate the symptoms and speed up recovery, but they can't fundamentally change the natural course of a cold.

Likewise, we can speak of the social course that diseases and disorders go through, a course

affected by sociological factors such as the ethnic background, culture, class, age, and sex of the people affected. The following example traces the social course of an injury and illustrates how that course is affected by class.

I recently injured myself while running when I should have walked, and I ruptured my Achilles tendon. During my initial trip to the hospital, my left leg was put in a cast, so that I could move only and equipment. Mothers had no chance to arrange for someone to care for their children or to sew and process the skins needed to keep the family warm. . . . Those needing hospital treatment were kept on board, the rest sent ashore, and on sailed the ship to the next settlement. (Grygier, 1994: p. 96)

The tuberculosis rate among the Inuit dropped during the 1950s to a low of 53 per 100,000 (just 5 actual cases) in 1959, but the effects of the separation lasted. Many families were never reunited, often because a sick loved one died but even in cases where the TB-suffering family member recovered.

Photo by Peter Power/The Globe and Mail/CP

Tuberculosis is still a problem among Inuit in Canada, as this sign at a nurses' station in Cape Dorset, Nunavut, makes clear. According to Canada's Public Health Agency, the tuberculosis rate in Canada reached an all-time low of 4.6 per 100,000 in 2010, yet there were 101 active TB cases in Nunavut that year, representing a rate of 304.0 per 100,000 (CCDIC, 2012). Is it possible that ethnicity is still a factor in the social course of this disease?

through the use of crutches. I was billed for both the fiberglass cast and the crutches, but because I was a full-time salaried employee with benefits, my employee health plan covered the cost of both. My middle-class job did not require heavy lifting or great physical exertion, so I continued to work, despite having to hobble around the campus on crutches for nine weeks. I could have decided not to work during that period, and a good disability

allowance would have ensured that I lost no significant income. The injury caused a deadly blood clot to develop, so my doctor prescribed a blood thinner. Fortunately, my drug plan covered almost the entire cost of this expensive drug.

My wife suffers from a disability that makes it very difficult for her to work full time. Because I was well paid, we could afford to live on one income. My wife was able to be at home and to take good care of me during my recovery period. It would have been much worse for my emotional state and physical health if she had not been so diligent in helping me. I owe her a lot.

Once the cast was removed, I began physiotherapy. The cost was covered almost completely by my insurance plan at work. It helped immeasurably. My recovery proceeded much more quickly than I had hoped.

I dread to think what the social course of my healing would have been if I had been an unskilled worker in a factory or warehouse. Other sociological factors that influenced the social course of my recovery include my marital status and the fact that I lived and worked near a large urban centre with abundant medical resources and facilities. What would the social course of my recovery have been like had I been living alone, or in a rural area without access to transportation? What other factors might have changed the course?

The Our Stories feature on pages 382–3 provides another example of factors that affect the social course of a disease. It's good to keep in mind that the sociological factors surrounding a patient, just like physical factors such as medicine, clean living conditions, and rest, can influence the social course of recovery in either a positive or a negative way.

Biomedicine

Biomedicine involves the application of standard principles and practices of Western scientific disciplines, particularly biology, in the diagnosis and treatment of symptoms of illness and disease. It uses physical tests to find defined, purely physical entities (such as bacteria, viruses, and trauma) and then applies purely physical medicines and therapies to counteract them. It is the dominant practice in Western society.

When, suffering from migraine headaches, you visit your family doctor and she prescribes medication to reduce the severity of your symptoms, you have experienced biomedicine. If you've grown up in Canada, this is likely the approach you expected when you booked your appointment. Other approaches to treatment fall outside of conventional medical practice. We refer to these approaches collectively as alternative (or complementary) medicine. Your doctor, for instance, might have recommended

acupuncture for your migraines. Or she might have recommended massage therapy or yoga as means of reducing the stress contributing to your headaches. She might have tried to discover environmental causes of your condition—bright lights in the area where you read or study, for example. These would all be considered alternative approaches.

Alternative approaches are used to treat many medical ailments. Recent research in psychoneuroimmunology—the study of the effect of the mind on health and resistance to disease—has shown links between a person's psychological state and his or her ability to fight diseases such as cancer. A study at the University of Texas monitored the spread of cancer in two groups of mice. One group was placed in small plastic chambers for several hours at a time, which caused a surge in their stress hormones. Tumours in these mice grew more quickly and in greater number than those in the mice that were not so confined, suggesting a link between stress and the spread of the disease. As the *Globe and Mail*'s Margaret Philip (2006) reports, the study is one of a number that have caused oncologists to consider more holistic approaches to treating cancer sufferers, using massage, meditation, music therapy, and support groups to help reduce tension.

A good example of divergent biomedical and alternative approaches to health is childbirth. Most North American women choose to give birth to their infants in a hospital, under the care of a team of medical professionals including an obstetrician, an anaesthesiologist, and several nurses. Increasingly, however, women are choosing to stay at home to give birth under the care of a midwife. There are good reasons to recommend the latter approach. Many people find hospitals uncomfortable. Some women do not want to be separated from their families, especially if they have other young children. Knowing they will remain at home eliminates stressful worries concerning the hurried trip to the hospital once contractions begin. Many mothers-to-be find that a midwife is more available to provide support and answer questions than is an obstetrician. And, it's important to point out, for thousands of years and in many parts of the world today, giving birth at home was and is the only option. On the other hand, there are many advantages to having a hospital birth, including ready access to doctors and medical equipment in the event that either the mother or the infant requires immediate care for life-threatening complications. Some women choose to combine these approaches by having a hospital birth attended by the midwife who has guided them through their pregnancy. In cases such as this, the term "complementary medicine" is really more apt: biomedicine and alternative medicine do not need to be mutually exclusive.

Biomedicine remains the norm in North American society, but it is increasingly called into question by those who endorse a more holistic approach to diagnosis and treatment. Biomedicine has been criticized for looking at health from a reductionist perspective that attributes medical conditions to single factors treatable with single remedies. It fails to take into account the broader set of circumstances surrounding a person's health or illness. Those involved in biomedicine are sometimes accused of being absolutist, of failing to recognize that just as there are different cultures when it comes to business, policing, or clothing, there are cultures of medicine, each with a unique approach to interpreting medicine in ways that reflect and reinforce other aspects of the culture from which it is derived. Every patient, critics argue, should be treated in the context of his or her culture. No single treatment should be applied universally across all cultures.

In Chapter 3 I brought up Anne Fadiman's study of the Hmong people living in the United States (Fadiman, 1997). Originally from China, the Hmong were forced to flee their homeland after resisting the Chinese government and encouraging the participation of the United States in the Southeast Asian wars of the 1960s and 1970s. Fadiman's study shows how Hmong refugees suffered because of narrow Western biomedical practices that did not respect their cultural beliefs. She cites, as just one example, the failure of North American doctors to take into account their fear—widespread among the Hmong people—of losing their soul. The Hmong wear (and put on their infants) neck-rings and cotton-string spirit bracelets to combat their fear of soul loss, and they rely on their spirit doctors or shamans, the *tsiv neebs*, to address and help them overcome these fears. Problems occurred when Hmong patients arriving at a refugee camp in Thailand had their spirit strings cut by American health workers, who claimed they were unsanitary. The neck-rings

thought to hold intact the souls of babies were also removed, placing this especially vulnerable group in graver danger of soul loss in the eyes of the Hmong.

Medicalization

An offshoot of the biomedical approach to medicine is a practice known as medicalization. Sociologists Chang and Christakis define medicalization as

> the process by which certain behaviours or conditions are defined as medical problems (rather than, for example, as moral or legal problems), and medical intervention becomes the focus of remedy and social control. (Chang & Christakis, 2002: p. 152)

Critics of the health industry's tendency to medicalize conditions describe the practice as a form of reductionism that reduces complex medical conditions to biomedical causes without examining possible sociocultural or political factors. A second, and related, criticism is that Western health professionals are too quick to situate the problem exclusively or primarily in the individual human body, rather than, say, in an oppressive social or political system. Medicalization, by ascribing conditions like alcoholism to genetic factors, does excuse the sufferer by removing individual blame, but at the same time it portrays the sufferer as a genetic "victim" who can be saved only by an intervention engineered by the medical profession. It takes away the individual's ability to make empowering choices that could affect the outcome of his or her condition. This leads to a further criticism: that medicalization promotes the commodification of health care by identifying certain normal conditions as diseases that may be treated with "commodity cures" (e.g. drugs or procedures). In sociological terms, this makes the normal seem deviant. Examples for the aging male include obesity, male pattern baldness, increasingly frequent nighttime trips to the bathroom, and erectile dysfunction. These are not diseases. They are relatively normal aspects of the aging process and do not need to be medicalized.

Government agencies and health professionals sometimes medicalize disorders traceable more to social or environmental factors than to purely medical factors. Medical journalist Lynn Payer offers an example in *Disease-Mongers: How Doctors, Drug Companies, and Insurers Are Making You Feel Sick* (1992):

> When . . . a child died of lead poisoning in Michigan, there was a call for screening for lead poisoning. But when you read the circumstances, you found that the child was homeless, living in an abandoned building. Calling for blood testing was obviously easier than calling for a policy of providing safe and low-cost shelter for the poor. . . . (Payer, 1992: p. 39)

Consider another condition that has been medicalized and commodified in North America: nicotine addiction. Since being conclusively linked to higher rates of lung and breast cancer, cigarette

A social determinist might argue that the upward trend in obesity rates is a societal problem having to do with the prevalence of fast food advertising and the ready availability of cheap, unhealthy food in our restaurants and supermarkets. So if our streets were lined with healthier options, would obesity rates decline? Is obesity a societal problem or an individual one?

smoking has gone from being portrayed as a cause of disease to a disease in its own right. Public health campaigns designed to get people to stop smoking have been replaced by advertising campaigns promoting a growing list of products you need in order to stop smoking. These ads sell several ideas. First, they sell the idea that smoking is the individual's problem, following the line of reasoning used by defenders of firearms: cigarettes don't cause cancer, smokers do. Then, they sell the idea that an addiction to smoking should be treated as a medical condition that requires medical help. Finally, they sell the idea that the medical help required is a drug, a patch, or a spray, and that you need their product. Distrust ads asking you to ask your health care professional.

Posttraumatic stress disorder is often medicalized (see Kleinman, 1995). Suffered especially by those who have experienced the extreme violence of warfare (as soldiers or civilians), violent political oppression, or crime, PTSD was first diagnosed by Western psychiatrists who traced its origins to bleak, unstable environments in countries such as Cambodia, El Salvador, Tibet, and the former Republic of Yugoslavia. Gradually, though, the focus of treatment has shifted from the pathology of the environment to the pathology of the individual. Patients are often treated as though their psychobiological reactions to these harrowing circumstances are not normal, as if a psychologically healthy person would not react that way. To be clear, it is not wrong to help people by recognizing that they have suffered psychological trauma, but it is misleading to remove from an individual's story the sickness of the social situation endured.

Ivan Illich: Pioneering Critic of Medicalization

Ivan Illich (1927–2002) introduced the notion of medicalization to sociology. Although Illich was trained as a medieval historian, theologian, and philosopher, sociologists stake claim to him as a public sociologist.

Illich developed the concept of medicalization as part of a general critique of radical monopolies in industrial societies:

> A radical monopoly goes deeper than that of any one corporation or any one government.

It can take many forms. . . . Ordinary monopolies corner the market; radical monopolies disable people from doing or making things on their own. . . . They impose a society-wide substitution of commodities for use-values by reshaping the milieu and by "appropriating" those of its general characteristics which have enabled people so far to cope on their own. Intensive education turns autodidacts [people who teach themselves] into unemployables, intensive agriculture destroys the subsistence farmer, and the deployment of police undermines the community's self-control. The malignant spread of medicine has comparable results: it turns mutual care and self-medication into misdemeanors or felonies. (1976: p. 42)

This passage comes from *Medical Nemesis: The Limits of Medicine*, which opens with the shocking claim: "The medical establishment has become a major threat to health" (1976: p. 1). In the book, Illich describes a "doctor-generated epidemic" that is harming the health of citizens in industrialized society by taking away people's freedom to heal themselves or prevent their illnesses, as well as their freedom to criticize industrial society for the ills of stress, pollution, and general danger that make people sick. Illich's term for this is iatrogenesis. He distinguished three different kinds:

- clinical iatrogenesis
- social iatrogenesis
- cultural iatrogenesis.

Clinical iatrogenesis refers to the various ways in which diagnosis and cure cause problems that are as bad as or worse than the health problems they are meant to resolve. This occurs when a patient enters hospital for treatment of one ailment and becomes

The Point Is . . .

Illich on Medicalization

What point do you think Illich was making with each of the following statements? Do you agree with him?

The fact that the doctor population is higher where certain diseases have become rare has little to do with the doctors' ability to control or eliminate them. It simply means that doctors deploy themselves as they like, more so than other professionals, and that they tend to gather where the climate is healthy, where the water is clean, and where people are employed and can pay for their services. (1976: pp. 21–2)

In a complex technological hospital, negligence becomes "random human error" or "system breakdown," callousness becomes "scientific detachment," and incompetence becomes "a lack of specialized equipment." The depersonalization of diagnosis and therapy has changed malpractice from an ethical into a technical problem. (1976: p. 30)

In every society, medicine, like law and religion, defines what is normal, proper, or desirable. Medicine has the authority to label one man's complaint a legitimate illness, to declare a second man sick though he himself does not complain, and to refuse a third social recognition of his pain, his disability, and even his death. It is medicine which stamps some pain as "merely subjective," some impairment as malingering, and some deaths—though not others—as suicide. (1976: p. 45)

Medicine always creates illness as a social state. The recognized healer transmits to individuals the social possibilities for acting sick. Each culture has its own characteristic perception of disease and thus its unique hygienic mask. Disease takes its features from the physician who casts the actors into one of the available roles. To make people legitimately sick is as implicit in the physicians' power as the poisonous potential of the remedy that works. (1976: p. 44) infected with a virus originating in the hospital. Social iatrogenesis occurs when political conditions that "render society unhealthy" are hidden or obscured (Illich, 1976: p. 9). In Canada this includes lax monitoring by government agencies of laws concerning workplace safety, for example. Cultural iatrogenesis takes place when the knowledge and abilities of the medical community are extolled or mythologized to the point where the authority of the health profession "tends to mystify and to expropriate the power of the individual to heal himself and to shape his or her environment" (Illich, 1976: p. 9). In other words, the patient is given no credit for his or her role in the recovery: it's all the result of the doctor's work.

Big Pharma: The Role of Drug Companies in Medicalization

The term "Big Pharma" is used to refer to the world's large pharmaceutical companies, which reap enormous annual profits from developing, manufacturing, and marketing the drugs used to fight and manage a range of medical conditions, some of them serious (such as HIV), some of them less so (such as insomnia, when this can often be cured through lifestyle changes).

Drug companies invest heavily in research and development. They recover those R&D costs by charging prices well beyond what it costs to manufacture a particular drug product. They can do this when they have a patent on the drug that prevents other companies from copying the product and selling a generic form at lower prices.

Consider the case of Roche, the owners of the patent for Tamiflu. Tamiflu is the proprietary term for oseltamivir, the main vaccine used against some strains of flu. In 2005, there was an international panic around a new strain of flu, officially known as H5N1 but more commonly known as avian flu or bird flu, because it was first found in birds. Soon after several cases were found in humans, Canada, the US, Britain, Israel, and Australia bought billions of dollars' worth of Tamiflu to stockpile just in case of a serious outbreak. The money was mostly wasted on a pandemic that never emerged (or, if you prefer, never lived up to the hype). Meanwhile, countries that couldn't afford the expensive patented vaccine, and companies that wanted to provide generic

versions of oseltamivir, had to fight to make those cheaper versions of the vaccine available. In 2009, an Indian company (Cipla Ltd) won the right to produce an alternative version of Tamiflu, called Antiflu, for the populace of India. Canadians were not so fortunate.

Consider another product: the EpiPen device. If you know someone with a serious allergy, or if you have one yourself, you have probably seen an EpiPen. It is used to administer a potentially life-saving dose of the drug epinephrine to someone experiencing a serious allergic reaction. In this case it is not the drug itself that is patented but the delivery method: an autoinjector, consisting of a spring-loaded syringe designed to inject the sufferer with the proper dosage of the drug. In the United States, Mylan Pharmaceuticals, which owns the patent, has raised the price of the EpiPen by over 400 per cent since 2009, despite the fact there have been no significant changes to the product to warrant such an increase ("EpiPen Price Furor," 2016). In this case, Canadians *are* lucky: Pfizer, the company with the licence to distribute the product in Canada, has kept the price consistent, partly because it must operate under the oversight of this country's Patent Medicine Prices Review Board.

Big Pharma lobbies hard against generic drugs, which cut into their massive profits, and fiercely defend their patents. Their lobby is strong in Canada, and affects policy. Big Pharma benefits when the media uncritically spread fear over pandemics, sending concerned citizens to the nearest public health clinic for an immunization shot. Curiously, the same drug companies that market and sell anti-viral drugs seem immune to media criticism. (Big Pharma spends a lot on advertising, in print and online news media, and with their advertising dollars comes some influence.) The flu shot sold in Canada hadn't been through a complete set of clinical trials when it was distributed in the fight against a strain of H1N1 known as swine flu in 2009. Possible side effects and risks to people with certain pre-existing conditions weren't completely known when the vaccine began to be used. Yet the Canadian government granted GlaxoSmithKline (GSK, a manufacturer of the anti–swine flu vaccine) indemnity, meaning that the government (that is, you, the taxpayer) would cover the cost of any lawsuit filed against the drug maker in the event the drug failed to work or produced fatal side effects. GSK might have invested heavily in developing the vaccine, but the government gave the company a deal that carried no financial risk and the promise of huge profits for the drug manufacturer, which currently earns an estimated $1.66 billion (US) a year on sales of vaccine.

Medical Sociology, "Race," and Ethnicity

Unemployed Immigrant Doctors: A Problem with Many Standpoints

The Canadian health care system is currently facing a shortage of doctors in communities far from large urban centres. At the same time, the country is welcoming immigrants with medical degrees and general credentials that are considered insufficient to qualify them to practise medicine in Canada. It is a perplexing issue, one that must be considered from a number of *standpoints*—perspectives shaped by social location. The sections that follow outline four of these differing standpoints.

1. Immigrant Doctors

As an immigrant doctor, you came to a country that offered a greater financial opportunity for you and your family. On the strength of skills and experience gained in your home country, you scored highly in the "point system" by which the worthiness of candidates for immigration is judged. The Canadian government seemed to be encouraging you to come.

As soon as you arrived in Canada, problems hit you in the face. If you chose to settle in Toronto—as many do—you encountered a two-step problem. First, your skills and knowledge were assessed through a training program. The Ontario International Medical Graduate Program takes 48 weeks—close to a year—to complete and has limited space. You managed to gain admission to the program and did well, but then you faced a second, even higher hurdle: a residency program of several years in which you would essentially re-learn everything

Public health campaigns appeal to civic duty when they encourage you to protect yourself *and others* by getting the annual flu shot. Yet since 2014, the vaccine's effectiveness in Canada has been disappointing (Crowe, 2016). Is getting the shot when your government tells you to the responsible thing to do?

you needed to know to earn your medical qualifications in the first place. As if that were not frustrating enough, you faced the largest problem: the small number of residency positions available. Until recently, you would have been one of more than 1,100 immigrant doctors in Ontario competing for just 36 spots open each year in the residency program. The number of spots has recently increased to 250. Still, the odds are not in your favour.

In the meantime, your family must eat. You might get a job in a medical field, possibly (with training) as a lab assistant. But it is more likely you will end up working as a telemarketer, driving a taxi, delivering pizza, or doing manual labour in factories. Your dream of practising your chosen profession in this country supposedly rich in opportunity has proven elusive.

2. Rural Communities

You live in a community that is home to fewer and fewer doctors. The older ones retire; the young graduates opt to take up medical work in the big city. Your family doctor has retired and closed her practice, and you, like her other patients, are scrambling to find another doctor to take you on. But most family doctors are already seeing more patients than they can handle. The trouble is that you're older and therefore are more likely to have complicated and time-consuming medical problems. You are more work for a new doctor, who can choose not to take you on as a patient. So you put up with minor complaints, knowing that anything more serious will require a trip down to the big city, where the bigger research hospitals and more lucrative practices are.

Occasionally you wonder whether there's something your town should be doing to attract doctors. You don't care where they come from. In Ontario, 214 communities have been designated as "underserved" by the provincial ministry of health. Saskatchewan and Newfoundland and Labrador have higher percentages of foreign-trained doctors than other provinces. The reason: not as many obstacles for immigrant doctors.

Keith Beaty/Toronto Star via Getty Images

Naseem Ahmed Pasha arrived in Toronto from India in 2006, having completed medical school at Mysore University and then having practised for 15 years in India and Saudi Arabia. Although he passed the Canadian exams, he wasn't able to get into the requisite residency program and was forced to take a minimum-salary job at a home improvement store. Do you think he was prepared for this when he came to Canada? What effect do you think the 10-year wait to practise his profession in this country has had on his morale? How do you think this type of situation can be changed (without taking away from residency opportunities for Canadian students)?

3. Countries of Origin of Internationally Trained Doctors

In developing countries, especially in rural areas, there are even fewer doctors per population than there are in Canada's rural communities. The cost of educating medical professionals is prohibitively high. It is much more likely that your country will lose trained doctors to emigration than benefit from an influx of health professionals. In post-apartheid South Africa, the government decided to block doctors immigrating from other African nations to halt the brain drain—the exodus of educated professionals—eroding the health care systems of those countries. Canada experiences a bit of that brain drain when some of its medical specialists go to the US, but it's nothing compared to the brain drain of doctors leaving developing countries for North America.

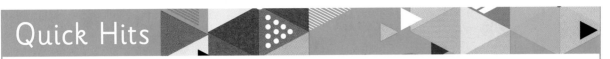

Quick Hits

Where Do You Go When You Don't Have a Family Doctor?

According to the Canadian Community Health Survey, in 2013, 4.6 million Canadians over the age of 12 were without a regular family doctor.

- In all age groups, men were more likely than women to report not having a regular family doctor.
- Among those who had looked for a family doctor,
  - 36.7 per cent said that doctors in their area were not taking new patients;
  - 29.7 per cent said their doctor had retired or left the area;
  - 25.2 per cent said that no doctors were available in their area; and
  - 21.2 per cent gave other reasons.

(These add up to more than 100 per cent because respondents were permitted to choose more than one option.)

- Of those without a regular family doctor, 80.6 per cent reported they had a place to go when in need of health advice; these included
  - walk-in clinics (58.9 per cent);
  - hospital emergency rooms (13.0 per cent);
  - community health centres (8.7 per cent); and
  - other facilities, including hospital out-patient clinics and telephone health lines (19.3 per cent).

Source: Statistics Canada, 2013c.

4. Doctors' Associations

Placing restrictions on internationally trained medical graduates gives Canadian-trained doctors more power as a sociopolitical body of professionals. As Linda McQuaig (a journalist who took a course in sociology: personal communication) explained in a commentary on the New Brunswick doctors' strike in 2004,

> Doctors have managed to maintain enormous bargaining power in Canada by threatening, from time to time, to abandon us for more prosperous climes. But these threats only have teeth because doctors can rely on the fact that there is no one here to replace them if they go—even when potential replacements are already here and desperate to get to work. (McQuaig, 2004)

On the other side, consider the Ontario Medical Association's "Position Paper on Physician Workforce Policy and Planning," dated April 2002. It addresses the OMA's concerns about "the problem of inadequate physician human resources, and the related consequences for public access to medical treatment." One of the 18 recommendations in the report was to "Temporarily increase the number of fully qualified international medical graduate (IMG) positions." In a 2004 speech, OMA president Dr Larry Erlick, addressing the same problems, noted:

> We . . . need more foreign-trained physicians to practise in Ontario. The fact that we have relied on foreign-trained physicians in the past should come as no surprise, as 25 per cent of physicians practising today in this province are in fact international medical graduates! Some of the red tape has to be cut.

Still, in both documents, helping foreign-trained physicians gain accreditation to practise in Canada was clearly viewed as a secondary solution. The words "temporarily" and "fully qualified" in the first statement leave holes in that support, and Dr Erlick's recommendation was one of a number of "short-term recommendations," given less priority than bringing back Ontario medical graduates now practising elsewhere.

The Racialization of Disease: The 2003 SARS Outbreak

A disease becomes racialized when it is strongly associated with people of a particular "race" or

Telling It Like It Is

An Account of Systemic Racism from a Black First-Year Nursing Student

I have had my first clinical experience in the nursing profession and I feel I have already been subjected to systemic racism. Examples of this include disciplinary actions that are different from other student nurses such as when myself and a non-Black student returned late from break. I was pulled aside and it was stated that the teacher felt sorry for the other student. When I asked "why," it was implied that I coerced her into returning late against her will. Also, vague work appraisals are given and no specific areas of improvement are suggested. Comments such as, "You seem like a very angry person," and "I have a hard time approaching you and can only imagine how the residents feel," or "Any monkey can be trained to take a blood pressure" are an everyday occurrence. There are many cases where my mistakes are far more noted and exaggerated than those of other students. When defending myself (as I feel I am performing equally well to everyone else), I am labelled as not being "self-aware" and not accepting feedback. Yet, when feedback is taken and changes are made, I am told I take things too literally. As a result, I can do no right.

Events like these are commonplace. As a result, promotions as well as workload may not be fairly distributed.

—Nadine Smith

What do YOU think?

1. In what ways might the social situation of the clinical experience lend itself to forms of systemic or personal racism? What recourse should a student nurse have to be able to address this kind of experience?
2. Why do you think a black nursing student might be more sensitive to the inequality of the relationship between the clinical supervisor and the student nurse?

ethnic background, and people of this background are treated negatively because of that association. A good example occurred in 2003, when an outbreak of severe acute respiratory syndrome, or SARS, afflicted Canadians of all "races" but became primarily associated with Asians.

Canadians began hearing about SARS in March 2003. They quickly learned that the highly contagious respiratory ailment with flu-like symptoms was serious, and in about 10 per cent of cases fatal. This made it the focus of widespread media attention throughout the spring and early summer. Over this period, the disease became racialized: because it originated in China, and because members of a Catholic Filipino community were among those who had contracted it, the disease took on a racial identity. Once cases of the disease began to appear in Canada, Chinese and Filipino Canadians became targets of discrimination.

In June 2004, a year after the World Health Organization had removed Toronto from the list of cities affected by SARS, researchers Carrianne Leung and Jian Guan noted how the mainstream media had racialized SARS by portraying Asians as carriers of disease in a way that spread fear among non–Asian Canadians. Table 13.1 summarizes Leung and Guan's findings about the content of pictures accompanying articles on the disease in four national newspapers and periodicals (Leung & Guan, 2004: p. 9, 10).

They found that photographs accompanying stories about SARS tended to feature Asians,

| Table 13.1 | Photographic Treatment of SARS in the National Media, 2003 | | | | | | |

Newspaper / Magazine	Number of SARS Photos	Showing People		Showing Asians		Showing Asians with Masks	
		#	%	#	%	#	%
National Post	120	95	82.0	65	54.2	60	50.0
The Globe and Mail	119	68	57.1	52	43.9	41	34.5
Maclean's	27	17	63.0	8	29.6	6	22.2
Time (Canada)	17	15	88.2	8	47.0	6	35.3

Source: Leung & Guan, 2004.

THURSDAY, APRIL 3, 2003 ★ TORONTO STAR ★ B3

SARS Outbreak

China admits wider spread of SARS

12 more deaths reported among inland provinces

First cases found in Latin America and Israel

ANN PERRY
STAFF REPORTER

The global death toll from Severe Acute Respiratory Syndrome jumped yesterday as China broke its silence and admitted it had more cases in more provinces than it had previously revealed.

The South China Morning Post reported today that the first victims of the deadly illness were people in China's southern province of Guangdong who ate or handled wild game, confirming earlier reports linking the disease to ducks.

China said it had 1,190 suspected cases through the end of March, and 46 deaths instead of the 34 it had admitted. Cases were reported in Guangxi, Hunan and Sichuan provinces as well as Guangdong for the first time.

In total, the World Health Organization estimated that SARS has infected more than 2,200 people worldwide and killed an estimated 78.

Brazil reported its first suspected case, which, if confirmed, would be the first in Latin America. Israel also reported its first suspected case.

China agreed yesterday to let a team of WHO investigators visit the southern province of Guangdong, where the disease is believed to have started.

The four-member international team, which will leave Beijing today, will take samples from suspected patients to help identify a culprit virus and assess how infectious and virulent it is.

And, for the first time in its 55-

REUTERS

With Hong Kong being the global centre of the SARS outbreak, face masks are common on the city's streets. Some residents strive for their own style amid the crisis. Chinese officials are reporting there are more cases and more deaths than they previously admitted.

year-history, WHO recommended that travellers avoid part of the world because of an infectious disease: Hong Kong and adjoining Guangdong province.

In the first public statement by a senior leader, Chinese Health Minister Zhang Wenkang said the outbreak was "under effective control."

He said 80 per cent of those diagnosed with SARS have recovered.

For weeks, U.N. agency officials have appealed for more cooperation from China.

"Because the mainland is not sharing information . . . the outbreak has been lengthened," Taiwan's Mainland Affairs Council said in a recent report.

Laboratories around the world are racing to come up with a test for SARS.

The U.S. Centers for Disease Control has issued two tests that health officials can give to patients with suspected SARS. Dr. Julie Gerberding, the director of the Atlanta-based centre, said until a large number of people are tested, no one can say whether the disease is caused by the main suspect — a coronavirus.

But she said so far 400 healthy people had been tested for the virus, a previously unknown relative of one of the common cold viruses, and all had tested negative.

Several patients with SARS have tested positive.

"It is not yet proof. There are other viruses still under investigation," she said. In Toronto, Dr. Raymond Tellier of the Hospital for Sick Children, has developed a test that detects this new species of coronavirus. It is currently being used here.

A top health expert in China told a newspaper the earliest SARS patients in Guangdong had close and continuous contact with chickens, ducks, pigeons and owls.

"We will explore further if the disease was passed to human beings from wild animals. You know, Guangdong people like eating exotic animals and I don't find it a healthy practice," said Bi Shengli, a vice-director at the Chinese Centre for Disease Control and Prevention.

The earliest cases of the disease were traced to either chefs or bird vendors, Bi said.

In Thailand yesterday, the government said it would turn back foreigners suspected of having SARS and would force those allowed in from affected countries to wear masks in public.

In the Philippines, which has no confirmed cases, President Gloria Macapagal Arroyo put in place a contingency plan — including air and seaport checks — to prevent an outbreak. Health officials in New Zealand urged indigenous Maori tribesmen to forgo their traditional "hongi" nose-rubbing greeting for visiting Chinese at a convention.

In Hong Kong, the Roman Catholic Church ordered priests to wear masks during Communion and put wafers in the hands of the faithful rather than on the tongue.

FROM STAR WIRE SERVICES

Toronto Star

particularly Asians wearing masks to reduce the spread of the disease. The researchers noted that the exaggerated use of frightening words and unreasonable parallels drawn between SARS and the Spanish influenza pandemic of 1918–19 (in which at least 20 million people died over an 18-month period) were also part of media fear-mongering. Fear surrounding the disease had a devastating economic impact on parts of Canada where the outbreak was prevalent, notably Toronto and, in particular, its various Chinatowns. Media commentators noted that many of the patrons suddenly avoiding Chinese business communities and restaurants were themselves Chinese, as though this fact somehow justified similar acts of discrimination on the part of non–Asian Canadians. But whether the economic losses can be attributed more to a drop in Chinese-Canadian patronage or to decreased patronage by non–Chinese Canadians makes little difference. The fact is that the loss of business occurred, and it did so because the disease was racialized to the point where many Canadians temporarily changed their purchasing habits as a precaution against contracting the virus in communities where it was thought to be prevalent.

What do YOU think?

1. Who is involved in racializing a disease like SARS? Whose role should it be to challenge the racialization of disease as it is occurring?
2. To what extent can we blame the media for exaggerating the association of SARS with Asians and spreading fear about the disease? Is it the media's responsibility to make people aware of the gravest possible outcomes of an event?
3. To what extent does blame lie with individuals, for succumbing to fear-mongering? Can regular patrons of Chinatown businesses be blamed for altering their purchasing habits if there's any chance at all that not doing so will increase their odds of contracting the virus? Should people be expected to weigh decisions about their personal health against the greater economic and social impact of their decisions?
4. Ultimately, what social effects result when a disease such as SARS is racialized?

Medical Sociology and Gender

Physicians and Gender

Both the number and the percentage of women in and graduating from medical schools in Canada are increasing. In 1959, women accounted for just 6 per cent of medical school graduates; in 2011, 62.2 per cent of 25- to 34-year-olds with a medical degree were women. Compare those with the data for older Canadians aged 55–64: among that group of medical degree–holders, just 28.0 per cent were women, showing that the preponderance of women with a medical degree is a significant change from the recent past (Statistics Canada, 2013b: p. 8). Most medical school graduates now are female. Clearly this is a significant trend.

How might this trend affect the profession? How do women physicians differ from their male counterparts? In a number of ways regularly noted in the relevant literature. Here are a few examples.

Women doctors are more likely to . . .

- screen their patients for preventable illnesses.
- spend time counselling patients about psychosocial issues.
- enter primary care (i.e. become family physicians).
- work fewer hours and see fewer patients.
- leave the profession sooner.

Women doctors are less likely to . . .

- become surgeons.
- be sued for malpractice.
- join professional organizations.

What do YOU think?

1. How much do you think this changing gender dynamic will affect the practice of medicine in Canada?
2. Do you think this could lead to a reduction in the power differential between doctors and nurses in Canadian hospitals?
3. Why do you think some students resist the idea that, on average, male and female doctors practise medicine differently?

Telling It Like It Is

SARS and Being Chinese

Around the time of the SARS crisis, being Chinese made people look at me in a different way, whether it was at school, at work, or in public places such as the subway and buses. It did not bother me at first, but as more and more individuals died due to SARS, the more I kept my eyes open for tainted looks darting in my direction.

Around that time in school, it wasn't so much the looks, but comments made in class about the situation. What I have learned and understood in this game we call life is that everyone is entitled to his or her opinion. I have also learned and understood that not all opinions are necessarily right or wrong. Unfortunately, not all people feel that their opinions are wrong, hurtful, disrespectful, condescending, and rude.

One incident happened in my math class at college. Our class got off topic, and our focus was turned from present and future value to SARS. Our teacher was reminding us that proper hand washing helps in preventing the spread of infection. One obnoxious fellow who felt he was the class clown replied to our teacher's comment and stated that to prevent the spread of infection, we need to stay away from all those darn Chinese people. His language use and vocabulary was a little cruder. Being the only Asian person in the class, everyone turned and looked in my direction as if they were expecting me to curse him. I decided to let the one and only authority figure take care of his biased opinion. However, our teacher said absolutely nothing, except to get on with the lesson. His comments offended me and our teacher not correcting him hurt my feelings. It made me pay more attention to the things that were being said in all the rest of my classes. The impact it had on my school life made me more defensive towards what my peers had to say about those of Asian descent. . . .

Ethnicity is a sociological factor that made an impact on my life within that year. Because I have been on the end of a biased opinion at school and indirect discrimination at work, I have further learned another aspect of the game of life: the value and meaning of equality and fairness and that even though there are different ethnicities and races, we are all part of one race called the human race.

—Karin Koo

What do YOU think?

1. What do you think motivated the student to say what he did in class? Why might he have thought that he was "just joking"?
2. How might you have responded to the student's comment had you been the instructor in charge of this class? What is the danger in saying nothing?

Male Nurses

Men have long been involved in the nursing profession, but their numbers have been small. In 2002, there were 219,161 women registered nurses (RNs) in Canada, compared with just 11,796 male registered nurses (about 5.4 per cent of the total). By 2011 the percentage of male RNs had grown to 9.0 per cent. Change is happening, but it is slow. This is largely because of the persistent stereotype of male nurses being gay. (Think of the movie *Meet the Fockers* (2004), in which the lead character, played by Ben Stiller, is a male nurse named Gaylord Focker.)

In my experience teaching introductory sociology to nursing students, almost every male in the program comes from a country outside of North America, where, I suspect, the male nurse is not seen as deviant the way it is here. Support for that

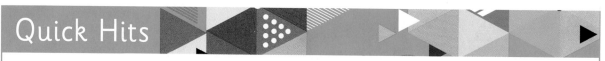

Quick Hits

How Female Nurses Interact with Male and Female Doctors

Female nurses at a hospital in Kingston, Ontario, completed a vignette-based survey in January 2000. Each questionnaire presented four clinical scenarios that had previously been identified as areas of strain in the doctor–nurse relationship. The aim was to study differences in responses to the scenarios based on the physician's sex. The researchers found that persistent sex-role stereotypes influenced the relationship between female nurses and physicians. Nurses were more willing to serve and defer to male physicians than to female physicians. They approached female physicians on a more egalitarian basis and were more comfortable communicating with them, but they were also more hostile toward them (Zelek & Phillips, 2003).

supposition comes from the fact that in 2002, almost half of the male nurses in Canada worked in Quebec, a province that often leads the way in progressive social change in Canada.

Medical Marginality: The Intersectionality of Gender and "Race"

In 1866, two First Nations men became the first Indigenous people in Canada to earn medical degrees. Both were more westernized than most Indigenous people of the time and yet were leaders of their people. Peter Edmund Jones, or Sacred Feathers, was a member of the Mississauga (Anishinabe) nation and was educated at the University of Toronto and Queen's University. Peter Martin, or Oronhyatekha ("Burning Sky"), was Mohawk and attended Oxford University (through contacts with Prince Edward and his personal physician) before completing his degree at the Toronto School of Medicine (TSM), later incorporated into the University of Toronto.

The first Canadian women to become doctors were Jennie Trout and Emily Stowe. Both went to the Toronto School of Medicine, where they were regularly harassed by their male colleagues with the encouragement of their male professors. Scottish-born Jennie Trout left Canada to complete her medical degree at the Women's Medical College of Pennsylvania in 1875, before returning to practise in Canada, becoming the first woman licensed to do so. She helped establish a women's medical college at Queen's University in 1883.

Emily Stowe was a woman of firsts, being the first female principal of a public school in Upper Canada (later Ontario). In 1865 she applied to the Toronto School of Medicine but was rejected because she was a woman. She then went to the United States, where she received a degree in homeopathic medicine at the New York Medical College in 1867. Because she was not licensed as a "regular" doctor, she practised homeopathic medicine in Toronto. In 1870 she and Jennie Trout were both accepted by special permission into the TSM. Frustrated by the persistent harassment she received and the unwillingness of administrators to intervene, she refused to take her exams. She was officially licensed in 1880. Her daughter, Ann Augusta Stowe-Gullen, was the first woman in Canada to be awarded a medical degree, in 1883 at the University of Toronto.

The first Indigenous woman to be licensed as a doctor in Canada did so in 1980, more than 100 years after Peter Jones and Peter Martin became the first licensed Indigenous doctors and Jennie Trout became the first woman doctor in Canada. Her name is Elizabeth Steinhauer, and she is Cree. The residential school had a devastating effect on the education young Indigenous people—men and women—received; it did not foster a desire to pursue higher education. Another factor in why it took so long for an Indigenous woman to become licensed is that the Indian Act forbade Aboriginal people to go to university unless they became enfranchised: a status Indian would have to voluntarily give up her Aboriginal and treaty rights, and perhaps be forced to leave her home reserve. For most Indigenous people this was simply too much to ask. Both Jones and Martin became doctors before the Indian Act was passed.

While the first formal nursing school in Canada was established in St Catharines in 1874, it wasn't until 40 years later that Canada had its first Indigenous nurse. Charlotte Edith Anderson Monture, a Mohawk of the Six Nations, graduated with a degree in nursing in 1914, but not from any school in Canada. After being turned down by Canadian nursing schools she was forced to pursue her degree at the New Rochelle Nursing School in New York, where she began her career as a public school nurse. During World War I she served in France in the US Army Nurse Corps (along with 13 other Aboriginal women). Upon her return she worked as a nurse at a hospital in Six Nations.

Canadian schools trained no black nurses until 1950. There was a formal ban in Canada on black nursing students until after World War II. Toronto-born Bernice Redmon, who was educated at St Philip Hospital Medical College in Virginia, having been refused entry at Canadian schools, was the first black woman licensed as a nurse in Canada. After graduating in 1945, she got a job with the Nova Scotia Department of Public Health, and later became the first black woman to become a member of the Victorian Order of Nurses.

Notice the patterns. Racialized people were discriminated against in Canada, so they had to be educated in the United States. Minoritized men broke the bar first, usually by a long stretch; this is generally true of any profession.

Although I have been engaged in Indigenous studies for over forty years, I was unaware of the history of Aboriginal women doctors until January 2015, when an Indigenous woman, Sally Simpson, who in her forties decided to enter university, compiled a list of "Indigenous Firsts" as a university project. Items from this list are presented in the Quick Hits feature on page 396. A link to the full list can be found at the end of the chapter.

What do YOU think?

When would you guess the first Canadian doctors of Chinese, Japanese, and South Asian descent were licensed? How easy do you think it would be to research this topic? (Hint: begin with the name Victoria Chung.)

© 2013 Waterloo Region Record, Ontario, Canada

Sally Simpson put together her list of "Indigenous firsts" in 2015. Why do you think it had taken so long for anyone to assemble a list of that kind?

Quick Hits

Medical Firsts in Canada

1860	first black male doctor	1893	first female dentist
1861	first Canadian-born black male doctor	1914	first Indigenous nurse
1866	first male Indigenous doctors	1945	first black nurse (note that nurse training had been available to black women in the US since the 1890s)
1867	first female doctor practising in Canada		
1874	first Canadian nursing school established		
1875	first woman licensed as a doctor	1980	first female Indigenous doctor
1883	first female doctor trained in Canada	1990	first female Indigenous dentist
1892	two male nurses in first graduating class at Victoria General Hospital (Halifax)		

Medical Sociology and Class

The Inverse Care Law

Dr **Julian Tudor Hart** studied medicine at Cambridge and interned at the equally prestigious St George's Hospital in London. A natural career move for a British doctor on that path would have been to serve the needs of the middle class or the rich in London or some other big city. Instead, he dedicated his life to helping the citizens of a working-class mining village in Wales. Dr Hart became famous among medical sociologists for an article he wrote in 1971. In it he introduced the idea of the inverse care law:

> The availability of good medical care tends to vary inversely with the need for it in the population served. This inverse care law operates more completely where medical care is most exposed to market forces, and less so where such exposure is reduced. The market distribution of medical care is a primitive and historically outdated social form, and any return to it would further exaggerate the maldistribution of medical resources. (Hart, 1971: p. 405)

Hart was describing a system that had, for almost 20 years, experienced socialized health care similar to the one existing today in Canada, a system markedly different from the private or market-force system found in the United States. What the inverse care law meant in terms of the Britain he was describing can be seen in statistics concerning infant mortality from the years 1949–53. From Hart's perspective, these statistics

> showed combined social classes I and II (wholly non-manual) with a standardised mortality from all causes 18% below the mean, and combined social classes IV and V (wholly manual) 5% above it. Infant mortality was 37% below the mean for social class I (professional) and 38% above it for social class V (unskilled manual). (Hart, 1971: p. 405)

In other words, the lower classes experienced a greater likelihood of infant mortality (i.e. death of an infant during the first year of life). This would reflect both the working and living conditions of the different classes, as well as differences in medical care in areas where the various classes live, work, and see doctors. Regarding doctors, Hart observed the following trends:

> In areas with most sickness and death, general practitioners have more work, larger lists [of patients], less hospital support, and inherit more clinically ineffective traditions of consultation [e.g. short visits with little listening to patients' problems] than in the healthiest areas; and hospital doctors

shoulder heavier case-loads with less staff and equipment, more obsolete buildings, and suffer recurrent crises in the availability of beds and replacement staff. (Hart, 1971: p. 412)

What do YOU think?

1. Do you think that the inverse care law holds in Canada? How would you, as a sociologist, go about trying to prove or disprove it?
2. How do you think class affects the social course of disease?
3. We know that certain classes of individuals are routinely allowed to "jump the queue" to receive medical procedures faster than most Canadians would normally be able to (when was the last time you heard of an NHL player having to wait four to six months for an MRI?). Who in your opinion is entitled to priority care? Professional athletes? High-ranking politicians, like the prime minister or a provincial premier? Emergency services professionals (paramedics, police officers, firefighters)? Hospital workers? Spouses and families of any of the above?

Rising Tuition Fees and Medical Students

Most students can relate to the effects of rising tuition fees. How does that affect medical students? A study conducted by Kwong et al. in early 2002 compared tuition costs in Ontario with costs in the rest of Canada (except for Quebec).

The reason for highlighting Ontario tuition costs is that medical students in that province had the greatest hike in tuition fees in Canada from 1997–8 to 2000–1. The cost of first-year tuition at the University of Toronto's school of medicine, for example, nearly tripled over that period, from $4,844 per year to $14,000. By 2010–11, it had risen to $18,424 for Canadian students. The researchers contrasted people in their fourth year with those in their first, because they represented the two extremes. They found that there were three differences between the two academic cohorts that were unique to Ontario. First, the proportion of respondents with a family income of less than $40,000 declined significantly between the first-year and fourth-year students, from

22.6 per cent to 15.0 per cent, respectively; the same figure among non-Ontario schools stayed just about the same (decreasing slightly from 16.0 per cent to 15.8 per cent overall). The figure of $40,000 was chosen to represent "low income," as it was beneath the median family income of $46,951 in Canada in 1996. Another difference between the two groups was that the median debt level anticipated upon graduation by first-year medical students in Ontario was $80,000; the debt anticipated by the graduating class was a lower, but still nasty, $57,000; no such contrast existed in the other provinces. The problem here for the sociologist is that there are no earlier studies with which to compare these findings. What if first-year medical students often project a higher figure than their more experienced graduating colleagues? Is the control group sufficient here for comparative purposes? What do you think?

Finally, first-year medical students in Ontario were more likely than fourth-year students to report that their financial situation was "very" or "extremely" stressful (20.5 per cent versus 17.5 per cent; the reverse was true in other provinces: 11.9 per cent versus 15.8 per cent). They were also more likely to cite financial considerations as having a major influence on their choice of specialty or practice location (25.4 per cent versus 13.3 per cent, compared with a reverse ratio of 21.4 per cent to 26.0 per cent in the other provinces). Again, is this a cohort problem or a stage problem somehow conditioned by being in Ontario?

Table 13.2	Average Annual Cost of Attending Medical School, by Province, 2010–11
Ontario	$18,420
British Columbia	15,547
Nova Scotia	13,818
Alberta	13,157
Saskatchewan	12,276
National average	**11,319**
Manitoba	7,499
Newfoundland and Labrador	6,250
Quebec	3,584

Source: Based on www2.macleans.ca/2010/09/16/how-much-they-pay-for-it/

Photo by Rene Johnston/Toronto Star via Getty Images

This medical student works 20 hours a week at his university's athletic complex to supplement the students loans that pay for his education. Part-time jobs are a reality for many medical students in Canada, but the added stress of a tenuous financial situation can be a barrier to success. Should medical students expect to graduate with higher debts given the greater earning potential their degree confers?

Final Thoughts: Twelve Tips for Better Health

In 1999, British sociologist David Gordon drew up the following list of "Alternative 10 Tips for Better Health." It was meant to present an alternative to the British Medical Officer's 10 health tips, which included the usual things about not smoking, eating healthy foods, drinking in moderation, driving safely, and so on. Although it's now over 15 years old, the list still applies:

1) Don't be poor. If you can, stop. If you can't, try not to be poor for long.
2) Don't have poor parents.
3) Own a car.
4) Don't work in a stressful, low-paying manual job.

5) Don't live in damp, low-quality housing.
6) Be able to afford to go on a foreign holiday and sunbathe.
7) Practise not losing your job and don't become unemployed.
8) Take up all benefits you are entitled to, if you are unemployed, retired, or sick or disabled.
9) Don't live next to a busy major road or near a polluting factory.
10) Learn how to fill in the complex housing benefit/asylum application forms before you become homeless or destitute. (cited in Pohlmann, 2002)

This tongue-in-cheek but accurate appraisal has been adapted a number of times. In a 2003 speech, Roy Romanow, author of the Romanow Report on the state of Canada's health care industry, expanded this list to include two additional items:

11) Graduate from high school and then go on to college or university. Health status improves with your level of education.

12) Be sure to live in a community where you trust your neighbours and feel that you belong. A civil and trusting community promotes health and life expectancy.

What do YOU think?

1. How do these "health tips" reflect William Ryan's idea of **blaming the victim** (see Chapter 7)?

2. Are there any items you can think of adding to this list?

WRAP IT UP

Summary

Sociology has an important role to play in the way health care is taught and delivered. Medical sociologists look carefully at the relationships between standard social factors such as class, gender, "race" and ethnicity, and location, and document inconsistencies in the way patients are treated. They study the social course of disease and record how different illnesses are portrayed in the media.

Canada has a public health care system, but make no mistake about it: it's a big business heavily influenced by big business interests. Hospitals grappling with barely adequate budgets make business decisions every day, deciding where best to allocate their funding, while companies ranging in size from huge multinationals selling pharmaceutical products to private clinics offering cosmetic procedures like tummy tucks have a vested interest in making us feel less healthy than we are, and incapable of improving our health without costly medical interventions. It is my firm belief that one of the best ways of improving the health care system in Canada, and the health of all Canadians, is to increase the amount of medical sociology being carried out in this country to bring a critical perspective to the way health care is delivered.

THINK BACK

Questions for Critical Review

1. Take a particular disease or injury that you have experienced and discuss the social course that you went through to have it diagnosed and treated. Where did you go? Who healed you? How were you socially processed?

2. Identify what biomedicine is and talk about its weaknesses and strengths. In what situations is biomedicine most successful? In what situations does it fail to serve the needs of patients as well as alternative medical approaches?

3. Define medicalization. How and why are certain physical conditions medicalized? When is medicalization more harmful than helpful?

4. Describe the situation that faces immigrant doctors upon arriving in Canada. What barriers do they face to practising medicine in this country? Why do these barriers exist? What would happen if they did not exist?

5. Give an overview of Ivan Illich's critique of modern medicine. Do you agree or disagree with his views? Why?

READ ON

Suggested Print and Online Resources

Online

"50 Years of Medical Sociology"

http://somatosphere.net/2010/12/50-years-of-medical-sociology-html

- Eugene Raikhel reviews the fiftieth anniversary issue of the *Journal of Health and Social Behavior*, which looked back at a number of issues that had been tackled in the 50-year history of the journal. It is effectively an overview of issues in the history of medical sociology in the United States. Raikhel provides titles and abstracts of the special issue's contents, and the issue itself is available online at http://hsb.sagepub.com/content/51/1_suppl.

Medical Sociology Fact Sheet

www.ndsu.edu/socanth/sociology/careers_in_sociology/

- The sociology department at North Dakota State University provides "occupational tracks" to help students understand what jobs are open to students interested in different areas of sociology and what courses they will need to take. Go to this page to view the occupational track for medical/aging sociology, or one of the other areas you might be interested in.

Medical Sociology online (MSo)

www.medicalsociologyonline.org

- The British Sociology Association's free-access online journal provides its own articles, commentaries, and reviews, and acts as a portal to other news and information in the wider world of medical sociology.

Nursing Education in Nova Scotia: Male Nurses

http://forms.msvu.ca/library/tutorial/nhdp/history/malenurses.htm

- Mount Saint Vincent University is home to a fascinating archive of Nova Scotia's nursing history. This link features a 21-minute recording by Frank Graham, who shares his experiences as a male nursing student in the 1930s.

Female, Indigenous, Born in Canada, and First to . . .

www.kickaction.ca/files/female_indigenous_born_in_canada_did_it_first_list_april_3.pdf

- Sally Simpson's list of Indigenous firsts is proof that a sociology assignment can inspire important scholarship that will broaden the knowledge of others.

In Print

Tania Das Gupta (2009), *Real Nurses and Others: Racism in Nursing* (Halifax: Fernwood Publishing).

- Tania Das Gupta is a professor in the Department of Equity Studies at York University. This book is her study of the racism experienced by visible-minority nurses in Canada.

Michel Foucault (1973), *The Birth of the Clinic: An Archaeology of Medical Perception*, trans. A.M.S. Smith (New York: Vintage Books).

- Foucault's work offers a good look at the social processes involving the development of roles and practices in a medical setting.

Pat Grygier (1994), *A Long Way from Home: The Tuberculosis Epidemic among the Inuit* (Montreal: McGill–Queen's).

- Grygier provides an enlightening (and alarming) examination of how Inuit with tuberculosis were treated in Canada during the 1950s.

PART FIVE

Global Perspectives

The Environment

The Gist

Reading this chapter will help you to . . .

- Understand the vested interests that come into play when "scientific judgements" are made about the health of the environment.
- Identify the environmental effects of the China price.
- Discuss how environmental disasters can lead to positive social change.
- Describe how "race" and environmental practices intersect.

Terms of the Trade

- China price
- community of scholars
- environmental racism
- environmental refugees
- epidemiology
- genetically modified
- intersectionality

- moral community
- operational definition
- organizational culture
- peer-review process
- red herring
- rotten apple approach
- social ecology

- sociological imagination
- standpoint
- tobacco strategy
- vested interests
- victimology

Names to Know

- Murray Bookchin
- Samuel Henry Prince
- Lloyd Tataryn

For Starters

Not in My Country: Rich Countries Dumping Waste in Poor Countries

You may be familiar with the acronym NIMBY. It stands for "not in my backyard," and it comes up in the news whenever a community group is attempting to stop an undesirable outsider from setting up shop in the neighbourhood. Group homes, halfway houses, and legal medical marijuana grow-ops are among the "social pariahs" that tend to find opposition from NIMBYism. The term is often applied derisively to self-interested residents concerned that their comfortable way of life may be threatened by a project that serves the greater good of the community. In the international context, it describes the very real victimization of vulnerable nations by well-developed countries, including Canada, that are looking for dumping grounds for toxic garbage.

The African coastline, especially the waters of some of the poorer and least powerful countries, has for some time experienced environmental damage resulting from the actions of more powerful countries of the developed North. One reason for the rise

of modern piracy off the Somali coast is the decline in the ocean food resources—once a staple of the Somali economy—due to the offshore dumping of toxic waste. In 2006, the small West African country of Côte d'Ivoire had a health crisis on its hands owing to massive amounts of toxic waste dumped by a local contractor in some 12 sites in the port city of Abidjan, the country's capital. The culprit was the Netherlands-based oil and commodity shipping company Trafigura Beheer BV, using a ship licensed in Panama.

The Canadian story (unsurprisingly not well reported in the Canadian media) involves the illegal dumping of a hundred 40-foot container vans filled with what was labelled "heterogeneous plastic scrap materials" but what was actually mixed waste that included rotting food and used diapers (Gutierrez, 2016). The made-in-Canada waste was shipped from Vancouver to the Philippines by a private firm based in Ontario between 2013 and 2014. The containers have been leaking and present an environmental health hazard. Despite international petitions (I signed one) and political pressure from the Philippines and the United Nations, the Canadian government has done nothing to remedy the situation or prosecute the offending Canadian company, which argues it was in compliance with Canadian (if not international) law. The Philippines, which has received millions of Canadian dollars in tourism grants and disaster relief (following a typhoon that devastated Southeast Asia in 2013) is understandably reluctant to press the matter in international courts (Gutierrez, 2016).

This is one example of what is called **environmental racism**, which sets a double standard for management of the environment depending on the part of the world affected and the ethnicity of the people harmed. We will see other examples—too many—throughout this chapter.

Environmental Sociology: Science or *Social* Science?

Environmental sociology is a fast-growing subdiscipline. It examines our relationship with the environment, focusing especially on where we have gone wrong and looking for ways to reverse our mistakes in the future.

There is a lot of science involved in environmental studies—in proving climate change, in tracking carbon emissions and weather patterns, in testing the safety of drinking water—but sociology teaches us that the science of the environment is deeply embedded in a social context. The scientific world is political. Scientific facts cannot "speak for themselves"—they have interpreters who are part of the social world and who cannot always be trusted to report "the facts" without a distorting bias based on their place in that world, their standpoint.

Lloyd Tataryn is a Canadian investigative journalist who has written about the dangers in our environment, from the formaldehyde found in home insulation (1983) to the uranium mined at Elliot Lake (1976). His investigations often feature places where environmental science and politics collide. Consider the following passage from *Dying for a Living* (1979):

> The scientific truth must first run a political gauntlet. For after the authorities give their advice, and all the technical data is in, the decision arrived at is ultimately a political verdict and merely masquerades as a purely scientific ruling.
>
> Politicians, corporations, and unions are aware of this environmental fact of life. And since in the long run they must rely upon the combined political and scientific judgement of their technical advisors, they tend to choose as advisors scientists whose biases are similar to their own—scientists who are prone to ask the type of questions that produce answers which most often serve the interests of their employers. . . .
>
> Unfortunately, the public is seldom informed of the political, economic, and scientific biases which scientists in environmental health conflicts bring to their investigations. Most of us have been led to believe that "science" and "scientists" are above such considerations. (Tataryn, 1979: p. 90)

This book, now close to 40 years old, was written well before climate change became a topic in the popular media, and before the Northern Gateway pipeline was a gleam in Stephen Harper's eye. Do you think the situation Tataryn describes has changed?

Assessing Environmental Arguments: Two Keys for Social Scientists

Operational Definitions

In Chapter 2, we looked at the importance of establishing clear operational definitions for variables in social research. Operational definitions are essential to the process of creating policies concerning social issues. But it can be difficult to take abstract concepts such as poverty and abuse, and turn them into concrete, countable entities. All operational definitions "leak": they are imperfect, and sociologists, as scientists, often disagree on the best definition of a term. Scholarly debate can bring clarity to an operational definition, especially during the peer-review process, when the draft of an article, report, or book written by an academic researcher undergoes rigorous assessment by other experts in the field to ensure that it is suitable for publication. The author must take into consideration any and all criticisms before the work can be published. Eventually, through this scientific social process, the best leaky term or terms win out.

The peer review and the author's follow-up work of addressing and incorporating feedback from the community of scholars are steps in the social process that helps to advance the discipline as a whole. This practice is a well-developed and effective method of reaching consensus on an idea. But while the process is known to most scientists, it is not as familiar to people outside the scientific community. Among the outsiders are journalists, politicians, and corporate interest groups, who are often guided by non-scientific social processes and ideas, like the notions that there are two equally valid sides to every story, and that presenting a "balance of views" is always necessary. A classic example is the persistent attempt by American Christian groups to provide "balance" to the discussion of evolution by bringing forward non-scientific arguments in support of creationism and intelligent design. Only evolution is scientific.

In the study of the environment, the same difficulties are involved, with critical arguments hinging on abstract terms that are difficult to define. How would you begin to devise an operational definition for "pollution"? Where do you set the limits on "safe" versus "dangerous" or "acceptable" versus "unacceptable" levels of exposure to a particular toxin? The stakes are high when millions of dollars and people's lives are involved. Consider the following statement from uranium miner Gus Frobel, who later died from the cancer that he rightfully believed was caused by his working conditions:

> When you read the scientific papers you find the really knowledgeable scientists, the experts in the field, don't use the term "safe" level of exposure. They know they can't defend it scientifically. They say that to their knowledge there is no "safe" level. Some use the term "acceptable level." Now what's an "acceptable level?" That means some men have to die—but how many? How many deaths are acceptable? (Tataryn, 1979: p. 100)

Pollution is like poverty. Just as you can tell when someone is very poor (a person sleeping on the street is definitely poor), so you can tell when water or air is extremely polluted: it smells bad, looks horrible, and makes you sick. Extremes are easy to identify. Finding the line that separates "polluted" from "not polluted" is not so easy—it takes a scientific approach to get there. It is especially difficult when the damaging effects of pollution may not become apparent for many years. If it takes 20 years for an asbestos mine worker to die from exposure to an unsafe level of asbestos in the air, it could take 20 years for a hypothesis of what constitutes an "unsafe level of exposure" to be proven true, although reasonably sound predictions can be made earlier.

Jan Will/iStockphoto

Ice-o-lation. How would you go about drafting an operational definition for "climate change"? Whom would you consult? Whom would you not consult? What vested interests might be involved in the varying answers you receive?

Operational definition thus becomes a key aspect of environmental debates. In any discussion of the environment, look closely for abstract terms. Are they carefully defined? Do the definitions look sound? How were the definitions arrived at? Do the people presenting the information use the words "significant" or "serious" without explaining what they mean by them? The answers to these questions will tell you a lot about whether a particular argument is being fought more on scientific grounds or political ones.

Vested Interests

Even when operational definitions of an environmental argument have been assessed, important sociological questions remain. Who paid for any research studies cited in the argument? Who stands to benefit or lose from a particular test result? Politics are involved in environmental research, especially when some social policy is being proposed, implemented, attacked, or defended. That's why it is important to identify the vested interests surrounding any argument about the environment.

A vested interest is any social or financial interest a party may have in the results of a scientific study and the way those results are interpreted, particularly if the interest is strong enough to override the interest of ensuring those results are accurate, or "truthful." Although scientific measurement can be precise, the interpretation of data can be highly subjective. Give two scientists the same numbers, and they may come up with two very different interpretations.

The way operational definitions are derived may be influenced by the vested interests of the person designing the study or interpreting the results. It is statistically predictable that if one scientist is paid by a mining company, that scientist is likely to have a lower threshold for what constitutes a safe level of exposure to the material being mined, and will be more likely than an impartial scientist to give workers a clean bill of health. A scientist paid by the miners' union or one who is an independent researcher at a local university or hospital will have a different view.

For example, by 1960, there were 63 published scientific papers on the effects of exposure to asbestos. Eleven of those papers were sponsored by the asbestos industry; 52 were published by hospital and medical school staff. The papers sponsored by the "industry 11" all claimed to show there was no relationship between asbestos exposure and cancer, and played down the seriousness of asbestosis. The papers published by the "independent 52" drew

Quick Hits

Oreskes and Conway on Two Scientific Mercenaries

In the following passage, Naomi Oreskes and Erik Conway describe the practices of Frederick Seitz and Siegfried Singer. Both were scientists who had produced legitimate research in physics before their connections with conservative American government administrations and industry interests seriously affected the scientific credibility of their work:

> From 1979 to 1985, Fred Seitz directed a program for R.J. Reynolds Tobacco Company that distributed $45 million to scientists around the country for biomedical research that could generate evidence and cultivate experts to be used in court to defend the "product." In the mid-1990s, Fred Singer co-authored a major report attacking the US Environmental Protection Agency [EPA] over the health risks of second-hand smoke. Several years earlier, the US surgeon general had declared that second-hand smoke was hazardous not only to smokers' health, but to anyone exposed to it. Singer attacked this finding, claiming the work was rigged, and that the EPA review of the science—done by leading experts from around the country— was distorted by a political agenda to expand government control over all aspects of our lives. Singer's anti-EPA report was funded by the Tobacco Institute, channeled through a think tank, the [conservative, climate change denying] Alexis de Tocqueville Institution. (Oreskes & Conway, 2010: pp. 5–6)

connections between asbestos and cancer, and made a strong case for the destructiveness of asbestosis on the human body. As Lloyd Tataryn concluded, "Clearly the perspectives of the doctors writing the reports were influenced by whether they were employed treating the victims of the diseases, or hired by the perpetrator" (Tataryn, 1979: p. 31).

An important work on the subject of vested interest is Naomi Oreskes and Erik Conway's *Merchants of Doubt: How a Handful of Scientists Obscured the Truth on Issues from Tobacco Smoke to Global Warming* (2010). They assert that the same tactics (often, the same scientists) are deployed to manufacture and market doubt about environmental concerns and health issues caused by huge multinational companies. These scientists can be considered *scientific mercenaries*. Their dedication to science is secondary to their dedication to

a conservative, pro-industry political agenda. They fight "good" science with "bad" science in the name of industry, following the blueprint of the tobacco strategy, an early large-scale application of the tactics. In the 1950s scientists began to understand how damaging cigarette smoking could be to one's health. By the 1960s the community of scholars knew it, but the tobacco industry successfully paid teams of scientists to combat the growing evidence, forestalling the onslaught of successful lawsuits against the industry until the 1990s.

When searching for vested interests, it is always important to trace the science back to its social location. Many of the think-tanks, institutes, and other organizations that publish reports are funded by large companies, so they tend to be conservative. For example, the climate change–attacking Friends of Science is an organization founded by oil industry

What do YOU think?

Imagine that a large petroleum-exporting company wanted to run a natural gas pipeline through your community. Who would you trust to give you reliable information on its safety: an engineer employed by the company? An environmental regulator working for the federal government (whose job status might be affected by a negative report)? A university professor whose research is funded by a grant? An activist working for a charitable organization dedicated to saving the environment? What are the vested interests of each party?

geologists and funded by oil companies. They generally take positions that support the big business agenda while downplaying or dismissing potential harm to the environment or industry-related health risks. University researchers are generally more reliable concerning environmental issues, but check first to see who funds their work.

The tobacco strategy has been used by other deniers of science, to dispute other facts including acid rain, ozone layer depletion, and, most recently, human-produced climate change.

Social Ecology

There is a growing awareness of the human role in environmental issues, from the importance of household recycling to the dangers of our carbon emissions. As is written in many self-help books, the first and hardest step is acknowledging you have a problem. This is a key tenet of social ecology, a school of thought founded by American thinker and ecologist **Murray Bookchin** (1921–2006). He explained social ecology as follows:

> What literally defines social ecology as "social" is its recognition of the often overlooked fact that nearly all our present ecological problems arise from deep-seated social problems. Conversely, present ecological problems cannot be clearly understood, much less resolved, without resolutely dealing with problems within society. To make this point more concrete: economic, ethnic, cultural, and gender conflicts, among many others, lie at the core of the most serious ecological dislocations we face today.... (Bookchin, 1996)

Stanford Research into the Impact of Tobacco Advertising (SRITA)

[*Opposite*] Having grown up in an age where the dangers of tobacco use are well established, you might find it easy to scoff at the naiveté of magazine readers in the first half of the twentieth century who found this kind of advertising compelling. But be honest: how often do you find yourself picking up the skincare product, toothpaste, or pain-relief medication that is advertised as "doctor-recommended" or "clinically proven"? [*Left*] The Scientific Division of the US Tobacco Institute put out this ad encouraging readers to get the whole story on second-hand smoke. Look at how the argument is crafted. Is it effective?

Our Stories

The Big Business behind the UFFI Disaster: A Case of Vested Interests

Citizens depend on their governments to protect them from the harmful effects of industrial pollution. Government agencies study the health impacts of different manufacturing materials, approving the ones that are safe and recommending bans on the ones that are not. The system fails when government has a vested interest in promoting an unsafe product. A Canadian case in point surrounds the widespread use of urea formaldehyde foam insulation (UFFI) during the late 1970s and 1980s.

Formaldehyde is a chemical with many uses. It is an ingredient of a glue used to bind wood fibres together in such products as particle board, chipboard, and plywood. In Canada in the 1960s, it was introduced as foam insulation.

Complaints about the formaldehyde-based insulation began to surface in the 1970s, primarily in northern European countries such as Denmark, Sweden, and the Netherlands, where governments were generally quick to respond to concerns around industrial pollution. There were reports that the foam encouraged harmful fungal growth. Also, the formaldehyde-based glue used in composite wood products was causing allergic reactions and respiratory problems among

In 1977, the same year as CHIP, Canadians had developed an energy-efficient solar-paneled better-insulated house that required very little energy input to heat. Why do you think the UFFI insulation took off instead of energy-efficient houses? How much of our purchasing decisions are influenced by corporations in ways we don't even realize?

people living in mobile homes, where particleboard and plywood were among the principal building materials. What's more, UFFI was not proving effective as an insulation material. Canada's own National Research Council (NRC) had tested the foam and found it liable

To get a better sense of how a social ecologist might view the relationship between social conflict and environmental issues, we will look at the role of class conflict in the context of industrial pollution.

Industrial Pollution and Social Ecology

We can adopt a social ecology approach to better understand how the exposure of workers to unsafe environmental conditions reflects larger trends in the issue of industrial pollution. First, in order for

workers to be placed in this situation, it requires the complicity of the employer—the company that requires the work—and sometimes the government, which is ultimately responsible for overseeing environmental protection as well as workplace safety. As Lloyd Tataryn notes:

> Today, people who work and live in contaminated environments serve as early warning systems for toxic substances, much like the ancient royal food tasters and the canaries the coal miners

to shrink, crack, and crumble, greatly decreasing its value as an insulator.

Why then, in the light of these ominous findings, did Canada's government continue to endorse the use of formaldehyde-based products?

A pivotal event occurred in the mid-1970s, when the Organization of Petroleum Exporting Countries (OPEC), representing the world's major oil-producing countries, declared an embargo against the West, creating an oil shortage that led to a sharp rise in North American and European gas and oil prices. The industry solution was to promote greater use of insulation to improve the efficiency of heating in homes and workplaces. Formaldehyde-based insulation was a key part of this proposal, which required the approval of various federal agencies, including the Canadian General Standards Board (CGSB) and the Canada Mortgage and Housing Corporation (CMHC). These government regulatory bodies were ill prepared to counter the strong-arm tactics of the chemical companies. Moreover, the government itself was in a conflict of interest, as the federally financed Canadian Development Corporation owned 40 per cent of one of the foam-producing chemical companies.

In 1977, the federal government announced the Canadian Home Insulation Program (CHIP), which provided financial incentives to homeowners to upgrade their insulation. Some 80,000 Canadian homeowners registered for CHIP. The government set standards on the percentage of formaldehyde that could be used in UFFI products, but these limits were voluntary, not enforceable, and therefore largely ignored. No consideration was given to the health of contractors installing the insulation.

By 1978, homeowners began to complain about the deteriorating quality of foam insulation and its effects on health. In 1979, Massachusetts became the first jurisdiction to ban UFFI, a move influenced by a scientific study that had found a link between formaldehyde and cancer. Chemical companies responded with an industry-funded conference in 1980, in which 22 of the 26 papers delivered were by industry "experts" who defended the safety and reliability of the product. They argued against any form of regulation.

In December 1980, urea formaldehyde foam insulation was banned in Canada. Homeowners and contractors installing the product were left stranded.

What do YOU think?

1. What should government agencies and the government have done in this situation?
2. Is there anything that personal consumers can do in this situation to protect themselves from being overly influenced by chemical corporations and big business? Is it realistic to expect individual consumers to take these precautions?

once trundled underground to test the air. Workers and those who live in the shadow of polluting industries are the first people to encounter intense and prolonged exposure to toxic wastes. Much of what is known about environmental health and the consequences of exposure to poisonous and cancer-causing materials has been learned from examining disease patterns among workers and exposed populations. Exposure standards are usually established once an unusual pattern of disease has been detected. In this way workers and people living in industrially contaminated environments act as guinea pigs for the rest of society. (Tataryn, 1979: p. 1)

There appear to be two different ways of interpreting workplace-related illness and injury. The first is the social ecology view, which sees these as essentially *social* in their origin and in the way that they are dealt with. Working conditions are set in place by a company and monitored in varying degrees by the political authorities in an area. This reflects C. Wright Mills's notion of the sociological imagination, in which individual problems and situations readily connect with the broader social structure and its processes. The workers are not in a position to oppose the company's unsafe environmental practices. This is essentially a class conflict. What does that say about industrial pollution on a larger scale?

A sociologically *uninformed* way of interpreting workplace illness is to keep it individual and personal, reflecting the individual choices and physical constitution of the person afflicted. Far from being symptomatic of broader social processes, a worker's disease is viewed as a result of personal choices taken by the individual worker: smoking, drinking, lack of exercise, and poor lifestyle choices in general. With this view, injuries happen at job sites because workers are careless (a viewpoint reflected in early commercials promoting workplace safety as an individual responsibility). It would be wrong to say that individuals are powerless to play a role in workplace safety; however, this second view leans too far in the direction of William Ryan's notion of blaming the victim. It's a recurring theme—watch for it in sections that follow.

What do YOU think?

1. Consider a common workplace setting, such as a warehouse, and a common workplace injury, such as lower back pain. Who should take the greater share of responsibility for ensuring worker safety in this context: the employer or the employee? Now apply the same question to carpal tunnel syndrome suffered by secretaries whose jobs consist mainly of keyboarding. Is your answer the same?
2. What does Tataryn mean when he calls people who work in or live near polluting industries "human canaries"?

The Asbestos Industry: Dying for a Living

It has long been known that asbestos is hazardous to human health. Roman writers in the second century CE noted that those who spun its threads into valuable robes often became sick. By the early twentieth century, some North American insurance companies were refusing to insure asbestos workers, recognizing that these employees had relatively low chances of long-term survival at the job. In 2012, a consortium of epidemiology organizations from around the world issued a position statement on asbestos, declaring their opinion that "all types of asbestos fibre are causally implicated in the development of various diseases and premature death" (JPC-SE, 2012: p. 2). These diseases include lung cancer, mesothelioma, and asbestosis.

Canada became a major producer of asbestos in 1879, when the fibrous mineral was first mined in Thetford Mines, Quebec. In the early twentieth century, other jurisdictions began to observe standards of what was considered "acceptable" risk of exposure, a figure first set at 35 fibres per cubic centimetre in 1938, before falling, with further study, to 12, then 5, then 2. By contrast, Thetford Mines, the world's largest producer of asbestos, observed no such standard until 1978, when it finally bowed to media and public pressure by adopting limits of "acceptable" exposure. In the mid-1970s, a worker at another Canadian mine, Paul Formby, discovered levels ranging from 30 to 50 fibres per cubic centimetre where he was working.

It is not just the miners who have been exposed to the environmental hazards of asbestos:

> Towering over the town of Thetford Mines are massive grey piles of asbestos tailings. These tailings poke their way like giant fingers into sections of the town, spilling asbestos waste into the yards of many of the homes. Positioned on top of the tailings are machines called swivel pilers, constantly spraying out clouds of asbestos waste, a practice that Mount Sinai's doctors say would be illegal in the United States. Thetford's tailings daily grow higher and higher, leaving the town covered in grey dust. (Tataryn, 1979: p. 23)

The prevailing attitude in a one-industry town like Thetford Mines is often one that defends the business that brings food to the table, even in the face of environmental health studies with grave conclusions about the health risks to the town's citizens. In a 2007 article, one retired miner, who had worked in the mines for 38 years, articulated this view:

> Those people who had their houses tested [for asbestos] are just whiners, looking for compensation. . . . We made a very good

The Point Is...

Does Disaster Bring Positive Social Change?

Central to the social ecology viewpoint is the idea that environmental problems reproduce—and even arise from—existing social problems. We can consider this idea in the context of "natural" environmental disasters. But can they produce positive social change?

Samuel Henry Prince (1886–1962) was an influential Canadian sociologist who taught in Halifax at King's University (now part of Dalhousie University) from 1924 until 1955. The breadth of his interests and the way they guided him along a path of policy sociology are summarized nicely by Leonard Hatfield:

> [T]he mental health movement, social planning in Halifax, housing reform, social work education, prison reform, juvenile corrections, family case work, and improved services for the mentally handicapped all became his special concerns and the centre of his activities for the most productive years of his life. (Hatfield, 1990: pp. 8–9).

An ordained Anglican minister, Prince received his PhD in sociology in 1919 from Columbia University, where his doctoral dissertation involved pioneering work on "disaster" as a sociological context for social change. His study dealt with the Halifax Explosion of 1917, in which a docked naval vessel carrying explosives caught fire and blew up in Halifax Harbour, rocking the city of some 50,000 with blast, fire, and floods that killed nearly 2,000 people. Prince's hypothesis was that a disaster can lead to significant social change. In Halifax,

> the shock resulted in disintegration of social institutions, dislocation of the usual methods of social control and dissolution of the customary; that through the catastrophe the community was thrown into the state of flux which . . . is the logical and natural prerequisite for social change. . . . [T]he shock was of a character such as "to affect all individuals alike at the same time," and to induce that degree of fluidity most favorable to social change. (Prince, 1920)

Prince demonstrated how this disaster led to a broad variety of changes, including the improvement of public transportation and a building code that would gradually replace the previous wood-dominated housing with building using materials less likely to burn. His argument that catastrophe can lead to positive social change is an important and contentious sociological point, and we will take it up in a moment in the context of Hurricane Katrina, which hit New Orleans in 2005. The Halifax Explosion was nothing like the natural event that Hurricane Katrina was, but it caused environmental devastation on a comparable scale, and Prince's work has great relevance in an investigation of the aftermath of Hurricane Katrina.

First, though, we should point out that Prince's work reflects a greater sense of positivism than one finds in current work taking the social ecology approach. Contemporary studies tend to support the hypothesis that there is a direct connection between social and environmental problems. So-called natural disasters occur in a social context. They have different impacts on groups of people occupying different social locations within the same basic geographical location. The effects of gender, "race," ethnicity, class, age, and (dis)ability are all felt by the victims of natural disasters. The greatest number of victims of Hurricane Katrina were black, female, poor, and disabled. The greater the number of those social features you possessed (remember the concept of intersectionality), the more likely you were to suffer, or even die, from the natural effects of the storm and the social response to the storm. It illustrates the concept of environmental racism introduced at the start of the chapter as well.

So what of Prince's hypothesis that disaster brings positive social change? Rebuilding in New Orleans tended to benefit large, well-connected companies that were able to obtain government reconstruction contracts. Privately run schools that best serve the well-to-do have secured education contracts in the city at a cost to the public system. Even though the city is now better protected and prepared for the natural aspects of a future hurricane (the damage from Hurricane Isaac in August 2012 was considerably less), it would be inaccurate to say that Hurricane Katrina has brought significant positive social change to New Orleans, or that the city is better off than it was before the storms of 2005.

living in the mines, and I don't regret it for a minute. . . . It's paranoia. It's just like smoking. I know lots of people who smoke and live to be 80 or 90 years old. (cited in Lalonde, 2007)

While some of his colleagues had died of asbestos-caused illnesses, the miner, according to the article, believed the deaths were owing to "a vulnerability on their part" (Lalonde, 2007).

While studies of the health risks of asbestos exposure were being carried out and debated, the provincial government of Quebec and Canada's federal government continued to promote the use of asbestos products, particularly in developing countries, the destination for 90 per cent of the 150,000 tonnes of asbestos produced in Canada. It was not until September 2012, shortly after the last Canadian asbestos mine closed, that the federal Conservative government announced it would no longer oppose global rules restricting the use and shipment of asbestos (CBC News, 2012).

The Canadian government still has not followed the lead of other countries by banning asbestos altogether. According to journalist Tavia Grant, Canada continues to import products containing asbestos, such as brake pads and pipes (Grant, 2015). However, in July 2015, Health Canada revised its long-held position that asbestos was dangerous only when inhaled "in significant quantities"; the agency now states plainly that "breathing in asbestos fibres can cause cancer and other diseases" (Grant, 2015).

What do YOU think?

Why do you think Canada's government promoted asbestos use primarily in developing countries? Can Canada's policy be characterized as an instance of environmental racism?

Paul Formby: Environmental Hero in the Fight against Asbestos

After graduating in philosophy from the University of British Columbia, Paul Formby felt the call of the Canadian north. In the early 1970s he travelled to Clinton Creek, Yukon, where he started work in the asbestos mine. He soon wound up in charge of the

Francis Vachon/TCPI/The Canadian Press

Rising majestically behind this row of houses in Thetford Mines is a large tailings pile from the town's asbestos quarry. How comfortable would you feel living in one of these houses? Describe the social profile of the typical resident of this street.

health and safety committee of the miner's union—an often thankless task—where he encountered significant resistance from the mining company. He explains:

> As far as the company was concerned, . . . asbestos dust levels were a taboo subject. From the company's point of view the most important safety measure was safety glasses. As long as we all wore safety glasses everything was supposed to be OK. It was almost as if it was more important to keep the stuff out of our eyes than out of our lungs. By arguing in this way, the company was trying to shift the responsibility for health and safety off of its shoulders and onto ours. The company refused to admit that the work environment it created could possibly be hazardous to its workers. (cited in Tataryn, 1979: p. 20)

At issue was the union's right to test the air for asbestos contamination, as well as the company's questionable claim that the white asbestos (chrysotile) that they were mining was far safer than the dangerous blue asbestos (crocidolite) found in the mines of South Africa and Australia. This is a red herring: a logical fallacy in which an irrelevant topic is introduced in an argument in order to divert attention from the original and more important issue (in this case, the hazards of chrysotile). Company management and physicians may have believed in the safety of white asbestos, but their lives were never endangered the way that those of the miners were:

> During contract negotiations the company absolutely refused to discuss the union's right to test the air. . . . The management stated emphatically that asbestos dust levels were not an issue in Clinton Creek. Furthermore, they assured me that the white asbestos found in Canada was so safe I could pour it on my breakfast cereal every morning and suffer no ill effects. The bad stuff, they said, was the blue asbestos that is mined only in South Africa. (Formby, in Tataryn, 1979: p. 21)

Formby remained unconvinced, and decided to take his inquires further afield. In early 1974

he expressed his concerns in a letter to Dr Irving Selikoff, the head of the environmental sciences laboratory at New York's Mount Sinai Medical School and a leading authority on asbestos-related lung cancer and asbestosis (the scarring of the lung by the body's reaction to the indestructible fibres of asbestos entering the lungs). Selikoff wrote back, confirming that Formby's concerns were valid, and taking issue with the supposed "safety" of the white asbestos.

Formby then asked for and received a leave of absence from work. He travelled across the continent to New York, and walked into Mount Sinai Hospital asking to be trained in taking air samples to test for asbestos fibres. Hospital officials were surprisingly sympathetic and accommodating. Rather than treating him like a fanatic, they agreed to train him.

Formby next went to Montreal to contact the union that represented the workers in Thetford Mines, home to Canada's largest asbestos mine. There he spoke with the union's health and safety representative about testing for asbestos particles in the air. Formby was well received, and was assisted in carrying out tests on the air quality at the mine.

For Formby, it was then back to Clinton Creek, where he secretly tested the air there—and then quit. After that he went south to conduct air quality tests at the mine in Cassiar, British Columbia (closed, since 1992, after 40 years in existence). Living out of a suitcase, and occasionally sleeping in his old car, Formby went back to Thetford Mines, where he trained the miners to collect air samples. They had to do this in secret, as their actions were considered by the company as grounds for suspension or dismissal.

Formby had samples from the three mines sent to Mount Sinai Hospital for testing. The union at Thetford Mines arranged to have a team of doctors and technical experts, Canadian and American, visit the mine to examine the workers for signs of asbestosis and cancer. Although the miners had previously received class "A" health ratings from the doctors who worked for the mining company, the independent experts found many sick, some dying.

Paul Formby significantly raised the profile of the dangers of asbestos, both for miners and for other workers (such as builders) exposed to the deadly material. His work spawned awareness-raising documentaries and government actions that have reduced (but not eliminated) the risks of human exposure to asbestos.

In July 2015, Health Canada finally changed the information on its website, which had long maintained that chrysotile was "less potent" and less dangerous than other forms of asbestos (Grant, 2015).

Industrial Communities and the Disposable People of Pollution

The story of Thetford Mines and Asbestos, Quebec—towns whose names are synonymous with the industry they revolve around—underline the fact that it is not just workers who are exposed to the hazardous pollutants produced by environmentally unfriendly companies. Also affected are the communities surrounding these dangerous enterprises. Again, we find the social ecology approach useful in examining how the poor and marginalized communities are usually the ones most powerfully affected. An illustrative case is that of the chemical giant Monsanto and the tiny city of Anniston, Alabama.

The Industrial Contamination of Anniston, Alabama

The following is a classic case of environmental racism. A little background information is necessary. Monsanto has, since its origin in 1901, manufactured and distributed some of the most toxic chemicals ever produced. Specifically, the company was involved in the production and sale of polychlorinated biphenyls, or PCBs, from 1929 until the early 1980s, when the substance was effectively banned through a series of regulations. What are PCBs? In the words of journalist Marie-Monique Robin, "for half a century they colonized the planet; they were used as coolants in electric transformers and industrial hydraulic machines, but also as lubricants in applications as varied as plastics, paint, ink, and paper" (Robin, 2010: p. 11).

Monsanto also produced the deadly compound dioxin. It was used as an ingredient in Agent Orange,

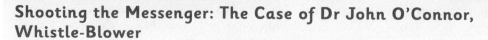

Our Stories

Shooting the Messenger: The Case of Dr John O'Connor, Whistle-Blower

John O'Connor served as a physician in northern Alberta from 1993, spending much of this time in the oil sands boomtown of Fort McMurray. In 2001 he started working with the Indigenous community of Fort Chipewyan, population 1,200, located a little way downriver from the sands. Shortly after beginning to work with the Fort Chipewyan community, whose elders told O'Connor about new deformities they were seeing in fish—a staple of their diet—along with a peculiar oily taste, the doctor began to notice evidence of health problems he hadn't seen in Fort McMurray. Specifically, he observed new cases of cholangiocarcinoma, a rare bile duct cancer that had killed his father, and that often showed up in bile ducts of fish swimming in oil-infested water. He also found a high incidence of liver cancers.

When Dr O'Connor began publicly articulating his concerns, Canada's federal agency, Health Canada, approached the community for its medical files. One government representative even made a very public

visit to declare the water fit for consumption. He demonstrated this with a rather unscientific gesture: at the local nursing station, he filled his mouth with water from a tap and announced to an attending *Globe and Mail* reporter: "There's nothing wrong with the water in Fort Chip."

Health Canada presented the findings of their report to the Alberta Energy and Utilities Board in Fort McMurray one week *before* they spoke with members of the Fort Chipewyan community about their experience. After a quick analysis of the data set, which mysteriously omitted statistics from 2004 and 2005, the agency gave the community a clean bill of health.

The agency's work didn't end there, as O'Connor, in a statement given in the House of Commons in June 2009, explained:

> In 2007 I got a large envelope in the mail from the College of Physicians and Surgeons

the notorious broad-based plant killer and defoliant that was dumped in massive quantities on the jungles and people of Vietnam by the US during the Vietnam War to deprive the enemy fighters of cover. So powerful was Agent Orange that plants still do not grow around an airport in western Newfoundland where the chemical was tested during the 1970s (personal observation, 2013). Then there are the other deadly D's, including 2-4-D (a component of Agent Orange, used for a time in household weed killers) and the environmentally toxic insecticide DDT. Monsanto also produces the controversial artificial sweetener aspartame. If you try to research aspartame to see whether or not it is carcinogenic, you will get two different kinds of responses: one from those friendly to Monsanto, and another from neutral scientists (see, for example, a 2010 article in the *American Journal of Industrial Medicine*, which presents a link between aspartame and cancers of the lung and liver in male mice: Soffritti et al., 2010).

And now I will tell the story of the small city of Anniston.

Situated in Calhoun County, Alabama, Anniston was home to a Monsanto production facility for PCBs beginning in 1929. Most of the workers at Monsanto's plant in Anniston were black. Many of them lived in the neighbourhoods surrounding the plant, which were likewise predominantly black. During the 1930s, Monsanto was already receiving and documenting warnings about the deadly nature of PCBs to anyone in close contact with the toxic compound, and the company continued to acquire and file away such information until they stopped producing PCBs in 1971. During this time, they did nothing to warn or protect either their workers or their Anniston neighbours.

The truth of Anniston's PCB contamination began to emerge in a series of news items in 2002. By 2005, the US Environmental Protection Agency (EPA) was reporting that 60 million pounds of PCBs

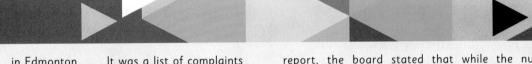

in Edmonton. . . . It was a list of complaints that Health Canada had laid about my activities in Fort Chip. They accused me of blocking access to files, billing irregularities, engendering a sense of mistrust in government in Fort Chip, and causing undue alarm in the community. (Canada, 2009)

It was the first time that a Canadian government agency had ever used a patient complaint process to attack a physician in this way. The charges were serious and could have led to the suspension—temporary or permanent—of O'Connor's licence to practise medicine. The first three charges were dismissed relatively quickly. The people of Fort Chipewyan, who hadn't been consulted concerning whether they felt "undue alarm," supported him, and in fact requested the dismissal of Health Canada's senior physician. Members of the Alberta Medical Association were unanimous in their support.

In 2008 the Alberta Cancer Board engaged in a more comprehensive study of the community, releasing their findings in February 2009. In their

report, the board stated that while the number of cases of cholangiocarcinoma and colon cancer were "within the expected range" during the period of investigation,

> [t]he number of cancer cases overall was higher than expected. In particular, increases of observed over expected were found for biliary tract cancers as a group and cancers of the blood and lymphatic system. These increases were based on a small number of cases and could be due to chance or increased detection. The possibility that the increased rate is due to increased risk in the community, however, cannot be ruled out. (Alberta Cancer Board, 2009: p. 10)

The board concluded that further study was warranted to see if there was any risk associated with living in Fort Chipewyan. In November 2009, the charge against O'Connor of "causing undue alarm" was dropped. In 2015, he was fired from the Nunee Health Board in Fort Chipewyan with no explanation.

had been emitted into the atmosphere surrounding Anniston. A nearly equivalent amount—68 million pounds—of PCB-contaminated waste had been dumped at a disposal site in Anniston, while 1.8 million pounds of PCBs had been poured into local streams, where the locals sometimes fished for food. The reported effects on the health of Anniston's residents included rare cancers, brain tumours, miscarriages, and brain damage to infants and children caused by contaminated breast milk.

Monsanto had taken steps to limit the legal damage it knew could result from any discovery of the extent of contamination. They had begun to buy up homes surrounding the disposal site, offering "good money" in exchange for a written promise from any seller not to sue the company. In 1997, Monsanto sold its industrial chemical division, which included the factory at Anniston, to another company, Solutia Inc., in a move widely seen as an attempt to evade financial liability in lawsuits the company was anticipating.

Nevertheless, in 2002, Monsanto and Solutia were successfully sued in a class action suit by former employees and the citizens of Anniston. Money was awarded to the individual plaintiffs based on the quantities of PCB in their blood, with the cutoff being 20 parts per million (ppm)—10 times the acceptable rate. Under these conditions, only 15 per cent of the plaintiffs qualified for compensation, up to a maximum of US$500,000. One of the leaders of the lawsuit, David Barker, whose brother had died of cancer at 17, had a bloodstream PCB level of 341 ppm—170 times the acceptable level—and was awarded $33,000.

As Marie-Monique Robin reports, the jury's decision was unequivocally condemning:

> The legal grounds for the verdict were "negligence, wantonness, fraud, trespass, nuisance, and outrage," and it included a harsh judgment of Monsanto's conduct, which was "so outrageous in character and

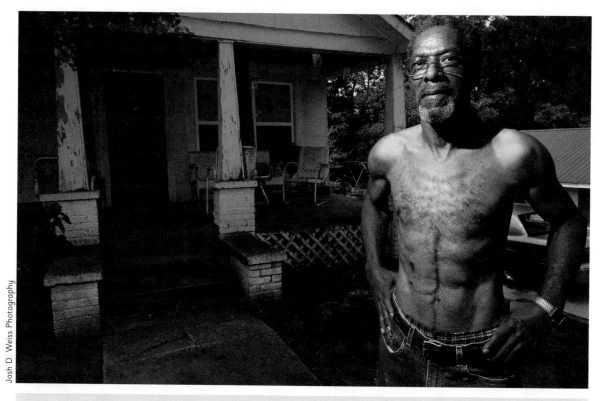

Josh D. Weiss Photography

Vernon Powell and his wife received about US$20,000 between them from the settlement of the lawsuit against Monsanto. He owes thousands in medical bills (remember this is the US—no publicly funded health care system), and his stomach bears the scars of surgeries he says were necessary because of PCBs. Looking at the community of Anniston, why do you think that Monsanto thought it was "safe" to pollute there?

extreme in degree as to go beyond all possible bounds of decency, so as to be regarded as atrocious and utterly intolerable in civilized society." (Robin, 2010: p. 27)

How could a company conduct business in this way? Is it arrogance, cynicism, or plain greed? Sociologists might look at the organizational culture of such a huge corporate entity, whereby the company and the work it does become a part of the individual identity of the employees working there, especially those at the upper level. They might draw on Durkheim's study of religions, drawing on his notion of a moral community, where individuals have shared mutual identities and a commitment to a common purpose. It's a situation that fosters group loyalty—the kind that is strengthened when the group with which you identify is threatened by outsiders. In war your first loyalty is to those beside you in the trenches. But the situation can also be viewed as a reflection of prevailing class and "race" relations, where the majority of those in positions of power—the scientists and administrators who

directed company policy—were white, while the non-corporate members, the "Other," were predominantly black and without power, and therefore more disposable.

Monsanto Again: A Canadian Connection

Consider for a moment the different ways of owning the environment. You can own a piece of property. You might own the rights to the resources beneath the surface, and to the plants growing on top. But what about owning an entire biology entity, patenting a life form? The following case involves a Canadian farmer and the chemical giant Monsanto. It's a David and Goliath story, only in this instance, Goliath wins.

Born in Bruno, Saskatchewan in 1930, Percy Schmeiser grows canola, the oily seed plant formerly known as rapeseed. He has been mayor of his small town and a local member of the Legislative Assembly. He has worked his 1,500 acre farm for over 50 years.

In 1997, Schmeiser sprayed the ditches bordering his land with Roundup, a trademarked weed

Quick Hits

Eight Questions about the Environment of the Workplace

At the end of his chapter on the dangers of working with asbestos, Lloyd Tataryn poses 10 questions applicable to all potentially unsafe workplace and living environments (Tataryn, 1979: pp. 58–60). I have cut the list down to eight and modified the questions to make them more relevant to the current context.

1. Is it important to prevent panic among people exposed or even possibly exposed to a health hazard?
2. How do you balance an employer's obligation to provide a safe working environment with a worker's willingness to accept certain risks (and "danger pay") for reasonably well-paying jobs?
3. Whose primary responsibility is it to oversee working conditions to ensure their safety? Does responsibility rest with the company, the industry, government protection agencies at the municipal, provincial, and/or federal level, the union, or an outside watchdog group? How might such groups work together?

4. What responsibility does the industry have regarding the health of those who do not work for the company but who live and work nearby?
5. As a city or town, how do you balance the benefits of hosting a large company that employs local citizens and pays salaries that are spent in the community with the need to guarantee safe working and living conditions by ensuring the company is environmentally responsible?
6. Economic risk is often presented as a reason that owners and executives receive much higher pay than ordinary workers. Should health risk be part of that equation?
7. Should decisions about what constitutes an "acceptable" level of health risk require the approval of those placed in situations of greatest risk?
8. How can it be guaranteed that industry-hired "experts" are objective and trustworthy in compiling and presenting their observations on a particular company's environmental practices?

killer produced by Monsanto. Unfortunately, he found that it was ineffective in killing the plants that were threatening to encroach on his canola fields. After consulting with a Monsanto representative, Schmeiser learned the source of his problem: the encroaching plants were a Monsanto-patented "Roundup-Ready Canola" meaning that they were grown from a Monsanto-engineered seed made to be resistant to a Monsanto-engineered weed killer.

The following year, Schmeiser replanted his fields using seeds from the previous year's crops, as is common practice. In August, around harvest time, he was contacted by a Monsanto representative who informed him that inspectors had, without notifying him (much less asking for permission), trespassed on Schmeiser's property and taken a sample of his crops. Laboratory analysis provided evidence that the canola crops were of the patented Monsanto variety. The representative proposed that

Schmeiser agree to a settlement for compensation or else be sued by the multinational company.

Schmeiser opted not to settle, and a court battle followed. "Experts" disagreed over the percentage of plants affected. Schmeiser lost the first case, with the judge ruling as follows:

> [A] farmer whose field contains seed or plants originating from seed spilled into them, or blown as seed, in swaths from a neighbor's land, or even growing from germination by pollen carried into his field from elsewhere by insects, birds, or by the wind, may own the seed or plants on his land even if he did not set about to plant them. He does not, however, own the right to the use of the patented gene or cell [since] growth of the seed, reproducing the patented gene and cell, and sale

Moe Doiron/The Globe and Mail/CP

This genetically modified pig, developed at the University of Guelph, provides a distinct advantage over regular pigs: its pig poo is environmentally friendly! If you're a bacon lover, would you have any reservations about eating meat from a genetically modified pig? If you're a vegetarian, how do you feel about the fact that many soy products are made with genetically modified soybeans? Overall, what are the benefits and dangers of consuming food with genetically modified ingredients?

of the harvested crop constitutes taking the essence of the plaintiff's invention and using it without permission. (as cited in Robin, 2010: p. 215)

Schmeiser's "crime," in other words, was not harvesting the Monsanto-patented canola plants that happened to be growing in his field, but inadvertently using seeds from those plants to plant his next year's crops. The company was awarded damages of $15,450 ($15 per harvested acre), plus the cost of their legal fees. Schmeiser's own legal fees were nearly $200,000. Schmeiser appealed his case to the Supreme Court, which supported the lower court's decision (by a 5–4 margin) but did not make Schmeiser pay the damages or Monsanto's legal fees.

What this means is that genetically modified plants, which have the capacity to spread like weeds and may have localized evolutionary advantages over traditional organic crops, are working for their masters (usually Monsanto, which owns about 90 per cent of the patents) by taking over the farmlands. The damage to the environment in this case is social and economic, although we haven't yet learned if genetically modified organisms pose significant biological dangers. Stay tuned.

What do YOU think?

Genetically modified plants may be stronger than traditional crops, being more resistant to drought, disease, and damage caused by insects. Farmers stand to gain from such improvements. Should the company that invents these tougher varieties be allowed to profit from their use, even if the plants grow by chance, winning out over inferior varieties? More generally, should companies hold patents on living things?

The Environment and "Race"

The principle of environmental racism is that pollution is racialized. As we have seen, rich white nations dump waste in poorer black and brown nations. Thetford Mines, as we saw earlier, ships most of its asbestos to developing nations, where the lethal health risks of the substance are not as widely understood or where safer alternatives are prohibitively expensive. The City of Halifax, before demolishing the Africville neighbourhood in the mid-1960s, located several major polluters and a dump site right beside the black community. And oil companies observe different environmental guidelines in Africa than they do in Europe and North America. Oil companies frequently do business with dictatorships that can readily oppress Africans who resist Western pollution. The story of Ken Saro-Wiwa is instructive in this regard.

Ken Saro-Wiwa: Resisting Pollution

It has been over 20 years since Ken Saro-Wiwa was hanged in Nigeria in 1995. He was a journalist, a publisher, the writer/producer of a popular Nigerian sitcom, and a successful entrepreneur. More than anything else, however, he was a man of his people, the Ogoni, for whom he was killed.

His story exemplifies the greatest ills of European colonialism in Nigeria specifically and Africa in general. Nigeria was artificially created in the twentieth century, when the British brought together into one massive country three large and very distinct peoples: the Muslim Hausa-Fulani in the north; the Yoruba, rooted in great kingdoms past, in the west; and the Igbo, who tried to separate as Biafra, in the east. Imagine forcing together under the roof of one nation Germany, France, and England. With a population of close to 160 million, Nigeria is the largest country in Africa.

Numbering about 500,000, the Ogoni are a minority people living in the once biologically diverse and still oil-rich Niger Delta. Since Nigeria became independent their territory has been dominated by the Igbo. After oil was discovered on the delta, the Ogoni territory was worked by the multinational oil producer Royal Dutch Shell. We could say that Shell's environmental practices in various countries are as different as black and white. Where the population is black, so is the soil; where the population is white, so is Shell's environmental reputation. Their work on the Niger Delta is characterized by gas flaring, oil spills, and irresponsible dumping of wastewater, which greatly affected the traditional way of life of the Ogoni, who depend on agriculture and fishing.

Oppressed under a succession of military dictatorships that were friendly to the oil companies, the

Ogoni had no voice, no ability to express their concerns, until Ken Saro-Wiwa created one. In October 1990, he helped launch the Movement for the Survival of the Ogoni People (MOSOP), and shortly afterward he composed the Ogoni Bill of Rights. Inspired by what he had read of Gandhi's non-violent protests, he led the Ogoni in peaceful protest to halt oil exploration and production on their land until something was done to improve the deteriorating living conditions of his people. Shell had soldiers brought in to protect their interests from "hostile villagers," with predictable results. Saro-Wiwa took his people's struggles to the United Nations and caught the fickle attention of the world's press. Shell armed itself with high-priced public relations firms, which, unable to attack his ideas, resorted to character assassination. Saro-Wiwa, along with eight other MOSOP members, was charged with inciting the mob killing of four conservative Ogoni chiefs; he was arrested, jailed for over a year, and found guilty and sentenced to death in a hasty trial. Shell had an opportunity to save Saro-Wiwa from execution. Strategically, however, the biggest oil company operating in Nigeria and in the world stated that they would not interfere in the politics of a host country. Ken Saro-Wiwa was hanged on 10 November 1995.

The poverty rate in Nigeria is growing, with almost 100 million of the country's population of 160 million living on less than a dollar a day (Brock & Cocks, 2012). Western oil workers, including Canadians, continue to reap economic benefits from the oppression of the Ogoni and other Nigerians. Shell promotes itself as a good corporate citizen, with website testimonials about its positive environmental practices and co-operation with communities affected by their work. In 2009, the company agreed to an out-of-court settlement of US$15 million to end lawsuits brought against it for alleged human rights violations. They denied any wrongdoing, calling the settlement a "humanitarian gesture" while suggesting that part of the sum be put into an educational trust fund for the Ogoni (Mouwad, 2009).

The Case of Grassy Narrows

In *A Poison Stronger Than Love: The Destruction of an Ojibwa Community* (1985), Anastasia Shkilnyk presents an often cited case study of how pollution is racialized. It is a sympathetic study of the plight of the Anishinabe, or Ojibwa, people of Grassy Narrows, a First Nations community in northwestern Ontario, near the city of Kenora. However, Shkilnyk's study is flawed in being entrenched in victimology: it portrays the people as hapless victims of an industrial attack on the environment, rather than as agents and leaders in the fight against such an attack (a fight that continues to this day). For this reason, the incident and Shkilnyk's role in reporting on it are worth studying together as an example both of how environmental issues intersect with "race" and of how knowledge is produced.

In the mid-twentieth century, fishing was vital to the community of Grassy Narrows, both as a source of food and as a source of income (largely through tourism). Between 1962 and 1970, Reed Paper Company, a British-owned multinational, began dumping huge amounts of mercury—about 20,000 pounds—into the English–Wabigoon river system, about 170 kilometres upstream from Grassy Narrows. In 1970, significantly high amounts of the deadly element were detected in the local fish. Two years later came the first human casualty, a 42-year-old fishing guide.

The people of Grassy Narrows knew that mercury was making the fish and the people who depended on them sick, but the provincial government, with significant financial interests at stake, downplayed the problem. The pulp and paper industry, which was the source of the mercury pollution, was a major employer in northwestern Ontario—so much so, in fact, that the government was supporting Reed Paper with tax rebates. Local tourism, another important industry, stood to suffer if concerns about mercury contamination of the river system became public. There, again, the Ontario government was a stakeholder, having invested large sums in Minaki Lodge, just 45 kilometres west of Grassy Narrows. In 1977 it was revealed that the government had spent about $7.5 million in its acquisition and renovation of the lodge.

The people of Grassy Narrows, led by Chief Andy Keewatin, were not afraid to pursue their case against the company and the government's negligence. In 1975, they contacted the people of Minimata, Japan, a fishing community whose name is now synonymous with the motor and nervous disorder resulting from mercury poisoning (Minimata disease). They paid to have experts from Japan come to assess their situation, and armed with evidence of the river's contamination, they took their fight to the courts. In December of that year, the chief and councillors of Grassy Narrows, along with those of neighbouring Whitedog, threatened to deliver poisoned fish to the homes of Ontario's premier, the ministers of natural resources and of health, the attorney general, the leaders of the opposition parties, and the president of Reed. In a letter sent to these individuals, the representatives of Grassy Narrows clearly articulated their determination not to be victims:

> We know that the fish are poisonous. We know that eating the fish can destroy the mind and health and take the life of Indians and whites. This cannot fail to be known

by anybody who, for five long years, has watched the growing violence, the deteriorating health, and the declining morale of our people. . . .

For five years, we have fought the bias, indifference and hostility of your minister of natural resources.

It is long enough. Enough people have died. Enough of our people have been destroyed. Enough lack of understanding. Enough pro-polluter bias. Enough indifference. (cited in Hutchison & Wallace, 1977: p. 140)

In 1976, Anastasia Shkilnyk was hired by the Department of Indian Affairs and Northern Development (DIAND) to study the community of Grassy Narrows, which she did over the next two

Krystalline Kraus/rabble.ca

The community of Grassy Narrows First Nation is fighting to prevent clearcutting on their territory, saying that commercial logging operations are infringing on their treaty-protected right to use and make decisions about that land. Why do you think the people of Grassy Narrows are depicted as victims, rather than activists, in most of the literature on the subject?

years, returning for follow-up research in 1981 and 1983. She had a genuine interest in helping the people, and her work produced some valuable insights. However, she failed to question seriously the destructive role of the multinational company then fighting the community in the courts and the weak response and motives of both the federal government (her employer) and the provincial government. Further, she failed to accurately represent the active role taken by the people in their effort to resolve the crisis. In her work, the people neither understand their situation nor mount any resistance to the large corporate and governmental players. They are merely victims. There is little Indigenous voice in this book.

Sociology textbooks addressing the circumstances of Grassy Narrows typically give equal weight to two other factors, abuse and alcoholism. They do not mention that the people eventually were able to win $8.7 million in an out-of-court settlement from Reed Pulp and Paper in 1985. They do not talk about the community's fight since 1993 against the environmental impact of the logging practices of Abitibi Consolidated Corporations. They are locked into a time zone of perpetual environmental victimhood.

In 2011, Grassy Narrows First Nation won an Ontario Supreme Court victory stating that the province could not authorize logging operations that would infringe on federal Indigenous rights to hunting and trapping. In spite of the ruling, the provincial government in 2014 denied the community's request to conduct an environmental assessment of Abitibi's commercial timber extraction, even though the people's concerns were supported by locally knowledgeable biologists working for the province.

Meanwhile, the fight over contaminated water is not over. An Ontario government report released in June 2015 revealed that waterways in and around the Grassy Narrows community continue to show high levels of mercury. One year later, another government-funded report acknowledged that there was "an ongoing, yet unknown, source of mercury in the water," rumoured to be a mercury disposal site where dozens of barrels of the poisonous substance are thought to have been dumped (Porter, 2016). In June 2016, the province committed $300,000 to testing the water and identifying the source of the contamination, a first step in remediation of the local English–Wabigoon River system. Meanwhile, Grassy Narrows remains under a "do not consume" water advisory, with water having to be trucked into the community from a local treatment facility (Klasing, 2016).

The Environment and Class

As we have seen already in this chapter, there is a fairly clear relationship between class and the environment. People from the lower classes are more likely than those of the upper classes to live and work in conditions characterized by high levels of pollution or environmental hazards. People from the higher socioeconomic classes can also better afford to eat foods that are healthier and less affected by pollution. The following sections provide two illustrations of the way that environmental issues intersect with class.

Walkerton and the Social Politics of Water

In May 2000, the town of Walkerton, Ontario, was hit by an epidemic of the bacterium *Escherichia coli*, commonly known as *E. coli*, which came from their main water supply. In total, an estimated 2,300 people were affected by the outbreak; just over half of them were residents of the town itself, meaning that roughly one-quarter of Walkerton's population became ill. Seven people died as a consequence of the infection.

The tragedy raised questions about whom to trust when it comes to the social management of pollution. The province's Conservative government had been pursuing a policy of privatizing public-sector government departments, including the one responsible for inspecting the water supply. As a result of granting contracts for testing the water to private companies, the province had drastically reduced its funding to the Ministry of the Environment. Journalist Colin Perkel, in his thorough investigation into the Walkerton tragedy, cites this as evidence of a lack of social responsibility, both on the part of the government and on the part of the American firm, A & L Canada Laboratories East, that filled the government-created vacuum:

Although A & L Canada Laboratories East, a US-based franchise operation, had never tested for bacteria and was not accredited to do so, it nevertheless accepted water samples from Walkerton. In the absence of updated guidelines or regulations the provincial government felt no need to implement, A & L followed private industry practice in deeming test results to be confidential, to be shared only with the client [i.e. the town workers responsible for monitoring the pollution levels of the water]. (Perkel, 2002: p. 35)

One social product of having a private company do this work was a breakdown in the chain of communication and responsibility between the town and Ministry of the Environment.

When the story hit the news, the media followed two main storylines. One focused on the personal incompetence and lack of responsibility shown by the Walkerton employee who was primarily responsible for monitoring the water and notifying the Ministry of the Environment of any problems. We can call this the rotten apple approach, which aims to argue that the fault lies not with the system but with the individuals who make it up. This non-sociological line of inquiry, which is typical of tabloid-style reporting (e.g. that found in any paper named "Sun"), dominated certain parts of the media coverage. A bumbling rural official is an easy target for big-city reporters.

Sociologists tend to believe that there are no rotten apples, just a bad orchard—the social system surrounding the situation. The second main storyline, exhibited in the work of journalists such as Perkel, took this view, arguing that the *E. coli* epidemic was an inevitable result of the Ministry of the Environment's loss of influence over water testing. The less oversight shown by a large and authoritative social body, the greater the chance that something important will go unnoticed—with tragic consequences, in the case of Walkerton.

What do YOU think?

What are the arguments that governments use to justify outsourcing public-sector responsibilities like water testing to private firms? What are the risks? How can they be overcome?

The China Price: The True Cost of Chinese Competitive Advantage

Does it seem like everything you buy is made in China?

In 2007, China exported US$1,218 billion worth of goods, making it the third-largest exporter in the world, not far behind the United States and Germany (Harney, 2009: p. 4). The US alone imported slightly more than one-third of those exports, valued at $321.5 billion (with at least $18 billion in merchandise imported by retail giant Walmart), while they exported only $65.2 billion in goods to China, resulting in a trade deficit of over $250 billion for the Americans (Harney, 2009: p. 5).

Canada is in a similar situation, albeit on a much smaller scale. In 2015, Canadians imported $38.9 billion worth of goods from China, with consumer electronics and industrial machines (reactors, boilers, and so on) each representing roughly 20 per cent of the imports. Only $21.5 billion worth of Canadian exports went the other way to China, the top four trade items being wood pulp, organic chemicals, nickel articles, and metal ores. As a result, there was a China–Canada trade imbalance of some $17.4 billion in 2015 (Statistics Canada, CANSIM Table 228-0069).

So how has China become the "workshop of the world"? Much of it has to do with what is often called the China price. China has a huge competitive advantage in the manufacture and assembly of just about any kind of goods, as it is incredibly cheap to have work done in China. This cheapness comes at the expense of exploited Chinese workers and the environment. Alexandra Harney (another journalist who appears to have a good background in sociology) used the concept of the China price and turned it around to consider it as the price that China is paying for its manufacturing success—a price too dear, as Harney showed.

The mechanism has been called the "survival of the cheapest" (Harney, 2009: p. 40). It has been estimated that the average wage for Chinese manufacturing workers in 2002 was 57 cents an hour. There are literally millions of migrant workers competing for these jobs. Tens of millions of them are from farming areas that have made their former villagers environmental refugees and the villages themselves "cancer villages" or "widow towns."

The few health benefits that workers can draw on are controlled by the household register, or *hukou*, who typically favour those from cities over those from villages.

The importance of health benefits to Chinese workers cannot be overestimated, since the workplace in China is a major source of pollution. Work-related lung diseases such as silicosis (producing scar tissue in the lungs, and often leading to tuberculosis) claim as many as one million new cases every year (Harney, 2009: p. 57), many of them found in industries relating to jewellery manufacture. Perhaps the greatest environmental villain is coal, used to provide power to the ever-growing number of Chinese industries (not to mention supplying fuel for heat and cooking in people's homes). China is the world's largest producer and consumer of coal, and because of that it emits more carbon dioxide and sulphur dioxide than any other country (Harney, 2009: p. 89). Corrosive acid rain soaks the ground in nearly all parts of the country.

It is not just the burning of coal but its extraction that makes it an environmental hazard. In 2006, according to official statistics, 4,746 people died in Chinese coal mines (Harney, 2009: p. 90). However, since much of the coal is produced in relatively small, private, often "illegal" mines, the actual number is probably higher. Owning a coal mine is a lucrative enterprise in China, making it one of the chief sources of millionaires in the country. While China still retains some of the political mechanisms of its earlier communist period, it is now very much a free-wheeling capitalist economy, with the free exploitative hand of the market wielding more power in some ways than in most countries of the West.

Shanxi province is the largest coal-producing area in China. Four of the world's 20 most polluted cities are in this province, including its capital, Taiyuan, which in 1998 was the city with the most polluted air in the world. A 2002 survey reported that 64 per cent of children tested in the city had "excessively high levels of lead" in the blood of their young veins. After a much publicized attempt by municipal officials to clean up the city's image, the title of city with the most polluted air was taken over by nearby Linfen.

Officially, China takes strong measures to control the pollution, and as the country demonstrated

Rob Wilkinson/Alamy Stock Photo

The last few decades seem to have brought a proliferation of dollar stores to urban centres. What do you think is the environmental impact of so many cheaply made, cheaply bought goods shipped from around the world?

during the 2008 Summer Olympics in Beijing, it does not lack the resources to improve its air quality when it is sufficiently motivated to do so. Too often, though, this is not the case, as there are huge financial benefits tied to the lack of effective supervision, both in terms of corporate profits and in personal gain for environmental regulators who take bribes to look the other way. It is easy to blame the Chinese government, but the truth is that Western companies that invest in profitable Chinese businesses regardless of their environmental records make it easy to justify lax oversight of environmental policies. Harney interviewed two women whose husbands (Feng Xingzhong and Deng Wenping) were victims of silicosis. When she asked them why it was that Chinese factories killed young, strong men, they answered:

"Isn't it because you Americans have brought all your bad factories to China?" Feng's wife asks me.

"I heard it's because China has so much corruption, and it needs the money so it wants foreign investment," Tang [Deng's widow] offers. (Harney, 2009: p. 86)

What do YOU think?

1. How well does the brief exchange of the two Chinese widows capture the issues involved in China's poor record of meeting reasonable standards on environmental protection?
2. In terms of the environment, what is the China price?
3. Are there environmental refugees in Canada?

WRAP IT UP

Summary

It is easy to find discouraging evidence concerning the state of the environment, but in this chapter we have tried to find some hope to balance any feelings of despair you might be feeling. Human action is the main cause of environmental degradation, but human action can play the most important role in reversing the process. Natural disasters typically bring about uneven results to different social groups, but they can, in theory, provide opportunities for development that will benefit different social groups equally.

It would take an entire book to provide a comprehensive account of the environmental issues of concern to sociologists today. "The environment" is a hot-button topic, with daily news items about the food we eat and where it comes from, about climate change, about environmental disasters and cleanup, all backed by the latest research and statistics. What I hope I have provided you with here are some sociological tools with which you can assess the issues surrounding the interaction between groups in society and the fate of the environment. These tools include the concepts of social ecology, environmental racism, vested interests, the tobacco strategy, the China Price and, as well, the example of people like Paul Formby and Ken Saro-Wiwa, demonstrating what individuals can do in the fight against socially powerful opponents.

THINK BACK

Questions for Critical Review

1. Discuss how pollution is a lot like poverty in terms of operational definitions.
2. What is wrong with the "rotten apple approach" to dealing with issues of pollution? Why does it not make for good sociology?
3. What is the tobacco strategy, and how does it affect social policy concerning the environment?
4. Why do you think that major polluting companies work so hard to deny the environmental impact of their products?
5. What is meant by the claim that there is no such thing as a (purely) natural disaster?

READ ON

Suggested Print and Online Resources

Online

Stanford Research into the Impact of Tobacco Advertising (SRITA)

http://tobacco.stanford.edu/tobacco_main/index.php

- This interdisciplinary research project draws contributions from Stanford faculty and students in the departments of medicine, history, and anthropology, all looking at the effects of advertising. If you've grown up in the age where tobacco advertising is absent from Canadian magazines and television, you'll likely be astonished by this site's gallery of print and TV ads—particularly those featuring doctor endorsements and those unabashedly targeting teens.

David vs Monsanto

www.journeyman.tv/film/4495

- This is a short documentary film about Saskatchewan farmer Percy Schmeiser's battle with Monsanto.

Environmental Sociology Research Cluster

www.csa-scs.ca/enviro-home

- The Canadian Sociological Association's environmental sociology website aims to provide information on research, events, and news to a varied audience that includes "academics, students, the media, policy-makers, and non-governmental organizations."

Grassy Narrows to Ontario: No Reconciliation without Clean Water

www.youtube.com/watch?v=B6J987kE4Ng

- Uploaded in June 2016, this seven-minute RealNews report reviews how the water around Grassy Narrows became contaminated while highlighting recent activism involving the young people of the community.

Alexandra Harney: The Chinese Competitive Advantage

www.youtube.com/watch?v=xMFp8feQbvc

- The author of *The China Price* is featured in this 20-minute TEDx talk.

In Print

Murray Bookchin (1996), *The Philosophy of Social Ecology: Essays on Dialectical Naturalism* (Montreal: Black Rose Books).

- This work contains the essential ideas of Bookchin's social ecology.

Alexandra Harney (2009), *The China Price: The True Cost of Chinese Competitive Advantage* (New York: Penguin Books).

- This is an important work outlining the social and environmental cost of the China price.

Ike Okonta & Oronto Douglas (2001), *Where Vultures Feast: Shell, Human Rights, and Oil* (San Francisco: Sierra Club Books).

- Written by Nigerian authors, this book tells the story of Royal Dutch Shell's involvement in environmental and socioeconomic disasters that have taken place in the African country.

Andrew Nikiforuk (2009), *Tar Sands: Dirty Oil and the Future of a Continent* **(Vancouver: Greystone Books).**

- A prominent Canadian journalist tells a rarely heard story about the devastating social and environmental effects of the Alberta tar sands.

Colin N. Perkel (2002), *Well of Lies: The Walkerton Water Tragedy* **(Toronto: McClelland & Stewart).**

- This book describes in great detail how the Walkerton tragedy was allowed to occur, and how the drama played out.

Naomi Oreskes & Erik M. Conway (2010), *Merchants of Doubt: How a Handful of Scientists Obscured the Truth on Issues from Tobacco Smoke to Global Warming* **(New York: Bloomsbury Press).**

- This book outlines how a few politically well-connected scientists assist polluting companies in resisting environmental policies.

Lloyd Tataryn (1979), *Dying for a Living* **(Ottawa: Deneau and Greenberg).**

- This is still an important work detailing the social situation surrounding the lethal effects of asbestos on people who work in the industry.

Lloyd Tataryn (1983), *Formaldehyde on Trial: The Politics of Health in a Chemical Society* **(Toronto: Lorimer).**

- An excellent study of how the ineptness of government agencies and the bullying of big chemical companies has polluting results on Canadians.

Social Change and the Future

The Gist

Reading this chapter will help you to . . .

- Outline and contrast five different models of social change.
- Apply the cycle of civilization to the United States and comment on its applicability.
- Summarize the social changes to which the Luddites were reacting and draw connections to contemporary society.
- Outline Arthur Kroker's idea of the virtual class and discuss its relevance today.

Terms of the Trade

- barbarism
- civilization
- conservatism
- cycle of civilization
- democracy
- digital divide
- evolution
- fashion
- Islamist

- Luddites
- manufacturing of need
- modernism
- narrow vision
- neoliberalism
- nihilism
- oligarchy
- particularist protectionist
- political globalization

- polyarchy
- postmodernism
- savagery
- slippery slope
- social change
- social Darwinism
- survival of the fittest
- universalist protectionist
- virtual class

Names to Know

- Noam Chomsky
- Auguste Comte
- Herbert Spencer

- Lewis Henry Morgan
- Robert A. Dahl
- George Grant

- Arthur Kroker
- Manfred Steger

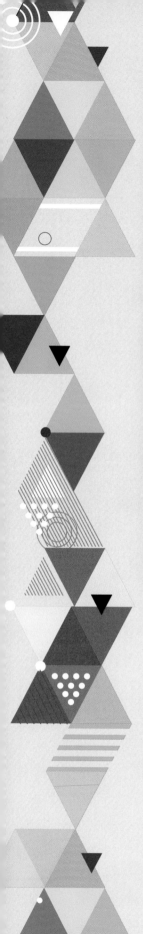

For Starters

Raging Against the Machine

The following words were used in 1802 by an English "cropper" (an independent producer of woollen cloth) to describe the desperate straits of people in his position, and what he wanted to do to the machines that were, in part, the cause of their difficulty:

> The burning of Factorys or setting fire to the property of People we know is not right but Starvation forces Nature to do that which he would not, nor would it reach his Thoughts had he sufficient Employ. We have tried every Effort to live by Pawning our Cloaths and Chattles so we are now on the brink for the last struggle. (cited in Sale, 1996: p. 71)

People sharing this view would later be known as Luddites, a term that has become synonymous with an opposition to industrialization or technology. But the Luddites weren't really raging against technology as much as they were raging against the social and political machinery of their time—the "system," in other words. To use an expression we will return to later, they knew that technology was not *socially neutral*, that it produces winners and losers. In this sense, the Luddites have much in common with those fighting to change the system today, from those who took part in the Quebec student protests in 2012 or the worldwide Occupy protests a year earlier to anti-racism groups like Idle No More and Black Lives Matter. These are the people bringing about social change in our time— maybe you're one of them.

Introduction: Why Predicting the Future is a Fool's Game

So what do we mean by social change? We mean that a group of people has experienced dramatic change in at least one part of their lives and must make adjustments in other areas of their lives in order to adapt. The central fact about society today is that it is changing. Things are not what they used to be, even just a few years ago. Think just of personal technology change: we only have to look back a few years to remember a time before smartphones and tablets, e-readers and Bluetooth headsets—and any of a number of items that first seemed gimmicky and are now indispensable to most people (not me). Some of us can even remember life before touching a computer keyboard.

Throughout much of this textbook I have presented trends and events that triggered, exemplified, or proceeded from social change. I have tried to show that these trends and events are subject to different and often equally valid interpretations by groups examining them from different standpoints, depending on such factors as gender, "race," class, and so on. In other words, examining social change in the past is no straightforward exercise. Imagine, then, the difficulty of predicting social change in the future.

Ultimately, it's a fool's game. In 1987, no one could have predicted that the divorce rate would peak that year, and then decline over the next 25 years. (For that matter, twenty years ago, I could not have predicted that I would get married for a third time—and have that marriage last!) At the start of the twenty-first century, no "futurist" (a consultant who is paid a lot of money to study trends and make predictions that generally don't come true) predicted that within 10 years there would be a black president of the United States, that General Motors would crash, that the Canadian and American governments would bail out and impose tight conditions on the automotive industry (once thought to be the ultimate capitalist industry), and that Ontario

would become one of Canada's "have-not" provinces. Of course, no one on New Year's Day 2001 could have foreseen the extraordinary set of social changes that would be set in motion by the events of that now infamous date just eight months and eleven days later.

Another cautionary note concerning any discussion of social change: it is important to recognize that as rapid as change is today, it would be wrong to say that earlier society was primarily static, sitting still. Think, for instance, of the Austronesian-speaking people, perhaps as far back as 2,000 years ago, who travelled from mainland Southeast Asia to the far-flung islands of Taiwan, Malaysia, Indonesia, Hawaii, Easter Island, New Zealand, and even Madagascar, hundreds of years before the era of modern travel—all in relatively small outrigger canoes. Think, too, of fourteenth-century China, Africa, and Europe, whose populations, recovering from the devastating effects of the Black Plague, saw their cultures change on a large scale. In Europe, surviving labourers of the plague-ravaged workforce were able to charge more for their work. Dramatic social change, certainly a defining feature of our present age, is nevertheless not unique to it.

Five Interpretations of Social Change

Any one instance of social change may be interpreted in a number of different ways. No single model of interpretation is the "right" one all the time. The five I will invite you to consider here have varying degrees of applicability to different situations. They are:

1) modernism
2) conservatism
3) postmodernism
4) evolution
5) fashion.

As I present each one, I will point out situations where it is and is not likely to apply. First, though, I offer a disclaimer concerning sociological models based on analogy. It comes from American sociologist Robert A. Nisbet (1913–1996), in *Social Change and History: Aspects of the Western Theory of Development*:

> No one has ever seen a civilization die, and it is unimaginable, short of cosmic disaster or thermonuclear holocaust, that anyone ever will. Nor has anyone ever seen a civilization—or culture or institution—in literal process of decay and degeneration, though there is a rich profusion of these words and their synonyms in Western thought. . . . Nor, finally, has anyone ever seen—actually, empirically seen, as we see these things in the world of plants and animals—growth and development in civilizations and societies and cultures, with all that is clearly implied by these words: change proceeding gradually, cumulatively, and irreversibly, through a kind of unfolding of internal potentiality, the whole moving toward some end that is presumably contained in the process from the start. We see none of these in culture: death, degeneration, development, birth. (Nisbet, 1969: p. 3)

1. Modernism

Modernism holds that change equals progress, that what is modern or new will automatically be better than the older thing it replaces. It views society as advancing along a straight path from primitive to more sophisticated, from out-of-date to up-to-date, from worse to better. This change is usually portrayed as a single, straight line, one that is not open to different paths of development.

Seen in its best light, the modernist view is the view of the future long envisioned by Gene Roddenberry, creator of *Star Trek*, and captured in the fictional space crew's stated mission "to boldly go where no man has gone before." Seen in a more sinister light, modernism reduces progress to a formula that equates "new" with "better" and simultaneously "more expensive." Education technology has co-opted the term "advanced learning" without even having to demonstrate that it is in any way more "advanced" or "better" than traditional methods of instruction. Teachers using older methods are portrayed as educational dinosaurs. "My name is John, but you can call me Professor T. Rex. Blackboards

and chalk are more reliable than any high-tech form of teaching."

French thinker **Auguste Comte** (1798–1857), often called the father of sociology, was a cheerleader for modernism:

> The true general spirit of social dynamics [i.e. sociology] then consists of each . . . social [state] as the necessary result of the preceding, and the indispensable mover of the following. . . . [T]he present is big [i.e. pregnant] with the future. In this view the object of science is to discover the laws which govern that continuity. (Comte, 1853)

Positivism, which characterized Comte's view and dominated much of the early history of sociology, is an aspect of modernism. Positivism, as defined in Chapter 2, involves a belief that the rules, methods, and presumed objectivity of the natural sciences can be applied to the social sciences with no accommodation made for the biases, or subjectivity, of the social scientist. This is why Comte, in the passage quoted above, feels it's within the sociologist's abilities to examine the course of social history to find the secrets behind the seemingly "inevitable" progress from one period to the next.

Along with Charles Darwin's theory of evolution came the idea, often referred to as social Darwinism, that societies naturally proceed from simple (and inferior) to complex (and superior), and that only the strongest societies triumph. This notion of progress was articulated by **Herbert Spencer** (1820–1903), who coined the phrase survival of the fittest to refer not to species (as is widely believed) but to societies. The idea that society progresses through distinct stages was developed and put forward by anthropologist **Lewis Henry Morgan** (1818–1881), who identified the three stages of savagery, barbarism, and civilization (Morgan, [1877]/1964: p. 12). The following passage from his study of human society lays the groundwork for his argument:

> The latest investigations respecting the early condition of the human race are tending to the conclusion that mankind commenced their career at the bottom of the scale and slowly worked their way up from savagery to civilization through the slow accumulations of experimental knowledge.

As it is undeniable that portions of the human family have existed in a state of savagery, other portions in a state of barbarism, and still other portions in a state of civilization, it seems equally so that these three distinct conditions are connected with each other in a natural as well as necessary sequence of progress. . . .

An attempt will be made in the following pages to bring forward additional evidence of the rudeness of the early condition of mankind, of the gradual evolution of their mental and moral powers through experience, and of their protracted struggle with obstacles while winning their way to civilization. It will be drawn, in part, from the great sequence of inventions and discoveries which stretches along the entire pathway of human progress; but chiefly from domestic institutions, which express the growth of certain ideas and passions. (Morgan, [1877]/1964: p. 11)

The influence of Morgan's three-tiered view of human development lasted well into the twentieth century. Vestiges of it can be seen in Durkheim's *Elementary Forms of Religious Life* (1912) and in the writings of Talcott Parsons. In *Societies: Evolutionary and Comparative Perspectives* (1966) Parsons divided societies into the supposedly less judgemental but nevertheless still misleading "primitive," "intermediate," and "modern."

Up until the mid-twentieth century, a key aspect of modernism was the belief that science and technology would combine to create a material heaven on earth. Science would become a rational, hard evidence–based religion to supersede the traditional religions built on faith. Technology would free people from having to perform hard physical labour on the job and at home. Thus liberated from drudgery and tedious labour, humans would have abundant leisure time for more worthwhile pursuits. It's easy to smirk at the idealism of the 1950s and early 1960s, but how different is that from the message we hear in TV and radio ads today about the newest form of techie toys?

Modernist theories of politics incorporate the idea that societies are constantly improving *politically*. According to this view, societies are becoming more democratic, with respect for human rights

Village Roadshow/The Kobal Collection

The modernist view of society's continued improvement is countered in popular culture by the popularity of post-apocalyptic dystopias presenting a future world that is much worse than the one we currently inhabit. (Think, for example, of book and movie franchises such as *The Hunger Games*, *Divergent*, and *Delirium*.) Why do you think we spend so much time contemplating society's inevitable demise?

on the rise and barriers between societies falling, all of which will help to eradicate the threat of war. Indeed, this was the optimistic premise behind the founding of the United Nations after World War II. A glimpse into that post-war feeling comes from the general introduction to a series of philosophical and religious works put together by liberal, religious-minded Oxford scholars during the 1950s:

[These readings] will help men and women to find "fullness of life," and peoples to live together in greater understanding and harmony. Today the earth is beautiful, but men are disillusioned and afraid. But there may come a day, perhaps not a distant day, when there will be a renaissance of man's spirit: when men will be innocent and happy amid the beauty of the world, or their eyes will be opened to see that egoism and strife are folly, that the universe is fundamentally spiritual, and that men are the sons of God. (The Editors, "Introduction," cited in Kaizuka, [1956]/2002: p. 8)

It is easy for the leaders of developing empires to use modernist principles to justify their decisions on the grounds that their latest achievement represents the culmination of progress and that whatever is in the best interests of their country is in the best interests of humankind. American public intellectual **Noam Chomsky** (b. 1928) has expressed his concern that American presidents and policy-makers have taken this approach, wrapping American policy in the flag of modernism. In *Hegemony or Survival: America's Quest for Global Dominance*, he describes the modernist thinking of the American power elite:

> [T]here is a guiding principle that "defines the parameters within which the policy debate occurs," a consensus so broad as to exclude only "tattered remains" on the right and left and "so authoritative as to be virtually immune to challenge." The principle is *"America as historical vanguard"*: "History has a discernible direction and destination. Uniquely among all the nations of the world, the United States comprehends and manifests history's purpose." Accordingly,

Rene Johnston/Toronto Star via Getty Images

Drawn by Toronto artist Ramon Perez, the cover of a special issue of the Marvel comic *Civil War II* features a confident-looking Justin Trudeau in the boxing ring, flanked by Sasquatch, Aurora, and other members of the Canadian peacekeeping force Alpha Flight. What does it say about the national political climate when the prime minister is portrayed on a comic book in the company of superheroes? Is Canada enjoying a modernist moment of optimism? Months later, do we see this optimism fading?

US hegemony is the realization of history's purpose, and what it achieves is for common good, the merest truism, so that empirical evaluation is unnecessary, if not faintly ridiculous. (Chomsky, 2004: pp. 42–3)

Chomsky here identifies one of the flaws of the modernist model, namely its narrow vision, roughly cast as "Whatever innovation benefits the dominant class is justifiable on the grounds of progress." Today, many are skeptical of modernism. Science, technology, and industry have created problems of pollution that we need to solve more by how we live than by adding more technology. Commercials for SUVs promise personal freedom, yet if we in North America did not manufacture vehicles with such poor fuel efficiency, if we depended less on automobiles and more on bikes and public transit to commute to work and to school, our demand for oil and the consequent damage to our environment would be less.

Meanwhile, human leisure time is not increasing. People with jobs seem to be working longer hours than in decades past in spite of labour-saving technology. The office is now a virtual space, as advances in telecommunications make it more difficult for people to leave their work at the office. Smartphones enable employers to stay in touch with their staff on weekends. In politics, governments with little respect for democracy, human rights, or peace abound in countries that talk of protecting those ideals.

Where might the modernist view be valid? When asked this question in the classroom, students typically point to medical technology. Certainly diagnostic and life-saving technology has become

Our Stories

The "Mincome": A Manitoba Town's Modernist Experiment

During the 1970s, the Manitoba town of Dauphin was home to a progressive social experiment around a simple idea: what if every family in the town received a guaranteed, unconditional annual income?

Would citizens become lazy, knowing their income was guaranteed no matter how hard they worked? Would they stop working altogether?

The pilot project was introduced in 1974 under the province's NDP government and the Liberal government of Canada. Under the plan, families were guaranteed a minimum income based on family size. The guaranteed income (or "mincome," as it came to be known) would be reduced by 50 cents for each dollar the household earned.

During the four years the project lasted it was studied by anthropologists, sociologists, and economists. It was stopped in 1979 by Conservative governments that came to power at the provincial and federal levels. As Dutch historian Rutger Bregman explains in his book *Utopia for Realists* (2016), hardly any of the results were analyzed by staff overseeing the project. Boxes of paper files and questionnaires were left to rot in the archives.

Twenty-five years later, University of Manitoba researcher Evelyn Forget unearthed the documents shortly before they were to be destroyed. She found that during the time of the study, the town recorded fewer work-related injuries, fewer mental health visits, and an 8.5 per cent drop in hospital visits overall (Forget, 2011). There were only minor reductions in the number of hours worked by Dauphin residents, except among young adults, where the decrease was greater. However, the decrease in hours worked meant that young adults were more likely to complete their high school educations and young families were likely to devote more time to the care of young children.

What do YOU think?

1. Forget attributes the demise of the project to "a change in the intellectual and economic climate" (Forget, 2011: p. 8). What do you think she means?
2. Do you think a guaranteed minimum income would be possible to implement today? Why or why not?

more sophisticated, and in this sense it validates a modernist view of progress. At the same time, in some senses reliance on this technology as an alternative to adopting preventative social practices is not a social improvement. The old saying "an ounce of prevention is worth a pound of cure" seems valid, even if it isn't metric.

> **What do YOU think?**
>
> 1. From the seventeenth century into the early 1920s in Canada, European explorers, trading companies, missionaries, and governments brought many changes they thought would improve the lives of people living here. From an Indigenous perspective, which "improvements" might in fact have seemed like the exact opposite?
> 2. Is there an example of social change that does not come at a cost? Consider the answer in terms of social institutions (family, religion, education, health) presented earlier in the book.

2. Conservatism

Conservative thinkers see social change as potentially more destructive than constructive, especially in emotionally charged areas of life such as family, gender roles, sexuality, and the environment.

It would be easy to dismiss conservatism as an "unrealistic" interpretation of social change held by old-timers or religious fanatics romanticizing the past, by red-necked reactionaries gazing down the gun barrel at anyone attempting to interfere with their rights, or by anti-business, tree-hugging nature "freaks." It would be wrong to do so. Some values and customs, such as community and "neighbourliness," need to be preserved. Their loss is neither inevitable nor desirable.

Conservatism as it relates to social change should not be confused with the political principles of right-wing, large-C Conservative parties in Canada, Britain, Australia, and New Zealand. An excellent example of small-c conservatism is found in the nationalist sentiment of **George Grant** (1918–1988), one of Canada's foremost conservative public intellectuals. Grant taught philosophy at McMaster, Dalhousie, and Queen's. His *Lament for a Nation*

(1965) is recognized as a landmark of Canadian writing. His concern, as expressed in *Lament* and in *Technology and Empire* (1969), was that the technology, culture, and sense of progress emanating from the US would lead to the destruction of Canada as a place that cultivated and cherished an alternative to the American vision. A man of deep religious convictions, he inspired Canadian nationalists across the political spectrum.

I mentioned earlier the modernist belief that science will ultimately replace traditional religion. So far this has not happened, and I bet on the side of it won't happen. Humans, it would appear, have spiritual needs, however defined, that science cannot completely address. We see, in the enduring strength of conservative religion in the United States and in the battles that proponents of non-scientific "intelligent design" or "scientific creationism" are mounting against the scientific fact of evolution, that the modernist vision of the new religion of science has not overcome the old religions of faith.

One of the ideas closely associated with conservatism is that of the cycle of civilization. This is the belief that civilizations rise and fall in a predictable cycle. It was early articulated by Greek historian Polybius (*c.* 200–*c.* 118 BCE) in explaining to his fellow Greeks how the Roman Empire came to have dominance over them, while warning the Romans about the potential for their collapse:

> [T]he destruction of the human race, as tradition tells us, has more than once happened, and as we must believe will often happen again, all arts and crafts perishing at the same time, then in the course of time, when springing from the survivors as from seeds men have again increased in numbers. (cited in Nisbet, 1969: p. 34)

Historian Oswald Spengler, in *The Decline of the West* (1918–22), took a similar view when he wrote that civilization was passing "through the age-phases of the individual man. It has its childhood, youth, manhood, and old age" (cited in Nisbet, 1969: p. 8). Adherents of conservatism are sometimes guilty of the logical fallacy known as slippery-slope reasoning. This occurs when they cite one instance of social change—say, for example, gay marriage—as evidence of the imminent collapse of the entire social order (including, to keep with this particular example, polygamy and bestiality). It is an overreaction.

Another pitfall of the conservative position is a tendency to project backwards an idealized picture of social life from which the modern world is said to have fallen. For instance, people who bemoan what they consider the rampant sexual promiscuity occurring today speak in idealized terms of a time when couples would not engage in sex before marriage. They are misinformed. British social historian Peter Laslett wrote about how it was common in the late sixteenth century for couples to contract marriage (like our engagement) and then immediately live together for months, with full sexual benefits. In his conclusion to a discussion of the county of Leicester, Laslett observes that "Brides in Leicestershire at this time must normally have gone to their weddings in the early, and sometimes in the late, stages of pregnancy" (Laslett, 1971: p. 150).

Sometimes modernism and conservatism combine in theories that view signs of decline as indications that progress is on the horizon. In Marx's thinking, the worse capitalism got, with the shrinking of the bourgeoisie and the growth of the proletariat to include a falling middle class, the more likely capitalism would collapse altogether, leading to the ultimate social change, the communist revolution. With a similar perspective, albeit from a very different position, conservative Americans who believe in fundamentalist Christianity often look upon environmental, economic, political, and social (i.e. moral) decline in their country as a sign that the world is on the verge of the apocalypse.

Crowds gather outside a life-size replica of Noah's Ark, which opened in July 2016 a short distance away from the Creation Museum in Kentucky. Both attractions are operated by Answers in Genesis, an apologetics ministry dedicated to helping Christians defend their faith. Visitors to the Ark Encounter can tour the Ark's interior, which displays representations of animals, including dinosaurs, believed to have been aboard the Biblical vessel. Which model of social change does this exhibit reflect?

Going Global

Political Globalization and the Spread of Democracy

Political globalization, as defined by **Manfred Steger** (b. 1961), is "the intensification and expansion of political interrelations across the globe" (Steger, 2003: p. 56). It is manifest in the United Nations and its affiliated organizations, as well as regional coalitions such as the European Union and NATO (the North Atlantic Treaty Organization). Political globalization also involves NGOs (non-government organizations) such as Amnesty International and Greenpeace.

Champions of globalization, taking a modernist view of change, argue that it benefits many countries by spreading democracy (Steger, 2003: p. 110). The validity of this claim depends on how broadly **democracy** is defined. At the foundation of a democracy is a government elected by its citizens. But this is a rather thin definition. Merely holding a vote for a leader does not guarantee democracy. In the former Soviet Union, citizens would go through the exercise of voting for the one name on the ballot. And how many people must be allowed to vote in order for there to be a true democracy? A broader definition of democracy might include such features as

- an electorate that is broad-based in terms of gender, class, ethnicity, and "race";
- freedom of the press and freedom of speech;
- freedom of association and of travel (within and between countries);
- the presence of a viable opposition (and one that does not literally fear for its life);
- a system of education in which people can teach and take courses critical of society's institutions;
- protection of the rights of minorities; and
- equality of men and women.

Thin democracy might be spreading, but broad democracy really is not.

Around the time of the US-led invasion of Iraq in 2003, there was a joke going around that George W. Bush was trying to bring democracy to Iraq—and if it worked there, he was going to try to bring it to Florida (the deciding state in the 2000 presidential election, which became the focus of allegations of voter fraud). The joke raises an interesting question: When do we have democracy? A typical definition of democracy involves some notion of government by citizens. Note the Greek root of the word, *demos–*, meaning "the people." But the ancient Greeks, who coined the term, can hardly be said to have had democracy themselves. Women and the large class of slaves were excluded from having a voice.

What are the analytical alternatives to "democracy" when describing a society? In *A Preface to Democratic Theory* (1956), American political scientist and sociologist **Robert A. Dahl** (1915–2014) suggested that modern industrial states were governed by **polyarchies**, shifting coalitions of powerful interest groups. In *Power Elite*, published that same year, C. Wright Mills disagreed, arguing that the power elite, who ran the big companies and had the most significant say in government, was not a shifting group but one that was relatively stable. In essence, he claimed that there was an **oligarchy**, rule by a few powerful individuals or groups. Russia is often said to be governed by oligarchs today. Kirkpatrick Sale (1980) has argued that democracy cannot exist in a population over 10,000, so that we can have only relative degrees of democracy in state-level societies. While the actual number can be debated, the basic premise seems sound.

What do YOU think?

1. What features would have to be in place in any society that can be considered relatively "democratic"? In what ways would you consider Canada "democratic" and "undemocratic"?
2. In 2016, the people of Britain voted to withdraw from the European Union, an economic association of countries promoting open borders and the free movement of goods and of people. What view of social change best characterizes the sentiment of those who voted to leave the EU?

American movies and TV shows often reflect an apocalyptic or dystopic view (the negative opposite of utopian view). Kirkpatrick Sale (2005) cites a survey, commissioned by conservative media *Time* and CNN, that indicates 59 per cent of Americans polled believed the apocalypse was just around the corner.

A Case Study in Social Change and Conservatism: The Luddites

From 1811 to 1813, beginning in the English industrializing area of Nottinghamshire and spreading to Yorkshire and Manchester, a group of independent textile workers took desperate measures into their hands by destroying what would today amount to millions of dollars' worth of property. In the words of American writer Kirkpatrick Sale, they were "rebels against the future" (Sale, 1996). Part of a larger movement occurring at the time in Britain, France, Germany, and the United States, they made nighttime raids to destroy machinery, sent anonymous threatening letters to known industrialists, stockpiled weapons, and participated in food riots in the marketplace.

They were called Luddites, after a mythical, Robin Hood–like figure, Edward (Ned) Ludd, whose precise origin is unknown. They were skilled tradesmen—croppers (finishers of wool cloth), wool combers, handloom wool weavers—who in the late eighteenth century worked out of their homes and made good wages. They had leisure time probably similar to that of most Canadians today, and were part of strongly linked small communities.

But the work of the Luddites was becoming obsolete. While in 1812, in Yorkshire, there were about 5,000 croppers, within a generation there were virtually none. Huge steam-driven machines owned by the rising class of factory owners, combined with new business practices, were changing the working and social world. Even with the earliest generation of machines, one person could do the work of five or six. Contrary to the tradition surrounding the old-fashioned machine-hating Luddites, the social practices accompanying the machines were just as much the enemy. A typical workday in the new factories averaged 12 to 14 hours in length, sometimes as many as 16 to 18, and people worked six days a week. Children as young as four and women were hired in preference to men, and they made up a great majority of the workforce (80 per cent, according to Sale). They received about a third of a man's wages, and were thought to be less likely than men to resist owner oppression.

Quick Hits

The Impending Collapse of the American Empire?

A good example of modern conservatist thinking is an argument Kirkpatrick Sale makes in his essay "Imperial Entropy: Collapse of the American Empire" (2005). Sale regards the United States as an empire, and therefore subject to what he believes is the inevitable fate of all empires: collapse.

Sale points to four things that have toppled empires of the past and could bring about the collapse of the American empire:

- environmental degradation
- economic meltdown (through excessive resource exploitation)
- military overstretch
- domestic dissent and upheaval.

I would add "decline in creativity" to this list, as evidenced in American television, movies, and music. Think of how many Hollywood movies in 2016 were remakes.

What do YOU think?

1. Do you think that the United States can be considered an empire akin to the Greek, Roman, Mongol, Ottoman, British, and Soviet empires?
2. Do you agree with Sale that the decline or collapse of the United States is inevitable? Given the divisiveness of the country's current political climate, could it be occurring right now?

Desperate poverty for millions of people resulted. Life expectancy dropped drastically. In the rough statistics for 1830, it was reckoned that 57 per cent of the people of Manchester died before the age of five. While the life expectancy at birth for people throughout England and Wales was 40, for labourers in the textile manufacturing cities of Manchester and Leeds, it was thought to be about 18 (Sale, 1995: p. 48).

Working conditions were not the only social change the Luddites rebelled against. They also opposed the manufacturing of need. One of the most profound social changes accompanying the Industrial Revolution and the manufacture of consumer goods was the sudden creation of a need where people had once been mostly self-sufficient. Food and clothing now had to be purchased rather than produced at home. The social change this brought about was neatly summed up by nineteenth-century British writer Thomas Carlyle in *The Gospel of Mammonism* (1843): "We have profoundly forgotten everywhere that *Cash-payment* is not the sole relation of human beings" (quoted in Sale, 1995: p. 39). This trend, described by French historian Fernand Braudel as "a revolution in demand," extended from Britain to the colonies—particularly India, where millions of consumers were created by the dumping of manufactured cloth from Britain. It was not until the 1930s and 1940s, with the peaceful intervention of Gandhi and the lesser-known Muslim Pathan Badshah Khan (leader of the Khudai Khidmatgar), that the people of India began to boycott British cloth and make their own, as had been their tradition.

A remarkable aspect of the Luddite social movement was its solidarity. Despite the rich rewards paid to those who would snitch on their neighbours, despite the torture alleged to have been used on those who were caught, there were few informers. In all, 24 Luddites were hanged, and about an equal number died in the raids; a similar number were put in prison, while at least 37 were sent to the prison colony of Australia.

What did they achieve? There were a few short-term gains for the Luddites. Wages were raised slightly in areas where the Luddites had been the most active. Social reform got on the political agenda, although it would be a long time before significant changes were made. And the "poor laws," which administered what we might today call social welfare, received more attention and greater funding, although charities continued to carry the greater part of the welfare load.

Perhaps the main accomplishment of the Luddites lies in what they can teach us today about social change and what Sale calls the "machine question." We need to realize that technology is not socially neutral. It creates certain kinds of jobs, but destroys others. The Luddites were not backward-looking "loonies" refusing to face the inevitability of technological "progress." They wanted an alternative future, an alternative modern. That progress can take many forms is perhaps the most important lesson of the Luddite movement. It's why I never bristle when my tech-addicted colleagues call me a Luddite.

What do YOU think?

1. Why can it be said that technology is not neutral in terms of social change?
2. The term "Luddite" today is most often applied to someone considered too small-minded to embrace change. Is this a fair way to characterize the original Luddites? Were they unable to understand "progress," or did they understand progress too well?
3. Forty years ago you could not pull your car into any gas station and fill it up yourself: you required an attendant to do this for you. Banking transactions were most commonly conducted in person, not through a machine. Today, self-serve checkout lines are replacing grocery store cashiers. If you have been through an airport recently, think of all the technology you were forced to interact with there. What are the benefits of these changes? Do they have negative impacts on society? Whom does this kind of change benefit the most? Whom does it harm?

3. Postmodernism

Postmodernism, as a social theory, relates largely to voice. It challenges the notion that researchers can speak for peoples that they study without letting the people studied themselves have a voice. Postmodernism challenges the notion that anyone can, with any authority, talk of progress or decline

Going Global

Opposing Globalization: A Conservatist Stance

There are fundamentally two kinds of opposition to globalization: particularist and universalist. **Particularist protectionist** opponents of globalization focus on the socioeconomic, political, and cultural problems caused in their home territory by increasing processes of globalization. In Steger's words:

> Fearing the loss of national self-determination and the destruction of their cultures, they pledge to protect their traditional ways of life from those "foreign elements" they consider responsible for unleashing the forces of globalization. (Steger, 2003: p. 114)

This is a mixed group. It includes **Islamists** who oppose globalization with narrow-minded and very distorted fundamentalist notions of Islam (al-Qaeda and IS(IL) are examples). It also includes European ethnic entrepreneurs, who use principles of particularist protectionism to defend their campaign for "racial/national purity." It includes those in Britain who voted in 2016 to leave the European Union in order to safeguard British jobs for British workers.

Particularist protectionists also include Americans who argue that skilled and unskilled trade workers are losing their jobs to citizens of the developing world, and are not benefiting from economic globalization the way the power elite are. While they sometimes identify "big business" as the culprit, it is often easier to blame Japanese-owned firms or outsourced workers in India. Sociologist Roland Robertson, who teaches in the United States, wrote the following for a Japanese publication in 1997:

> I can assure you that the *anti*-global sentiment is very, very strong in the United States of America. It is playing a key part in the current campaign to decide which candidate should run for president from the Republican Party; the phrase "anti-globalism" is a significant one in American politics; there are numerous movements which are directed in opposition to the teaching of the subject of globalization, to so-called "international education"; there have been people protesting at school boards all over America about American children learning about other countries; they fear that if they learn about ancient Greek philosophy or about Japanese religion or French philosophy, that their minds will be destroyed, in other words, that their views will be relativized. (Robertson, 1997)

That was in 1997. Much more recently, the same anti-globalism sentiment (except in the military sense) was central to both the Republican and the Democratic races. Opposition to free trade, and to foreigners generally, helped push Donald Trump to victory in the campaign for the Republican Party nomination. On the Democratic side, the particularist-protectionist ideas of Bernie Sanders kept him in the race against Hillary Clinton long after pundits thought he would disappear.

Is particularist protectionism a bad policy? From a Canadian perspective, a certain amount of particularist protection would seem necessary. Only about 2 per cent of the movies we watch are Canadian, despite the fact that there is a relatively successful movie production business in Toronto and Vancouver. Think of how often you have seen someone play the part of an American president in a movie. Can you ever remember seeing a movie with someone cast as the Canadian prime minister? Our stories are not being told on film, except in Quebec, where French-language films are being produced for the domestic market. Canadian content rules and specially funded programs have helped many of our musicians begin careers in the face of the competition from the loud voices to the south.

While particularist protectionists argue that globalization causes social, cultural, and political problems in their own countries, **universalist protectionists**, as Steger describes them, promote the interests of the poor and marginalized groups worldwide (Steger, 2003: p. 115). Amnesty International, Doctors Without Borders, and similar organizations can be seen as universalist protectionist, taking up the cause of those hurt by globalization worldwide.

The Point Is...

The Radical Politics of Nihilism

In an editorial for a January 2015 issue of the *New York Times*'s Sunday Review, political philosopher Kenan Malik characterized Islamist attacks like the one on the editorial offices of *Charlie Hebdo*, Taliban attacks on schools in Pakistan, and the Boko Haram kidnapping of schoolgirls in Nigeria as examples of nihilism. Central to nihilism is the rejection of traditional moral principles, including those articulated in the Qur'an. Malik points out that nihilism was not always a feature of the radical politics of Africa and Asia. For most of the twentieth century the radical politics of the region embodied a Marxist stand against imperialism and a desire to bring the non-Western world into modernity. However, when that failed, modernity itself became the target of hatred and anger. The result, as Malik contends, is "the transformation of anti-Western sentiment from a political challenge to imperialist policy to an inchoate [i.e. just begun, not fully formed] rage against modernity" (Malik, 2015).

Many people in the West would agree that anti-West radicalism is to be expected given the way North American and European powers have exploited the people of these areas. Islamic extremism stands as the only radical ideology that can present a meaningful challenge to Western ideals. It succeeds by virtue of its apocalyptic nature, according to which every disruption to society can be seen as a distorted form of victory. When the West responds by bombing targets in Syria, Iraq, and Afghanistan, these acts are used in recruitment propaganda around the message, "the West hates us."

What do YOU think?

1. How would people interpret nihilist movements from a modernist, conservatist and postmodernist perspective?

2. Do you think that the Islamist movement will be replaced by some other form of anti-West ideology in the future. Bear in mind: nihilism, as a political movement, has never lasted for any great length of time.

3. What could change the West's continued exploitation of Asian and African nations?

AP Photo/Sunday Alamba

Nigerian refugees of Boko Haram, mostly children, welcome visitors to their camp. If these children are left to grow up in a refugee camp, who do you think they will blame? Is the "West" complicit in the terrorist attacks against it?

across all society. Instead, a sociologist with a post-modernist perspective might ask, Progress *for which group(s)*? Decline *for which group(s)*? The same sociologist, hearing conservatives complain about how Canadian values are eroding, might wonder if what they really mean is that *their* ethnic group with *its* set of values is no longer dominating as it once did.

Think of how modernist media usually present computers and computer-related products and services as bringing about benefits to everyone. But how often do you hear or read the opinions of those, even within Canada, who cannot afford a (decent) computer or the education necessary to make use of one? This is creating a situation that has been called the digital divide, a socioeconomic gap separating those who are "haves" from those who are "have-nots" where modern computer technology and reliable Internet access are concerned. One person known for thinking this way is Arthur Kroker.

Arthur Kroker and the Virtual Class

Arthur Kroker, of the University of Victoria's political science department, is a Canadian futurist who advanced the notion of the virtual class in the mid-1990s as part of his conservatist position. His writing combines Marxist views on class with a lot of postmodernist wordplay (which can make him hard to read). His work is difficult to summarize in an introductory textbook because it depends on a great deal of jargon. However, we can give you a taste of what Kroker has to say.

The virtual class, according to Kroker, is a class of visionary capitalists or, as he calls them:

> visionless-cynical-business capitalists, and the perhaps visionary, perhaps skill-oriented, perhaps indifferent techno-intelligentsia of cognitive scientists, engineers, computer scientists, video-game developers, and all the other communication specialists, ranged in hierarchies, but all dependent for their economic support on the drive to virtualization. (Kroker & Weinstein, 1995: pp. 15–16)

We will briefly outline three ways in which this diverse group acts like a class.

First, says Kroker, this class is responsible for the loss of jobs by those who do not belong to the class. This group supports the goals of a neoliberalism that promotes the interests of big business. This is how Kroker accounts for the corporate downsizing that became a widespread cost-saving strategy among North American businesses during the early 1990s:

> Against economic justice, the virtual class practices a mixture of predatory capitalism and gung-ho technical rationalizations for laying waste to social concerns for employment, with insistent demands for "restructuring economies," "public policies of labor adjustment," and "deficit cutting," all aimed at maximal profitability. (Kroker & Weinstein, 1995: p. 5)

Another example of the virtual class's move for power has to do with its role in the way the Internet, once democratic and freely accessible, became restricted by the authoritarian "digital superhighway" ever more controlled by what Kroker calls "privileged corporate codes." To use an example close to my own heart, online access to sociology journals is being more and more limited to those who possess expensive memberships and those who are affiliated with universities and not community colleges. Another example: several online newspapers have begun erecting paywalls to charge for content that was once free. The *Globe and Mail*, a source of information for sociology instructors and textbook writers, is one of those that has ended the free availability of articles online.

The third defining characteristic of the virtual class is the way this group, according to Kroker, restricts the freedom of creativity, promoting instead "the value of pattern-maintenance (of its own choosing)" (Kroker & Weinstein, 1995: p. 5). Have you ever noticed how computer-generated zombies, ghosts, and aliens all look remarkably alike? How often have you seen black smoke issuing from people possessed by demons? This is an example of "pattern maintenance": the tools of the trade are controlled by a few companies.

What do YOU think?

1. How does Kroker portray the virtual class as a class in the Marxist sense?
2. Do you think that Kroker leans a little too far toward conspiracy theory in his worldview?

4. Evolution

Evolution is perhaps the most misused of all scientific concepts. The biological term does not refer to general progress or improvement of a species. What it means is adapting well to particular circumstances. Darwin's use of Spencer's phrase "survival of the fittest" is best interpreted as "survival of the *best fit*"—the one best suited to the environment. It was not about the biggest, the meanest, the fastest, and so on.

Jonathan Weiner, in *The Beak of the Finch: A Story of Evolution in Our Time* (1995), provides an example of evolution when he explains that guppies swimming in the rivers of Venezuela come in two basic colour patterns. High in the hills, where the rivers are little more than streams, the guppies are brightly coloured. They compete in terms of sexual selection, with the most colourful having the greatest chance of attracting a mate. The bright colours are the result of the competition. In the waters down in the valleys, the guppies swim where predators feed upon those guppies that are easily seen. Not surprisingly, the guppies there are less brightly coloured. The competition has less to do with attracting a mate and more to do with not being seen by predators. Neither colour pattern represents an improvement in the species. Each is a better fit in the local environment.

How does this apply to social change? We can look at the history of the family structure in Canada as an example. At different times, the number of children born to parents has varied. In times and places where agriculture was the primary source of income, the number of children was relatively high, since children grow up to be good unpaid help to work the land. During the 1950s and early 1960s, the number of children went up, going against the trend of previous decades, because it was a time of prosperity. People could afford to have more children. Today, with increasing urbanization, Canadian families are less likely to require children as labour; well-paying jobs require more postsecondary education, delaying the point at which young families are in a comfortable position to start having children, and it is generally more expensive to raise children today. Hence, the birth rate has declined. The "ideal" number of children changes with the circumstances—just like the colours of the Venezuelan guppies.

5. Fashion

Sometimes a change is just change solely for its own sake. We seek novelty, and the result is neither an improvement nor a turn for the worse. And it does not reflect some deeper meaning, or a value shift. In this case, we have the fashion model of change. Stanley Lieberson (2000) has argued that the change in North American baby names falls into the category of fashion. Consumer companies likewise profit from this desire for the new, and it's not just clothing companies, either. Tweaking an automotive design, or the "look" of a team uniform can help a company make money on people's desire for the new.

Education involves fashion changes, too. Catchy phrases such as "whole language," "collaborative learning," and "adaptive learning" are used to promote new styles in education, but they often reflect people's need to feel they have a fresh approach to an age-old problem. Education fashions come and go, but real improvement or decline is hard to measure. The culture around education changes and has an impact on the scores that quantify educational "excellence." Declining marks in North American literacy tests may reflect educational changes, but they might also reflect an increase in the number of students whose first language is not English, and a decrease in reading as a leisure activity.

Tattoos

The American poet T.S. Eliot (1888–1965) once wrote, "Art never improves, but . . . the material of art is never quite the same."

The number of people who have tattoos has increased greatly over the last two decades. Estimates have it that one in five adults in the West has at least one, whether it is boldly presented on an arm or neck or tucked away secretly in a place far from public view. How would a sociologist look at that aspect of social change? Here are several ways.

First, there is a traditional association of tattoos with marginalized people: prisoners, sailors, prostitutes, and people in circus sideshows (also sometimes called "freak shows"). Second, it is generational: people in their twenties and thirties (and increasingly "their forties and fifties") are the most likely to have tattoos in the highest numbers. Third, it is gender-related: more women than men sport body art.

A public school student in Nicaragua looks at his new laptop, courtesy of a local investment group, the Fundacion Zamora Teran. They have partnered with the international non-profit One Laptop Per Child, which strives to provide affordable educational devices to schoolchildren in the developing world. The program has been criticized by those who think the funds would be better spent on schools or on children's public health and by those who think that sending older, recycled computers to developing countries is a more cost-effective (and environmentally friendly) solution. Are these petty complaints about a well-meaning initiative to bridge the digital divide? Or are these students being locked into the "after three years it breaks, and the parts to repair it aren't available" cycle?

What happens when the tattoo, a traditional demonstration of deviance, comes into conflict with mainstream values and attitudes? It becomes a social issue, as we have seen in the hiring practices of many employers, particularly those in retail. Andrew Timming, a sociologist teaching in the School of Management at the University of St Andrews, Scotland, presented a paper at a 2013 conference of the British Sociological Association (BSA). He had interviewed 15 managers (aged 30–60+) with responsibility for hiring about how they reacted to job candidates with visible tattoos. His findings:

"Most respondents agreed that visible tattoos are a stigma," Dr Timming told the conference. One woman manager told him that "they make a person look dirty." Another male manager told him "subconsciously that would stop me from employing them." Another male manager said "tattoos are the first thing they [fellow recruiters] talk about when the person has gone out of the door."

The managers were concerned about what their organisations' customers might think, said Dr Timming. "Hiring managers realise that, ultimately, it does not matter what they think of tattoos—what really matters, instead, is how customers might perceive employees with visible tattoos.

"Respondents expressed concern that visibly tattooed workers may be perceived by customers to be 'abhorrent', 'repugnant', 'unsavoury' and 'untidy'. It was surmised that customers might project a negative service experience based on stereotypes that tattooed people are thugs and druggies."

One woman manager told him: "We all judge people on first impressions and what we sum up is quite quick. When they [customers] walk in the door and see that there's a receptionist with guns or knives tattooed, or 'hate' tattooed, I think that is something that would be uncomfortable." (SAGE, 2013)

There are a few things I can add to this. One, as we can see from the last sentence, responses are based at least partly on the nature of the tattoos. The more aggressive the tattoo, the less acceptable it is. This can give a hiring advantage to women, who *typically* sport more modest decorations. Second, there are cases where having a tattoo would be an advantage, something Timming also noted. He mentioned people who work with prisoners as an example. Third—and this is a question closely tied to our interpretations of social change—as time passes, a tattoo in the workplace will become more and more acceptable, given that older people are more likely than younger people to judge tattoos negatively.

This woman's tattoo is likely not a barrier to being employed; is that a gender bias that she is benefiting from, or did she just make more informed choices about the image on her body?

Primeop76/iStockphoto

What do YOU think?

1. A similar stigma was once attached to men with long hair (personal experience). In what ways would this be similar to having a tattoo? In what ways different?
2. In what other workplaces might there be an advantage to having visible tattoos? What workplaces would show the greatest resistance to tattooed employees?
3. Do you agree that women are more likely than men to have tattoos? Why do you think this is?
4. Some people have argued that we have reached "peak tattoo"—that it's a fad nearing its end now that the novelty, and perhaps the stigma, of having a tattoo is fading. Can you see a time where tattoos are once again viewed more negatively than positively?

Social Change in Canada: Two Case Studies

Canadians have been and are experiencing social change in many forms. In earlier chapters we have looked at how social change is playing out in all aspects of life, from the family and education to health and culture. The following sections present two striking, and very different, examples of recent social change in Canada.

Social Change and the Decline of the Cod Fishery in Newfoundland and Labrador

One of the most devastating social changes to hit any part of Canada in recent decades is the loss of the cod fishery in Newfoundland and Labrador. Sociologists Lawrence Hamilton and Cynthia Duncan and biologist Richard Haedrich have described how that change has affected communities along the province's Northern Peninsula (2004).

As the three researchers explain, the most fisheries-dependent part of the province, the Northern Peninsula was hardest hit by the closure of the cod fishery, which had sustained the region for centuries. The first signs of trouble appeared in the 1970s, when it became apparent that cod stocks were diminishing, owing largely to overfishing by foreign vessels and mismanagement of the resource. When, in 1976, the 200-mile economic exclusion zone was declared, reserving waters within 200 nautical miles of the shore for Canadian fishers, many in the province thought that the troubles were over. People who had left returned, and the fishing population grew.

Sociologically and technologically, there were two different cod fisheries in Newfoundland: the dragger, or long-liner, fishery, and the in-shore fishery. The first made use of larger boats, more technology, and longer trips. Traditionally, both were profitable, and the fishing community overall was very egalitarian. And in the "glory years" following the establishment of the 200-mile line, the dragger fleet increased, as did the catch, which reached unprecedented levels. Dragger captains made huge profits, some as much as $350,000–600,000 a year, and even sharemen (often the teenage sons of dragger boat owners) could earn $50,000 a year. But the in-shore fishery started to suffer. In the words of one fisher, "Guys were makin' big bucks and the other guys were just survivin'. Just livin' from day to day, where the other guys were drivin' fancy skidoos and two vehicles" (cited in Hamilton, Duncan, & Haedrich, 2004). The community was more financially divided than ever before.

Eventually, the cod fishery crashed. In 1992, the federal government declared a two-year moratorium on the fishery from the Labrador coast to the southeastern tip of Newfoundland, temporarily suspending cod fishing in this part of the province; the following year the closure area was expanded to include the southern shore of the island. Although it was supposed to be in effect for just two years, the moratorium has yet to be lifted.

It was not just fishers and their families who were hit by the moratorium but others along the chain of the fishing industry. At a local fish-processing plant on the Northern Peninsula, 400 workers were laid off.

Different adaptations occurred among the people in the area. For instance, the birth rate went down, from one of the highest in Canada to just slightly above the national average. Some of the dragger captains were well placed to shift their prey species from fish to invertebrates, such as snow crab, northern shrimp, and the more traditional lobster. Fortunately for them, government money was available to make the transition easier. This new fishery brought revenues comparable to those of the glory days of the cod fishery, but these were distributed across a much smaller segment of the local population.

Many, forced out of their livelihoods, had to leave the province to look for a new line of work. Young people especially travelled west to find work in Alberta's oil fields, and you can see the oil field money in some parts of the province, where earnings made outside of the province have been returned to family members left behind.

Others who remained could not afford to become involved in the new fishery, yet refused to move off the island because they didn't feel they could leave their home. The province invested heavily in its own offshore oil industry, but a growing percentage of the local income came from government transfer payments in the form of employment insurance and welfare. The most recent hope, at least for the provincial government, lies with Muskrat Falls, a huge energy project to harvest hydroelectric power in the lower Churchill River in Labrador.

What do YOU think?

What adaptations did the people of Newfoundland and Labrador make with the loss of the cod fishery? What social change did these adaptations bring about?

Telling It Like It Is

Four-Letter Words and Social Change, or How I Learned to Love the F-Bomb

I don't remember the first time I heard the "f-word" used, but I do recall that in the suburban, middle-class junior high school that I attended in the early 1960s, there was one really tough guy, feared by everyone, who seemed to use it in every sentence he spoke. He was eventually expelled for hitting a teacher.

The first movie I heard the f-word uttered in was the 1970 film *Joe*. It was carefully and deliberately used for shock effect by Peter Boyle's character, a working-class guy who stuns his polite upper-middle–class companions by shouting, "Fucking right!"

The one and only time I heard the word spoken in a university classroom was when a very well-spoken classmate of mine used it (with implied quotation marks around it) after the word "mind," to refer to someone trying to psyche someone out. Her male classmates were dumbstruck.

As far as I can remember, the mores, or customs, surrounding the use of the word as I was growing up in my middle-class neighbourhood were these: I could, as a teenage boy, use the word (but not too frequently) with my buddies, but never with my parents or teachers (no matter how tempted I was on occasion to tell them all to f— off). I would not use the word in front of a girl or woman, ever. Generally, use of the f-word in front of a woman was considered a vile offence committed by a man too drunk, too stoned, or too angry to realize what he was doing. Use of the word *by* a woman would normally elicit shock and disgust.

That was a different time. Now, and in the Toronto college where I teach, use of the word seems to depend on social location. It was in the general concourse that I first started hearing the word regularly, between 10 and 15 years ago, and it is where I still hear it used most often. True, it is on the premises of the college, but it isn't really a site of education; it is more of a public place. Recently I've begun to

Religious Change: Islam as a Canadian Religion

As we saw in Chapter 11, Islam is Canada's fastest-growing organized religion. From 1991 to 2001, the number of Canadian Muslims rose by 128.9 per cent—more than twice the increase for the period 1981–91. In 2001, Canada's 579,640 Muslims made up 2 per cent of the country's total population. Most of them (352,525) were living in Ontario, where the province's Muslim population had grown by 142.2 per cent over the same 10-year period. Islam was the sixth largest religion in the country, just a little behind the Baptist and Lutheran churches, and way behind the "big three"—the Catholic Church, the United Church, and the Anglican Church. But in contrast to these, Islam was the religion with the youngest median age: its followers averaged just 28.1 years. Muslims come from a broad variety of ethnic backgrounds and countries, including Iran, Iraq, Pakistan, India, Afghanistan, Turkey, Somalia, Bosnia, and Indonesia.

By 2011, Muslims had surpassed Baptists and Lutherans to become the fourth largest religious denomination in Canada, according to the National Household Survey. Between 2001 and 2011, their numbers nearly doubled, from 579,640

What do YOU think?

1. Canada's Muslim population represents a variety of ethnic backgrounds. Do you think this will lead to the development of "Canadianized" multicultural mosques?

2. Canadian introductory sociology textbooks often present Muslims, even those living in Canada, as "them," or an "Other." What do you think is the effect among non-Muslim Canadians of reading this treatment of Muslim Canadians?

An Author's POV

Ugurhan Betin/iStockphoto

hear the f-word in the halls between classrooms. Five years ago I heard the word spoken for the first time in my classroom. It wasn't spoken in anger, but it was used for effect by someone with a reputation for brash attention-seeking behaviour.

Over the past five years, I've found that the f-word is relatively commonplace in the concourse and still not infrequent in the halls, used with no apparent concern that "the teacher walking past might hear." I have heard it in the classroom in general conversation during breaks, and used about as often by women as by men.

What do YOU think?

1. How have the rules, or mores, surrounding use of the f-word changed, according to this narrative? What changes have you noticed?
2. What would it take for these mores to change back? Could they change back?
3. Could this kind of language use be considered a verbal "fashion statement"?

to 1,053,945, and from 2.0 per cent of all Canadians to 3.2 per cent.

While there isn't what could be called a "Muslim tradition" in Canada, the faith is not entirely new to the country. In 1871, according to that year's census, there were 13 Muslims living in Canada. The first mosque in Canada—in all of North America, in fact—was Al Rashid, built in Edmonton in 1938, funded by local Muslims, Arab Christians, and Jews.

Social Change and Sociology in Canada

Like all academic disciplines, sociology must change, and it must do so in a way that involves all five of the models of change discussed above. It needs to improve, to get better, in a modernist sense. Perhaps some of this improvement will come in the way sociology is presented to students of the

discipline, just as I've tried to fashion something a little different with this textbook. But sociology also needs a touch of conservatism to ensure that it does not stray too far from the early vision that gave it perception; otherwise, it will diminish. It must constantly have postmodern eyes, using fly-like, multi-dimensional perception to look at who has benefited and who hasn't from sociology as it has been traditionally practised and written about. And it must adapt, evolve.

Concerning that last point, sociology in Canada is facing some serious challenges. In 2003, in the *Canadian Journal of Sociology*, Robert Brym remarked on the fact that while the Canadian Sociology and Anthropology Association (CSAA) was the official organization of Anglo-Canadian sociology, it was losing members, even while the number of faculty members in sociology and anthropology was growing. Membership had peaked at 1,165 in 1993 and within 10 years had dropped by

Mombasa is an amateur boxer and PhD candidate. Does she fit your idea of a young Canadian Muslim woman? What do you think it will take for Canada to be considered, at least in part, a "Muslim country"?

39 per cent. Brym has his explanations for this phenomenon, including (1) external competition from American sociological organizations, (2) internal competition from the *Canadian Journal of Sociology*, (3) a changing organizational environment, and (4) unprofessionalism. On the second-to-last point, he notes reform movements that are "left-leaning" and "feminist." Those he names might argue that they left or never even joined because the organization had become an old boys' club that failed to represent their interests. Whichever way you interpret it, Canadian sociology needs to change. In the personal narrative that ends this introduction to the discipline, I suggest one way I would like to see sociology change.

Concluding Narrative: Where Does Sociology Go from Here?

In a book that emphasizes the importance of personal narratives that highlight unique perspectives on our social world, it is only fitting that we should end with a narrative.

In the conclusion to my doctoral dissertation on how Canadian introductory sociology textbooks present information about Indigenous people, I argued that in order for textbook writers to present the information in a way that is worthy of the best

Telling It Like It Is

Irshad Manji on the Gender Challenge for Canadian Muslim Women

A few years ago, the Ontario government considered allowing Islamic *sharia* law to be applied in family law cases involving Muslims. It was strongly opposed by most Muslim women as well as by more liberal Muslim groups. The Canadianization of Islam poses a considerable gender challenge, as the Muslim writer of the excerpt below, Irshad Manji, explains. Born in Uganda in 1972, Manji and her family emigrated to Canada when she was four, during the expulsion of Uganda's South Asian population under Idi Amin. As an activist and a lesbian, Manji has faced considerable opposition from within her Muslim community. In her provocative book *The Trouble with Islam: A Wake-Up Call for Honesty and Change* (2003), Manji describes how she discovered, at the madressa (the Muslim school she attended on weekends), that the separation and inequality of the genders found in strict Muslim countries were being reproduced in Canada. That this situation was not being challenged but obeyed without question conflicted with what she was learning about the importance of individuality and equality taught to her in the regular school system. In the following, she describes the conflict that led her to leaving the madressa:

> The trouble began with *Know Your Islam*, the primer that I packed in my madressa bag every week. After reading it, I needed to know more about "my" Islam. Why must

girls observe the essentials, such as praying five times a day, at an earlier age than boys? Because, Mr Khaki [her nickname for her teacher] told me, girls mature sooner. They reach the "obligatory age" of practice at nine compared to thirteen for boys.

> "Then why not reward girls for our maturity by letting us lead prayer?" I asked.
> "Girls can't lead prayer."
> "What do you mean?"
> "Girls aren't permitted."
> "Why not?"
> "Allah says so."
> "What's His reason?"
> "Read the Koran." (Manji, 2003: pp. 13–14)

She did not find an answer there that satisfied her Western-trained (and somewhat Western-biased) mind. Still, she remains a Muslim. Later in the book, she writes the following:

> Had I grown up in a Muslim country, I'd probably be an atheist in my heart. It's because I live in this corner of the world, where I can think, dispute, and delve further into any topic, that I've learned why I shouldn't give up on Islam just yet. (Manji, 2003: p. 228)

aims and works of the discipline, they must engage in what can be called "Aboriginal sociology." We could generalize this approach to a broader category of "minorities sociology," but here I will speak in terms of the minority I know best.

This Aboriginal sociology, as I envisioned it, must begin by recognizing the inadequacy of traditional methods of producing sociological knowledge concerning Indigenous people. The voices of the people need to be heard. I warned that if the writers

of these textbooks continued to ignore Indigenous voices in their knowledge production, they would continue to be complicit in the colonialist practices of governments. They were not being neutral, objective, or distanced. They were taking a side.

Equally important is the related recognition that the non-Indigenous cultural background of the writers of introductory sociology textbooks permits them but a limited perspective, one that, as Dorothy Smith (1990) informs us, will miss core concepts that are intrinsically important to understanding Indigenous people from an Indigenous standpoint. The important place of elders in Aboriginal society is one of these core concepts. Elders are involved in all the social institutions of Indigenous life—education, justice, religion, and politics, for example—and anyone in any way involved in Aboriginal society is aware of their significance. But people coming from other cultures that diminish the role of the elderly could easily miss this important point. Indeed, they *have* missed it. Spirituality is another core concept, one that tends to be erased in sociology textbooks. The reserve is a spiritual centre, often (one can probably say *usually*) the location of a number of sacred sites of significance, and yet in sociology textbooks it is only a site for sorry statistics and horror stories.

More generally, the development of an Aboriginal sociology entails the recognition that non-sociologists have authority in talking about Indigenous life. There are very few Aboriginal sociologists, something that the discipline should note and rectify. For the Aboriginal standpoint

to be represented, the knowledge production of Indigenous journalists, educators, filmmakers, elders, and literary writers should be sought out and respected. All of them have voices that are valued in Aboriginal society. That alone should guarantee their inclusion in introductory sociology textbooks.

In my first year of university, sociology opened my eyes to a world of understanding that changed my perception forever. Every semester that I have taught introductory sociology, I have told my students that my goal in teaching the course is to change how they think. I quote, with pride, a former sociology student of mine—a Brazilian nun—who said that my course had "ruined her" by forcing her (enabling her?) to question her previous perceptions of society.

I am a believer in the discipline. But I strongly believe that it needs to change its textual presentation of Indigenous people, as well as its presentation of other groups that do not belong to the dominant culture, in ways as radical as how the discipline itself altered my viewpoint. It requires more voices to thrive in Canada in the twenty-first century.

© Sonny Assu; photo by Guy Letts

"Coke Salish" is a Coast Salish parody displayed at the UBC Museum of Anthropology in Vancouver. What is the artist trying to communicate with this piece of work?

THINK BACK

Questions for Critical Review

1. Compare and contrast the five different models of social change presented in this chapter.
2. Outline the features of the cycle of civilization, and discuss the degree to which it might apply to the United States.
3. Explain who the Luddites were, and outline the social changes to which they were reacting. Do you see parallels between history's Luddites and today's proponents of food-related trends such as urban farming, craft beer (three cheers!), and free-range and other anti-industrial farming movements?
4. Outline Arthur Kroker's idea of the virtual class.
5. How can sociology be made to appeal to Indigenous students, to encourage the growth of Indigenous sociology in Canada?
6. In North America we have cultivated a workplace culture that encourages people to work longer hours in the name of "greater productivity." Smartphones keep us tethered to the office during the supposed off hours from work. Meanwhile, some social reformers, including author and historian Rutger Bregman, are advocating a 15-hour work week. Provided the pay remains roughly the same, is a shorter work week the way of the future?
7. It is common today for a video or picture to go viral. What does that mean? Does it have relevance only for the moment, before it is quickly forgotten? Does it have significance in terms of long-term social change? A similar term is "trending," with reference to the prevailing but fleeting patterns in the Twitterverse. Do "trending" issues ever have long-term significance?
8. As English becomes the world's global language, we are losing other languages at an alarming rate. Do you think that attempts by Indigenous people to preserve their languages is an impractical conservatism or an important measure for maintaining a strong sense of their Indigenous identity?
9. In Chapter 1 I said that by the time you reached the end of this book, you should have a better sense of what sociology is. So, here we are: what is sociology?

READ ON

Suggested Print and Online Resources

Online

Canadian Centre for Policy Alternatives: Commentary and Fact Sheets
www.policyalternatives.ca/publications/commentary
- The CCPA is a liberal think-tank headquartered in Ottawa. This page provides commentaries on a range of current issues that reflect the centre's approach to influencing social policy in an attempt to make Canada more democratic.

Gay Marriage Plan: Sign of Sweeping Social Change in Canada
www.nytimes.com/2003/06/19/world/gay-marriage-plan-sign-of-sweeping-social-change-in-canada.html
- This *New York Times* article by Clifford Krauss may seem a little out of date, having been published in 2003, when the legalization of gay marriage was still a hot topic here in Canada. But gay marriage is just a point of departure for a look at the pace and scale of social change taking place in Canada, in

comparison with the US.

Interview—Kirkpatrick Sale

www.primitivism.com/sale.htm

- This online interview with Kirkpatrick Sale examines the author's views on Luddites, industrialism, and the dangers of new technology.

Why We Should Give Everyone a Basic Income

www.youtube.com/watch?v=aIL_Y9g7Tg0

- In this TEDx talk, Dutch historian and author Rutger Bregman discusses the ideas behind his book *Utopia for Realists*, which makes the case for a universal basic income and a 15-hour work week.

In Print

George Grant (1965), *Lament for a Nation* **(Toronto: McClelland & Stewart).**

- A classic Canadian work "lamenting" the changes taking place in mid-twentieth-century Canadian society.

Arthur Kroker & Michael A. Weinstein (1995), *Data Trash: Theory of the Virtual Class* **(Montreal: New World Perspectives).**

- It is in this now classic work that the Canadian technology and cultural theorist Arthur Kroker expounds his theory of the virtual class.

Kirkpatrick Sale (1996), *Rebels against the Future: The Luddites and Their War on the Indutrial Revolution—Lessons for the Computer Age* **(Cambridge, MA: Perseus).**

- An elegant case study of an epic fight against the destruction of a social class by technology.

John Steckley (2003), *Aboriginal Voices and the Politics of Representation in Canadian Introductory Sociology Textbooks* **(Toronto: Canadian Scholars' Press).**

- This is my doctoral dissertation made readable. It argues for the need to develop a stronger Aboriginal sociology in Canada.

Glossary

Abell, Helen C. (1917–2005) Canadian sociologist considered a founding figure of rural sociology in Canada, particularly regarding the roles women played on the farm.

Aboriginal *see* **Indigenous**.

Abrahamic religions the three major religions—Judaism, Christianity, and Islam—that trace their origin to the biblical patriarch Abraham.

absolute poverty poverty calculated in absolute material terms. To exist in absolute poverty is to be without sufficient nutritious food, clean and safe shelter, access to education, etc. *Compare* **relative poverty**.

absolutist holding or having to do with the view that certain things are always right, good, moral, modern, or beautiful. Ethnocentrism is a negative example of an absolutist position.

access (without mobility) a buzzword in postsecondary education referring to the availability of online courses to those who would not otherwise be able to attend a college or university because of factors such as cost and family situation. The "without mobility" part is my own addition to the buzzword.

achieved denoting a **status** that a person has earned but was not born into. Professional titles are an example. *Compare* **ascribed**.

actual (or real) culture social life and institutions as they actually exist. *Compare* **ideal culture**.

adjunct professor a college or university professor who is employed on a contract basis and who does not enjoy the benefits and job security of a full-time member of staff.

age group a group composed of people of a particular age (e.g. teenagers, "tweens," twentysomethings), studied over time.

agency the capacity to influence what happens in one's life. *Compare* **victimology**.

agent a person who takes or is capable of taking an active role in the events and circumstances that shape her or his life.

agents of socialization the groups that have a significant influence on a person's socialization. Examples include family, **peer group**, community, school, mass media, the legal system, and culture generally.

aid evangelism the practice of sending religious missionaries into developing countries in need of financial assistance, and using their need as a tool for trying to convert them.

Algonquian the largest family of Indigenous languages in Canada, including Abenaki, Algonquin, Blackfoot, Cree, Delaware, Maliseet, Mi'kmaq, and Ojibwa.

alienation (in Marxist theory) a condition experienced by workers in a capitalist economy when they feel a lack of identity with the products of their labour and a sense of being controlled or exploited.

alternative medicine any medical treatment or remedy that falls outside of conventional Western medical practices. Examples include traditional Chinese medicine, healing techniques such as acupuncture and massage therapy, and herbal remedies. *See* **biomedicine**, **complementary medicine**.

American dream the mostly unrealistic belief that one can become rich and successful through hard work and determination alone. A naive belief in the American dream is sometimes used to justify punishing others for being poor (the "American nightmare").

Ames, Herbert Brown (1863–1954) Canadian businessman and politician who engaged in a detailed sociological study of poor areas of Montreal.

anomie **Durkheim's** term for a societal state of breakdown or confusion, or a more personal one based on an individual's lack of connection or contact with society.

anti-colonialism *another term for* **postcolonialism**.

Anyon, Jean (1941–2013) American critical education researcher involved with studying the intersection between "race," class, and educational policy.

archaeology of knowledge **Foucault's** term for the process of "digging down" to find out how a piece of information was constructed, typically in order to discover or expose flaws in the way supposed facts or truths were established.

aristocrats (in Marxist theory) the landowner class of feudal times, who owned the land worked on by the class of **peasants**.

ascribed denoting a **status** that a person is born into (female, daughter, older sister) or has entered involuntarily (adult, diabetic). *Compare* **achieved**.

assimilation the process by which minorities, indigenous peoples, and immigrants lose their distinctive cultural characteristics to become like members of the dominant culture. It is a key principle of **melting pot** societies.

authenticity the quality of being true to the traditions of a people. Authenticity is often **contested** by the modern representatives of the people themselves and "experts" from outside the community.

autism spectrum disorder a broad range of neurodevelopment disorders that involve a relative lack of ability to communicate and generally interact with others. It is also associated with restricted repetitive behaviours, interests, and activities. While it was once attributed to socialization (*see* **refrigerator mothers**), it is now believed to be primarily genetic.

average a statistical figure determined by adding up the numbers for a given phenomenon and dividing the sum by the number of individuals in the statistical population. Five squirrels picked up 24 peanuts from my front porch. The average number of peanuts per squirrel is $24 \div 5 = 4.8$.

back stage (as described by **Goffman**) the site of private, personal, or intimate encounters between individuals. *See* **dramaturgical approach**, **front stage**, **impression management**.

bakla in Tagalog (the national language of the Philippines), a word referring to the cultural configuration of someone who is assigned male gender at birth but is usually attracted to other males and typically engages in cross-dressing and behaviour deemed more "feminine" than "masculine."

Bales, Robert F. (1916–2004) American social psychologist who taught at Harvard and developed **interaction process analysis**, a framework for studying social interaction in small groups.

barbarism (as described by **Morgan** in the nineteenth century) the second stage of social evolution on the way to modern civilization. It was identified as one of a series of stages all societies were thought to pass through in their natural development. *Compare* **civilization**, **savagery**.

bar mitzvah a Jewish **rite of passage** in which a boy becomes a man.

bat mitzvah   a Jewish **rite of passage** in which a girl becomes a woman.

Battiste, Marie (b. 1949)   Canadian Mi'kmaq educator who specializes in the sociology of anti-colonialism and decolonization in education and knowledge.

Baudrillard, Jean (1929–2007)   French sociologist, political commentator and postmodernist cultural theorist, associated with the term **simulacrum**.

Beaujot, Rod (b. 1946)   Canadian demographer specializing in the sociology of the family.

Becker, Howard (b. 1928)   American sociologist specializing in the sociology of deviance, particularly with regard to **labelling theory**.

behaviourism   a school of thought in psychology, which emphasizes that behaviour can be studied and explained scientifically not in terms of internal mental states (unlike **psychoanalysis**) but through observing how people's actions are supposedly conditioned by earlier actions and reactions.

behaviour modification   an approach to changing someone's behaviour by giving rewards for behaviour that one wishes to encourage and, sometimes, issuing sanctions for behaviour one wishes to discourage. *See* **law of effect**.

best practices   strategies with a demonstrated history of achieving desired results more effectively or more consistently than similar methods used either in the past by a particular organization or currently by other organizations in the same industry.

Bettelheim, Bruno (1903–1990)   Austrian-born American child psychologist who, before both his credentials and his work were discredited, became famous for his work with autistic children. *See* **refrigerator mothers**.

Big Pharma   the pharmaceutical or drug manufacturing industry, especially when viewed as a large, lucrative industry ultimately more concerned with generating corporate profits than with improving public health.

biomedicine   the application of standard principles of Western scientific disciplines (particularly biology) in the diagnosis and treatment of symptoms of illness. *Compare* **alternative medicine**.

bisexual   a person who is sexually attracted to people of both sexes.

blaming the victim   William Ryan's term for the process of assigning responsibility to individuals for events or circumstances that have broader social or genetic causes. Example: ascribing unemployment to laziness on the part of unemployed people while failing to consider that job creation is not keeping pace with population increases.

Blumer, Herbert (1900–1987)   American sociologist who was a pioneer in **social interactionism**, as well as a critic of positivist sociological research.

bodily stigma   *see* **stigma**.

Bookchin, Murray (1921–2006)   American thinker prominent in the ecology and anarchism movements.

Bott, Elizabeth (Spillius) (1924–2016)   Canadian-born anthropologist and social psychologist who specialized in the study of family networks. She is best known for formulating the theory that came to be known as the Bott hypothesis.

Bott hypothesis   the theory that when a husband's and wife's separate social networks are dense and closely connected, the husband and wife are likely to take on segregated, rather than joint, conjugal roles in the household; joint conjugal roles are more likely to exist where husband and wife do not have close social networks outside of the household.

Bourdieu, Pierre (1930–2002)   French sociologist and social critic, who introduced the concepts of **cultural capital** and **habitus** to sociology.

bourgeoisie   *see* **capitalists**.

boyah (plural boyat)   a woman living in an Arab country of the Middle East who adopts a masculine style of dress and appearance (e.g. by cutting her hair short) as a way of defying gender norms.

brain drain   the exodus of scientists, doctors, and other skilled professionals from a country.

branding   the corporate use of marketing as an instrument of socialization to encourage teens and younger children to covet brand-name products linked, via advertising, to the cool or fashionable identity of the day.

broad socialization   socialization in which individualism and independence are promoted. *Compare* **narrow socialization**.

Butler, Judith (b. 1956)   American feminist theorist who examined the way people perform gender roles in an effort to meet society's expectations of what it means to be "male" or "female."

capital   Marx's term for the funds and properties necessary for the large-scale manufacture and trade of goods.

capitalists   Marx's term for the owners of the means of production (or capital, as these were known during the industrial era). *Also called* **bourgeoisie**.

case study approach   a research design that explores a social entity or phenomenon by examining a single representative case or a few selected examples.

catharsis   emotional relief through the release of built-up energy or tension.

Catholic-Traditionalists   Angela Robinson's term for Mi'kmaq who adopted Catholicism but incorporated non-Christian elements into their religious practices.

causation   the relationship between cause and effect.

China price   the true cost of China's competitive advantage in manufacturing, which takes into account the harm done to exploited workers and damage caused to the environment.

Chomsky, Noam (b. 1928)   American theoretical linguist, social critic, and activist who demonstrated that language is innate, not learned.

cisgender   a term used for people who identify with the gender corresponding to their biological sex. *Compare* **transgender**.

civilization   (as described by **Morgan** in the nineteenth century) the third and final stage of social evolution of all societies, viewed by European and North American thinkers as best exemplified by European and North American culture. *Compare* **barbarism**, **savagery**.

Clark, Samuel Delbert (1910–2003)   Canadian sociologist whose writings about Canada's social development helped sociology gain respectability in Canada. He founded the sociology department at the University of Toronto.

class   Marx's term for a socioeconomic group defined either relationally—that is, in Marxist terms, with respect to their relationship to the **means of production** (e.g. owner, worker)—or absolutely, in terms of access to socially valued goods such as money, education, and respect.

class consciousness   Marx's term for the awareness of what is in the best interests of one's social class.

class reductionism   the intellectual fallacy that all forms of oppression are just about class and class differences, a view that wrongly downplays the role of factors such as "race," ethnicity, gender, and age.

clinical iatrogenesis   Illich's term for the ways in which diagnosis and cure cause problems that are equal to or greater than the health problems they are meant to resolve. An example would be catching a virus while in hospital for minor surgery.

cluttered nest   a situation in which adult children continue to live at home with their parents. *Compare* **empty nest**.

cohabiting union (*or* **couple**)   *see* **common-law union**.

Cohen, Albert (1918–2014)   American sociologist specializing in criminology. He is most famous for his **subcultural theory** of delinquents (or **delinquent subculture**).

cohort   a group of people with a common statistical characteristic. Examples include baby boomers, who were born during the same period, and the frosh of 2017, who entered college or university in the same year.

collective   *another term for* **small group**.

collective consciousness   Durkheim's term for shared feeling and understanding among people belonging to a particular religion, fostered by group experiences and rituals.

Collins, Patricia Hill (b. 1948)   American critical sociologist who is best known for her work on feminist standpoint theory and **intersectionality**.

colonialism   the policy or practice of acquiring full or partial control over another country, occupying it with settlers, and exploiting it economically or culturally.

commodification   the tendency to treat something as though it were an object to be bought or sold. For example, the commodification of medicine involves identifying certain conditions that might be normal (though slightly regrettable) as diseases that may be treated with "commodity cures" (such as drugs or surgical procedures).

common-law union (*or* **couple**)   two people of the same or opposite sex who are living together as a couple but who are not legally married to each other. *Also called* **cohabiting union**.

community of scholars   the people associated with a particular academic discipline, including researchers and instructors.

companionate roles   the overlapping **conjugal roles** of partners in a marriage who both work outside the home and do work around the house. *Compare* **complementary roles**.

complementary medicine   alternative medicine practised in conjunction with conventional medicine. *See* **alternative medicine**, **biomedicine**.

complementary roles   the **conjugal roles** of partners in a marriage when one (traditionally the husband) does paid work, while the other (traditionally the wife) does the unpaid work of child care and housework. *Compare* **companionate roles**.

complex household   a household in which there are two or more adults who are related but not married to each other.

complicit masculinity   forms of masculinity that do not contribute to or embody male hegemony yet still benefit from it.

Comte, Auguste (1798–1857)   French proponent of **positivism** who aimed to develop a truly scientific social science that could be used for social reconstruction.

confirmation   a Christian **rite of passage** in which an adult who was baptized as a child or an infant affirms Christian belief and is admitted as a full member of the church.

conflict deviance   behaviour that is subject to debate over whether or not it is deviant. Examples: marijuana use; "creative accounting" on tax returns.

conflict theory (*or* **approach**)   a sociological perspective espousing the view that complex societies are made up of groups in conflict, with one or more groups dominating or oppressing the others.

conjugal roles   the distinctive roles of spouses that result from the division of labour within the family.

conservatism   a view of social change as potentially more destructive than constructive, especially in emotionally charged areas of life such as family, gender roles, sexuality, and the environment.

content analysis   a study of a set of cultural artifacts (e.g. children's books, newspaper articles, Internet memes) or events by systematically counting them and interpreting the themes they reflect.

contested   describing a practice whose moral goodness or badness, normalcy or deviance, or general predominance is disputed by some members of society.

control   one of four main elements of **Weber's** model of **formal rationalization**, having to do with the use of rules, regulations, and a hierarchical structure to keep workers in line. *See* **efficiency**, **predictability**, **quantification**.

Cooley, Charles Horton (1864–1929)   American sociologist who was an early proponent of **symbolic interactionism**, reflected in his introduction of the concept of the **looking-glass self**.

corporate crimes   (as described by Clinard & Quinney) (1) offences committed by corporate officials on behalf of the corporation they represent, or (2) the offences of the corporation itself. *Compare* **occupational crimes**.

corporate identity   the shared sense of common membership and common purpose that a social group can have. *Also called* **organic identity**.

corporatization of education   significant corporate investment in research funding that conditions the direction that academic research takes, potentially restricting the intellectual freedom of the researchers and their department. Under the corporatization of education, postsecondary institutions follow a model of policies and practices more typical of a business than of a place of higher education.

correlation   a mutual relationship or interdependence among **variables**. *See* **direct correlation**, **inverse correlation**.

cosmology   an account or theory of the origin of the universe.

countercultures   groups that reject selected elements of the dominant culture, such as clothing styles or sexual norms. *Compare* **subculture**.

counter-ideology   a set of beliefs that challenges or contests the **dominant ideology** put forward by the dominant culture and the ruling classes.

covert characteristics (**of deviance**)   the unstated qualities that might make a particular group a target for sanctions. *Compare* **overt characteristics** (**of deviance**).

credentialism   a bias in favour of job candidates with academic degrees, diplomas, or certificates over those without, regardless of their demonstrated knowledge, ability, and experience.

Crenshaw, Kimberlé W. (b. 1959)   American legal theorist who helped develop critical race theory and who introduced the term **intersectionality** to refer to the linking forms of prejudice based on "race" and gender.

criminology   the study of crime in terms of such key sociological elements as causation, prevention, management, or control, and the statistical patterning among certain groups and geographical areas.

critical education   an education model that involves the analysis and discussion of ideas. *Compare* **instrumental education**.

critical management studies   research that challenges traditional theories of management by examining previously neglected factors such as the effects of gender, "race," and class on groups and organizations.

critical sociology sociology that challenges both established sociological theories and the research that sociologists do.

crude marriage rate the number of marriages per 1,000 people in a population.

cultural artifact an item produced for mass cultural consumption, with value to a researcher engaged in content analysis. Cultural artifacts can include books, articles, websites, advertisements, and other items created to be seen but not specifically to be studied.

cultural capital (as described by **Bourdieu**) the knowledge and skills required to develop the sophisticated taste that mark someone as a person of high culture and upper class.

cultural globalization (as described by **Steger**) the intensification and expansion of the flow of culture across the world in a process that involves media and patterns of consumption.

cultural iatrogenesis (as described by **Illich**) a situation in which the knowledge and abilities of health professionals have become so mythologized that individuals lose the capacity to heal themselves.

cultural mosaic a metaphor for any society in which individual ethnic groups are able to maintain distinctive identities. *Compare* **melting pot**.

cultural norms generally expected or explicitly stated rules of behaviour. These may reflect the **ideal culture** more than they do the **real culture**.

cultural relativism the view that any aspect of a culture, including its practices and beliefs, is best explained within the context of the culture itself, not by the standard or ways of the researcher's own culture.

cultural reproduction theory the theory that the education system reproduces and reinforces the inequality of the surrounding society.

cultural studies a field of study drawing on both the social sciences (primarily sociology) and the humanities (primarily literature and media studies) to cast academic light on the meanings expressed in popular culture and their significance.

culture a social system (sometimes **contested**) comprising behaviour, beliefs, knowledge, practices, values, and material such as buildings, tools, and sacred items.

culture and personality (as described by R. **Benedict**) a now discredited school of thought that argued that every culture has a distinct personality that is encouraged by its cultural practices and beliefs.

culture industry an industry that produces commodities and services that in some way express a way of life (such as the film and TV industry) or that occupy a special place in the social communications system (such as advertising or the media).

cultures of education the attitudes toward education and educational practices associated with different cultural groups (e.g. European, Indigenous, black).

cultures of medicine the recognition that different cultures have different ways of practising medicine, including different **social courses of disease**, different techniques, and different physical remedies.

cycle of civilization the supposed rise and fall of **civilizations** in somewhat predictable cycles. The term has been applied to the Roman empire, the Mongol empire, the Ottoman (Turkish) empire, and the American empire.

Dahl, **Robert A.** (1915–2014) American political scientist who specialized in looking at types of power or influence. He discussed this in terms of **oligarchy** and **polyarchy**.

Dawson, **Carl Addington** (1887–1964) Canadian sociologist trained at the University of Chicago, formed Canada's first postsecondary department of sociology, at McGill University.

d'Eaubonne, **Françoise** (1915–2014) French feminist and prolific writer who introduced the term ecofeminism.

decipherment the process of examining a text to discover its true meaning, which often involves looking beyond the explicit message to discover the intent (conscious or unconscious) of the individual or organization that produced it.

definition of the situation (in symbolic-interactionist thinking) the notion that different individuals will define a given situation differently, possibly in contradictory ways, based on their own subjective experiences. As a result, understanding how an individual defines a situation is crucial to understanding the individual's actions and responses to it.

degradation ceremony a **rite of passage** designed to strip a person of his or her individuality. Hazing is an example of a degradation ceremony.

delinquent subculture (as described by A. **Cohen**) the **subordinate culture** of teenage gangs. *See* **subcultural theory**.

democracy a political system that involves a broad-based voting electorate, an opposition that is free to criticize the group in power without fear, freedom of the press and of speech, protection of the rights of minorities, and relative equality of men and women.

dependent variable a **variable** that is assumed to be affected by an **independent variable**.

desensitization theory the idea that increased exposure to media violence (e.g. from television, movies, and video games) blunts, or desensitizes, natural feelings of revulsion at the sight or thought of violence.

determinism the belief that personal characteristics, including behaviour and attitudes, are shaped by forces beyond the control, or **agency**, of the individual.

developed nations the wealthier nations of the world, typically including the United States, Canada, the western European nations, and the more financially successful countries of Asia, Africa, and the Americas.

developing nations poorer nations of the world that are seeking to become more advanced economically and socially. The label is **contested** by some critics of globalization, who prefer the term "underdeveloping nations" to better reflect the status of these countries as they become poorer as a result of exploitation by **developed nations**.

deviance straying from or different to what is considered usual or normal.

dialect a version of a language, usually with a unique set of features (in terms of vocabulary, grammar, and pronunciation) and a socially identifiable group of speakers. Newfoundland English is an example of a dialect (even though technically there are several Newfoundland dialects).

digital divide the situation in which citizens of the world's wealthier nations, as well as richer citizens of the poorer nations, have an access to computers and related technology that gives them an enormous social, economic, and political advantage over the poorer citizens of the richer nations and most people in the poorer countries.

direct correlation a relationship between two **variables** in which an increase (or decrease) in one causes a corresponding increase (or decrease) in the other. *Compare* **inverse correlation**.

disabled family the family of a person with a disability. As noted by W. Hower, the disability of an individual can become a kind of **ascribed status** for the individual's entire family, which may lead to discrimination against all family members by others within the community.

discourse a conceptual framework with its own internal logic and underlying assumptions. Different disciplines, such as sociology and psychology, have their own discourses.

discourse analysis an approach to analyzing a conversation, a speech, or a written text. The scope of discourse analysis has broadened recently to encompass entire academic disciplines, such as sociology and political philosophy.

discrimination acts by which individuals are differentially rewarded or punished based on their membership in a social group defined by class, sexual orientation, ethnicity, and so on.

disenchanted lacking in magic, fantasy, or mystery. **Weber** used the term to characterize the secular, rationalized West.

disjuncture a gap between knowledges produced from two or more different perspectives (e.g. those of management and employees).

disproportionate representation a situation that occurs when an atypically high or low number of a particular social group is associated with a specific situation. South Asian men are over-represented in the population of cricket players in Canada but are underrepresented in the population of professional hockey players: in both cases, disproportionate representation exits.

disqualified knowledges **Foucault**'s term for knowledge that is discredited on the grounds that it lacks the trained, objective, scientific basis of knowledges considered superior. The exclusion of Indigenous voices from the coverage of First Nations history in Canadian sociology textbooks can be considered a case of disqualified knowledges.

docile body **Foucault**'s term for a group that has been conditioned, through a specific set of procedures and practices, to behave in a particular, pre-programmed way.

dominant capitalist class the social class composed primarily of those who own or control the **means of production**.

dominant culture the culture that through its political and economic power is able to impose its values, language, interpretations of events, and ways of behaving on a given society.

dominant ideology a set of beliefs put forward by and in support of the dominant culture and/or ruling classes within a society, to help them justify their dominant position and dominating practices.

dominants the group within a society that has the most political and social power, whose culture or subculture is seen as "the" culture of a country. They make up the **dominant culture**.

double burden (*or* **ghetto**) a term used to characterize the imbalance in gender roles in situations where a married woman works a paid job during the day and is expected to perform the unpaid domestic work (cleaning house, preparing meals, looking after children, etc.) traditionally associated with women when she comes home. *See* **second shift**.

Dragon Lady (as described by Tajima & Das Gupta) a stereotype of East Asian women as tough, ruthless, and mercenary. The stereotype is seen in film and TV portrayals of hardened prostitutes and madams, and women who fight with nasty, angry facial expressions. *Compare* **Lotus Blossom Baby**.

dramaturgical approach (as described by **Goffman**) a way of approaching sociological research as if everyday life were taking place on the stage of a theatre. *See* **back stage, front stage, impression management**.

dual colonialism a situation that occurs when the most oppressed groups (e.g. Rwanda's Hutu) are colonized both by the colonizing outsider group (the Belgians) and by a local group that is given privilege and power by the outsider group (the Tutsi).

Du Bois, W.E.B. (1868–1963) African-American social philosopher, who was among the first to document the experience of American blacks from a sociological perspective.

Duffy, Ann Canadian sociologist who works from a feminist political economy perspective, and who has a long history of studying the sociology of families.

Durkheim, Émile (1858–1917) French founding figure of sociology, who studied society in terms of **social facts** such as ethics, occupations, religion, and suicide.

dynamic denoting a social situation in which groups are subject to change. *Compare* **static**.

Ebaugh, Helen Rose Fuchs (b. 1942) American sociologist, who specializes in organizational sociology and the sociology of religion. She has studied and written about **role exit**.

Edwards, Henrietta Muir (1849–1931) Canadian political activist, one of the **Famous Five**, who fought for the rights of women, especially working women and those in prison.

efficiency one of four main elements of **Weber**'s model of **formal rationalization**, having to do with the streamlined movement of people and things. *See* **control, predictability, quantification**.

egalitarianism (*adj*. **egalitarian**) the principle that all people are equal and deserve equal rights and opportunities.

ego (as described by **Freud**) the conscious aspect of the individual personality. *Compare* **id, superego**.

Elkind, David (b. 1931) American child psychologist, who has studied culture as an agent of child socialization. He developed the concept of **hurried child syndrome**.

embedded journalist a journalist who travels with the military to report objectively on their activities. In exchange for protection, the journalist may be persuaded to present an impression sympathetic to the military's purposes.

empty nest a situation in which the children of an older couple have grown up and moved out of the family home. *Compare* **cluttered nest**.

endogamy the practice of marrying within one's class, "race," or ethnic group. *Compare* **exogamy**.

Engels, Friedrich (1820–1895) German economist, who co-wrote, with **Marx**, *The Communist Manifesto* (1848).

environmental racism a double standard in attitudes around environmental protection, depending on which "race" or ethnicity prevails in the threatened region. "White" places generally attract a high level of concern and care, while places associated with racial minorities are often neglected.

environmental refugees people forced to leave their home region owing to sudden changes to the local environment (e.g. drought, melting land ice, polluted water) that pose a threat to their livelihood or survival.

epidemiology the study of public health, specifically the incidence and spread of diseases in a population.

epiphenomenal denoting a factor of secondary significance to a more significant cause. For **Marx**, "race" and ethnicity were epiphenomenal to economic structure.

eros (as described by **Freud**) the "sexual" or "life" instinct within the **id**.

essentialism the view that every ethnic group is made up of a set of readily identifiable traits that have been passed down from the past to the present with little or no change. *Also called* **primordialism**.

essentialist feminism a feminist approach that involves looking at differences between the way women and men think while arguing for the equality—and sometimes female superiority—in that difference.

ethics the honourable moral principles that govern sociological research, including respect for the privacy and the rights and concerns of the research subjects.

ethnic class (as described by Dofny & Rioux) the situation that exists when members of different ethnic groups adopt occupations that are ranked differently (e.g. administration versus labourers). An ethnic class system existed in Quebec for most of the twentieth century.

ethnic entrepreneurs individuals who manipulate symbols with strong meaning to their ethnic group in order to gain and wield personal power. Examples include Adolf Hitler and Slobodan Milošević.

ethnocentrism the belief that one culture (often one's own, occasionally another considered more powerful or respect-worthy) is the absolute standard by which other cultures should be judged.

ethnography a research method, shared by sociology and social anthropology, in which communities or groups are studied through extensive fieldwork. Ethnography requires the researcher to participate daily in the lives of the subjects, observing their actions and asking questions. *See* **institutional ethnography**.

eugenics the science of improving a population by controlled breeding. The idea was especially popular in the early twentieth century, when people believed that "good traits" and "bad traits" were inherited, and that the poor, the colonized, and other marginalized people should be sterilized to prevent them from reproducing.

Eurocentrism (*adj.* **Eurocentric**) generally, the belief that "European" (i.e. western and northern European, plus North American) culture is superior to other cultures; more specifically in sociology, the use of a European viewpoint to address others, often with the assumption that the audience shares (or would like to share) that viewpoint.

evolution a model of **social change** in which change is seen as an adaptation to a set of particular circumstances, an idea captured by the expression **survival of the fittest**. *See* **social Darwinism**.

examination a form of disciplinary control that combines the methods of **hierarchical observation** and **normalizing judgement** to condition group behaviour; it is part of a set of tactics used to produce what **Foucault** called a **docile body**.

exogamy the practice of marrying outside of one's class, "race," or ethnic group. *Compare* **endogamy**.

exoticism the process of making peoples from other cultures seem more exotic or "strange," more different from one's own culture than they actually are or were.

experiential based on or acquired through one's own experience.

extended family the family beyond mother, father, and children. Use of this term reflects the user's belief that the **nuclear family** is the model of a "normal" family.

fact something that has been observed, and that as far as can be proven is believed to be true.

false consciousness (as described by **Marx**) the belief that something (e.g. capitalism, religion) is in the best interests of one's class when it is not.

Famous Five, The five Canadian women (Henrietta Muir **Edwards**, Nellie **McClung**, Louise **McKinney**, Emily **Murphy**, and Irene **Parlby**) who fought for equal social rights for women (including obtaining the vote and being able to run for political office) during the first half of the twentieth century.

Fanon, Franz (1925–1961) Afro-Caribbean thinker from Martinique, who engaged in pioneering work in **anti-colonialism**.

fashion a model of **social change** that promotes change for its own sake, not for better (**modernism**), not for worse (**conservatism**), nor even for adaptation (**evolution**). Fashion change may occur because a manufacturer wants consumers to believe a product has been improved (though it hasn't), or it may occur because people desire something different.

fecundity a woman's ability to conceive, which changes with age.

feminist organization an organizational form based on principles different to those underlying more patriarchal organizational structures, including inclusiveness, an absence of hierarchy, and a more equitable distribution of power.

feminization the process whereby an occupational sphere becomes dominated by and associated with women (e.g. secretarial work, clerical work). Feminized occupations are usually rewarded with lower salaries and fewer benefits.

First World a term used prior to the collapse of the USSR in the late twentieth century to refer to the world's rich, capitalist countries.

folk society (as described by R. Redfield) a rural, small-scale, homogeneous society imbued with a strong sense of the sacred and the personal, usually in contrast to an urban society.

folkways (as described by **Sumner**) **norms** that in the usual course of events one *should* not (rather than *must* not) violate. They are the least respected and most weakly sanctioned norms.

food bank a central clearing house run by a non-profit organization to collect, store, and distribute food free of charge to the poor.

formal rationalization (*or* **rationality**) (as described by **Weber**) a model of improving the effectiveness of an organization or process based on four elements: (1) efficiency, (2) quantification, (3) predictability, and (4) control. Weber was critical of the concept, believing that it led to **disenchantment** and alienation of the individuals involved in the rationalized process or organization.

formal social movement organization (as described by C. Mueller) a type of **feminist organization** characterized as professionalized, bureaucratic, and inclusive.

Foucault, Michel (1926–1984) French social theorist who studied and wrote about the relationship between power and the acceptability of different socially placed knowledges. His methodology, known as **archaeology of knowledge**, is a valuable sociological tool.

Frankfurt school a school of social philosophers (including Adorno, Horkheimer, and Marcuse) who, beginning in the 1920s, applied the insights of Nietzsche, Marx, and Freud to their critical writing on fascism, communism, and capitalism.

Franklin, Frazier E. (1894–1962) African-American sociologist who is best known for his research on the subject of the "Negro family" in the United States.

free-floating statistic a statistic created in a particular context of time and place but that is repeated outside of that context.

Freud, Sigmund (1856–1939) Austrian neurological doctor who founded the psychological methodology of **psychoanalysis**.

friendly racism (as described by H. Codjoe) a form of racism that is subtle and seemingly (to the perpetrator) harmless.

front stage (as described by **Goffman**) the site of social interactions designed for public display. *See* **back stage**, **dramaturgical approach**, **impression management**.

functionalism a sociological approach that involves explaining social structures in terms of their functions, i.e. what they do for society.

Galton, Francis (1822–1911) English statistician who coined the terms **eugenics** and **correlation**, as well as the phrase "nature vs nurture" (with reference to the two influences of genetics and society).

game stage (as described by **Mead**) the third stage of intellectual development, in which the child considers simultaneously the perspective of several roles. *Compare* **play stage**, **role-taking**.

gay an informal term for someone (male or female) who is sexually attracted to people of the same sex.

gender (as described by A. Oakley) the socially constructed and socially unequal division of masculinity and femininity, as opposed to the biological division of **sex**.

gendered denoting occupations or postsecondary programs dominated either by men or by women. Examples include early childhood education and interior design for women, firefighting and industrial design for men.

gender role the role that a culture or society assigns as "normal" for boys/men and girls/women.

gender strategy (as described by A. Hochschild) a way of dealing with situations in different areas of life (work, family, etc.) based on culturally defined **gender roles**. For example, in a dual-income household, the typical gender strategy for caring for infants is for the mother to take time off of work.

genealogy a form of **discourse analysis** that involves tracing the origin and history of modern **discourses** (e.g. the importance of light-coloured skin in South Asian culture). The term is sometimes considered interchangeable with the **archaeology of knowledge**.

general intelligence the mistaken idea that people have a single intelligence level that applies to many areas of life, skills, and abilities. Belief in general intelligence would lead one to conclude that a boy or girl who does not earn high marks at school but has other skills is stupid.

generalized others (as described by **Mead**) the attitudes, viewpoints, and general expectations of the society that a child is socialized into.

generation gap significant cultural and social differences that produce a lack of understanding between members of different generations.

genetically modified denoting a plant, animal, or micro-organism whose genetic material has been artificially manipulated in order to produce a desired characteristic. Genetically modified varieties of certain food crops are more resistant to plant diseases and insects, but that may exhibit unplanned features that cause yet unknown problems among consumers. *Compare* **transgenic**.

genocide a set of social practices designed to eliminate or exterminate a people. These practices include warfare, displacement from a homeland, enforced sexual sterilization, separation of family members, and banning languages and other culturally identifiable features, all of which were committed against Indigenous people in Canada.

Gilligan, **Carol** (b. 1936) American educational psychologist and feminist theorist, who identified stages of moral development in girls and women.

globalism (as described by **Steger**) an ideology that links **globalization** with **neoliberalism**.

globality (as described by **Steger**) a set of social conditions of globalization at a particular time and place.

globalization the process or policy of removing barriers to the free passage of goods and individuals in order to make commerce more international in scope.

glocalization (as described by R. Robertson) the process of tailoring globalization to local needs and tastes. Glocalization is done either by **transnational companies** bent on increasing their globalized sales and influence, or by the local culture filtering the effects of globalization.

Goffman, **Erving** (1922–1982) Alberta-born sociologist, best known for his work on **total institutions**, **stigma**, social roles, and **impression management**.

Gramsci, **Antonio** (1891–1937) radical Italian Marxist thinker and politician, best known for his concept of **hegemony**.

Grant, **George** (1918–1988) Canadian philosopher and nationalist who warned against cultural absorption by the United States and the excesses to technologically-driven modernity.

Great White Man a biased portrayal of history that records and values almost exclusively the lives and historical contributions of white men in positions of leadership (e.g. prime ministers, governors, missionaries, traders, and explorers).

habitus Bourdieu's term for a set of class-affected or culturally affected and socially acquired characteristics (e.g. opinions, definitions of "manners" and "good taste," leisure pursuits).

haram forbidden or proscribed under Islamic law.

Hart, **Julian Tudor** (b. 1927) British doctor who served the working classes and introduced the **inverse care law**.

hegemonic masculinity (as described by R. Connell) practices and beliefs that normalize and naturalize men's dominance and women's subordination.

hegemony (as described by **Gramsci**) a set of relatively non-coercive methods of maintaining power used by the dominant class (e.g. through the various media and the legal system). Often the terms *hegemony* and *hegemonic* are used to refer just to the possession and exercise of power (see, for instance, **hegemonic masculinity**).

heteronormative denoting or relating to the norms, mores, rules, and laws that uphold heterosexual standards of identity and behaviour and heterosexuality as natural and universal.

heterosexual a person who is sexually attracted to people of the opposite sex.

hidden curriculum the unstated, unofficial agenda of school system authorities, including such elements as obedience and ranking.

hierarchical observation a form of disciplinary control in which group behaviour is conditioned through observation and surveillance; it is one of three tactics used to produce what **Foucault** called a **docile body**. *Compare* **examination**, **normalizing judgement**.

high culture the culture within a society that is deemed to be sophisticated, civilized, and possessing great taste.

Highland Clearances the eviction by land-owning aristocrats of tenant farmers in Scotland in the late eighteenth and early nineteenth centuries. The clearances, which were carried out to make room for sheep, helped aristocrats capitalize on the rapidly growing textile industry while sending many peasant farmers abroad to find work.

Hill, **Daniel G**. (1923–2003) American-born Canadian sociologist, who specialized in human rights and black Canadian history, later becoming ombudsman of Ontario.

Hitchcock, **John T**. (1917–2001) American anthropologist who specialized in South Asian studies. His classic work is of the family **socialization** of the Rajput of Khalapur.

homosexual a person (male or female) who is sexually attracted to people of the same sex.

Hughes, **Everett C**. (1897–1983) American sociologist, trained at the University of Chicago, who while working at McGill University explored the ethnic division of labour between French and English in Quebec.

human capital thesis the theory that marginalized groups earn less money than dominant groups because they possess less human capital in the form of education, skill, and experience.

Humphreys, **Margaret** (b. 1944) English social worker and social activist who drew public attention to the British government's program of forcibly relocating the children of poor families to Australia, Canada, and other countries of the British Commonwealth.

hurried child syndrome   (as described by **Elkind**) a situation in which a child, pushed to high levels of accomplishment in school and in after-school activities (such as extracurricular sports and clubs), experiences adult-like levels of stress, guilt, and inadequacy.

Husain, **Mir Zohair**   American Muslim academic, who writes about the politics of Islam worldwide.

hyperglobalists   people who are uncritical of globalization and dismissive of its negative effects; they champion the process of globalization as good for everyone.

hypothesis   a statement that is verifiable/falsifiable (i.e. that can be proven true or false) and that proposes a specific relationship between or among **variables**. Example: "Playing violent video games makes a person more violent or anti-social."

iatrogenesis   (as described by **Illich**) health problems that are supposedly caused by health professionals. *See* **clinical iatrogenesis**, **cultural iatrogenesis**, **social iatrogenesis**.

Ibn Khaldûn   (1332–1406)   Arab scholar who presented early, insightful analyses of Middle Eastern societies.

id   (as described by **Freud**) the instinctive part of the subconscious. (Remember it by the term *inner demons*.)

ideal culture   social life and institutions as they ought to exist based on our social norms, values, and goals. *Compare* **actual culture**.

ideology   (*adj.* **ideological**) a relatively coherent set of inter-related beliefs about society and the people in it. Examples include **dominant ideology**, **counter-ideology**, and **liberal ideology**.

ideology of fag   (as described by G. Smith) the use of such labels as "gay" and "lesbian" pejoratively as a way to make people conform to strictly prescribed gender roles (e.g. telling a young man who expresses interest in poetry, "You're so gay.").

Illich, **Ivan**   (1926–2002)   Austrian philosopher who was a social critic of the **institutions** of modern Western society, especially those of education and medicine.

impression management   (as described by **Goffman**) the ways in which people present themselves publicly in specific roles and social circumstances. *See* **back stage**, **dramaturgical approach**, **front stage**.

independent variable   a **variable** that is believed to have some effect on another variable. *Compare* **dependent variable**.

Indian Princess   an Indigenous woman portrayed or seen as beautiful, submissive to white men, and ready to betray her nation for the love of a European man. The classic example is Disney's Pocahontas. *Compare* **squaw**.

indigeneity   the end-result of the process of refashioning Indigenous identities according to alternative knowledges rather than those traditionally produced by outsider experts.

Indigenous   denoting the First Nations, Inuit, and Métis people collectively. The term is an increasingly common synonym for **Aboriginal**.

indirect rule   a colonial policy in which a European nation uses members of a particular ethnic group as its intermediaries in ruling an area. The policy often leads to **dual colonialism** and **internal colonialism**.

Indo-European   (1) a language family that includes almost every language spoken in Europe, as well as the languages of Iran, Afghanistan, Pakistan, and India. (2) the prehistoric peoples that swept from a presumed location in Ukraine to where these languages are spoken today.

informant   a person knowledgeable in his or her own culture who provides his or her views of the culture to an outside researcher (a sociologist, an anthropologist, or another ethnographer).

informed consent   the process whereby fully informed research subjects indicate their understanding and acceptance of the research conditions and formally agree to be studied. Informed consent includes the understanding that permission can be revoked at a later time.

Innis, **Harold**   (1894–1952)   Canadian pioneer of **political economy**, who examined the influence of staples (e.g. fish, fur, minerals, wheat) on the economic and social development of Canada.

insider perspective   the viewpoint(s) of those who experience the subject being studied or written about. *Compare* **outsider perspective**. *See also* **standpoint theory**, **subjective**.

institution   an enduring set of ideas, established by law, custom, or practice, about how to accomplish goals that are deemed important within a society or culture. Marriage is an institution, as are education and religion.

institutional ethnography   a form of ethnography that challenges the need for a neutral stance in sociological research, claiming instead that any institution or organization can be seen as having two sides: one representing the **ruling interests** of the organization, one representing the interests of those working for the organization (typically in a non-administrative capacity).

institutional racism   *another term for* **systemic racism**.

instrumental education   an education model in which courses are narrowly directed to particular sets of tasks or outcomes, and do not involve challenging or being critical of information received. *Compare* **critical education**.

instrumentalism   a sociological approach that focuses on situations in which ethnic leaders mobilize groups in order to develop the groups' political and social strength.

intellectual property   intangible property items such as ideas or artistic works (e.g. literary products, music, films, videos, photographs, drawings, and sculptures) that are the result of a person's creativity.

intelligences   a term that expresses the idea that we have different levels of intelligence in different areas of life (e.g. mathematical, computer-related, literary, musical, artistic, culinary, architectural, etc.).

interaction process analysis (IPA)   a method pioneered by **Bales** and used in the experimental study of small groups; it codes observations in terms of task vs relationship orientation, dominant vs submissive approach, acceptance vs rejection of authority, and so on.

interlocking matrix of domination   the effect on an individual or group of gender-based stereotypes when combined with other minoritizing social factors, such as class or ethnicity.

internal colonialism   a situation that occurs when people within a country are colonized or put in a subordinate position (e.g. Indigenous people in Canada, the Karen in Myanmar).

internalize   incorporate the norms and values that one observes.

intersectionality   the way different social factors—"race" and ethnicity, gender, sexual orientation, class, age, and disability—combine to shape the negative experience of a minoritized group. The greater the number of negatively valued social locations you have, the greater the degree of discrimination you are likely to experience.

intersectionality theory   the theory that the experience of a group that is minoritized because of one social factor (e.g. "race") is shaped by the way that factor combines, or "intersects," with other social factors (e.g. sex, class, age, etc.).

intersex a person with both male and female sexual characteristics, as a result of a biological condition that produces either an atypical combination of male and female chromosomes or both male and female genitals/secondary sexual characteristics.

Inuit (*singular* **Inuk**) a people indigenous to Canada, Alaska, Greenland, and Siberia, who have been in Canada for a shorter time (between 5,000 and 10,000 years) than earlier Indigenous people. They speak related languages and share various aspects of an Arctic-adapted culture.

inverse (*or* **negative**) **correlation** a relationship between two **variables** in which an increase in one variable causes a decrease in the other, or vice versa. *Compare* **direct correlation**.

inverse care law the theory, articulated by **Hart**, that good medical care is most available in populations where it is needed the least and least available in populations where it is needed the most.

Islamists people who oppose globalization and Western culture generally with narrow-minded and distorted fundamentalist notions of Islam.

Islamophobia fear or hatred of Muslims or of Islam, especially when viewed as a political or social force.

jihad a term generated from an Arabic word meaning "to struggle, strive"; it has several different forms and interpretations. *See* **jihad-i-akbar, jihad-i-asghar, ummaic jihad**.

jihad-i-akbar the personal **jihad**, which represents the perpetual struggle to purge oneself of baser instincts such as greed, racism, hedonism, jealousy, revenge, hypocrisy, lying, and cheating.

jihad-i-asghar literally "the smaller, lower, or lesser jihad," it is the struggle against aggressors who are not practising Muslims. Islamists practise a distorted version of this.

joint conjugal roles **conjugal roles** in which many tasks, interests, and activities are shared. *Compare* **segregated conjugal roles**.

Kachuck, Beatrice (1926–2014) American educational psychologist and feminist researcher who identified four categories of feminism: **liberal, essentialist, socialist,** and **postmodernist**.

Keneally, Thomas (b. 1935) Australian writer of plays, novels, and non-fiction surrounding social issues; he is known as the author of *Schindler's Ark* (1982), adapted for the screen as *Schindler's List*.

Kirkby, Mary-Ann Canadian Hutterite author who has written and lectured about her upbringing as a Hutterite.

Kroker, Arthur (b. 1945) Canadian political scientist, whose work explores the relationship between technology and culture.

labelling theory (as described by **Becker**) the theory that individuals and groups outside the mainstream internalize the labels applied to them by the dominant class. The label may, in this way, cause labelled people to act in a way consistent with the label.

latent dysfunction (as described by **Merton**) the unintended negative consequence of a social process or institution. Example: the latent dysfunction of religion is that it divides people into violently opposed groups. *Compare* **manifest function**.

latent function (as described by **Merton**) the largely unintended and unrecognized positive consequence of a social process or institution. Example: a latent function of religion is that it provides social opportunities for older people who might otherwise be socially isolated. *Compare* **manifest function**.

law of effect (as described by **Thorndike**) the principle that the likelihood of a person's repeating an action increases if the action is rewarded, while the likelihood decreases if the action is punished or ignored. The law of effect is central to **behaviour modification**.

legitimization of inequality (in **cultural reproduction theory**) the validation of streaming that occurs when students accept their categorization as, say, "basic" or "advanced" (a

judgement that may reflect that person's class or "race"), thereby reproducing social inequality within the school system.

lesbian a woman who is sexually attracted to other women.

LGBTTQ an abbreviation for *lesbian, gay, bisexual, transgender, two-spirited, queer/questioning*, serving as an all-encompassing term for anyone who is not heterosexual.

liberal feminism a feminist approach that typically involves working toward **pay equity** for women. This form of feminism is criticized as reflecting the concerns of white middle-class Western women while overlooking the concerns of women of different ethnicities and classes.

liberal ideology a set of beliefs that focuses on the individual as an independent player in society, not as a member of a class or an ethnic group. Components of this set include a strong belief in the potential for **social mobility** in the individual (as seen in the **American dream**).

liberalism (as described by **A. Smith**) the belief that "the market" should be completely free to expand and grow without any government interference. In the writing of nineteenth-century thinker J.S. Mill, it referred to a belief in the freedom of the individual from both government and the dominant culture (the "tyranny of the majority").

liberation theology a political movement based on a progressive school of Christian thought, rooted in the Catholic Church in Latin America, which advocates social justice for the poor, especially in the developing world.

linguistic determinism (*or* **causation**) the theory that the way an individual understands the world is shaped by the language he or she speaks. *See* **Sapir–Whorf hypothesis**.

living wage generally, a salary sufficient to pay for housing, food, and other basic necessities. Any specific definition of this term will be **contested**.

longitudinal study a study that continues over time to track changes in the research subjects as they get older.

looking-glass self (as described by **Cooley**) the self as defined and reinforced through interactions with others.

Lotus Blossom Baby (as described by Tajima & Das Gupta) a stereotype of East Asian women as childlike, sexually available, and respectful of men. Evidence of this stereotype may be found in the China doll and in Western notions of the Japanese geisha. *Compare* **Dragon Lady**.

low income cut-off (LICO) a measure of poverty derived by calculating the percentage of a family's income spent on food, clothing, and shelter.

Luddites British members of an early anti-industrial movement in Europe, in which craftspeople who had lost their work with the introduction of labour-saving machines protested by destroying the new machinery. The term is used today to refer to people who resist new technology.

lumpenproletariat (as described by **Marx**) the group of people in capitalist society who neither own capital nor participate in wage labour. For the most part they get by with casual/occasional labour, scavenging for food and articles to sell, and crime.

McClung, Nellie (1873–1951) early Canadian feminist and member of the **Famous Five** who fought for women's rights to vote and run for political office.

McDonaldization (as described by Ritzer) the application of principles of formal rationalization seen in the fast-food industry to other sectors of society.

McJob a low-paying, unskilled job in the service industry (e.g. at a store or fast-food restaurant).

McKay, Colin (1876–1939) prolific early Canadian socialist writer on issues of **class**.

McKinney, Louise (1868–1931) Canadian women's right activist and politician, the first woman to be elected in a legislature in Canada and the British Commonwealth, and a member of the **Famous Five**.

MacLean, Annie Marion (1869–1934) Canadian sociologist, the second woman to receive a PhD in sociology, and a pioneering researcher in using **participant observation**.

macrosociology an approach to sociological inquiry that involves looking at the large-scale structure and dynamics of society as a whole.

Malthus, Thomas (1766–1834) English minister whose contribution to the study of **political economy** and demography was his view that population growth would inevitably be checked by the opposing impact of famine and disease.

Mandell, Nancy Canadian sociologist who specializes in the study of family and gender.

manifest function (as described by **Merton**) the intended and widely recognized function of a social process or institution. *Compare* **latent function**.

manufacturing of need the creation of consumer demand for (1) items that were once produced in the home, or (2) products that were once considered inessential.

marginalization the experience of being treated as insignificant or of being moved beyond the margin of mainstream society.

marginalized masculinity (as described by R. Connell) those forms of masculinity that, owing to class, "race," sexual orientation, and ethnicity, are accorded less respect than other forms of masculinity.

marital roles *another term for* **conjugal roles**.

marked term a term with a qualifying or distinguishing label added to it (e.g. *field hockey* or *Aboriginal sociologist*), showing that it is not the usual or commonly accepted form. *Compare* **unmarked term**.

Market Basket Measure (MBM) an estimate of the cost of a specific basket of goods and services for a given year, assuming that all items in the basket were entirely provided for out of the spending of the household. Having an income lower than the MBM constitutes low income or poverty.

Marsh, Leonard (1906–1983) British-born sociologists who, while working at McGill University, produced groundbreaking work on **class** in Canada.

Martineau, Harriet (1802–1876) British sociologist who is generally considered to be the first woman in the discipline.

Marx, Karl (1818–1883) influential German economist and thinker, who viewed society primarily in terms of **class** and **social change** in terms of economic factors; he was the founder of modern communism.

mass culture the **culture** of the majority, when that culture is produced by big companies and powerful governments.

master narrative a story that a nation or a people constructs about itself. A master narrative typically makes one group (the group that produced it) look heroic while casting other peoples, including minorities within the group, as bad or invisible.

master status the **status** of an individual that dominates all of his or her other statuses in most social contexts, and plays the greatest role in defining the individual's social identity.

matrilineal denoting kinship determined along the mother's line.

matrilocal denoting a situation in which a man and a woman live together in or near the mother's family residence(s).

Mead, George Herbert (1863–1931) American founding figure of **symbolic interactionism** looked at how the self is constructed through personal exchanges with others.

mean a statistical figure usually calculated in the same way as the **average**, but for some purposes determined by taking the sum of the highest and lowest figures only and dividing by two. If I have six coffees one day, then two coffees another, and three another, the mean is $(6 + 2) \div 2 = 4$.

means of production (as described by **Marx**) the social means required for producing wealth (e.g. land in feudal times; capital—wealth, machinery—during the industrial period).

median the number that falls in the middle of a series of figures for a given population or group. I worked ten hours on Monday, ten hours again on Tuesday, five hours on Wednesday, two hours on Thursday, and one hour on Friday. The median of the set 10, 10, 5, 2, 1 is 5.

medical sociology the use of sociological research and data to analyze and improve public health, focusing primarily on how health care is administered and whether the medical system adequately supports both the providers and the recipients of health care and health services.

medicalization the process by which certain behaviours or conditions are defined as medical problems (rather than, say, social problems), and medical intervention becomes the focus of remedy and social control.

melting pot a metaphor for a country in which immigrants are believed or expected to lose their cultural distinctiveness and assimilate into the dominant society. *Compare* **cultural mosaic**.

Memmi, Albert (b. 1920) French social philosopher of Tunisian-Jewish origin, who is one of the foundational writers on the subject of **anti-colonialism**.

meritocratic describing the tendency to award power or rewards to people based on their demonstrated ability or achievements.

Merton, Robert K. (1910–2003) American sociologist whose many contributions to the discipline include his work in the sociology of science and his coining of important terms such as **reference group**, **role model**, and **status set**.

Métis a people of mixed First Nations and European ethnicity (usually Cree or Saulteaux and French) who took on a sense of nationality as well as a distinct legal status.

metrosexual a man (usually a heterosexual man) whose lifestyle, spending habits, and concern for personal appearance are likened to those considered typical of a fashionable, urban, homosexual man.

microsociology an approach to sociology that focuses not on the grand scale of society but on the plans, motivations, and actions of the individual or a specific group. *Compare* **macrosociology**.

middle class the social class made up primarily of small-scale businesspeople, educated professionals, and salaried employees possessing certifiable credentials.

Mills, C. Wright (1916–1962) influential American sociologist engaged in issues of class, whose work embraced **public sociology**, and who introduced the important concept of the **sociological imagination**.

Miner, Horace (1912–1993) Chicago School American sociologist and anthropologist whose work put the study of French Canada at the forefront of Canadian sociology.

minoritized denoting an identifiable social group that is discriminated against by mainstream society or the **dominants**.

Minturn, Ann Leigh (1928–1999) American social psychologist involved with cross-cultural studies of family and child-rearing.

mismatch a situation in which a person with postsecondary education is working at a job that requires a high school education or less. *See* **underemployment**.

misogyny (*adj.* **misogynous** *or* **misogynistic**) practices or beliefs in a patriarchal culture that show contempt for women.

mobility sports sports such as soccer and boxing that provide access to socioeconomic mobility for the poorest groups in society. These sports do not require significant funds or access to resources and can be played with little or no equipment.

modernism an optimistic view of **social change** that sees change as producing circumstances better than those that preceded them.

monoculturalism. promotion of just one culture. *Compare* **multiculturalism**.

moral community (as described by **Durkheim**) a group of individuals sharing a commitment to a common moral (usually religious) worldview Durkheim differed from his contemporaries in viewing religion as a communal rather than individual experience.

moral entrepreneur someone who tries to convince others of the existence of a particular social problem that he or she has defined.

moral panic widespread concern over an issue believed to threaten both society and the individuals in it. It is typically the product of exaggeration on the part of a manipulative **moral entrepreneur** (e.g. Donald Trump) or sensationalistic mass media (e.g. Fox News).

moral stigma *see* **stigma**.

mores (as described by **Sumner**) rules that one *must not* violate. Some of these are enshrined in the criminal code as laws; violation of mores often results in shock, severe disapproval, or punishment.

Morgan, **Lewis Henry** (1818–1881) pioneering American anthropologist best known for his work with the Haudenosaunee (Iroquois) in the areas of kinship and social structure.

multiculturalism the set of policies and practices directed toward the respect for cultural differences in a country.

Murphy, **Emily** (1868–1933) Canadian women's rights activist and member of the **Famous Five**, she was also a writer and **moral entrepreneur** on the subject of drug culture and "race."

Nakhaie, **M. Reza** Arab-Canadian sociologist involved with a broad range of study areas, including studies of gender and housework.

narratives stories that reflect the lives and views of the tellers.

narrow socialization socialization in which obedience and conformity to the standards and expectations of the community are emphasized, and punishment for deviation is practised. *Compare* **broad socialization**.

narrow vision (as described by **Chomsky**) a short-sighted view, held by those who believe in **modernism**, that whatever innovation benefits the dominant class is justifiable on the grounds of progress.

national character a now discredited belief, belonging to the culture and personality school of thought, that people of different countries have distinct personalities unique to their country (e.g. Italians are passionate, Germans are cold).

negative correlation *See* **inverse correlation**.

negative sanctions ways of punishing people who contravene cultural norms. Examples include laughing at, isolating, or shaming an individual.

neoliberalism a set of financial policies designed to free (i.e. *liberate*) big businesses through tax cuts, deregulating the economy, eliminating tariffs and other barriers to free trade, and weakening labour unions. *Also called* **neoconservatism**.

neotraditionalism (among some Indigenous peoples) a religious movement that involves the reinterpretation of traditional beliefs and practices in ways that incorporate elements unique to one's own culture and others borrowed from Native cultures elsewhere.

Nietzsche, **Friedrich** (1844–1900) German philosopher championed the "will to power" of the *Übermensch* ("Superman"), who could rise above the restrictions of ordinary society and its morality.

nihilism the extremely pessimistic position that traditional moral principles and values are unimportant or non-existent. It is often accompanied by actions aimed at destruction for its own sake.

niqab an article of clothing that covers the head and face, with a narrow opening for the eyes, worn by some Muslim women for religious and cultural reasons.

non-utilitarian denoting actions that are not designed to gain financial rewards or desired possessions.

normalized made to seem "normal," "right," and "good."

normalizing judgement a form of disciplinary control in which group behaviour is conditioned through a judging system that ranks individual performance in relation to the performance of others, rather than on its intrinsic merits; it is one of three tactics used to produce what **Foucault** called a **docile body**. *Compare* **examination**, **hierarchical observation**.

norms rules or standards of behaviour that are expected of a group, society, or culture.

North, the the wealthiest nations of the world, previously termed the **First World** or the **developed nations**. The term derives from the fact that the majority of rich countries are located in the northern hemisphere.

nuclear family a family comprising a mother, a father, and children. The term is used to describe what is typically considered a "normal" family in North American society.

Oakes, **Jeannie** American academic specializing in education, especially of inequality in education.

Oakley, **Ann** (b. 1944) British feminist sociologist and novelist, who was among the first to distinguish the concepts of **sex** and **gender** in a sociological context.

objectivity (*adj.* **objective**) a supposed quality of scientific research that is not influenced by emotions, personality, or particular life experiences of the individual scientist. It better applies to the physical sciences—physics, chemistry, biology, etc.—than to the social sciences.

observational learning theory the theory that children acquire "aggressive scripts" for solving social problems through watching violence on television.

occupational crimes (as described by Clinard & Quinney) offences committed by individuals for themselves in the course of their occupations, or by employers against their employees. *Compare* **corporate crimes**.

occupational segregation (as described by **Beaujot**) the situation in which women choose (or end up in) occupations that afford them some flexibility and greater tolerance of child care–related **work interruptions**.

oligarchy rule of a country by a few powerful individuals or groups.

operational definition the definition of an abstract quality (e.g. poverty, pollution) in such a way that it can be counted for statistical purposes.

organic identity *see* **corporate identity**.

organizational behaviour the study of organizations in terms of the way the individuals within organizations interact.

organizational culture the dynamics of an organization studied in terms of the ritual and symbolic acts carried out by its members.

organizational theory   the study of the way organizations operate.

Orientalism   (as described by **Said**) a romanticized **discourse** about the Middle East and the Far East constructed by outsider "experts" from the West.

Other, the   an exotic, often fearful image of a racialized subordinate culture conjured up by the dominant culture.

outsider perspective   the viewpoint(s) of those outside of the group or culture being studied. The outsider perspective was once considered a privileged position, with the outsider viewed as an expert. *Compare* **insider perspective**.

oversocialized   (as described by **Wrong**) a misleading conception of humans as passive recipients of socialization.

overt characteristics (of deviance)   actions or qualities taken as explicitly violating the cultural norm. *Compare* **covert characteristics**.

Park, Robert (1864–1944)   American urban sociologist who was a founding member of the Chicago School of sociology.

Parlby, Irene (1868–1965)   British-born Canadian women's rights activist and a member of the **Famous Five**. She advocated for women's rights in rural areas especially and was the first female cabinet minister in Alberta.

Parsons, Talcott (1902–1979)   influential conservative American sociologist linked with **structural functionalism**.

participant observation   a form of research in sociology and anthropology that entails both observing people as an outsider would and actively participating in the various activities of the studied people's lives. It is often used in **ethnographic** research.

particularist protectionist   describing policies (or those who promote them) designed to protect the culture, politics, and economy of a country from foreign competition and the forces of globalization in general. *Compare* **universalist protectionist**.

passing   the practice of downplaying or disowning an ascribed status (typically "race" or sexuality) by claiming a dominant status. Indigenous people, for example, may try to pass for white to avoid discrimination; likewise, gay people may pass for straight for the same reason.

patriarchal construct   a set of social conditions structured in a way that favours men and boys over women and girls.

patriarchy   a social system in which men hold political, cultural, and social power. Patriarchy is visible in societies where only male political leaders are elected and where the media and the arts are dominated by male views.

patrilineal   kinship determined along the father's line.

pay equity   compensation paid to women in traditionally female-dominated industries (e.g. child care, library science, nursing, and secretarial work) where salaries and benefits have been lower than those given to employees in comparable (in terms of educational qualifications, hours worked, and social value) professions dominated by men.

peasants   (in Marxist thinking) the people who in feudal times worked the land but did not own it.

pecking order   a hierarchical arrangement of people or animals within a group.

peer group   the social group to which one belongs, or to which one wishes to belong, as a more-or-less equal.

peer pressure   the social pressure put on an individual to conform to the ways of a particular group that the individual belongs to or wishes to belong to.

peer-review process   the rigorous assessment by academic experts of the draft of a scholarly article or book to ensure that the research findings are sound and the work overall is suitable for publication.

petty bourgeoisie   (as described by **Marx**) the sub-class made up of small-time owners with little capital.

phantom aid   *see* **tied aid**.

plagiarism   a serious form of academic misconduct in which another person's ideas are presented as one's own, whether knowingly or unknowingly.

play stage   (as described by **Mead**) the second developmental sequence for child socialization, in which pretending is involved. *See* **game stage**, **role-taking**.

policy sociology   the use of sociological research and data to produce social change, especially through government or corporate policy.

polite racism   *another term for* **friendly racism**.

political economy   an interdisciplinary discipline that involves sociology, political science, economics, law, anthropology, and history. It looks primarily at the relationship between politics and the economics surrounding the production, distribution, and consumption of goods.

political globalization   (as described by **Steger**) the intensification and expansion of political connections across the world.

polyarchy   literally, government by many people. As described by **Dahl**, this refers to government by changing coalitions of powerful interest groups.

polygamy   the practice of having more than one husband or wife at the same time. A situation in which a woman has more than one husband at the same time is **polyandry**; the analogous situation in which a man has more than one wife at the same time is **polygyny**.

popular culture   commercial culture based on popular taste.

Porter, John (1921–1979)   influential Canadian sociologist who engaged in foundational work looking at social stratification as it relates to ethnicity. His *Vertical Mosaic* is a classic work in Canadian sociology.

positive correlation   *another word for* **direct correlation**.

positive sanctions   ways of rewarding people for following the norms of a society (e.g. inclusion into a desired group, career success).

positivism   the belief that every rational assertion can be verified by scientific proof.

postcolonialism   a theoretical framework developed by **Fanon** and **Memmi** to analyze the destructive impact colonialism has on both the colonizer and the colonized. *Also called* **anti-colonialism**.

postmodernism   a model of **social change** that recognizes that change can benefit some while harming others (e.g. a **digital divide**).

postmodernist feminism   a feminist approach that involves looking at women more as subjects (i.e. people with **voices** and **standpoints** of interpretation) who guide research, rather than as objects being researched.

posttraumatic stress disorder (PTSD)   a condition in which the sufferer experiences serious psychobiological symptoms stemming from his or her experience of harrowing events, such as warfare, political oppression, or crime. The condition is often medicalized, so that treatment focuses on the pathology of the individual rather than the pathology of the social environment that provides the context for the event experienced by the sufferer. *See* **medicalization**.

potlatch   any of various traditional ceremonies of Indigenous groups of the Northwest Coast. It involves reaffirming traditional values and stories through speaking, acting, dancing, and singing important stories, and reflecting the traditional value of generosity through large-scale giveaway of cherished items.

poverty   a state of doing or being without what are considered essentials.

poverty line   the arbitrary dividing point, usually based on household income, that separates the poor from the rest of society. It can differ according to the cost of living in the studied environment, and it may differ for urban and rural communities. It can also vary according to the political biases of the person drawing the line.

power elite   Mills's term for the people wielding significant economic and political power.

predictability   one of four main elements of **Weber**'s model of **formal rationalization**, having to do with setting clear expectations for both the employee and the consumer. *See* **control, efficiency, quantification.**

prejudice   the pre-judging of people based on their membership in a particular social group.

preparatory stage   (as described by **Mead**) the first developmental sequence of child socialization, which involves pure imitation.

preventive war   a military campaign justified on the grounds of preventing an attack on one's own country.

primary socialization   the earliest socialization that a child receives.

primordialism (*or* primordiality)   *another term for* **essentialism**.

Prince, Samuel Henry (1886–1962)   early Canadian sociologist involved with research of a practical application. His study of the Halifax Explosion of 1917 is a classic work on the sociology of disasters.

profane   not sacred or concerned with religion. *Compare* **sacred.**

professionalization   the process of turning work done by volunteers into paid work.

professional sociology   sociology that involves research typically designed to generate highly specific information, often with the aim of applying it to a particular problem or intellectual question. Its usual audience is the academic world of sociology departments, academic journals, professional associations, and conferences.

proletariat   *see* **workers.**

Protestant (work) ethic   (as described by **Weber**) a set of values embodied in early Protestantism, believed to have led to the development of modern capitalism.

psychoanalysis   (as described by **Freud**) an approach to psychological study that involves hypothesized stages of development and components of the self (*see* **ego, eros, id, superego,** and **thanatos**). It is used by sociologists to look at individual relationships to society and at cultural expression.

psychoneuroimmunology   the study of the effect of the mind on health and resistance to disease.

public sociology   (as described by H. Gans) sociology that addresses an audience outside of the academy. It is presented in a language that can be understood by the college-educated reader, without the dense style of the academic paper or journal, and expresses concern for a breadth of sociological subjects.

purple-collar   modelled on the analogy of white-collar office work, blue-collar manual work, and pink-collar clerical work, this is Emmanuel David's term to describe the work role of transgender women in the Philippines, which involves lightening the mood of colleagues in an environment where the work can be repetitive, dull, or demoralizing. *See* **queer value.**

qualitative research   the close examination of characteristics that cannot be counted or measured.

quantification   one of four main elements of **Weber**'s model of **formal rationalization**, having to do with breaking a process down into a number of quantifiable tasks that can be easily measured to gauge success. *See* **control, efficiency, predictability.**

quantitative research   the close examination of social elements that can be counted or measured, and therefore used to generate statistics.

queer   an informal term for someone (male or female) who is sexually attracted to people of the same sex.

queer theory   (as described by **Butler**) an approach that rejects the idea that gender identity is connected to some biological essence, proposing instead that gender reflects social performance on a continuum, with "male" and "female" at opposite poles.

queer value   Emmanuel David's term for the benefits **purple-collar** transgender employees bring to an office where dull, repetitive, and sometimes demoralizing work is performed. These benefits include the trans women's ability to entertain and boost the morale of their co-workers.

quintile   each of five ranked groups making up 20 per cent of a total population, used for statistical analysis of such things as household income.

racial bigotry   the open, conscious expression of racist views by an individual.

racialization (*adj.* racialized)   a social process in which groups of people are viewed and judged as essentially different in terms of their intellect, morality, values, and innate worth because of differences of physical type or cultural heritage.

racializing deviance   the creation of a connection, through various media (television, movies, textbooks), between a racialized group and a form of deviance or crime (e.g. Latinos and drug dealing, black people and prostitution).

racial profiling   actions undertaken supposedly for reasons of safety, security, or public protection, based on racial stereotypes, rather than on reasonable suspicion.

radical monopoly   (as described by **Illich**) a situation in which professional control work is deemed socially important (e.g. teachers in education; doctors/nurses in health care).

reading   the process of analyzing or interpreting narrative texts produced by the culture industry, often in ways not necessarily intended by the creators of the text.

real culture   *See* **actual culture.**

red herring   a logical fallacy in which a fundamentally irrelevant topic is presented in an argument in order to divert attention from the original and more important issue. Red herrings also occur in literature, as an apparent villain who isn't really that bad. Snape, in the *Harry Potter* series, is an example—his character diverts the reader's attention from other, real villains.

reductionist   denoting any unrealistic statement or theory that attempts to explain a set of phenomena by referring to a single cause. In sociology, this includes **class reductionism**, or reducing all inequality to gender, "race," or ethnicity.

reference group   a group perceived by another group to be equal but better off.

refrigerator mothers   women whose lack of maternal affection was thought to be a cause of autism in their sons. The refrigerator mother was a central component of **Bettelheim**'s outdated and now disproven hypothesis surrounding the causes of autism.

refugees   people who for political, religious, or environmental reasons are forced to leave their homeland in fear for their lives.

registered Indian   an Indigenous person who bears federal government recognition of his or her legal right to the benefits (and penalties) of being "legally Indian." *Formerly called* **status Indian**.

relational   denoting the relationship between a class and the means of producing wealth.

relational accountability   an approach that balances the social portrayal of a people so that both strengths and weaknesses, problems and successes are seen.

relations of ruling   (as described by **D. Smith**) the dominance of the individual or group by large government and large business. Smith argues that these are reinforced by uncritical sociological analysis.

relative deprivation   a situation in which an individual or the members of a group feel deprived compared to a **reference group** that they see as having no greater entitlement to their relatively better situation.

relative poverty   a state of poverty based on a comparison with others in the immediate area or country. *Compare* **absolute poverty**.

replacement rate   the rate at which children must be born in order to replace the generation before them.

reproduction (of social structure)   (as described by **Bourdieu**) the means by which classes, particularly the upper or dominant class, preserve status differences between classes.

research methodology   the system of methods a researcher uses to gather data on a particular question.

residential schools   a system of educating Indigenous children that involved removing them from their homes and communities, isolating them from their culture, and often abusing them physically, emotionally, and sexually. Underfunded by the federal government, the schools were run by a number of church groups, primarily the Roman Catholic, Anglican, and Presbyterian churches. The system, which began in the late nineteenth century and was formalized in 1910, ended slowly between the 1960s and the 1980s.

resocialization   the process of unlearning old ways and learning new ways upon moving into a significantly different social environment.

reverse ethnocentrism   a situation in which individuals set up a culture other than their own as the absolute standard by which to judge their own culture. *Compare* **ethnocentrism**.

rhetoric   the study of how people use language to persuade others or to put together an argument.

risk behaviour   activities and habitual practices with a high chance of bringing harm to those who engage in them. Examples include driving at unsafe speeds, engaging in unprotected sex, gambling above one's financial means, and using illegal drugs.

rite of passage   a ceremony or ritual that marks the passage from one stage of life to another. A wedding is a rite of passage marking the passage from single to married.

ritual degradation   a **rite of passage** in which a person being initiated into a new group is stripped of his or her individuality through activities such as hazing.

role   the function assumed or the part played by a person holding a particular status.

role conflict   a situation that occurs when the demands of two separate roles a person has are incompatible. Example: a father who works as a city bus driver cannot pick his sick daughter up from daycare because the demands of his job prevent him from leaving work early.

role exit   the process of disengaging from a role that has been central to one's identity and establishing a new role. Role exit occurs, for example, when a person leaves a long-held job or a marriage.

role model   an influential person whose patterns of behaviour are observed and imitated by others.

role set   all of the roles attached to a particular **status**. For example, attached to the status of "professor" are the roles of educator, colleague, writer, and employee.

role strain   a situation that occurs when two or more roles associated with one **status** come into conflict. A nurse may experience role strain when his duty to his employer (the hospital) may come into conflict with his obligations to a patient.

role-taking   (as described by **Mead**) the developmental stage at which children assume the perspective of **significant others**, imagining what they are thinking as they act the way they do. *Compare* **game stage**, **play stage**.

Ross, Aileen (1901–95)   first Canadian woman hired as a sociologist at a Canadian university. Her *The Lost and Lonely* is a classic work in employing **narrative** as a sociological tool.

Rossmo, D. Kim   Canadian criminologist and former police officer who engages in innovative work in geographical profiling.

rotten apple approach   an attempt to downplay the systemic problems in a process or an organization by placing the blame on individuals.

ruling interests   the interests of an organization, particularly its administration, or the interests of those who are dominant in society, particularly when these trump the interests of the indivdual.

ruling relations   the conformity of workers to the rules and practices of the organization they work for; ruling relations are activated when workers fulfill the organization's **ruling interests**.

sacred   describing an act or experience that is positively regarded and deemed worthy of respect and veneration, being associated with religion and set apart from ordinary acts and experiences. *Compare* **profane**.

Said, Edward (1935–2003)   Palestinian-American cultural critic and public intellectual whose classic work *Orientalism* describes the West's romanticized perception of the Middle East.

sanctions   *see* **negative sanctions**, **positive sanctions**.

Sapir–Whorf hypothesis   the theory that the structure of a language determines a person's perception of experience. A milder version argues for linguistic relativity, the view that language and culture have a unique relationship in each society. *See* **linguistic determinism**.

savagery   (as described by **Morgan**) the supposed first stage of social evolution toward modern civilization. *Compare* **barbarism**, **civilization**.

Schecter, Stephen   Canadian sociological theorist, as well as poet and performance artist, who applies systems theory to the study of society, which he sees as functionally differentiated and highly complex.

scientific classism   the use of flawed, pseudoscientific ideas (e.g. eugenics) to justify discriminatory actions against poor people.

scientific management   *see* **Taylorism**.

scientific racism   the use of flawed, pseudoscientific ideas (e.g. eugenics, measuring brain sizes) to justify discriminatory actions against certain racialized groups.

scrips   certificates issued to Métis in the latter part of the nineteenth century, which declared that the bearer could receive payment in land, cash, or goods. The legal status of these certificates was abused by government officials and land speculators.

secondary socialization   any socialization that occurs later than the **primary socialization** in the life of a child.

second shift   the household labour a woman is expected to perform in addition to the labour she performs in the workplace. *See* **double burden**.

Second World (prior to the collapse of the USSR in the late 1980s) a term used to refer to the Soviet Union and the eastern European countries under its power.

segregated conjugal roles **conjugal roles** in which tasks, interests, and activities are clearly differentiated. *Compare* **joint conjugal roles**.

semiotics the study of signs, symbols, and signifying practices.

semi-structured interview an informal, face-to-face interview designed to cover specific topics without the rigid structure of a questionnaire but with more structure than an open interview.

service-provider organization (as described by C. Mueller) a type of **feminist organization** that combines elements of **formal social movement organizations** and **small groups**.

sex the biological differences between boys/men and girls/women, as opposed to the sociological differences (which come under the term **gender**).

sexuality feelings of sexual desire and attraction and how these are expressed.

sick role (as described by **Parsons**) the set of expectations that surround a sick person and the experience of being sick.

Siddiqui, **Haroon** (b. 1942) Indian-born Canadian journalist whose work *Being Muslim* provides an excellent account of Islam for non-Muslims.

sign communication made up of a signifier, which carries meaning, and a signified, the meaning that is carried.

significant others (as described by **Mead**) those key individuals—primarily parents, to a lesser degree older siblings and close friends—whom young children imitate and model themselves after.

Simmel, **Georg** (1858–1918) German sociologist and initiator of **microsociology**, which involves studying the way people experience the details of daily life.

simple household a household consisting of unmarried, unrelated adults with or without children.

simulacra (as described by **Baudrillard**) cultural images, often in the form of stereotypes, that are produced and reproduced like material goods or commodities by the media and sometimes by academics.

Sixties Scoop the removal, between the 1960s and the early 1980s, of thousands of Indigenous children from their families, their communities, their home provinces (particularly Manitoba), and sometimes their home country, to place them in non-Indigenous homes.

skeptical globalizers those who see globalization as a process that is potentially dangerous to the environment and to the economies and social welfare of the "have-not" countries.

slippery slope the logical fallacy that one small change will automatically snowball into the collapse of the entire social order. Slippery-slope arguments are often voiced by adherents of **conservatism**.

small group (as described by C. Mueller) a type of **feminist organization** with an informal structure, which typically requires large commitments of time and resources from its members. *Also called* **collective**.

smiling racism *another term for* **friendly racism**.

Smith, **Adam** (1723–1790) Scottish founder of modern economics, who advocated minimal state interference in business, making him a pioneer of **neoliberalism**.

Smith, **Dorothy** (b. 1926) British-born Canadian feminist sociologist, who pioneered **standpoint theory** and **institutional ethnography**.

social change the set of adjustments or adaptations made by a group of people in response to a dramatic change experienced in at least one aspect of their lives.

social constructionism the idea that social identities such as gender, ethnicity, and "race" do not exist naturally but are constructed by individuals or groups for different social purposes; **instrumentalism** is an example of social constructionism.

social course of disease the social interactions that a sick person goes through in the process of being treated.

social Darwinism the application to human groups of the principle of **survival of the fittest** in the late nineteenth and early twentieth centuries; it was used to justify the power wielded by Europeans and the upper classes on the grounds that they were the strongest and the "best fit" to hold power.

social distance a lack of personal familiarity that exists when individuals do not have face-to-face interactions, or any interaction at all. Social distance may exist between students of online courses and their instructors.

social ecology a school of thought, founded by **Bookchin**, that recognizes the link between environmental issues and social problems, including economic, cultural, ethnic, and gender conflicts.

social fact **Durkheim**'s term for a patterned way of acting, thinking, and feeling that exists outside of the individual but that exerts control over all people.

social gospel a movement in the late nineteenth and early twentieth centuries in Canada, the United States, and various European countries to apply the human welfare principles of Christianity to the social, medical, and psychological ills brought on by industrialization and uncontrolled capitalism.

social iatrogenesis (as described by **Illich**) the deliberate obscuring of political conditions that render society unhealthy.

social inequality the long-term existence of significant differences in access to goods and services among social groups defined by class, ethnicity, etc.

social location a unique vantage point influenced by the important social characteristics of an individual, including class, "race," age, gender, sexual orientation, and degree of ability, that inform the individual's perspective and shape his or her experience.

social mobility the ability to move from one social class into another (usually higher) class.

social movement a group of people organized and working together to achieve a common social goal through activism, protest, volunteer work, etc.

social order the network of human relationships within society or, more generally, the way society is structured or organized.

social organization the social and cultural principles around which things are structured, ordered, and categorized.

social resources the knowledge and ability required to get what one needs from the system. In the context of law, for example, social resources include knowledge of the legal system, the ability to pay for legal advice, and the ability to present oneself as respectable in a courtroom.

social segregation either a deliberate strategy to separate groups of individuals based on social characteristics such as sex, ethnicity, and class, or the outcome of feeling marginalized as a result of this strategy.

socialist feminism a feminist approach that involves looking at the intersections of oppression between class and gender, focusing mainly on the struggles faced by lower-class women.

sociolinguistics (as described by W. Labov) the study of language (particularly **dialect**) as a social marker of status or general distinctiveness, or the study of how different languages conceptualize the world. *See* **Sapir–Whorf hypothesis**.

socialization involves a learning process in which individuals learn to members of a given society or sub-group (e.g., college or university student).

sociological imagination (as described by **Mills**) the capacity to shift from the perspective of the personal experience to the grander, societal scale that has caused or influenced that personal experience.

sociological poetry (as described by **Mills**) the writing of sociology in such a way that it is beautifully crafted and readily understood. *Compare* **public sociology**.

sociology the social science that studies the development, structure, and functioning of human society.

South, the the poorer nations of the world, previously known either as the **Third World** or the **developing nations**.

Spencer, Herbert (1820–1903) British social thinker who believed that societies evolved like plants and animals do. He coined the term **survival of the fittest** and applied it both within and between societies.

spurious reasoning the perception of a correlation between two factors that are wrongly seen as cause and effect.

squaw an offensive stereotype of the Indigenous woman as lazy, drunken, and available for abuse by Indigenous men. *Compare* **Indian Princess**.

standpoint the unique perspective of an individual based on a set of sociological characteristics including age, sex and gender, social class, "race" or ethnic background, employment status, family situation, degree of physical ability, etc.

standpoint theory (as described by **D. Smith**) the view that knowledge is developed from a particular lived position, or "standpoint," making **objectivity** impossible.

static a social situation in which a culture or group does not change significantly over time. It is reasonable to state that this is more often hypothesized than actual exists (e.g., with Indigenous cultures). *Compare* **dynamic**.

statistical norms norms that reflect, statistically, what people actually do, in distinction to **cultural norms**, which are what people claim to do.

statistics a science that, in sociology, involves the use of numbers to map social behaviour and beliefs.

status the relative social standing of a person or group, typically when it is highly regarded.

status consistency *see* **status inconsistency**.

status frustration (as described by **Cohen**) a feeling of failure to succeed in middle-class terms or institutions, leading to participation in **delinquent subculture**. *See* **subcultural theory**.

status hierarchy the ranking of **statuses** within the categories of ethnicity, class, age, etc., based on the degree to which they are favoured by society generally. Heterosexuality, for example, is generally ranked above homosexuality and bisexuality in the status hierarchy associated with sexual preference.

status inconsistency a situation in which the **statuses** a person holds do not align in terms of how they are generally ranked by society. A successful First Nations businessman may experience status inconsistency because his ethnic status is not favoured the way his professional and economic statuses are. When an individual's statuses do align, the result is **status consistency**.

status Indian *a former term for* **registered Indian**.

status set the complete set of **statuses** held by an individual.

Steger, Manfred (b. 1961) Austrian-born sociologist who specializes in the study of **globalization**.

stigma (*plural* **stigmata**) (as described by **Goffman**) a human attribute that is seen to discredit an individual's social identity: **bodily stigmata** are any of various physical deformities; **moral stigmata** are perceived flaws in the character of an individual; **tribal stigmata** relate to being of a particular lineage or family that has been stigmatized (e.g. the family of a murderer or gang member).

strain theory (as described by **Merton**) the theory that individuals are drawn to crime because of the frustration they feel at being prevented by their real-life circumstances from attaining society's culturally defined goals (expressed as the **American dream**).

strata (*sing.* **stratum**) social classes in ranked layers, with no specific relationship to the means of producing wealth.

streaming *another term for* **tracking**.

structural functionalism a sociological approach that examines the way social systems operate by viewing those systems in terms of the various parts or structures of which they are made. The structural-functionalist approach views society as being like a human body, made up of different structures, with each having a vital function in ensuring the survival of the whole body.

subcultural theory (as described by **Cohen**) the theory that youths drawn to crime are those who, having failed to succeed in middle-class institutions (specifically school), become socialized into a **delinquent subculture** in which the values of middle-class institutions are inverted. Cohen's theory builds on Merton's **strain theory**.

subculture a group that is organized around occupations or hobbies differing from those of the dominant culture but that is not engaged in any significant opposition to the dominant culture. People involved in furry fandom, a fascination with anthropomorphic animal characters and costumes, constitute a subculture.

subjective denoting theories, beliefs, and opinions influenced by emotions, personality, and particular life experiences of the individual. The term is used in opposing ways: some sociologists discredit observation that is "merely subjective" rather than "objective fact"; others argue that all "facts" are to some degree subjective but hide behind the mask of objectivity.

subordinate cultures groups that feel the power of the dominant culture and exist in opposition to it.

subordinate masculinity (as described by **R. Connell**) behaviours and presentations of self that can threaten the legitimacy of hegemonic masculinity. The usual examples given are gay or effeminate men, and those whose lives and beliefs challenge traditional definitions of male success.

substantive rationalization (*or* **rationality**) a model of corporate rationality that emphasizes values and ethical norms, rather than the efficiency of business practices. *Compare* **formal rationality**.

Sumner, William Graham (1840–1910) the first American professor of sociology, who introduced to the discipline such terms as **ethnocentrism** and **folkways**.

superego (as described by **Freud**) the human conscience or moral sense.

survival of the fittest (as described by **Spencer**) the principle, wrongly attributed to Darwin, that only the biggest and strongest survive, both in nature and in human society.

Sutherland, Edwin (1883–1950) American criminal sociologist and **symbolic interactionist**, who introduced the idea of **white-collar crime**.

swaddling hypothesis (as described by Richman & Gorer) a hypothesis that attributed the presumed "moodiness" of Russian citizens to their having been too tightly swaddled or wrapped up as infants.

symbol an aspect of a culture that has many strings of meaning that are unique to that culture. Examples include the flag for Americans, hockey for Canadians, songs of the early fourteenth century for Scots.

symbolic interactionism a view of social behaviour that looks at the meaning of daily social interactions, including the words and gestures we use and how these are interpreted by others.

systemic racism racist practices, rules, and laws that have become institutionalized or made "part of the system." People who benefit from this type of racism tend to be blind to its existence. *Also called* **institutional racism**.

taboo a **norm** so deeply ingrained that the mere thought or mention of it is enough to arouse disgust or revulsion. Examples: incest, cannibalism.

tabula rasa the idea that every human is born as a "blank slate" upon which the culture writes or inscribes a personality, values, and/or a set of abilities.

Tataryn, Lloyd Canadian writer and documentary producer who is primarily involved with the sociology of pollution.

Taylor, Frederick W. (1856–1915) American mechanical engineer who developed what is termed **scientific management** or **Taylorism**.

Taylorism an approach to workplace efficiency that involves studying the least amount of time, methods, and tools required for a proficient worker to complete a specific task in order to determine the single best way of doing that job (typically from a management perspective, not the worker's). Named for American mechanical engineer Frederick **Taylor**. *Also called* **scientific management**.

team approach a business approach that encourages workers to feel greater involvement in the operation of the company by inviting their ideas and input.

terrorism the intentional use or threat of violence against civilians in order to attain political objectives (e.g. freeing political prisoners, establishing an independent country, or destabilizing a political regime in another country in order to produce a regime change).

thanatos (as described by **Freud**) the violent death instinct within the **id**.

theory an attempt to explain something that has been observed.

third variable a variable that explains the connection or correlation between two other variables.

Third World a twentieth-century term used to refer to the poorer nations of the world. *Compare* **First World**, **Second World**.

Thomas theorem the notion that individuals interpret shared experiences differently, and that an individual's view of a particular situation will influence the way she reacts to it.

Thorndike, Edward (1874–1949) American psychologist involved in the establishment of the psychological school of **behaviourism**, largely through his development of the **law of effect**.

Thrasher, Frederic M. (1892–1962) American sociologist, part of the University of Chicago school of sociology, involved with studying gangs and juvenile delinquency.

tied aid financial assistance given to a developing country with conditions attached (e.g. that the developing country must spend a portion of the money on products purchased from the donor country). This is sometimes called **phantom aid**, which captures the idea that the aid is not real but rather a form of investment on which the donor country expects to realize a significant return.

tobacco strategy a marketing strategy in which a medical professional or other scientific "expert" is paid by a company to endorse the company's product on scientific grounds. The tactic was first used by tobacco producers, who hired medical researchers to combat public concerns about the health risks of cigarettes.

total fertility rate an estimate of the average number of children that a woman between the ages of 15 and 49 will have in her lifetime if current age-specific fertility rates remain constant during her reproductive years.

total institutions (as described by **Goffman**) institutions such as the military, hospitals, and asylums that regulate all aspects of an individual's life.

totalitarian discourse any **discourse** that makes a universal claim about how all knowledge and understanding can be achieved.

totem from the Ojibwa word *ndotem*, meaning "my clan," an animal or natural object that has spiritual significance for a group and is adopted as the group's emblem. **Durkheim** viewed the totem as symbolic both of a particular society and of its god, leading him to conclude that *god = society*.

tracking the process in which students are assigned to different groups according to their aptitude (based on marks) and projected outcomes (e.g. whether they are expected to pursue postsecondary education). *Also called* **streaming**.

transgender a person (male or female) who either (a) does not conform to the gender role associated with his or her biological sex, or (b) does not self-identity with the biological sex assigned to him or her at birth.

transgenic denoting a plant or animal that has been engineered by having genes from one species inserted into another. Transgenic plants include flowers that have been genetically modified to alter or "improve" their colour. Transgenic animals have been used in biomedical research. *See* **genetically modified**.

transnational corporation a company operating in countries around the world, typically based in the United States, Europe, or Japan.

transsexual a person who either (a) has the physical characteristics of one sex and a persistent desire to belong to the other, or (b) has had surgery (or is undergoing surgery) to have his or her sex changed surgically.

triangulation the use of at least three narratives, theoretical perspectives, or investigators to examine the same phenomenon.

tribalism a movement to promote the cause of a small nation that is usually not represented as having a country of its own.

tribal stigma *see* **stigma**.

trickle-down theory the misleading notion that if wealthy corporations are permitted to operate unfettered by trade restrictions and high corporate taxes, they will generate greater revenues, some of which will "trickle down" to society's poorer citizens in the form of more jobs and higher wages. It is a central pillar of **neoliberalism**.

ummaic jihad the non-violent struggle for freedom, justice, and truth within the Muslim community. *Compare* **jihad-i-akbar**, **jihad-i-asghar**.

underemployment a situation in which a person does not have enough paid work or else has paid work that does not make full use of the person's abilities and experience. A person with a medical degree earned outside of North America who earns a living as a cab driver because he or she has not been licensed to practise medicine in Canada may be considered underemployed. (It does make a taxicab a good place to give birth.)

universalist protectionist describing policies (and those who support them) that shield the domestic culture, politics, and economy of poorer countries from foreign competition and the processes of globalization in general. Universalist protectionists are motivated to promote the interests of poor and other marginalized groups and greater social, economic, environmental, political, and cultural equality worldwide. *Compare* **particularist protectionist**.

unmarked term a term without any distinguishing or delimiting term added; the usual form, as opposed to a **marked term**. Example: *hockey* is an unmarked term, in contrast to the marked terms *ice hockey*, *field hockey*, *table hockey*, etc.

urban reserve a parcel of land within an urban area reserved for businesses and services run by Indigenous people.

values those features held up by a culture as good, right, desirable, and admirable. Values are typically **contested**.

variable a factor or element that is likely to vary or change according to the circumstances governing it. *See* **dependent variable**, **independent variable**.

Veblen, Thorstein (1857–1929) American economist and social critic best known for critiquing *conspicuous consumption* in the United States. *See* Chapter 1.

vertical mosaic **Porter**'s metaphor to describe a society or nation in which there is a hierarchy of higher and lower ethnic groups. *See* **cultural mosaic**.

vested interest a personal interest in a situation from which an individual or group stands to gain in some way. A vested interest can contribute to bias if it is strong enough to override an individual's interest in learning and presenting the truth.

victimology generally, the study of victims of crime and the psychological effects on them of their experience; in sociology, it often refers to the way a person is portrayed as the victim of some event or situation in a way that downplays or denies the person's **agency**.

virtual class **Kroker**'s term for a **class** of people who control and are dependent for their jobs and economic well-being on digital technologies and the Internet.

visible minorities according to Canadian law, people of non-Caucasian ethnicity, non-white skin colour, and non-Indigenous ancestry. As of the 2011 National Household Survey, the three largest visible-minority groups in Canada are South Asians, Chinese, and blacks.

vision quest in traditional Indigenous culture, a **rite of passage** in which an adolescent leaves the community for a brief period in the hopes of having a vision that will reveal his or her guardian spirit, personal songs, and other things.

voice the expression of *a* (not *the*) viewpoint that comes from occupying a particular **social location**.

Watson, John B. (1878–1958) American psychologist and researcher was a pioneer in **behaviourism**, which he applied to the study of animal behaviour, the raising of children, and advertising.

Weber, Max (1864–1920) German founding figure in sociology, best known for identifying a set of values, the **Protestant** (**work**) **ethic**, to which he identified as central to the rise of capitalism.

white-collar crime (as described by **Sutherland**) non-violent crime committed by a person of the middle or upper middle class in the course of his or her job. Examples include embezzlement and fraud. *See* **corporate crimes**, **occupational crimes**.

workers (as described by **Marx**) the people who work for wages and do not own capital, the means of production, in an industrial, capitalist society. *Also called* **proletariat**.

working class the social class made up primarily of those who lack resources or skills apart from their own labour power.

work interruptions (as described by **Baudrillard**) time taken off work, typically by a woman, to care for an infant (i.e. during maternity or paternity leave) or a child who is sick.

Wrong, Dennis H. (b. 1923) Canadian-born sociologist who has specialized in writing about the nature of power and of socialization.

xenocentrism a preference for foreign goods and tastes based on the belief that anything foreign must be better than the same thing produced domestically.

XYY males men and boys who differ from the "normal" XY chromosome pattern. They are associated with above-average height, a tendency to have acne, impulsive or anti-social behaviour, and slightly lower intelligence than "normal" men and boys.

References

Adachi, Ken (1976). *The Enemy That Never Was: A History of Japanese Canadians*. Toronto: McClelland & Stewart.

Adams, Howard (1975). *Prison of Grass: Canada from the Native Point of View*. Toronto: New Press.

Adams, Michael (2003). *Fire and Ice: The United States and the Myth of Converging Values*. Toronto: Penguin Canada.

——— (2014). Fire and Ice Revisited: American and Canadian Social Values in the Age of Obama and Harper. Speech presented at the Woodrow Wilson Center, Washington, DC, 14 March.

Aguiar, Luis (2001). "'Whiteness' in White Academia." In Carl James & Adrienne Shadd (eds), *Talking About Identity: Encounters in Race, Ethnicity and Language*, 2nd edn, pp. 177–92. Toronto: Between the Lines.

Albanese, Patrizia (2009), *Child Poverty in Canada*. Toronto: Oxford.

Alberta Cancer Board (2009). *Cancer Incidence in Fort Chipewyan, Alberta, 1995–2006*. Alberta Cancer Board: Division of Population Health and Information Surveillance (online).

Alexander, Doug, & Scott Deveaux (2015, Sept. 28). "Hydro One CEO's Pay of $4 Million with Bonus Approaches Top End." *Financial Post* (online).

Allen, Mary (2015, June 9). "Police-Reported Hate Crime in Canada." *Juristat*. Statistics Canada cat. no. 85-002-X.

Ames, Herbert Brown (1972). *The City Below the Hill*. Toronto: University of Toronto. (Original work published 1897)

Anderson, Karen L. (1991). *Chain Her by One Foot: The Subjugation of Women in Seventeenth-Century New France*. London: Routledge.

——— (1996). *Sociology: A Critical Introduction*. Toronto: Nelson.

Anyon, Jean (1980). "Social Class and the Hidden Curriculum of Work." *Journal of Education* 162 (1), pp. 67–92.

Aristotle (2000). *Politics*. Mineola, NY: Dover Publications.

Armstrong, Karen (2005). *Through the Narrow Gate: A Memoir of Life In and Out of the Convent*. Toronto: Vintage Canada. (Original work published 1982)

Armstrong, Pat, & Hugh Armstrong (2010). *The Double Ghetto: Canadian Women and Their Segregated Work*. Don Mills, ON: Oxford University Press. (Original work published 1978)

Arnett, Jeffrey (1995). "Broad and Narrow Socialization: The Family in the Context of a Cultural Theory." *Journal of Marriage and the Family* 57 (3), pp. 617–28.

Arnett, Jeffrey, & Lene Balle-Jensen (1993). "Cultural Bases of Risk Behavior: Danish Adolescents." *Child Development* 64, pp. 1842–55.

Aujla, Angela (1998). "The Colour Bar of Beauty." *The Peak* 1 (99), pp. 1–5.

Axelrod, Paul (1982a). "Businessmen and the Building of Canadian Universities." *Canadian Historical Review* 63, pp. 202–22.

——— (1982b). *Scholars and Dollars: Politics, Economics, and the Universities of Ontario, 1945–1980*. Toronto: University of Toronto.

Backhouse, Constance (1999). *Colour-Coded: A Legal History of Racism in Canada, 1900–1950*. Toronto: University of Toronto.

Bales, Robert F. (1950). *International Process Analysis: A Method for the Study of Small Groups*. Chicago: University of Chicago Press.

Banerjee, Mukulika (2000). *The Pathan Unarmed*. Karachi & New Delhi: Oxford University Press.

Barber, Benjamin (1992, March). "Jihad vs McWorld." *The Atlantic Monthly*.

Barrowcliffe, Mark (2009). *The Elfish Gene: Dungeons, Dragons and Growing Up Strange—A Memoir*. London, UK: Soho.

Barthes, Roland (1957). *Mythologies*. London: Paladin/HarperCollins.

Baskin, Cyndy (2003). "Structural Social Work as Seen from an Aboriginal Perspective." In W. Shera (ed.), *Emerging Perspectives on Anti-oppressive Practice*. Toronto: Canadian Scholars' Press.

Battiste, Marie (1997). "Mi'kmaq Socialization Patterns." In L. Choyce & R. Joe (eds), *Anthology of Mi'kmaq Writers*. East Lawrencetown, NS: Pottersfield.

Baudrillard, Jean (1983). *Simulations*. Trans. Paul Foss, Paul Patton, & Philip Beitchman. New York: Semiotext[e].

Bauer, Greta R., Ayden I. Scheim, Jake Pyne, Robb Travers, & Rebecca Hammond (2015). "Intervenable Factors Associated with Suicide Risk in Transgender Persons: A Respondent Driven Sampling Study in Ontario, Canada." *BMC Public Health* 15: 525.

Beaujot, Rod (2000). *Earning and Caring in Canadian Families*. Peterborough, ON: Broadview.

——— (2002). "Earning and Caring: Demographic Change and Policy Implications." *Canadian Studies in Population* 29 (2), pp. 195–225.

——— (2004, June 15). "Delayed Life Transitions: Trends and Implications." *Vanier Institute of the Family*. Retrieved: www.vifamily.ca/library/cft/delayed_life.html

Becker, Howard (1963). *Outsiders: Studies in the Sociology of Deviance*. New York: The Free Press.

Bellegarde-Smith, Patrick (2004). *Haiti: The Breached Citadel*. Toronto: Canadian Scholars' Press.

Benton-Banai, Edward (1988). *The Mishomis Book: The Voice of the Ojibway*. St Paul, MN: Red School House, Indian Country Communications.

Best, Joel (2001). *Damned Lies and Statistics: Untangling Numbers from the Media, Politicians, and Activists*. Berkeley and Los Angeles: University of California.

Bibby, Reginald Wayne (1995). *The Bibby Report: Social Trends Canadian Style*. Toronto: Stoddard.

Binelli, Mark (2013). *Detroit City Is the Place to Be: The Afterlife of an American Metropolis*. London: Picador.

Bingham, Russell (2013). "Viola Desmond." Rev. Eli Yarhi (2016). *The Canadian Encyclopedia* (online). Toronto, ON: Historica Canada.

Bissell, Tom (2003). *Chasing the Sea: Lost Among the Ghosts of Empire in Central Asia*. New York: Pantheon.

Blatchford, Andy (2015, Feb. 1). "'Middle-Class' Politics: Who Belongs to this Vote-Rich Group?" *CBC News* (online).

Bloom, Allan (1988). *The Closing of the American Mind*. New York: Simon & Schuster.

Blum, William (2003). *Killing Hope: US Military & CIA Interventions since World War II*. London: Zed Books.

Blumer, Herbert (1969). *Symbolic Interactionism: Perspective and Method*. Englewood Cliffs, NJ: Prentice-Hall.

Bogaert, Laura, Jeff Whitehead, Miriam Wiens, & Elizabeth Rolland (2013, March). *Suicide in the Canadian Forces 1995–2012*. Surgeon General doc. no. SGR-2012-011. Ottawa, ON: Minister of Defence.

Bohannan, Laura (1966). "Shakespeare in the Bush." *Natural History* (Aug./Sept.). Reprinted in E. Angeloni (ed.), *Annual Editions Anthropology, 1995/1996*, pp. 65–9.

Bolaria, B. Singh, & Peter S. Li (1985). *Racial Oppression in Canada*. Toronto: Garamond.

Bookchin, Murray (1996). *The Philosophy of Social Ecology: Essays on Dialectical Naturalism*. Montreal: Black Rose.

Bothelo-Urbanski, Jessica (2016, July 11). "Baby Storm Five Years Later: Preschooler on Top of the World." *The Star* (Toronto) (online).

Bott, Elizabeth (1957). *Family and Social Networks: Roles, Norms, and External Relationships in Ordinary Urban Families*. London: Tavistock.

Bourdieu, Pierre (1970). *La reproduction: Eléments pour une théorie d'enseignement*. Paris: Éditions de Minuit.

—— (1988). *Homo Academicus*. Trans. P. Collier. Stanford, CA: Stanford.

—— (1996). *On Television*. New York: New.

Bourdieu, Pierre, & Jean-Claude Passeron (1990). *Reproduction in Education, Society and Culture*. Thousand Oaks, CA: Sage.

Bowles, S., & H. Gintis (1976). *Schooling in Capitalist America: Educational Reform and Contradictions of Economic Life*. New York: Basic.

Boyd, Monica, & Doug Norris (1995). "Leaving the Nest? Impact of Family Structure." *Canadian Social Trends* 38, pp. 14–17.

Brean, Joseph (2014, Jun. 17). "Vancouver School Board's Genderless Pronouns—Xe, Xem, Xyr—Not Likely to Stick, If History Is Any Indication." *National Post* (online).

Bregman, Rutger (2016). *Utopia for Realists: The Case for a Universal Basic Income, Open Borders, and a 15-Hour Workweek*. The Correspondent (Kindle edition).

Briggs, Jean (1970). *Never in Anger: Portrait of an Eskimo Family*. Cambridge: Harvard.

—— (1998). *Inuit Morality Play: The Emotional Education of a Three-Year-Old*. New Haven, CT: Yale.

Brightwell, Laura (2016, May 10). "Attack on Canada's Only Surgery Clinic for Trans People Elicits 'Zero Reaction.'" *Rabble.ca* (online).

Brignall, Richard (2010). *China Clipper: Pro Football's First Chinese-Canadian Player, Normie Kwong*. Toronto: James Lorimer and Company

Brill, A.A. (1913). "Piblockto or Hysteria among Peary's Eskimos." *Journal of Nervous and Mental Disease* 40, pp. 514–20.

Brock, Joe, & Tim Cocks (2012). "Nigeria Oil Corruption Highlighted by Audits." *Reuters* (online).

Brouchu, Pierre, Marie-Anne Deussing, Koffi Houme, & Maria Chuy (2013). *Measuring Up: Canadian Results of the OECD PISA Study*. Toronto, ON: Council of Ministers of Education, Canada.

Brownlee, Jamie (2015). *Academia Inc.: How Corporatization Is Transforming Canadian Universities*. Black Point, NS: Fernwood Publishing.

Bruemmer, René, & Kevin Dougherty (2012, May 3). "CLASSE Student Group Presents Counter Proposal to End Boycott." *The Gazette* (online).

Brym, Robert J., ed. (1985). *The Structure of the Canadian Capitalist Class*. Toronto: Garamond.

—— (2000). "Note on the Discipline: The Decline of the Canadian Sociology and Anthropology Association." *Canadian Journal of Sociology* 28 (3), pp. 411–26.

Budgell, Janet (1999). *Our Way Home: A Report to the Aboriginal Healing and Wellness Strategy: Repatriation of Aboriginal People Removed by the Child Welfare System: Final Report*. Prepared by Native Child and Family Services of Toronto, Sevenato and Associates. Toronto: Native Child and Family Services of Toronto.

Burawoy, Michael (2004). "The World Needs Public Sociology." *Sosiologisk tidsskrift* (*Journal of Sociology*) 3.

Burnet Jean R., & Howard Palmer (1988). *"Coming Canadians." An Introduction to a History of Canada's Peoples*. Ottawa: Ministry of Supply and Services.

Burton, Kirsteen R., & Ian K. Wong (2004, April 17). "A Force to Contend With: The Gender Gap Closes in Canadian Medical Schools." *Canadian Medical Association Journal* 170 (9).

Bushman, Brad J., & L. Rowell Huesmann (2001). "Effects of Televised Violence on Aggression." In D. Singer & J. Singer (eds), *Handbook of Children and the Media*, pp. 223–54. Thousand Oaks, CA: Sage.

Butler, Judith (1990). *Gender Trouble: Feminism and the Subversion of Identity*. London: Routledge.

Buttel, Frederick, & Kenneth Gould (2004). "Global Social Movement(s) at the Crossroads: Some Observation on the Trajectory of the Anti-corporate Globalization Movement." *Journal of World Systems Research* 10 (1), pp. 51–2.

Cameron, Linda, & Lee Bartel (2008). *Homework Realities: A Canadian Study of Parental Opinions and Attitudes*. Technical Report. Toronto: University of Toronto, Ontario Institute for Studies in Education.

Cameron, Darla, & Bonnie Berkowitz (2016, June 14). "The State of Gay Rights around the World." *Washington Post* (online).

Campbell, Marie, & Frances Gregor (2002). *Mapping Social Relations: A Primer in Doing Institutional Ethnography*. Aurora, ON: Garamond.

Canada (1884). *An Act to Further Amend the Indian Act 1880*. Statutes of Canada, 47 Vict. c 27.

Canada (Attorney General) *v* Bedford (2013). SCC 72, [2013] 3 S.CR. 1101.

Canada, Department of Immigration, Refugees, and Citizenship (2015). "Facts and Figures 2015—Immigration Overview: Permanent Residents" (online).

Canada, Department of Justice (2014). Technical Paper: Bill C-36, *Protection of Communities and Exploited Persons Act* (online).

Canada, 40th Parliament, 2nd Session (2009). Standing Committee on Environment and Sustainable Development: Evidence (11 June). Retrieved: www.parl.gc.ca/House Publications/Publication.aspx?DocId=3983714&Language=E&Mode=1

"Canada's Top CEOs Leave the 99% in Their Gold Dust" (2012, Jan. 3). *The Star* (Toronto) (online).

Canadian Academy of Health Sciences (2014). Improving Access to Oral Health Care for Vulnerable People Living in Canada. Ottawa, ON: Canadian Academy of Health Sciences.

Canadian Association of Food Banks (2004). *Poverty in a Land of Plenty: Towards a Hunger-Free Canada*. Toronto.

Canadian Dental Association [CDA] (2016a). Population to Dentist Ratios, Canadian Provinces, 1997–2013 Trend [figure]. www.cda-adc.ca/en/services/fact_sheets/dentist_pop_ratios.asp

—— (2016b). Publicly Funded Share of Total Expenditures for Dental Services—Canada, Provinces, and Territories 2010 [figure]. www.cda-adc.ca/en/services/fact_sheets/2010ExpendituresforDentalServices.asp

—— (2016c). Gender of Canadian Dentists by Age Range, January 2012 [figure]. www.cda-adc.ca/en/services/fact_sheets/dental_gender.asp

Canadian Press (2012, July 24). "Girls in Ontario More Likely to Be Bullied than Boys." *CBC News* (online).

Cardinal, Harold (1969). *The Unjust Society: The Tragedy of Canada's Indians*. Edmonton: New Press.

—— (1977). *The Rebirth of Canada's Indians*. Toronto: New Press.

Casey, Liam (2015, June 9). "Ontario Teachers Need More Training on Aboriginal Issues: Report." *CBC News* (online).

Cavan, Ruth (1965). *Suicide*. New York: Russell and Russell. (Original work published 1928)

CBC News (2012, Sept. 14). "Canada Won't Oppose Asbestos Limits. Federal Tories Reverse Course and Won't Veto Substance's Listing in Rotterdam Convention" (online).

Central Intelligence Agency (2009). *The World Factbook*. Retrieved: www.cia.gov/library/publications/the-world-factbook.

Centre for Communicable Diseases and Infection Control (CCDIC) (2012, April 30). "Tuberculosis in Canada 2010, Pre-release." Retrieved: www.phac-aspc.gc.ca/tbpc-latb/pubs/tbcan10pre/index-eng.php

Chang, Virginia, & Nicholas Christakis (2002). "Medical Modelling of Obesity: A Transition from Action to Experience in a 20th Century American Medical Textbook." *Sociology of Health and Illness* 24 (2), pp. 151–77.

Chen, Anita Beltran (1998). *From Sunbelt to Snowbelt: Filipinos in Canada*. Calgary: Canadian Ethnic Studies Association.

Chodrow, Nancy (1978). *The Reproduction of Mothering: Psychoanalysis and the Sociology of Gender*. Berkeley: University of California.

—— (1994). *Femininities, Masculinities, Sexualities: Freud and Beyond*. Lexington, KY: University of Kentucky.

Chomsky, Noam (2004). *Hegemony or Survival: America's Quest for Global Dominance*. New York: Henry Holt.

Chrétien, Jean-Pierre (1997). *Le defi de l'ethnism: Rwanda et Burundi, 1990–1996*. Karthala.

Clark, S.D. (1962). *The Developing Canadian Community*. Toronto: University of Toronto.

—— (1976). *Canadian Society in Historical Perspective*. Toronto: McGraw-Hill.

Clarke, George Elliot (1997, Winter). "The Complex Face of Black Canada." *McGill News: Alumni Quarterly* (online).

Clinard, M., & R. Quinney (1973). *Criminal Behavior Systems: A Typology*, 2nd edn. New York: Holt, Rinehart, and Winston.

Codjoe, Henry M. (2001). "Can Blacks Be Racist? Further Reflections on Being 'Too Black and African.'" In Carl James & Adrienne Shadd (eds), *Talking About Identity: Encounters in Race, Ethnicity and Language*, pp. 277–90. Toronto: Between The Lines.

Cohen, Albert K. (1955). *Delinquent Boys: The Culture of the Gang*. Glencoe, IL: Free Press.

Colapinto, John (2000). *As Nature Made Him: The Boy Who Was Raised as a Girl*. New York: HarperCollins.

Coleman, James William (2002). *The Criminal Elite: Understanding White-Collar Crime*, 5th edn. New York: Worth.

Comaskey, Brenda, & Anne McGillivray (1999). *Black Eyes All of the Time: Intimate Violence, Aboriginal Women, and the Justice System*. Toronto: University of Toronto.

Comte, Auguste (1830–42). *Cours de Philosophie Positive*. Paris: Librairie Larousse.

—— (1851–4). *Système de Politique Positive*.

—— (1853). *The Positive Philosophy of Auguste Comte*. Trans. & ed. Harriet Martineau. London: Longmans.

—— (1877). *The System of Positive Polity*. London: Longmans, Green.

Connell, R.W. (1995). *Masculinities*. Berkeley: University of California.

Conrad, Margaret R., & James K. Hiller (2001). *Atlantic Canada: A Region in the Making*. Don Mills, ON: Oxford.

Contenta, Sandro & Jim Rankin (2009, June 6), "Suspended Sentences: Forging a School-to-Prison Pipeline?" *The Star* (Toronto) (online).

Cordell, Arthur J. (1993). "The Perils of an Information Age." In P. Elliot (ed.), *Rethinking the Future*. Saskatoon: Fifth House.

Côté, James, & Anton Allahar (2007). *Ivory Tower Blues: A University System in Crisis*. Toronto: University of Toronto.

—— & —— (2011), *Lowering Higher Education: The Rise of Corporate Universities and the Fall of Liberal Education*. Toronto: University of Toronto.

Court Brown, W. Michael (1968). "Males with an XYY Sex Chromosome Complement." *Journal of Medical Genetics* 5 (4), pp. 341–59.

Crehan, Kate (2002). *Gramsci, Culture and Anthropology*. Berkeley: University of California.

Cross, Philip, & Peter John Mitchell (2014). *The Marriage Gap Between Rich and Poor Canadians: How Canadians Are Split into Haves and Have-Nots along Marriage Lines*. Ottawa: Institute of Marriage and Family Canada.

"Cross about Cross-Dressing: Is It a Wicked Western Habit that Should Be Stopped?" (2010, Jan. 28). *The Economist* (online).

Crowe, Kelly (2016, July 10). "Flu Shot Effectiveness for 2015–16 Disappointing, Data Shows." *CBC News* (online).

Curtis, James, Edward Grabb, & Neil Guppy, eds (1999). *Social Inequality in Canada: Patterns, Problems and Policies*, 3rd edn. Scarborough, ON: Prentice Hall.

Daily Bread Food Bank (2012). *Who's Hungry: Faces of Hunger. 2012 Profile of Hunger in the GTA*. Retrieved: www.dailybread.ca/wp-content/uploads/2012/09/WhosHungryReport2012LowRes.pdf

Dasgupta, Sathi (1992). "Conjugal Roles and Social Network in Indian Immigrant Families: Bott Revisited." *Journal of Comparative Family Studies* 23 (3), p. 465.

Das Gupta, Tania (1996). *Racism and Paid Work*. Toronto: Garamond.

Dauvergne, Mia, & Shannon Brennan (2011). "Police-Reported Hate Crime in Canada, 2009." *Juristat*. Statistics Canada cat. no. 85-002-X.

David, Emmanuel (2015). "Purple-Collar Labor: Transgender Workers and Queer Value at Global Call Centers in the Philippines." *Gender & Society* 29 (2), pp. 169–194.

Davis, Lennard J. (2006). "Constructing Normalcy: The Bell Curve, the Novel, and the Invention of the Disabled Body in the Nineteenth Century." In Lennard J. Davis (ed.), *The Disability Studies Reader*, 2nd edn, pp. 3–16. New York: Routledge.

Dawson, Carl A., & Warren E. Getty (1948). *An Introduction to Sociology*, 3rd edn. New York: Ronald.

d'Eaubonne, Françoise (1974). *Le féminisme ou la mort (Feminism or Death)*. Paris: P. Horay.

de Certeau, Michel (1984). *The Practice of Everyday Life*. Trans. S. Rendell. Berkeley, CA: University of California.

"Defying Gender Expectations through Gender Performance: Boyat in the UAE" (2009, Feb. 23). *Globe and Mail* (online).

Dei, George (1996). *Anti-racism Education: Theory and Practice*. Halifax: Fernwood.

Dei, George, & Agnes Calliste (2000). *Power Knowledge and Anti-racism Education: A Critical Reader*. Halifax: Fernwood.

Dei, George, Irma James, L. Karumanchery, S. James-Wilson, & J. Zine (2000). *Aboriginal Margins: The Challenges and Possibilities of Inclusive Schooling*, Toronto: Canadian Scholars' Press.

Demerson, Velma (2004). *Incorrigible*. Waterloo: Wilfrid Laurier.

Dempsey, L. James (1995). "Alberta's Indians in WWII." In Ken Tingley (ed.), *King and Country, Alberta in the Second World War*. Edmonton: Provincial Museum of Alberta.

Dick, Lyle (1995). "'Pibloktoq' (Arctic Hysteria): A Construction of European–Inuit Relations?" *Arctic Anthropology* 32 (2), pp. 1–42.

Dofny, Jacques, & Marcel Rioux (1962). "Les classes sociales au Canada français." *Revue français de sociologie* 111 (3), pp. 290–303.

Dollard, John (1937). *Caste and Class in a Southern Town*. New Haven, CT: Yale.

Dosman, Edgar J. (1972). *Indians: An Urban Dilemma*. Toronto: McClelland & Stewart.

Du Bois, W.E.B. (1896). *The Suppression of the African Slave Trade in America*. New York: Longmans, Green.

—— (1903). *The Souls of Black Folk*. Chicago: A.C. McClurg.

—— (1935). *Black Reconstruction: An Essay toward a History of the Part which Black Folk Played in the Attempt to Re-construct Democracy in America*. New York: Harcourt Brace.

—— (1940). *Dusk of Dawn*. New York: Harcourt, Brace & World.

—— (1967). *The Philadelphia Negro: A Social Study*. New York: Schocken Books. (Original work published 1899)

Dubson, Michael, ed. (2001). *Ghosts in the Classroom: Stories of College Adjunct Faculty—and the Price We All Pay*. Boston: Camel's Back.

Dumas, Jean, & Alain Bélanger (1996). *Report on the Demographic Situation in Canada, 1995*. Statistics Canada cat. no. 91-209. Ottawa: Minister of Industry.

Dunfield, Allison (2005, March 15). "Why Do Women Always Pay More?" *Globe and Mail* (online).

Durkheim, Émile (1938). *The Rules of Sociological Method*. Chicago: University of Chicago. (Original work published 1895)

—— (1951). *Suicide: A Study in Sociology*. Trans. John A. Spaulding & George Simpson. New York: The Free Press of Glencoe. (Original work published 1897)

—— (1965). *The Elementary Forms of Religious Life*. New York: Free Press. (Original work published 1912)

—— (1995). *The Elementary Forms of the Religious Life*. Trans. Karen Fields. New York: Simon & Schuster. (Original work published 1912)

Dusenberry, Verne (1998). *The Montana Cree: A Study in Religious Persistence*. Norman, OK: University of Oklahoma.

Ebaugh, Helen Rose Fuchs (1988). *Becoming an Ex: The Process of Role Exit*. Chicago: University of Chicago.

"Editorial: The Loss of Spontaneous Play from Childhood" (2012, June 1). *Globe and Mail* (online).

Eichler, Margrit (2001). "Women Pioneers in Canadian Sociology: The Effects of a Politics of Gender and a Politics of Knowledge." *Canadian Journal of Sociology* 26 (3) (Summer), pp. 375–404.

Elkind, David (2001). *The Hurried Child: Growing Up Too Fast Too Soon*, 3rd edn. Cambridge, MA: Perseus. (Original work published 1981)

—— (2003). "The Reality of Virtual Stress." *CIO* (fall/winter). Retrieved: www.cio.com/archive/092203/elkind

Emke, Ivan (2002). "Patients in the New Economy: The 'Sick Role' in a Time of Economic Discipline." *Animus: A Philosophical Journal for Our Time* 7.

"EpiPen Price Furor Heats up in US" (2016, Aug. 24). *CBC News* (online).

Esar, Evan (1943). *Esar's Comic Dictionary of Wit and Humour*. New York: Horizon.

Etzioni, Amitai (1964). *Modern Organizations*. Englewood Cliffs, NJ: Prentice-Hall.

Fadiman, Anne (1997). *The Spirit Catches You and You Fall Down. A Hmong Child, Her American Doctors, and the Collision of Two Cultures*. New York: Farrar, Straus and Giroux.

Fanon, Franz (1965). *The Wretched of the Earth*. New York: Grove. (Original work published 1961)

—— (1967). *Black Skin, White Masks*. New York: Grove. (Original work published 1952)

Fields, Karen (1995). Introduction. In Karen Fields (trans.), *The Elementary Forms of the Religious Life*, by Émile Durkheim. New York: Simon & Schuster.

Fiske, John (2010). *Understanding Popular Culture*, 2nd edn. London: Routledge.

Flavelle, Dana (2003, Jan. 3). "Canada's 0.01%." *The Star* (Toronto), pp. B1–B3.

Fleras, Augie, & Jean Elliott (1999). *Unequal Relations: An Introduction to Race, Ethnic, and Aboriginal Dynamics in Canada*, 3rd edn. Scarborough, ON: Prentice-Hall, Allyn & Bacon.

Fletcher, S.D. (2000). "Molded Images: First Nations People,

Representation and the Ontario School Curriculum." In T. Goldstein & D. Selby (eds), *Weaving Connections: Educating for Peace, Social and Environmental Justice*. Toronto: Sumach.

Flint, David (1975). *The Hutterites: A Study in Prejudice*. Don Mills, ON: Oxford.

Food Banks Canada (2004). *HungerCount 2004: A Comprehensive Report on Hunger and Food Bank Use in Canada, and Recommendations for Change*. Mississauga, ON: Canadian Association of Food Banks.

——— (2015). *HungerCount 2015: A Comprehensive Report on Hunger and Food Bank Use in Canada, and Recommendations for Change*. Mississauga, ON: Food Banks Canada.

Forbes (2016). The World's Highest-Paid Athletes: 2016 Ranking. Retrieved: www.forbes.com/athletes/list/

Forget, Evelyn L. (2011). "The Town with No Poverty: Using Health Administration Data to Revisit Outcomes of a Canadian Guaranteed Annual Income Field Experiment" (online). University of Manitoba.

Foucault, Michel (1961). *Madness and Civilisation: A History of Insanity in the Age of Reason*. New York: Vintage.

——— (1975). *Discipline and Punish: The Birth of the Prison*. New York: Vintage.

——— (1977). *Discipline and Punish: The Birth of the Prison*. New York: Pantheon.

——— (1978). *The History of Sexuality. Vol. 1: An Introduction*. New York: Pantheon.

——— (1980). "Two Lectures." In Colin Gordon (ed.), *Power/Knowledge*, pp. 78–108. New York: Pantheon.

——— (1994). *The Archaeology of Knowledge*. London: Routledge. (Original work published 1972)

Fournier, S., & E. Crey (1997). *Stolen from Our Embrace*. Vancouver: Douglas & McIntyre.

Fowles, Jib (1999). *The Case for Television Violence*. London: Sage.

——— (2001, March). "The Whipping Boy: The Hidden Conflicts Underlying the Campaign against TV." *Reason*.

Frank, David, & Nolan Reilly (1979). "The Emergence of the Socialist Movement in the Maritimes, 1899–1916." In Robert J. Brym & R. James Sacouman (eds), *Underdevelopment and Social Movements in Atlantic Canada*, pp. 81–106. Toronto: New Hogtown.

Frazier, E. Franklin (1939). *The Negro Family in the United States*. Chicago: University of Chicago.

Freud, Sigmund (1977). *On Sexuality*, vol. 7. London: Penguin. (Original work published 1916–17)

Gallagher, James E., & Ronald D. Lambert, eds (1971). *Social Process and Institution: The Canadian Case*. Toronto: Holt, Rinehart and Winston.

Gans, Herbert (1989, Feb.). "Sociology in America: The Discipline and the Public." *American Sociological Review* 54, pp. 1–16.

Garigue, Philippe (1964). "French Canada: A Case-Study in Sociological Analysis." *Canadian Review of Sociology and Anthropology* 1 (4), pp. 186–92.

Gaul, Ashleigh (2014, Sept. 20). "Between the Lines: Tracing the Controversial History and Recent Revival of Inuit Facial Tattoos." *Up Here* (online).

Gephart, Robert (1988). *Ethnostatistics: Qualitative Foundations for Quantitative Research*. London: Sage.

Gilbert, Dennis (1988). *Sandanistas: The Party and the Revolution*. Oxford: Basil Blackwell.

Giles, Philip (2004). "Low Income Measurement in Canada." Retrieved: www.statcan.ca/english/research/75F0002MIE/75F-0002MIE2004011.pdf

Gilligan, Carol (1982). *In a Different Voice: Psychological Theory and Women's Development*. Cambridge, MA: Harvard.

——— (1990). *Making Connections: The Relational Worlds of Adolescent Girls at Emma Willard School*. Cambridge, MA: Harvard.

Giroux, Henry (2001). *The Mouse that Roared: Disney and the End of Innocence*. New York: Rowman & Littlefield.

Goffman, Alice (2006). *Beyond the Spectacle of Terrorism: Global Uncertainty and the Challenge of the New Media*. Boulder, CO: Paradigm.

——— (2014). *On the Run: Fugitive Life in an American City*. Chicago: University of Chicago Press.

Goffman, Erving (1959). *The Presentation of Self in Everyday Life*. New York: Anchor.

——— (1961). *Asylums: Essays on the Social Situation of Mental Patients and Other Inmates*. New York: Anchor.

——— (1963). *Stigma: Notes on the Management of Spoiled Identity*. Englewood Cliffs, NJ: Prentice-Hall.

——— (1976). *Gender Advertisements*. New York: Harper Torch.

Goldscheider, Frances, & Regina Bures (2003). "The Racial Crossover in Family Complexity in the United States." *Demography* 40 (3), pp. 569–87.

Gorer, Geoffrey, & John Rickman (1949). *The People of Great Russia: A Psychological Study*. New York: Norton.

Grabb, Ed, & Neil Guppy, eds (2008). *Social Inequality in Canada*, 5th edn. Toronto: Pearson.

Gramsci, Antonio (1992). *Prison Notebooks*, vol. 1. Ed. Joseph A. Buttligieg. New York: Columbia.

Grant, George (1965). *Lament for a Nation: The Defeat of Canadian Nationalism*. Toronto: McClelland & Stewart.

——— (1969). *Technology and Empire: Perspectives on North America*. Toronto: House of Anansi.

Grant, Tavia (2011, July 20). "Statistics Canada to Stop Tracking Marriage and Divorce Rates." *Globe and Mail* (online).

——— (2015, July 1). "Ottawa Reverses Stand on Health Risks of Asbestos in 'Landmark Shift.'" *Globe and Mail* (online).

Grattan, E. (2003). "Social Inequality and Stratification in Canada." In Paul Angelini (ed.), *Our Society: Human Diversity in Canada*, 2nd edn, pp. 61–86. Scarborough, ON: Thompson-Nelson.

Grisham, John (2008). *The Appeal*. New York: Doubleday.

Griswold, Wendy (1994). *Cultures and Societies in a Changing World*. London: Sage.

Gross, Bertram (1980). *Friendly Fascism: The New Face of Power in America*. Montreal: Black Rose.

Grygier, Pat (1994). *A Long Way from Home: The Tuberculosis Epidemic among the Inuit*. Montreal: McGill–Queen's.

Gutierrez, Richard (2016, March 2). "Canada's Waste Trade Policy: A Global Concern." *Philippine Daily Inquirer* (online).

Haedrich, Richard L., & Cynthia M. Duncan (2004). "Above and Below the Water: Social/Ecological Transformation in Northwest Newfoundland." *Population and Environment* 25 (3), pp. 195–215.

Hale, Sylvia (1992). "Facticity and Dogma in Introductory Sociology Texts: The Need for Alternative Methods." In William K. Carroll, Linda Christiansen-Ruffman, Raymond F. Currie, & Deborah Harrison (eds), *Fragile Truths: 25 Years of Sociology and Anthropology in Canada*, pp. 135–53. Ottawa, ON: Carleton.

Hall, Elaine J. (1988). "One Week for Women? The Structure of Inclusion of Gender Issues in Introductory Textbooks." *Teaching Sociology* 16 (4), pp. 431–2.

Halsall, Jen (2015, Dec. 18). "One Year Later: Looking Back on the Dalhousie Dentistry Scandal." *Rabble.ca* (online).

Hamilton, Lawrence, Cynthia Duncan, & Richard Haedrich (2004). "Social/Ecological Transformation in Northwest Newfoundland." *Population and Environment* 25 (3), pp. 195–215.

Hamilton, Roberta (1996). *Gendering the Vertical Mosaic: Feminist Perspectives on Canadian Society.* Toronto: Pearson.

Hanemaayer, Ariane, & Christopher J. Schneider (2014). *The Public Sociology Debate: Ethics and Engagement.* Vancouver: UBC Press.

Hango, Darcy (2013, Dec.). "Gender Differences in Science, Technology, Engineering, Mathematics and Computer Science (STEM) Programs at University." *Insights on Canadian Society*, Statistics Canada cat. no. 75-006-X. Ottawa, ON: Minister of Industry.

Hanson, Glen R., Peter J. Hanson, Peter J. Venturelli, & Annette E. Fleckenstein (2009). *Drugs and Society*, 10th edn. New York: Jones and Bartlett.

Harney, Alexandra (2009). *The China Price: The True Cost of Chinese Competitive Advantage.* New York: Penguin.

Harrison, Deborah (1999). "The Limits of Liberalism in Canadian Sociology: Some Notes on S.D. Clark." In Dennis W. Magill & William Michelson (eds), *Images of Change.* Toronto: Canadian Scholars' Press.

Hart, Julian Tudor (1971, Feb.). "The Inverse Care Law." *The Lancet* 27, pp. 405–12.

Hatfield, Leonard Fraser (1990). *Sammy the Prince: The Story of Samuel Henry Prince.* Hantsport, NS: Lancelot.

Hegel, Georg Wilhelm Friedrich (1956). *The Philosophy of History.* Trans. J. Sibree. New York: Dover.

Helmes-Hayes, Rick (2010). *Measuring the Mosaic: An Intellectual Biography of John Porter.* Toronto: University of Toronto.

Helmes-Hayes, Rick, & James Curtis, eds (1998). *The Vertical Mosaic Revisited.* Toronto: University of Toronto.

Henry, Frances, & Carol Tator (2006). *The Colour of Democracy: Racism in Canada.* Toronto: Nelson Thomson.

Hicks, Denver (2014, Nov. 25). "Confessions of Lumbersexual." *Time* magazine.

Hill, Daniel (1960). *Negroes in Toronto: A Sociological Study of a Minority Group.* Unpublished doctoral dissertation.

—— (1981). *The Freedom Seekers: Blacks in Early Canada.* Agincourt, ON: Book Society of Canada.

Hiller, Harry H., & Linda Di Luzio (2001). "Text and Context: Another 'Chapter' in the Evolution of Sociology in Canada." *Canadian Journal of Sociology* 26 (3), pp. 487–512.

Hiller, Harry H., & Simon Langlois (2001). "The Most Important Books/Articles in Canadian Sociology in the Twentieth Century: A Report." *Canadian Journal of Sociology / Cahiers canadiens de sociologie* 26 (3), pp. 513–16.

Hitchcock, John T., & Leigh Minturn (1963). "The Rajputs of Khalapur." In B. Whiting (ed.), *Six Cultures: Studies of Child Rearing*, pp. 203–362. New York: John Wiley & Sons.

Hochschild, Arlie Russell, & Anne Machung (1989). *The Second Shift: Working Parents and the Revolution at Home.* New York: Viking Penguin.

Hodges, David, & Mark Brown (2015, Jan. 27). "Are You in the Middle Class?" *Maclean's* magazine (online).

Hodkinson, Paul (2011). "Ageing in a Spectacular Youth Culture: Continuity, Change and Community in the Goth Scene." *British Journal of Sociology* 62, pp. 262–82.

—— (2013). "Family and Parenthood in an Ageing 'Youth' Culture: A Collective Embrace of Dominant Adulthood?" *Sociology* 47 (6) pp. 1072–1087.

Hoebel, E. Adamson (1965). *The Law of Primitive Man, A Study in Comparative Legal Dynamics.* Cambridge, MA: Harvard. (Original work published 1954)

Hofley, John R. (1992). "Canadianization: A Journey Completed?" In William K. Carroll, et al. (eds), *Fragile Truths: 25 Years of Sociology and Anthropology in Canada*, pp. 102–22. Ottawa: Carleton.

Hoodfar, Homa (2003). "More Than Clothing: Veiling as an Adaptive Strategy." In Sajida Alvi, H. Hoodfar, & Sheila McDonough (eds), *The Muslim Veil in North America: Issues and Debates*, pp. 3–40. Toronto: Women's Press.

Horowitz, Irving Louis, ed. (1971). *People, Power and Politics: The Collected Essays of C. Wright Mills.* New York: Oxford.

Hower, Wayne (2006). *Does a Disabled Child = A Disabled Family?* Bloomington, IN: AuthorHouse.

Huesmann, L. Rowell, & L.D. Eron (1986). *Television and the Aggressive Child: A Cross-national Comparison.* Mahwah, NJ: Lawrence Erlbaum.

Huesmann, L. Rowell, & L. Miller (1994). "Long-Term Effects of Repeated Exposure to Media Violence in Children." In L.R. Huesmann (ed.), *Aggressive Behavior: Current Perspective*, pp. 153–86. New York: Plenum.

Huesmann, L. Rowell, J. Moise, C.P. Podolski, & L.D. Eron (2003). "Longitudinal Relations between Childhood Exposure to Media Violence and Adult Aggression and Violence: 1977–1992." *Developmental Psychology* 39 (2), pp. 201–21.

Hughes, Everett C. (1945). "Dilemmas and Contractions of Status." *American Journal of Sociology* 50 (5), pp. 353–9.

—— (1963). *French Canada in Transition.* Chicago: University of Chicago. (Original work published 1943)

Human Resources and Skills Development Canada (HRSDC) (2003). "Market Basket Measure Report." Retrieved: www.hrsdc.gc.ca/eng/cs/comm/news/2003/030527.shtml

Human Rights Watch (1999, April 1). *Broken People: Caste Violence against India's "Untouchables."* Retrieved: www.unhcr.org/refworld/docid/3ae6a83f0.html

Humphreys, Margaret (1995). *Empty Cradles.* London: Transworld.

Hunter College Women's and Gender Studies Collective, & Simalchik, Joan (2017). *Women's Realities, Women's Choices: An Introduction to Women's and Gender Studies.* Don Mills, ON: Oxford University Press.

Hurst, Mike (2009, Sept. 11). "Caster Semenya Has Male Sex Organs and No Womb or Ovaries." *Daily Telegraph* (London, UK) (online).

Husain, Mir Zohair (1995). *Global Islamic Politics*. New York: HarperCollins.

Hutchison, George, & Dick Wallace (1977). *Grassy Narrows*. Toronto: Van Nostrand Rinehold.

Ibn Khaldûn (1981). *The Muqaddimah: An Introduction to History*. Trans. N.J. Dawood. Princeton, NJ: Princeton.

Illich, Ivan (1976). *Medical Nemesis: The Limits of Medicine*. London: Penguin.

Iker, Jack (2003, Aug 1). "A Church's Choice." *WCNY Online NewsHour*. Retrieved: www.pbs.org/newshour/bb/religion/july-dec03/episcopalian_8-1.html

Isajiw, Wsevolod W. (1999). *Understanding Diversity: Ethnicity and Race in the Canadian Context*. Toronto: Thomson.

Islam, Gazy, & Michael J. Zyphur (2009). "Rituals in Organizations: A Review and Expansion of Current Theory." *Group Organization Management* 34 (114): pp. 114–39.

Jacobs, Patricia A., Muriel Brunton, Marie M. Melville, Robert P. Brittain, & William F. McClemont (1965). "Aggressive Behaviour, Mental Sub-normality and the XYY male." *Nature* 208 (5017), pp. 1351–2.

Jacobsen, Michael Hviid, ed. (2009), *The Contemporary Goffman* New York: Routledge.

Jenkins, Richard (1992). *Pierre Bourdieu*. London: Routledge.

Jenness, Diamond (1932). *Indians of Canada*. Ottawa: King's Printer.

Jenness, Stuart (1991). *Arctic Odyssey: The Diary of Diamond Jenness, 1913–1916*. Ottawa: Canadian Museum of Civilization.

Jhally, Sut (1990). *The Codes of Advertising: Fetishism and the Political Economy of Meaning in the Consumer Society*. New York: Routledge.

Jocas, Yves de, & Guy Rocher (1957). "Inter-generation Occupational Mobility in the Province of Quebec." *Canadian Journal of Economics and Political Science* 25 (1), pp. 57–68.

Johnson, Allan G. (1997), *The Blackwell Dictionary of Sociology: A User's Guide to Sociological Language*. Oxford: Blackwell.

Johnston, Hugh (1989). *The Voyage of the Komagata Maru: The Sikh Challenge to Canada's Colour Bar*. Vancouver: University of British Columbia.

Joint Policy Committee of the Societies of Epidemiology (JPC-SE) (2012). "Position Statement on Asbestos" (4 June). Retrieved: www.jpc-se.org/documents/01.JPC-SE-Position_Statement_on_Asbestos-June_4_2012-Summary_and_Appendix_A_English.pdf

Kachuck, Beatrice (2003). "Feminist Social Theories: Themes and Variations." In Sharmila Rege (ed.), *Sociology of Gender: The Challenge of Feminist Sociological Knowledge*. New Delhi: Sage. (Original work published 1995)

Kaizuka, Shigeki (2002). *Confucius: His Life and Thought*. Mineola, NY: Dover. (Original work published 1956)

Kane, P.R., & A.J. Orsini (2003). "The Need for Teachers of Color in Independent Schools." In P.R. Kane & A.J. Orsini (eds), *The Colors of Excellence: Hiring and Keeping Teachers of Color in Independent Schools*, pp. 7–28. New York: Teachers College.

Kanigel, Robert (1997), *The One Best Way: Frederick Winslow Taylor and the Enigma of Efficiency*. New York: Viking.

Keay, John (2000). *India: A History*. London: HarperCollins.

Kehoe, Alice (1995). "Blackfoot Persons." In L. Klein & L. Ackerman, *Women and Power in Native North America*. Norman, OK: University of Oklahoma.

Keleta-Mae, Naila (2016, Feb. 8). "Get What's Mine: 'Formation' Changes the Way We Listen to Beyonce Forever." *Vice.com* (online).

Kelly, Mary Bess (2012). "Divorce Cases in Civil Court, 2010/2011." *Juristat*, Statistics Canada cat. no. 85-002-X. Ottawa: Minister of Industry.

Kimelman, Edwin C. (1985). *No Quiet Place: Review Committee on Indian and Metis Adoption and Placements*. Manitoba Community Services.

King, Alan, Wendy Warren, & Sharon Miklas (2004). "Study of Accessibility to Ontario Law Schools." Executive Summary of the Report Submitted to Deans of Law at Osgood Hall, York University; University of Ottawa; Queen's University; University of Western Ontario; University of Windsor. Queen's University: Social Program Evaluation Group.

Kinsman, Gary (1995). *The Regulation of Desire: Homo and Hetero Sexualities*. Montreal & New York: Black Rose. (Original work published 1987)

Kirkby, Mary-Ann (2007). *I Am Hutterite*. Prince Albert SK: Polka Dot.

Klasing, Amanda (2016, Aug. 30). "Why Is Canada Denying Its Indigenous Peoples Clean Water?" *Globe and Mail* (online).

Klein, Naomi (2000). *No Logo*. Toronto: Vintage.

——— (2002). *Fences and Windows: Dispatches from the Frontlines of the Globalization Debate*. Toronto: Vintage.

Kleinman, Arthur (1995). *Writing at the Margin: Discourse Between Anthropology and Medicine*. Berkeley: University of California.

Klopfenstein, Kristin (2005). "Beyond Test Scores: The Impact of Black Teacher Role Models on Rigorous Math-Taking." *Contemporary Economic Policy* 23, pp. 416–28.

Knockwood, Isabelle (1992). *Out of the Depths: The Experiences of Mi'kmaw Children at the Indian Residential School at Shubenacadie, Nova Scotia*. Lockeport, NS: Roseway.

Koos, E.L. (1954). *The Health of Regionsville: What the People Thought and Did About It*. New York: Columbia.

Kramer, Laurie (2009, Winter), *Siblings as Agents of Socialization: New Directions for Child and Adolescent Development* 126. Hoboken, NJ: Jossey-Bass.

Krause, Elliott (1980). *Why Study Sociology?* New York: Random House.

Kroker, Arthur, & Michael A. Weinstein (1995). *Data Trash: The Theory of the Virtual Class*. Montreal: New World Perspectives.

Kruijver, FP, J.N. Zhou, C.W. Pool, M.A. Hofman, L.J. Gooren, & D.F. Swaab (2000, May). "Male-to-Female Transsexuals Have Female Neuron Numbers in a Limbic Nucleus." *Journal of Clinical Endocrinology and Metabolism* 85 (5), pp. 2034–41.

Kushner, David (2009). *Levittown: Two Families, One Tycoon, and the Fight for Civil Rights in America's Legendary Suburb*. New York: Walker & Company.

Kwong, J.C., I.A. Dhalla, D.L. Streiner, R.E. Baddour, A.E. Waddell, & I.L. Johnson (2002). "Effects of Rising Tuition Fees on Medical School Class Composition and Financial Outlook." *Canadian Medical Association Journal* 166 (8), pp. 1023–8.

Lalonde, Michelle (2007, Nov. 9). "Town Built on Asbestos Downplays Health Risks." Montreal *Gazette*.

Lammam, Charles, & Hugh MacIntyre (2016, January). *An Introduction to the State of Poverty in Canada*. Toronto, ON: Fraser Institute.

Langlois, Simon (1999). "Empirical Studies on Social Stratification in Quebec and Canada." In Y. Lemel & N. Noll (eds), *New Structures of Inequality*. Montreal: McGill–Queen's.

Larkin, Philip (1974). "This Be The Verse." *High Windows*. London: Faber and Faber.

LaRocque, Emma (1975). *Defeathering the Indian*. Agincourt, ON: Book Society of Canada.

——— (1993). "Three Conventional Approaches to Native People." In Brett Balon & Peter Resch (eds), *Survival of the Imagination: The Mary Donaldson Memorial Lectures*, pp. 209–18. Regina: Coteau.

Laslett, Peter (1971). *The World We Have Lost*. London: Methuen.

Lawrence, Bonita (2004). *"Real" Indians and Others: Mixed-Blood Urban Native Peoples and Indigenous Nationhood*. Vancouver: University of British Columbia.

Leah, Ronnie, & Gwen Morgan (1979). "Immigrant Women Fight Back: The Case of the Seven Jamaican Women." *Resources for Feminist Research* 7 (3), pp. 23–4.

Lebkowsky, J. (1997). "It's Better to be Inspired than Wired: An Interview with R.U. Sirius." In A. Kroker & M. Kroker (eds), *Digital Delirium*. Montreal: New World Perspectives.

Le Bourdais, C., & N. Marcil-Gratton (1996). "Family Transformations Across the Canadian/American Border: When the Laggard Becomes the Leader." *Journal of Comparative Family Studies* 27 (3) (Fall), pp. 417–36.

Leffingwell, William (1925). *Office Management: Principles and Practice*. Chicago: A.W. Shaw.

Leiss, William, Stephen Kline, & Sut Jhally (1988). *Social Communication in Advertising: Persons, Products, and Images of Well-Being*. Toronto: Nelson.

Lemieux, Thomas, & W. Craig Riddell (2015, July 9). "Who Are Canada's Top 1 Percent?" (online). Montreal: Institute for Research on Public Policy.

Leung, Carrianne, & Jian Guan (2004). "Yellow Peril Revisited: Impact of SARS on the Chinese and Southeast Asian Canadian Communities." Toronto: Canadian National Council, www.ccnc.ca

Lieberman, Jay A., Christopher Weiss, Terence J. Furlong, Mati Sicherer, & Scott H. Sicherer (2010, Oct.). "Bullying among Pediatric Patients with Food Allergy." *Annals of Allergy, Asthma & Immunology* 105 (4), pp. 282–6.

Lieberson, Stanley (2000). *A Matter of Taste: How Names, Fashions and Cultures Change*. New Haven, CT: Yale.

Lipset, Seymour Martin (1990). *Continental Divide: Values and Institutions of the United States and Canada*. New York: Routledge.

Livingstone, David W. (2004). *The Education–Jobs Gap: Underemployment or Economic Democracy*, 2nd edn. Toronto: Garamond.

Love, John F. (1986). *McDonald's: Behind the Arches*. Toronto: Bantam.

Lowe, Kevin, Stan Fischler, & Shirley Fischler (1988). *Champions: The Making of the Edmonton Oilers*. Scarborough, ON: Prentice-Hall.

Lundy, Katherina, & Barbara Warme (1990). *Sociology: A Window on the World*. Toronto: Methuen. (Original work published 1986)

McClintock, Walter (1910). *The Old North Trail. Life, Legends, and Religion of the Blackfeet Indians*. London: Macmillan.

McGillivray, Anne & Brenda Comaskey (1999). *Black Eyes All of the Time: Intimate Violence, Aboriginal Women, and the Justice System*. Toronto: University of Toronto.

McInnis, Opal A., Matthew M. Young, & Student Drug Use Surveys Working Group (2015, Sept.). *Urban and Rural Student Substance Abuse: Technical Report*. Ottawa, ON: Canadian Centre on Substance Abuse.

McIntosh, Peggy (1989, July/Aug.). "White Privilege: Unpacking the Invisible Knapsack." *Peace and Freedom Magazine*, pp. 10–12. Philadelphia, PA: Women's International League for Peace and Freedom.

McKay, Ian (1998). "Changing the Subject(s) of the 'History of Canadian Sociology': The Case of Colin McKay and Spencerian Marxism, 1890–1940." *Canadian Journal of Sociology* 23 (4).

McKenna, Barrie (2014, Feb. 24). "White-collar crime hits more than a third of Canadian organizations". *Globe and Mail* (online).

MacLean, Annie Marion (1897–8). "Factory Legislation for Women in the United States." *American Journal of Sociology* 3, pp. 183–205.

——— (1898). "Two Weeks in a Department Store." *American Journal of Sociology* 4, pp. 721–41.

——— (1899–1900). "Factory Legislation for Women in Canada." *American Journal of Sociology* 5, pp. 172–81.

——— (1903–4). "The Sweat Shop Summer." *American Journal of Sociology* 9, pp. 289–309.

——— (1908–9). "Life in the Pennsylvania Coal Fields." *American Journal of Sociology* 14, pp. 329–51.

——— (1909–10). "With the Oregon Hop Pickers." *American Journal of Sociology* 15, pp. 83–95.

——— (1910). *Wage-Earning Women*. New York: Macmillan.

——— (1923). "Four Months in a Model Factory." *Century* 106 (July), pp. 436–44.

McQuaig, Linda (2004). "Closed Shop Gives Doc the Hammer in New Brunswick Strike." *Straight Goods*. Retrieved: www.straightgoods.com/McQuaig/010122.shtml

Maines, D.R. (1993). "Narrative's Moment and Sociology's Phenomena—Toward a Narrative Sociology." *Sociological Quarterly* 34 (1), pp. 17–37.

Maioni, Antonia (2004, Aug.). "New Century, New Risks: The Marsh Report and the Post-war Welfare State in Canada." *Policy Options*, pp. 20–3.

Malacrida, Claudia (2015). *A Special Hell: Institutional Life in Alberta's Eugenic Years*, Toronto: University of Toronto Press.

Malik, Kenan (2015, Jan. 3). "Radical Islam, Nihilist Rage." *New York Times* (online).

Mandell, Nancy, & Ann Duffy (1995). *Canadian Families: Diversity, Conflict and Change*. Toronto: Harcourt, Brace.

Manji, Irshad (2003). *The Trouble with Islam: A Wake Up Call for Honesty and Change*. Toronto: Random House.

Maracle, Brian (1996). *Back on the Rez: Finding The Way Home*. Toronto: Viking Penguin.

Maracle, Lee (1992). *Sundogs*. Penticton, BC: Theytus.

Marshall, Gordon (1998). *Oxford Dictionary of Sociology*. New York: Oxford.

Martelle, Scott (2014). *Detroit: A Biography*. Chicago, IL: Chicago Review Press.

Marx, Karl (1967). *Capital: A Critique of Political Economy*. Ed. F. Engels. New York: International. (Original work published 1867)

Marx, Karl, & Friedrich Engels (1967). *The Communist Manifesto.* New York: Pantheon. (Original work published 1848)

——— (1970). *The German Ideology*, part 1. Ed. C.J. Arthur. New York: International. (Original work published 1845–6)

Matthews, Jason (2016). "Black Kickers in the NFL 1966 to 2015–16: Final Prejudice or Rarest Athlete?" Retrieved: www.thebigbangauthor.com/2011/11/black-kickers-in-nfl-final-prejudice-or.html (Original work posted 22 Nov. 2011)

Mazón, Mauricio (1984). *The Zoot-Suit Riots: The Psychology of Symbolic Annihilation.* Austin, TX: University of Texas.

Mead, George Herbert (1934). *Mind, Self, and Society.* Chicago: University of Chicago.

Memmi, Albert (1991). *The Colonizer and the Colonized.* Boston: Beacon. (Original work published 1957)

Merton, Robert K. (1938). "Social Structure and Anomie." *American Sociological Review* 3 (5), pp. 672–82.

——— (1968). *Social Theory and Social Structure.* New York: Free Press. (Original work published 1949)

Michaels, Eric (1986). *The Aboriginal Invention of Television in Central Australia, 1982–6.* Canberra: Australian Institute of Aborigine Studies.

Milan, Anne (2013, July). "Fertility: Overview, 2009 to 2011." Statistics Canada cat. no. 91-209-X.

Milan, Anne, Hélène Maheux, & Tina Chui (2012). *A Portrait of Couples in Mixed Unions.* Statistics Canada cat. no. 11-008-X. Ottawa, ON: Minister of Industry.

Milan, Anne, & Kelly Tran (2004, spring). "Blacks in Canada: A Long History." *Canadian Social Trends*, pp. 2–7.

Miller, J.R. (1996). *Shingwauk's Vision: A History of Native Residential Schools.* Toronto: University of Toronto.

Mills, Albert J., & Tony Simmons (1995). *Reading Organization Theory: A Critical Approach.* Toronto: Garamond.

Mills, C. Wright (1948). *The New Men of Power: America's Labor Leaders.* Harcourt, Brace.

——— (1951). *White Collar: The American Middle Classes.* New York: Oxford.

——— (1956). *The Power Elite.* New York: Oxford.

——— (1958). *The Causes of World War Three.* London: Secker & Warburg.

——— (1959). *The Sociological Imagination.* New York: Oxford.

——— (1960). *Listen Yankee: The Revolution in Cuba.* New York: Ballantine Books.

——— (1962). *The Marxists.* New York: Dell Publishing.

——— (2000). *Letters and Writings by C. Wright Mills.* Eds. Kathryn Mills and Pamela Mills. Berkeley and Los Angeles: University of California.

Miner, Horace (1963). *St Denis: A French Canadian Parish.* Chicago: University of Chicago. (Original work published 1939)

Montagu, Ashley (1942). *Man's Most Dangerous Myth: The Fallacy of Race.* New York: Columbia.

Morissette, René, Garnett Picot, & Yuqian Lu (2013). "The Evolution of Canadian Wages over the Last Three Decades." Statistics Canada Analytical Studies Branch Research Paper Series, cat. no. 11F0019M, No. 347. Ottawa, ON: Minister of Industry.

Morgan, Lewis Henry (1964). *Ancient Society or Researches in the Lines of Human Progress from Savagery through Barbarism to Civilization.* Cambridge, MA: Harvard. (Original work published 1877)

Mouwad, Jad (2009). "Shell to Pay $15.5 Million to Settle Nigerian Case." *New York Times* (8 June) (online).

Mueller, Carol (1995). "The Organizational Basis of Conflict in Contemporary Feminism." In Myra Marx Ferree & Patricia Yancey Martin (eds), *Feminist Organizations*, pp. 263–75. Philadelphia: Temple University.

Muir, Leilani (2014). *A Whisper Past – Childless After Eugenic Sterilization in Alberta.* Calgary: Friesen Press.

Murphy, Emily (1973). *The Black Candle.* Toronto: Coles. (Original work published 1922)

Muzzin, Linda J. (2001). "Powder Puff Brigades: Professional Caring vs Industry Research in the Pharmaceutical Sciences Curriculum." In Eric Margolis (ed.), *The Hidden Curriculum in Higher Education*, pp. 135–54. London: Routledge.

Myers, S.A., trans. (1862). *Martin's Natural History,* first series. New York: Blackeman & Mason.

Naidoo, Amelia (2011, April 21). "Shedding Light on the 'Boyat' Phenomenon." *GulfNews.com* (online).

Nakhaie, M. Reza (1995). "Housework in Canada: The National Picture." *Journal of Comparative Family Studies* 23 (3), pp. 409–25.

Newbury, Catharine (1993). *The Cohesion of Oppression.* New York: Columbia. (Original work published 1988)

Newson, Janice, & Howard Buchbinder (1988). *The University Means Business: Universities, Corporations and Academic Work.* Toronto: Garamond.

New York City Department of Consumer Affairs (2015, Dec.). *From Cradle to Cane: The Cost of Being a Female Consumer.* New York: Department of Consumer Affairs.

Nicolosi, Joseph, & Linda Ames Nicolosi (2002). *A Parent's Guide to Preventing Homosexuality.* Downers Grove, IL: InterVarsity Press.

Nightengale, Bob (2016, April 15). "As MLB Celebrates Jackie Robinson, Dearth of Black Pitchers Concerns Many." *USA Today* (online).

Nikiforuk, Andrew (2009). *Tar Sands: Dirty Oil and the Future of a Continent.* Vancouver: Greystone.

Nisbet, Robert A. (1969). *Social Change and History: Aspects of the Western Theory of Development.* Oxford: Oxford University Press.

Noble, David (1998). "Digital Diploma Mills: The Automation of Higher Education." *Science as Culture* 7 (3), pp. 355–68.

——— (2002). *Digital Diploma Mills: The Automation of Higher Education.* Toronto: Between the Lines.

Nonaka, K., T. Miura, & K. Peter (1993). "Low Twinning Rate and Seasonal Effects on Twinning in a Fertile Population, the Hutterites." *International Journal of Biometeorology* 37 (3), pp. 145–50.

Nova Scotia Communities, Culture and Heritage (2015). Nova Scotia Heritage Day: Viola Desmond, 1914–1965 (online). Halifax: Province of Nova Scotia.

Oakes, Jeannie (2005). *Keeping Track: How Schools Structure Inequality*, 2nd edn. New Haven: Yale.

Oakley, Ann (1972). *Sex, Gender and Society.* London: Temple Smith.

Ontario Human Rights Commission (OHRC) (2003). *Paying the Price: The Human Cost of Racial Profiling.* Inquiry Report. Toronto: OHRC. Retrieved: www.ohrc.on.ca/en/paying-price-human-cost-racial-profiling

Ontario Soccer Association (OSA) (2015). The Ontario Soccer Association Grassroots Festival Guide. Retrieved: www.ontariosoccer.net/images/publications/2015/about/employment/Grassroots_Festival_Guide_2015.pdf

Oreskes, Naomi, & Erik M. Conway (2010). *Merchants of Doubt: How a Handful of Scientists Obscured the Truth on Issues from Tobacco Smoke to Global Warming*. New York: Bloomsbury.

Ortiz, Isabel, & Matthew Cummins (2011, April). *Global Inequality: Beyond the Bottom Billion: A Rapid Review of Income Distribution in 141 Countries*. New York: UNICEF.

O'Sullivan, Patrick, with Gare Joyce (2015), *Breaking Away: A Harrowing True Story of Resilience, Courage, and Triumph*. Toronto: HarperCollins.

Owusu-Bempah, Akwasi, & Scot Wortley (2014). "Race, Crime, and Criminal Justice in Canada." In Sandra Bucerius & Michael Tonry, eds, *The Oxford Handbook of Ethnicity, Crime, and Immigration*. New York: Oxford.

Palmay, Frank (2015, Sept. 16). "Canada Acted Differently to Hungarian Refugees in 1956." *The Star* (Toronto) (online).

Park, Robert, & Ernest Burgess (1921). *Introduction to the Science of Sociology*. Chicago: University of Chicago.

—— (1967). *The City*. Chicago: University of Chicago. (Original work published 1925)

Parsons, Talcott (1951). *The Social System*. New York: Free Press.

—— (1966). *Societies: Evolutionary and Comparative Perspectives*. Englewood Cliffs, NJ: Prentice-Hall.

Patai, Raphael (2014). *The Arab Mind*, updated edn. New York: Recovery Resources Press. (Original work published 1973)

Payer, Lynn (1992). *Disease-Mongers: How Doctors, Drug Companies, and Insurers Are Making You Feel Sick*. New York: Wiley.

Penny, Laura (2005). *Your Call Is Important to Us: The Truth About Bullshit*. Toronto: McClelland & Stewart.

Perkel, Colin N. (2002). *Well of Lies: The Walkerton Water Tragedy*. Toronto: McClelland & Stewart.

Pew Research Center (2015, Dec. 9). "The American Middle Class Is Losing Ground: No Longer the Majority and Falling Behind Financially." Washington, DC: Pew.

Philip, Margaret (2006, Dec. 9). "Cancer in the Mind's Eye." *Globe and Mail* (online).

"Plural Wife Describes Life in Bountiful Commune" (2011, Jan. 27). *CTV News* (online).

Pohlmann, Lisa (2002). "Inequality is Bad for your Health." Retrieved: www.mecep.or/MEChoices02/ch_029.htm

Poirier, Agnes (2016, Aug. 17). "Burkini Beach Row Puts French Values to Test." *BBC News* (online).

Poisson, Jayme (2013, Nov. 15). "Remember Storm? We Check in on the Baby Being Raised Gender-Neutral." *The Star* (Toronto) (online).

Porter, Jody (2016, June 20). "'Guilt' Drives Former Dryden, Ont. Mill Worker to Reveal His Part in Dumping Toxic Mercury." *CBC News* (online).

Porter, John (1965). *The Vertical Mosaic: An Analysis of Social Class and Power in Canada*. Toronto: University of Toronto.

Price, William H., & Peter B. Whatmore (1967). "Behaviour Disorders and Pattern of Crime among XYY Males Identified at a Maximum Security Hospital." *British Medical Journal* 2 (5601), pp. 533–6.

Prince, Samuel Henry (1920). *Catastrophe and Social Change: Based Upon a Sociological Study of the Halifax Disaster*. New York: Columbia.

Quan, Douglas (2015, 12 Feb.). "Harper Vows to Appeal Court Ruling Allowing Women to Wear Niqab during Citizenship Oath, Calls It 'Offensive'." *National Post* (online).

Rajulton, Fernando, T.R. Balakrishnan, & Zenaida R. Ravanera (1990). "Measuring Infertility in Contracepting Populations." Presentation, Canadian Population Society Meetings (Victoria, BC, June 1990).

Ramraj, C., E. Weitzner, R. Figueiredo, & C. Quiñonez (2014, July). "A Macroeconomic Review of Dentistry in Canada in the 2000s." *Journal of the Canadian Dentistry Association* 80.

Reiman, Jeffrey (2007). *The Rich Get Richer and the Poor Get Prison: Ideology, Class, and Criminal Justice*, 8th edn. Boston: Allyn & Bacon.

Reinharz, Shulamit (1992). *Feminist Methods in Social Research*. New York: Oxford.

Rennie, Steve (2012, Sept. 19). "Boomerang Kids Mean Empty Nests Not Quite So Empty." *Globe and Mail* (online).

Richards, John, Jennifer Hove, & Kemi Afolabi (2008, Dec.). *Understanding the Aboriginal/Non-Aboriginal Gap in Student Performance: Lessons from British Columbia*. Commentary 276. Toronto: C.D. Howe Institute.

Ritzer, George (2004). *The McDonaldization of Society*, rev. edn. Newbury Park, CA: Pine Forge Press.

Robin, Marie-Monique (2010). *The World According to Monsanto: Pollution, Politics, and Power; An Investigation into One of the World's Most Controversial Companies*. Melbourne: Spinifex.

Robinson, Angela (2002). "Ta'n Teli-ktlamsitasit ('Ways of Believing'): Mi'kmaw Religion in Eskasoni, Nova Scotia." *Open Access Dissertations and Theses*, Paper 1477. Retrieved: http://digitalcommons.mcmaster.ca/opendissertations/1477

—— (2005). *Ta'n Teli-ktlamsitasit (Ways of Believing): Mi'kmaw Religion in Eskasoni, Nova Scotia*. Toronto: Pearson.

Robson, Wanda, & Ronald Caplan (2010). *Sister to Courage: Stories from the World of Viola Desmond, Canada's Rosa Parks*. Sydney, NS: Cape Breton Books.

Rosario, M., E. Scrimshaw, J. Hunter, & L. Braun (2006). "Sexual Identity Development among Lesbian, Gay, and Bisexual Youths: Consistency and Change Over Time." *Journal of Sex Research* 43 (1), pp. 46–58.

Roscoe, Will (1998). *Changing Ones: Third and Fourth Genders in Native North America*. Palgrave/St Martin's Press.

Ross, Aileen (1962). *The Hindu Family in Its Urban Setting*. Toronto: University of Toronto.

—— (1976). "Changing Aspirations and Roles: Middle and Upper Class Indian Women Enter the Business World." In Giri Raj Gupta (ed.), *Main Currents in Indian Sociology*, 103–32. Bombay: Vikas.

—— (1977). "Some Comments on the Home Roles of Businesswomen in India, Australia and Canada." *Journal of Comparative Family Studies* 8 (3), pp. 327–40.

——— (1979). "Businesswomen and Business Cliques in Three Cities: Delhi, Sydney, and Montreal." *Canadian Review of Sociology and Anthropology* 16 (4), pp. 425–35.

——— (1982). *The Lost and the Lonely: Homeless Women in Montreal.* Montreal: Canadian Human Rights Commission.

Rossmo, Kim D. (1995). "Place, Space and Police Investigations: Hunting Serial Violent Criminals." In D. Weisburd & J.E. Eck (eds), *Crime and Place*, pp. 217–35. New York: Criminal and Justice Theory.

——— (1999). *Geographic Profiling.* Boca Raton, FL: CRC Press.

Rotenberg, Cristine (2016, 12 April). Aboriginal People Survey, 2012: Social Determinants of Health for the Off-Reserve First Nations Population, 15 Years of Age and Older, 2012. Statistics Canada cat. no. 89-653-X2016009. Ottawa, ON: Minister of Industry.

Ruddick, Sara (1989). *Maternal Thinking: Toward a Politics of Peace.* Boston: Beacon.

Rush, Joan (2014, Dec. 24). "Dentistry Has a Far Larger 'Boys' Club' Problem." *Globe and Mail* (online).

Russell, George (2001, June 24). "Cover Stories Taming the Liberation Theologians." *Time Magazine World.* Retrieved: www.time.com/time/magazine/article/0,0171,141037,00.html

Rutherford, Kate (2016, April 9). "Attawapiskat Declares State of Emergency over Spate of Suicide Attempts." *CBC News* (online).

Ryan, William (1976). *Blaming the Victim.* New York: Pantheon. (Original work published 1971)

Saewyc, Elizabeth, Chiaki Konishi, Hilary Rose, & Yuko Homma (2014). "School-Based Strategies to Reduce Suicidal Ideation, Suicide Attempts, and Discrimination among Sexual Minority and Heterosexual Adolescents in Western Canada." *International Journal of Child, Youth, and Family Studies* 5 (1).

SAGE Publications (2013, Sept. 4). "Tattoos Reduce Chances of Getting a Job." *Science Daily* (online).

Said, Edward (1979). *Orientalism.* New York: Pantheon.

Sale, Kirkpatrick (1980). *Human Scale.* New York: Coward, McCann & Geoghegan.

——— (1996). *Rebels Against the Future: The Luddites and Their War on the Industrial Revolution—Lessons for the Computer Age.* Cambridge, MA: Perseus.

——— (2005, Feb.). "Imperial Entropy: Collapse of the American Empire." *CounterPunch* 22.

Sapers, Howard (2015). Annual Report of the Office of the Correctional Investigator, 2014–15. Ottawa, ON: Ministry of Public Safety.

Sargent, Paul (2005, Feb.). "The Gendering of Men in Early Childhood Education." *Sex Roles: A Journal of Research.*

Sarlo, Christopher (2013, Nov.). "Poverty: Where Do We Draw the Line?" Toronto, ON: Fraser Institute.

Schecter, Stephen (1977). "Capitalism, Class, and Educational Reform in Canada." In L. Panitch (ed.), *The Canadian State: Political Economy and Political Power.* Toronto: University of Toronto.

Scoffield, Heather (2011, Nov. 29). "Locals Disagree on Who's to Blame for Attawapiskat Crisis." *Globe and Mail* (online).

Scull, Andrew (2009). *Hysteria: The Disturbing History.* Oxford, UK: Oxford University Press.

Seeley, John, R. Alexander Sim, & E.W. Loosely (1956). *Crestwood Heights: A Study of the Culture of Suburban Life.* Toronto: University of Toronto.

Service Canada (2015, May). Dental Hygienists and Dental Therapists. Retrieved: www.servicecanada.gc.ca/eng/qc/job_futures/statistics/3222.shtml

Sherrod, Katie (1998, July 30). "First Female Bishops Find Warm Welcome at Lambeth Conference." *ACNS: Anglican Communion News Service* (online).

Shkilnyk, Anastasia M. (1985). *A Poison Stronger Than Love: The Destruction of an Ojibwa Community.* New Haven, CT: Yale.

Siddiqui, Haroon (2006). *Being Muslim.* Toronto: Groundwood Books.

Simmel, Georg (1890). *On Social Differentiation.* Leipzig: Duncker & Humbolt.

——— (1908). *Sociology: Investigations on the Forms of Socialization.* Lepizig: Duncker & Humbolt.

——— (1990). *The Philosophy of Money.* Ed. David Frisby. New York: Routledge. (Original work published 1900)

Simon, Michele (2014, Nov.). "Walmart's Hunger Games: How America's Largest Employer and Richest Family Worsen the Hunger Crisis." Eat Drink Politics. Retrieved: www.eatdrinkpolitics.com/wp-content/uploads/Walmarts_Hunger_Games_Report.pdf

Singh, Sundar (1912, Jan. 25). "The Sikhs in Canada. An Address Delivered before the Empire Club of Canada." Retrieved: http://speeches.empireclub.org/62324/data?n=15

Smith, Adam (1976). *The Theory of our Moral Sentiments.* Ed. D.D. Raphael & A.L. Macfie. Oxford: Oxford University Press. (Original work published 1759)

Smith, Dorothy (1987). *The Everyday World as Problematic: A Feminist Sociology.* Boston: Northeastern University.

——— (1990). *The Conceptual Practices of Power: A Feminist Sociology of Knowledge.* Toronto: University of Toronto.

Smith, George W. (1998). "The Ideology of 'Fag': The School Experience of Gay Students." *Sociological Quarterly* 39 (2), pp. 309–35.

Smith, James M. (2007). *Ireland's Magdalen Laundries and the Nation's Architecture of Containment.* Notre Dame, IN: University of Notre Dame.

Smith, Joanna (2015, Feb. 8). "High-Paid Chiefs are Outliers, Data Shows." *The Star* (Toronto) (online).

Smith, N. (2009). "Beyond the Master Narrative of Youth: Researching Ageing Popular Music Scenes." In D. Scott (ed.), *The Ashgate Research Companion to Popular Musicology.* Farnham, UK: Ashgate.

Smits, David D. (1982). "The 'Squaw Drudge': A Prime Index of Savagism." *Ethnohistory* 29 (4), pp. 281–306.

Soffritti, Morando, Fiorella Belpoggi, Marco Manservigi, Eva Tibaldi, Michelina Lauriola, Laura Falcioni, & Luciano Bua (2010, July 30). "Aspartame Administered in Feed, Beginning Prenatally Through Life Span, Induces Cancers of the Liver and Lung in Male Swiss Mice." *American Journal of Industrial Medicine.* DOI:10.1002/ajim.20896

Spencer, Herbert (1862). *First Principles.* Retrieved: http://praexology.net/HS-SP-FP-pref1.htm

——— (1896). *Social Statics, Abridged & Revised Together with Man Versus the State.* New York: D. Appleton.

——— (1896). *The Study of Sociology.* New York: D. Appleton. (Original work published 1880)

Spengler, Oswald (1918–22). *The Decline of the West*. New York: Alfred A. Knopf.

Statistics Canada (1992). *Marriage and Conjugal Life in Canada*, cat. no. 91-534E. Ottawa, ON: Minister of Industry.

—— (2001). "Religions in Canada: Highlight Table, 2001 Census," cat. no. 97-F0024-XIE2001015.

—— (2004, Dec. 7). "Performance of Canada's Youth in Mathematics, Reading, Science, and Problem Solving." *The Daily* (online).

—— (2009). "Household Size Declining." *Canada Year Book Overview. 2008*. Retrieved: www41.statcan.gc.ca/2008/40000/ceb40000_000-eng.htm

—— (2010, Jan. 29). "Study: The Financial Impact of Student Loans." *The Daily* (online).

—— (2011a). "Low Income Cut-Offs." *Low Income Lines, 2009–2010. Income Research Paper Series*. Retrieved: www.statcan.gc.ca/pub/75f0002m/75f0002m2011002-eng.htm

—— (2011b). "Women in Canada: A Gender-Based Statistical Report," cat. no. 89-503-X. Ottawa, ON: Minister of Industry.

—— (2011c). "Access to a Regular Medical Doctor, 2010." Retrieved: www.statcan.gc.ca/pub/82-625-x/2011001/article/11456-eng.htm

—— (2011d). Canadian Vital Statistics, Marriage Database and Demography Division (population estimates). Ottawa, ON: Minister of Industry.

—— (2012a). *Portrait of Families and Living Arrangements in Canada: Families, Households, and Marital Status, 2011 Census of Population*, cat. no. 98-312-X2011001). Ottawa, ON: Minister of Industry.

—— (2012b). *Live Births, by Age of Mother, Canada, Provinces and Territories, Annual*, CANSIM Table 102-4503. Ottawa, ON: Minister of Industry.

—— (2012c). *Mental Health Profile, Canadian Community Health Survey*, CANSIM Table 105-1101. Ottawa, ON: Minister of Industry.

—— (2013a). Immigration and Ethnocultural Diversity in Canada: National Household Survey, 2011. Cat. no. 99-010-X2011026-28. Ottawa, ON: Minister of Industry.

—— (2013b). Education in Canada: Attainment, Field of Study and Location of Study, National Household Survey, 20111, Ministry of Industry

—— (2013c). "National Household Survey Dictionary, 2011," cat. no. 99-000-X2011001. Ottawa, ON: Minister of Industry.

—— (2013d). "Aboriginal Peoples in Canada: First Nations People, Métis, and Inuit." *National Household Survey, 2011*, cat. no. 99-011-X2011001. Ottawa, ON: Minister of Industry.

—— (2014). "Mixed Unions in Canada." *National Household Survey (NHS), 2011*, cat. no. 99-010-X2011003. Ottawa, ON: Minister of Industry.

—— (2015a, Dec. 24). *Aboriginal Statistics at a Glance*, 2nd edn, cat. no. 89-645-x2015001. Ottawa, ON: Minister of Industry.

—— (2015b, Jun. 24). "Study: Employment Patterns of Families with Children, 1976–2014." *The Daily* (online).

—— (2016a, May 26). "Census Family Structure Including Intact Families and Stepfamilies for Couple Families with Children in Private Households, 2011 Counts, All Couples, for Canada, Provinces and Territories, and Census Metropolitan Areas and Census Agglomerations" (table). *Families and Households Highlight Tables, 2011 Census.*

—— (2016b). "Fertility: Fewer Children, Older Moms." *The Daily: Canadian Megatrends*, cat. no. 11-630-X.

Steckley, John L. (1999). *Beyond Their Years: Five Native Women's Stories*. Toronto: Canadian Scholars' Press.

—— (2003). *Aboriginal Voices and the Politics of Representation in Canadian Introductory Sociology Textbooks*. Toronto: Canadian Scholars' Press.

—— (2008). *White Lies About the Inuit*. Toronto: University of Toronto.

—— (2013). *Learning from the Past: Five Cases of Aboriginal Justice*. Whitby, ON: de Sitter Publications.

Steckley, John, & Bryan Cummins (2001). *Full Circle: Canada's First Nations*. Toronto: Prentice-Hall.

—— & —— (2008). *Full Circle: Canada's First Nations*, 2nd edn. Toronto: Pearson.

Steckley, John, & Brian Rice (1997). "Lifelong Learning and Cultural Identity: A Lesson from Canada's Native People." In Michael Hatton (ed.), *Lifelong Learning: Policies, Programs & Practices*, pp. 216–29. Toronto: APEC.

Steger, Manfred B. (2003). *Globalization: A Very Short Introduction*. Oxford, UK: Oxford.

Stewart, Susan (1996, March). "A Day in the Life of Two Community Police Officers: The Aboriginal Police Directorate Takes a Look at the First Nations Policing Policy in Action." *First Nations Policing Update* 4. Retrieved: www.sgc.gc.ca/whoweare/aboriginal/newsletter/no4/no43.htm

Stiglitz, Joseph E. (2003). *Globalization and Its Discontents*. New York: Norton.

Sumner, William Graham (1906). *Folkways: A Study of the Sociological Importance of Usages, Manners, Customs, Mores, and Morals*. Boston: Ginn and Co.

Sutherland, Edwin (1940). "White Collar Criminality." *American Sociological Review* 5 (1), pp. 1–12.

—— (1949). *White Collar Crime*. New York: Holt, Rinehart and Winston.

Tajima, E. Renee (1989). "Lotus Blossoms Don't Bleed: Images of Asian Women." In Asian Women United of California (ed.), *Making Waves: An Anthology of Writings by and about Asian American Women*, pp. 305–9. Boston: Beacon.

Talbot, Yves, E. Fuller-Thomson, F. Tudiver, Y. Habib, & W.J. McIsaac (2001, Jan.). "Canadians Without Regular Medical Doctors: Who Are They?" *Canadian Family Physician* 47, pp. 58–64.

Tataryn, Lloyd (1979). *Dying for a Living*. Ottawa: Deneau and Greenberg.

Tatum, Beverly Daniel (2003). *"Why Are All the Black Kids Sitting Together in the Cafeteria?" and Other Conversations about Race*, rev. edn. New York: Basic Books.

Telfer, Mary A. (1968). "Are Some Criminals Born That Way?" *Think* 34 (6), pp. 24–8.

Tepperman, Lorne, & Michael Rosenberg (1998). *Macro/Micro: A Brief Introduction to Sociology*, 3rd edn. Scarborough, ON: Prentice Hall, Allyn & Bacon.

Thiessen, Victor, & Christy Nickerson (1999). *Canadian Gender Trends in Education and Work*. Ottawa: Human Resources and Development Canada, Applied Research Branch.

Thomas, W.I. (1966). *W.I. Thomas on Social Organization and Social Personality. Selected Papers*. Ed. Morris Janowitz. Chicago: University of Chicago.

Thomas, W.I., & Florian Znaniecki (1996). *The Polish Peasant in Europe and America*. Urbana, IL: University of Illinois. (Original work published 1918–20)

Thompson, Carol (2006). "Unintended Lessons: Plagiarism and the University." *Teachers College Record* 108 (12), pp. 2439–49.

Thorndike, Edward (1999). *Animal Intelligence: Experimental Studies*. Piscataway, NJ: Transaction. (Original work published 1911)

Thrasher, Frederic M. (1927). *The Gang: A Study of 1,313 Gangs in Chicago*. Chicago: University of Chicago.

Torczyner, Jim, Wally Boxhill, Carl James, & Crystal Mulder (1997). *Diversity, Mobility, and Change: The Dynamics of Black Communities in Canada*. Montreal, QC: McGill Consortium for Ethnicity and Strategic Social Planning.

Totten, Mark, (2014). *Gang Life: 10 of the Toughest Tell Their Stories*. Toronto: James Lorimer.

Totten, Mark, & Daniel Totten (2012). *Nasty Brutish and Short: The Lives of Gang Members in Canada*. Toronto: James Lorimer.

Truth Commission into Genocide in Canada (2001). *The Untold Story of the Genocide of Aboriginal Peoples by Church and State in Canada*. Retrieved: http://canadiangenocide.nativeweb.org/genocide.pdf

Tuck, Eve, & K. Wayne Yang (2012). "Decolonization Is Not a Metaphor." *Decolonization: Indigeneity, Education & Society* 1 (1): pp. 1–40.

Tuhiwai Smith, Linda (1999). *Decolonizing Methodologies: Research and Indigenous Peoples*. London: Zed Books.

Ubelacker, Sheryl (2015, April 17). "Health Care System Can Often Be a Challenge for Transgender Patients." *Global News* (online).

Umutesi, Marie Beatrice (2004). *Surviving the Slaughter: The Ordeal of a Rwandan Refugee in Zaire*. Madison, WI: University of Wisconsin Press.

Ungerleider, Charles, Terri Thompson, & Tracy Lavin (2012, Dec. 26). "No Quick Fix for Gender Gap in Education." *The Star* (Toronto) (online).

Uppal, Sharanjit, & Sébastien LaRochelle-Côté (2014, April). "Changes in the Occupational Profile of Young Men and Women in Canada." *Insights on Canadian Society*, Statistics Canada cat. no. 75-006-X. Ottawa, ON: Minister of Industry.

Urmetzer, Peter, & Neil Guppy (1999). "Changing Income Inequality in Canada." In J. Curtis, et al. (eds), *Social Inequality in Canada*, pp. 56–65. Scarborough, ON: Prentice Hall.

Van Poppel, Frans, & Lincoln H. Day (1996). "A Test of Durkheim's Theory of Suicide—Without Committing the 'Ecological Fallacy.'" *American Sociological Review* 61, pp. 500–7.

Van Tubergen, Frank, Manfred te Grotenhuis, & Wout Ultee (2005). "Denominatino, Religious Context, and Suicide: Neo-Durkheimian Multilevel Explanations Tested with Individual and Contextual Data." *American Journal of Sociology* 111 (3), pp. 797–823.

Veblen, Thorstein (1904). *The Theory of Business Enterprise*. New York: Charles Scribner's Sons.

——— (1912). *The Theory of the Leisure Class*. New York: Macmillan. (Original work published 1899)

Vermond, Kira (2016, Jan. 19). "Small Change: Women Can Beat the 'Pink Tax' by Buying Guys' Supplies." *Globe and Mail* (online).

Walla, Harsha (2008, Sept. 11). "*Komagata Maru* and the Politics of Apologies." *The Dominion: News from the Grassroots*. Retrieved: www.dominionpaper.ca/articles/2014

Warner, Jessica (2002). *Craze: Gin and Debauchery in an Age of Reason*. New York: Basic.

Watson, John B. (1925). *Behaviorism*. New York: Norton.

Watson, John B., & R. Rayner (1920). "Conditioned Emotional Reactions." *Journal of Experimental Psychology* 3, pp. 1–14.

Weber, Max. (1930). *The Protestant Ethic and the Spirit of Capitalism*. Trans. Talcott Parsons. New York: Charles Scribner's Sons. (Original work published 1904)

——— (1958). "Essays in Sociology." In M. Weber, H. Gerth, & C.W. Mills (eds), *From Max Weber*. New York: Oxford. (Original work published 1946)

——— (1968). *Economy and Society: An Outline of Interpretive Sociology*. New York: Bedminster. (Original work published 1914)

Weiner, Jonathan (1995). *The Beak of the Finch: A Story of Evolution in Our Time*. New York: Alfred A. Knopf.

Weyer, Edward M. (1962). *The Eskimos: Their Environment and Folkways*. Hamden, CT: Archon Books. (Original work published 1932)

Whitfield, Harvey Amani, (2004). *From American Slaves to Nova Scotian Subjects: The Case of the Black Refugees, 1813-1840*, Toronto: Pearson Canada

Whiting, Beatrice B. (1963). *Six Cultures: Studies of Child Rearing*. New York: John Wiley.

Whyte, William F. (1955). *Street Corner Society: The Social Structure of an Italian Slum*, 2nd edn. Chicago: University of Chicago.

Williamson, Judith (1978). *Decoding Advertisements: Ideology and Meaning in Advertising*. London: Marion Boyars.

Willis, Paul E. (1977). *Learning to Labor: How Working Class Kids Get Working Class Jobs*. New York: Columbia.

Wrong, Dennis (1961). "The Oversocialized Conception of Man in Modern Sociology." *American Sociological Review* 26 (2), pp. 183–93.

Yalnizyan, Armine (1998). *The Growing Gap: A Report on Growing Inequality between the Rich and Poor in Canada*. Toronto: Centre for Social Justice.

York, Geoffrey (1990). *The Dispossessed: Life and Death in Native Canada*. Toronto: Lester & Orpen Dennys.

Young, Egerton R. (1974). *Stories from Indian Wigwams and Northern Campfires*. Toronto: Coles. (Original work published 1893)

Zelek, Barbara, & Susan P. Phillips (2003, Feb. 11). "Gender and Power: Nurses and Doctors in Canada." *International Journal for Equity in Health* 2 (1).

Index